ZakkaSewn

Stitch, Quilt, Share & Love

20+ PROJECTS

Rashida Coleman-Hale

an imprint of C&T Publishing

Text copyright © 2025 by Rashida Coleman-Hale

Photography and artwork copyright © 2025 by C&T Publishing, Inc.

Publisher: Amy Barrett-Daffin

Creative Director: Gailen Runge

Senior Editor: Roxane Cerda

Technical Editor: Debbie Rodgers

Cover/Book Designer: April Mostek

Production Coordinator: Tim Manibusan

Illustrator: Aliza Shalit

Photography Coordinator: Rachel Ackley

Front cover photography by Jodi Foucher

Lifestyle photography by Jodi Foucher, unless otherwise noted

Subjects photography by C&T Publishing, Inc., unless otherwise noted

Published by Stash Books, an imprint of C&T Publishing, Inc., P.O. Box 1456, Lafayette, CA 94549

All rights reserved. No part of this work covered by the copyright hereon may be used in any form or reproduced by any means—graphic, electronic, or mechanical, including photocopying, recording, taping, or information storage and retrieval systems—without written permission from the publisher. The copyrights on individual artworks are retained by the artists as noted in *Zakka Sewn*. These designs may be used to make items for personal use only and may not be used for the purpose of personal profit. Items created to benefit nonprofit groups, or that will be publicly displayed, must be conspicuously labeled with the following credit: "Designs copyright © 2025 by Rashida Coleman-Hale from the book *Zakka Sewn* from C&T Publishing, Inc." Permission for all other purposes must be requested in writing from C&T Publishing, Inc.

Attention Copy Shops: Please note the following exception—publisher and author give permission to photocopy pages 118–127 for personal use only.

Attention Teachers: C&T Publishing, Inc., encourages the use of our books as texts for teaching. You can find lesson plans for many of our titles at ctpub.com or contact us at ctinfo@ctpub.com.

We take great care to ensure that the information included in our products is accurate and presented in good faith, but no warranty is provided, nor are results guaranteed. Having no control over the choices of materials or procedures used, neither the author nor C&T Publishing, Inc., shall have any liability to any person or entity with respect to any loss or damage caused directly or indirectly by the information contained in this book. For your convenience, we post an up-to-date listing of corrections on our website (ctpub.com). If a correction is not already noted, please contact our customer service department at ctinfo@ctpub.com or P.O. Box 1456, Lafayette, CA 94549.

Trademark (™) and registered trademark (®) names are used throughout this book. Rather than use the symbols with every occurrence of a trademark or registered trademark name, we are using the names only in the editorial fashion and to the benefit of the owner, with no intention of infringement.

Library of Congress Control Number: 2025003447

Printed in China

10 9 8 7 6 5 4 3 2 1

Dedication

To Tomorrow, Elijah, Matthew, and Cassandra, my precious, beloved children. My raison d'etre. I do all of this for you. Thank you for all you have taught me as your mother. I love you to the moon and back. Remember—Fall seven times, get up eight. Love, Marmee

Acknowledgments

An extra special thank you to my daughter, Tomi. You're my little rock and I could not have done this without you by my side.

To Grandma Sybil, Mommie, Dad, Sabin, Fernando, Rosalinda, Donna, and Gretta: You all are my heart and your love and support mean the world to me. Thank you.

My Ruby Star Society sisters, Alexia, Kim, Sarah, and Melody. My second family. I love you down! Thank you for your love, support, friendship, fabric, and especially all of the laughing. XO

A special thank you to Roxane Cerda, my editor. Thank you for your guidance and encouragement to get to the finish line! To the amazing C&T Publishing team, thank you for all of your hard work and dedication to making my little dream a reality.

A huge thank you to Moda Fabrics, Oliso, Pellon, and Robert Kaufman for sending fabric and supplies for this project!

Thank you to the lovely Mindy at Wild Phil Quilting for making my quilts sparkle!

CONTENTS

Introduction 6

Tools and Materials 8
Machine Feet 8
Sewing Machine Needles 9
Straight Pins 10
Hand Sewing Needles 10
Thread 10
Seam Ripper 10
Loop Turner 11
Scissors 11
Rotary Cutter and Self-Healing Mat 12
Clear Gridded Acrylic Ruler 12
Water-Soluble Fabric Pen 12
Point Turner 12

The Stash: Fabrics and Care 13
Linen 13
100% Cotton 14
Cotton Cord 15
Storage 16
Choosing Colors and Prints 16

Techniques 17
Squaring Up 17
Cutting Shapes 18
Pinning 19
Hand Sewing 20
Machine Sewing 22

Home 26
Kitchen 57
Accessories 76
Templates 118
About the Author 128

Home 26
Obround Pillow 27
Onigiri Pillow 30
Quatrefoil Pillow 33
Scrappy Wall Hanging 36
Floral Wall Hanging 40
Dune Door Stop 44
Knotted Door Decor 47
Brilliance Quilt 50
Circle Gets a Square Quilt 53

27

44

Kitchen 57
Kaya Produce Bags 58
Orange Peel Trivet 62
Half Moon Oven Mitt 65
Crossroads Placemat 69
Roundel Napkin Ring 73

58

Accessories 76
Favorite Project Pouch 77
Honeycomb Pencil Case 82
Capsule Bag 86
Ingot Pincushion 91
Hey, Lady Sewing Case 93
Knotted Headband 101
Glow Up Pouches 104
Tomorrow Tote 108
Cassandra Crossbody Bag 113

77

101

 30

 33

 36

 40

 47

 50

 53

 62

 65

 69

 73

 82

 86

 91

 93

 104

 108

 113

INTRODUCTION

When your life is turned upside down, sometimes you lose yourself or your sense of purpose. At the end of my marriage a few years ago, I found myself suddenly a single mom of four, laid off from my day job, trying to figure out how to pick up the pieces of my life and stand on my own two feet. Not just for myself, but mainly for my children who I now had to care for alone. Divorce left me feeling like I was drifting; like I had lost not just my sense of purpose but also my creative spark. That spark had always driven my passion for making things. When I thought about my work as a designer, I wondered how I would continue to make art when my creative spark felt lifeless.

During the quiet times, I'd think back on my blogging days when I was constantly sewing, sharing the things that I had made, and connecting with an amazing community of people who shared my love of sewing and quilting. My very first blog entry was back in January of 2007 and I remember feeling unsure and uncertain of what the act of posting that first entry would mean for me. I wrote, "I know there are already a gajillion blogs based on the same type of subject matter. But everyone's different and each brings something special to the table. Even if no one reads my blog, I know it has something special to offer. Just not sure what it is yet! Haha!"

Blogging was where my career in the sewing and quilting industry started. One that I couldn't have imagined at the time but here I am, some 18 years later, 35 fabric collections in, writing the introduction for my third book. You truly never know where life will take you! Over the years, my focus shifted to fabric design, and I realized that I had drifted away from the hands-on creative work that had always brought me so much joy. I just HAVE to create with my hands and I love the process of figuring out how to build things, but I'm equally curious about how things work and I love to take things apart. Writing *Zakka Sewn* felt like a way to come full circle, to return to my roots as a maker and a quilter. The bonus was that I had my own fabric to use as I wasn't yet a fabric designer when I wrote my first two books! Yay! Writing *Zakka Sewn* has been quite a journey of rediscovery for me and it reminded me why I fell in love with this craft and my creative spark is now a huge fireball. Through these pages, I hope to inspire others to find their creative spark or perhaps even rediscover it as I have.

Zakka is a Japanese word that means "miscellaneous goods," but it is so much more than that! The concept of zakka combines functionality and beauty to bring joy and style to your daily life. It's about finding happiness in the little things in life such as handmade crafts, cozy home décor, and random items that just make you happy when you look at them. I truly enjoyed the process of sketching out these projects and I wanted to create some fun and unusual shapes and details in my designs that speak to this concept.

I hope the projects in this book will inspire you to make them your own and that you can think of them as a starting point and a launchpad for your creativity! Add some patchwork, or maybe some quilting, or just add some pom-pom trim! Whether you're crafting for your home, for a loved one, or simply for the pleasure of sewing, I hope you embrace the freedom to explore and experiment. The goal isn't just to sew but to create with character, charm, and delight. Make your projects a reflection of you and make them *Zakka Sewn*!

With love and creativity,

Rashida

TOOLS AND MATERIALS

Every sewist needs what seems like an arsenal of tools and materials for successful stitching. This is an overview of the essential tools and materials for creating the projects in this book, as well as a few nonessential, but very helpful, tools.

You should always have the following items on hand before beginning any of the projects in this book. Anything further that is needed will be listed with each project.

- Sewing machine, with assorted needles and presser feet (see Machine Feet, below)
- Hand sewing needles
- Assorted sewing thread, to match or coordinate with your fabric
- Straight pins

- Pincushion
- Fabric scissors
- Craft scissors
- Embroidery scissors or other small, sharp scissors
- Rotary cutter and self-healing mat

- Seam ripper
- Loop turner
- Clear gridded acrylic ruler
- Tape measure
- Iron and ironing board
- Water-soluble fabric pen
- Pencil

TIP Be sure to clean your sewing machine often, freeing it from dust and lint that can accumulate from regular use. Your machine should come equipped with tools for cleaning, and the manual will instruct you on how to keep it in tip-top shape. Finally, take your machine to the dealer or shop for a tune-up once a year. These simple tasks can help your machine live a longer, happier sewing life.

Machine Feet

Your sewing machine likely came with the zigzag foot already on the machine. This foot is usually the standard presser foot and can be used for most sewing tasks. However, there are a few specialty feet that can make certain tasks simpler.

Walking foot: This foot grips multiple layers of fabric, which is helpful for quilting and sewing on binding.

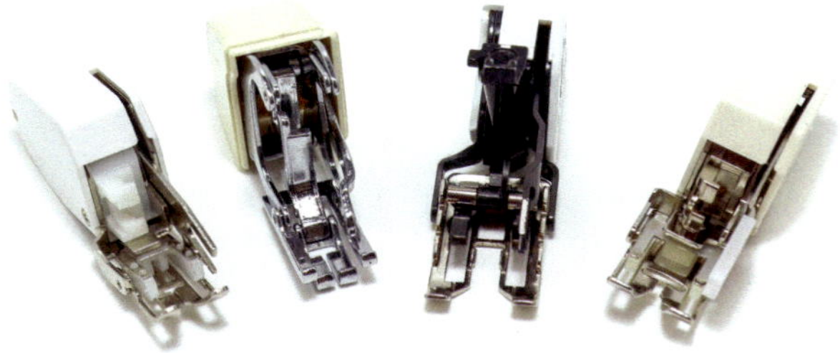

Machine feet photos on pages 8-9 by Bernie Tobisch

ZAKKA SEWN

Blind hem foot or edgestitch foot: Both of these have a metal guide that can be placed along an edge or a fold, making edgestitching easier (a blind hem foot comes with some machines).

Zipper Foot: This foot makes sewing on zippers super simple. The foot features notches on either side of the foot that allow your needle to get as close as possible to the edge of the zipper.

TIPS

- To learn how to get the most out of all of your sewing machine feet, check out *The Ultimate Guide to Sewing Machine Feet* by Shelley and Bernie Tobisch (C&T Publishing).

- Because every machine is a little different, be sure to always refer to your sewing machine manual for information about settings, using the different functions on your machine, and using various machine feet.

Sewing Machine Needles

These needles come in a variety of sizes, each for a specific task; refer to your sewing-machine manual for information on the needles that came with your machine and/or specialized needles. Universal point needles are the all-purpose needle, good for just about any type of sewing.

It's important that you change your needle often. I've found that a good rule of thumb is to change your needle before each project.

Keep extra needles handy because needles get dull and sometimes even break. Check your sewing-machine manual to be sure you're buying the right type for your machine.

Straight Pins

Straight seams make for happy patchwork, and pinning is the key to straight seams. There are several types of straight pins available, but glass-head pins are my hands down favorites. You can press over them with a hot iron and they flow through fabric with brilliant ease. Glass-head pins may cost a little more, but to me they're well worth it. They are available in a variety of colors, but I'd avoid buying the clear ones, as they are difficult to find if you lose one.

Hand Sewing Needles

There are so many types of hand-sewing needles, all with a different use. Sharps are a great general-purpose needle to have in your sewing arsenal. They can be used for general sewing, appliqué, and even quilting. Although a thimble isn't essential, it's a nice thing to have around for hand sewing. If you need to push the needle through several layers of fabric, your finger will thank you for using a thimble.

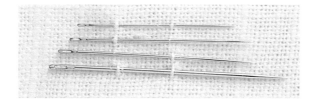

Thread

I typically only use cotton or linen fabric for my projects, so I stick to cotton thread. Although polyester thread is strong, it can cut through the fibers in cotton fabric. The only brand of cotton thread that I use is Mettler Silk-Finish Cotton. I find it to be superior to other brands, and I love how it looks on my projects. Test out a few brands and see which ones tickle your fancy. Avoid cheap thread as it tends to break easily and can get a little fuzzy during use.

Seam Ripper

Having to undo a seam is something we all wish we could avoid, but mistakes do happen. You'll need a sharp seam ripper to cut through the threads of the faulty seam. I prefer the larger more heavy-duty seam rippers because I'm the person who always ends up breaking the small plastic ones. You don't want to be that sewist. The point of a heavy-duty seam ripper can also be used in place of an awl to create a hole through layers of fabric to install a Chicago screw.

TOP (LEFT TO RIGHT): point turner, loop turner, water-soluble fabric pen, straight pins and pincushion, seam ripper, hand-sewing needles, sewing machine needles, rotary cutter, clear gridded acrylic ruler, self-healing cutting mat, assorted threads, and tape measure.
BOTTOM (LEFT TO RIGHT): embroidery scissors, fabric scissors, craft scissors, and thread nippers.

Loop Turner

Trying to turn narrow fabric tubes right side out without using a loop turner can be very frustrating. Fortunately, loop turners are inexpensive and easy-to-find tools. They are long thin metal rods with a hook on one end and a loop on the other. To use a loop turner, feed the tool through the fabric tube, use the hook to grab the far fabric edge of the tube, and use the loop on the other end to gently pull the opposite end of the tube through the middle, turning it right side out.

Scissors

Most crafters have several pairs of scissors and use each for a different purpose. I have three pairs that I use most frequently:

- Knife-edge bent shears for cutting fabric.

- Embroidery scissors for cutting thread and clipping fabric in tight spots.

- Craft Scissors for cutting paper and everything else.

Find scissors that are comfortable and feel good in your hand. You may want to splurge a little when buying scissors because you'll be using them quite a bit. Better-quality scissors will also last longer, and they won't dull as quickly as the lower-quality ones. Scissors will dull over time, so you will need to be sure to have them sharpened now and then.

THREAD NIPPERS

Although not essential, thread nippers are handy for clipping threads when you've finished a seam. If you're as graceful as I am, you'll probably like to have a pair of these to avoid regrettable mistakes that can happen when trying to use regular scissors for such close snipping.

Rotary Cutter and Self-Healing Mat

Sometimes I think I use my rotary cutter even more than my scissors. This tool makes sewing life easier by allowing you to cut quickly through several layers of fabric at a time. There are a variety of rotary cutters available, in a variety of sizes. I have an Olfa 45mm, which is a good all-purpose size. I also have an Olfa 18mm, which is better for cutting smaller pieces and curves. These blades are super sharp, so make sure that the one you choose has some type of safety feature. Keep a few replacement blades handy. The cutter blades can get dull with use. Pinking blades are also available from some brands, and I tend to use them more often than pinking shears.

Remember to protect your cutting blades and tabletops from damage with a self-healing mat. They come in several sizes and can sometimes be bought as a kit with the rotary cutter. An 18″ × 24″ (45 × 60cm) mat is a good size for starting out, but you may soon find that you'd prefer a larger one for various projects.

Clear Gridded Acrylic Ruler

You'll need one or two of these to use with your rotary cutter to make straight cuts. It is an indispensable tool for creating beautiful patchwork. They come in various sizes and colors, but I find the Omnigrid 6″ × 12″ (15 × 30cm) and 6″ × 24″ (15 × 60cm) versions to be the most useful. Try a few out and see which ones suit you best.

Water-Soluble Fabric Pen

To transfer templates and pattern markings to fabric I prefer using a water-soluble fabric pen. These are easy to use and create temporary marks on fabric that disappear with water.

Point Turner

A point turner is a tool with a pointed end that is used to push out corners and smooth out seams for crisp, neat edges and corners. A bluntly pointed object, such as a knitting needle, can also be used for this purpose.

THE STASH: FABRICS AND CARE

Ah, fabric. It's the real reason we all love to sew so much, isn't it? I have to admit that I really, really have to show some restraint when it comes to fabric shopping. Fabric Addicts Anonymous anyone?

My favorite fabrics by far are 100% linen and 100% cotton; they are what I use for all of my projects. Feel free to experiment with different types of fabrics to achieve a look that's all your own as you create the projects in this book.

Linen

Linen, how do I love thee? Let me count the ways. Working with linen just makes me divinely and utterly happy. This fabric, much like cotton, is very easy to work with and can be used for just about any project. Natural linen comes in lovely subtle shades of beige and cream, which looks wonderful paired up with some colorful patchwork. Linen and cotton make a great team!

Made from the stalk of the flax plant, linen is two to three times stronger than cotton and is also extremely absorbent. Linen can absorb 30% or more of its weight in moisture, which makes it especially useful for making things like kitchen towels and summer clothing (it will pull moisture away from the skin during the hotter seasons).

Should you decide to buy your linen online, I suggest ordering swatches before you buy several yards. It's hard to see the quality of the linen in photos. Lower quality linen tends to be a bit slubby, meaning there are lumps and bumps in the threads. Higher-quality linen is very smooth and consistent in texture and appearance throughout.

You can buy linen in the same types of cuts as cotton quilting fabric. It is also available in the following weights and is typically 60˝ (152 cm) wide.

Handkerchief-Weight: 3 to 4 oz Slightly sheer, this weight is suitable for handkerchiefs, sheer curtains, and light blouses.

Medium-Weight: 4½ to 6½ oz My favorite weight to work with, this weight can be used for almost any type of project from clothing to interior projects. Both medium- and heavyweight are excellent choices for embroidery. Medium-weight linen is appropriate for any of the projects in this book.

Heavyweight: 7 to 8 oz Suitable for upholstery and curtains, I like to use this weight for tote bags.

CARE

If the project you are making is going to be washed a lot, I highly recommend preshrinking your fabric in the wash before sewing, as linen will definitely suffer initial shrinkage.

For maximum shrinkage, linen should be washed on a hot setting and then dried on a low setting or line dried. You may want to wash it a few times to make sure it won't shrink more. You'll be happy that you did.

You'll notice when purchasing linen that it has a very stiff and crisp hand when it's fresh off of the bolt. This can be great for certain projects, and if you'd like the fabric to maintain that feel, then washing isn't recommended, and dry cleaning would be the better choice. The more linen is hand- or machine-washed the softer and less stiff it becomes. I've found that linen also responds well to spray starch which can help it retain some of the original stiffness, if that's what you prefer. When washing a finished project, wash it in cold water.

Linen wrinkles quite easily, and some people feel the wrinkles add to its charm. But, I like my work to be wrinkle-free, so I iron it like mad. To iron linen, dampen it with a spray bottle of water and iron it on a high steam setting. Don't worry about scorching it, linen has a very high resistance to heat, but it does tend to develop a shine when ironed too much. To remedy that, simply use a press cloth over the linen to protect it as you iron (muslin or scrap cotton fabric works well for this, cotton press cloths are also available for purchase at many fabric stores).

100% Cotton

Plain-weave quilter's cotton is, in my opinion, the easiest cotton to work with. It feels great to the touch, can be washed easily, is very easy to cut and sew, and is great for patchwork. It does like to wrinkle, so be sure to have your iron ready!

This cotton can be bought in 42" (106cm), 44" (112cm), or 54" (137cm) widths, but you'll probably find that 44" (112cm) is the most common width.

In addition to fabric by the yard (and/or fractions of a yard), many shops also have fat cuts available. These are regular cuts of fabric, cut off of the bolt and then cut in half, parallel to the selvedge. There are two types of fat cuts: **fat quarters**, which are 18" × 22" (45 × 56cm) and **fat eighths**, which are 9" × 22" (23 × 56cm). Some fabric shops sell these in sweet little bundles, which are great for stash building.

If you're like me, you probably like to buy fabric whether you need it or not, but if shopping for a particular project, try to determine how much fabric you will need in advance. It's never a bad idea to buy a little more than what you need in case of mistakes and that darn shrinkage! The wonderful thing about the projects in this book is that many of them require various small pieces, so you'll probably be able to use up lots of scraps from your current stash.

CARE

Cotton fabric likes to shrink! It is essential to wash your fabric before you begin cutting it. This will allow you to avoid any disappointment that would likely be the result of waiting to wash a finished project, only to find that it's become warped. Cold water works best for cotton as hot water can be damaging to the color or finish.

Cotton Cord

Several projects in this book call for cotton cording. This is a type of cotton cord made by braiding multiple strands of cotton together. It works well for drawstrings and also has many decorative uses. It can be used to fill a fabric tube to create a 3D circular effect.

THE STASH: FABRICS AND CARE

Storage

Keeping your stash clean and dust free is important for the longevity of the fabric. Avoiding direct sunlight is important as well to prevent fading. The linen closet at my house has been turned into the "fabric-stashery." The sheets and towels will just have to fend for themselves. I like to keep my fabrics folded neatly and color coordinated on a shelf. Having my fabric folded and organized makes it much easier to see what I have when choosing fabric for a new project. The color coordination aspect is helpful as well. If I have color combinations in mind, I don't have to spend much time searching. This method may not work for you, just find a storage place that is clean and dry and organize according to your own preferences.

Choosing Colors and Prints

Selecting colors is one of the best parts of starting a new project—it's just so much fun! I simply choose one print fabric as my base, and I select the other colors based on those in the base fabric. The colors you choose don't have to exactly match the colors in your base fabric. I've always been pleased with the results I get by choosing several fabrics in varying shades of the same or similar colors.

There is no written rule for choosing prints, at least not to my knowledge. With the growing number of fabric designers and different prints available, you can go to town mixing and matching all the prints you want. I'm especially fond of polka dots, stripes, and gingham prints. I find that they help the other prints really pop on a project, so I typically use them as accent fabrics or as a lining for my pouches and bags.

Don't be afraid to experiment with color combinations and prints, try something unexpected—you'll be pleasantly pleased by the results.

TECHNIQUES

Before you begin the projects in this book there are a few basic techniques that you should learn for creating beautiful patchwork projects. Just remember, it takes some practice—take your time, there's no rush!

Squaring Up

One of the first things you need to do with your fabric is straighten the edges so that you can make nice straight cuts. Squaring up is essential for accurate patchwork piecing and will save you a lot of heartache later on. Grab your rotary cutter, self-healing mat, two clear acrylic rulers (the 6″ × 12″ [15 × 30cm] and the 6″ × 24″ [15 × 60cm]) and your fabric, then follow the instructions below for squaring up.

1. Iron your fabric to ensure that it is nice and flat when you're ready to cut.

2. Fold the fabric in half, wrong sides together, matching up the selvages and adjusting the layers side-to-side until there are no diagonal ripples; place it on the self-healing mat.. The fold should be toward the bottom of the mat, with the selvages toward the top.

3. Place the 6″ × 24″ (15 × 60cm) ruler (or the larger of the two that you own) on top of the fabric at one side (the left or right cut edge), overlapping the edge of the fabric by 1″ (2.5cm). Line up one of the horizontal grid lines on the ruler with the fold of the fabric.

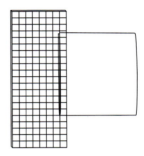

4. Place the second ruler right next to the first, on top of the fabric. The edges of the rulers should be touching, and a horizontal line on each should be in line with the fold. Adjust the placement of fabric as necessary until the fold is in line with both of the grid lines.

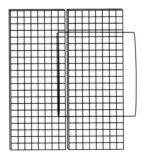

5. Remove the second ruler and place your hand firmly on top of the first ruler to keep it in place. Use the edge of the ruler as a guide to make a straight cut (mind your fingers!) by running your rotary cutter flush against the edge. Cut the fabric all the way from the folded edge to the selvage. Voila! You now have a perfectly squared edge. You'll want to start your cutting from this edge, cutting strips to the necessary width (see Cutting Shapes at right). Check to make sure that the cut edge of the fabric is at a perfect right angle to the fold before cutting each strip. If not, you'll need to square up again before cutting.

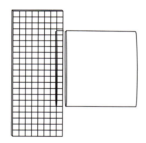

Cutting Shapes

For some of the projects in this book, you'll need to cut squares and rectangles. Several squares and rectangles can easily be cut with accuracy from strips of your squared-up fabric.

> **NOTE** The following instructions for cutting shapes include adding seam allowance. The templates and cutting measurements for the projects in this book already have seam allowance added, so you don't need to worry about adding it when you are cutting your shapes. Simply use the templates and/or measurements as given.

SQUARES

1. Cut strips of squared-up fabric to the width you'd like your finished squares to be plus ½" (1.2cm) for seam allowance. For example, if your finished squares need to be 5" × 5" (12.5 × 12.5cm), you'll cut your strips 5½" (14cm) wide.

2. Now, use your ruler to measure the length of the squares (desired finished length plus ½" (1.2cm) seam allowance) along the squared-up edges of the strip and cut (use the edge of your ruler as a guide to make straight cuts with the rotary cutter).

RECTANGLES

1. Cut strips of squared-up fabric to the width you'd like your finished rectangles to be plus ½″ (1.2cm) seam allowance. For example, if your finished rectangles need to be 5″ (12.5cm) long x 7″ (18cm) wide, you'll cut your strips 7½″ (19cm) wide.

2. Now use your ruler to measure the length of the rectangles (desired finished length plus ½″ (1.2cm) seam allowance) along the squared-up edges of the strip and cut (use the edge of your ruler as a guide to make straight cuts with the rotary cutter).

Pinning

Pinning is something that I really didn't enjoy doing until I began my love affair with patchwork. Now, I've come to realize that it's an absolute must for perfect patchwork seams. It's a simple task that sometimes gets overlooked, but pinning properly before you begin to sew will make all the difference. There may be times when you don't need to pin, but be sure to pin when matching seams to ensure accurate patchwork. Keep your pincushion nearby and remember to remove the pins as you sew. You can easily damage your sewing machine or break a needle by sewing over a pin.

BASIC PINNING

Place your fabric right sides together, lining up the raw edges, then insert your pins through all layers, perpendicular to the raw edges.

A good rule of thumb is to place your pins about 2″ (5cm) apart on straight edges, moving them a little closer together on curved edges. Be sure that the ball ends of the pins are pointing away from the fabric for easy removal as you sew.

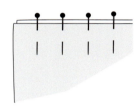

PATCHWORK PINNING

1. Before you begin stitching 2 pieced units together, press the corresponding seam allowances on the seam(s) of each unit in opposite directions. This will ensure that the two edges will meet perfectly when you pin and stitch them together.

2. Place the 2 units right sides together and line up any corresponding seams (you can feel with your fingers if the seams are touching).

3. Pin the 2 units together, with the pins perpendicular to the raw edge and be sure to pin about ⅛" (3mm) to each side of the matched seams to hold them firmly in place. Leave the ball ends of the pins out of the fabric a bit for easy removal as you sew.

Hand Sewing

Hand sewing isn't very difficult to learn and can be enjoyable as well as relaxing. I learned how to hand sew from my grandmother who sewed her own curtains, pillows, school uniforms for her children, and even mattresses—all by hand!

In this section, I'll cover some of the hand sewing basics that you'll need to complete the projects in this book.

PREPARING YOUR THREAD

With sharp scissors, cut one strand of thread, no longer than the length of your arm (or about 18" [46cm]). Cutting it any longer than that will most likely cause your thread to get unpleasantly tangled. Using some thread conditioner or beeswax to coat the thread can help make the thread less likely to tangle and will make threading a little easier. (Thread conditioner and beeswax can both be found packaged in small containers that are designed for coating the thread. Follow the manufacturer's instructions to coat the thread.)

Pass the thread through the eye of the needle and pull several inches of thread through the eye, creating a tail. You should thread your needle with one strand of thread for most handstitches, but when the sewing requires stronger stitching you should use the thread doubled by knotting the ends together.

KNOTTING THE THREAD

My grandmother taught me one way to knot the end of my thread, and the quilter's knot is an alternative that I've picked up in the last couple of years. You can use either method, try them both and see which you prefer.

Grandma's Knot

1. Hold the tail of your thread between your thumb and your forefinger and wrap the thread around your finger. Cross the thread over the end you're holding and slip it between your thumb and forefinger.

2. Begin rolling the thread up your finger with your thumb until it slips off of your finger, then slide the knot toward the end of the thread (it will tighten into a secure knot at the end of the thread).

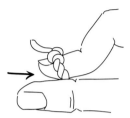

Quilter's Knot

1. Thread the needle and then grasp the eye of the needle with the thumb and forefinger of your nondominant hand. Bring the long end of the thread up so that the point of the needle and the end of the thread are facing each other and then slip the end of the thread between the fingers that are holding the eye of the needle (you now have a loop of thread hanging from the needle).

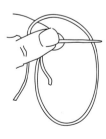

2. With your free hand, wrap the tail of the longer thread around the needle three times.

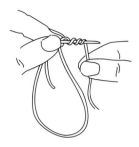

3. Slide the wound thread down and lodge it between the fingers holding the eye of the needle and then, with your free hand, slowly pull the needle from the pointed end, until the entire length of thread has passed through your thumb and forefinger (still grasping the wound thread). The wound thread will form a small knot at the base of the thread.

SLIP STITCH

Take a stitch, about ½" (1.2cm) long, into the folded edge of one piece of fabric and then bring the needle out. Insert the needle into the folded edge (or the fabric surface) of the opposite piece of fabric, directly across from the exit point of the thread in the previous stitch. Repeat by inserting the needle into the first piece of fabric, as before. This will create small, almost invisible stitches.

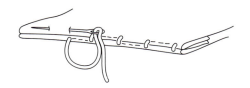

Machine Sewing

Machine sewing can bring you so much joy, as it enables you to create projects quickly and with ease. Take some time to sit and read your sewing machine manual so that you can really get to know your machine and all of its many functions. The more familiar you are with your machine and how it operates, the easier it will be for you to sew with speed and accuracy.

SOME NOTES ABOUT SEAM ALLOWANCE

Patchwork uses ¼" (6mm) seam allowances and ensuring that your seam allowances remain accurate will allow your pieces to be smooth and fit together nicely. There are a couple of ways you can be sure to have the perfect ¼" (6mm) seam allowances:

The Throat Plate

The throat plate of your sewing machine (the plate, usually metal, that lies directly beneath your presser foot and needle) typically has marks on it that you can use as a guide while sewing. If your machine does not have these marks, you can use a piece of masking tape to create a seam guide on the throat plate. This guide will help you sew a straight seam, exactly ¼" (6mm) from the raw edges.

Create a Seam Guide

1. Take a piece of ¼" (6mm) graph paper (four squares to an inch) and trim it along the edge of one of the graph lines at the right side of the paper to ensure an accurate grid.

2. Place the paper under the presser foot and lower your needle onto the first ¼" (6mm) line from the right edge of your paper.

3. Place a piece of masking tape on the throat plate right next to the edge of the paper.

4. Remove the paper. The edge of the masking tape can now serve as a ¼" (6mm) guide.

THE PRESSER FOOT

Most sewing machines come with a presser foot that is the proper width to easily sew ¼" (6mm) seam allowances by lining up the raw edges against the side of the presser foot. To test your presser foot, simply line up the edge of a scrap of fabric with the right edge of your presser foot. Stitch down the edge of the fabric, then take a ruler or tape measure and measure the seam allowance.

If you don't have a ¼" (6mm) presser foot you can purchase a patchwork presser foot for your machine, which will make sewing for patchwork and quilting easier.

SEWING A CORNER

1. About 1" (2.5cm) before you reach the corner, stop stitching with the needle still down, then shorten the stitch length setting on your machine to about 15–20 stitches per inch (1.7–1.3mm; this will reinforce your corner). Continue stitching until you are ¼" (6mm) from the edge.

2. When you are ¼" (6mm) from the edge of the fabric, stop sewing with the needle down in the fabric, lift the presser foot and pivot the fabric so that the adjoining edge is now vertical in front of you. Lower the presser foot.

3. Sew for about 1" (2.5cm), then stop stitching (with the needle still down) and return your stitch length to the regular setting (10–12 stitches per inch [2.5–2.1mm]), then continue stitching.

4. Repeat Steps 1–3 for each corner, then remove the fabric from the machine and clip the corners before turning the piece right side out.

SEWING A CURVE

1. When your seam begins to curve, stop sewing, with your needle still down, and shorten the stitch length on your machine to about 15 stitches per inch (1.7mm).

2. Stitch slowly around the curve as you guide the fabric with your hands, keeping your seam allowances constant. Going slowly will give you better control to keep your stitching smooth and even.

3. Once you have finished sewing the curve, stop stitching (with the needle still down) and return your stitch length to the regular setting (10–12 stitches per inch [2.5–2.1mm]), then continue stitching.

4. Once you are done stitching, remove the fabric from the machine and clip the curves before turning the piece right side out.

MAKING BINDING

1. Square up your fabric and cut the indicated number of strips. The project instructions will indicate what width to cut for your binding.

2. Place the ends of 2 of the binding strips right sides together perpendicularly to form an L shape. Then, stitch the 2 strips together diagonally and trim the seam allowances to ¼″ (6mm).

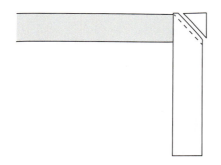

3. Open up the strips so they are lying flat and press the seam allowances open.

4. Repeat Steps 2 and 3 until you've stitched all of your strips together, forming one long strip of fabric.

5. Fold the strip in half lengthwise with wrong sides together and press. Then, unfold the strip and fold over each long edge, toward the wrong side, by ½″ (1.2cm) so that the raw edges meet at the center crease; press.

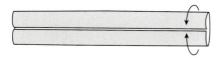

6. Refold the binding along the center crease, enclosing the raw edges, and press again.

MAKING BIAS BINDING

1. Square up your fabric. Using a ruler, find a 45-degree angle. Cut the indicated number of strips at this angle (the bias), being sure not to stretch or distort your fabric. The project instructions will indicate what width to cut for your binding.

2. Place the ends of 2 of the binding strips right sides together perpendicularly to form an L shape, rotating the strips to match the diagonal ends if possible. Then, stitch the 2 strips together diagonally and trim the seam allowances to ¼″ (6mm).

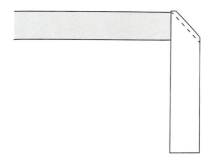

3. Open up the strips so they are lying flat and press the seam allowances open.

4. Repeat Steps 2 and 3 until you've stitched all of your strips together, forming one long strip of fabric.

Follow steps 5–6 under Making Binding (to the left) to complete the binding preparation.

ATTACHING BINDING WITH MITERED CORNERS

1. Unfold the binding completely and then fold under one short end of the binding strip, toward the wrong side by 1″ (2.5cm) or as directed by the pattern, and press.

2. Starting from the bottom center of the project (with the right side facing up), place the folded-under end of the binding on top of the project, lining up the raw edge of the binding with the raw edge of the project (right sides will be together); pin in place to the first corner.

3. Start sewing the binding to the project along the first crease (closest to the raw edge), about 2″ (5cm) from the folded-under edge, through all layers.

4. Stop stitching about ¼″ (6mm) from the first corner and backtack. For extra security you can backtack twice.

5. To form a mitered corner, rotate the project 90 degrees so that the adjoining edge of the project is now vertical in front of you. Fold the binding fabric up, away from the project, at a 45-degree angle.

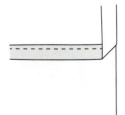

6. Fold the binding back down to match the raw edge of the project and align the raw edges as before. Beginning at the top edge of the folded binding, stitch the binding to the project, and sew until you are ¼″ (6mm) away from the next corner.

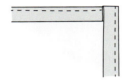

7. Repeat Steps 4–6 to bind the remaining edges and miter the corners. When you reach your starting point, overlap the folded-under edge by about 1″ (2.5cm) or as directed by the pattern, and then trim the binding if necessary. Continue stitching until you have reached the beginning of your stitch line.

8. Refold the binding along the bottom crease and then fold the binding over the edge of the project from front to back, placing the folded-under edge on the back of the project (it should be directly across from the bottom of the binding on the opposite side and should cover the stitches). Handstitch the binding to the back of the project using a slip stitch; make sure to cover the machine stitches and fold each corner into a miter as before.

HOME

Obround Pillow

Finished pillow: 8″ × 16″ (20.3 × 40.6cm)

This trio of modern throw pillows features some delightful shapes that are easy to make and can brighten up your space in a flash! Mix and match them to your heart's desire. Using heavier canvas or linen fabric will help these hold up to everyday wear and tear. Best of all, they are all easy to make!

Start with this simple pill-shaped pillow for an added touch of softness.

MATERIALS

Yardages are based on 40″ (1m)-wide fabric.

Cotton, linen, or canvas: ½ yard (45.7cm)

Cotton print for buttons: 2 scraps at least 3″ × 3″ (7.6 × 7.6cm)

Cover buttons: 2, size 45 (1⅛″ [2.9cm])

Buttons: 2 standard, ½″ (12mm)

Pearl cotton thread

Fiber fill: 12 ounce bag

Obround Pillow template (page 118)

Paper or cardstock for templates

Cutting

COTTON, LINEN, OR CANVAS
Cut 2 rectangles 9″ × 17″ (22.9 × 43.2cm).

Construction

Seam allowances are ½″ (12mm) unless otherwise noted.

PREPARING PATTERN PIECES

1. Press the fabric.

2. Trace the template onto paper or cardstock and cut out.

3. Fold the fabric pieces in half, widthwise. Align the template along the fold, as indicated on the template. Trace the template onto the wrong side of each fabric piece using a water-soluble fabric pen and then cut out along the traced lines. Cut out 2 pieces for the pillow body.

4. Transfer markings for button placement.

ASSEMBLING THE PILLOW

1. Line up the edges, right sides together, and pin.

2. Stitch together around the perimeter of the pillow, leaving a 3″ (7.6cm) opening for turning. Make sure to start and stop with a backstitch.

3. Clip seam allowance along the curves. Turn pillow right side out.

4. Fill with fiber fill really well so that the pillow is solid and firm.

FINISHING

1. Fold in the seam allowances at the opening and pin together. Hand stitch closed with a slipstitch.

2. Cover your buttons following the manufacturer's instructions.

3. Tie a knot at the end of the pearl cotton thread and loop it through the shank of the covered button to secure it.

4. Using the marking on the front as a guide, push the needle through to the back of the pillow to create the tuft in the front. Pull it taught, but not too taught!

5. Thread the needle through the regular button on the back to create an anchor and stitch the buttons securely.

6. Wrap the thread around the button's stitches a few times and end with a few knots.

7. Repeat this step with the remaining button and your pillow is complete!

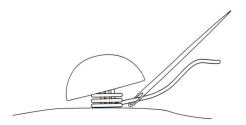

Onigiri Pillow

Finished pillow: 15″ × 15″ (38.1 × 38.1cm)

This triangular pillow is reminiscent of the beloved Japanese rice snack of the same name. It's definitely my favorite shape of the lot! Make this in a larger scale as a fun floor pillow!

MATERIALS

Yardages are based on 40″ (1m)-wide fabric.

Cotton, linen, or canvas: ½ yard (45.7cm)

Cotton print for bottoms: 1 scrap at least 3″ × 3″ (7.6 × 7.6cm)

Dritz cover button: 1, size 45 (1⅛″ [2.9cm])

Button: 1 standard, ½″ (12mm)

Pearl cotton thread

Fiber fill: 20 ounce bag

Onigiri Pillow template (page 118)

Paper or cardstock for templates

Cutting

COTTON, LINEN, OR CANVAS

Cut 2 squares 17″ × 17″ (43.2 × 43.2cm).

Construction

Seam allowances are ½″ (12mm) unless otherwise noted.

PREPARING PATTERN PIECES

1. Press the fabric.

2. Trace the template onto paper or cardstock and cut out.

3. Fold the fabric squares in half, lengthwise. Align the template along the fold, as indicated on the template. Trace the template onto the wrong side of each square using a water-soluble fabric pen and then cut out along the traced lines. Cut out 2 pieces for the pillow body.

4. Transfer markings for button placement.

ASSEMBLING THE PILLOW

1. Line up the edges, right sides together, and pin.

2. Stitch together around the perimeter of the pillow, leaving a 3″ (7.6cm) opening for turning. Make sure to start and stop with a backstitch.

3. Clip seam allowance along the curves. Turn pillow right side out.

4. Fill with fiber fill really well so that the pillow is solid and firm.

FINISHING

1. Fold in the seam allowances at the opening and pin together. Hand stitch closed with a slipstitch.

2. Cover your buttons following the manufacturer's instructions.

3. Tie a knot at the end of the pearl cotton thread and loop it through the shank of the covered button to secure it.

4. Using the marking on the front as a guide, push the needle through to the back of the pillow to create the tuft in the front. Pull it taught, but not too taught!

5. Thread the needle through the regular button on the back to create an anchor and stitch the buttons securely.

6. Wrap the thread around the button's stitches a few times and end with a few knots.

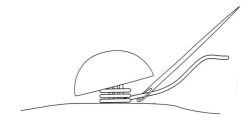

Quatrefoil Pillow

Finished pillow: 18″ × 18″ (45.7 × 45.7cm)

Round out your trio of pillows with a quirky shape and a quick pop of color.

MATERIALS

Yardages are based on 40″ (1m)-wide fabric.

Cotton, linen, or canvas: ⅝ yard (57.2cm)

Cotton print for buttons: 4 scraps at least 3″ × 3″ (7.6 × 7.6cm)

Dritz cover buttons: 4, size 45 (1⅛″ [2.9cm])

Buttons: 4 standard, ½″ (12mm)

Pearl cotton thread

Fiber fill: 32 ounce bag

Quatrefoil Pillow template (page 118)

Paper or cardstock for templates

Cutting

COTTON, LINEN, OR CANVAS

Cut 2 squares 19″ × 19″ (48.3 × 48.3cm).

Construction

Seam allowances are ½″ (12mm) unless otherwise noted.

PREPARING PATTERN PIECES

1. Press the fabric.

2. Trace the template onto paper or cardstock and cut out.

3. Fold the fabric squares in half. Align the template along the fold, as indicated on the template. Trace the template onto the wrong side of each square using a water-soluble fabric pen and then cut out along the traced lines. Cut out 2 pieces for the pillow body.

4. Transfer markings for button placement.

ASSEMBLING THE PILLOW

1. Line up the edges, right sides together, and pin.

2. Stitch together around the perimeter of the pillow, stopping to pivot at the corners, leaving a 3″ (7.6cm) opening for turning. Make sure to start and stop with a backstitch.

3. Clip seam allowance along curves and trim the corners. Turn pillow right side out.

4. Fill with fiber fill really well so that the pillow is solid and firm.

FINISHING

1. Fold in the seam allowances at the opening and pin together. Hand stitch closed with a slipstitch.

2. Cover your buttons following the manufacturer's instructions.

3. Tie a knot at the end of the pearl cotton thread and loop it through the shank of the covered button to secure it.

4. Using the markings on the front as a guide, push the needle through to the back of the pillow to create the tuft in the front. Pull it taught, but not too taught!

5. Thread the needle through the regular button on the back to create an anchor and stitch the buttons securely.

6. Wrap the thread around the button's stitches a few times and end with a few knots.

7. Repeat this step with the remaining buttons and your pillow is complete!

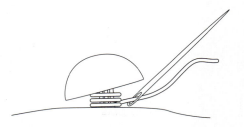

Scrappy Wall Hanging

Finished quilt: 24″ × 24″ (61 × 61cm)

This modern patchwork wall hanging design features a vibrant, geometric circle divided into four quadrants, each showcasing a different color palette. Set against a light background, the contrasting colors and clean lines make this piece a striking statement in any space. This project is perfect for using up some of those scraps you have in your stash!

MATERIALS

Yardages are based on 40″ (1m)-wide fabric.

Cotton print: 20 scraps, at least 3″ × 5″ (7.6 × 12.7cm)

Cotton print: 44 scraps, at least 3″ × 3″ (7.6 × 7.6cm)

Cotton for background: ¾ yard (68.6cm) solid color

Cotton for backing: ¾ yard (68.6cm) solid color

Batting: ¾ yard (68.6cm)

Scrappy Wall Hanging templates (page 119)

Paper or cardstock for templates

SCRAPPY WALL HANGING

Cutting

COTTON PRINT

Cut 20 strips 2½" × 4¼" (6.4 × 10.8cm).

Cut 44 squares 2½" × 2½" (6.4 × 6.4cm).

COTTON BACKGROUND

Cut 4 squares 12½" × 12½" (31.8 × 31.8cm).

COTTON BACKING

Cut 1 square 24½" × 24½" (62.2 × 62.2cm).

BATTING

Cut 1 square 24½" × 24½" (62.2 × 62.2cm).

Construction

Seam allowances are ¼" (6mm) unless otherwise noted.

PREPARING PATTERN PIECES

1. Press the fabric.

2. Trace each template onto paper or cardstock and cut out.

3. Trace the template B pieces 4 times onto the wrong side of the background fabric with a water-soluble fabric pen and then cut them out along the traced lines.

4. Set aside.

CREATE THE PATCHWORK PIE SECTIONS

1. Arrange your squares and rectangles as shown.

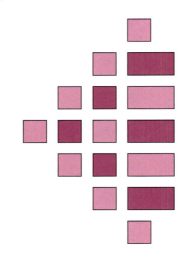

2. Sew the squares and rectangles into rows, then press the seam allowances in each row in opposite directions.

3. Sew the rows together, pressing the seams open.

4. Using the template A, trim the section as shown, being sure to cut ¼" (6mm) away from the center points where the patchwork meets.

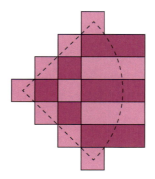

ZAKKA SEWN

ASSEMBLE THE BLOCKS

The straight edges of the templates have an extra ¼″ (6mm) of seam allowance to allow a bit of wiggle room when trimming to the final block size.

1. Align the curved edge of the colored pie shape with the curved edge of the background piece. Pin or clip the curves to keep everything aligned as you sew.

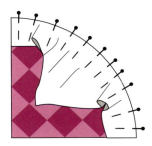

2. Carefully sew the two pieces together.

3. Press the seam allowance toward the colored fabric. Trim to measure 12½″ × 12½″ (31.8 × 31.8cm).

4. Repeat Steps 1–3 to create the other 3 blocks.

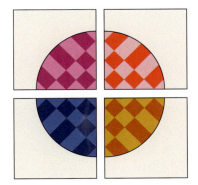

ASSEMBLE THE QUILT TOP

1. Lay out the 4 blocks in the correct orientation to form the center circle.

2. Sew the blocks together as shown to complete the quilt top. Press the seams open.

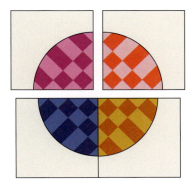

3. Layer in this order: batting, quilt top (right side up), and backing (right side down). Line up all of the edges and pin or clip the layers together.

4. Stitch around the perimeter, leaving at least a 3″ (7.6cm) opening along one side for turning.

5. Clip the corners and then turn the wall hanging right side out. Push out the corners using a point turner, knitting needle, or similarly-shaped object.

FINISHING

1. Tuck in the opening seam allowances ¼″ (6mm), and press. Hand sew the opening closed using a slipstitch.

2. Quilt as desired.

Floral Wall Hanging

Finished quilt: 10″ × 18″ (25.4 × 45.7cm)

A modern wall hanging with a floral design. If you follow my fabric design work, you'll know that I love to include geometric-inspired florals. This favorite flower shape will pretty up your wall and is so simple to make.

MATERIALS

Yardages are based on 40″ (1m)-wide fabric.

Solid color cotton for appliqué:
3 off-white scraps at least 3″ × 5″ (7.6 × 12.7cm),
1 gold scrap at least 3″ × 3″ (7.6 × 7.6cm),
1 orange scrap at least 7″ × 10″ (17.8 × 25.4cm)

Linen or cotton for background and backing:
½ yard (45.7cm), or 2 fat quarters

Batting: ½ yard (45.7cm)

MATERIALS continued

Binding: ⅛ yard (11.4cm)

Hera marker

Matching thread

Appliqué needle

Floral Wall Hanging templates (pages 119-121)

Freezer paper

Basting glue

Spray starch

Paintbrush

Small bowl

NOTE In place of the circle templates, I used Perfect Circles brand templates to make the dots on these flowers. Made of heat-resistant plastic, they make creating circles for appliqué much easier.

Cutting

LINEN OR COTTON FOR BACKING AND BACKGROUND

Cut 2 rectangles 11″ × 20″ (27.9 × 50.8cm).

BINDING

Cut 2 strips 1½″ (3.8cm) x width of fabric.

BATTING

Cut 1 rectangle 11″ × 20″ (27.9 × 50.8cm).

Construction

Seam allowances are ¼″ (6mm) unless otherwise noted.

PREPARING APPLIQUÉ SHAPES

1. Press the fabric.

2. Trace the templates onto the paper side of the freezer paper.

3. Carefully cut out the shapes from the freezer paper. To create a more sturdy template, layer 2 more pieces of freezer paper underneath your shapes, paper side up and iron them together with a hot, dry iron.

4. Place the freezer paper shiny side down onto the wrong side of your appliqué fabric. Press it with a hot, dry iron to temporarily fuse it to the fabric.

5. Cut the fabric around the freezer paper template, adding a ¼″ (6mm) seam allowance around the edges.

6. Clip the seam allowance slightly around the curves and especially in the valleys of the petals to help them lay flat. Be careful not to clip too close to the freezer paper.

7. Spray a little starch into a small bowl (or even the cap). Using a small paintbrush, lightly apply the starch to the seam allowance.

8. Gently fold the seam allowance over the edge of the freezer paper template. Press the folded seam with a hot iron to hold it in place. Continue folding and pressing the fabric around the entire shape.

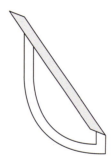

9. Carefully peel the freezer paper away from the fabric and press the fabric again to help it retain its new shape.

PREPARING THE BACKGROUND

1. Layer in this order: backing (right side down), batting, and quilt top (right side up). Line up all of the edges and baste or pin the layers together.

2. Using a Hera marker and an acrylic ruler, mark vertical lines approximately every ¾″ (1.9cm) on the assembled top.

3. Beginning at the center, use a walking foot and a straight stitch to machine-quilt the wall hanging along the center line you just marked. Then, work your way out toward the edges. Remove the basting stitches with a seam ripper.

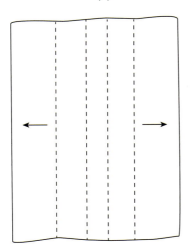

4. Square up the edges and set aside.

5. Trim the wall hanging to 10″ × 18″ (25.4 × 45.7cm).

ADDING THE APPLIQUÉ SHAPES

1. Using the appliqué placement guide, position the appliqué shapes starting with the leaves, then the stem, and lastly the petals and the dots onto your background fabric.

2. Use tiny dots of basting glue to hold them in place. Press the appliqué onto the background fabric with a warm iron to temporarily secure it.

3. Thread an appliqué needle with matching thread and knot the end. Be sure to use matching thread for each portion of the flower. Stitching only through the top layer of the quilted background, bring your needle up through the fold of the appliqué shape.

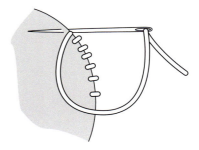

4. Using a small, invisible stitch such as a slip stitch, hand stitch around the entire shape, keeping your stitches about ⅛″ (3mm) apart. Repeat this with all of the remaining flower sections and end with a knot. Bury the knot under the shape.

ADDING THE BINDING

1. Following the instructions in Making Binding (page 23) to make the binding for your quilt.

2. Following the steps in Attaching Binding with Mitered Corners (page 25), attach the binding to the quilt.

Dune Door Stop

Finished door stop: 5″ wide x 3½″ tall x 2″ deep (12.7 × 8.9 × 5.1cm), not including handle

With a fun little shape and a convenient handle this door stop shows off a favorite print while serving a useful purpose. Even if your doors stay open on their own, you'll want to make a few of these to brighten up your space. It would make a great pattern weight as well!

MATERIALS

Yardages are based on 40″ (1m)-wide fabric.

Cotton or canvas fabric: ¼ yard (23cm) or one fat quarter

Leather strap: 5½″ × ¼″ (14 × 6mm)

2½ cups (6.25ml) rice, dried beans, or poly beads

2 Chicago screws, 6mm with 5mm posts

Pencil or leather marking pen

Awl

Optional: leather screw punch

Dune Door Stop template (page 120)

Paper or cardstock for templates

Cutting

COTTON OR CANVAS PRINT FABRIC
Cut 1 rectangle 7″ × 16″ (17.8 × 40.6cm).

Construction

Seam allowances are ¼″ (6mm) unless otherwise noted.

PREPARING PATTERN PIECES

1. Press the fabric.

2. Trace each template onto paper or cardstock and cut out.

3. Trace each template onto the wrong side of the fabric using a water-soluble fabric pen. Repeat for the number of fabric pieces indicated on the template and then cut out along the traced lines.

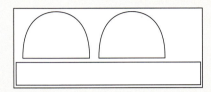

4. Label each piece of fabric on the wrong side and transfer all markings using a water-soluble fabric pen.

DUNE DOOR STOP

PREPARING THE OUTER STRIP

1. With an awl, make the holes for the Chicago screws on the fabric strip using your pattern markings as a guide.

2. Fold the strip right sides together, lining up the short edges. Stitch about ½" (12mm) on each edge and backstitch, which leaves a 1½" (3.8cm) opening for turning. Press the seams out flat.

ASSEMBLING THE DOOR STOP

1. Pin 1 outer panel A to the strip, lining up the markings. Stitch around the perimeter removing pins as you go. Repeat with the second panel A.

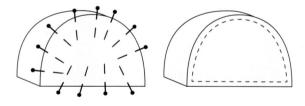

2. Clip the seam allowance of the curves and trim the corners.

3. Turn the door stop inside out and poke out the corners.

ATTACHING THE LEATHER STRAP

1. Using the Dune Door Stop template as a guide, mark the holes ¾" (1.9cm) from each end on the leather strap piece with a pencil or leather marking pen.

2. Cut the holes using an awl or a leather screw punch.

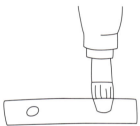

3. Following the manufacturer's directions, attach the leather handle to the door stop body by inserting the top of the Chicago screws through the holes in the leather strap and the backs through the door stop body.

FINISHING

1. Fill the bag with rice, dried beans, or poly beads through the opening at the bottom. Be sure to fill really well so that the doorstop is solid and firm.

2. Hand stitch the opening closed using a slip stitch.

Knotted Door Decor

Finished size: 2½″ × 11½″ (6.4 × 29.2cm)

Door knobs need love too! This simple, yet complex-looking project adds a touch of movement to a plain door and can help tie your decor together. The fun and flirty pom poms lend a little playfulness.

MATERIALS

Yardages are based on 40″ (1m)-wide fabric.

Cotton fabric: ⅛ yard (11.4cm)

Cotton cording: 1¼ yards (1.2m) of ⅜″ (1cm) cord

Matching yarn: approximately 30 yards (27.6m) worsted weight

Loop turner

Tape

1⅝″ (4.1cm) pom pom maker, I used the small 45mm Clover Pom Pom Maker

Cutting

COTTON PRINT FABRIC

Cut 1 strip, 2″ (5.1cm) x width of fabric (WOF).

COTTON CORDING

Cut a 40″ (1m) piece of cord.

Wrap tape around one end of the piece of cord to keep the end from fraying. This will make it easier to insert the cording into the casing.

Construction

Seam allowances are ¼″ (6mm) unless otherwise noted.

COVERING COTTON CORDING

1. Fold the fabric strip in half lengthwise, right sides together. Line up the long edges and pin together. Stitch along the long edge of the fabric strip.

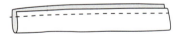

2. Turn the casing right side out using a loop turner and press to remove any wrinkles.

3. Insert the loop turner into one end of the casing, thread it through the casing, and out the other end.

4. Hook the end of the loop turner onto the taped end of the cording and pull the cord all the way through the casing.

CREATING THE DECORATIVE KNOT

Fold the fabric-covered cord in half and carefully tie into a decorative knot using the illustration as a guide. Allow enough of a top loop to fit your door handle.

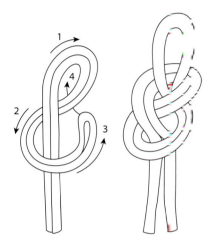

FINISHING THE DOOR DECORATION

1. Following the manufacturer's instructions create 2 pom poms using the pom pom maker. Trim the pom pom to even it out.

2. With needle and thread, attach the pom poms to both ends of the door decoration.

3. Hook it onto your doorknob and enjoy!

49

KNOTTED DOOR DECOR

Brilliance Quilt

Finished quilt: 60″ × 60″ (1.9 × 1.9m)

I was so excited to use my newest Ruby Star Society Speckled fabric colors for this! You could turn a stack of solids into a collage of checkerboards and stipes that provide a burst of color.

MATERIALS

Yardages are based on 40″ (1m)-wide fabric.

Cotton solids or blenders: ⅔ yard (61cm) each of 9 various dark and light color pairs (18 colors total)

Backing: 4 yards (3.7m)

Batting: 4 yards (3.7m)

Binding: ⅝ yard (57.2cm)

Matching thread

Cutting

COTTON SOLIDS OR BLENDERS

Cut each color into a rectangle 15″ × 24″ (38.1 × 61cm).

Subcut each rectangle into 5 strips 2½″ × 24″ (6.4 × 61cm).

BINDING

Cut 7 strips 2½″ (6.4cm) x width of fabric.

Construction

Seam allowances are a scant ¼″ (6mm) unless otherwise noted.

CREATE THE BLOCKS

1. Sew 5 pairs of matching 2½″ × 24″ (6.4 × 61cm) strips to form a set of 10 alternating stripes. It will measure 24″ × 20½″ (61 × 52.1cm).

BRILLIANCE QUILT

2. Repeat Step 1 with the remaining strips to create 9 striped strip sets 24˝ × 20½˝ (61 × 52.1cm).

3. From each strip set cut 6 strips 2½˝ × 20½˝ (6.4 × 52.1cm). Trim the remaining panel to 8½˝ × 20½˝ (21.6 × 52.1cm).

4. Join 3 strips 2½˝ × 20½˝ (6.4 × 52.1cm), flipping the center strip so that the colors alternate like a checkerboard to create a new 30 patch block that will measure 6½˝ × 20½˝ (16.5 × 52.1cm).

5. Repeat step 4 with the remaining sets of 3 strips.

6. From each dark and light color pair you will have 2 checkerboard blocks and 1 striped block.

7. Using the quilt assembly diagram as a guide, sew together 2 checkerboard blocks and 1 striped block to form one block 20½˝ × 20½˝ (52.1 × 52.1cm). Make 9 blocks.

QUILT ASSEMBLY

1. Lay out the 9 blocks as shown in the quilt assembly diagram. Sew together the blocks to form horizontal rows and press the seam allowances to opposite sides.

2. Sew the rows together and press the seam allowances to one side.

3. Layer in this order: backing (right side down), batting, and quilt top (right side up). Baste. Quilt as desired.

ADDING THE BINDING

1. Follow the instructions in Making Binding (page 23) to make the binding.

2. Follow the instructions in Attaching Binding with Mitered Corners (page 25), to attach the binding to your quilt.

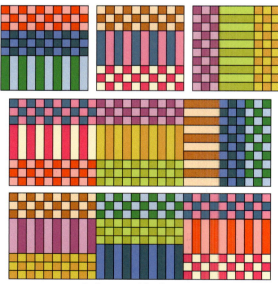

Quilt assembly diagram.

Circle Gets a Square Quilt

Finished quilt: 68˝ × 68˝ (173 × 173cm)

This simple yet stunning quilt is the perfect way to showcase some favorite scraps. It features fabric from all of the designers and guest designers of Ruby Star Society!

MATERIALS

Yardages are based on 40˝ (1m)-wide fabric.

Cotton print for accent fabric: 36 various scraps at least 4˝ × 14˝ (10.2 × 35.6cm)

Background fabric: 4⅛ yards (3.8m)

Backing: 4⅜ yards (4.1m)

Batting: 4⅜ yards (4.1m)

Binding: ⅝ yard (57.2cm)

Matching thread

Circle Gets a Square Templates (pages 120–121)

Cutting

BACKGROUND FABRIC

Cut 9 squares 12½″ × 12½″ (31.8 × 31.8cm).

Cut 16 squares 8½″ × 8½″ (21.6 × 21.6cm).

Cut 24 rectangles 8½″ × 12½″ (21.6 × 31.8cm).

COTTON PRINT FABRIC

Cut 36 rectangles 4″ × 14″ (10.2 × 35.6cm).

BINDING

Cut 8 strips 2½″ (6.4cm) x width of fabric.

Construction

Seam allowances are ¼″ (6mm) unless otherwise noted.

PREPARING PATTERN PIECES

1. Press the fabric.

2. Trace each template onto paper or cardstock and cut out. You can use template plastic in place of cardboard for increased durability.

PREPARING THE BACKGROUND PIECES

1. Take 12 rectangles 12½″ × 8½″ (31.8 × 21.6cm) and trace template A onto the wrong side of the fabric using a water-soluble fabric pen and then cut out along the traced lines. Set aside.

2. Take 12 rectangles 12½″ × 8½″ (31.8 × 21.6cm) and trace template B onto the wrong side of the fabric using a water-soluble fabric pen and then cut out along the traced lines. Set aside.

PREPARING THE ACCENT PIECES

Take the 36 rectangles 4″ × 14″ (10.2 × 35.6cm) and trace template C onto the wrong side of the fabric using a water-soluble fabric pen and then cut cut along the traced lines. Set aside.

BLOCK ASSEMBLY

1. Fold 12 A and C pieces in half widthwise to find the center. Finger press to make a crease.

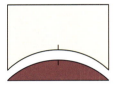

2. Line up the center creases edges of an A and a C right sides together and pin.

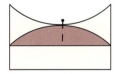

3. Match the ends and pin in place along the curve.

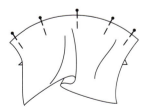

4. Set your stitch length to 1.5 to 1.8 (17–14 stitches to the inch) and if possible, set your machine to a needle down position.

CIRCLE GETS A SQUARE QUILT

Place piece A on top and stitch slowly and carefully with a scant ¼″ (6mm) seam allowance to allow for a little wiggle room to smooth the gathers. Take your time and stop to raise your presser foot and smooth out and gathers if necessary.

5. Repeat Step 4 with the 11 remaining A and C pairs to create a total of 12 A/C blocks. Press the seam allowances toward the accent piece C. Sew slowly and accurately and your blocks will measure 8½″ × 12½″ (21.6 × 31.8cm).

6. Repeat Steps 1–5 with the remaining B and C pieces, sewing an accent to both sides of the rectangle to create a total of 12 B/C blocks. Press the seam allowances toward the accent fabric. Sew slowly and accurately and your blocks will measure 8½″ × 12½″ (21.6 × 31.8cm).

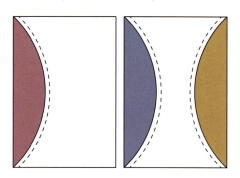

QUILT ASSEMBLY

1. Lay out the blocks and the 12½″ × 12½″ (31.8 × 31.8cm) and 8½″ × 8½″ (21.6 × 21.6cm) background squares as shown in the quilt assembly diagram. Sew together the blocks to form horizontal rows and press the seam allowances to one side, alternating each row.

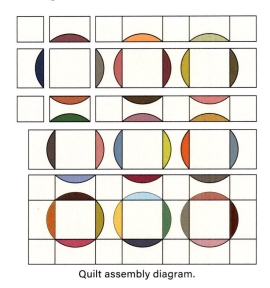

Quilt assembly diagram.

2. Sew the rows together and press the seam allowances to one side to finish the quilt top.

3. Layer in this order: backing (right side down), batting, and quilt top (right side up). Baste. Quilt as desired.

ADDING THE BINDING

1. Follow the instructions in Making Binding (page 23) to make the binding.

2. Follow the instructions in Attaching Binding with Mitered Corners (page 25), attach the binding to your quilt.

KITCHEN

Kaya Produce Bags

Finished bag:
Large 12″ × 14″ (30.5 × 35.6cm) • Medium 10″ × 12″ (25.4 × 30.5cm) • Small 8″ × 10″ (20.3 × 25.4cm)

Using the Japanese mosquito netting allows your produce to breathe. The colorful casings make them a pretty addition to any shopping trip.

MATERIALS

Yardages are based on 40″ (1m)-wide fabric.

Japanese cotton mosquito net fabric (Kaya cloth): Large ½ yard (45.7cm), medium and small ⅓ yard (30.5cm)

Cotton print fabric: ¼ yard (23cm) all sizes

Cotton cord: ⅛″ (3mm) cord, large and medium ½ yard (45.7cm), small ⅓ yard (30.5cm)

Cutting

JAPANESE COTTON MOSQUITO NET FABRIC

Large: Cut 1 rectangle 13″ × 27½″ (33 × 69.9cm).

Medium: Cut 1 rectangle 11″ × 23½″ (27.9 × 59.7cm).

Small: Cut 1 rectangle 9″ × 19½″ (22.8 × 49.5cm).

COTTON PRINT

Large: Cut 2 strips 2½″ × 13″ (6.4 × 33cm).

Medium: Cut 2 strips 2½″ × 11″ (6.4 × 27.9cm).

Small: Cut 2 strips 2½″ × 9″ (6.4 × 22.9cm).

COTTON CORD

Large: Cut a 16″ (40.6cm) piece.

Medium: Cut a 14″ (35.6cm) piece.

Small: Cut a 12″ (30.5cm) piece.

Construction

Seam allowances are ½″ (1.2cm) unless otherwise noted.

MAKING THE CASINGS

1. Fold the long edge of one strip under ½″ (1.2cm) toward the wrong side of the fabric and press. Repeat with the second strip.

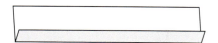

2. Place the 2 strips right sides together with the folded edges at the bottom. Pin the short ends together.

3. Stitch each end together at the top and bottom about ⅜″ (1cm), backstitching to secure, leaving an opening in the middle for the cording. Press the seam allowances open. Topstitch along either side of the openings.

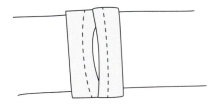

4. Set the casings aside.

MAKING THE BODY

1. Fold the mesh in half widthwise, lining up the sides and top edges; pin together along the sides.

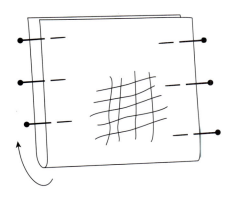

2. Stitch the side seams and then stitch a zig zag stitch along the seams to finish the raw edges.

3. Turn the bag right side out and push out the corners.

ADDING THE CASING

1. Pin the casing to the bag, placing right sides together and lining up the seams. Stitch around the perimeter of the bag.

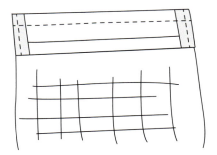

2. Fold the casing up, away from the bag, and press.

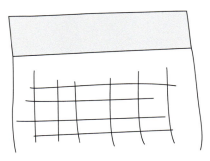

3. Fold the casing down over the raw edges of the bag and pin. Topstitch around the perimeter of the casing.

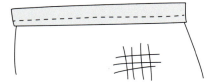

FINISHING

1. Use a loop turner to pull the cording through the casing and tie a knot on the end.

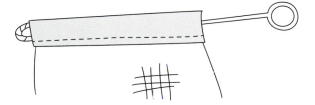

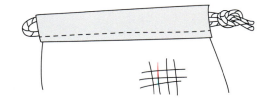

Orange Peel Trivet

Finished trivet: 8˝ (20.3cm) diameter

This lovely little trivet is the perfect way to use up those last scraps of treasured fabric and small pieces of leftover linens. It's also a fun way to feature a beloved traditional quilt design during tea time!

MATERIALS

Yardages are based on 40˝ (1m)-wide fabric.

2 Cotton prints for front piecing: 2 scrap rectangles at least 8˝ × 7˝ (20.3 × 17.8cm)

Linen for background and backing: ⅓ yard (30.5cm)

Batting: ⅓ yard (30.5cm) high loft

Orange Peel Trivet templates (page 120 and 122)

Paper or cardstock for templates

Cutting

COTTON PRINTS FOR FRONT

Cut 2 rectangles 3½″ × 7½″ (8.9 × 19.1cm) from each print.

LINEN

Cut 1 square 11″ × 11″ (30.5 × 30.5cm) for background.

Cut 1 square 9″ × 9″ (22.9 × 22.9cm) square for backing.

BATTING

Cut 2 squares 9″ × 9″ (22.9 × 22.9cm).

Construction

Seam allowances are ¼″ (6mm) unless otherwise noted.

PREPARING PATTERN PIECES

1. Press the fabric.

2. Trace each template onto paper or cardstock and cut out.

3. Trace the peel template onto the wrong side of each cotton print rectangle 2 times using a water-soluble fabric pen and then cut out along the traced lines.

4. Trace the background block template onto the wrong side of a linen background square 4 times using a water-soluble fabric pen and then cut out along the traced lines.

5. Label each piece of fabric on the wrong side and transfer all markings using a water-soluble fabric pen.

ORANGE PEEL TRIVET

CREATE THE BLOCKS

1. Fold a linen background piece and a cotton peel in half making a crease at the center points.

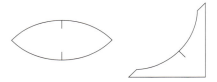

2. Lay one linen piece on top of one cotton piece, right sides together, lining up the creased middle points. Pin or clip together at the center and at the ends. Pin along the seam.

3. Adjust your machine's stitch length to about 1.85 (14 stitches to the inch) and slowly stitch along the curve, removing pins as you go. Clip the seam allowance and press the seam toward the cotton print. Repeat this with the remaining pieces to create a total of 4 units.

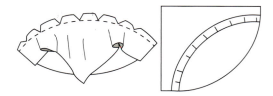

ASSEMBLE THE TRIVET TOP

Square up the blocks and sew each of the units together, pressing the seams open.

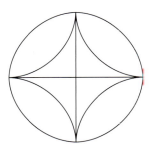

FINISHING

1. Layer in this order: batting pieces, trivet top (right side up), and backing (right side down). Line up all of the edges and pin or clip the layers together.

2. Stitch around the perimeter, leaving at least a 2″ (5.1cm) opening for turning.

3. Trim the batting and clip the seam allowance along the curves and then turn the trivet inside out.

4. Tuck in the seam allowance ¼″ (6mm) at the opening, and press. Hand sew the opening closed using a slipstitch.

5. Hand stitch tufting onto the trivet.

Half Moon Oven Mitt

Finished mitt: 6″ × 6½″ (15.2 × 16.5cm)

Why not protect your hands with a favorite linen print while you bake? This oven mitt comes together quickly and is easier to slip on and off by avoiding a shaped thumb.

MATERIALS

Yardages are based on 40″ (1m)-wide fabric.

Cotton or canvas fabric for outside:
⅜ yard (34.3cm)

Cotton or canvas fabric for lining: ⅜ yard (34.3cm)

Batting: ⅜ yard (34.3cm)

Half Moon Oven Mitt templates (page 122)

Cutting

OUTER FABRIC
Cut 1 rectangle 11″ × 22″ (27.9 × 55.9cm).

LINING
Cut 1 rectangle 11″ × 22″ (27.9 × 55.9cm).

BATTING
Cut 2 rectangles 11″ × 22″ (27.9 × 55.9cm).

BINDING
Cut 2 strips 2″ × 6½″ (5.1 × 16.5cm).

Construction

Seam allowances are ¼″ (6mm) unless otherwise noted.

MAKING A QUILT SANDWICH

Layer in this order: outer fabric (right side down), 2 pieces of batting, and the lining fabric (right side up). Pin or baste the layers together and quilt as desired.

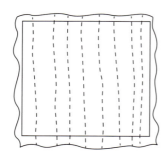

PREPARING PATTERN PIECES

1. Trace each template onto paper or cardstock and cut out.

2. Trace the pattern pieces onto the lining side of the quilt sandwich using a water-soluble pen.

3. Label each piece of fabric on the wrong side and transfer all markings using a water-soluble pen.

4. Cut out the 3 pieces for the oven mitt.

ATTACHING THE BINDING

1. Pin the binding in place, aligning the raw edges of the binding and the bottom of one outer piece of the oven mitt, with right sides together. Sew the layers together.

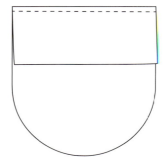

2. Press the binding up toward the seam and then fold it to the back, folding the raw edge under the same width as the seam allowance.

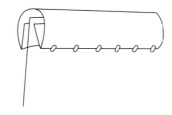

3. Hand stitch the binding to the back.

4. Repeat Steps 1–3 on the second outer oven mitt piece.

ASSEMBLING THE OVEN MITT

1. Place the A and B pieces of the mitt right sides together and pin. Stitch along both sides from the bottom to the notch mark, ending with a backstitch.

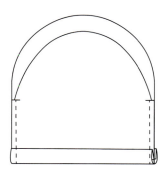

2. Fold back one of the unsewn parts of the oven mitt and align the third oven mitt piece along the top, right sides together, lining up the curves. Pin together. Repeat with the other outer oven mitt piece.

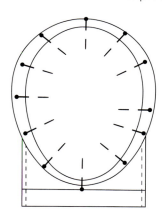

3. Starting at one side, stitch all the way around the curve to the other side.

Repeat to stitch the other curve.

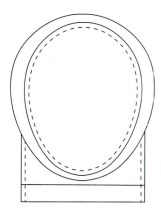

4. Turn the mitt inside out and press.

Crossroads Placemat

Finished placemat: 12˝ × 18˝ (30.5 × 45.7cm)

The patchwork on these placemats is deceptively simple and will add a spot of color to your table. Mix and match the colors on each placemat to really make them unique!

MATERIALS

Yardages are based on 40˝ (1m)-wide fabric.

These instructions will make 4 placemats.

Four cotton prints: ¼ yard (22.9cm)

Linen for background and backing: 1¾ yards (1.7m)

Batting: ⅞ yard (80cm)

Crossroads Placemat template (page 122)

Paper or cardstock for templates

Cutting

COTTON PRINTS

From each print:

Cut 4 strips 1″ × 14″ (2.5 × 35.6cm)

Cut 4 strips 1″ × 8″ (2.5 × 20.3cm)

Cut 8 strips 1″ × 5″ (2.5 × 12.7cm)

Cut 4 squares 1″ × 1″ (2.5 × 2.5cm)

LINEN BACKGROUND AND BACKING

Cut 4 rectangles 13″ × 19″ (33 × 48.3cm)

Cut 4 rectangles 8″ × 14″ (20.3 × 35.6cm)

Cut 4 rectangles 5″ × 14″ (12.7 × 35.6cm)

Cut 4 rectangles 5″ × 8″ (12.7 × 20.3cm)

Cut 4 squares 5″ × 5″ (12.7 × 12.7cm)

BATTING

Cut 4 rectangles 13″ × 19″ (33 × 48.3cm)

Construction

Seam allowances are ¼″ (6mm) unless otherwise noted.

PREPARING PATTERN PIECES

1. Press the fabric.

2. Trace each template onto paper or cardstock and cut out.

3. Set aside.

CREATE THE PATCHWORK SECTIONS

1. Divide each group of strips and squares from 1 print into sets:

A. A 14″ (35.6cm) strip, an 8″ (20.3cm) strip and a 1″ (2.5cm) square

B. An 8″ (20.3cm) strip, a 5″ (12.7cm) strip and a 1″ (2.5cm) square

C. A 14″ (35.6cm) strip, a 5″ (12.7cm) strip and a 1″ (2.5cm) square

D. 2 strips 5″ (12.7cm) and a 1″ (2.5cm) square

2. Select 4 different A, B, C, and D sets for each placemat so that all 4 fabrics will be in each placemat.

3. Place the linen squares and rectangles along with the sets of strips and small squares as shown in the patchwork assembly diagram below.

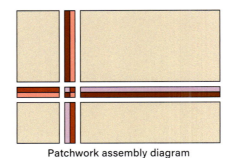

Patchwork assembly diagram

4. Following the diagram, sew the top row together, pressing the seam allowances all to one side.

5. Repeat Step 4 for the remaining 3 rows, pressing the seam allowances in opposite directions so that they nest.

6. Repeat Steps 2–5 for the remaining 3 placemats.

CROSSROADS PLACEMAT

ASSEMBLE THE TOP

1. Sew the rows together pressing the seams toward the cotton print fabric.

2. To find the middle, fold the placemat in half, right sides together and pinch at the top and bottom to create a temporary crease.

3. Place the template on top, lining it up along the folds just created. Trace the template pieces onto the wrong side of the placemat top using a water-soluble fabric pen and then cut out the top along the traced lines.

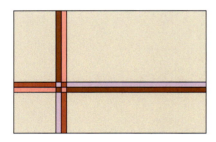

4. Repeat Steps 1–3 for the other three placemat tops.

CREATE THE BACK

1. To find the middle, fold the placemat back in half, right sides together, and pinch at the top and bottom to create a temporary crease.

2. Place the template on top, lining it up along the folds just created. Trace the template pieces onto the wrong side of the placemat back using a water-soluble fabric pen and then cut out the top along the traced lines.

3. Repeat Steps 1–2 for the other three placemat backs.

FINISHING

1. Layer in this order: batting, placemat top (right side up), and backing (right side down). Line up all of the edges and pin or clip the layers together.

2. Stitch around the perimeter, leaving at least a 2″ (5.1cm) opening along the bottom edge for turning.

3. Clip the seam allowance along the curves and then turn the placemat right side out. Push out the edges using a point turner, knitting needle, or similarly-shaped object.

4. Along the opening, tuck in the seam allowance ¼″ (6mm) and press. Hand sew the opening closed using a slipstitch. Topstitch around the perimeter of the placemat.

5. Quilt as desired.

Roundel Napkin Ring

Finished size: 3″ × 2″ (7.6 × 5.1cm)

These harvest-colored napkin rings are so quick to whip up that you'll find yourself assembling a set for every get together. You could even make them to match your Crossroads Placemats.

MATERIALS

Yardages are based on 40″ (~m)-wide fabric.

Makes 4 napkin rings.

Cotton print fabric: 1 fat quarter

Batting: 18″ × 11″ (45.7 × 27.9cm) rectangle

8 Chicago screws, 6mm with 5mm posts

Roundel Napkin Ring template (page 123)

Cutting

COTTON PRINT FABRIC
Cut 8 strips 3″ × 9″ (7.6 × 22.9cm).

BATTING
Cut 4 strips 3″ × 9″ (7.6 × 22.9cm).

Construction

Seam allowances are ¼″ (6mm) unless otherwise noted.

NAPKIN HOLDER ASSEMBLY

1. Press the fabric.

2. Trace the template onto paper or cardstock and cut out.

3. Trace the template onto the wrong sides of 2 of the 3″ × 9″ (7.6 × 22.9cm) strips using a water-soluble marker.

4. Place 2 of the strips right sides together and then layer them on top of a strip of batting. Sew on the traced line, leaving a 2″ (5.1cm) opening for turning. Stitch slowly around the curves.

5. Trim the seam allowance to ⅛″ (3mm) and clip the curves carefully. Turn right side out and press.

6. Hand sew the opening closed.

7. Repeat for the remaining 3 napkin rings.

FINISHING THE NAPKIN RING

1. Quilt the napkin ring as desired.

2. Using an awl, make holes on the napkin holder using the pattern as a guide.

3. Overlap the two ends of the napkin ring and install the Chicago screws, following the manufacturer's instructions.

75
ROUNDEL NAPKIN RING

ACCESSORIES

Favorite Project Pouch

Finished pouch: 10″ diameter × 10½″ tall (25.4 × 26.7cm)

The plethora of pockets is what will make this bag your favorite. It keeps all your tools handy without having to disturb your work in progress looking for what you need.

MATERIALS

Yardages are based on 40″ (1m)-wide fabric.

Canvas for exterior: 1⅛ yard (1.1m)

Cotton print for lining: ⅜ yard (34.3cm)

Cotton print for casing: ⅛ yard (11.4cm)

Cotton cording: 2¼ yards (2.1m)

4 snaps, ½″ (12mm)

Awl

Favorite Project Pouch template (page 123)

Paper or cardstock for templates

Cutting

COTTON PRINT FOR LINING

Cut 2 rectangles 9½″ × 16¾″ (24.1 × 42.5cm).

COTTON PRINT FOR CASING

Cut 2 rectangles 3½″ × 16½″ (8.9 × 41.9cm).

CANVAS

Cut 2 rectangles 3″ × 19½″ (7.6 × 49.5cm) for straps.

Cut 2 rectangles 9½″ × 16¾″ (24.1 × 42.5cm) for exterior.

Cut 2 rectangles 12½″ × 16¾″ (31.8 × 42.5cm) for pockets.

COTTON CORDING

Cut 2 pieces 40″ (1m).

Construction

Seam allowances are ¼″ (6mm) unless otherwise noted.

PREPARING PATTERN PIECES

1. Press the fabric.

2. Trace the template onto paper or cardstock and cut out.

3. Trace the pouch bottom template onto the wrong side of lining and exterior fabrics using a water-soluble fabric pen and then cut out along traced lines. Set aside.

CREATE THE EXTERIOR POCKETS

1. Fold a 12½″ × 16¾″ (31.8 × 42.5cm) canvas rectangle lengthwise wrong sides together and press. Fold again, short ends together, to find the middle and finger press to form a crease down the center.

2. Place folded pocket on top of one 9½″ × 16¾″ (24.1 × 42.5cm) canvas rectangle, lining up the bottom edges, and pin together.

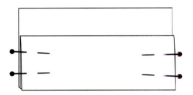

3. Starting from the top of the pocket, make a straight stitch down the middle of the pocket using the crease you made earlier as a guide. Repeat with the remaining 12½″ × 16¾″ (31.8 × 44.5cm) and 9½″ × 16¾″ (24.1 × 42.5cm) canvas rectangles.

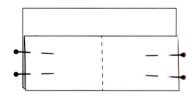

ADDING THE SNAPS

1. Place the exterior panel right side up. Using a water soluble pen, mark a dot ½" (12mm) from the top edge in the center of each pocket for snap placement.

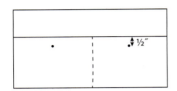

2. Using an awl, punch a hole on each mark through all layers. Install the snap tops and bottoms following the manufacturer's instructions.

CREATE THE BODY

1. Place the exterior rectangles right sides together, line up all edges, and pin. Stitch together along the short ends using a ½" (12mm) seam allowance.

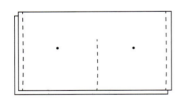

2. Take the round canvas pouch bottom and fold in half to find the center. Finger press along the fold to make a crease. Repeat the the canvas exterior bottom.

3. Line up the canvas bottom and exterior, right sides together, matching the creases and pin together.

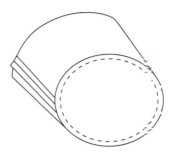

4. Stitch around the perimeter of the bag bottom, removing pins as you go.

5. Repeat steps 1–4 with the lining pieces but leave an opening along one of the side seams for turning.

6. Set the exterior and lining aside.

CREATE THE CASINGS

1. Hem the short ends of the 3½" × 16½" (8.9 × 41.9cm) strips by folding ¼" (6mm) to the wrong side, then fold again. Press and topstitch along the folded edges.

2. Fold in half lengthwise, wrong sides together. Press. Set aside.

CREATE THE STRAPS

1. Take the 19½" × 3" (49.5 × 7.6cm) canvas pieces and fold lengthwise ¾"

(1.5cm) on either side and press. Fold in half lengthwise again and press to create a 19½" × ¾" (49.5 × 1.9cm) strap.

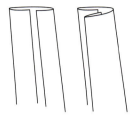

2. Topstitch along both long edges of the straps.

ASSEMBLING THE POUCH

1. Pin the casings to the top edges of the pouch exterior, lining up the raw edges.

2. Next, pin the straps to the exterior on top of the casings and extend the ends about ½" (1.2cm) beyond the raw edges. Make sure to space them out evenly about 4½" (11.4cm) away from the sides seams.

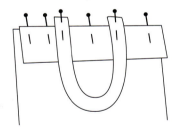

3. Turn the lining wrong side out and slip it over the exterior, lining up the sides seams and the raw edges. Clip or pin together along the top edges.

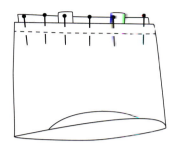

4. Stitch around the top edge of the bag.

5. Turn right side out through the opening and press. Handstitch the opening closed.

6. Topstitch around the top edge of the pouch below the casing.

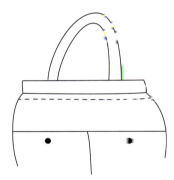

7. Using a loop turner thread the cording through the casing and then back around the other side so that both ends of the cording are on one side. Repeat with the other cord starting on the opposite side of the bag. Tie the ends in a knot.

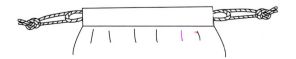

Honeycomb Pencil Case

Finished case: 8″ × 5½″ (20.3 × 14cm)

Keep your writing utensils handy in this subtle yet elegant case. Try your hand on English paper piecing without the headache of tiny pieces when you add the hexagons to the pouch exterior.

MATERIALS

Yardages are based on 40″ (1m)-wide fabric.

Pre-quilted fabric: ⅓ yard (30.5cm)

Linen or cotton print: ⅓ yard (30.5cm) assorted scraps

Optional: Silk thread

1 snap, ½″ (12mm)

Honeycomb Pencil Case template (page 123)

Paper or cardstock for templates

Cutting

PRE-QUILTED FABRIC

Cut 1 rectangle 8½″ × 14½″ (21.6 × 36.8cm).

LINEN OR COTTON PRINT

Cut 3 squares 4¼″ × 4¼″ (10.8 × 10.8cm).

Cut 1 rectangle 14½″ × 8½″ (36.8 × 21.6cm).

Construction

Seam allowances are ¼″ (6mm), unless otherwise noted.

CREATE THE EXTERIOR

1. Take the 8½″ × 14½″ (21.6 × 36.8cm) linen or cotton print and pre-quilted rectangles and place them right sides together, lining up all of the edges.

2. Starting and ending with a backstitch, stitch around the perimeter of the rectangle, leaving an opening for turning on one of the long edges.

HONEYCOMB PENCIL CASE

3. Clip the corners and turn inside out. Push out the corners with a point turner or similarly shaped object. Press.

4. Handstitch the opening closed using a slip stitch. Press and set aside.

PREPARING PATTERN PIECES

1. Press the fabric.

2. Trace each template onto paper or cardstock and cut out.

CREATE THE HEXAGONS

1. Pin one paper template to the wrong side of the desired fabric scrap and cut around the template, leaving ¼″ (6mm) seam allowance on all edges.

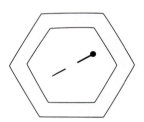

2. Fold the seam allowance over the template at each edge and begin hand-basting the folded edges together. Keep the folded edges neat and the corners crisp, being careful not to sew the fabric to the paper (your stitches should only catch the layers of fabric). You can simply carry the thread between the corners, there is no need to knot and cut the thread until you have completed the stitching. Complete the last fold and baste it in place, then knot and trim the thread; be sure to remove the pin.

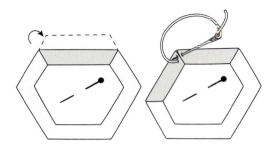

3. Repeat Steps 1 and 2 with the remaining paper templates and fabric squares.

CREATE THE HEXAGON ROW

1. To stitch the shapes together, place 2 of the finished shapes right sides together, aligning them along the edge to be attached.

2. With your needle and thread, whipstitch the 2 shapes together along the edge, being sure to pick up only two or three threads of the fabric with each stitch. Using such tiny stitches will keep the stitching virtually invisible. Do not stitch through the paper and try to keep the stitching as close to the edge of the shapes as possible. I like to use silk thread for this. It's finer, stronger, and the stitches are almost invisible.

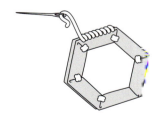

3. When you get to a corner make a few extra stitches to reinforce the seam. Once you've finished stitching all the shapes together, press them and then remove the paper templates.

ATTACHING THE HEXAGONS

1. Place the 8″ × 14″ (36.2 × 21.6cm) quilted exterior quilted side up. Pin the hexagons to the panel on the lower right side, lining up the bottom edges and about ½″ (12mm) in from the right.

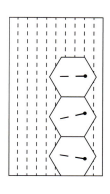

2. Hand sew the hexagon row to the pencil case, using a blindstitch around the outer edges to secure it to the case. Remove the pins.

FINISHING

1. Place the quilted exterior right side up. Using a water soluble pen and a ruler, find the center of the pencil case and mark with a dot ⅝″ (1.6cm) from the top and a dot 1¾″ (4.4cm) up from the bottom.

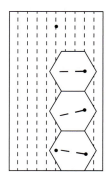

2. Use an awl to punch a hole at the marks through all of the layers.

3. Turn the pouch over, lining side up and fold the bottom up in the center of the middle hexagon and pin or clip on the sides.

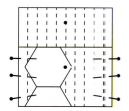

4. Topstitch the pouch on three sides through all layers creating the pencil pouch.

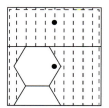

5. Finish by installing the snaps on the front of the exterior panel and the interior pocket following the manufacturer's instructions.

Capsule Bag

Finished bag: 17″ wide x 13″ tall x 7¼″ deep (43.2 × 33 × 18.4cm) (not including straps)

Sometimes you need an extra bag for all of that fabric you buy. This compact travel bag folds into itself making it easy to have just in case!

MATERIALS

Yardages are based on 40″ (1m)-wide fabric.

Canvas or linen for exterior: 1 yard (91.4cm)

Canvas or linen for outer pocket: ¼ yard (23cm)

Cotton for binding: ½ yard (45.7cm)

Webbing for handles, 1½″-(3.8cm) wide: 1 yard (91.4cm)

Zipper, 25″ (63.5cm)

Reversible Zipper, 17½″ (44.5cm)

Capsule Bag templates (page 124)

Paper or cardstock for templates

Cutting

COTTON OR LINEN FOR EXTERIOR

Cut 2 rectangles 14″ × 18″ (35.6 × 45.7cm) for the body.

Cut 1 rectangle 7¾″ × 30½″ (19.7 × 77.5cm) for bag bottom.

Cut 2 rectangles 4″ × 25″ (10.2 × 63.5cm) for zipper panel.

Cut 1 rectangle 8″ × 9″ (20.3 × 22.9cm) for pocket.

Cut 2 squares 1½″ × 1½″ (3.8 × 3.8cm) for tabs.

CANVAS OR LINEN FOR OUTER POCKET

Cut 1 rectangle 8″ × 9″ (20.3 × 22.9cm) for pocket.

Cut 2 squares 1½″ × 1½″ (3.8 × 3.8cm) for tabs.

BINDING

Cut 6 strips 2″ (5.1cm) of bias binding; subcut 2 pieces 7¾″ (19.7cm).

WEBBING

Cut 2 pieces 1½″ × 18″ (3.8 × 45.7cm).

Construction

Seam allowances are ¼" (6mm) unless otherwise noted.

PREPARING PATTERN PIECES

1. Press the fabric.

2. Trace each template onto paper or cardstock and cut out.

3. Trace the templates onto the wrong side of the fabric using a water-soluble fabric pen and then cut out along the traced lines. Repeat for the number of fabric pieces indicated on the templates. Set aside.

4. Transfer the markings for the pocket and handle placement onto the right side of the exterior panels.

MAKE THE HANDLES

1. Fold the 1½" × 18" (3.8 × 45.7cm) webbing pieces in half lengthwise.

2. Starting 4" (10.2cm) from one end, topstitch each webbing handle together along the outer edge for 10" (25.4cm). Set aside.

CREATING THE ZIPPER PANEL

1. Take a 4" × 25" (10.2 × 63.5cm) rectangle and fold back one long edge ⅜" (1cm) and press.

2. Place the folded edge on top of the 25" (63.5cm) zipper and pin. Using a zipper foot, topstitch the rectangle to the zipper along the folded edge, removing pins as you go.

3. Repeat along the other side of the zipper with the other 4¾" × 25" (12.1 × 63.5cm) rectangle.

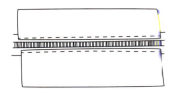

ASSEMBLE THE BOTTOM PANEL

1. Place the short ends of the zipper panel and the 7¾" × 30½" (19.7 × 77.5cm) rectangle right sides together and pin. Stitch each end together, removing pins as you go.

2. Attach the short bias binding strips to the 7¾" (19.7cm) raw edge seams. Set aside.

ADDING TABS TO THE REVERSIBLE ZIPPER

1. Place 1 outer tab square 1¾" × 1¾" (4.4 × 4.4cm) right side up.

2. Place the end of the reversible zipper, right side up, on top, lining up the bottom and right edges so that there is a ½" (12mm) of seam allowance of the tab exposed at the top.

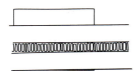

3. Place 1 inner tab square 1¾" × 1¾" (4.4 × 4.4cm) on top of the zipper, right side down, lining up the edges as before, making a sandwich.

4. Stitch the 2 tabs together, just outside the edge of the zipper making sure not to stitch through it. Stop about a ¼" (6mm) away from the end. With the needle down, raise the presser foot and turn the zipper. Lower the presser foot and finish stitching, this time through all the layers being careful not to hit the teeth with the needle.

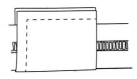

5. Pull the tabs right sides out over the end of the zipper.

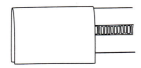

6. Repeat Steps 1-5 on the other end of the zipper with the remaining tabs.

CREATING THE ZIPPER POCKET

1. Fold the inner pocket and outer pocket pieces crosswise and fold them in half lengthwise to find the center. Make a tiny snip at the top. Place them right sides together.

2. Fold the zipper in half to find the center. Pin the zipper in between the pocket pieces, matching the center marks and the raw edges, and placing the side of the zipper with the finished seam facing away from the pocket pieces.

3. Stitch the zipper sandwich together using a ¼" (3mm) seam allowance. Open the zipper. I find it easier to stitch and pin zippers on curves with the zipper open. Take your time and stitch slowly. It may help to use a tool, for example a tweezer, to grip the pocket as you sew. I also prefer to stitch from the center top out towards one side and then flip it and repeat on the other side. Stop sewing ½" (12mm) from the ends of the zipper. With the needle down, lift the presser foot and pull the pocket pieces and pivot the zipper to form a corner. Place the presser foot down again and then finish the stitching the last ½" (12mm) of the zipper.

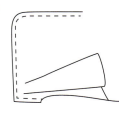

4. Turn the pocket right side out. Fold in the raw edges of the pocket ¼" (6mm) at the bottom and press.

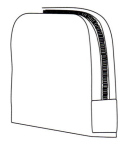

ATTACHING THE POCKET

1. Using the marking on the front as a guide, pin the pocket to the front of the exterior panel with your desired side facing out. Make sure to line up both of the pocket's bottom edges.

2. Topstitch the pocket to the front panel pivoting at the bottom corners with the needle down.

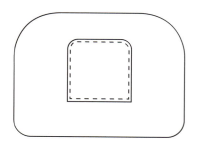

FINISHING

1. Fold the exterior panels and the zipper panels in half to find their centers and make a tiny clip.

2. Using the markings as a guide, pin the webbing handles to the exterior panels of the bag.

3. Next pin the zipper panel to the exterior panels right sides together using the tiny clip as a centering guide.

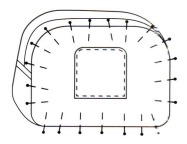

4. Stitch the bag together around the perimeter of the two panels and remove pins as you go.

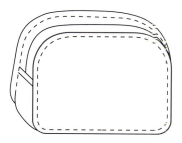

5. Piece the 6 strips of bias binding to make 116" (1.9m) of 2" (5.1cm)-wide bias binding See Making Bias Binding (page 24). Attach the bias binding to cover both of the raw edge seams on the interior of the bag.

Ingot Pincushion

Finished: 4˝ long x 2¼˝ deep x 1¾˝ tall (10.2 × 5.7 × 4.4cm)

Shaped like a tiny gold treasure, this pincushion isn't just practical, it's perfect for holding your pins and needles in style. This pattern is simple but could be upgraded a notch with some patchwork and/or quilting. This one is filled with emery to add weight, but you could certainly use ground walnut shells.

MATERIALS

Yardages are based on 40˝ (7m)-wide fabric.

Cotton canvas or linen: 1 scrap at least 8˝ × 9˝ (20.3 × 22.9cm)

Emery sand or ground walnut shells for filling: 1 cup

Ingot Pincushion template (page 124)

Cutting

COTTON CANVAS OR LINEN

Cut 1 square 8″ × 9″ (20.3 × 22.9cm).

Construction

Seam allowances are ¼″ (6mm) unless otherwise noted.

PREPARING PATTERN PIECES

1. Press the fabric.

2. Trace each template onto paper or cardstock and cut out.

3. Trace the pattern piece onto the wrong side of the fabric using a water-soluble pen.

ASSEMBLING THE PINCUSHION

1. Line up the short sides, right sides together, and pin.

2. Stitch the 4 short sides together starting from the top of the pincushion making sure to stop and backstitch ¼″ (6mm) away from the bottom edge.

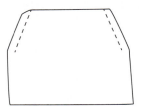

3. Pin the bottom edges and stitch around the bottom of the pincushion stopping and pivoting at the corners. Leave one end open for turning and filling.

FINISHING

1. Turn the pincushion right side out. Finger press the top and bottom edges to create a crease.

2. Fill with emery sand or ground shells. Be sure to fill really well so that the pincushion is solid and firm.

3. Pinch the opening together and hand stitch closed with a slipstitch.

Hey, Lady Sewing Case

Finished case (unfolded): 16½″ × 9″ (16.5 × 22.9cm)

Compact and classy, this little sewing case keeps your supplies at hand then folds up to slip inside your project bag. The drawstring pouch can also be removed! On the go or on the couch, this will be your new favorite accessory.

MATERIALS

Yardages are based on 40″ (1m)-wide fabric.

Cotton print for exterior: 1 fat quarter

Cotton print for interior: ¼ yard (23cm) total assorted scraps (see cutting list for specific dimensions)

Linen for interior: ⅜ yard (34.3cm)

Cord for pouch drawstring: ⅛″ (3mm)-diameter, 1 yard (91.4cm)

Single-sided fusible foam stabilizer for batting: ⅓ yard (30.5cm) (I used Pellon FlexFoam)

Cotton print for bias binding: ½ yard (45.7cm)

Zipper, 9″ (22.9cm)

2 snaps, ½″ (12mm)

1 sew-in magnetic plastic snap

Sashiko thread

Fiber fill

Awl

Hey, Lady Sewing Case templates (page 125)

Paper or cardstock for templates

Cutting

COTTON PRINT

Cut 1 rectangle 10″ × 17″ (25.4 × 43.2cm) for the exterior.

COTTON PRINT SCRAPS

Cut 2 strips 1¼″ × 9″ (3.2 × 22.9cm) for the zipper panel.

Cut 1 rectangle 2½″ × 3½″ (6.4 × 8.9cm) for the needle minder.

Cut 1 rectangle 2¾″ × 5″ (7 × 12.7cm) for the pin cushion.

Cut 2 rectangles 4″ × 6″ (10.2 × 15.2cm) for the pouch exterior.

Cut 1 square 6″ × 6″ (15.2 × 15.2cm) for the pouch interior.

Cut 2 strips 2″ × 7½″ (5.1 × 19.1cm) for the pouch casing.

LINEN

Cut 1 rectangle 2½″ × 3½″ (6.4 × 8.9cm) for the needle minder.

Cut 2 rectangles 5½″ × 9″ (14 × 22.9cm) for the interior panel and zipper pocket interior.

Cut 1 rectangle 5½″ × 10″ (14 × 25.4cm) for the folded pocket.

Cut 1 rectangle 5½″ × 7½″ (14 × 19.1cm) for the folded pocket.

Cut 1 rectangle 6½″ × 9″ (16.5 × 22.9cm) for the middle panel.

Cut 1 rectangle 3½″ × 9″ (8.9 × 22.9cm) for the zipper pocket exterior.

STABILIZER

Cut 1 rectangle 10″ × 17″ (25.4 × 43.2cm).

CORDING

Cut 2 pieces 17″ (43.2cm).

BINDING

Cut 3 strips of 2″ (5.1cm)-wide bias binding.

Construction

Seam allowances are ¼″ (6mm) unless otherwise noted.

PREPARING PATTERN PIECES

1. Press the fabric.

2. Trace each template onto paper or cardstock and cut out.

3. Trace the templates onto the wrong side of the fabric using a water-soluble fabric pen and then cut out along the traced lines. Repeat for the number of fabric pieces indicated on the templates. Set aside.

CREATE THE EXTERIOR

Following the manufacturer's instructions, fuse the foam stabilizer to the back of the 10″ × 17″ (25.4 × 43.2cm) cotton print exterior. Quilt as desired. Trim the exterior panel to 9″ × 16½″ (22.9 × 41.9cm) and using the template as a guide, trim the corners.

Create the Zipper Pocket Panel

1. Place one cotton print 1¼˝ × 9˝ (3.2 × 22.9cm) strip right side down along the zipper and pin or clip to the zipper.

2. Switch to a zipper foot and stitch the strip to the zipper. Fold the strip back and press. Topstitch along the folded edge.

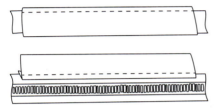

3. Repeat Steps 1 and 2 with the other cotton print 1¼″ × 9″ (3.2 x 22.9cm) strip.

4. With the zipper full on the left, place the 3½″ × 9″ (8.9 × 22.9cm) linen rectangle along the edge of the bottom cotton piece, right sides together, and pin or clip. Stitch the pieces together. Press the seam toward the cotton print. Edge stitch along the seam.

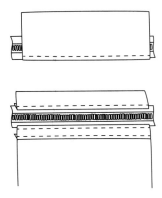

5. Place the top zipper panel cotton piece along the edge of the 5½″ × 9″ (14 × 22.9cm) linen rectangle and line up the edges. Pin or clip together along the short edges and set aside.

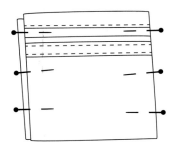

Create the Middle Panel

Measure 3″ (7.6cm) from the bottom of the 6½″ × 9″ (16.5 × 22.9cm) rectangle and place a magnet in the marked position. Stitch around the perimeter of the magnet making a 1″ (2.5cm) square. Set aside.

Create the Pocket Panel

1. Place the remaining 5½″ × 9″ (14 × 22.9cm) linen rectangle right side up.

2. Fold the 5½″ × 10″ (14 × 25.4cm) linen rectangle in half and press to be the upper pocket.

3. Fold the 5½″ × 7½″ (14 × 19.1cm) linen rectangle in half and press to be the lower pocket.

4. Stack the pockets onto the rectangle as shown, lining up the bottom edges and pin or clip together. Stitch through all layers down the middle of the two pockets.

Assemble the Interior

1. Place the middle panel right side down on top of the zipper panel, line up the right edges, and pin or clip together. Stitch together through all of the layers. Press the seam toward the cotton print. Edge stitch along the top of the cotton print.

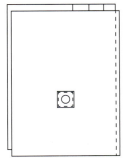

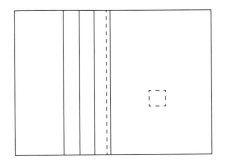

2. Place the pocket panel on top of the middle panel, line up the right edges, and pin or clip together. Stitch together through all of the layers. Press the seam toward the middle panel.

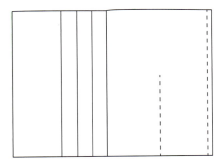

3. Stitch through all layers 1″ (2.5cm) from the left edge of the zipper panel to close the pocket.

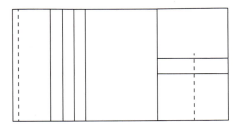

CREATE THE POUCH

1. Take the 2 half-circle pouch exteriors and place them right sides together. Stitch down the flat side leaving a 1½″ (3.8cm) opening at the center. Press the seam open. Set aside.

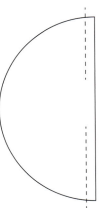

2. Hem the short ends of both of the 2″ × 7½″ (5.1 × 19.1cm) casing strips by folding to the wrong side ¼″ (6mm), then again. Press and topstitch along the folded edges.

3. Fold casing strips in half lengthwise, wrong sides together. Press.

4. Pin the long sides of the casing to the pouch interior, lining up all edges, and pin. There should be a ¼" (6mm) space between the two casing ends. Stitch together using a ⅛" (3mm) seam allowance.

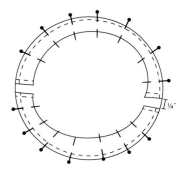

5. Place the pouch exterior on top, right sides together and pin. Stitch together using a ¼" (6mm) seam allowance. Turn right side out.

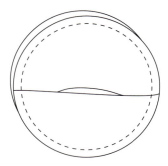

6. Place a magnet inside the open seam at the bottom of the pouch. Close up the open seam with a handstitch.

7. Position the magnet in the center of the pouch bottom and stitch through both cotton layers through the pvc around the magnet to secure it.

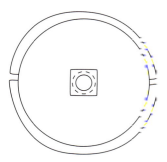

8. Thread each piece of cording through both casings in opposite directions using a loop turner or safety pin and knot the ends.

CREATE THE NEEDLE MINDER

1. Place the 2½" × 3½" (6.4 × 8.9cm) cotton and linen rectangles right sides together and stitch around all sides, leaving an opening for turning.

2. Clip the corners of the seam allowance and turn inside out. Poke out the corners and press.

3. Fold in the seam allowance of the opening and hand stitch closed with a slipstitch.

4. Measure 1½" (3.8cm) down from the top of the middle panel and 1" (2.5cm) from the left seam. Pin the needle minder in this position. Edge stitch the minder along the right side to the middle panel.

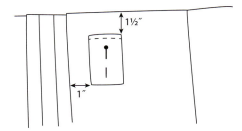

CREATE THE PIN CUSHION

1. Fold the 2¾" × 5" (7 × 12.7cm) cotton print rectangle in half, right sides together, aligning the short ends. Stitch together, leaving an opening 1¼" (3.2cm) wide.

2. Crease the top to find the center. Match the seam to the center and press the seam open.

3. Stitch along the remaining open sides.

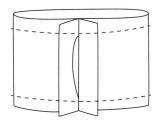

4. Flatten the corners to form a triangle as shown.

5. Stitch ¼" (6mm) across the corner. Repeat on the remaining corners. Trim the corners off.

6. Turn the pincushion inside out and gently poke the corners out.

7. Stuff with fiber fill and hand stitch the opening closed using a slipstitch.

8. Measure 2½" (6.4cm) down and 2" (5.1cm) in from the right side of the middle panel of the case and mark with a dot.

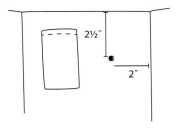

9. Using a needle and sashiko thread, attach the pincushion to the panel. From under the linen panel go through the bottom of the pincushion up through the middle and pull the thread through. Then go back down and pull it taught. Repeat this, making an X on the top of the pin cushion. Make a strong knot on the backside of the panel, tufting the pincushion and securing it to the case.

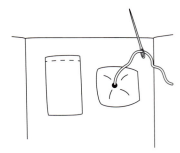

ADDING THE SNAPS

1. Place the exterior panel right side up. Using a water soluble pen, mark 2 dots on the left side 2½" (6.4cm) from the edge and 2" (5.1cm) from the top and bottom.

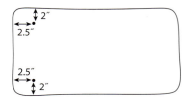

2. Punch a hole through each mark using an awl. Install the snap bottoms to the front of the exterior panel following the manufacturer instructions.

3. Place the exterior right side down and place the interior on top right side up. Lining up all the edges. Using a water soluble pen, mark 2 dots on the left side of the zipper panel, right on top of the stitching line 1" (2.5cm) inside the left edge and 2" (5.1cm) from the top and bottom.

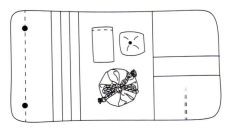

4. Using an awl, punch a hole through each mark, through all layers. Install the snap tops following the manufacturer instructions.

ATTACHING THE BINDING

1. Piece the 3 bias strips to make at least 56" of bias binding. Pin or clip the binding right sides together all the way around the interior edges of the case. Fold under the overlapping end of the binding and trim the excess.

2. Stitch the binding to the case being sure to go slowly around the curved edges.

3. Fold the binding over the seam allowance and press. Hand stitch the binding to the front of the case.

Knotted Headband

Finished headband: 17˝ × 2˝ (27.9 × 5.1cm), not including elastic

Although this headband might look complex it is actually a cinch to assemble. To switch up the look use 2 different fabrics instead of just one.

MATERIALS

Yardages are based on 40˝ (1m)-wide fabric.

Cotton print fabric: ⅓ yard (30.5cm)

Cotton cording, ¼˝ (6mm): 3¼ yards (3m)

Braided elastic: 3½˝ (8.9cm) of ⅜˝ (1cm) elastic

Cutting

COTTON PRINT FABRIC

Cut 4 strips 1⅜″ × 28″ (3.5 × 71.1cm)

Cut 1 strip 2½″ × 7½″ (6.4 × 19.1cm)

COTTON CORDING

Cut 4 pieces of cord 28″ (71.1cm).

Wrap tape around one end of each piece of cord to keep the end from fraying. This will make it easier to insert the cording into the casing.

Construction

Seam allowances are ¼″ (6mm) unless otherwise noted.

COVERING COTTON CORDING

1. Fold a 1⅜″ × 28″ (3.2 × 71.1cm) fabric strip in half lengthwise, right sides together. Line up the edges and pin together. Stitch along the edge of the fabric strip to make the casing.

2. Turn the casing right side out using a loop turner and press with an iron to remove any wrinkles.

3. Insert the loop turner into one end of the casing and out the other.

4. Hook the end of the loop turner onto the taped end of the cording and pull the cord all the way through the casing.

5. Repeat Steps 1–4 to create 4 fabric-covered cords.

CREATING THE DECORATIVE KNOT

Lay the cords out together and carefully tie into a decorative knot following the illustration. If necessary, trim the ends to ensure that they are even.

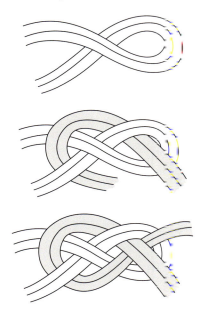

FINISHING THE HEADBAND

1. Take the 2½″ × 7½″ (6.4 × 19.1cm) cotton strip and fold together lengthwise, right sides together.

2. Stitch along the edge leaving a 2″ (5.1cm) opening for turning. Press the seam allowances open.

3. Through the opening, slide one end of the knotted headband into the casing right sides together, sandwiching one end of the elastic in between. Stitch through all of the layers.

4. Repeat Step 3 with the other end of the headband, stretching the elastic through the casing, too.

5. Flip the casing right side out through the opening. Handstitch the opening closed.

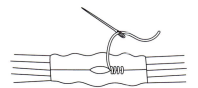

Glow Up Pouches

Finished pouch: Large 7½″ tall x 10½″ wide x 3″ deep (19.1 × 26.7 × 7.6cm)
Medium: 6″ tall x 8½″ wide x 3″ deep (15.2 × 21.6 × 7.6cm)

You can never have enough pouches. Take your pick of two different sizes or mix and match fabrics and make a set. For added detailing you can quilt the sides.

MATERIALS

Yardages are based on 40″ (1m)-wide fabric.

Cotton print for side and zipper panels:
1 fat quarter

Cotton print for bottom: ⅛ yard (11.4cm)

Cotton print for lining and bias binding:
¾ yard (68.6cm)

Foam stabilizer: ½ yard (45.7cm) (I like Soft and Stable or Pellon Flex-Foam.)

Zipper, 13″ (33cm)

Zipper foot

Glow Up Pouches templates (page 125)

Paper or cardstock for templates

Cutting

COTTON PRINT FOR SIDE AND ZIPPER PANELS

Large: Cut 2 rectangles 9″ × 12″ (22.9 × 30.5cm).

Medium: Cut 2 rectangles 8″ × 10″ (20.3 × 25.4cm).

Both sizes: Cut 2 rectangles 1⅞″ × 13¾″ (4.8 × 34.9cm) for zipper panel.

COTTON PRINT FOR BOTTOM

Large: Cut 1 rectangle 3½″ × 21¼″ (8.9 × 54cm).

Medium: Cut 1 rectangle 3½″ × 15″ (8.9 × 38.1cm).

COTTON PRINT FOR BIAS BINDING AND LINING

Both sizes: Cut 4 bias strips 1½″ (3.8cm)-wide.

Large: Cut 2 rectangles 9″ × 12″ (22.9 × 30.5cm).

Medium: Cut 2 rectangles 8″ × 10″ (20.3 × 25.4cm).

Both sizes: Cut 2 rectangles 4″ × 15″ (10.2 × 38.1cm) for zipper panel.

Both sizes: Cut 2 rectangles 1⅞″ × 13¾″ (4.8 × 34.9cm) for lining.

Cutting continued on next page

Cutting continued

FOAM STABILIZER

Large: Cut 2 rectangles 9″ × 12″ (22.9 × 30.5cm).

Large: Cut 1 rectangle 3½″ × 21¼″ (8.9 × 54cm).

Medium: Cut 2 rectangles 8″ × 10″ (20.3 × 25.4cm).

Medium: Cut 1 rectangle 3½″ × 15″ (8.9 × 38.1cm).

Both sizes: Cut 2 rectangles 1⅞″ × 13¾″ (4.8 × 34.9cm).

Instructions

Seam allowances are ⅜″ (1cm) unless otherwise noted.

ATTACHING FOAM STABILIZER

1. Following the manufacturer's instructions, fuse the stabilizer to the backs of the exterior cotton pieces.

2. If you'd like to quilt the sides of your pouch, now would be the time to do so. Quilt as desired.

PREPARING PATTERN PIECE

1. Press the fabric.

2. Trace the template onto paper or cardstock and cut out. You can use template plastic in place of cardboard for increased durability.

3. Trace the template onto the wrong side of the fabric using a water-soluble fabric pen and then cut out along the traced lines. Repeat for the number of fabric pieces indicated on the template.

4. Stitch around the side panels with ⅛″ (3mm) seam allowance.

CREATE THE ZIPPER PANEL

1. Line up the zipper and the edge of an exterior zipper panel right sides together, add the lining zipper panels, right side to the back side of the zipper. Pin or clip as needed. Using a zipper foot, sew along the edge with a ¼″ (6mm) seam allowance. Fold the panel back and press. Topstitch along the edge of the seam. Repeat along the other side of the zipper with the second set of zipper panels.

2. Place the completed zipper panel and the bottom right sides together, lining up the short edges and pin. Sew the edges together.

3. Cut 2 pieces of bias binding 3¾″ (9.5cm).

4 Line up a piece of bias binding along one of the 3¾" (9.5cm) raw edges of the zipper panel, right side of the bias binding and lining side together. Stitch together, being careful when sewing over the zipper teeth.

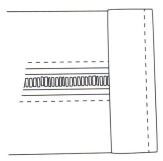

5 Fold the bias binding over the raw edge and topstitch the binding to the zipper panel.

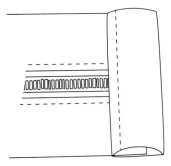

6 Repeat steps 4–5 with the other end of the zipper panel.

ASSEMBLING THE POUCH

1. Fold the exterior panels in half to find the center and make a tiny clip at the top and bottom of the panels to mark the center. Repeat with the zipper panels.

2. Line up a side panel with a zipper panel right sides together and matching the center. Clip or pin together all the way around the perimeter. Make sure your zipper is open!

3. Stitch around the perimeter of the pouch, taking your time around the curves.

4. Repeat steps 2–3 on the other side of the pouch with the other side panel.

ATTACHING THE BINDING

1. Cut 2 strips of bias binding 41" (104.1cm) for the large pouch or 35" (88.9cm) for the medium pouch. Pin or clip the binding all the way around the edges of the pouch with the right sides together. Fold under the overlapping end of the bias tape and trim the excess.

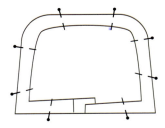

2. Stitch the binding to the case being sure to go slowly around the curved edges.

3. Fold the binding over the seam allowance and press. Hand stitch the binding to finish.

4. Repeat Steps 2–3 for the other side of the pouch.

5. Turn the pouch inside out and press.

Tomorrow Tote

Finished: 14¾″ × 14″ (37.5 × 35.6cm) (not including straps)

This casual, but sophisticated tote is great for everyday use or for a special day out. I love using canvas fabric, especially for bags! Large scale prints would make this bag sing!

MATERIALS

Yardages are based on 40″ (1m)-wide fabric.

Cotton print or canvas for exterior: ¾ yard (68.6cm)

Cotton print for lining: ½ yard (45.7cm)

Cotton print for pocket: ⅜ yard (34.3cm)

Fusible interfacing (20″ (50.8cm)-wide): 1 yard (91.4cm) (I used Pellon SF101)

Zipper, 10″ (25.4cm)

14mm magnetic snap: 1

8 Chicago screws, 8mm with 5mm posts

2 squares 2″ × 2″ (5.1 × 5.1cm) batting

Tomorrow Tote templates (page 127)

Paper or Cardstock for templates

Cutting

EXTERIOR FABRIC

Cut 2 rectangles 16″ × 17″ (40.6 × 43.2cm) for the body.

Cut 2 strips 3½″ × 31″ (8.9 × 78.7cm) for handles.

LINING FABRIC

Cut 2 rectangles 16″ × 17″ (40.6 × 43.2cm) for the body.

POCKET FABRIC

Cut 1 rectangle 10½″ × 20½″ (26.7 × 52.1cm).

INTERFACING

Cut 2 rectangles 16″ × 17″ (40.6 × 43.2cm) for the body.

Cut 2 strips 3½″ × 31″ (8.9 × 78.7cm) for handles.

Construction

Seam allowances are ½" (1.2cm) unless otherwise noted.

PREPARING PATTERN PIECES

1. Print each pattern piece onto paper or card stock and cut them out.

2. Trace the pattern pieces onto the wrong side of the fabric with a water-soluble fabric pen and then cut them out along the traced lines.

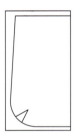

3. Fuse the interfacing to the wrong side of the exterior pieces following the manufacturer's instructions.

4. Transfer the pattern markings (darts, zipper placement, etc.) to the fusible interfacing and the wrong side of the lining fabric using a water soluble marker.

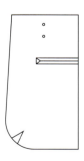

5. Using the markings as a guide, pinch each dart right sides together. Starting and stopping with a backstitch, sew the darts on the marked line from the raw edge to the end of the dart. Repeat for the lining pieces.

6. Press the darts out towards the sides. Set the exterior and lining pieces aside.

MAKE THE HANDLES

1. Fold a 3½" × 31" (8.9 × 78.7cm) strip in half lengthwise, right sides together.

2. Sew around all edges leaving an opening for turning. Clip the corners.

3. Turn the handle right side out, pushing out the corners and press it flat. Press the edges at the opening to the inside.

4. Handstitch the opening closed.

5. Pinch the handle to fold it in half down the middle. Pin in place to hold about 4" (10.2cm) from both ends of the handle. Beginning and ending at the 4" (10.2cm) marks with a backstitch, topstitch along the edge of the handle.

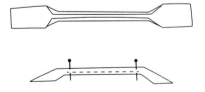

6. Repeat Steps 1–5 for the other handle.

ADDING THE HANDLES

1. Using the pattern markings as a guide, pin the ends of the handles in place to the bag exteriors.

2. Stitch the handles to the bag exteriors by sewing a rectangle through the ends of the bag handles.

3. Using the markings as a guide, punch holes in the straps and the bag through all layers using an awl or a leather punch.

4. Line up the holes on the handles and bag. (The bottom of the straps should be 2¾" (7cm) from the top of the bag.) Install the Chicago screws through all layers using the manufacturer's instructions.

MAKE THE ZIPPER POCKET

1. Place the 10½" × 20½" (26.7 × 52.1cm) pocket piece on top of the front exterior piece right side down. Line up the centers and the raw edges along the top.

2. Measure 5" (12.7cm) down from the top edge and, using the template as a guide, mark the ⅝" × 8½" (1.6 × 21.6cm) rectangle and center lines on the wrong side of the pocket with a water soluble pen.

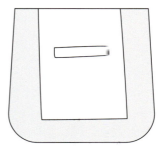

3. Sew around the perimeter of the marked rectangle through all of the layers.

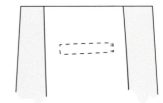

4. Cut through the lines being careful not to clip through the stitching you just made.

5. Pull the zipper pocket rectangle through to the wrong side of the exterior. Press to crease the rectangle and make it nice and flat.

6. Switching to a zipper foot. Place the closed zipper behind the rectangular opening and pin or tape in place. Topstitch around the rectangle through all layers.

7. Fold the zipper pocket rectangle up so that the raw edges meet. Stitch around the sides and top of only the pocket.

INSTALLING THE SNAP

1. Using a water soluble pen mark about 2″ (5.1cm) down and centered from the raw edge of the lining.

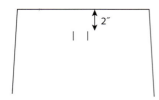

2. Fuse a small square of fusible interfacing over the spot where the snap will go.

3. Using the snap's washer as a guide, mark the prong placement of the snap. Cut small slits along the marks. Mark and snip the 2″ × 2″ (5.1 × 5.1cm) squares of batting also.

4. Push the snap through from the right side of the fabric and place one the batting scrap over the prongs. Place the washer on top and bend the prongs back to secure. You can cover the back of the snap with another scrap of fusible interfacing if you desire.

5. Repeat steps 1–4 with the other lining piece and snap.

ASSEMBLING THE EXTERIOR AND INTERIOR

1. Place the exterior pieces right sides together and stitch along the sides and bottom. Press and turn right side out.

2. Place the lining pieces right sides together and sew together along the sides leaving a 4″ (10.2cm) opening at the bottom for turning.

3. Pull the lining up over the exterior right sides together and sew together along the top.

4. Turn the bag right sides out through the opening in the lining. Handstitch the opening closed.

5. Press the bag and topstitch along the top edge.

Cassandra Crossbody Bag

Finished: 10″ × 8½″ (25.4 × 21.6cm) (not including straps)

I love a good crossbody bag, so including one was a must! It has a zippered pocket inside and is perfect for a night out or running errands around town. Also, Kimberly Kight's Strawberries!

MATERIALS

Yardages are based on 40″ (1m)-wide fabric.

Cotton print or canvas for exterior: ⅝ yard (57.2cm)

Cotton print for lining: ⅜ yard (34.3cm)

Cotton print for pocket: ⅜ yard (34.3cm)

Fusible fleece: ⅜ yard (34.3cm)

Fusible interfacing: ⅜ yard (34.3cm) (I used Pellon SF101)

Zipper, 7″ (17.8cm)

1 magnetic snap, 14mm

5 Chicago screws, 8mm with 5mm posts

2 squares 2″ × 2″ (5.1 × 5.1cm) batting

2 D-rings, 1″ (2.5cm)

1 strap slider adjuster, 1″ (2.5cm)

Cassandra Crossbody Bag templates (page 127)

Paper or cardstock for templates

Cutting

EXTERIOR FABRIC

Cut 2 rectangles 10″ × 12″ (25.4 × 30.5cm) for the body.

Cut 2 rectangles 9″ × 11″ (22.9 × 27.9cm) for the flap.

Cut 2 strips 40″ × 4″(1m x 10.2cm) for handles.

LINING FABRIC

Cut 2 rectangles 10″ × 12″ (25.4 × 30.5cm) for lining.

POCKET FABRIC

Cut 1 rectangle 9″ × 10½″ (22.9 × 26.7cm).

FUSIBLE FLEECE

Cut 2 rectangles 10″ × 12″ (25.4 × 30.5cm) for the body.

Cut 2 rectangles 9″ × 11″ (22.9 × 27.9cm) for the flap.

FUSIBLE INTERFACING

Cut 2 rectangles 10″ × 12″ (25.4 × 30.5cm) for the body.

Construction

Seam allowances are ½″ (1.2cm) unless otherwise noted.

PREPARING PATTERN PIECES

1. Press the fabric.

2. Trace the template onto paper or cardstock and cut out.

3. Fuse the fleece to the wrong side of the exterior fabric following the manufacturer's instructions.

4. Fuse the interfacing to the wrong side of the lining fabric following the manufacturer's instructions.

5. Trace the pattern pieces onto the wrong side of the fabric with a water-soluble fabric pen and then cut them out along the traced lines.

6. Transfer the pattern markings (darts, zipper placement and snap) to the fusible interfacing and the wrong side of the lining fabric using a water soluble marker.

7. Using the markings as a guide, pinch each dart right sides together. Starting and stopping with a backstitch, sew the darts on the marked line from the raw edge to the end of the dart. Repeat for the lining pieces.

8. Press the darts out towards the sides. Set the exterior and lining pieces aside.

MAKE THE STRAP

1. Place 2 ends of the 4″ × 40″ (10.2 × 1.02m) right sides together perpendicularly to form an L shape. Stitch together and trim the seam allowance to ¼″ (6mm) and press the seam allowance open.

2. Fold the strap in half lengthwise and press. Fold in both raw edges toward the

center and press. Fold again lengthwise and topstitch along both edges to form the strap. Set aside.

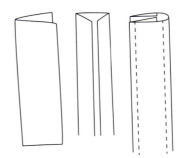

MAKE THE ZIPPER POCKET

1. Place the 9″ × 10½″ (22.9 × 26.7cm) pocket piece right sides together with a lining piece. Center the 9″ (22.9cm) edge of the pocket to the top edge of the lining and match the raw edges.

2. Using the template as a guide, mark the ⅝″ × 7″ (1.6 × 17.8cm) rectangle and center lines on the wrong side of the pocket fabric with a water soluble pen. (It's 2½″ [6.4cm] down from the raw edge.)

3. Sew around the perimeter of the marked rectangle through all of the layers.

4. Cut through the lines, being careful not to clip through the stitching you just made.

5. Pull the zipper pocket lining through to the wrong side of the lining. Press to crease the rectangle and make it nice and flat.

6. Place the closed zipper behind the rectangular opening. Switching to a zipper foot, topstitch around the rectangle through all layers.

7. Fold the zipper pocket lining up so that the raw edges meet. Stitch around the sides and top of only the lining to close the pocket.

8. Place the lining pieces right sides together and stitch along the sides leaving an opening at the bottom for turning and press.

INSTALLING THE SNAP

1. Fuse a small square of fusible interfacing over the dot where the snap will go.

2. Using the snap's washer as a guide, mark the prong placement of the snap. Cut small slits along the marks as well as some scraps of batting.

3. Push the snap through from the right side of the fabric and place one of the batting scrap over the prongs. Place the washer on top and bend the prongs back to secure. You can cover the back of the snap with another scrap of fusible interfacing if you desire.

ADDING THE STRAP TABS

1. Take the bag strap and cut 2 pieces off that measure 2½" (6.4cm).

2. Loop one strap piece through each D-ring. Using a ¼" (6mm) seam allowance, stitch together along the raw edges.

ASSEMBLING THE EXTERIOR AND INTERIOR

1. Place the bag exteriors right sides together and stitch together. Press and turn right side out.

2. Pull the lining up over the exterior right sides together. Pin or clip the raw edges of the strap tabs centered over either side seam, in between the lining and exterior. Sew together along the top.

3. Turn the bag right sides out through the opening in the lining. Handstitch the opening closed.

4. Press the bag and topstitch along the top edge.

ASSEMBLING THE FLAP

1 Place the flap pieces right sides together. Starting on the top straight edge, stitch all the way around the perimeter of the bag flap, leaving an opening for turning. Trim the seam and clip the curves.

2. Turn the flap right side out and press, tucking seam opening inside. Handstitch the opening closed.

3. Using the pattern markings as a guide, mark the position for the Chicago screws and the magnetic snap on the flap and the back of the bag body with a water-soluble fabric pen.

4. Using an awl or a leather punch, make the holes.

5. Attach the flap to the bag with the Chicago screws following the manufacturer's instructions.

6. Attach the snap to the flap following the manufacturer's instructions.

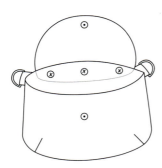

ADDING THE STRAPS

1. Take the bag strap and thread it through the slide adjuster. Fold the raw edge under and punch a hole through all of the layers. Install the Chicago screw through all layers following the manufacturer's instructions.

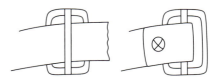

2. Thread the other end of the strap through one of the D-rings, then up through one side of the slide adjuster and down through the other side.

3. Loop the end through the other D-ring. Fold under the raw edge and punch a hole through all of the layers. Install the Chicago screw through all layers following the manufacturer's instructions.

4. Adjust the strap to your preference.

TEMPLATES

Many of the projects in this collection include templates, which you can find here. For your convenience we've also provided these templates as downloadable PDFs.

To access the pattern through the tiny url, type the web address provided into your browser window. To access the pattern through the QR code, open the camera app on your phone, aim the camera at the QR code, and click the link that pops up on the screen.

You can then print the selected template directly from the browser window or download the pattern. To print at home, print the letter-size pages, selecting 100% size on the printer. Use dashed/dotted lines to trim, layer, and tape together pages as needed. To print at a copyshop, save the full-size pages to a thumb drive or email them to your local copyshop for printing.

For complete instructions, go to: https://tinyurl.com/11602-patterns-download

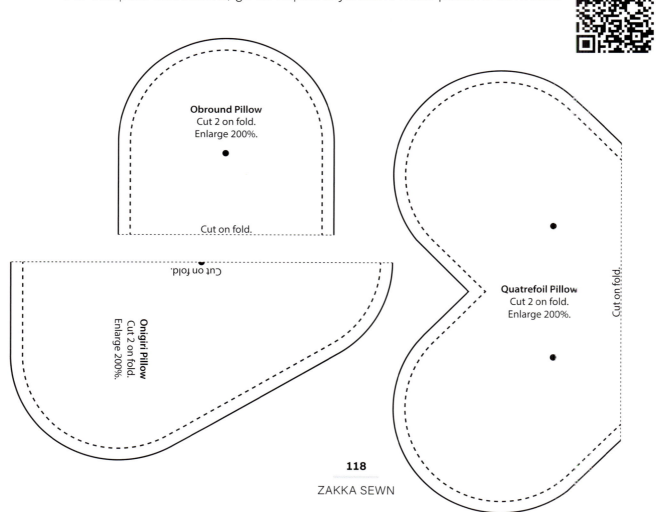

ZAKKA SEWN

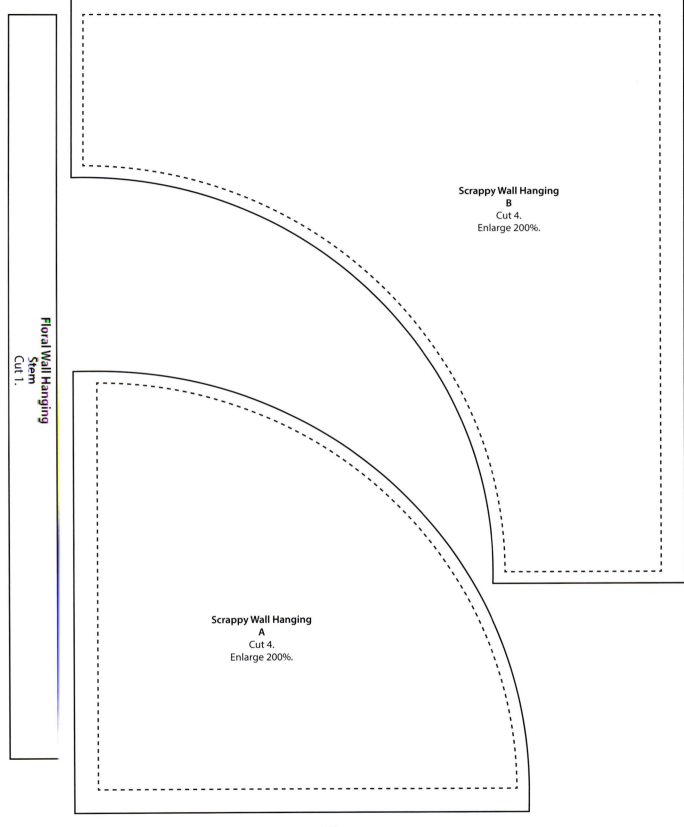

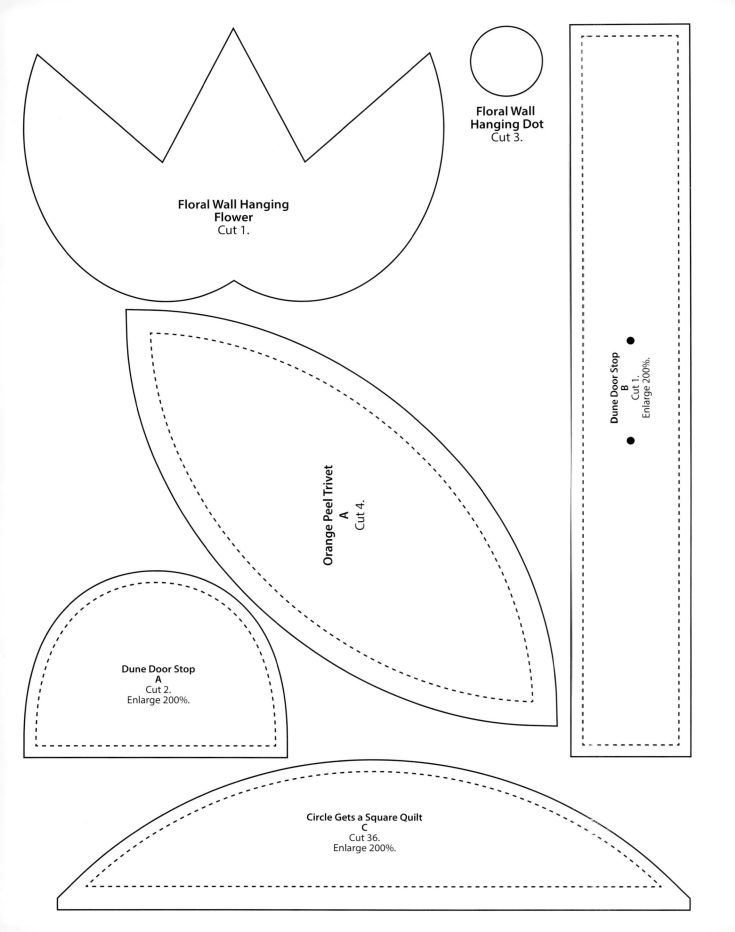

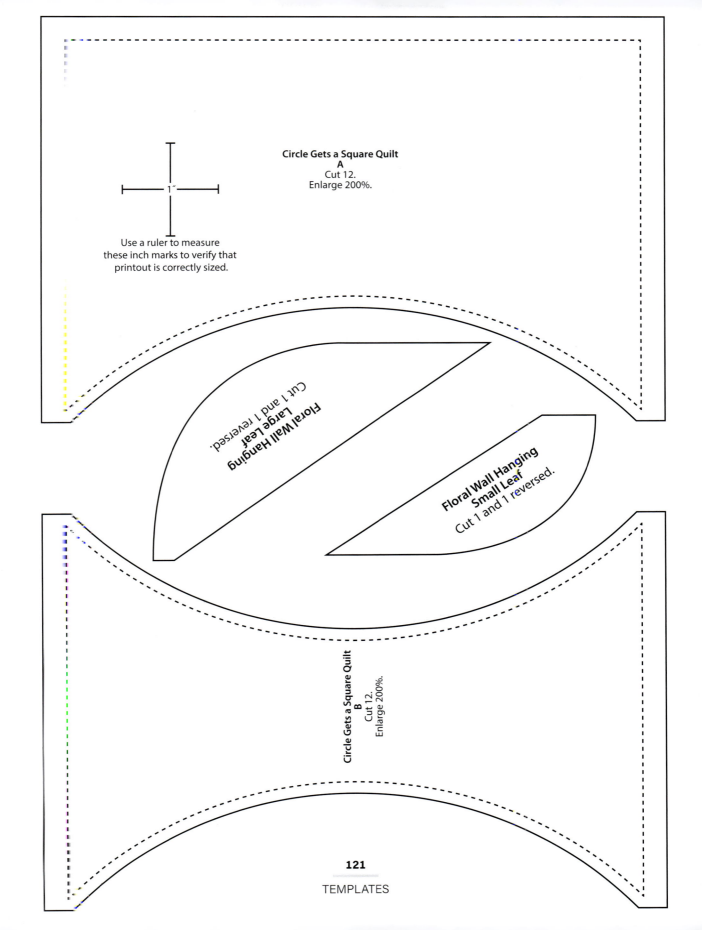

121
TEMPLATES

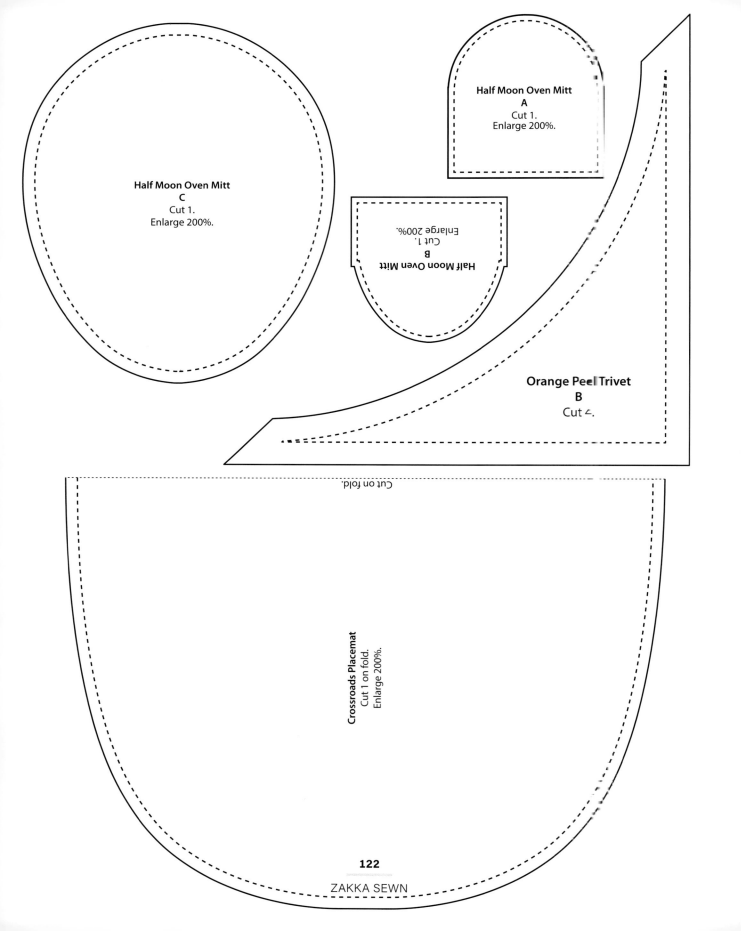

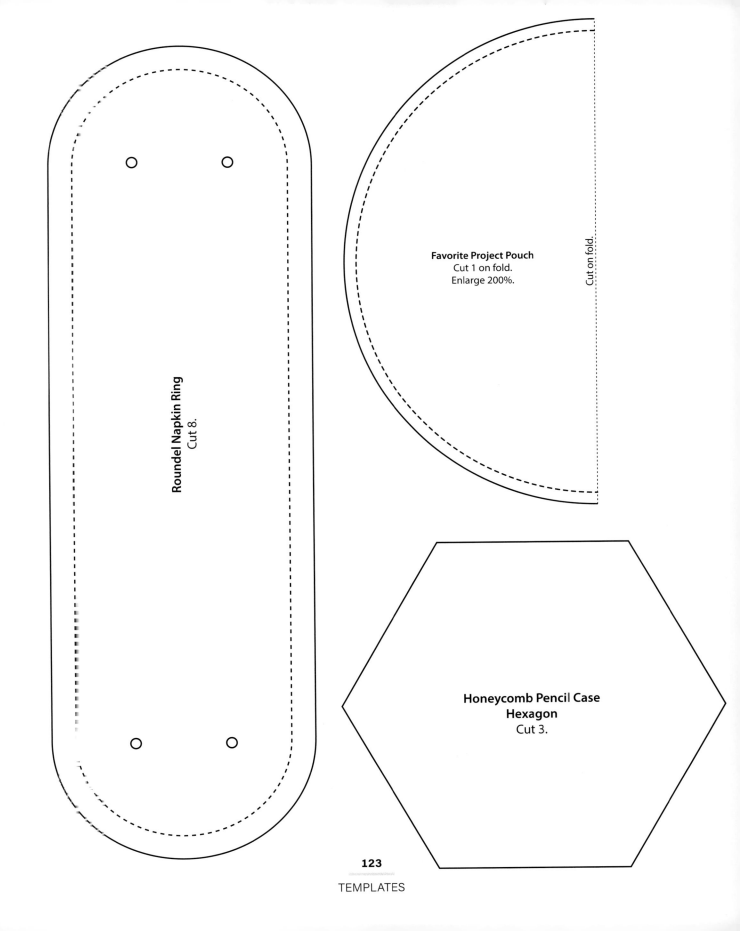

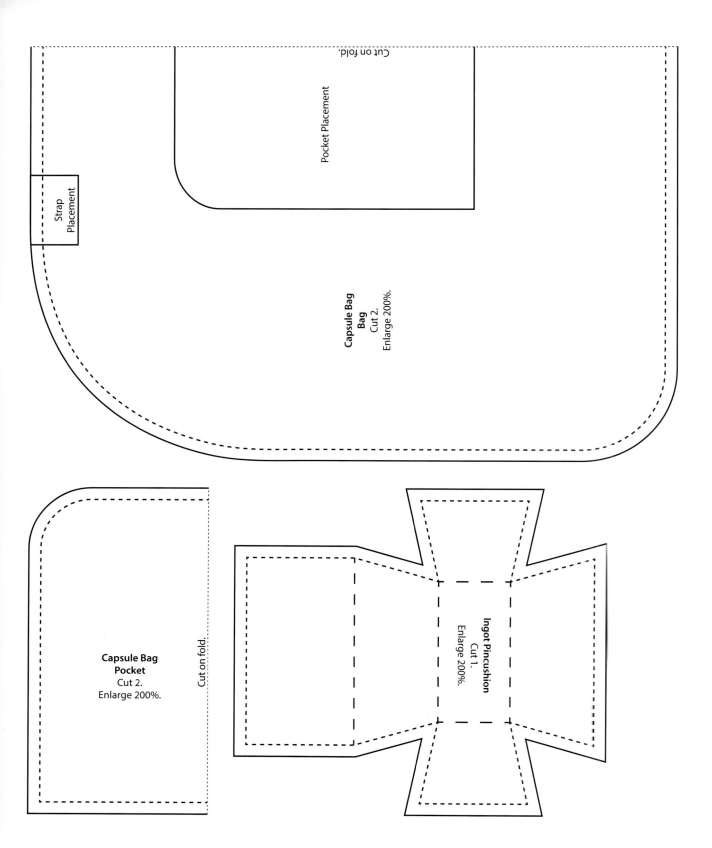

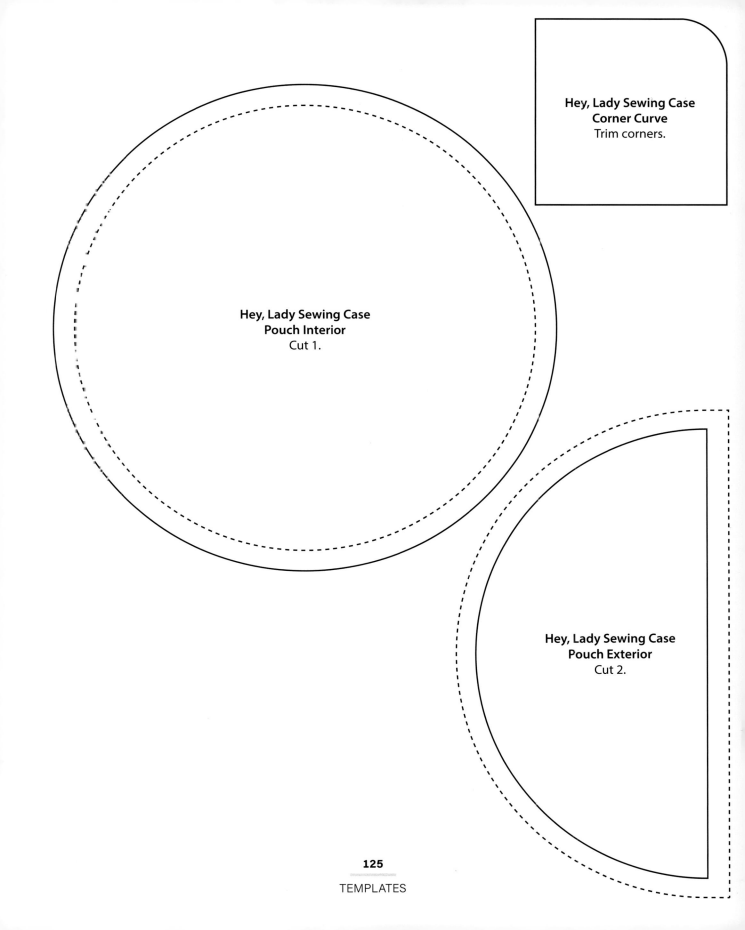

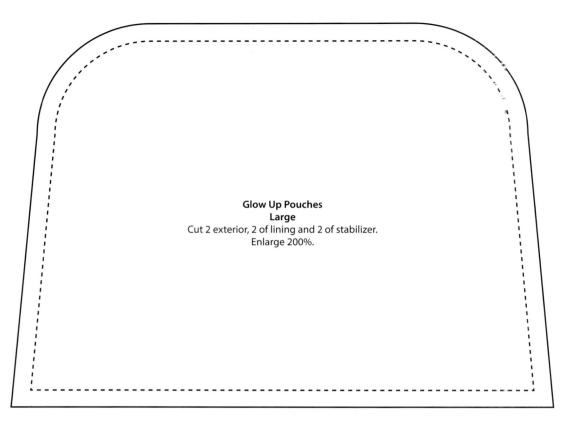

**Glow Up Pouches
Large**
Cut 2 exterior, 2 of lining and 2 of stabilizer.
Enlarge 200%.

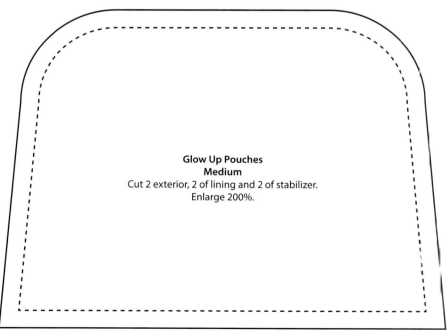

**Glow Up Pouches
Medium**
Cut 2 exterior, 2 of lining and 2 of stabilizer.
Enlarge 200%.

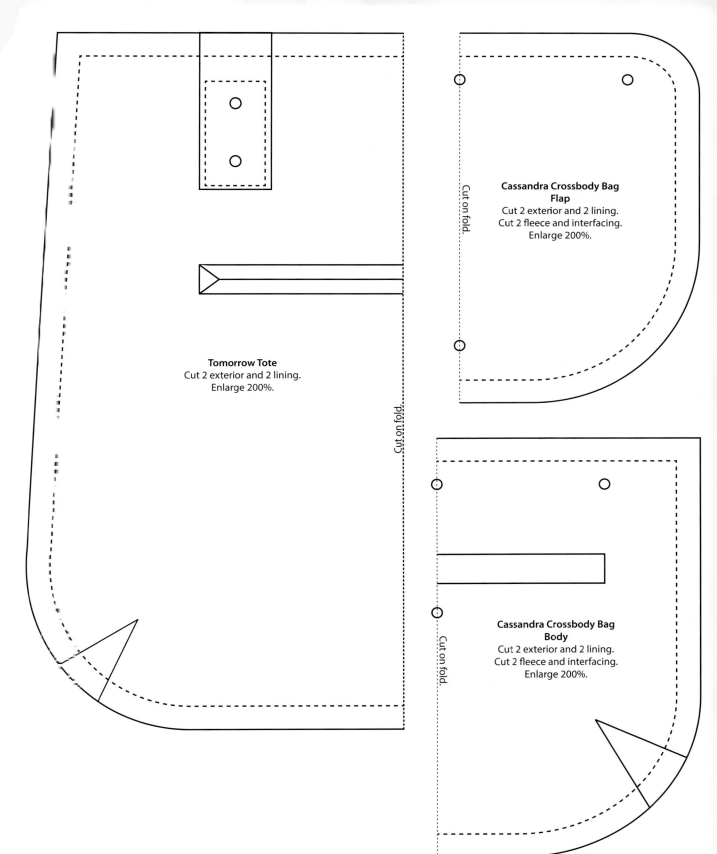

ABOUT THE AUTHOR

Rashida Coleman-Hale has been drawing ever since she could pick up a pencil and her passions include illustration, textile design, surface pattern design, and fiber arts. Inspired by countless summers in Japan with her fashion model mother, the California-based designer has lived a life brimming with excitement and inspiration.

After attending FIT in New York, she ended up trading the fashion world for design, teaching herself Photoshop and Illustrator and dabbling in freelance graphic design, but she can actually credit motherhood for her segue to fabric design.

In the twelve years since Rashida Coleman-Hale became a fabric designer, she's worked with Cloud9 Fabrics, co-founded Cotton + Steel, and landed as a designer at Ruby Star Society. She has also authored two award winning sewing how-to books, *I Love Patchwork* and *Zakka Style*.

Rashida's work is a visual treat, a modern collection of lines and movement in a color spectrum that soothes the soul. Her illustration style tends to be colorful, playful, and graphic.

Her work has been featured at Target, Blue Sky Planners, Maisonette, Petite Plume, Flow Magazine, Moda Fabrics, Cloud9 Fabrics, Bloom Baby, Winter Water Factory, and Hazel Village.

You can follow her creative journey on Instagram @iamrashidacolemanhale and her website www.rashidacolemanhale.com

Trolleybus
miniatures, models and the real things

Ashley Bruce
with Gottfried Kuře

Copyright Notice © Ashley Bruce 2012
ISBN 978-0-904235-23-4
"Trolleybooks" has endeavoured to correctly attribute the photographs used in this book to the copyright holder in compliance with legal provisions. Anyone who believes that copyright has been wrongly attributed or not acknowledged is invited to contact the publisher. All rights reserved. Nothing in this book may be reproduced, stored in any kind of retrieval system or made public in any form or by any electronic, mechanical or other means without the prior written consent of the publisher.

Published by
Trolleybooks
4 Borderside,
Yateley,
Hampshire,
GU46 6LJ
www.trolleybooks.co.uk

Graphics and Book design by eQdigital,
156 High Street, Bildeston, IP7 7EF, UK

Typesetting by Sherbert Design,
sherbertdesign@googlemail.com

Cover by Lateral Concepts,
Church Lane, Langtree, Torrington, EX38 8NS, UK

Printed by Hunan Tianwen Xinhura Printing Co. Ltd.
Brokered by BookSpan, Northampton, NN6 0HA

Trolleybooks is the Joint Publications Panel of:
British Trolleybus Society and
National Trolleybus Association.
For further information on the activities of these organisations please contact:

Mr A J Barton
Membership Secretary
British Trolleybus Society
2 Josephine Court
Southcote Road
READING
RG30 2DG
www.britishtrolley.org.uk

Mr I G Martin
Membership Secretary
National Trolleybus Association
2 St John's Close
Claines
WORCESTER
WR3 7PT
www.trolleybus.co.uk/nta

Front cover: from top left,
Bradford 754, BUT 9611T/Weymann/EE by Bradford City Transport, 1:12, wood, metal. (Mike Bruce)
Generic green Alfa Romeo 110AF and overhead by Rivarossi, 1:80, injection plastic.
London trolleybuses by Pirate Models, 1:76 cast, Taylor & Barrett, 13cm, cast, Betal, 18cm, tinplate and St. Petersburg Tram Collection, 1:43, resin.
Paris style 3 axle single decker by Joustra, 30cm, tinplate.
Beijing BJD-WG120EK by CM Model, 1:64, diecast.

Title page:
Dresdner Haide-Bahn Stoll/AEG by Axel Dopperphul, 1:25, wood, plastic

London Transport 3 axle double decker by Taylor & Barrett, 13cm, cast lead.

Contents

Acknowledgements			4
Preface – How this book is organised			5
Chapter 1 – Introduction Why we like trolleybuses and collect the models: a history			7
Chapter 2 – Professional model trolleybuses Manufacturers' models and models in museums.			17
Chapter 3 - One offs, specials and making them steer The story of modellers and their powered model trolleybuses			35
Chapter 4 – Commercial motorised model trolleybuses The history and development of model trolleybuses that move and you could buy			55
Chapter 5 – Toy and Model trolleybuses by country and prototype			
	1	Austria	75
	2	Belarus	83
	3	Belgium	87
	4	Canada	91
	5	China	97
	6	Czech Republic	107
	7	Denmark	131
	8	Finland	135
	9	France	137
	10	Germany	155
	11	Hungary	193
	12	Italy	203
	13	Japan	219
	14	Mexico	225
	15	Netherlands	227
	16	Poland	233
	17	Russia	239
	18	Spain	261
	19	Sweden	267
	20	Switzerland	269
	21	Ukraine	273
	22	United Kingdom	277
	23	United States	355
Chapter 6 – The future and new directions			377
Bibliography			383
Appendix 1 – Model listing alphabetically by maker			385
Appendix 2 – Suppliers			410

Acknowledgements

One acknowledgement now almost taken for granted is the internet, without which the four years it has taken to produce this book would have at least doubled, with all the attendant risk of collectors and contributors having shuffled off this mortal coil. Both website and email ability have made the task often dauntingly fast. So too has eBay, which is a surprising, if fleeting, historical resource, where items have appeared that might otherwise have had no record, especially in the global context. Traditional methods have been used, such as auctions and plain paper letter writing, but to a surprisingly slight extent.

This electronic connectivity has led to conversations with well over a hundred people, all of whom we gratefully acknowledge, but ask forgiveness for not listing all of them – many are duly acknowledged in the credits to their, by and large, freely given photographs. We also thank museums and professional sources mentioned in the text as well as Danmarks Tekniske Museum, Stockholm Spårvägsmuseet and Musee Montreux for additional assistance and research.

We should also thank various couriers who managed to find their way through the trees to the studio in Bildeston where most of the work was done, laden with small model packages from exotic places – they got to know what and why they were bringing them.

Amongst those whom we have had protracted dealings or who have given time and generous help, are

Benny Aalbers, Laurence Ahearn, Ken Allborn, Luca Angerame, Petr Babayev, Stefan Baguette, Paul Bennett, Grahame Bilbé, Rod Blackburn, David Bowler, David Bradley, Mike Bruce, Antonio Bruck, Roland Le Corff, André Corteil, John Couser, Greg Diffen, Fabio Dobran, Andras Ekkert, Vincent Espinasse, Nigel Frampton, John Fuller, Martin Harák, Ronald Helder, Andrew Henbest, Ed Humphreys, Barbara Hünike, Zachary Jiang, Leonid Khoykhin, Ronald Kiebler, Nigel Leahy, Jürgen Lehmann, Peter Lepino, Robin Male, Barry Marsden, Stephan Mashevich, Albert Maslip, Enrico Mittiga, Phillipe Morro, Vittorio Naldini, Palle Nilsson, Larry Noades, Dave O'Connor, Alexander Olajos, Zbynek Ondryás, Konrad Pernetta, Ray Piesciuk, Wim van der Plaats, Thierry Portman, Tony Price, Roger Pride, John Priestley, Terry Russell, Karlheinz Salzer, Stephen Scalzo, Rudiger Schreiber, Peter Short, Liu Shuang, Simon and Ian Smiler, Peter Smith, Daniel Steiner, Robin Symonds, Pavel Trávníek, Keith Turner, Christian Vana, Frantisek Vecernik, David Voice, Dave Wall, David Wallace, Dewi Williams, David Wood and Andreas Zietemann.

Because of their unstinting assistance in knowledge and/or providing help we'd like to especially thank

Jon Dockendorf, Emídio Gardé, John Gay, Bruce Lake, Harry Porter, Mattis Schindler, Gunter Mackinger and Dave Wilshire.

Ed Humphreys acted as an inspiring editor and Ian Blee an untiring proof reader. Andrew Braddock and Carl Isgar never faltered in supporting this rather unusual Trolleybook.

Ashley Bruce
Gottfried Kuře

July 2011

Generic Alfa Romeo 110AF by Rivarossi, 1:80, injection plastic

Preface

Organising this book

In writing this book about model and toy trolleybuses, we were faced with the problem of how to organise the volume in the most logical and user friendly way. We have written the first four chapters in a conventional way but when it came to the world's models, and realising how we all like to dip in, here and there, it became obvious that we should accommodate two ways of finding what you're looking for – one is by model maker, and this is what we have done in the appendix, and one is by a way that you should find easy and more interesting to use. This results in a number of assumptions on our part, but we have ordered the models in chapter 5 and its sections by -

- Chassis/ lead manufacturer country
- Alphabetical listing by chassis builder
- Chronological listing by chassis type

One assumption is that categorisation by country comes first, as we all, like it or not, tend to think in a nationalistic way. Second comes alphabetical ordering of chassis maker or lead producer. This may not sound logical, but it is the way we tend to think about real trolleybuses, when identifying them, and so we've applied this to the models. It has to be added that this is truer of the British than of the world at large, but we hope, it is a recognisable method. Third, comes a chronological order, just because it's the only universally applicable way to sort chassis types. There are two points about this ordering scheme; these days trolleybuses tend not to have chassis, so the rule becomes 'lead manufacturer', which often, and possibly confusingly, means the body builder. Second is the problem of toys, which may or may not have a recognizable real equivalent. So each country chapter first deals with toy trolleybuses in chronological order according to when the toy was made and then goes on to look at the models in alphabetical chassis/lead manufacturer order and then chronological order. Some chapters break this order, mainly because we also, to some extent, want to relate the history of trolleybus development – for example, the US chapter puts Vesare at the front because they only built in the early days, albeit innovatively, and it would be odd to deal with them alphabetically. Denmark had no indigenous makers but an intriguing history. There's both models and toys and unique imported trolleybuses that merit breaking the chassis country 'rule'. Interrupting the Leyland story in the British chapter for such idiosyncratic Copenhagen trolleybuses felt odd, in any case.

There is, inevitably, some blurring of what constitutes a toy or a model, so much so that, in the case of commercial motorized model trolleybuses, we've decided to give them a whole chapter on their own, not least because the story is international and has a fascinating historical development that is particular to them.

To find models by their model maker/manufacturer tends, sometimes, to be a little tricky in the main text of this book, but can always be cross checked by using the appendix which lists all model makers alphabetically. In the text, finding particular models only becomes a problem where a model maker makes a model that isn't from his country; say a model maker from Russia making models of American trolleybuses, but then in this particular case, you'll find that there are so many of them, you'll know where to look!

Organising the book in this way has the main advantage of being able to compare different models of the same prototype (or should that be prototypical example?). We have made a rather large assumption that our readers are enthusiasts of full-size trolleybuses and that their interest is reflected in toys and models as surrogates for the real thing. Hopefully, if this is not the case for you, you will find the comparison exciting and see that the interpretation of reality on a small scale is an act of creativity that usually equates to being a motivation and solution for the need to express enthusiasm for trolleybuses. We have also included mention of preserved full size equivalents, many of which can be publicly inspected. One other point – we couldn't resist including scratch built or adapted one-offs, and these are included where we think them relevant. Whilst we hope we've included all commercially produced models and toys, we obviously can't make the same claim for the hundreds of miniature trolleybuses around the world that have been produced by their owners for their own delight – and we apologise for not including those masterpieces we didn't know about. We would be pleased to hear about any omissions or errors at trakless@trolleybus.co.uk.

Finally, all pictures are by the author, except, and there are quite a few, where noted in brackets as a credit to the photographer.

Praha Tatra T401 by RA Model Petr Dosly, 1:87, resin.

San Francisco 621, Twin Coach 44TTW by St.Petersburg, 1:48, resin

Chapter 1
An introduction

Trolleybus Nostalgia

In September 1923, brand new 'trackless trams' were being tested conspicuously by Ipswich Corporation Transport Department between Cornhill and the Station along Princes Street. The local newspaper sensed the excitement of the rate-paying public who saw this new 'toy' being driven without passengers, and so published a cartoon of a Corporation official re-poling a model of Railless no.2. (The real thing is, today, in Ipswich Transport Museum). The young 'ratepayer' is innocently asking "May I play with it soon, please, Papa?" Much can be read into this cartoon, the paternalism of officials, officialdom and their toys and the way professionals, like toy makers and cartoonists, seem unable to get the precise details of the vehicle quite right! But the real point is that there's nothing new about the idea of model trolleybuses signifying delight.

We also get the point that the reason for the delight is in the nostalgia, the fascination and the need to interact with the technology, in this case, of a trolleybus. Few can be surprised by an image of a be-capped four-year old standing erect and intent at the wonderful machine before him. We don't imagine for a second that the picture needed posing. Did he grow up to be a trolleybus driver and collect model trolleybuses? Growing up with the daily sight of big, whooshing people carriers, sparking on their overhead lines, sometimes whisking us away to relatives and later, to school and then to work, could hardly fail to make trolleybus enthusiasts of us all who had them in our towns, cities and even, in a few cases, villages. If we're old enough, and lucky enough, we remember them as the only way we wanted to travel the streets, aloof from those noisy, smelly diesel buses. There was something marvellous about the wonderful silence of a trolleybus, and by the time we knew about positive and negative currents, we appreciated the brilliant simplicity of how they worked – you could almost see it happening; electricity up and down those amazing swinging arms on the roof. And, of course, we all delighted in their inability to always stay attached to the wires. But it has to be admitted that the trolleybus mostly was and is a pretty rare thing compared to motor buses. All the more surprising then, considering their relative rarity, that there are so many toy and model versions, throughout the world.

Scale fascination

There must be a uniting characteristic amongst us that, in appreciating these artefacts, almost doesn't distinguish between the size of a model

Ipswich Corporation Railless Cartoon "The New Toy", 1923 (c/o Ipswich Transport Museum)

Ipswich 34, Garrett/Strachan and Brown/Bull, 1926   (c/o Ipswich Transport Museum)

Brno Skoda 22Tr by Marek Bures, 1:13, brass, copper, plastic   (Marek Bures)

Reading Corporation Sunbeam F4A/Burlingham by Peter Lepino, 1:3, Aluminium and wood

Des Moines 239, ACF-Brill T-46 (Illinois Railway Museum)

Des Moines 245, ACF-Brill T-46 by St.Petersburg, 1:43, resin (SPTC)

and the real thing. There are models that need a magnifying glass to appreciate their detail and others that carry people. Some are approximate symbols and others are almost indistinguishable from those that are full size or one to one scale. But there must be underlying reasons for this appreciation, this fascination. According to Claude Lévi-Strauss, "the intrinsic value of a small scale model is that it compensates for the renunciation of sensible dimensions by the acquisition of intelligible dimensions" or, as Will Self puts it, "reductions in size enable us to grasp things in their totality". So much for the philosophy, but what about the nostalgia? Bill Bryson in his book "The Life and Times of the Thunderbolt Kid" has this paragraph – "Buses in Des Moines in those days were electrically powered and drew their energy from a complicated cats cradle of overhead wires, to which each was attached by means of a metal arm. Especially in damp weather, the wires would spark like fireworks at a Mexican fiesta as the arm rubbed along them, vividly underscoring the murderous potency of electricity. From time to time the bus-arm would come free of the wires and the driver would have to get out with a long pole and push it back into place – an event that I always watched with keenest interest because my sister assured me that there was every chance he would be electrocuted".

8 An introduction

Just to set the record straight, Des Moines "Curbliners" could go for 18 months without de-wiring according to the roll call records. 239 is preserved at Illinois Railway Museum and, like very many Brill trolleybuses, has been modelled by the St Petersburg Tram Collection.

Bill Bryson's memories evoke the excitement of experiencing the real thing. And for some of us, that encounter goes further. A fascination is born (I was going say sparked) that can last the rest of our lives. The way in which we all play as children, and have a need for substitute objects, not only protects us from the dangers of the real thing, in this case around 600 volts of direct electric current, but also helps our growing minds to absorb concepts and gain some sort of understanding and control over the underlying technology. So toy trolleybuses don't need to be particularly realistic to act as symbols as we rehearse reality at a more convenient scale, just as long as we can play with them. Of course, as our minds develop so we demand greater realism and tinplate or diecast toys are relegated to just that, toys, without any important function any more, other than indulgent playthings. By now, as we pass our first decade, we want motorized trolleybuses, which emulate more fully the real thing. Not many of us achieve this, though it's interesting that the famous Eheim models were in production, in some form or another for over 50 years, enough for three generations of model trolleybus childhoods. Phillip Hanson recalls 'seeing a Rivarossi trolleybus layout in a Bradford toyshop around 1950/51 and marvelled at its ingenuity, but the cost was way beyond my reach as a boy with a shilling for pocket money!' Asked if he remembered the name of the shop, Phillip replied 'Could I forget! ... I used to drool over the contents in the window which I could never afford. The shop was Carters, in Bridge Street, Bradford, opposite Brown and Muffs, itself an upmarket department store and a mere stone's throw from the City terminus of the Duckworth Lane and Allerton trolleybus routes. Just a very few of us had fathers who built us large scale remote controlled trolleybuses, whether we liked it or not, even if father was really doing it for himself.

Horam Transport Leyland TB10 by BW Francis, 1:43, wood   (BW Francis)

Model History

Later on, model trolleybuses become artefacts or depending on your appreciation, even objects d'art. And as we reach our latter years, those toys become items of nostalgia, to be appreciated differently, for the creativity of their designers or the skill of their craftsmen builders. Models become important for their ability to evoke the real thing or to substitute our not being able to see and experience the full sized reality any more. They even help some of us indulge in fantasies of what might or could have been. They are also ornaments to decorate our homes. Some function to educate in museums, or even to test concepts for manufacturers and, exceptionally, to train trolleybus drivers.

Trolleybus models have varying heritages in

Kingsland Corporation Crossley TDD6 'Dominion'/MV by Anbrico (conversion), 1:76, diecast kit

Salzburg Steyr STS 11HU and Henschel/Urdingen ÜH IIIs, layout by Gunter Mackinger, 1:87, resin   (Gunter Mackinger)

Zlin Skoda 8Tr by Willi Schincke, 1:63, plasticard, tin, balsa   (Willi Schincke)

different parts of the world. Many are adjuncts or alternatives to model railway layouts, usually within the strict confines of 00 (1:76) scale in the UK or H0 (1:87) in more or less the rest of the world. Some, particularly in Britain, are in the tradition of diecast toys, developing from Dinky toys to toys for adults. Others, though less prevalently, are hand-crafted models in their own right, usually from Eastern Europe for the more affluent Western market. These rarefied models are usually around 0 (1:43 or 1:48) scale and are expensive. Then there are home made models, reflecting their builder's obsession with the real thing, whether built uniquely from the ground-up or by adapting existing models to local liveries or particularly favourite vehicles. Some have gone to extraordinary lengths to recreate the trolleybus in miniature.

Much of the above applies equally to model cars or trucks or trams or buses, where the extent and variety of available choices is now vast, as if almost any wheeled vehicle, old or new, can now find its miniature equivalent. Over the last decade or so, there has been an exponential explosion in the numbers of models available and that is perhaps why it is now possible to not just write this book, but to do so as an encyclopaedia, listing over 1200 examples of toy and model trolleybuses.

A bit of toy history

It's first worth looking at the history of toys because it has relevance to what, in the case of trolleybuses, only really started in the 1930s. Wheeled toys have existed at least since Egyptian times, during the early Dynastic Period from whence toy carts, pulled along by asses and oxen on wheels have been found. Plato in his "The Laws" says that parents rearing children "must provide each child with toy tools modelled on real ones". Later, in Greece, racing chariots were modelled, pulled by horses made of clay with terracotta wheels. By the 8th century BC they boasted painted patterns, liveries, hair and manes, doubtless reflecting the most famous race winners of the day. The Romans continued the tradition, with wooden pull along horses and chariots and toys of vehicles that could be seen everyday on city streets – a practice that continues to this day.

Trade in toys was happening by at least 1000 BC, with Phoenician merchants exporting from what is now Lebanon to the whole of the Mediterranean. And the business of trade in miniatures for children, usually carried out along the major trade routes, continued until industrialisation and then globalisation created greater universality. Down the centuries, toys made in family workshops on a small scale became centralised and increasingly mechanised. 13th Century city fairs in London and Leipzig, for example, included toys, and they were starting to reflect places that were specializing in toy manufacture. All sorts of materials were used at this time, including pewter, bronze and brass for making moulded miniatures in batches. Moulds, as a specialist skill, were often produced separately, to be sold on to toy manufacturers. Typically, toy makers kept up with the times, for example, replica miniature moulded warships were made to commemorate the defeat of the Spanish Armada in the year it happened, in 1588.

Major toy making centres

The most important place of toy making was already established around Nuremberg in the centre of Germany by the 16th century. There was already supply of wood and skilled craftsmen and many traders passed by; it was a combination of factors that has made the area pre-eminent right up to the present day.

Nuremberg was later to have a small trolleybus system of 8 MAN vehicles and 2 routes, between 1948 and 1961, but whether this had any influence on German toymakers is not known. The famous Nuremberg Toy Fair though, has been the scene of many model trolleybus announcements.

As manufacture became more concentrated into workshops, so the arrival of the lathe from France in the 1560s made production faster and more uniform. Nuremberg, which also had a clock making tradition, was making sheet metal toys with clockwork motors by the 1840s. It's hardly surprising that when the very first steam railway in Germany, running the Stephenson locomotive "Adler" between Nuremberg and Fürth, opened in 1836, local manufacturers faithfully produced models of the engine and carriages, but, apparently, without tracks. It marked the beginning of toy trains the world over, including the USA where tinplate clockwork trains appeared in 1856. Workshops were becoming large factories with names like Bing, Lehmann and Märklin becoming famous. By 1875 the artisan skills of airbrushing and hand painted details were being replaced by offset lithographic printing and mechanical industrialisation was all-prevailing, able to reproduce whatever famous invention came along (the real Adler has been replicated at full size twice, by the way, in 1935 and 2008).

Despite the profusion of novelties, there's no evidence that Werner von Siemens 'Elektromote' trolleybus of 1881/2 was ever modelled commercially, though it could be argued that it was itself an experimental 'model' for something larger. The electrified horse carriage ran from von Siemens house in Halensee near Berlin, on a 540m installation above cobbled streets near the railway station. 25 different designs of current collector were tried over the six week period of the experiment, but Siemens wasn't satisfied with any of them. Although the invention was publicly announced, the trolleybus wasn't yet 'out there', and wasn't to be, for nearly another twenty years.

Nuremberg Adler full size replica, 2008   (Magnus Kertkemper)

Siemens Elektromote by Siemens, 1:10, wood, metal (Siemens)

Siemens Elektromote, Berlin 1882 (Siemens)

Today, the Elektromote is modelled in the Siemens Museum in Munich, at tenth scale.

Meanwhile, in France and Britain, toys remained part of the product range of craftsmen, rather than the specialty of growing enterprises that distinguished those in and around Nuremberg. The progression to factories wasn't to happen beyond Germany until the 20th century, mostly because German industry before the World Wars, was so efficient at exporting its huge range. In Britain, toys were bought from retailers like William Hamley who had set up shop in High Holborn in 1760 to sell the latest from around the world and later, Arthur Gamage who set up his bazaar nearby. Both imported from the likes of Bing and Lehmann as well as selling home produced products. By the 1850s there were around 3500 toymakers and sellers in England and Wales. Not included in that figure were children selling 'penny toys' from trays on the streets. Specialist warehouses had grown up near London Docks to stock vast quantities of toys from Germany, France, Japan, China and India and it was here that street hawkers would go, doubtless by foot, to stock up for the day and eke a poor living. Their wares, by Edwardian times, included "racing motor cars, taxi cabs, motor ambulances and airships" – there was "hardly a modern invention of which you cannot buy a copy for a penny" said The Strand Magazine at the time. You can still see the huge variety of penny toys in Ernest Kings collection at the Museum of London. It includes many from the J. Meir company of Nuremberg, who made a 1905 double deck bus with 'Electric Omnibus Company' printed on the side. The real London Electric Omnibus Co Ltd. had existed up until 1899, though the toy looks more like a petrol bus. Battery electric buses didn't run in service in London until 1907, so Johann Meir was certainly up-to-the minute, even predating reality. Such modernity shows a sophistication that must have involved a quick turn round between the very latest vehicles hitting the streets of London and German toy factories designing, building and exporting miniature equivalents back to the child hawkers in Ludgate Hill, who were then able to sell the very latest. It was about this time that motor buses, whose number had risen tenfold in just one year (1905) were sited as making Ludgate Hill too dangerous for the hawkers. They were moved on to Holborn and so further away from their suppliers, making their existence even more precarious. At the other extreme, the rich could buy incredibly detailed and large models of almost anything that moved. The fabulous tinplate ships that would have dwarfed any child suggest that even at the turn of the 20th century, toys were no longer just for children. Expensive toys, particularly railway models, were becoming ever more accurate representations of the real thing. Only rich adults were going to appreciate the makers skill and be able to buy them.

First public trolleybuses

As aeroplanes started to take to the skies, and toymakers echoed the headlines of future transport with miniature versions, so trolleybus development was starting to happen. North east of the Nuremberg toy manufacturing heartland, at Bielathal, near Dresden, history was being made in 1901 with the opening of an overhead electric road passenger service. There are two myths about Max Schiemann's Bielathalbahn - it wasn't the world's first passenger trolleybus service (Eberswalde had a public service 6 months earlier) and it didn't get to Bielathal, stopping shorter than planned at Königsbrunn.

Today, and only 20km away, Herr Lorenz's 2005 model of Schiemann's trolleybus runs around Dorf Wehlen Miniature Park and has been operating for longer than the original. Not the oldest model trolleybus in this book but the oldest service trolleybus to be modelled, and a significant one. By the standards of the time, Schiemanns original was a relative success and ran from July 1901 until September 1904 when bad roads and less than expected patronage led to its closure. But this operation led to a whole series of attempts to bring overhead electric road public transport to the world. The trolleybus, albeit in small numbers, was now 'out there'. The influence spread to Klotzsche, even nearer to Dresden, where the affluent village had been thwarted in its rather grand attempt to build a power station for a tram extension from the city line at Arsenal. Carl Stoll stepped in with his newly patented current collection system of a 4 wheeled 'trolley' that ran on top of the double overhead. He built and operated the 5.4km line and initially had to double the frequency to 6 per hour. But the onset of winter in 1903-4 and the dirt road caused accidents, breakdowns and ultimately bankruptcy.

The Electric Omnibus Company
Penny toy by J. Meir, (no scale), tinplate
(Museum of London)

Schiemann Bielathalbahn by Lorenz, 1:10, wood, metal (Kleine Sächsische Schweiz)

Schiemann Bielathalbahn 1901 (Werner Stock arckiv)

Dresdner Haide-Bahn Stoll/AEG, 1903 (werkphoto)

Dresdner Haide-Bahn Stoll/AEG by Axel Dopperphul, (1:25), wood, plastic

Marseilles CGFT Electrobus Lombard-Gerin by ARTM, (approx. 60cm), wood, metal

Lloyd-Kohler Brush advertisement, 1913 (Brush)

12 An introduction

Siena STE Turrinelli by Giuliano Càroli, 1:43, wood, plasticard (Giuliano Càroli)

Siena STE Turrinelli, 1907 (Francesco Rizzoli col.)

Carl Stoll, sadly, committed suicide, such was the stress he suffered, but his son Ludwig was to continue what became the "Cedes-Stoll" system. The Dresden Verkehrsmuseum has a fine model of the "Dresdner Haide-Bahn" in bright yellow that clearly shows the flexible cable that connected the trolley to the 3 axled articulated carriage.

Between 1901 and 1914 there were 24 demonstrations and 61 installations around the world, with at least 5 different collector systems, operating sometimes for only months and mostly in out-of-town locations. It's hardly surprising the trolleybus wasn't yet featured on toymakers most wanted lists. Max Schiemann described his vehicles as 'village trams', intended for "the poorer rural communities". "The 'Trackless' was only planned to be used with low traffic density where a tram on tracks would not be economic". Perhaps, as well as being hidden in the countryside, the trolleybus at the turn of the century was not sufficiently visually different from buses of the time, or else the current collector mechanisms, especially the Cedes-Stoll or the Lloyd-Kohler systems that were very flimsy looking affairs, were not easily included in a toy. The nearest of these early systems to Nuremberg was Heilbronn, a one route, 4 vehicle Cedes-Stoll system that was an adjunct to the trams and lasted for only five years between 1911 and 1916. Heilbronn, 140km south of Nuremberg, is known for wine growing and had a population of just over 40,000 souls at the time, so hardly likely to be influential to the global thinking toy entrepreneurs of Germany's heartland. But we digress.

There are at least two other models of trolleybuses of this period. The city of Marseilles had a pioneer system on its outskirts between La Croix-Rouge and Allauch that ran from June 1903 until September 1905 using the complex motorized Lombard-Gerin system of current collection. To celebrate the fact, a model of one of the vehicles is on display in the Marseilles Noailles Metro station.

There was a nationalistic dimension to current collector designs at the turn of the century and the Italians used a single pole design, known as Filovia or Cantano-Frigerio. Giuliano Caroli has recently made a 1/43 scale model of Impresse Elettriche Di Siena's no.12, clearly showing the 4 wheeled collector pressed against the underside of the overhead wiring. The system, like a number of others in Italy, was promoted by Società per la Trazione Elletrica (STE) of Milan. The five diminutive vehicles of Siena, built by Turrinelli and seating only 12, ran from March 1907 to October 1917, by which time the First World War had ended this and most of the early systems.

The toy industry continued, despite the war, with patriotism not stopping Arthur Gamage buying up large stocks of banned German toys and selling them for the duration. Whilst banned German companies meant no spares were available for Aberdare, Keighley and Stockport trolleybuses with their Cedes-Stoll and Lloyd – Kohler systems in the UK, they somehow managed to survive the war - just. The same cannot be said of Bradford trolleybuses, which were to operate for over 60 years. In 1949 Eric Thornton built a 1/30 scale model of the very first, no.240, a Railless with its British version of the Schiemann under-running trolley. The Model Engineer magazine put the model on its front cover. It was exhibited at Cartwright Memorial Hall and supposedly went on to Bradford Industrial Museum, but, unfortunately no sign of it can now be found. Which is a pity, as the model certainly looks to be very accurate. It would have been built from wood and metal, virtually in the

Bradford 240, Railless/Hurst Nelson/Siemens, 1911   (Bradford Corporation)

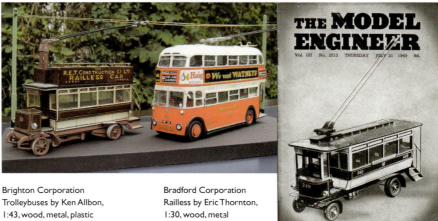

Brighton Corporation Trolleybuses by Ken Allbon, 1:43, wood, metal, plastic (Andrew Henbest)

Bradford Corporation Railless by Eric Thornton, 1:30, wood, metal (Model Engineer)

An introduction   13

same way as the original, with a lathe and possibly castings, as there were few off-the-shelf model parts in the late 1940s, at least for model trolleybuses. Another Railless model, of the 1913 double deck prototype and demonstrator that was built for the Leeds Morley routes that never happened, has been modelled by Ken Allbon. The Railless original was sent to Brighton and later had its booms moved back towards the rear of the upper deck. It ran for 2 months in the middle of winter along London Road in 1913/4. The Brighton Railless has been lovingly crafted by hand in 1:43 scale of card and wood to create a scene never possible in reality – a side by side time leap of 26 years with a 1939 AEC 661T model, also made of wood and card.

Industrialisation

The toy industry had long gone down another path, ruthlessly using materials that produced the most profit. The last development in this regard, was the introduction of plastics. Celluloid was used from its introduction in 1871 but being highly inflammable, its use was severely limited. Bakelite, invented by Leo Baekeland in the early years of the twentieth century was much more suitable, but needed careful moulding and could crack. Polyurethane, polystyrene and then polypropylene, all developed after the Second World War, completely revolutionised toy making. They are unbreakable, hard wearing, very mouldable and reproducible in an almost infinite number of colours. Rubber was quickly replaced, but tinplate lasted a little longer, into the late 50s. Zamak, an alloy of zinc, aluminium, magnesium and copper was patented in 1929 and used to diecast toys in their thousands. Only the UK mass toy market continues using whitemetal (as its commonly known and can contain tin, lead and zinc), although some Russian and lately Chinese models use the material, instead of the more usual polyurethane resin or injection moulded plastic. Some larger Ukrainian models use electroplated copper on moulds to give a very effective modelling solution.

German domination of toy manufacture faltered after 1918, but quick recovery meant products from Nuremburg could again flood the UK market by the 1920s and 30s, mainly because raging domestic inflation in Germany meant cheap selling prices. There was also a UK public perception of superior German craftsmanship. Elsewhere, Hong Kong was already making toys and Japan was becoming a leading manufacturer in the 1920s. This didn't stop the three Lines Brothers from setting up Tri-ang in the Old Kent Road in 1920 and Alfred Wells setting up his Walthamstow factory to make pressed tin mechanical toys in 1926.

Meanwhile, the 1920s were a lean time for trolleybus development. Most of the early systems had failed by 1918 and of those that didn't, one imagines determined managers and exceptional engineers who doggedly produced essential spare parts themselves when little else was available. Of the 61 early systems of the

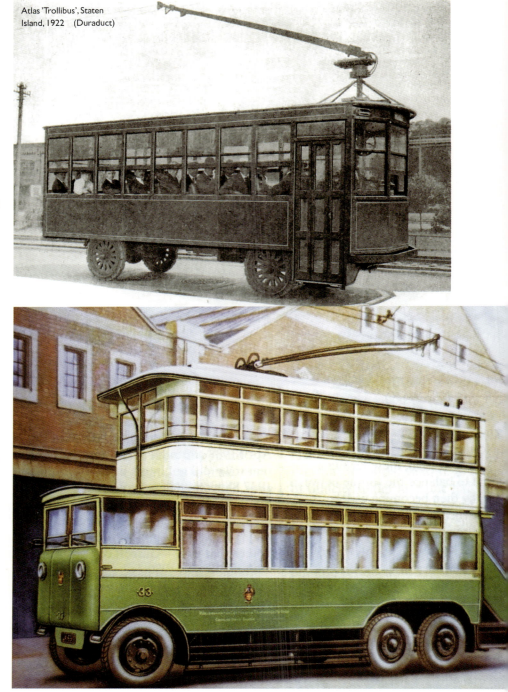

Atlas 'Trollibus', Staten Island, 1922 (Duraduct)

Wolverhampton 33, Guy BTX/Dodson/Rees Roturbo, 1926 (Guy Motors)

world only 10 survived the 1920s. There were no systems in Germany during the entire decade. Globally, there were 48 new systems in the twenties but 11 of those didn't survive the decade and others only just lasted into the 30s. In the UK just 7 new trolleybuses were delivered in 1920 and only 83 in 1929. The problem was that the function and the technology of the trolleybus hadn't quite been decided. Were they to be tram-like or based on buses? Should they be an adjunct to the tram or replace it? And which collector system should they use? With the visual identity of the trolleybus in doubt and so few around the world, it's hardly surprising that, as far as we know, no model trolleybuses were produced in the twenties. There is a mystery contender however.

An almost unbelievable reference to a 1920s Dayton toy trolleybus, when the US had extremely few real ones operating, is made by Geoff Price in Model Auto Review number 4. Dayton Toys did make a Faegol Observation bus according to C.E.Moate, who was quoting from their catalogue, and there were to be similar trolleybuses. There's no doubt Dayton Friction Toy Works existed, from 1897 until the 1930s, inventing the friction drive and making many novelties, including a Trolley Car in 1900. But only 55 trolleybuses were delivered in the USA in the 1920s and few lasted into the 30s. By 1927 Philadelphia's 8 Brills were the only trolleybuses operating in whole country. Assuming the reference is correct, the prototype could have been the single boomed Atlas 'Trollibus' that

Garrett OS prototype doubler decker, 1927 (Garrett)

operated on Staten Island - at least its simple box shape would have been easy to reproduce in tin. Dayton itself didn't have trolleybuses until April 1933, when the first Brill T-40 entered service.

At least one trolleybus was modelled by a trolleybus manufacturer at this time. Richard Garrett and Sons, of Suffolk, built a model of their open staircase double decker of 1927 and exhibited it, and the real thing, at the Commercial Motor Show. The factory had intended to build a single decker but speculatively built a demonstrator with common parts and an extra deck. It went to Southend on hire, stayed, and led to an order for 5 more, albeit with enclosed staircases. The model, which for many years resided in the Garrett boardroom, may have been built to gauge the directors' styling opinion but, more likely, was for exhibition and sales purposes. With the breakup of Garretts in 1985 the model went missing but was later returned to the East Anglia Transport Museum at nearby Carlton Colville, where the London Trolleybus Preservation Society restored it before presenting it to the Long Shop Museum where it now resides, back in a large glass case in the preserved Garrett directors boardroom. Garretts actually had the largest share of the tiny

Garrett OS double decker by Garrett, 1:10, wood, metal

UK trolleybus market at this time – which, considering the UK market was the largest in the world in 1927, made Garretts arguably the worlds leading supplier, for just one year. But they were desperate to procure business and, as well as the model, produced lavish brochures and an early film commercial. It was all to no avail - the receiver was called in during 1932 and Garretts was taken over by Beyer, Peacock. They never again built a trolleybus.

With Paris, Manila and Wien, the only capital cities with trolleybuses in the twenties, and then only on the outskirts, there was still little to attract toy makers. But there had been very significant trolleybus developments in the twenties. In Britain's Birmingham, very tall, tram-like vehicles had replaced tramcars with great success, at least operationally – the solid tyres on cobbled streets must have given a rough ride. Nearby, in Wolverhampton, four years later in 1926, Guy Motors produced the world's first 3 axle pneumatic tyred double deck trolleybus. The trade press went to town, so to speak, with colour illustrations (see page 14) and feature articles detailing its smooth riding and better traction. Within another year, subsequent deliveries had enclosed staircases. The three causes of the trolleybus identity crisis had been solved; their function, at least for now, was to replace tramcars and their technology was firmly based on bus practise with, usually, two under-running trolley booms as promoted by Max Schiemann. By the end of the decade, and from then on, the trolleybus became a recognised weapon in the transport planners armoury.

3 axle double decker by Günthermann, (no scale), tinplate, 1938

Finally, toy trolleybuses

Trolleybuses in the 1930s were suddenly being introduced at almost an exponential rate and toy makers, at long last, noticed. With the staggering 'trolleybusification' of London from 1931, and especially after 1934, no less than four toy manufacturers produced toy versions of London's impressive trolleybuses. It could hardly have been otherwise. In just four years, between 1935 and 1939, over 1500 trolleybuses swept aside tramcars from all of west, east and most of north London. The fleet in London in 1939 represented something like a quarter of all trolleybuses in the world. Günthermann in Germany, Joustra in France, Wells and Betal made tinplate toy London trolleybuses in response, in 10 versions of which, bizarrely, seven had only four wheels. This demonstrates an essential quality of toys – their makers take liberties with reality – only one, out

Wells Catalogue 1951, 2 axle double decker, (Wells-Brimtoy)

Joustra catalogue 1949, 3 axle double decker, (Joustra)

of 1,891 London trolleybuses, had two axles.

Now that model trolleybuses were historically 'out there', we can now concentrate on the subject of this book, but before going on in subsequent chapters to itemise model and toy trolleybuses, we look at models that had a public or industrial purpose but which weren't necessarily produced commercially.

Young and old; a two year old and a seventy something share the fascination of miniature trolleybuses. Like much else, the absorption is seemingly innate and can last a lifetime.

Nye Davison, aged 2

Larry Noades, aged 72

Chapter 2
Professional model trolleybuses

London experiments

George Sinclair, Rolling Stock engineer of London Transport, and Theodore Thomas, General Manager, went to the United States in 1934 to see trolleybuses in Chicago, Indianapolis and Cleveland, where the latest models by ACF and Twin Coach were on display. All were chassisless and so lighter and stronger. Sinclair, a formidable Scottish designer, who developed the London trolleybus throughout the thirties, returned to build 754 as a prototype over a period of two years at LT Charlton Works. Two and a half inches lower, six cwt. lighter and with a second door at the front, 754 was a success, but needed to be replicated by trolleybus manufacturers. AEC and MCW, the preferred suppliers, had their own thoughts on the best solution and produced large, detailed models to convince the London Transport Board of their merits. Both models can be seen today at the Trolleybus Museum at Sandtoft.

London Transport 953, AEC unit construction/ Weymann/MV by AEC, 1:8, wood, metal

London Transport 953, AEC unit construction/ Weymann/MV, 1937 (AEC)

London 953, AEC unit construction/Weymann/MV, 1937 (AEC)

Professional model trolleybuses 17

London Transport 954, AEC chassisless/MCCW/MV by MCW, 1:5, wood, metal

John Rackham, AECs Chief engineer proposed a lighter chassis that lined up with the strengthened uprights of a Weymann body to produce a more integrated whole that avoided the differing flexing of standard chassis and body combinations. The 1:8 scale model includes the uprights of the 'unit construction' design and closely follows the structure that became no.953; regarded by Ken Blacker in "The London Trolleybus" as one of the best looking trolleybuses ever produced. She led to 25 M1 class trolleys being built in late 1939 but was sadly destroyed by fire during the war.

Metro Cammell followed Sinclair's more radical chassisless principles but with the addition of 16 gauge steel waist-rail flanged girders along the length. These can be seen on the surviving 1:5 scale model, which includes lower deck roof cross pieces but leaves out the side welded seat

London 954, AEC chassisless/MCCW/MV, 1937 (LT Museum)

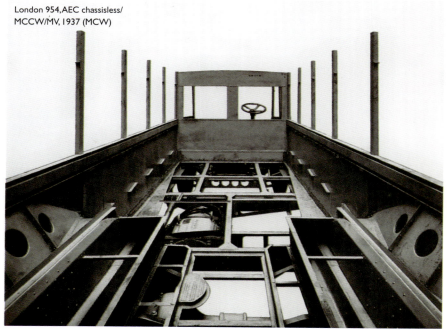

London 954, AEC chassisless/MCCW/MV, 1937 (MCW)

brackets of the original. Integration extended to one piece sheeting on the front panel of what became 954, although an access panel was later added. She served for 23 years on some of the busiest routes, which certainly proved the validity of her pioneering design. 175 L class trolleys had followed in 1939, but without the distinctive cream band under the windscreen. Quite what role the models played in the chassisless saga isn't known, but manufacturers being able to produce such large and accurate artefacts do reflect London Transport's ability at the time to commission thoroughly engineered high quality solutions almost without restraint.

Škoda's models

Another manufacturer, apart from Garrett in the twenties, who used models, was Škoda. They had produced their first trolleybus, the 1Tr, in 1936 for Prague (and modelled by Petr Došlý for RA model – see page 109). This was followed by the similar 2Tr in 1938. Under German occupation,

18 Professional model trolleybuses

Škoda produced 34 3Trs for their home town of Plzeň from 1941 onwards but for their first two axle trolleybus, the 5Tr of 1943, the factory produced a model, prepared drawings and did structural analysis for management's perusal but built no full size trolleybus. The model was highly detailed and included the interior seating arrangement and cab, right down to dials on the dashboard. Photographs are all that survive of the metal and plastic model. This careful retention of historic company documents and the making of models was to be become a Škoda tradition. Today the Škoda Works Museum in Plzeň houses

Škoda 9Tr prototype, 1961 (Škoda)

Generic Škoda 5Tr by Škoda, unknown scale, wood (Škoda)

not only real vehicles but a number of meticulous model trolleybuses illustrating the long history of this prodigious manufacturer.

On view is a wonderfully detailed, 1:18 scale metal model of a prototype 9Tr, with roof lights, built in 1961. It also has an inductive steering coil at the front and is electrically powered. A second 9Tr, in local Plzeň colours, is also to be seen. Interestingly, both of these models are too low, with the lower panel only a little higher than the wheel arches, unlike the real thing where panels are almost twice as high as the wheel intrusion. Perhaps the apprentices who made them, were being tested for their skill to work in miniature rather than their model accuracy. The models, however, were used by Škoda for over 30 years at international trade fairs.

Škoda kept strictly to its trolleybus designation scheme, including numbers for designs that were never to see the light of day. The 13Tr was one

Plzen Škoda 9Tr prototype by Škoda, 1:18, metal (Škoda)

Plzen Škoda 9Tr by Škoda, 1:18, metal (Škoda)

Generic Škoda 13Tr by Škoda, unkown scale, wood (Škoda)

Generic Škoda 16Tr by Škoda, unkown scale, wood (Škoda)

Generic Škoda 13Tr by Škoda, unkown scale, wood (Škoda)

norm, it would have been seen as fashionable. There was hardly the need for a new model at this time – the 14Tr was still selling in the thousands throughout the world.

The Škoda Works Museum houses a model of a standard 14Tr, the version adapted for San Francisco and the articulated version, the 15Tr. All are 1:16 scale and were made in the pattern shop of Škoda Steelwork. There are also working models, running under scale overhead, steered by a slot.

Despite both the 14Tr and the 15Tr selling so well, the management kept thinking ahead and had a model made of a 17Tr in 1988 to test, amongst other ideas, the use of small wheels to try to get round the high floor problem that was starting to make Škoda trolleybuses look dated. It

such, dating from 1969 and was more advanced than the design that was to follow in 1972, the ubiquitous 14Tr. The pictures of the first wooden model show three entrances and a deep curved windscreen, which may have been ambition rather than practicality, although the 21Tr of 30 years later is stylistically similar. A second, two entrance, model was produced, that looked a little more practical. The design was to have had a capacity for 69 passengers and a top speed of 65km/hr.

Another model was of the radical 16Tr with much squarer styling. This proposal is less documented, just stating that the motor was to have a rating of 120kW. One can imagine some would regard the 16Tr as ugly, with a backward canted windscreen and rather brutal front bumper, but for the 1980s with high floors still the

Generic Škoda 16Tr by Škoda, unkown scale, wood (Škoda)

had a more practical wrap around windscreen and the idea became built prototypes, but with added rear windows. The project was part of a government initiative to unify buses, coaches and trolleybuses using common parts from Škoda and the Karosa bus company. But the project was cancelled and the three prototypes, each with a capacity of 80 passengers and a motor rated at 100kw, ended up on the Ostrava system, in the town in which they were built. Only one

Generic Škoda 14Tr by Škoda Museum, 1:16, metal (Škoda)

San Francisco Municipal Railway Škoda 14Tr by Škoda, 1:16, metal (Škoda)

Ostrava Škoda 17Tr (Harold17)

Ostrava Škoda 17Tr by Škoda, 1:16, wood (Škoda)

remained in service by 2007.

The latest scale model produced by the Škoda factory is the 21Tr of 1996. With the rationalisation of Škoda into an electrical parts manufacturer rather than a vehicle producer, it may be the last. This, of course, hasn't stopped the many modellers of the Czech Republic from making a great number of Škoda trolleybus models, which we review from page 108.

Professional model trolleybuses 21

Szegred SZKV Škoda 21Tr by Škoda, 1:13, metal (Škoda)

motors, with rather solid 1:50 scale models.

Vossloh-Kiepe, long specialising in trolleybus control and collection equipment, recently commissioned a model of the latest Hess Swisstrolley3, an 18m version of the 25m long 'Lightram' for exhibition purposes. Hess similarly have a model of their prototype of this articulated trolleybus (see overleaf).

Public trolleybus models

Museums and public exhibitions, meanwhile,

Other Manufacturers

Thought to have been built by the original bodybuilder, Verheul, at the time of delivery of the BUT prototypes in 1949, this magnificent 1:12 scale model has resided in operator Gemeente Arnhem's canteen and bar ever since. Perhaps it was this model that secured the order. The 5 visible sides are carved in wood, with the windows represented by printed graphics, and chrome work, bumpers and trolley gear attached. The wheels are integrally carved with the body sides.

We can speculate that historic manufacturers of trolleybuses may have produced models. One can imagine a bodied model of say, the 'ahead of its time' low floor Leyland TB10 to go with the demonstration of its chassis to London Transport at Fulwell Depot in 1935, but that's (almost) certainly wishful thinking. Obscure documentation or somebody's elderly memory would need to (miraculously) surface with new evidence. By way of at least contributory evidence, competitor AEC did produce models of their radical Q type at this time.

Today, models are still used to sell trolleybuses. A user of Škoda electrical parts is the Polish firm of Solaris. New and rather energetic, the company has offices all over Europe, including Switzerland, where their salesman Hans Thommen, can be seen on occasion, proudly holding their 1:20 scale model of a Trollino 12T.

Ganz Transelectro, the Hungarian electrical company that's been in existence for 130 years, recently presented customers of Solaris Trollino trolleybuses, incorporating their traction

Generic Solaris Trollino SGT 12 by Solaris, 1:30, wood

Arnhem BUT 9721T/Verheul/EE by Verheul, 80cm, wood, metal

Budapest BKV Solaris Trollino 12T by Ganz, 1:50, wood (Andras Ekkert)

Roma ATAC Solaris Trollino 18T by Ganz, 1:50, wood (Andras Ekkert)

Professional model trolleybuses

Generic Hess SwissTrolley3/2 by Vossloch, 1:20, wood

Zurich 76, Hess LighTram/Vossloch, 2008

24   Professional model trolleybuses

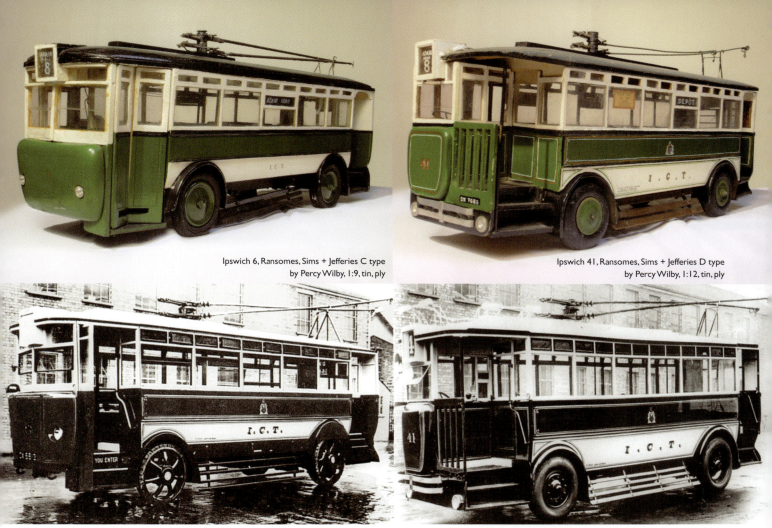

Ipswich 6, Ransomes, Sims + Jefferies C type
by Percy Wilby, 1:9, tin, ply

Ipswich 41, Ransomes, Sims + Jefferies D type
by Percy Wilby, 1:12, tin, ply

Ipswich 12, Ransomes, Sims + Jefferies C type, 1926 (Reavels/Langford)

Ipswich 41, Ransomes, Sims + Jefferies D type, 1928 (Ransomes)

inevitably have need of models. Amongst the earliest are a set of four trolleybuses from Ipswich, made by Percy Wilby from 1948 onwards and now in the Ipswich Transport Museum. Chronologically the oldest vehicle modelled was Ipswich's second 6, a Ransomes, Sims and Jefferies "C" type of 1926. It was originally fitted with solid tyres on cast seven spoke wheels and had a spat covering the rear pair. Pneumatics were fitted in 1932 and the class had billboards added to the roof. Percy Wilby's model faithfully reproduces the later incarnation and the Estler trolleybases, but the wooden front panel is less accurate, and the working headlights are not recessed as on the original. The model has a Government war surplus 12 volt motor driving a tiny differential through a universal coupling, but there is no steering mechanism. Percy Wilby wrote an article in the March 1956 issue of the 'Model Railway Constructor' entitled "The Upside Down Railway" where he appealed for "anyone (who) has already tackled this problem, I would like to know how they overcame the difficulties of running driverless trolleybuses". There were several replies, which we have detailed in the next chapter about powered trolleybuses.

Percy Wilby also wrote "Ever since I was a child, trolleybuses have been a favourite with me, and as I grew older, my interest deepened to a point where I could no longer just study them as a working public undertaking: I wanted to reproduce them as a working model and what better prototype could I use than that running in my own home town?". Ipswich Corporation had, until 1950, owned only trolleybuses and until 1944 only owned locally built ones, so "Here then, was the final spur to build a model trolleybus, particularly as the diesel-driven bus was now encroaching our trolleybus depot".

Percy built three more local model trolleybuses including 41 as she had appeared when new, with the unique open dual entrance configuration that lasted just 4 years in service, before conversion to a more conventional frontal arrangement was carried out in 1932. It seems Percy repainted this model, adding the fine lining that was used before the war. The sign in the window says 'Visit the Co-Op Fete July 6th'. The wheels are 3 inch, so the scale is about 1 inch to the foot or 1:12. Missing items seem to be the wonderful hooter that protruded from under the windscreen and the handle to the right of the front entrance. Unfortunately, no full size original of this eccentrically designed class now survives.

Next came 47, a Ransomes "D" type but with a double deck body in the so-called "piano front" style. By using 3"'Airyda' model wheels with 'Sorbo' rubber tyres on hardwood hubs, made by the Modellers Supply Limited of Aspley, Huddersfield, Percy Wilby again had the scale of an inch to the foot dictated to him. The rubber of the tyres is now, 50 years later, about the only

Ipswich 47, Ransomes, Sims + Jefferies D type
by Percy Wilby, 1:12, tin, ply

Ipswich 52, Ransomes, Sims + Jefferies D type, 1933
(JH Meredith)

Professional model trolleybuses 25

Ipswich 68, Ransomes, Sims + Jefferies Light 2 by Percy Wilby, 1:9, tin, ply

'contraptions' as anachronistic, but at least they know about the concept.

Also across the Atlantic, a working model layout was built in 1952 for an exhibition as Seattle Transit's contribution to Seattle's centennial year celebrations with model Twin Coach Model 44GTTs whizzing round beneath accurately modelled overhead, guided by a pin that followed a slot in the road. The layout was built by the men of the transport authority, which would explain the accuracy. The exhibit has now gone missing, but 955 is preserved by Seattle Metro Transit and St Petersburg Tram Collection has modelled Seattle's 875 and 976 in O scale. Seattle still has its trolleybuses, which, hopefully, are not regarded as anachronisms.

A similar model guidance system is used at Aston Manor Transport Museum in Birmingham where Dave Wall's wonderful layout is on long

Ipswich 77, Ransomes, Sims + Jefferies Light 2, 1937 (C Carter)

Inset: St Louis Car Job 1754, 1948 (GE)

New York City Transit St Louis Car Job 1754 by NY Transit Museum, 1:12, wood, metal (Martin Sustina)

sign of deterioration. The rubber on the preserved full sized 46 is also of concern, and restoration of this nationally important relic is estimated to cost of the order of £80,000 – she too is at the Ipswich Transport Museum.

Percy Wilby was a railway engineer by trade and built his models from 5-ply plywood and angled aluminium. He used greaseproof paper as a mould for plastic wood to form the back rounded corners of the bodies. Ransomes 68 was modelled in this way with the radialised lower windows that had been added to the originals in 1949. This model uses four inch wheels which equate to an approximate 1:10 scale.

Not dissimilar in model construction technique, in New York's Transit Museum, there's a large model of 3124, a St. Louis Car trolleybus. 200 were delivered in 1948 and ran on 6 routes in and around Brooklyn. There had been grandiose plans for 435 'trolley coaches' to replace 13 tram routes but in the event electric traction only lasted until 1962. The model appears very accurate, except for the rather poor understanding of trolleygear and the missing shroud. Younger visitors seem to regard such

BUT S641T/East Lancashire/GEC, 1955 (David Bradley)

26   Professional model trolleybuses

Seattle Transit Twin Coach 44GTT by SeattleTransit, 1:87, metal, wood (Ohio Brass)

Cardiff Corporation BUT 9641T/East Lancashire/GEC by Dave Wall, 1:18, card, wood, plastic & metal

Professional model trolleybuses

Twin Coach 44GTT, 1943 (Twin Coach)

term loan. Built over a period of 40 years to a scale of 1:18 with a guidance groove between the tram tracks, there's a pin soldered to the steering tie bar of each trolleybus model. The models concentrate on robustness for demonstration circumstances so don't conform to highest representational standards, though you'd never know – they have a genuine feel of realism about them. Hidden underneath each is a Meccano chassis and sturdy ex-government surplus 24volt motors, whilst on top are bodies built of cardboard, plywood, plasticard and Perspex. The models include Birmingham's 90, a rarely modelled vehicle and numerically that city's last trolleybus – it lasted only 11 years in service, which makes Dave's model longer lasting. The real thing was a Leyland TB7 with a MCCW body and

Leyland TB7/MCCW/GEC, 1940 (AD Packer)

General Electric electrical equipment.

Next is Walsall Corporation 877 a Sunbeam F4/Park Royal trolleybus of 1950 that could, just as easily, have been painted in Ipswich Corporation colours. That's where the vehicle first saw service (and where sister vehicle 126 is preserved), but, as this is a Midlands Museum,

Birmingham Corporation Leyland TB7/MCCW/GEC by Dave Wall, 1:18, card, wood, plastic & metal

Sunbeam F4/Park Royal, 1950 (John Law)

28 Professional model trolleybuses

Walsall Corporation Sunbeam F4/Park Royal/MV by Dave Wall, 1:18, card, wood, plastic & metal

London United AEC 663T/Union Construction/EE by London Transport, 1:8, wood, metal

AEC 663T/Union Construction/EE, 1931 (LT Museum)

Walsall blue seems more appropriate. Future plans include modelling Wolverhampton 616, a similar Sunbeam that is also preserved, but not yet restored, at the nearby transport museum at Wythall.

Glasgow Corporation TBS13 was an example of a unique design, the only 35 foot (10.5m) trolleybuses in Britain, which had to have special legal dispensation to operate. The real TBS13 is preserved in the Glasgow Museum of Transport. Our picture of the model shows how Dave Wall's overhead is constructed, with piano running wire slotted into brass tubing ears that are soldered to a wire hoop that pinches the insulating cross bar on the span wires. The dumbbell insulators add realism.

Cardiff Corporation 243 is the newest model and has the same Meccano based trolleybooms as the rest of the fleet. The wheels too use Meccano parts, though the tread is a little narrow and rubber bands have been added for better traction, especially on the curves at either end of the loop layout.

Other museum trolleybus models of note include the AEC 663T "Diddler" 1:8 scale model at the London Transport Museum. The model was built before 1951 probably for the Festival of Britain, by apprentices at London Transport's Chiswick Works. With a registration plate of HX2756 at the back making this the first pre-production prototype no.1, the real vehicle never existed in the same state as the model. At the inauguration of London's vast system on 16th May 1931, London United's no.1 still retained the experimental black on white route indicators, an uplighting lamp on the cab roof and a rooftop route stencil sign. It had also acquired its iconic central headlamp and an AEC badge beneath. The first 8 Diddlers all underwent considerable modification in the first year of their lives, including, at the behest of drivers, the moving of the windscreen back to give greater width and leave a longer protuberance of 'bonnet'. The revised windscreen, the normal destination aperture, the narrower front chrome grill and

BUT RETB1/Burlingham/MV, 1958 (Martin Smith)

Glasgow Corporation Transport BUT RETB1/Burlingham/MV by Dave Wall, 1:18, card, wood, plastic & metal

Professional model trolleybuses 29

beading added at the join of the two decks all suggest the model is based on nos. 3-8, which were delivered without the front headlamp. The real surviving "Diddler" I can be seen on Acton Town Museum Depot open days, where, hidden away on the shelves are a couple of 00 gauge layouts with model trolleybuses of the London Transport rather than London United generations.

Built a little later in 1956, is the fantastically detailed and stunningly accurate 1:12 scale model of Bradford 754 – amongst the last traditional rear entrance, open platform trolleybuses built in the British Isles. Unfortunately not currently on public view, so you'll have to take our word for it, this must rate as the finest trolleybus model constructed. Getting the conservators at the Science Museum's reserve collection to turn her on her side took special pleading and separating her into fully detailed chassis and body sections, as is possible, was deemed out of the question. Suspending references to scale, it was hard to see that this is indeed a miniature, such is the very high modelling quality. And looking under simulated daylight makes the experience even better. There really is little more to say, except to convince the Science Museum to again put her on public show. We've included our portraits of 754 on page 294.

The Stephenson Museum in North Shields has a trolleybus model to illustrate what it calls "The Electric Century" because local Tyneside

Bradford City Transport BUT 9611T/Weymann/EE by Bradford City Transport, 1:12, wood, metal

engineers were pioneers of electric traction in the early 20th Century. The model is a meticulously made large scale representation of a Newcastle double decker – vehicles that were much loved and appreciated in the city. And Nottingham's Industrial Museum has a model of a 1927 Railless open staircase double decker, rather strangely painted in the local tram livery of maroon and cream, instead of the green and cream actually used.

At in the Musée AMTUIR, at Colombes, north west of Paris, there's a very detailed model of a Parisian Vetra CS60 of 1943, together with a real example from Marseilles and a CB60 version from Limoges amongst its preserved trolleybuses. There's also the guided Civis trolleybus promotional model of 2000 (see page 152).

In Spain, there are models of BUT single deckers, where the real no. 14 is still kept by its operator, Zaragoza T.SS. At least two models of one body design for the 40 BUT 9614T chassis imported to Spain in 1950-1, survive from the period and are thought to have been made by the bodybuilder, Carde y Escoriaza, as mock-ups for the full size bodies. One model is still exhibited and is now well over fifty years old. It has been restored, with added detail. Unlike nearly every

Zaragoza T.SS.T. BUT 9641T/Escoriaza by Carde y Escoriaza, unknown scale, metal (Mariano Gonzalvo)

BUT 9641T/Escoriaza, 1951 (Carde y Escoriaza)

from motor buses in 1940. Owner Albert Gonzalez has managed to include interior and exterior lighting in his 1:16 model.

At the Musée des Transports en commun du Pays de Liège there's a fine collection of the generations of trolleybuses that served here, starting with Ransomes, Sims and Jefferies trolleys, locally designated T30, that ran until 1961 and ending, for now, with the FN T54 the impressive single deckers for which so much development work had been done. We've described the models in the UK and Belgian chapters on pages 335 and 89, respectively.

In Dresden, at the Verkehrsmuseum, as well as the Dresdner Haide-Bahn Cedes-Stoll of 1903, there's a 1:25 scale model of a Lowa W602a, East Germany's workhorse trolleybus of the mid-fifties. And there's another under detailed yellow overhead. 125 of these single deckers were built and usually hauled a trailer. There have been quite a few commercial models made of the W602a, reflecting the 12 operators that used them, page 176 where we also include the Siemens Museum's Electromote of 1882 and Dorf Whehlen's Schiemann of 1901.

One museum that is dedicated to the trolleybus rather more than most is in Ukraine. The Crimean Trolleybus Museum, celebrating the much loved and socially important interurban line between Simferopol and Yalta with local services at each end, first opened in 1977. The museum is based at the former tram depot and trolleybus workshops in Simferopol. The line itself, at 86km in length, the longest in the world, opened between 1959 and 1961 with Russian MTB-82 trolleys and then 74 Škoda 8Trs. The museum's 8Tr model is, it has to be said, a little amateur, but reflects the enthusiasm of the company

Dresdner Haide-Bahn Cedes-Stoll by Axel Dopperphul, 1:25, wood, plastic

model in this book, the window pillars are actually thinner than the real thing and made of sheet steel. The models may predate real production and don't include the front cream droop below the windscreen of the original.

At Tramvies de Gratallops, a tiny tram museum in Catalonia, there's a model of one of the wonderful Tilling-Sevens double deck trolleybuses that operated in Barcelona after being converted

Barcelona CGA 551, Tillings Stevens/CGA by Albert Gonzalez, 1:16, wood, card (Albert Gonzalez)

Tillings Stevens/CGA, 1941 (CAP)

Liège trolleybus models by Musée des Transports, Liège, 1:43, wood, metal (André Corteil)

Dresden Lowa W602a by Axel Dopperphul, 1:43, resin

Simferopol 103, Škoda 8Tr, 1959-61 (unknown)

Simferopol KTU Škoda 8Tr by KTU, 1:20, wood, metal (Palmer)

particularly well suited to the long and spectacular journeys up and over the Yaila mountains beside the Black Sea.

192 Škoda 14Trs arrived between 1980 and 1991, but as the break-up of Comecon meant hard currency was needed for new vehicles, no more could be bought. In any case, the 14Trs have proved less reliable on this demanding system, with windscreen failures and problems with their more complex thyristor control. The museum model, however, is every bit as good as that in Plzeň, at Škoda's own museum, detailed above. There are more models on show, including KTG trolley-lorries and the 1995 YMZ-T2, a gift from the manufacturer (Yuzhmash) representing another (unsuccessful) attempt to finally retire the workhorse Škoda 9Trs. Hopefully, funding crises will be overcome.

We end this chapter with an admittedly crude model of Hastings 45 that was built "in a couple of evenings" in 1994 by Mick Sherwood of Hastings Trolleybus Restoration Group to

volunteers who created it. It stands surrounded by memorabilia, medals and certificates of the 'glorious' Soviet era. The trolleybus operation still needs nearly a thousand drivers, employed at four depots with headways during the tourist laden summers of two minutes.

Deliveries of Škoda 9Tr trolleybuses arrived in Crimea almost annually between 1962 and 1982 and some are still in service after 30 years – the engineers (who also created the museum) have become adept at repairing and keeping them going. The museum's model 9Tr is altogether more accurate than its predecessor and is thought to be built at 1:12 scale. Simferopol had 580 9Trs which were unusual in having two doors rather than the far more common three door variety. Despite attempts with Ukrainian and Russian trolleybuses, the Czech 9Tr has been

Simferopol 1990, Škoda 14Tr, 1984 (Aztec)

Simferopol 404, Škoda 9Tr, 1962-1981 (Kpost)

Simferopol KTU Škoda 9Tr by KTU, 1:20, wood, metal (Andrew Nechesin)

32　Professional model trolleybuses

Simferopol KTU Škoda 14Tr by KTU, 1:20, wood, metal (Andrew Nechesin)

demonstrate what a rebuilt original should look like. 80 year old Hastings 45 was, at that time, rather the worse for wear, after 21 years in service, serving as a ticket office for a further two decades and then stored for another 20 or so years. The model, though, was put on "Happy Harold" the preserved open-top double deck sister vehicle and attached to a collection box to gather public donations for the restoration that is to follow. This book serves a similar function, to raise money for the preservation of the "real things", including Hastings 45.

Hastings 45, Guy BT, 1929

Hastings Tramways Co. Guy ET by Mick Sherwood, 46cm, wood, plasticard

Professional model trolleybuses 33

Bradford 754, BUT 9611T/Weymann/EE by Bradford City Transport, 1:12, wood, metal (Mike Bruce)

Chesterfield Straker Squire by Eric Chambers, (AR Kaye)

Chapter 3
One offs, specials and making them steer

Eric Chambers, son of an engineer at Sheepbridge Steel Works, Chesterfield, made a model of the Straker Squire trolleybuses that had started turning outside his house at Brampton terminus in 1927. The sixth scale model is the earliest enthusiasts model trolley we know of. Perhaps his father helped make it, even if the wheels are obviously too small, and perhaps he sent the photograph to Model Engineer magazine. It appeared in a 1929 issue with editor Percival Marshall commenting "I do not know whether the builder intends to put down a miniature power plant and trolley wire system so that his model may be run, but this would be an interesting thing to do". Whether Eric or even his audience took this to heart isn't known, but plenty have tried.

Over the years, enthusiasts have gone their own ways to produce trolleybuses that move - hardly surprising, as one of the attractions of trolleybuses is their simplicity and the obvious, visible demonstration of their working by using overhead collectors. While the trolleybooms present a surmountable modelling challenge, steering, especially at smaller scales, always seems to have been a bit more of a hurdle. In this chapter we look at various modellers' attempts to come to terms with this desire. The commercial solutions and the story of toys produced for sale, most notably by Eheim/Brawa, is told in the next chapter.

The Biggest
We start with the most radical solution – make the trolleybus model so big that you can get in it and steer it yourself! Peter Lepine-Smith of Great Bookham, UK, built a 1:3 scale Sunbeam F4A Reading model trolleybus, based on coloured drawings supplied by the then transport manager at Reading Corporation, WJ Evans. He built it mainly between 1962 and 1964 but didn't manage to finish what must be the worlds largest trolleybus model until 2006 when he finally added the nearside mudguards.

Despite 44 years in the building, no. 182 still operates impeccably, with characteristic electrical whine, around the 100m loop of overhead equipped garden pathway. The wheels, steering and braking mechanisms, and parts of the chassis survive from a "Jobs Diary" battery milk float,

Reading 182, Sunbeam F4A/Burlingham/AEI by Peter Lepino, 1:3, Aluminium and wood

Reading 186, Sunbeam F4A/Burlingham/AEI, 1961 (Geoff Lumb)

Reading 182, Sunbeam F4A/Burlingham/AEI by Peter Lepino, 1:3, Aluminium and wood (P. Lepino)

powered by a 10hp Harbilt traction motor. One contactor supplies the 110volt 30 amp supply to a large variable resistor that is operated by the foot pedal. The aluminium panelled body is pop riveted to aluminium angle sections and plywood components. The trolleybus carries the driver and at a squeeze, three adult passengers. Interior lighting, like the original, is fluorescent and there are head and side lights for running at night.

The miniature trolley bases are by Brecknell Willis, suppliers of most of the full size equivalents used by UK operators. The brass trolley heads have carbon inserts from Morgan Crucible, just like the real thing. The overhead is supplied from an auto-transformer and silicon rectifier fed from the mains through a full size ex-London Transport feeder pillar. 10swg copper running wire is held by thin copper sheet that's bolted to old pattern mains electric plugs that serve as insulators. Erection and maintenance is carried out from a red tower wagon cart, suitably inscribed with "Danger Overhead Repairs". After a number of years gathering dust, Peter has restored his system, built a new depot and again provides visitors with an inspiring ride. The full size Reading trolleybus, no. 182, was built in 1961, and provided inspiration to build the model, but it only survived seven years of service. Today, sister vehicles no. 186 and 193 survive into preservation at Sandtoft Trolleybus Museum.

Remote control by cable

Apart from making it big enough to get in and steer, one of the earliest 'driveable' models we know of was BW Francis's 'remotely controlled model trolley bus' written up in Model Engineer in 1950. Painstakingly precise about the 1:18 scale 24-gauge tinplate body construction, rewiring the 6v Lucas SW4 wiper motor to make it reversible (!) and how the turned oak wheels were mounted, the article says little about the remote control aspect, mentioning only 'a speedo cable'.

Reading 182, Sunbeam F4A/Burlingham/AEI by Peter Lepino, 1:3, Aluminium and wood

Reading 182, Sunbeam F4A/Burlingham/AEI by Peter Lepino, 1:3, Aluminium and wood

Reading 182, Sunbeam F4A/Burlingham/AEI by Peter Lepino, 1:3, Aluminium and wood

Horam Transport Leyland TB10 by BW Francis, 1:43, wood   (BW Francis)

London Transport 1525, AEC 664T/MCCW/MV by WLC Jeffery, 1:6, wood, metal

There was a steering wheel that could be mounted inside, on the roof or used remotely, presumably acting mechanically. So there was no overhead, just details of the 'M/C' battery and how it was fitted. It did look rather modern though - was Mr. Francis inspired by the low floor Leyland of 1935 in his look through 'commercial vehicle magazines'? We trust, the then 6 year old DR Francis of Horam, Sussex, was pleased with the result, built by his father.

Another remotely controlled model trolleybus is the 1:7.5 scale London L3 class 1525 AEC/MCCW built by WLC Jeffery in 1960-64. Mystery had surrounded the origins of rather spectacular model until reference was found in Model Engineer magazine. According to its builder it had an 8-way cable that allowed forward and reverse motion, steering by servo motor, working bells, lights and windscreen wiper. The wheels were supplied by Goodyear, which dictated the odd scale. For some unexplained reason, Mr Jeffery removed the traction motor and the servo, perhaps he was planning to rework the mechanicals to include powering the 122cm model from scale overhead. Not knowing about such detail when I saw the model, I didn't think to investigate further, either way Mr. Jeffery built an amazing, if slightly flawed, replica (there's more on page 300).

The Great Steering Debate

Percy Wilby, a railway engineer of Ipswich, mentioned in the introduction, built four model trolleybuses in 1:10 and 1:12 scales between 1948 and 1956. He had powered them with ex-

Leyland TB10, 1934   (Leyland)

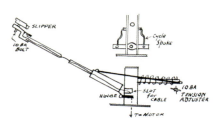

Trolley boom diagram by Percy Wilby, (MRC)

38   One offs, specials and making them steer

London Transport 1525, AEC 664T/MCCW/MV by WLC Jeffery, 1:6, wood, metal

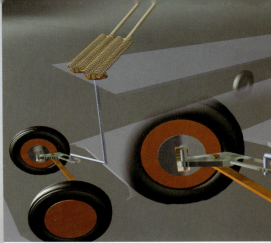

Trolley boom steering design by JA Vincent

government surplus 12 volt motors, (specifically ex-RAF camera motors) driving spur geared differentials made for model racing cars. He'd wired them to working trolleybooms and built a short straight section of overhead. The booms were made of brass tube with single PVC telephone cable inside and 0 gauge railway fishplates, cut in half, to form the slipper trolley heads. But, in his March, 1956 article in Model Railway Constructor magazine, he bemoaned the difficulty of producing a solution as to how the models might be steered. Mr. JA Vincent B.Eng replied 2 months later with a design that apparently took "quite a long time adjusting wires" and said "Patience is needed to get results". One trolleyboom, via a vertical rod, turned a lever that, at its other end, was slotted into an extension of an Ackermann steering mechanism, which reacted by turning to counter the deviation of the trolleyboom from the overhead. Similar in principle to the Smallwood, Eheim and Rivarossi designs (described in the next chapter), but the offset vertical rod, down from one boom would have led to inaccurate steering. The design did

Ipswich 6, Ransomes, Sims + Jefferies C type by Percy Wilby, 1:9, tin, ply

have the advantage of enabling the booms to be more realistically placed further back along the roof, but they would be 'late' in reacting to the overhead. What this shows, however, is that the Continental model trolleybuses such as Eheim, weren't widely available in the UK then or even much known about.

London Transport 2 axle double decker by (unknown), (no scale), wood, metal (John Couser)

Built by an unknown maker, there is a powered model of 155mm in length, in balsa and ply with an EverReady vertical placed motor and well engineered brass fittings that seem to emulate Eheim or Rivorossi steering mechanisms. The Dinky wheels would date it to late 50s or early 60s. Unfortunately the booms are missing but would have been attached and wired to an oversize block on the roof at the top of the steering column that operated the front axle. Whether inspiration was drawn from continental manufacturers or even the Smallwood patent of 1938 can only be conjecture, as can how well it worked. Mounting the booms behind the steering wheels may again have made anticipation of the overhead's direction a little late and adherence to the "line" a little erratic.

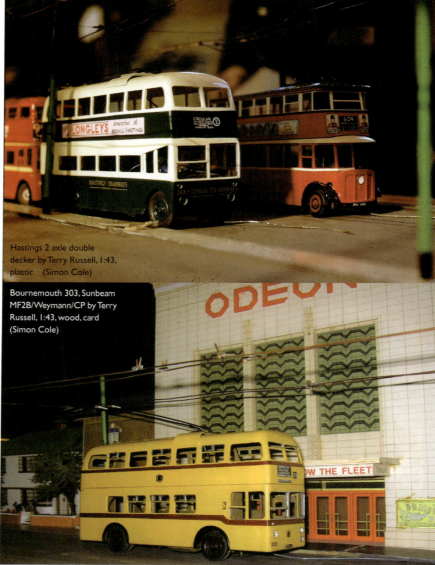

Hastings 2 axle double decker by Terry Russell, 1:43, plastic (Simon Cole)

Bournemouth 303, Sunbeam MF2B/Weymann/CP by Terry Russell, 1:43, wood, card (Simon Cole)

Glasgow BUT 9461T/MCCW by Nigel MacMillan, 1:72, diecast zinc (Nigel MacMillan)

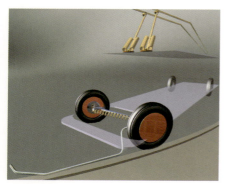

Feeler steering mechanism by Nigel MacMillan

Back to the public debate. Two months after Vincent's article, in September 1956 Model Railway Constructor, a simpler solution was recorded. Nigel MacMillan had tried JA Vincent's design in 1948 and in almost slandering him, said his model ran in "a series of wild oscillations, ... until it de-wired with a gesture like a double barrelled Roman catapult." He tried shorter booms but it was "still not docile enough to be let loose in traffic". In the style of bus modellers to this day, Nigel MacMillan talks in a parallel reality sort of way and the trolley "lay for years in the scrap yard next to the depot". Then, "when transport was required for the aspiring suburb of Blews Park" a new trolleybus route had vehicles with steering that used an 8mm kerb hugging feeler to counter the left full lock of the tensioned front wheels. This apparently worked well enough for trolleybuses to be left alone to run around a loop with four isolated sections, that stopped them catching up with each other. 'BTC' kits were used, adapted to Glasgow colours, but whether they were trolleybus kits or adapted bus kits wasn't mentioned.

Newcastle 620, BUT 9641T/MCCW/EE by Terry Russell, 1:43, wood, card (Simon Cole)

A layout that still uses the feeler idea is Terry Russell's 0 scale model street that has recently been refurbished after 40 years of storage in the attic. Terry remembers Geoff Sawland had devised the feeler idea whilst in a Bradford hospital bed in 1942 and he'd based his models on Nigel Macillan's MRC article. A commercial version for cars, called 'Roadedge' and 'Pathfinda' was produced by Victory Industries between

London Transport 12, AEC 663T/Union Construction/EE by Terry Russell, 1:43, wood, metal (David Bradley)

London Transport 78, Leyland TTB2/BRCW/MV by Terry Russell, 1:43, wood, card (David Bradley)

1956 and 1958. Terry Russell exhibited his layout a lot in the 70s until after the London Transport Museum showing in 1978, when he relegated it to the loft. At a 2007 showing in Brighton, a resurrected collection of 10 trolleybuses in the liveries of 8 operators, built by three modellers ran from a depot to a turning loop beyond the Odeon Cinema and Red Lion pub. They run about 25mm from the kerb with a long feeler, the same length again as the model. The only problem is tight left-hand turns, where the rear wheels tend to mount the kerb! Terry freely admits these are not 'true-to-scale' models, but include adaptations of plastic 'push n' go" Routemaster toys of the 1960s. – the Bradford, Derby and Hastings models were built in this way. The Bournemouth and Hull MF2Bs took slightly more surgery, and the use of Atlantean fronts ends to get the front entrances right. All are roughly 1:43 scale, including the rather more realistic London, Ipswich and Newcastle scratch built models. Particularly fine is a London Leyland TTB2 "B1" class. The trolleys run on 12v overhead, powering open frame Tri-ang X04 type motors with 30:1 worm and pinion gearing to the wheels. Axles came from Airfix slot racer steering units with racer rubber tyres. The trolleys also have flywheels to help them over inevitable breaks in the overhead at crossings and junctions. Assembling a 16 foot model layout with 2 way overhead and a full compliment of street side buildings takes some doing and isn't likely to be seen too often in public, especially as Terry Russell's speciality is model trams and supplying their model parts. But ever willing to help modellers, and aware that the parts he used 40 years ago are no longer available, Terry suggests using 1:32 scale slot racing car parts to power scratch-built bodies, based on any one of his 69 scale trolleybus drawings.

AC current modulation

The debate in model railway magazines about steering a model trolleybus wasn't yet over when, in 1971, John Edgar described his clever 'hot-wire' idea. To understand this concept is a little tricky. The need is to transmit variable power for the traction motor and some sort of control signal to steer the front wheels at the same time, sent along the overhead wires. Purist trolleybus modellers, at least in Britain, wanted to avoid the easy answer, radio control, because of the attraction of using two overhead wires for power and control. John used alternating current from a 7-15 volt transformer with the tapings selected by a foot pedal to get a range of power settings. On the model, a rectifier converted this to direct current for the Tri-ang motor. But he also added a rheostat, controlled by a steering wheel, that shifts the AC wave up or down relative to zero volts. On the trolleybus, one or other of two resistance wires get hot as a result of the DC bias, and expand, turning a pulley that has an arm attached, that in turn, moves the tie bar of the Ackermann steering. The components are otherwise the same as Terry Russell's, making use of slot car racing

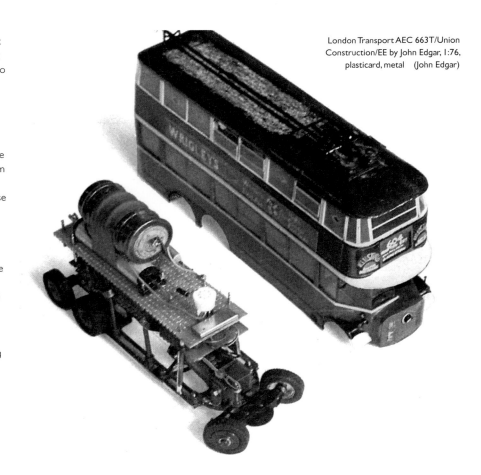

London Transport AEC 663T/Union Construction/EE by John Edgar, 1:76, plasticard, metal (John Edgar)

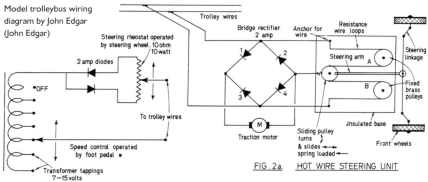

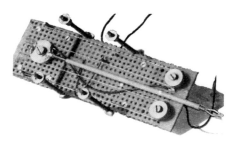

Hot wire steering by John Edgar (John Edgar)

parts. But just to add sophistication, a battery replaces the flywheel, not least because of space, but also to allow lighting to be added, as well as carrying the model through any breaks in the overhead. The model is a 1:76 scale London "Diddler" in wartime livery which rather conveniently allows the use of anti-splinter netting over the windows to hide the workings. John Edgar went on to refine the mechanisms and to add a way of reversing.

At around this time the author was inspired to develop a larger scale solution. Using the control part of 'radio control' but without the radio, the system uses a standard 10ms square wave mark space waveform to instruct an onboard RC servo to steer the front wheels. The digital signal also varies in an analogue way to provide variable power to the motor. A large resistor formed a voltage divider to ensure the 20 volt supply never reached the 5 volt servo. Having learnt this necessity the hard way, and the vision of smoke and melting plastic is still vivid after 35 years, there was, after corrective measures, nothing quite as satisfying as seeing a model trolleybus

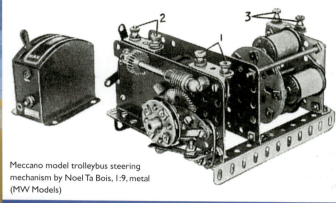
Meccano model trolleybus steering mechanism by Noel Ta Bois, 1:9, metal (MW Models)

London Transport AEC 664T/BRCW by Noel Ta Bois, 1:9, metal (unknown)

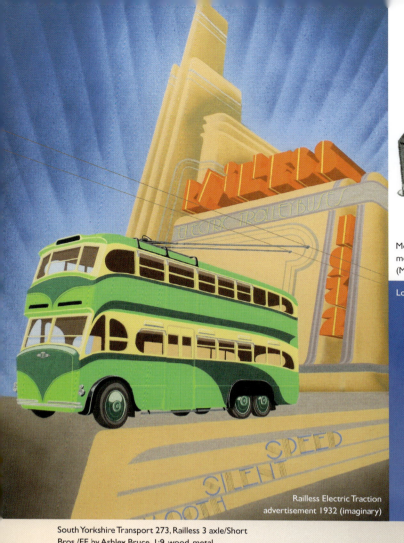
Railless Electric Traction advertisement 1932 (imaginary)

South Yorkshire Transport 273, Railless 3 axle/Short Bros./EE by Ashley Bruce, 1:9, wood, metal

Arnhem 2 axle single decker by Meccano, 1:9, metal (Meccano Ltd)

weaving from side to side as directed as if avoiding parked cars, all under straight overhead wiring. Today there are more sophisticated ways of dividing voltages than having miniature heaters inside your flammable model! The 1:9 scale model is pure fanatasy; as if, in an alternative universe, Railless had not gone bankrupt in 1927 and Rotherham and Doncaster Corporations had installed an inter-urban trolleybus line in 1932, using centre entrance, piano fronted 'trolley coaches'. The long planned around the garden layout, has, it must be admitted, still to be built and, for that matter, the electrics revived.

A similar solution, without electronics has been tried before. Noel Ta Bois built a large model trolleybus from Meccano parts and had a picture reproduced in the March 1946 issue of Meccano Magazine. Powered by a vacuum cleaner motor, the model also had a second motor for steering and ran under overhead wiring. The traction motor used AC current but, via a low resistance relay, wired in series, the steering motor turned when DC was applied, steering according to the polarity of the direct current. The mechanism was described in the October 1942 issue as "A full wave alternating current rectifier". The model, nominally based on a London C3 class without wheel spats, has been reconstructed since (without the electrics) and compiled into a set of plans, available as 'MB132' from The Meccanoman's Club. Meccano outfit no.9, issued between 1958 and 1961, included instructions for building a trolleybus. And S. Reid of Aberdeen won 10 shillings (50p) consolation prize in the 1952 Meccano Magazine Christmas competition for his model of what looks like an exported BUT trolleybus, but it's not known if it was steered.

Using a slot

In the late 1960s Les Brunton, an engineer with Parsons in Newcastle and proselytiser for the trolleybus (he wrote for the Institution of Electric Engineers in 1992) built a slot guided layout that, apart from Manchester, Ashton and London vehicles included Bradford's 522, the world's first 3 axle double deck trolleybus of 1922. The late Bill Avery also modelled this amazing pioneer in N gauge and had wished to power it.

Hidden away in his garage, Peter Smith keeps a fleet of scratchbuilt Cardiff 3 axle single deckers. The quite heavy vehicles are steered by a Scalextrix style slot but the power comes, rightly, from the overhead. Peter says previous use of the Faller system gave 'odd' results. The trolleys go around a loop circuit and represent "what-might-have-been". The English Electric trolleybus is a modernised version of the ex-Pontypridd vehicles that arrived in Cardiff in 1946, without the "one on top of the other" Estler trolleyboom mechanisms. The BUT 9641T represents a cut-down version of no.277, an East Lancs bodied double decker, and finally no.238, based on the real BUT 9641T, with dual entrance arrangement. The models are built from dissected Corgi diecast parts with plasticard and balsa wood. The rugged brass model trolley gear supplies 12volts to the 'large' motors.

Bradford 522, Bradford-Brown/EE by Bill Avery, 1:160, Balsa, card

Ashton-under-Lyne 77, Crossley TDD42/2/MV by Les Brunton, 1:50, wood, metal (c/o Carl Isgar)

Cardiff English Electric SD6W/EE by Peter Smith, 1:76, diecast and plastic (P Smith)

Pin and slot steering mechanism diagram

We mentioned Dave Wall's slot guided exhibition layout in chapter 2, where the inner tram rail of his Aston Manor Museum exhibit provides a handy slot for guidance and also includes a Cardiff single decker, no. 243, the last 3 axle of the type built for service in the UK. Dave uses dependable 24 volts to ensure reliability, sufficient to arc past minor ingressions of dust.

Cardiff 243, BUT 9641T/East Lancs/GEC by Dave Wall, 1:18, card, wood, plastic & metal

FBW/BBC, 1944   (Dr. Fritze Todta)

Zlín in minature

A layout that does stay assembled, also not in public and uses a slot with race car parts has been built by Willi Schincke. Willi remembers trolleybuses starting in his home town of Zlín, in the Czech Republic, in 1944 at the age of 7 and went on to make his first model trolleybus from plywood when he was 13. The 60th anniversary of the system saw the publication of a brochure with side views of all his favourite trolleys and the modelling passion was reborn. Willi devised a slot system of steering his powered models that cleverly doubles as the return path for the electrical current and thus avoids the problems of shorting, especially at junctions and frogs in the 1:63 scale overhead. A copper clad slide brushes along a metal strip set below the roadway slot.

Willi has faithfully modelled all the generations of Zlín's highly successful system, that today provides up to 80% of the town's public transport needs. He started with his beloved Swiss FBW/BBC, the mainstay of the fleet in the 1950s, that had surprisingly inaugurated the system in a then occupied, war torn, Czechoslovakia. They served the factory of the famous Bata shoe brand, and the model

Zlin FBW/BBC by Willi Schincke, 1:63, plasticard, tin, balsa   (Willi Schincke)

Zlin 335, Škoda 15Tr by Willi Schincke, 1:63, plasticard, tin, balsa   (Willi Schincke)

Zlin 16 Vetra VBR/Renault/CKD by Willi Schincke, 1:63, plasticard, tin, balsa   (Willi Schincke)

Brno 31, Škoda 7Tr, 1951   (Harold17)

Zlin 20 Škoda 7Tr by Willi Schincke, 1:63, plasticard, tin, balsa   (Willi Schincke)

Vetra VBR/Renault/CKD, 1949   (Jinho Hertia)

authentically displays its logo on the side. Few pictures survive of the real things, except rather modernist images of the inauguration. Is that the girl in the picture opposite, getting on board, he's admiring or a brand new Swiss trolleybus?

The FBWs were very quiet and aesthetically more pleasing to Willi's eye than the 8 Vetra VBR/ČKDs that followed in 1948, when Zlín was renamed Gottwaldov by the communists. The bombed-out national factories couldn't produce trolleybuses at the time so the Vetras were imported and given local CKD electrical equipment. With even fewer pictures surviving of the Vetras, (we only know of one) Willi's model stands as a more colourful evocation of the class.

10 Škoda 7Trs followed in 1951 and Willi has just finished the model. He has also completed a Škoda 8Tr, in the red livery that was applied to the fleet in 1957.

In the early 60s operating headway on some routes decreased from 30 to 3 minutes and, together with the need to replace older vehicles, the authorities ordered a total of 96 Škoda 9Tr trolleybuses between 1963 and 1980 – some 9Trs replaced 9Trs. Willi's model is of 62 which replaced an 8Tr in 1975.

62, in turn, was replaced by a Škoda 14Tr in 1988, though Willi's is of the very last of the type to be delivered to Zlín – 170. It looks a little narrow, but includes all the detail of the real thing.

At around this time the largest fleet of the Škoda-Sanos trolleybuses, 31 in all, were being delivered. The width of the window pillars on Willi's version shows a perennial problem for modellers; plasticard doesn't have the strength of steel or aluminium and so parts have to be 'thickened', especially at smaller scales.

The latest of Willi's recreation of the Zlín fleet is the articulated version of the 14Tr, the 15Tr, in its 'as delivered' livery. Willi's scale is dictated by the truck slot-car wheels he uses. He includes drivers and even a few passengers, such is his meticulous attention to detail. His model making is old school, inventive, skilled and all by hand – the very incarnation of fascination translated into miniature. Willi has yet to model the very latest, 4th generation 24Tr and 25Tr vehicles that have replaced the 14Tr and 15Trs. Meanwhile, a real 8Tr, a 9Tr and the prototype Škoda-Sanos from Zlín are all preserved.

Radio controlled trolleys

Another Škoda 15Tr trolleybus has been rather spectacularly modelled and offers yet another solution to the steering 'problem'. At 1:10 scale,

One offs, specials and making them steer   47

Zlin 30 Škoda 8Tr, 1958 (trolejbus.cz)

Ondřej Spáčila's model qualifies for the second biggest model trolleybus prize, but, (and there are other contenders, see below) it also qualifies for the most complete reproduction of a scale trolleybus. There's room on board for radio control, servo operated Ackermann steering and some serious model engineering. It contains a computer that monitors and manages various functions and weighs 22kg. The model represents a test vehicle, a subtle variation on the real thing, making it a Škoda 15Tr ASY-K13/6M, with the

Zlin 30 Škoda 8Tr by Willi Schincke, 1:63, plasticard, tin, balsa (Willi Schincke)

Zlin 329 Škoda Sanos S200Tr, 1986 (dszo.cz)

Zlin 329 Škoda Sanos S200Tr by Willi Schincke, 1:63, plasticard, tin, balsa (Willi Schincke)

Zlin 170 Škoda 14TrM, 1995 (Andras Ekkert)

Zlin 170 Škoda 14TrM by Willi Schincke, 1:63, plasticard, tin, balsa (Willi Schincke)

Zlin 1 Škoda 9Tr, 1975 (Vit Chrastina)

Zlin 62 Škoda 9Tr by Willi Schincke, 1:63, plasticard, tin, balsa (Willi Schincke)

never-allocated Brno fleet number of 3509. Built from copper section, welded to form the box skeletons, with plasticard body panels, the model is supported on two aluminium rails that give reinforcement and mounting points for the axles, electrical and electronic components. Four channels of radio control command two traction motors, the steering and a horn. There's working indicators, brake lights, air suspension, shock absorbers, windscreen wipers, changeable route displays, servo-operated doors with warning lights, interior and exterior lighting, audible stop announcements and even an on-board computer that records time, speed and distance. In fact, there's more - air conditioning, a lit dashboard, a ticket system and, of course, everything that ought to be physically adjustable, is – driver's side windows, wing mirrors and the electrically connected trolley booms. Literally everything, only one tenth the size! Ondřeje's amazing model can operate from model overhead but is usually powered by traction batteries. Not surprisingly, the model has appeared on television and so, inevitably, on YouTube. This is a whole new generation of model making – the trolleybus as an entire complex entity, seen as reproduceable in miniature, making use of the myriad possible components that have only recently become available, both small enough and affordable.

Only slightly smaller at 13:1 scale, is Marek Bureš Škoda 22TR, again from Brno, and carefully

Brno 3504 Škoda 15Tr, 1990 (Harold17)

Brno 3509 Škoda 15Tr by Ondreje Spáaila, 1:10, metal, plastic, wood (Ondreje Spáaila)

Brno 3509 Škoda 15Tr by Ondreje Spáaila, 1:10, metal, plastic, wood (Ondreje Spáaila)

One offs, specials and making them steer

Brno 3604 Škoda 22Tr, 2003 (Harold17)

Brno Škoda 22Tr by Marek Bures, 1:13, metal (Marek Bures)

documented as a build process. Construction started in 2003, as a Škoda 21Tr, but lack of space for batteries and equipment, meant a change of plans and the addition of a trailer section. The design includes opening doors, audible stop reports, interior and exterior lighting, reversing alarm and working trolleybooms. Construction is of 10x10mm steel section frames with copper sheet and tin body panels soldered together. Several layers of polyester cement are then built up to give a very strong final surface. The Brno municipal operator (DPMB) has an official colour chart, to which the paint conforms and the interior uses Altro flooring, just like the real thing. Electrically, the model uses a 12volt motor and eleven Li-ion batteries giving a capacity of 7.2Ah. Electronically the radio control has 4 channels and 16 switches which are all decoded on-board by four PIC microcontrollers which means the model can be operated entirely by a PC computer to test its operations and monitor voltages, settings and status. Marek has developed dedicated software to, for instance, make sure the trolleybus doesn't run with the doors open

Huddersfield 631, Sunbeam S7A/East Lancs/MV by Bruce Lake, 1:76, plasticard

Brno Škoda 22Tr by Marek Bures, 1:13, metal (Marek Bures)

Brno Škoda 22Tr by Marek Bures, 1:13, metal (Marek Bures)

and stop properly if the transmitter fails. The axles are adapted Tamiya model truck units, with ball bearings added and differential gearing reduced. Originally the middle and rear axles were powered, like their prototypes, but as that drained the batteries pretty quickly, the middle axle was disconnected. Braking now acts on this

Generic Škoda 21Tr by Marek Bures, 1:6, metal (Marek Bures)

axle and actually follows full size practice, with electrical and finally mechanical systems operated by a dedicated servo. The result of all this precision modelling is an object almost too difficult to discern from the real thing, unless you put the two together and then it's only size that differentiates the two.

Marek hasn't given up on building a Škoda 21Tr though, but has doubled the scale to 1:6, which means the model can just about fit in to his workshop. (Third prize in the largest model trolleybus stakes?) It's being built a similar way, except the larger size allows for riveting instead of soldering and even greater adherence to modelling reality. Just what is it about the Czech Republic and fantastically modelled trolleybuses? The energy of Škoda and a number of well run

trolleybus systems doubtless has a lot to do with it, but then Switzerland has many impeccably run systems and we've not been able to find a single indigenous Swiss model.

The Faller System

Another layout that stayed hidden is 'Walford Arches' by the late Tony Chlad, a well known system amongst bus modellers that had at least five London trolleybuses and a Bournemouth, hardly surprising for a scene based on East End London in the late forties (Bournemouth trolleybuses were lent during the war when nobody was going on seaside holiday and factories in London were working full time). Walford, by the way, is the fictitious name used by the long running British television soap opera, 'East Enders'. The 1:76 scale models use the Faller proprietary guidance system of steering with a wire set 0.5mm under the roadway and a magnet on the trolleybus that follows it. It was this layout that inspired Bruce Lake to further refine the Faller system for model trolleybus use – he rescued the layout and has worked to revive it to show condition.

Around 2000, Bruce was planning "Ridings", based on Yorkshire in general and Armley Moor in particular. It was always intended to be, first and foremost, a Huddersfield trolleybus layout of the 1960s. And rarely has a model trolleybus

Magnetic under road wire guidance system by Faller

Hudersfield 631, Sunbeam S7A/East Lancs/MV, 1959, with model on the drivers entrance step (Bruce Lake)

London Transport AEC 661T/English Electric/EE by Tony Chlad, 1:76, balsa, card. (Bob Heathcote)

been given such an extensive landscape to operate in. From the town centre, out through the suburbs and into the countryside, all in 10m × 2m and seven baseboards. Bruce went through three attempts at steering, first with electronic guidance from a wire carrying a high-frequency signal (which needed a radio license), then a suspended magnetic system that, for a while, sapped Bruce's enthusiasm because of the complexity and the need for specialist engineering tools, and then, finally, the Faller system. The main problem has been creating a point system that allows for various routes to be followed within what can best be described as quintuple loop layout. There are an amazing 36 points, though half that number are trailing and eighteen are selectable, by mechanical rods. All this has to happen under the road surface, and took years to build and perfect. In fact no overhead was erected until the steering problem had been solved. Trolleybus overhead, referred sometimes as an upside-down-railway, created a particular set of modeling difficulties. The first facing frog (the trolleybus term for a point), took three attempts to get right. In some ways Bruce's involvement with real trolleybuses (he part owns Huddersfield 619, and drives it at Sandtoft Museum), has been a great help in knowing how to model overhead (and being an electrical engineer helps too) but such detailed knowledge is also a hindrance. His frogs were sprung, like the real thing, but Bruce now thinks they should be "pull both ways", to relieve stress and reduce unnatural looking bulk. Despite the adoption of the Faller system which could have meant the trolleybus was battery powered, the overhead is live and powers the motor to give realistic acceleration and braking. It also means it has to be insulated across frogs and crossings and sectioned to avoid everything running at once. Sectioning in particular proved hard and led to the adoption of 'Digital Command Control' or DCC, developed for model railways, which means each trolleybus can be driven independently. Although there was only one trolleybus, with so much else to develop and build, 'Ridings' has to be a contender for the most complex model overhead award. Bruce has designed it to all come apart so that it can be shown in public, not least for the annual model day at Sandtoft, where two 631's, in both one to one and one to seventy six scales, can be seen side by side.

Like real operations, model fleets acquire secondhand vehicles and Tony Chlad's Bradford 704, (see overleaf) getting on for ten years of age, now rides around Ridings, with new chassis, motor, trolleygear and DCC chip to cope with differing overhead and layout. Doubtless, many more exhibition miles will result.

David Wood of Pontypridd has evolved his tram layout in keeping with historical trends with a scheme of replacement by trolleybuses. Like Bruce Lake, the learning process has been steep and the technology has moved on from Eheim/Brawa mechanical guidance (see next chapter) to Faller magnetic guidance. The transformation can rather neatly be seen in two AEC Q types adapted from Corgi models, that use the two

Huddersfield 631, Sunbeam S7A/East Lancs/MV by Bruce Lake, 1:76, plasticard

Huddersfield 631, Sunbeam S7A/East Lancs/MV by Bruce Lake, 1:76, plasticard

One offs, specials and making them steer 51

London Hess lighTram3 by Robin Male, 1:30, wood, metal

Bradford 704, Karrier W/East Lancs/MV by Tony Chlad, 1:76, resin

London Hess lighTram3 by Robin Male, 1:30, wood, metal

West Porton Corporation 3 axle articulated single decker by Brawa (conversion), 1:87, plastic

West Porton Corporation AEC 'Q' types by Corgi (conversion), 1:76, diecast zinc   (David Wood)

systems. David's layout is of fictitious West Porton and the fleet includes a motorised Little Bus Co. Sunbeam MS2, visiting trolleys from London and Derby plus a Brawa articulated single decker converted to Faller steering There's more on David's scale models on page 349. Suffice it to say, the steering problem has been sufficiently solved to allow all day running at public exhibitions.

One person who has extended the magnetic guidance system is Robin Male in Somerset. Wanting to use a bigger scale, Robin is dictated by the wheel size, in this case Meccano no. 20c 1" pulley and 142c tyre, to give gauge 1 or 10mm to the foot or 1:30.5. He's evolved his system over 10 years to use brass chassis, Hornby DCC control and an enlarged Faller type magnetic feeler that pivots on the front axle to turn the steering tie-bar as guided by the iron wire under the road surface (see page 413). Each model costs about a year in time and £100, of which £30 goes on passengers! The 140 foot of overhead has been by far the most tedious job, he says, but the result is well worth it. After two nostalgic Bournemouth trolleybuses, Robin built a bi-articulated Hess lighTram3, in London colours which, with the first and fourth axles steered and the middle two powered, not only proves the validity of the guidance but is almost uncanny to see operating. The destination blind reads Heathrow to City, an inter-airport trolleybus route that could conceivably see the light of day!

In Australia, Laurence Ahern has also scaled up the Faller system by doubling the size of everything to model a Perth Leyland TB5 of 1939. These trolleybuses had been ordered by Canton but were diverted and bodied by the operator, Western Australia Government Tramways in

Bournemouth Sunbeam MF2B/Weymann/CP by Robin Male, 1:30, metal, plasticard (Jane Saker)

Bournemouth Sunbeam MF2B/Weymann/CP by Robin Male, 1:30, metal, plasticard

1941. 38 has been lovingly restored and is on display at the BPSWA Museum Whiteman Park. Laurence's 0 scale model of 27 is turned on a working turntable of his developing layout with an ingenious overhead arrangement that includes two sets of 'pans', 3 rubber tyres underneath and a pulley arrangement.

We know of other modellers who have powered trolleybus layouts, Phil Carver's model of Sandtoft shown at the 2004 Festival of Tramways for instance, Phil Bertram's motorized Corgi Q1 layout and Graeme Bennett's "Tottenham Trackless Transit", both in Australia. Doubtless there are many more around the world, but for most of us, commercially available electric trolleybus models have been the way to pacify longings to be trolleybus drivers. After the war, as detailed in the next chapter, manufacturers in five countries, Austria, Britain, France, Germany and Italy, answered the call.

Perth 38, Leyland TB5/WAGT/GEC, 1939 (CW Davison)

Perth 27, Leyland TB5/WAGT/GEC by Laurence Ahearn, 1:43, wood, metal (Laurence Ahearn)

South Yorkshire Transport 273, Railless 3 axle/Short Bros./EE by Ashley Bruce, 1:9, wood, metal, plastic

Chapter 4
Commercial motorised model trolleybuses

We've seen how the urge to power and steer model trolleybuses has led many to try their hand at building their own systems and inevitably re-inventing the wheel, as it were. But the idea had commercial credence almost as soon as the first tinplate toys became available in the late 30s. In this chapter we chart chronologically the evolution of the commercial motorised model, by which we mean electrically powered and automatically steered trolleybus, something that has almost entirely been the preserve of German makers Eheim and their successor, Brawa, but with interesting and rather rare exceptions, that can be traced through the relevant patents.

Perhaps the first thing to say is that the earliest commercial powered model trolleybuses were very expensive to buy and were produced in very small numbers, the prospect of which might explain why the very earliest never entered production.

patentee	date	origin	company	model	page
George Smallwood	1937	United Kingdom	Triang Minic (?)	double decker	55 (286)
Karl Kreibich	1947	Austria	Kreibich	Minobus	56 (156)
			Rivarossi	Minobus	61 (204)
			Rico (?)		61 (262)
Erich Fischer	1948	Germany	Europabahn	EWF	61 (173)
			Eheim	2 axle	63
Gunther Eheim	1959	Germany	Eheim	3 axle	64
				articulated	66 (171)
				Minibus	67 (188)
	1963	Germany	Brawa	(as above)	68
Roland Longarzo	1955	USA	Polks Model Craft Hobbies Inc	Export	69
				Conversions	70 (180)
	1955	Germany GDR	VEB Dresdner Blech und Spielw	2 axle	70
	1968	Japan	Sakai	2 axle	71
(No known patent)	1950	France	SCMS	Vetra	71 (146)
	1950	France	Le Jouet Troll	Vetra	72 (146)
	1958 (?)	United Kingdom	Turner & Sanders	double decker	73 (287)
	1981	Germany	Mobatech	HAG Modelleisenbahn	74 (270)
	2003	Germany	Marks Metllmodellclassics	Henschel	74
	2006	Netherlands	Train PCB	Grell	74 (167)

The Smallwood patent 1937

The patent granted to George Edward Smallwood of London on February 10, 1937 covers several application possibilities including a trolleybus model. The drawing looks remarkably like the Triang Minic (Miniature Clockwork) tinplate double decker that had been produced since 1935. At 19cm in length it was big enough to accommodate an electric motor and steering mechanism. And the 1939 Triang catalogue included a trolleybus (which has since been recreated, also on page 286).

All this, of course, is anecdotal; we don't know if GE Smallwood had anything to do with Triang Toys or if they had plans to motorize a tinplate trolleybus that was never produced. Triang, while in many ways an archetypal traditional toy maker, certainly had an eye for all the latest developments.

As far as we can tell from the patent, the mechanical steering used similar principles to those used by all manufacturers of powered toy trolleybuses. There was an assumption of rigid overhead wiring that was strong enough to act

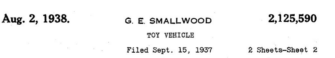

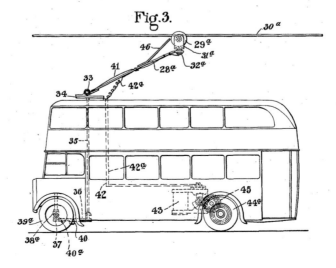

Patent for Toy Vehicle, inventor - George Edward Smallwood of London, 1938 (US Patent Office)

London Transport 3 axle double decker by Minic (Tri-ang conversion), 18cm, tinplate

3 axle double deck trolleybus, Tri-ang catalogue, 1939 (Tri-ang)

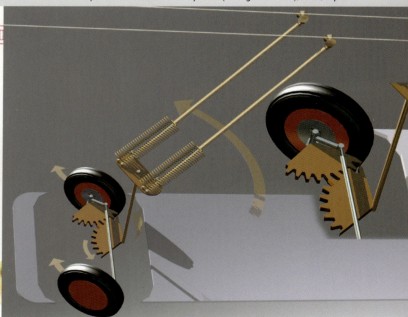

Steering mechanism diagram, derived from Smallwood Patent, 1938

on the two booms that were mechanically linked to the front wheels so that they always tried to steer back to directly underneath the overhead, whereupon the steering became aligned to straight ahead. In the Smallwood case, this used two quadrant gears, one at the end of a vertical shaft beneath the booms and one on the kingpin of one of the front wheels. There's no reason to suppose it wouldn't work, but there are simpler solutions.

The Kreibich patent 1947
Almost exactly 10 years later, and after a World War, Karl Kreibich in Austria patented an elegant solution that used a pin in a carefully shaped hole to more subtly steer according to the amount

56   Commercial motorised model trolleybuses

of deviation away from the overhead centre line. The patent covered model as well as real applications for trolleybuses, such as vehicles for mining, industrial and amusement purposes. Claimed advantages for additional steering sited use in bad weather conditions, darkness and fog. Kreibich also invented a spring system for trolley shoes on real trolleybuses but we don't know if any of these ideas were ever taken up. What was pursued was the model application, by Karl Kreibich himself, at the 1948 Vienna commercial fair, with an electrically operated "Minobus" trolleybus on display that looked just like the drawing in his patent.

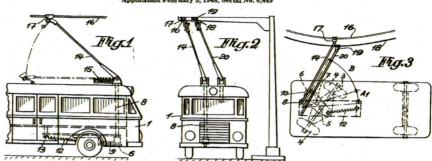

The Kreibich patent for Trackless vehicle driven by electric motors, 1948   (US Patent Office)

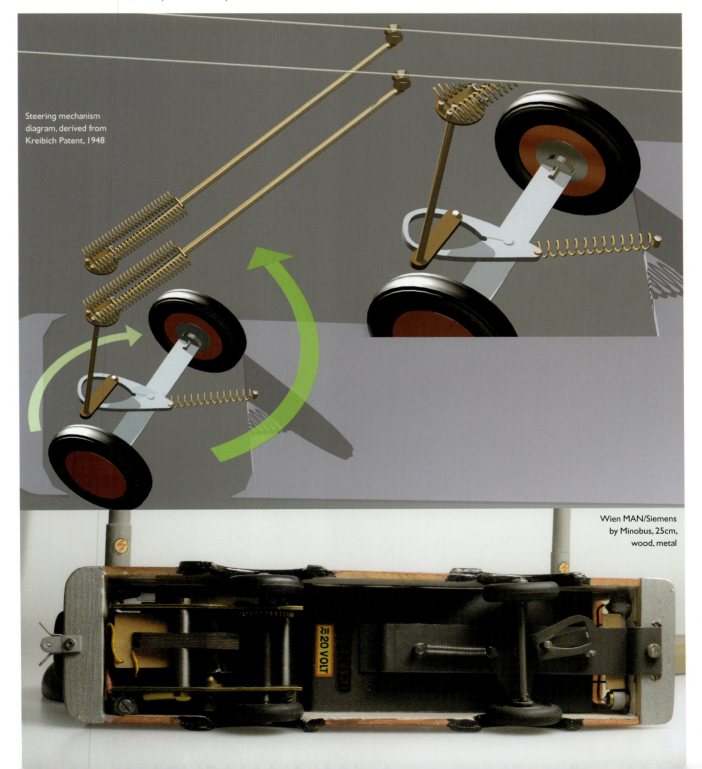

Steering mechanism diagram, derived from Kreibich Patent, 1948

Wien MAN/Siemens by Minobus, 25cm, wood, metal

Wien MAN/Siemens by Minobus, 25cm, wood, metal

Kreibich Minobus

1948 was not a very auspicious time to be considering producing a luxury toy trolleybus product. Vienna was occupied by France, the Soviet Union, UK and USA (and would be until 1955). For most people the issues were finding enough to eat and a place to sleep. But persevere Kreibich did, and his intention was mainly export, specifically to the USA. Some of the claimed 200 Minobus sets that were apparently produced came to UK, where at least one example is preserved, unused and in its original box. Another survives in Italy – needless to say an extant Minobus today is extremely rare.

Karl Kreibich is thought to have taken his inspiration from Bratislava, where he was living at the end of the war. One of the first things the capital of the Nazi Slovak state did in 1940 was import the first MAN trolleybuses built at the Josef Sodomka plant. Nos. 61-74 had the centre entrance, front grille, circular route indicator

Bratislava 125, MAN/Siemens, 1940 (unknown)

Wien MAN/Siemens by Minobus, 25cm, wood, metal

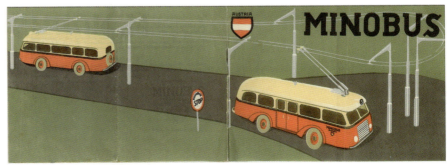

Cover of the Minobus instruction booklet, 1948 (c/o G Mackinger)

and the flared wheel arches that are echoed in the Minobus. Kreibich didn't manage the Estler style trolley base or the straight slopping front on his wonderful model trolleybus, but he did employ impeccable engineering. The electrically illuminated model had a body made of wood, wheels with full rubber tyres and a motor powered at 20v AC or DC. A coupling for trailer operation was announced in the 1948 one page report of the Austrian railway magazine "Eisenbahn" and there were rumours that trailers were offered but we haven't so far found a model or any photograph. There is, however, a picture of the layout at the Vienna toy fair showing a figure of 8 loop with an extra turning, intended to demonstrate the models' reliability, robustness and climbing ability. The Minobus was also reviewed in the German "Mechanikus" magazine in 1955 by Günther Stetza, who states that the control unit was operated by a pedal that looked like a small copy of the original. Five

Rivarossi model steering mechanism

Salerno 181, Alfa Romeo 110AF, 1945 (Paulo Gregoris)

Generic Yellow Alfa Romeo 110AF by Rivarossi, 15cm, plastic, metal

Generic Blue Alfa Romeo 110AF by Rivarossi, 1:80, plastic, metal

Generic Red Alfa Romeo 110AF by Rivarossi, 15cm, plastic, metal

Generic Alfa Romeo 110AF
by Rivarossi, 1:80, plastic, metal

different speeds were possible. Some examples were probably painted in the red and white of the Bratislava or Wien liveries of the time, as shown on the instruction brochure. The scale was 1:40, although some sources state 1:45.

Rivarossi Minobus

Rights to the patent and indeed the name were bought by Rivarossi in 1950, when production is thought have started on their '1:80' scale model of the Alfa Romeo 110AF. The compromise scale was intended to reflect American H0 (1:86) and European H0 (1:78) at a time when neither had been decided upon. In fact the scale is nearer to 1:72. The design was revised to use a lighter body and a black pressed steel chassis plate in 1952 and was listed in Rivarossi catalogues up until 1957. The Italian Minobus used the same Kreibich steering mechanism, albeit smaller, and was just as well engineered. It was also expensive and not many are thought to have been produced, which is why boxed sets can change hands at over €1200 each today.

The Rivarossi catalogues always mentioned the Alfa Romeo 110AF as the inspiration which has always struck us as odd as the only fluted 110AFs were just 3 examples, at Venezia-Lido, whereas Como, where Rivarossi was based, had visually identical fluted 140AFs. Venezia-Lido 215-218 had bodies by SIAI Marchetti who had formerly built aircraft – presumably they thought the bodies needed strengthening in this aeronautic way.

The trolley mechanism is inherited from the Austrian Minobus, pretty literally, with horizontal springs acting on pivoted booms. Only one boom activates the steered front wheels which turn tractor style rather than Ackermann. The booms can deviate more than the action on the front axle, which is the purpose of the cunning oval cutout plate in the steering mechanism. The all metal overhead was similar to the Minobus, but was sold pre-formed as a straight, curve or half curve, rather like the rails that Rivorossi was more used to making. The traction poles had substantial diecast bases.

Rico

An English collector has a blue and white Rico diecast trolleybus that has been adapted to run under overhead wiring mostly with Rivarossi parts. Whether this is a factory 'trial', as he fondly likes to think, is impossible to say – the circumstantial evidence is stronger than at first glance (more on page 262) but we can be pretty certain it didn't go into commercial production.

Nearly all conceptual development of commercial powered miniature trolleybuses occurred between 1948 to 1950, not only in Austria and Italy but also in France, perhaps Spain and more lastingly in Germany where production of models by Europabahn, Eheim and later on Brawa, started as the result of a patent filed on October 3, 1948 by Erich Fischer, of Wagenreith, south east of München, Germany.

The Fischer patent 1948

Where a real trolleybus, with booms set back to be accessible, has a driver to predict a coming curve, a model, unless guided by track in the road, has to have the booms as far forward as possible to follow the line without de-wiring. The Fischer patent provided for this even more than the Kreibich patent filed the year before. The mechanism varied a little during its long production run (1949-2001), most especially with the N-gauge version introduced in 1968 (see below). Both booms were originally mounted on an insulating phenolic paper bar which turned a vertical rod that pivoted a bracket which connected two tie rods and pivot points and thus steered the front wheels. Unlike the Kreibich mechanism, the deviation of the booms is rigidly limited by the turning circle of the wheels, but this doesn't have much of a deleterious effect

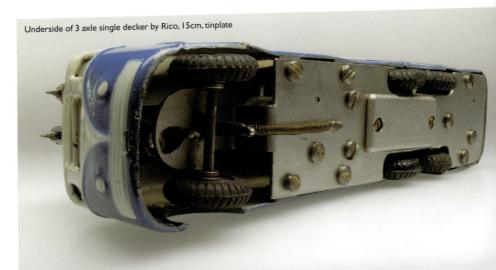

Underside of 3 axle single decker by Rico, 15cm, tinplate

Patent granted to Erich Fischer for a "Trackless electric toy vehicle with automatic steering", 1948-51 (Deutsches Patentamt)

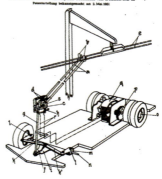

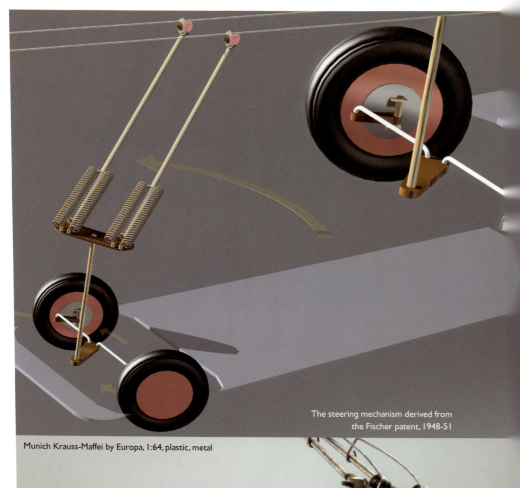

The steering mechanism derived from the Fischer patent, 1948-51

Munich Krauss-Maffei by Europa, 1:64, plastic, metal

on using the models. The original overhead used metal strips 2.7mm deep (the scale equivalent of 0.2m) and tends to capsize the trolleybus before de-wiring. Overhead parts were sub-contracted to Vollmer, who had patented a way of inserting metal into plastic. Vollmer still produces overhead for model railways.

Fischer – Europabahn EWF trolleybus

Engineer Günther Eheim of Esslingen developed Fischers patent into a product, produced by Europa Technische Spielwaren GmbH, successors to Löhmann-Präzix-Bahn model trains and was distributed by toy merchant Artur Braun. It was launched at the Leipzig fair in 1950. Inspiration is usually taken as the 1948-50 batch of 15 Krauss-Maffei KME-130 trolleybuses delivered to München, the nearest city to where Erich Fischer lived. On the box and underneath it was called the 'EWF Trolley Bus' and in the manual the name was the 'Europa-Trolley-Bus'.

Europabahn was founded by Heinrich Watter a producer of cardboard packages and Eugen Schurr a producer of transformers with Gunther Eheim as production manager in 1949, but was declared bankrupt by 1953. The toy trolleybus was taken over by Eheim's company,

Munich 15, Krauss-Maffei, 1950 (Ludger Kenning)

62 Commercial motorised model trolleybuses

Munich Krauss-Maffei by Europa, 1:64, plastic, metal

Eheim GmbH, founded in 1949 (originally as EEE Eheim Esslinger Elektrospielwaren) and had probably been acting as the manufacturing sub-contractor. Although intended for use with 00/H0 railways, the trolleybus was nearer to 1:64 than 1:76 and disproportionately wide. Available in natural maroon Bakelite or painted blue, yellow or ivory, there was also a maroon and ivory edition and the earliest versions had oversized front headlights. In keeping with German operating practices, there was also a trailer available. Today the robust motor (a Märklin SK800) is still likely to run and the Bakelite (Catalin) plastic survives well. Europabahn models do very occasionally appear for sale, usually for many hundreds of euros. Eheim continued production in 1953, apparently assembling the models at home until that year's Nuremberg Toy Fair, where he introduced his smaller, but more to scale (approximately 1:78) 2 axle single decker.

Eheim 2 axle trolleybus

Although the traction poles and insulated brackets were replaced by more realistic plastic, the same oversized overhead and heavy bases were retained. So too was the motor and the trolleygear. Originally there were no boom hooks on the roof. The Eheim was available first in ivory or red and ivory, then in subsequent years, red, blue, yellow and green. School teacher Richard Menzies, writing in Trolleybus Magazine, noted that the boom coil springs carry current and after prolonged use could heat up sufficiently to melt the roof plastic. The large motors also deformed the relatively thin cellulose acetate body of many an Eheim trolleybus.

Despite often being referred to as based on a Büssing trolleybus (of which there were few) perhaps because of the emblematic front horizontal stripes, the first catalogue showed Esslingen 11, the first of five Uerdingen-Henschel ÜH 111s delivered to Gunther Eheim's home town in 1952, just as he was re-tooling for his new model. Esslingen 6-10, MAN KPE4500

Commercial motorised model trolleybuses 63

Generic Büssing by Eheim, 1:87, plastic, metal

Eheim Catalogue cover, 1960 (Eheim)

Esslingen 10, MAN KPE4500/ Kässbohrer 1944 (Ludger Kenning)

trolleybuses with Kässbohrer bodies built in 1944, it has to be said, look like more of an inspiration – at least they had the doors in the right place. Models in the early 50s rarely copied reality, but interpreted it, to take account of differing materials and ease of production.

Eheim 3 axle trolleybus

The 2 axle Eheim sold well, and led to the 3 axle version in 1956, based loosely on the next generation Henschel 6500-IIB, with a prominent Henschel badge on the front. Larger in all 3 dimensions than the 2 axle, and always significantly more expensive, this more realistic Eheim is harder to find today, partly because it was discontinued in 1966.

Interestingly, there were no real 3 axle Henschel single deckers built, let alone any with roof lights. Seven 2 axle versions were delivered to Ulm in 1954 with rooflights and 3 axle one and a half deckers went to Aachen, Osnabrück and Wuppertal around 1956. Also Neuss, in the Ruhr, received Germany's first articulated PSV, a 4 axle Henschel trolleybus in 1955. Perhaps Gunther Eheim had seen Henschel's design plans, where, in the mid-50s, a rooflit 6 wheeler was possible but, as far as we know, there was no real prototype.

The steering mechanism was amended with the introduction of the 3 axle model to use a

Generic 3axle Henschel by Eheim, 1:87, plastic, metal

Generic Henschel by Eheim, 1:87, plastic, metal

Neuss 106, Henschel/ Kässbohrer, 1955 (Werner Stock arckiv)

Generic Henschel by Eheim, 1:87, plastic, metal

Ulm 111, Henschel HS56/ Kässbohrer, 1950 (Kässbohrer)

central pin on the tie rod and a 'U' plate that slotted around it, rather than the rigid pair of tie rod wires. The 2 axle was also amended. A new German version of the Fischer patent, assigned to Gunther Eheim, was applied for in 1959 to cover the new design.

The 3 axle trolleybus later used a new type of plastic and was less prone to the tendency for the body to deform and the 2 axle followed suit. The 3 axle was also unique in having a separate chrome front bumper – something which frequently goes missing. The model could

Commercial motorised model trolleybuses 65

Eheim's second steering mechanism, 1959

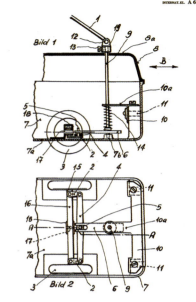
Gunter Eheim's patent, 1959   (Deutsches Patentamt)

also be supplied with a luggage trailer and still had individual headlights. The trolley collectors lost their wheels and gained shoes with the introduction of the third and final trolleybus model.

Eheim articulated trolleybus

In 1961 the articulated Eheim trolleybus was introduced, based, more closely than before, on a specific prototype, the Henschel HS160 OSL, then in production and successor to the ÜH 111s. Of the real trolleybuses, 35 singles and 32 in articulated form were built between 1959 and 1963 for 11 operators. 8 are preserved, including 4 singles (one of which is in England) and 4 artics. The model has a black ribbed cylinder as the bellows, held loosely between the two body sections and re-designed trolleygear that moved the spring mechanism to inside the roof. As far as we know, none, except maybe inside Eheim's factory, had the first external trolleygear originally fitted, but such examples do exist, an indication of the fascination collectors hold for these alluring models.

Generic articulated Henschel HS160 OSL by Eheim, 1:87, plastic, metal

Preserved Trier 28, Henschel HS160 OSL/Henschel, 1962 (Berthold Werner)

Generic articulated Henschel HS160 OSL by Eheim, 1:87, plastic, metal

66   Commercial motorised model trolleybuses

Generic 2axle Büssing by Eheim, 1:87, plastic

Overhead electric frog by Eheim, (Ronald Helder)

Overhead electric crossing by Eheim, (Ronald Helder)

A circular nylon plate now held both booms with long horizontal extension springs under the roof and a slotted plate, instead of the open 'U' bracket, now encircling the tie rod pin. The articulated Eheim had headlights inside the body and new sliding trolley shoes in place of the oversize pulley-like brass wheels. And for the one and only time in the 50 year history of these models, the motor was changed from a universal series to a permanent magnet type with a diode so it could still run from AC or DC and in one direction only. The 2 axle and 3 axle models followed suit, and also adopted the trolley shoes, but not yet the enclosed trolleygear. This never appeared on the 3 axle, which was discontinued in 1966, the year the 2 axle was finally converted to the new steering system and gained extra graphic detail.

To coincide with the release of the articulated version, with its new trolleygear, the overhead was redesigned in 1961 to use wire and better traction poles. To some extent the overhead was more limited than previously, with fewer accessories available, but looked more realistic. Gone was the admittedly massive crossing with traffic lights and the relay driven frog, replaced by a simpler, more lightweight crossing and a frog powered more realistically from a pole mounted actuator. Gone too were the double span three way poles and other variants that probably had few sales.

Eheim N scale trolleybus

Plans for an N gauge powered model trolleybus appeared in the 1963 Eheim catalogue, with an artists impression of a Mercedes O321, a type never to be adorned with trolleybooms. But the 'Minibus' didn't go on sale until 1968, soon after long-time distributor Artur Braun and his new company, Brawa, had taken over Eheim's trolleybuses. The real Mercedes-Benz OE302 bus, on which the model is based (it says O302 in relief, on the side) was announced in 1969, as a hybrid, but didn't go on trial as a Duo-bus in Esslingen with trolley booms until 1975. Perhaps Eheim waited until the real thing existed, but how did he pre-empt Mercedes-Benz with a model that was on sale 7 years before the real 'Obus' appeared in public? The Esslingen Duo-bus trial led to a large investment in Eheim's local system and quite possibly saved the trolleybus system from otherwise closing. Did Gunther Eheim know Dr. Volker Hauff, the Esslingen MP who, as a Federal Minister, was behind the Duo-bus project? So much mystery for such a small model. Meanwhile, Ing. Eheim, had, by the mid-70s, moved into bringing technology to aquariums, and still does.

All three colour versions of the 'Trolley-Minibus', usually with a silver roof, are on a fictitious route 3 going to Altstadt (Old Town). Esslingen has an Altstadt, but not directly served by trolleybuses.

The 'Minibus' has 50 listed parts including a

Generic Mercedes Benz O321 by Eheim, 1:160, plastic, metal (Eheim)

Esslingen demonstration Mercedes Benz O302 duo-bus, 1975 (W van der Plaats)

Commercial motorised model trolleybuses

Generic Mercedes Benz OE302-12R Duo-Bus by Brawa, 1:160 plastic, metal

N gauge Eheim steering mechanism

further revision of the steering system. Instead of a tie rod there's a torsion spring which keeps each of the steering arms in contact with a nylon bracket that's turned by the vertical shaft coming from the booms. The trolleygear assembly is under the roof. The 6.5cm 'toy' must have taken watchmaker skills to make.

Brawa

The Minibus was the last development as Eheim passed the models on to Brawa, and Artur Braun, who did not fundamentally change the range for the next 33 years. Production finished in 2001. Brawa did produce a special edition of the only 'Verkehrsbetriebe Kaiserslautern' Henschel HS160 OSL 115 which was delivered new to the operator in 1962, as a response to the German ban on the use of trailers and was almost the last Henschel trolleybus ever made. But quite why Brawa produced a special model is unclear - the Kaiserslautern system closed in the year the model was released, 1985, after a vote of 28 to 24 in the City Council. Unless the model was commissioned, Brawa was by now appealing to the nostalgia market rather than what had been the latest technology. Examples of the Kaiserlautern model attract a premium price, as do Eheims over Brawas.

In 2009, Esslingen City Museum displayed an Eheim trolleybus as an 'Historical Treasure'. And

Kaiserlauten articulated Henschel HS160 OSL by Brawa, 1:87, plastic, metal

the city operator presented plans to extend their trolleybus system. The spiritual home of the commercial model trolleybus remains wedded to the real thing and mindful of a heritage that includes its model equivalent.

Exported Eheims

In the UK, Edward Exley Ltd., well known model train distributor and model railway coach maker, of Baslow, Derbyshire, is thought to have started importing Eheims around 1956. My father, Alan Bruce, bought me my first in, I think, 1958, from either Bassett-Lowke at 202 High Holborn, London (later Beatties) or Gamages, further along the road. In 1967 Robin Hannay reviewed the range in Buses magazine. He mentions the articulated model at £6 17s (£95 today), the N gauge set at £5 15s (£80) and details the 'large' range of accessories that are 'impossible to list here'. By 1971, Exley quoted £3 8s for the 2 axle trolleybus and £2 15s for it as a kit. Ernest Rozsa of the Kivoli Centre in North Wales was one of a number of distributors who supplied the Brawa range in the UK up until production finished.

The 2 axle Eheim trolleybus was exported to the potentially lucrative United States market from about 1953. There is some evidence that the Europabahn predecessor had also been imported to the US by Aristo-Craft. Apart from red, blue and yellow editions, there was a simplified export version for the US in grey without rear lights or a connector for a trailer. The models were packed in special boxes with Aristo-Craft logos and a mention of the German manufacturer, "Made in Western Germany by G. Eheim Ing. exclusively for Aristo-Craft Miniatures, Newark 5, N.J., U.S.A.". The re-branding was to avoid a protectionist $300 levy placed on importers and applied to each line of toys. The 1960 catalogue prices the 4 wheeler at $7.50 ($55 today) and the 6 wheeler at $12.50 ($90).

Roland Longarzo of Polks Model Craft Hobbies Inc., who own Aristo-Craft, patented additional

Generic Büssing by Eheim (Aristocraft), 1:87, plastic, metal

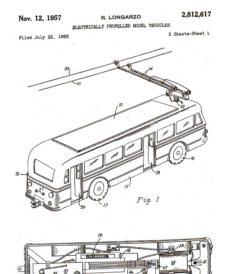

Longarzo's patent for an amended Eheim model, 1:87, plastic   (US Patent Office)

features for the Eheim model in 1955, such as operating doors that were never implemented. Polks still trades but unfortunately Lewis Polk, son of the founder now can't remember when his late father started importing, but it's thought to have finished around the mid-60s as Eheim handed over to Brawa.

US imports were also handled by Associated Hobby Manufacturers Inc. (AHM) of Philadelphia from the change over to Brawa around 1963, and they re-branded Eheim then Brawa boxes as the 'Minibus' Electric Trolleybus System. (AHM carried lines of "Minicars", Minitanks" and Minitrains" at this time). They imported only the 2 axle version with internal trolleygear and neither the trailers nor the N gauge Minibus. There is confusion as to whether they were concurrent with Aristo-Craft or if they also imported the Japanese clone (see below) at the same time.

Commercial motorised model trolleybuses   69

Silvine trolleybus made by Sakai

It's possible that Silvine Model Importer Inc. of Glenside, PA. commissioned long established toy maker Sakai (Seisakusho Ltd, Tokyo) to virtually clone the first generation Eheim overhead and produce a copy of the trolleybus at the time of the Brawa takeover, because the Fischer/Eheim patents didn't apply in the USA and the Longarzo patent applied only to details. Sakai is thought to have directly imported the trolleybus sets into the USA together with overhead that was virtually identical to Eheims, but designed for a model tram. The trolleybus is 'Americanized' with a mass of rivets reminiscent of US school buses. It's 1mm higher than the Eheim but is otherwise the same size, making it rather more 00 gauge than the 'accurate H0 scale' claimed. The motor and gearing is different, although similarly able to operate from AC or DC. You were supposed to run off 'your model train' controller, as no transformer was supplied. Silvine operated from a suburb north of Philadelphia and their trolleybus is regarded as 'coming' from this trolleybus pioneering city. Although yellow, as a few Philadelphia trolleys were in the 60s, the model looks nothing like the Marmon Herringtons then in service. Successors, Hobby Imports of Baltimore, then imported the Sakai and branded it "South Street", using the same box as Sakai themselves with the same illustration as Silvine. Baltimore really did have a 2133 fleet numbered

Philadelphia Transport Co. 2 axle single decker by Sakai, 1:87, plastic, metal

Hobby Imports Inc. box cover for 2 axle single decker by Sakai, 1:87, plastic

Baltimore 2101, Pullman/GE, 1944 (Scalzo coll. trolleybus.net)

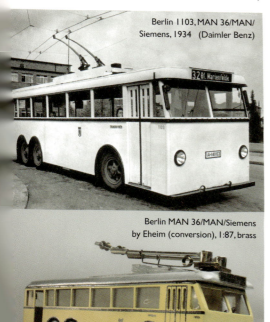

Berlin 1103, MAN 36/MAN/Siemens, 1934 (Daimler Benz)

Berlin MAN 36/MAN/Siemens by Eheim (conversion), 1:87, brass

Deutsche Bundesbahn Büssing 6500T by Brawa/Brekina (conversion), 1:87, plastic, metal

70 Commercial motorised model trolleybuses

trolleybus that was yellow with a silver roof and at least some rivets showing, but it, like the rest of system, had been scrapped in 1959. So 1960s America had two powered model trolleybuses on sale, but, reflecting the trends of the real things, they were mostly gone from the shelves by the 1970s.

Eheim/Brawa trolleybuses and hobbyists
Worldwide, there still are those devoted to Gunther Eheim's trolleybus creations. Large layouts have been built, mostly adjuncts to model railways but some, like John Huddlestones Cronenburg and Ruud van Houten's Dutch layout, are dedicated specifically to Eheims. Richard Menzies discovered with his layout that the motor diodes could be reversed to provide independent control of two trolleybuses on one section – one goes forward by turning the controller forward and the other goes forward by reversing the controller! Jörg Schmitz of Saarbrücken still produces scale overhead in brass for Eheims including a beautiful but expensive 7 segment turning loop.

Modellers have converted Eheims, to, for instance, the stoically styled 1934 SSW-MAN36 of Berlin. Bought in a second hand shop and made of brass, this rather expert conversion must rate as one of the earliest conversions of an Eheim trolleybus. Rather in the spirit of Gunther Eheim's taste in trolleybuses, a Büssing 6500T has been produced by rebodying a Brawa with a Brekina bus although none ever ran as trolleybuses in Deutsche Bundesbahn livery.

VEB Dresdner Blech- und Spielwarenfabrik, East Germany
At the Leipziger Spring Fair in 1955 the East German VEB Dresdner Blech- und Spielwarenfabrik launched a trolleybus model

Leipzig 126, Lowa W602a, 1954 (David Pearson)

Lowa W602a by VEB Dresdner Blech und Spielwarenfabrik, 1:87, plastic (Modelleisenbahner)

in H0 scale, looking mechanically very similar to an Eheim with, apparently, every intention of production. It was based, fairly accurately, on a Lowa 602a of 1954, then entering service in Dresden and other cities. The East German railway model magazine "Modelleisenbahner" pictured the model, announced it would be exhibited running on a layout and be available at the 1955 autumn fair. It never materialized, although the company did present an excellent model tram and trailer set – the worlds first plastic tram model in exactly H0 scale. So the company had the ability to produce a trolleybus model, but why it never reached the marketplace is not known, perhaps the steering mechanism infringed the Fischer Patent of 1948 and the GDR authorities didn't want to risk East/West political embarrassment. Or perhaps the tram was given priority as indigenous trolleybus production was about to cease in preference for the Škoda 8Tr in 1957.

La Société de construction de matériel scientifique (SCMS)
The gloriously named La Société de construction de matériel scientifique or SCMS as it says on the side, produced an intriguing 25cm powered toy trolleybus in 1950 (according to Phillip Morro).

Based in Saint Etienne, where 20 Vetra CB-45 and CS-60 trolleybuses had arrived between 1944 and 1947, SCMS based their petite looking toy on these omnipresent French trolley types. The mechanical steering was unique, and seems to have had no patent applied for. There are two vertical rods from the two booms that each

Amiens Vetra CS60, 1943 (P. Bouillion)

Generic Vetra CS60 by SCMS, 25cm, aluminium

SCMS model steering arrangement 1943

Underside of the trolleybus model by SCMS, Aluminium

section of overhead. There is no evidence of more than one wire passing down the un-sprung single boom that deviates only horizontally. You can see the problem we face with this model – how on earth did it work? Constant examination hasn't helped, but seemingly a single wire feeds a DC motor which drives the rear axle through a worm gear. Return current was presumably through the aluminium boom, although we can't quite see how this was achieved at the roof/boom interface, perhaps wires are missing on our model.

There is also a wonderful control panel that has a speed control (or is that for direction or both?) plus a big (15cm) steering wheel. Our best guess is that this controller generates a variable AC frequency, to differentiate it from the traction

Generic Vetra CS60 by SCMS, 25cm, aluminium   (Philippe Morro)

Generic Vetra CS60/Renault Scemia by Le Jouet Troll, 28cm, aluminium

Le Jouet Troll set box

turn forked pieces and act on pins attached to triangular plates that act on the king pins of the Ackermann style steering. Quite why both booms are connected is hard to fathom, as they could be in contradiction via the cross bar. Without trying to get one these museum pieces to run, we don't know how well they worked, although turning the booms by hand does indeed effectively steer the front wheels.

Each of the five examples we know of have different trolleygear mechanisms and none look as though they would apply sufficient upward pressure. Apparently, the trolley shoes "realistically flash during vehicle operation". Speed control was by a "low voltage rheostat". The model is big, diecast in aluminium and fairly heavy – it's difficult to imagine it performing other than a little ponderously. And the only two that survive compete are too precious to try applying the required 24 volts. The instructions talk of 30 watts and anyway, we didn't have the right transformer to hand!

Le Jouet Troll

Possibly the most bizarre powered model trolleybus was the large, 28cm long, Le Jouet Troll of around 1950. Claimed to have been patented (though we've been unable to find any record), it was produced in Paris and cost 14,000 francs (approximately £360). It uses a unique power collection system that owes very little to actual trolleybus technology. The first problem is the Bakelite cross bar that has two 1mm tubes through which passes what can only be a single

Le Jouet Troll steering and control box, aluminium and plywood

Disassembled Le Jouet Troll, 28cm, aluminium (Plilippe Moro)

DC, that drives the second onboard motor which outputs via a governor to a shaft that is thereby pushed or pulled to operate a bracketed kingpin and so steer. Pretty sophisticated stuff for 1950. The instruction sheet shows a depot with overhead that 'pulls out smoothly' and can be fixed to 'the foot of a piece of furniture'. A child can then 'reverse the vehicle out of the depot', although he'd not then be able to do much else. The controller is connected to '110/130AC mains' but there's no mention of the operating voltage (or the extreme hazard to children!) We know of three examples in varying degrees of completeness and degradation, especially to the rubber wheels and bumpers, but have no idea of how many Le Jouet Trolls were produced or exactly when.

Turner & Sanders (Models) Ltd.

Recently discovered at an auction in Devon was the previously unknown "Tee-an-Ess" motorized model trolleybus made by Turner & Sanders (Models) Ltd., of whom we have been able to find little record, other than company no. 00450128, of unknown address and now dissolved. The design used slot guidance and power pick-up while the overhead was passive. A date of the late 50s is conjecture, based on the injection molded plastic battery plug and the possibly concurrent production of electric slot cars by Minimodels of Havant that had started in 1957 and became Scalextric. 1957 also saw Victory Industries of Hampton Wick introduce their very similar VIP Roadway for 1:32 scale cars also with all-metal track but using wire pickups. There was nothing new about this idea of power collection for models – Lionel in the USA had marketed electric 'slot' cars in 1912. The "Tee-an-Ess" set must pre-date the similar scaled Minic Motorways of 1963 and the proliferation of 60s slot car systems. Judging by its crudity and rarity, it can not have been in commercial production for very long. It owes nothing to European commercial model trolleybus developments.

Quite why Turner and Sanders should choose a trolleybus to model, and one that owes none of

Model trolleybus chassis by Turner & Sanders, 1:72, diecast

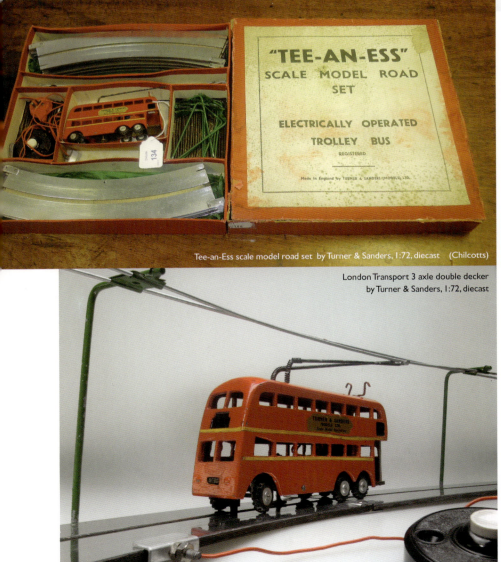

Tee-an-Ess scale model road set by Turner & Sanders, 1:72, diecast (Chilcotts)

London Transport 3 axle double decker by Turner & Sanders, 1:72, diecast

its power collection or steering to the overhead wires, is a mystery and hardly presented a 'sure fire' business opportunity. London Transport had already announced the replacement of its trolleybuses in 1954. The considerably more sophisticated Eheim models were already being imported into the UK by the late 50s. Seemingly Messrs. Turner and Sanders were letting their indulgent hearts rule their heads and thank goodness they did – it's hard to imagine a more archetypally 1950s British model trolleybus.

The rather heavy 12.5cm model is of diecast zinc and power collection is through two brass studs in contact with a chromed roadway while steering, tractor style, is via a peg beneath a self-centering front axle. An EverReady TG18 motor drives the rear axle vertically through a worm gear supplied, via the track, from a 12V EverReady Toy battery. The trolleybooms have a similarity to Taylor & Barrett toy trolleybuses, relying on just springs rather than any sprung pivot mechanism. Presumably other types of "Tee-an-Ess" vehicle could have used the 'scale model road' but no other 'starter' sets have been seen. Apart from not knowing when, we also don't know where in England the product was produced and just remain grateful that we still have the article itself, which, as far as we know, is the only one in existence.

Mobatech

The Miba model railway magazine's report on the 1981 Nuremburg Toy Fair included mention

Neuchatel 171, FBW 91 GTS/Hoch/SAAS, 1975 (Stephan Baguette)

Basle FBW/Hoch/SAAS by Mobatech, 1:87, brass (Miba)

of an H0 scale Basel trolleybus developed by Ivo Hügli, to be produced by Mobatech of Munich and distributed via HAG Miniaturbahnen of Mörschwil, the Swiss model railway company – their second attempt at marketing a model trolleybus. "Modelleisenbahner" magazine tantalizingly mentions a Swiss model trolleybus in 1955, to be made by HAG Modelleisenbahn, but nothing materialized. Apparently the 12v model which looks to be based on FBW/Hoch/SAAS Basel 911-20 of 1975, was a brass casting and enamel coated, but there was no indication of how the steering mechanism worked. The overhead looks similar to that of the concurrent Brawa type but has additional flexibility which might have made steering imprecise even if the booms had been at the front. With the booms on the trailer section Eheim type steering would have been impossible. Perhaps there was mechanical roadway guidance but the surviving image is indistinct. There were further model variants which were announced at the same time but nothing was subsequently heard of any production.

Marks Metallmodellclassics

The Marks Metallmodellclassics N gauge powered representation of a Henschel/Uerdingen ÜH IIIs that was announced at the 2003 Nuremberg toy fair, with what looks like a version of the Brawa N gauge mechanism, has yet to go into production. In 2006, Marks produced a brochure saying the body would be in whitemetal on a brass chassis with working lights and scale overhead. Prices were to be €396 for the Faulhaber motored trolleybus and €448 for a start set, based on a small production quantity. The prototype certainly looks good but it does sound rather heavy and expensive. Like the real things, hand making in small numbers is costly. It seems there's been no serial production so far.

TrainPCB

The only current commercial powered model we know of is another Henschel/Uerdingen ÜH IIIs. TrainPCB in the ex-trolleybus town of Nijmegen, in the Netherlands, has been producing powered Grell plastic trolleybuses with full digital encoding and Faller roadway electromagnetic guidance, since 2006. The fine trolleygear is spoilt a little by booms that have an exaggerated right angled turn towards the trolley heads. The kits are distributed by Eisner & Stahlhaus, an electrical retailer of Solingen, who thinks there's a special market in Germany's main trolleybus town. The kits have been available on eBay with a starter kit costing €245, not so expensive considering the large amount of re-engineering involved. The overhead is compatible with, and indeed very similar to Eheim/Brawa, and available individually.

Motorised commercial trolleybuses always suffered from the need to have the booms unrealistically placed at the very front of the bus, something that made them more toy-like than models. As an accessory to model railways they have suffered from the relentless push towards more realism, but the more flexible Faller roadway system can now provide moving model traffic on a layout, including model trolleybuses with more realistically positioned trolleybooms. In many ways it was incredible that Brawa was able to sell their Henschels right up until 2001. There remains a special fascination for them, and a brisk trade in second hand or even rediscovered 'new' stock. Perhaps the inherent connection with rigid overhead and mechanically linked steering still "does it" for so many.

Salzburg 123, (Solingen 40) Henschel/Uerdingen ÜH IIIs, 1959 (J Ward)

Generic Henschel/Uerdingen ÜH IIIs by Marks Metallmodellclassics, 1:160, plastic, metal (Marks)

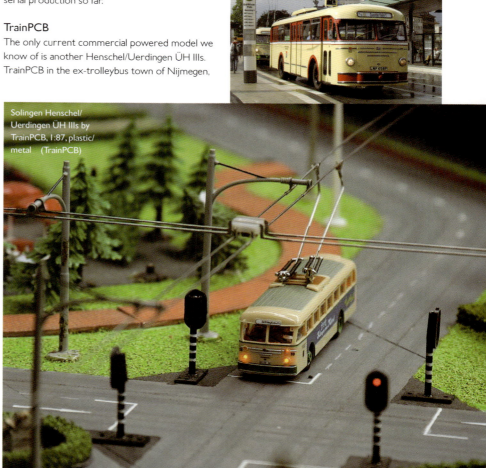

Solingen Henschel/Uerdingen ÜH IIIs by TrainPCB, 1:87, plastic/metal (TrainPCB)

Wien 3, Perl EPO/Cedes-Stoll, 1929 (Wiener Linien)

Chapter 5.1
Austria

Minobus	powered	75 (56)
Henschel	OM 5-1/Lohner	76
Gräf & Stift, 1948-1986	EO I	77
	EO II	77
	EO VI	78
	GEO	78
	OE 105/54	79
	GE 110 M 16	79
	GE 112 M	81
Steyr, 1988-1990	STS 11HU	81

Today there are two trolleybus cities in Austria, at Salzburg and Linz. Previous operations in Graz, Innsbruck, Kapfenberg, Klagenfurt, Leoben and Wien had mostly opened during WW2 and closed in the 1960s and 70s. A freight trolleybus line at St. Lamprecht to a dynamite factory also operated during the 1940s. Innsbruck had two installations, the second running from 1988 to 2007. But Austria, so closely allied to Germany, had Mercédès-Électrique-Stoll systems from the turn of the century in Gmünd, Judenburg, Kalksburg and Weidling (both close to Wien) and Wien Pötzleinsdorf – Salmansdorf which, incredibly, operated with progressively rebuilt and rebodied Cedes-Stoll trolleybuses from 1908 until 1938. If you count by the Austro-Hungarian border of the time, there were five more early systems, including a Schiemann system in Pirano, now Slovenia, and an AEG-Stoll system in Hermannstadt, (Sibiu) now in Romania. Two trolleybus pioneers, Hans-Ludwig Stoll (son of Carl) and Ferdinand Porsche (of car fame) worked together in Wien from 1907 onwards, building, with Austro-Daimler and Jacob Lohner & Co., ten of the early systems. There have been about 450 trolleybuses in Austria since 1904 and more than half of those have been used in Salzburg.

Stadtbus Salzburg AG is one of the world's most enthusiastic users of trolleybuses. In addition to the core network of the 1970s several new lines have been built and further extensions are planned. The General Manager, Gunter Mackinger, a keen collector of trolleybus models, likes to ensure the support of his ratepayers and often issues card kits to celebrate the arrival of new vehicles and anniversaries. The basement information centre of the Salzburg Lokalbahn in the Salzburg Hauptbahnhof (central railway station), usually has all available Salzburg trolleybus models. We've listed those based on German chassis from page 167 onwards, while all known Austrian chassis based models are listed here.

There is one very remarkable trolleybus model that we can't help but mention again here. The Austrian Minobus motorized trolleybus toy/model in near 0 scale manufactured from wood. They were first launched in 1948 at the Wien trade fair by Karl Kreibich and used a patented steering principle that was later used by Rivarossi for their trolleybus models. More details are on page 56.

Wien MAN/Siemens by Minobus, 25cm, wood, metal

Henschel OM 5-1/Lohner

model maker	ref.	issued	total	scale	construction	operator	fleet#	route	destination	built
ALO Alexander Olajos	ALO500-01	2004		1:87	resin, metal	Wien	6390-9	22	Salmannsdorf	1946
Technisches Museum Wien		1953		1:10(?)	wood, metal	Wien		3	Salmannsdorf	1943

Wien 395, Henschel OM 5-1/Lohner, 1946 (Mag. Alfred Luft)

Wien Henschel OM 5-1/Lohner by ALO Alexander Olajos, 1:87, resin, metal

Wien started test operation of their second generation trolleybuses in 1944. Ten trolleybus bodies were built in Austria by Lohner using Henschel II chassis. They had to be rebuilt between 1946 and 1949 because of considerable war damage so the single route 22 could re-open in 1946. As an isolated operation it closed in 1958 and the trolleybuses were sold to Kapfenberg, whence one survives, back in Wien, awaiting restoration.

Wiennese goldsmith Alexander Olajos, under his ALO Busmodelle brand name, offered a hand made trolleybus model of these rebuilt Henschels, made from resin in 1:87 scale for a price of €120. The very solid model has moveable and realistic trolley booms that are metal castings.

A much larger celebration of Wien's short lived use of trolleybuses is stored at the local Technisches Museum where a 1:10 scale model is inevitably more accurate than at 1:87.

Wien Henschel OM 5-1/Lohner by Technische Museum Wien, 1:10(?), wood, metal (Technische Museum Wien)

Lohner

model maker	ref.	issued	total	scale	construction	operator	fleet#	route	destination	built
Gottfied Kure		2009		1:87	resin, metal	St Lambrecht				1945

Dynamit Nobel AG Lohner, 1945 (Sammlung Jörg Prix)

Dynamit Nobel AG Lohner by Gottfried Kuře, 1:87, plastic

Rather rare is the modelling of trolley lorries, especially powered ones, but we include one here, using Eheim mechanicals and based on Lohner vehicles that used second-hand Italian trolleybus parts from a system in the Alto Adige of South Tyrol. The Dynamit Nobel AG factory at St. Lambrecht in central Austria desperately needed transport to Mariahof railway station 10kms away in 1945 when oil was virtually unobtainable. The solution was 3 lorries that used simple overhead strung between mostly wooden poles. What must have been fairly treacherous journeys lasted until 1951, when the system closed and one of the lorries was reportedly converted to a trolleybus and used at Kapfenberg.

Gräf & Stift

Of the 386 indigenously built Austrian trolleybuses, 322 were made by Gräf & Stift. Founded 1901 to make cars, Gräf & Stift. started trolleybus production in 1948 to supply the small home market as systems expanded after the war. The largest single batch numbered 20 (Linz 13-32) and exports included 28 to Bergen and Eberswalde. In 1971 the company was taken over by MAN but continued to manufacture trolleybuses, badged as Gräf & Stift. They also built bodies for MAN trolleybuses, which are included in the German chapter, from page 180 onwards.

Salzburg 115, Gräf & Stift EO 1, 1948   (Ernst Plefka)

Gräf & Stift EO1

model maker	ref.	issued	total	scale	construction	operator	fleet#	route	destination	built
ALO Alexander Olajos	ALO700-01	2005		1:87	resin, metal	Salzburg	122			1948
ALO Alexander Olajos	ALO700-02	2005		1:87	resin, metal	Linz	700-2			1950

Salzburg SSV Gräf & Stift EO 1 by ALO Alexander Olajos, 1:87, resin, metal

Linz ESG Gräf & Stift EO 1 by ALO Alexander Olajos, 1:87, resin, metal

The first model was originally designated EO ("Elektrischer Obus"), an integrated vehicle with both the body and chassis sub frames being made by Gräf & Stift. BBC (Brown Boveri) supplied the electrical equipment for the first 6 trolleybuses that went to Salzburg and later versions were delivered to Linz, Graz, Innsbruck, Kapfenberg and Leoben. By the 80s all EO types had been withdrawn but Leoben 4 of 1950 was saved by the Nostalgiebahnen in Kärnten (NBiK) and is now in Salzburg to be completely rebuilt and ultimately form part of the Salzburg museum trolleybus collection.

Alexander Olajos started making Austrian bus models in 2003 and produced his EO1 in Salzburg and Linz liveries two years later. Despite a relatively high price of €120, the EO1 models are now sold out. Only a few, about 20 of each, were made. Salzburg 121-7 had headlights that were further apart. The EO became the EO1 with the introduction of the EO11.

MAN MPE/Gräf & Stift EOII

model maker	ref.	issued	total	scale	construction	operator	fleet#	route	destination	built
ALO Alexander Olajos		2010		1:87	resin	Salzburg	128-30			1956

Alexander spent 2010 developing his model of the 1956 MAN MPE/Gräf & Stift, a type of which only 3 were built, for Salzburg, as shortened versions of the EOII that were supplied to Leoben and Linz. For the model to represent the prototype Linz delivery, with 6 prominent chrome strips at the front and a centre door towards the rear axle, the casting would have to be considerably re-worked. There can be few instances of commercial models being made of such rare trolleybuses.

Salzburg Gräf & Stift EO II master model by ALO Alexander Olajos, 1:87, brass, plastic   (Alexander Olajos)

Salzburg 130, Gräf & Stift EO II, 1956 (unknown)

Salzburg Gräf & Stift EO II by ALO Alexander Olajos, 1:87, resin

Gräf & Stift EO IV

model maker	ref.	issued	total	scale	construction	operator	fleet#	route	destination	built
V/R (conversion)				1:87	resin	Linz	43			1960

In 1959, Linz received EOIV trolleybuses and TSH158 buses with virtually identical bodies. V/R, the Czech Republic model maker modelled the bus batch (30-35) with a grille between chrome strips instead of none at all. But it's hard for local collectors not to add booms to these curvaceous shapes for the sake of nostalgia!

Linz 37, Gräf & Stift EO IV, 1960 (Linz AG)

Linz ESG Gräf & Stift EO VI by V/R (conversion), 1:87, resin

Gräf & Stift GEO

model maker	ref.	issued	total	scale	construction	operator	fleet#	route	destination	type	built
HB Model				1:87	resin	Salzburg	136-142			GEO-II	1961
HB Model				1:87	resin	Leoben	8			GEO-I	1960

Gräf & Stift built 29 of the articulated version of the EO series, prefaced with a G for Gelenkbus, one for Leoben, 21 for Linz and 7 for Salzburg. HB Models versions have an incorrect front slope and find the subtle relationship between windscreen pillars impossible to emulate, which is a pity, given the rather impressive shape of these trolleybuses. Missing too, is the articulation mechanism on top of the bellows.

Salzburg Gräf & Stift GEO II by HB Model, 1:87, resin   (Mattis Schindler)

Leoben Gräf & Stift GEO I by HB Model, 1:87, resin   (Mattis Schindler)

Salzburg 136, Gräf & Stift GEO II, 1961 (werkephoto)

Gräf & Stift OE 105/54

model maker	ref.	issued	total	scale	construction	operator	fleet#	route	destination	built
ALO	900/01	2006		1:87	resin	Salzburg	101-102			1971

Gräf & Stift OE 105/54 trolleybuses, with Kiepe electrical equipment went into operation in 1971 in Salzburg as 101 and 102 to replace the original two EOIs. The similar OE 105/54/2 trolleybuses of 1974 (103-112) replaced the rest of the batch. They all served until 1986-90. ALO Busmodelle's model, now sold out, is of the first two, with the large front badge and round headlights.

Salzburg 102, Gräf & Stift OE 105/54, 1974 (Walter Kramer)

Salzburg SSV Gräf & Stift OE 105/54 by ALO Alexander Olajos, 1:87, resin

Gräf & Stift GE 110 M 16

model maker	ref.	issued	total	scale	construction	operator	fleet#	route	destination	built
(unknown)				1:87	resin	Salzburg	136-47/161-78			1982-85
HB Model				1:87	resin	Salzburg	136-47/161-78			1982-85
HB Model				1:87	resin	Salzburg	129-135			1978-80
HB Model				1:87	resin	Linz				11979
HB Model				1:87	resin	Kapfenberg				1979
Salzburger Stadtwerke				1:50	card	Salzburg	129-135	6	Plainbrücke - Parsch	1978-80
Salzburger Stadtwerke				(no scale)	card	Salzburg	178			1985
Salzburger Stadtwerke				1:32	card	Salzburg	179			1986

Articulated Gräf & Stift GS GE 110 M 16 trolleybuses were delivered to Salzburg between 1981 and 1985 with Kiepe electrical equipment (136-147 and 162-178). Some were sold to Perm (Russia) in the late 1990s but 178 remains as a museum trolleybus, used for special trips and has the nick name "Trolli".

Trolleybus driver Andreas Zietemann used Alexander Olajos's diecast booms to convert a bus model to one of the batch, though he can't now remember who made it. HB Model of the Czech Republic has also, a little simplistically, modelled the batch as well as the two front door variants of the earlier 129-135 batch and those supplied to Linz ESG in 1979 (type GE 150 M 16). The model of the Kapfenberg 20-24 batch correctly looses the drivers kerb window on the front doors. HB Models are distributed by MMR in Czech Republic or Konrad Pernetta in Germany.

Salzburg SSV Gräf & Stift GE 110M16 by (unknown), 1:87, resin   (Andreas Zietemann)

Salzburg Gräf & Stift GE 110M16 by HB Model, 1:87, resin

Salzburg Gräf & Stift GE 110M16 by HB Model, 1:87, resin

Kapfenburg Gräf & Stift GE 105M16 by HB Model, 1:87, resin   (Mattis Schindler)

Salzburg 163, Gräf & Stift GE 110M16, 1983 (G Mackinger)

Linz Gräf & Stift GE 150M16 by HB Model, 1:87, resin

Over the years Salzburger Stadtwerke has offered free trolleybus card kits in different scales. The quite detailed 1:50 card kit of the GE 110 M 16 came with several destination boards but was issued when the 12 km long trolleybus line 7 was opened in 1983. A much simpler Salzburg card kit of 178 was given away at an open day in 2005.

Salzburg Gräf & Stift GE 110M16 by Salzburger Stadtwerke, (no scale), card

Salzburg Gräf & Stift GE 110M16 by Salzburger Stadtwerke, 1:50, card

Gräf & Stift GE 112 M 16 & OE 112 M11

model maker	ref.	issued	total	scale	construction	operator	fleet#	route	destination	built
Salzburger Stadtwerke				1:32	card	Salzburg	179			1986
Wiking (conversion)				1:87	plastic	Kapfenberg	15,16		Hauptbf	1986

The next Gräf & Stift trolleybuses, type GE 112 M16, were based on the standardised German VÖV II design which seems to have applied rather more to trolleybuses than buses. Between 1986 and 1994 Salzburg had two batches, 179-190 with DC traction motors and 191, 9161-9169, 9370-9374 and 9451-9468 with AC traction motors. A large 1:32 scale card kit was given away by Salzburger Stradtwerke to celebrate the 50th anniversary of trolleybus operation in 1990, when the rather boxy vehicles were being delivered. The model is agreeably more curvaceous than the real thing.

Salzburg SSV Gräf & Stift GE 112M16 by Salzburger Stadtwerke, 1:32, card

Gräf & Stift also produced eight of the single version, type OE 112 M11, for Salzburg and Kapfenberg. Andreas Zietemann has added booms to the Wiking model of the LH200 M12 bus on which they were based and painted it in Kapfenberg colours.

Kapfenberg Gräf & Stift OE 112M11 by Wiking (conversion), 1:87, plastic (Andreas Zietemann)

Salzburg 9167, Gräf & Stift GE 112M16, 1986   (G Mackinger)

Steyr Bus

The Steyr Bus GmbH was a part of the large Steyr Daimler Puch conglomerate. Originally a gun factory, then into cars, trucks and motorcycles, they had built Cedes-Stoll trolleybuses as the Austro Daimler company between 1907 and 1912. Just before being broken up in 1990, the company built 12 more trolleybuses.

Steyr STS 11HU

model maker	ref.	issued	total	scale	construction	operator	fleet#	route	destination	built
ALO Alexander Olajos	ALO200-01	2004		1:87	resin	Linz		45	Froschberg	1988
ALO Alexander Olajos	ALO200-02	2004		1:87	resin	Salzburg	107-114	1	Bahnhof	1989-90
ALO Alexander Olajos (repaint)	ALO200-02			1:87	resin	Salzburg		1	Bahnhof	1989-90
ALO Alexander Olajos (repaint)	ALO200-02			1:87	resin	Salzburg		6	Parsch	1989-90
Salzburger Stadtwerke				1:87	card	Salzburg			Sonderfahrt	1989-90

Steyr's final trolleybuses were based on the Austrian "Österreich Bus" platform (type SS11 HU) and were delivered 1988 – 1990 with Kiepe electrical equipment to Salzburg and Linz. Salzburg trolleybus 113 remains at the depot in 2010 and 209 is used as a "Museums-Obus" for special tours. The pair that went to Linz were sold in 2002 to Rostow in Russia.

Salzburg Steyr STS 11HU by Salzburger Stadtwerke, 1:87, card

Salzburg 109, Steyr STS 11HU, 1989 (Andras Ekkert)

Salzburg Steyr STS 11HU by ALO Alexander Olajos, 1:87, resin

Linz ESG Steyr STS 11HU by ALO Alexander Olajos, 1:87, resin

3 variants of Salzburg SSV Steyr STS 11HU by ALO Alexander Olajos, 1:87, resin

ALO Busmodelle sold hand made Steyr trolleybus models to order – Alexander only makes his models in July and August, so you might have to wait! Both trolleybuses from Salzburg and Linz were produced. Andras Ekkert, a meticulous modeller from Solingen, has repainted the Salzburg Steyrs in the three livery versions that were applied (and has been known to accept commissions to repaint models). Salzburger Stadtwerke produced a not very convincing card model when the Steyrs first arrived in 1989.

Austria was a trolleybus pioneer, mainly because Ferdinand Porsche built his hub-mounted electric motors in Wien, although both they and the Cedes-Stoll over running trolley system that used them were technologically flawed.

In recent times, Austria's heavy dependence on hydropower seems not to have influenced trolleybus use in the way it has in Switzerland and the small system of Linz has been through years of uncertainty. See page 268 for the current fleet. Innsbruck preferred trams and scrapped its system in 2007 but Salzburg remains an inspirational trolleybus network, much appreciated by its residents.

Chapter 5.2
Belarus

Minsk Radio Technical Factory	tinplate	83
Belkommunmash, 1995 - current	AKSM-101	84
	AKSM-201	84
MAZ, 2002	AKSM-221 (103T)	85
	AKSM 300 series	85
	AKSM 400 series	86

Minsk 01, MTB-82M, 1946 (Redline)

Belarus remains strongly tied to Russia and still has most of its industry owned by the state. Minsk still has the third largest trolleybus system in the world, and possibly the densest; 1022 vehicles serve 643 km of route and 901 trolleybuses have been delivered since 2002. None of the 7 systems that have existed in Belarus have closed and all are receiving the latest Belkommunmash 3 series trolleybuses. 1751 trolleybuses are in daily service (as of May, 2010)

Just worth a quick mention is the MTB-82 toy by the gloriously named Minsk Radio Technical Factory, possibly made when Minsk first introduced the ubiquitous Russian design as its first trolleybus in 1952. If originally white and red, like the proudly preserved original that today has its own plinth, then paint of the former Byelorussian SSR certainly doesn't keep its colour!

The Minsk system developed rapidly in the 50s and 60s in much the same way as Kiev (see page 273) and for the same reasons – the trolleybus had become the preferred mode of official state policy for urban street public transport. Deliveries of the MTB-82 started slowly but grew to 105 by 1960. 280 ZiU-5s followed in the late 60s, one of which was restored in 2003 with a rather exuberant paint job. 1,112 ZiU-9 (ZiU682) trolleybuses were delivered from 1972 onwards and survived until 2009. All three of these Soviet stalwarts have been variously modelled (see page 253). The six other systems of Belarus followed suit on a smaller scale, opening mainly in the 1970s and likewise following the party line of near total adherence to the ZiU-9, in all its many variants, up until the fall of Communism; some would say, and beyond. There had been the odd dalliance with Ukrainian trolleybuses (the abortive Kiev-11 especially) but the Minsk Tram and Trolleybus Overhaul Plant made a large scale living out of keeping thousands of the Soviet standard trolleybus on the road. In 1995, Belkommunmash, as the plant became known, started production of the first Belarus trolleybuses with the 101 series that were improved clones of the ZiU-682 and were exported to Russia.

Minsk MTB-82M by Minsk Radio Technical Factory, (no scale), tinplate

Belkommunmash AKSM-101

model maker	ref.	issued	total	scale	construction	operator	fleet#	route	destination	built
Mungojerrie		2008		1:87	card	Moscow	1806	70	Bratsevo	1995

Mungojerrie, aka. Andrey Kuznetsov of Moscow, at papertrolley.ucoz.ru has produced over a hundred image files that can be downloaded and made up as trolleybus models. There are two of the AKSM-101, as Moscow's 1806 and 4801, both withdrawn in 2008. The card models are photographic, and show the trolleybuses later in life - that's to say a little battered!

Moscow 1806, Belkommunmash AKSM-101, 1995 (Mungojerrie)

Moscow Belkommunmash AKSM-101 by Mungojerrie, 1:87, card (Mungojerrie)

Belkommunmash AKSM-201

model maker	ref.	issued	total	scale	construction	operator	fleet#	route	destination	built
Mungojerrie		2008		1:87	card	Moscow	1815	70	Bratsevo	1996

The following year, 1996, came the AKSM-201, a further development of the ZiU-682, with a modernized front and, for the first time, thyristor control. Andrey has produced 4 card models including Moscow 1815, built in 2003 and currently in service. There was also an articulated version, the AKSM-213, but using the ZiU-682 or ZiU-683 as an ancestor was becoming untenable, as progress toward low floor designs was seen as a necessity.

Moscow 1815, Belkommunmash AKSM-201, 1996 (Mungojerrie)

Moscow Belkommunmash AKSM-201 by Mungojerrie, 1:87, card (Mungojerrie)

MAZ 103T

model maker	ref.	issued	total	scale	construction	operator	fleet#	route	destination	built
Kimmeria		2007		1:43	electroformed copper	Minsk				2002
Kimmeria		2007		1:43	electroformed copper	Moscow				2002

The indigenous bus manufacturer MAZ (Minsk Automobile Factory) had built the first low floor buses in Belarus in 1996 and Belkommunmash took over production of the trolleybus version to supply over 200 of the type both to the (guaranteed) home market and as exports.

Kimmeria Models in Kherson, Ukraine, doubtless because 66 examples had been delivered to Kiev, has modelled the MAZ 103T (or AKSM-221) with commendable accuracy although lacking lettering detail. The booms are especially well handled. You could also buy one online in Moscow blue for 6750 roubles.

Minsk 5196, MAZ 103T, 2004 (Redline)

Minsk MAZ 103T by Kimmeria, 1:43, electroformed copper (ritmonexx.ru)

Moscow MAZ 103T by Kimmeria, 1:43, electroformed copper (Moscow Tram Collection)

Belkommunmash 300 series

model maker	ref.	issued	total	scale	construction	operator	fleet#	route	destination	built
Viva Scale Models		2008		1:20	plastic, wood, metal	Minsk				2004
Belkommunmash		2006		1:20	plastic, wood, metal	Minsk				n/a
Viva Scale Models		2008		1:20	plastic, wood, metal	Minsk				2006

Belkommunmash's third generation trolleybus, the AKSM-321, was their first proper in-house design and rather 'retro' to look at, with a smaller windscreen than their contemporaries and a droopy front that takes a 'stuck on' destination box. But the vehicle has gone down well with the operator in Minsk – 552 have been delivered so far – and more have followed to all of Belarus's other six systems. More have been exported to Russia, Serbia and Hungary, as a result of a new found marketing aggression that saw the company commission Viva Scale Models of Minsk to produce a deadly accurate 1:20 scale model, complete with the as-originally-fitted chrome wheels. The model is used to market the AKSM-321 at exhibitions.

Minsk Belkommunmash AKSM-321 by Viva Scale Models, 1:20, plastic, wood, metal (Viva)

Minsk 4624, Belkommunmash AKSM-321, 2004 (Edward Kravchenko)

The company has thought about a 15m rigid three axle variant, as had been developed by Solaris in Poland at the time, and had a model made to test the concept. Nothing, so far, has come of the unofficially called AKSM-331. Interestingly, the side glazing is deeper than the AKSM-321, an indication of the design prerogatives that were being thought about in 2006. Meanwhile, an articulated three axle version was and is being produced, the AKSM-333, which does, at least over the first axle, inherit deeper glazing. 51 have been supplied to Minsk and one, with supercapacitors and a 100kw diesel generator set has been used to test off-wire adaptability. Viva's model again has chrome wheels and rather eye-catching turquoise articulation bellows but not the white doors of the production versions. The model and the prototype have the rather dated black rubber extrusions above and below the glazing, around the windscreen and the wheels, something the latest examples have now lost.

Minsk Belkommunmash AKSM-331 by Belkommunmash, 1:20, plastic, wood, metal (Belkommunmash)

Minsk 3600, Belkommunmash AKSM-333, 2007 (Edward Kravchenko)

Minsk Belkommunmash AKSM-333 by Viva Scale Models, 1:20, plastic, wood, metal (Viva)

Belkommunmash 400 series

model maker	ref.	issued	total	scale	construction	operator	fleet#	route	destination	built
Viva Scale Models		2008		1:20	plastic, wood, metal	Minsk				2007

Minsk Belkommunmash AKSM-420 by Viva Scale Models, 1:20, plastic, wood, metal (Viva)

As if to make amends for their rather dated design thinking, Belkommunmash unleashed a radical fourth generation trolleybus in late August 2007 with a very flush fitting body and no hint of molded rubber. Based, as all agreed, as the images of AKSM-420 flashed around cyberspace, on the Dutch Phileas design and so a self conscious retro tram look, it has inherited something of the latter's misfortune. Despite being trumpeted as state-of-the-art and expected to sell to Russia, the AKSM-420 suffers from having only two doors where three are the norm. As a result, only eight have been built, despite Viva Scale Models wonderfully accurate showcase model being shown at many exhibition appearances. The model, like the real thing, was produced rather quickly, in 5 weeks – the real and entirely new prototype took 12 months.

Perhaps the AKSM-420 changes perceptions about Belarus's major trolleybus supplier, depending on your point of view. Either way, Belkommunmash have virtually renewed the country's entire fleet in less than a decade and broken into export markets. Despite murmurings, the trolleybus seems secure in Belarus for another generation.

Minsk prototype, Belkommunmash AKSM-420, 2007 (Redline)

Chapter 5.3
Belgium

Brossel Frères, 1936 - 1956	DE	87
	500	88
FN, 1932 - 1957	T54	89
Van Hool, 1989-current	AG 300T	89

Liège 403, Brossel Frères & D'Heure, 1936   (JH Rennard)

The small, linguistically split country of Belgium has had only 5 trolleybus networks, 4 between 1929 and 1971 and one, Gent, between 1989 and 2009. Altogether 227 vehicles saw service, while more, 300 plus, have been built on Belgian soil for export since 1994, by the Van Hool Company.

The first Belgian trolleybuses were 16 Straker Squire, Guy and Ransomes, Sims & Jefferies trolleys, imported from the UK between 1928 and 1930 and used at Antwerpen, Bruxelles and Liège. The Strakers dated from 1923 and were converted motor buses. The first indigenous trolleybus was built by luxury car maker Minerva in 1930, trying to find alternative markets at a time of financial crisis by diversifying its product range. The second was built in 1932 by FN (Fabrique Nationale), a motor cycle and small arms maker, also trying to diversify. One of the resulting batch, Liège 425, is preserved in running order at The Trolleybus Museum at Sandtoft in the UK (432 is also preserved). FN was to build trolleybuses for the local market until 1957, supplying 153, two thirds of all those supplied. The sudden interest in trolleybuses apparently had to do with the "big capitalists", the Englebert family who were busily exploiting the colonies for rubber and had set up a tyre factory in Herstal, home of the FN plant and CEB (Construction Electrique de Belgique). Electric traction on rubber tyres was seen as having potential in the hilly streets of nearby Liège and elsewhere. But one route in the suburb of Seraing was problematic. Hemmed in by a river and railway crossings, the turning of trolleybuses needed a double-ended vehicle with two sets of booms on three axles; an exuberant solution that can only reflect the Englebert pressure to use trolleybuses at all costs. The one preserved example, converted back to its original state and still on Englebert tyres (it says so on the bumper), is in the Musée des Transports en commun du Pays de Liège.

Brossel Frères

model maker	ref.	issued	total	scale	construction	operator	fleet#	route	destination	built
HB Model				1:43	resin	Liège RELSE	402		Yvoz depot	1936
HB Model				1:87	resin	Liège RELSE	402		Yvoz depot	1936
Liège				1:87	resin	Liège RELSE	402			1936

Truck maker Brossel Frères of Bruxelles built the four double ended trolleybuses (together with two smaller 2 axle versions with one set of booms) with bodies by Paul D'Heure. They were converted in 1949 to single ended layout and lasted until 1963. A terrific 1:43 version of the reconverted museum exhibit was made for HB Model and distributed by Konrad Pernetta. Not only are the inevitably long overhanging booms faithfully reproduced but also the doors on both sides as originally built. HB also made a 1:87 version. Belgian Trucks is reputed to have made a version in 1:50, but this is not confirmed.

Liège 402, Brossel Frères/D'Heure, 1936   (André Corteil)

Liège 402, Brossel Frères/D'Heure/CEB by HB Model, 1:43, resin

Brossel Frères 500

model maker	ref.	issued	total	scale	construction	operator	fleet#	route	destination	built
André Dessart				1:30	wood, metal	Liège	499	35	Robermont	1939
Belgium Trucks		1980	100	1:43	diecast whitemetal	Brussells	6023			1956

Liège 495, Brossel Frères 500/D'Heure/CEB T38, 1939 (col. Robert Fonteyne)

Three years later Brossel Frères produced a much more conventional trolleybus, based on their 500 chassis, again with bodies by D'Heure. The batch of six, 495-500 served until 1961 and were convincingly modelled using sheet metal and wood by André Dessart and now in the Musée des Transports en commun du Pays de Liège.

Bruxelles operator STIB received Brossel Frères trolleybuses in 1956 that were very similar to the initial batches delivered in 1939-45. They had locally produced electrical equipment by ACEC and bodies by D'Heure. The one route system had the vehicles turning with traction batteries and needing a tram skate at the depot. It closed in 1964. Having only seen eight years service, 6023 survives in running order as

demonstrated by its much noticed appearance at the closure of the Gent system in 2009. Model car maker Belgium Trucks (Gaston Thiry of Bruxelles) produced a heavy diecast 1:43 scale model in the late 1980s that survives the transition into miniaturisation rather well – the thick window pillars being the most obvious compromise.

Liège 499, Brossel Frères 500/D'Heure/CEB T38 by André Deassart, 1:30, wood, metal (André Corteil)

Bruxelles 6023, Brossel/ACEC, 1956 (Carl Isgar)

Bruxelles 6023, Brossel/ACEC by Belgium Trucks, 1:43, diecast whitemetal (Fabio Dobran)

FN T54

model maker	ref.	issued	total	scale	construction	operator	fleet#	route	destination	built
Belgium Trucks		1980		1:43	diecast whitemetal	Liège	544	12	Ans Loncin	1954
André Dessart				1:20	metal, wood	Liège	523	8	Fleron	1954

By far the largest supplier of trolleybuses in Belgium, arms manufacturer FN, delivered most of its trolleybus output to their local operator Liège TULE, the largest and most comprehensive network in Belgium. The great majority were supplied between 1936 and 1938 with electrics from local supplier CEB. A new generation arrived in 1954. Logically designated the T54, they replaced trams on three routes, and were built under licence from Marmon-Harrington of the United States. In 1980 Belgium Trucks modelled 544, the example preserved in the Liège Transport Museum. It's a very heavy model as expected of a 1:43 diecast and the soft metal booms are prone to bending out of shape. Detailing is very good with the inclusion of accurate window framing and full lettering down to entrance graphics and registration number. Well managed is the painting of the window rubbers although, 20 years on, the blue centre band can sometimes flake.

Twice as big is André Dessart's model that predates it. Like Percy Wilby at Ipswich, a local enthusiast had recreated the generations of his town's trolleybuses with evocative skill, to be inherited by the local transport museum. The models (and they include FN classes T32 and T38 of 1931-4 and 1939 respectively) are built in similar way, with cutout metal and carved wood.

FN reworked its unsuccessful T48 prototype in 1957 in anticipation of first generation trolleybus replacement, but despite considerable investment in the overhead network in 1956, the earliest trolleys, the much rebuilt Ransomes, lasted until 1961 and the pre-war FNs until 1965, by which time the Liège TULE system was winding down. Belgium lost its last service trolleybus of the first generation in 1971, just as oil was about to cause global crisis.

Liège 540, FN T54, 1954 (John Veerkamp)

Liège 544, FN T54 by Belgium Trucks, 25cm, diecast whitemetal

Liège 523, FN T54 by André Dessart, 1:20, wood, metal (André Corteil)

Van Hool AG 300T

model maker	ref.	issued	total	scale	construction	operator	fleet#	route	destination	built
Salzburger Stradtwerke				1:87	card	Salzburg SSV			Sonderfahrt	2000-5
Salzburger Stradtwerke				1:87	card	Salzburg SSV			Stadtbus	2000-5
Andras Ekkert				1:87	injection plastic	Solingen	268	684	Hassel Str	2002

18 years later environmental concerns saw the State government fund a new system in Gent, pretty much against the operator's wishes, with 20 locally built Van Hool trolleybuses that ran intermittently, it has to be said, until 2009. Models of the AG280T could and probably were made from Ferivan's A120 1:87 bus. The funding also foresaw the export potential of trolleybuses, so from a situation of parochial procurement, the Belgian trolleybus story moves to international markets with over 300 vehicles, mostly the AG300T type, exported to Austria, Holland, Italy, Germany, Greece and Switzerland.

While commercial models did exist of the bus version (as resin kits by EuroH0, Bram Osbourne) and perhaps as a trolleybus, the AG300T has certainly been modelled as a Code 3 by enthusiasts such as Andras Ekkert who has converted off-the-shelf model buses into his local Solingen 268 of 2002. Commemorative card models have also been issued by operator Salzburg SSV to celebrate their 65th anniversary of 'Obus' operation, when Van Hool AG300Ts were still being delivered.

Solingen 265, Van Hool AG 300T, 2002

Solingen Van Hool AG 300T by Andras Ekkert, (conversion), 1:87, injection plastic (Andras Ekkert)

Salzburg 280, Van Hool AG 300T, 2003 (Dave Wilsher)

Salzburg SSV Van Hool AG 300T by Salzburger Stadtwerke, 1:87, card

Today the A330T and the AG300T trolleybuses are being built in a country without a trolleybus service. Kiepe, the trolleybus electrical control manufacturers, made a model of their first Van Hool for Lecce, painted to celebrate their 100th anniversary - as it says on the side, "Made with eMotion".

Lecce Van Hool 330T, 2009 (Marcus Fey)

Windsor 1, St. Louis Car Co, 1922 (St. Louis Car Co)

Chapter 5.4
Canada

CCF-Brill, 145 - 1954	T-44	92
GMC, 1982	Brown Boveri	94
Flyer, 1974-1987	F700	95
	F800	95

From the very start, trolleybus operations in Canada mirrored those of the United States. In 1922, St. Louis Car Co. sent 3 "Trollicars" to Windsor, Ontario, together with the prototype that had been demonstrated in Detroit. They ran until 1926 and generated enough patronage to be replaced by an extended streetcar line. The following month, May 1922, remarkably similar American Packards with Brill bodies were tried in Mount Pleasant, Toronto for 3 years and had the same effect, being replaced by a rail service (No.23 survives at Halton County Railroad Museum).

Canada waited until the late 30s before importing AEC and Leyland six wheelers from Britain to start services in Montreal and Edmonton in 1937 and 1939 respectively. Winnipeg imported 29 Macks in 1938 and had a local company, Motor Coach Industries, build a trolleybus.

The real explosion in trolleybus usage in Canada started after the war, when the Canadian Car and Foundry Co. using its ACF-Brill franchise built the first Canadian T-44 for Edmonton. From 1945 until 1951, 12 trolleybus systems opened, mostly replacing tramcar core routes at a time when dependence on public transit still needed some heavy carrying power, that, arguably, could only be provided by electric traction. Nearly all Canadian trolleybuses were provided by CCF-Brill, with some second-hand US trolleybuses imported when the opportunity arose.

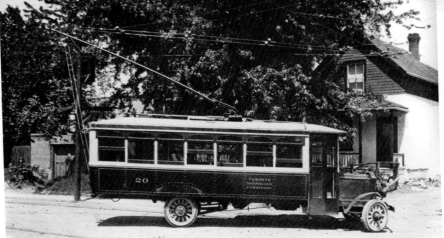

Toronto 20, Packard/Brill, 1922 (Brill)

Montreal 4003, AEC 664T/MCCW, 1937 (AEC)

CCF-Brill

Between 1945 and 1954, CCF-Brill built 1,098 trolleybuses and virtually monopolised the market. There was only one design, the T-44 which when lengthened in 1949 become the T-48 and which held sway until the last deliveries in 1954.

5.4 Canada   91

CC&F-Brill T-44

model maker	ref.	issued	total	scale	construction	operator	fleet#	route	destination	built
St.Petersburg	175	1999	100	1:48	resin	Toronto Transportation Commission	9000-9049	61		1947
St.Petersburg	175-1	1999	50	1:48	resin	Toronto Transportation Commission	9073		Nortown	1947
St.Petersburg	175a	1999	25	1:48	resin	Edmonton ETS	131-177			1947
St.Petersburg	175b	1999	50	1:48	resin	Vancouver BCER	2001		Stanley Park	1947
St.Petersburg	175c	1999	5	1:48	resin	Bogota	43831			1947
St.Petersburg	175d	1999	12	1:48	resin	Vancouver BCER	2042	25	Victoria	1947
St.Petersburg	175d-1	1999	12	1:48	resin	Vancouver BCER	2040	10	Tenth	1947
St.Petersburg	175e	1999	50	1:48	resin	Montreal Tramways	4042	26	Beabien	1947
St.Petersburg	175f	1999	25	1:48	resin	Halifax NSL&P	201	10	Howe Ave.	1947
St.Petersburg	175g	1999	10	1:48	resin	Calgary Transit System	422		Elbow Drive	1947
St.Petersburg	175h	1999	special	1:48	resin	Winnipeg Metro	1600		Osborne	1947
ETS					card	Edmonton ETS	148			1947
Roberts Miniature Transports				1:87	plaster	Toronto Transportation Commission	1925		Larden	1948

Vancouver 2416, CC&F-Brill T-44, 1947 (Dennis Tsang)

The St. Petersburg Tram Collection (SPTC) has impeccably modelled 7 of the 12 operators that had Canadian made Brill T-44s. Vancouver's 2040 is also impeccably preserved in running order. The lengthened version, the T-48 with an additional window ahead of the rear door, has yet to be produced (202 is preserved). All the Canadian SPTC models are now sold out, such has been the huge demand for such high quality modeling.

David Roberts of Florida has produced a T-44 Brill that resides in the Hershey, Penn. Bus Museum, a part of John Dockendorf's extensive collection, but whether it's a CCF-Brill of Toronto is a little open to doubt — Toronto's trolleys had fleet numbers in the 9000s not the no.1925 shown on the model. David Roberts, as Roberts Miniature Transports, produced many plaster models of buses, some that could easily be converted to trolleys.

Edmonton Transit System produced a card model of their CCF-Brill T44 back when they had faith in trolleybuses; a fact, sadly, no longer true. Trolleys 148 and 191 are, however, preserved.

Vancouver 2042, CC&F-Brill T-44 by St.Petersburg, 1:48, resin (SPTC)

Vancouver 2040, CC&F-Brill T-44, 1947 (Dennis Tsang)

GMC/Brown Boveri

model maker	ref.	issued	total	scale	construction	operator	fleet#	route	destination	built
Busch				1:87	plastic	Edmonton ETS	158			1982

Edmonton ordered 100 trolleybuses in 1981, rather more than it needed, at a time of expansion for electric traction, under the auspices of Llew Lawrence, the operations manager. It was not an easy time to buy home grown trolleys, but a combination of traction equipment by Brown Boveri Canada and 'New Look' body structures from General Motors Canada created the unique batch. Number 158 received an all-over 'Enviro Bus' livery in 1990, extolling the virtues of zero emission trolleybuses. It's ironic that German model bus maker Busch should choose to produce a version, accurate in many ways, that didn't have trolley booms. That, of course, is corrected here, with a pair by Eric Courtney of Alberta added and a cowling built to suit. Edmonton regrettably chose to abandon trolleybus operation in 2009. Sister vehicle 189 now runs at Sandtoft Trolleybus Museum in the UK.

Edmonton 158, GM/Brown Boveri, 1982 (Ashton Wong)

Edmonton 158 GM/Brown Boveri by Busch (conversion), 1:87, plastic

Flyer F700/800

model maker	ref.	issued	total	scale	construction	operator	fleet#	route	destination	built
Roberts Miniature Transports				1:87	plaster	Toronto Transportation Commission	9232	76	Mt. Pleasant	1979
3dTransit.com				any scale	virtual	Boston MTA	4002	73	Waverly Sq.	1979

Toronto 9200, Flyer E700, 1979 (skaliwagg66)

As the post war generation of trolleybuses neared the end of their lives, operators wanting to continue with trolleybuses could turn to Flyer Industries of Winnipeg who had an agreement with American Motors to produce bus shells either as diesels or trolley coaches. Toronto led the way in 1969 and went on, like others, to re-use motors and controls from 1940s Brills. In fact, Toronto specifically bought second hand trolleys to be able to re-use their traction equipment. The plaster model by David Roberts, at least the one in John Dockendorf's collection has the upright windows of the E800 type but the fleet number of an E700.

While some might scoff at the inclusion of a 'virtual' computer model, 3dTransit.com makes freely available an E800 of Boston that could have its left hand door removed and the livery of Philadelphia or San Francisco applied at the click of a few buttons. Rather more virtual engineering would be required to convert to a current generation New Flyer E40LF trolleybuses of Vancouver.

Toronto Flyer E700 by Roberts Miniature Transports, 1:87, plaster

Boston 4005, Flyer E800, 1979 (Bradlee9119)

Boston 4002, Flyer E800 by 3dTransit.com, any scale, virtual

Edmonton 158, GM/Brown Boveri by Busch, 1:87, injection plastic

Chapter 5.5
China

2 axle single decker	toy	98
3 axle single decker	toy	99
3 axle double decker	toy	99
4 axle double decker	toy	100
Beijing, 1956 - current	BK560	100
	BD562	101
	BK540	101
Shanghai, 1950 - 1990	SK5105GP	102
	SK561	102
Sunwin, 2000 - current	SWB5115GP	104
Beijing, 1956 - current	BJD-WG120N	104
	BJD-WG120EK	105

Shanghai B309, AEC 603T, 1925 (unknown)

Shanghai AEC 603T by Shanghai Living Museum, 1:1, Fibreglass (Zhong Wei)

Shanghai 341, AEC 603T, 1930 (c/o Mattis Schindler)

The trolleybus in China starts and continues to this day, in Shanghai, the world's oldest operating trolleybus system. 6 chain-driven Railless trolleys were sent in 1914 from the UK, plus the first shaft-driven Railless. All had a huge headlight and no driver protection – a tradition that continued through many of the 200+ AEC's supplied to Shanghai (and Singapore) up until 1939 - by far the largest ever British trolleybus export order. There's an appalling recreation of one at the Shanghai Living Museum.

Quite what filled the gap between the twenties and the post revolution era of the 50s and 60s is not clear, apart, presumably, from struggling on with rebodied AECs, - at least one, 341 of the 1930 delivery, was still running in 1960.

The Shanghai Trolleybus Plant started producing a wide variety home grown vehicles from 1951 onwards that initially looked like Russia's MTB-82, itself strongly influenced by America's GM bus of the time. Other places, such as Tianjin and Shenyang also built their own trolleybuses. Beijing followed in 1956, displacing the trams, and they also commission 1:64 scale models.

Until relatively recently China had only produced archetypal tinplate toys, not models.

Shanghai Trolleybus Plant single decker, 1951 (unkown)

Starting in the 1900s and taking over the market vacated by Japan, China is now estimated to provide 75% of the world's toys. The struggle to become the world's workshop is well beyond the scope of this book, but China's toy trolleybuses reflect the changes. By the 60s China's toy industry had broken into the international market, producing some sophisticated items cheaply, although most were rather primitive.

2 axle single decker

model maker	ref.	issued	total	scale	construction	operator	fleet#	route	destination	built
F Toys	F1208			(no scale)	tinplate	Generic				1982
Fairylite	MS705	1950s		(no scale)	tinplate	Generic				
Fairylite		1960s		(no scale)	tinplate	Generic				
M.F	MS705	1968		(no scale)	tinplate	Generic	426	ME634		
Wang Feng	SH-860			(no scale)	plastic	Generic	860			

Owing nothing to any real prototype, unless you want to conjecture a similarity, "F Toys" produced a simple 19cm red trolley in the 60s with a friction drive. The cut and bent windows have sharp edges that would not be recommended for children today.

Typically large is the 27cm 2 axle tinplate trolleybus, produced as China was introducing trolleybuses all over the country. The manufacturer has been stated as Fairylite (by John Gay) because of the logo on the box of a variant with neutral coloured plastic booms. There is no proper indication on versions with turquoise booms. The plainer version was sold in Britain in the 60s at a cost of 9s 11d (50p) the equivalent of £8 today. Mint condition examples include 5 front roof lights, something that sometimes go missing.

Generic 2 axle single decker by F Toys, 19cm, tinplate

Generic 2 axle single decker by Fairylite, 27cm, tinplate

Generic 2 axle single decker by Fairylite, 27cm, tinplate

Shanghai Trolleybus Plant SK560, 1983   (Yintai Ying)

Shanghai 2 axle single decker by M.F, 37cm, tinplate

Generic 2 axle single decker by Wang Feng, 20cm, plastic

There never was a rear bumper however, even on the more exuberant version with passenger graphics that are a wonderful mix of Chinese nationalities. The booms are spring mounted, the wheels have rubber tyres and both the windows and the waistband are separate tin plate pressings. The clockwork motor powers a small fifth wheel to make it run in circles.

Superficially owing a similarity to Shanghai's SK560 series and Beijing's BK560 series (and even more to the unlikely and bizarre North Korean trolley coach prototypes), the large 37cm toy trolleybus by "M.F" is thought to have been offered in the late 60s. There are red bus versions but this one with its sprung booms, battery powered motor and hidden two wheel undercarriage to make it spin, has an impressive presence.

By the 80s tinplate had all but gone, replaced by plastic fantasies that defy physics. Wang Feng made green and red articulated toy trolleybuses that are missing an axle, despite a plethora of sticky labels that include one at the front saying "uptodate"!

3 axle single decker

model maker	ref.	issued	total	scale	construction	operator	fleet#	route	destination	built
Wang Feng				35cm	plastic	Generic				
Wang Feng				35cm	plastic	Generic			Luxury bus	

Wang Feng have also made plastic concoctions that do have the missing centre axle but have booms on the front section. There are blue and green versions, with or without chrome "mag" wheels and integrated or attached windscreen wipers.

Generic 3 axle single decker by Wang Feng, 35cm, plastic

Generic 3 axle single decker by Wang Feng, 35cm, plastic

3 axle double decker

model maker	ref.	issued	total	scale	construction	operator	fleet#	route	destination	built
Wang Feng				25cm	injection moulded	Generic				

With their propensity for the extreme, Wang Feng have produced a 3 axle double-decker that just about constitutes a trolleybus with a chrome contraption that looks more like a tuning fork than booms sticking out of the top. At least the glazing is a subtle shade of blue.

Generic 3 axle double decker by Wang Feng, 30cm, plastic

4 axle single decker

model maker	ref.	issued	total	scale	construction	operator	fleet#	route	destination	built
Wang Feng				56cm	injection moulded	Generic				

The ultimate creation, not unlike a PCC tram but justified only because it has two booms and rubber tyres, is an eight wheeler thought to be by Wang Feng that reassuringly says it is a "21st Century grand bus to warm the cockles of ones heart". We'll leave you to decide whether it does or whether you'd rather quickly move on from the ridiculous to the sublime!

Generic 4 axle single decker by Wang Feng, 60cm, plastic

Beijing BK560

model maker	ref.	issued	total	scale	construction	operator	fleet#	route	destination	built
Beijing		2010		1:64	diecast zinc	Beijing	1128			1959

Beijing 2053, Beijing Trolleybus Plant BK560, 1958

Chinese toy and model makers still remain reticent about their identity, perhaps because they are subcontractors to the likes of Corgi and EFE. Despite our best efforts, the manufacturer of Beijing's articulated BK560 of 1958 (also known as the Jing 1) appears to be called Beijing whether full size or to 1:64 scale. China had imported 52 Skoda 8Trs in the 50s which doubtless served as the major design influence. The model is named after the commissioner (the Beijing operator, Beijing Public Transport) rather than the actual manufacturer and is reassuringly solid and large enough at this scale to not need proportional compromises, apart from the oversize driving mirrors. The model and the real thing obviously evoke nostalgia to the extent that a full size working replica has recently and painstakingly been built by a group of workers at the Beijing Trolleybus Company. In service, the originals lasted until 1991, more than thirty years, but none were preserved. The replica is now in the Beijing Public Transport Museum, hopefully available for tours. It is reassuring that there are like minded trolleybus people throughout the world.

Beijing 108, Beijing Trolleybus Plant BK560, 1958 (China Government)

Beijing BK560 by Beijing Public Transport Group, 1:64, diecast zinc

Beijing BD562

model maker	ref.	issued	total	scale	construction	operator	fleet#	route	destination	built
Beijing		2009		1:64	diecast zinc	Beijing	1039	108		1956

The single version of the BK560 was the BK540 the prototype of which was developed by 86 workers, sent to Beijing from the Shanghai Fu factory, in three months during the summer of 1956. Series production of 83 vehicles, for an 11 km new route followed in 1957. The Beijing Public Transport model, unlike that above, was made, apparently, by Beijing Bashi Media Co. Ltd. or so it says on the box and follows the impeccable quality of the articulated version.

Beijing 1039, BK540 by Beijing Public Transport Group, 1:64, diecast

Beijing BK540

model maker	ref.	issued	total	scale	construction	operator	fleet#	route	destination	built
Beijing		2010		1:64	diecast zinc	Beijing	2819	108		1978

The 178 Skoda influenced BK560s were replaced by 261 boxy BD562s from 1978 onwards as the Beijing system moved entirely to 3 axle articulated trolleys. Beijing has modelled these workhorses that had cousins all over China; some of which are still in service. And again the model, made for the Beijing Public Transport Group, to use its full title, is all the better for being 1:64. The models have appeared with various fleet numbers eg. 2600, 2819 and 2830, on various routes; 103, 108 and 111.

Feicheng, Beijing Trolleybus Plant BD562, 1978 (Liu Shuang)

Beijing 2819, Beijing BD562 by Beijing Public Transport Group, 1:64, diecast zinc

5.5 China   101

Shanghai SK5105GP

model maker	ref.	issued	total	scale	construction	operator	fleet#	route	destination	built
52Bus	52002-A	2009	1000	1:76	diecast zinc	Shanghai	100	14		1997
52Bus	52002-B	2009	1000	1:76	diecast zinc	Shanghai	1	15		1997
52Bus	52002-C	2009	1000	1:76	diecast zinc	Shanghai	80	11		1997

Representing only the fifth generation of Shanghai trolleybuses in 75 years, (strictly the 6th in 83 years) the SK5101GP replaced the SK562GP (or Beijing BD562) in the late nineties, keeping to a 20 year life cycle. A decidedly unprepossessing design, it followed a European look of at least a decade earlier. 52Bus issued three model versions in rapid succession in 2009-10, representing colour coded workings on routes 14, 15 and 11. Perhaps 19 and 14, the oldest trolleybus route in the world, will follow. The model is accurate enough, with commendable lettering detail, even if the name plate between the headlights is in gold rather than embossed. At 1:76 and diecast, the doors suffer 'scale compromise' but the insert window framing makes for realism, especially around the tricky windscreen. The manufacturer is referred to as 52Bus but, typically, this is who commissioned the set, a large forum and website based in Shanghai, rather than the modeller.

Shanghai 263, Shanghai Trolleybus Plant SK5105GP, 1997 (Richard Dearmond coll.)

Shanghai SK5105GP by 52Bus, 1:76, diecast zinc

Shanghai SK5105GP by 52Bus, 1:76, diecast zinc

Shanghai SK5105GP by 52Bus, 1:76, diecast zinc

Shanghai SK561

model maker	ref.	issued	total	scale	construction	operator	fleet#	route	destination	built
Beijing Public Transport Group		2010		1:64	diecast zinc	Shanghai				1983
Beijing Public Transport Group		2010		1:64	diecast zinc	Shanghai				1980
China Model		2010	1000	1:76	diecast zinc	Shanghai				1980
Imperssion Model	imbus1001	2010	150	1:76	resin	Guangzhou	1-151			1980

A little earlier, in 1980, Shanghai Trolleybus Co. produced the fondly remembered SK561 and variants, F,G, and GF, to replace the SK663, the first generation articulated trolley that was used widely in southern China and was similar to the BD560 (see above). A company called Imperssion Model brought out their first product in May 2010 – a 1:76 resin casing of a SK561G in the livery of Guangzhou, their home town and limited to 150 examples. Is this the beginning of Chinese modellers following those of the Czech Republic in using resin for small limited editions? The model is very good and includes etched brass details such as the windscreen wipers and boom retainers. China Model has produced a Shanghai livered SK561G, in 1:76 in diecast zinc, which really only goes to demonstrate how much better metal is as a modelling medium. Beijing Public Transport Group has also done the same, except it's at 1:64 and it's even better. 2010 certainly seems to have been the year of the SK561G model.

SK561s were amended to lose the unnecessary radiator, arguably improving the look, and Beijing Public Transport Group has

Shanghai 241, Shanghai Trolleybus Plant SK561G, 1980 (unknown)

Guangzhou Shanghai SK561G by Imperssion Model, 1:76, resin

Shanghai SK561G by China Model, 1:76, diecast zinc

Shanghai Shanghai SK561G by Beijing Public Transport Group, 1:64, diecast zinc (unknown)

Niushikou 3128, Shanghai Trolleybus Plant SK561, 1980, (Leroy W. Demery, Jr.)

Shanghai Shanghai SK561 by Beijing Public Transport Group, 1:64, diecast zinc (unknown)

duly done the same. Confusingly, not only were 1980s Shanghai trolleybuses painted in blue as well as red, but the similar SK570 of 1979 and the SK562/3 of 1986, also ran in green and yellow liveries. Hopefully, the issuing of a profusion of models covering all 5 types, 4 variants and liveries, from 3 makers in 2 scales and 2 materials is set to continue.

Sunwin SWB5115GP

model maker	ref.	issued	total	scale	construction	operator	fleet#	route	destination	built
Creative Master Northcord	CN2005	2004	2000	1:76	diecast	Shanghai	166	20	Sunwin	2001

In 2004, Creative Master Northcord issued a very precise model that marked China's conversion to producing high quality model trolleybuses. Built in collaboration with Volvo, the real Sunwin SWB5115GP trolleys formed part of a renewal of the Shanghai trolleybus system. Some of the batch run with super-capacitors that can drive for 3km without wires and recharge in 10 minutes at the bus stops of specially equipped route 18. The obsession with so-called "overhead visual pollution" by the authorities has led to a diminution of a system that once had nearly a thousand trolleybuses and now has about 400. The model is hard to fault, apart from the limitations imposed by the structural necessities of diecast moulding – the thicker front pillars would, perhaps, now be made thinner, relieved of their need to maintain integrity by an glazed pillar above the front wheels, rather like the real thing. A specially commissioned version of the model, ref. CN2007, was commissioned by the Ba-Shi Bus Group with added graphic detail including fleet number KGP-168.

Shanghai 166, Sunwin SWB5115GP-3, 2001 (Zheng Han) Shanghai Sunwin SWB5115GP-3 by Creative Master Northcord, 1:76, diecast

Beijing BJD-WG120N

model maker	ref.	issued	total	scale	construction	operator	fleet#	route	destination	built
CM Model		2007	3000	1:64	diecast	Beijing	852200	103	Zoo Beijing West Road	2006

Bus maker Jinan Youngman teamed up with Neoplan (and Lotus) in 1999 to produce Neoplan designs including the Electroliner. After a subtly different prototype that had rear wheel spats, 100 of the type (also known as the Beijing BJD-WG120N) were introduced as part of the Olympics Green City programme in 2006.

Completion of the first low floor trolleybuses in China and testing of the indigenous Zhuzhou electrics was done by development partner the Beijing Trolleybus Company. 20 more (of an order for 200) were sold to Kazakhstan. CM Model, commissioned by the Beijing Public Transport Group, has produced a terrifically detailed

Beijing 85228, Beijing-Neoplan WG120N, 2006 (Tony Luan)

Beijing-Neoplan WG120N by CM Model, 1:64, diecast

model with full lettering, impressive destination indicators and accurate glazing. It's hard to imagine how you could make a more faithful reproduction in diecast zinc at 1:64 scale for around £35. Oh, the wonders of computer CAD/CAM technology! Mind you, Chinese collectors have pointed out the differences to the booms, which, as so often on trolleybus models, are not correct, not least because they should be yellow.

Beijing BJD-G120EK

model maker	ref.	issued	total	scale	construction	operator	fleet#	route	destination	built
CM Model		2010	3000	1:64	diecast	Beijing			BJD-WG120EK	2008

CM Model, amongst their many bus models, has now produced a model of the latest Beijing BJD-WG120EK trolleybus; which reverts to a semi-high floor layout. Again built for the Olympics, between 2007 and 2008, this design includes battery bus versions (Beijing BK6122EV2) which perhaps explains the high floor. At least some of the 50 built were later converted to trolleybuses of which 160 single and articulated versions (the BJD-WG160B) are in service following on from 118 essentially similar but stylistically different vehicles delivered two years previously.

Seven versions with various all-over adverts of the ill fated battery bus were modelled by CM for Beijing Public Transport Group (as it says on the display stand). The mould, with the flourishes over the wheel arches, has been used incorrectly to depict the trolleybus. (Only the prototype Beijing BK6122EV2 had these embellishments and they made aesthetic sense with the squared cut-out for the wheels that went with them). The model again suffers from boom misrepresentation which probably has to do with master bodybuilder blueprints often not detailing bought-in trolleygear parts. The front doesn't quite reflect the appealing bulbousness of the original and the close tolerances of headlight fittings within the body are becoming tricky to replicate in diecast models.

Whether the impetus of the Olympics and green awakening in China will continue to see trolleybuses flourish here, (200 more are due in Beijing) or the perceived need to do without wires prevails remains to be seen. Either way, it's likely that more models will follow, and, judging by recent trends, pretty quickly at that.

Beijing BJD-WG120EK, 2007-8
(Li Yilin)

Beijing BJD-WG120EK by CM Model, 1:64, diecast zinc

Beijing 1039, Beijing BK540 by Beijing Public Transport Group, 1:64, diecast

Praha 303, Praga TOT 430 by HB Model, 1:43, resin

Chapter 5.6
Czech Republic

Praga, 1936	TOT	107
Škoda, 1936 - 2004	1Tr	108
	3Tr	109
	5Tr	110
	6Tr	110
Tatra, 1956-1958	T400	111
	T401	112
Škoda, 1936 - 2004	7Tr	113
	8Tr	115
	9Tr	116
	T11	120
	13Tr	121
	Sanos	121
	14Tr	122
	15Tr	124
	17Tr	125
	21Tr	125
	22Tr	127
	24Tr	129
SOR, 2008 - 2010	TN12	130

Praha 304, Praga TOT 430, 1936   (Praga)

More than its former partner Slovakia, the Czech Republic has perhaps more trolleybus fans than anywhere else, per head of the population; and certainly more model producers. Almost every major city has or has had a trolleybus system, partly because Škoda, the indigenous producer, became such a major supplier and exporter in Soviet times and partly because of strong national feelings toward the environment. All systems except Praha and Plzeň are post war, with the interesting exception of České Budějovice, formerly known as Budweis, home of the famous beer, where there have been three installations, starting in 1909 using the Stoll system. Budweis was part of Austria at the time, once the Kingdom of Bohemia. By 1948, the date of the second installation, the city was part of Czechoslovakia SSR. By 1991, the third installation mirrored coming independence and environmentalism, and has since been extended courtesy of the EU Structural Fund. 3156 locally built trolleybuses have operated in the former Czechoslovakia and the republic, and 10495 have been exported. Just 68, including 11 'purloined' trolleybuses from Milano, were imported between 1941 and 1949 when Škoda's facilities were limited. But even these mostly had indigenous ČKD electrical equipment and true to form, many have been modelled.

Trolleybus operation proper started in independent Czechoslovakia in 1936 in the capital, Praha, with three prototypes from 3 manufacturers – quite an achievement for a country of only 14 million people, nearly half of whom lived in the countryside in the 1930s. Such is the Czech (perhaps that should be Bohemian) cultural need to document, that (almost) the entire history of the country's trolleybuses has been preserved and built in model form.

Praga

model maker	ref.	issued	total	scale	construction	operator	fleet#	route	destination	built
HB Model				1:43	resin	Praha	303		Baba	1936

Praha 308, Praga TOT 430 3 axle by HB Models, 1:43, resin

At 13.30 on April 24th 1936 the first Czech built trolleybus drove along the ČKD test track at Vysočany. Prototype Praga TOT no.303 used a chassis from a TOV bus, had a wooden body and electrical equipment by ČKD, using adapted tram equipment. Withdrawn in 1959, she was discovered on a farm in 1995 and is now in Praha Public Transport Museum, awaiting restoration. Konrad Pernetta commissioned HB Model to make a 1:43 model of 303 as she looked after her conversion to right hand drive – one of the very few examples of trolleybuses being regarded as worth the considerable expense to convert. Praga, a small car and truck company that now makes gearboxes, went on to make nos.304-14 and never realised plans for a 2 axle variant. 303 had toplights for only a few months in 1936 before conversion to closed rain deflectors, as on the production batch (and so never existed as modelled). 308 has also been modelled by HB Model for Foxtoys in Praha where these imposing trolleybuses appeared after conversion to right hand drive in 1948 (although, by then, the waistband band gold lettering had gone). The model has the air vent and access doors that were added to the front of the production batch in a subtle re-working of the mold.

HB Model get their name from Havlíčkuv Brod, a town in the centre of the Czech Republic, where, from a nearby village, Jiri Plodik has produced a plethora, and steadily improving, series of Czech, Austrian, German and Dutch models over the years in 1:87 and 1:43 scales.

Škoda 1Tr

model maker	ref.	issued	total	scale	construction	operator	fleet#	route	destination	built
RA Model Petr Došlý	1210 00	2006		1:87	resin	Praha				1936

The first route in Praha ran 3.5km from the depot at Střešovice to Hanspaulka, a new housing estate and opened with the Praga, Tatra and Škoda prototypes on 28th August 1936. Production variants of all three followed, although the Tatra T86 failed within two years. The first Škoda trolleybus was shapelier than the others, was based on the 355 truck and had Škoda electrical equipment. 301 lasted in service until 1955 and was sent to the Technical Museum but was broken up in 1961.

Praha 301, Škoda 1Tr, 1936 (Škoda)

Petr Došlý, aka. RA Model, has modelled the only 1Tr built, complete with flag masts on the front bumper. Petr is a so-called 'artisan' modeller, working in Starý Šachov, a village of 198 souls, 32km east of the trolleybus system at Ústí Nad Labem in northern Czech Republic.

Praha 301, Škoda 1Tr by RA Model Petr Došlý, 1:87, resin

Škoda 3Tr

model maker	ref.	issued	total	scale	construction	operator	fleet#	route	destination	built
Ivan Staněk				1:43	wood, plastic	Plzeň	106			1941
MMR Modely	087 117CS01			1:87	resin	Plzeň				1941
MMR Modely	0871 117 CS02			1:87	resin	Plzeň				1941
RA Model Petr Došlý	1212 00			1:87	resin	Plzeň	106			1941

Unfortunately the Škoda 2Tr, which was a considerable refinement and resulted in a production batch of five, hasn't (yet) been modelled. Neither has the Tatra T86, of which a further 5 were also built. But the Škoda 3Tr has, at least four times! Further refinements to the 2Tr were the two compound motors. They were built in Plzeň for delivery there between 1941 and 1948. 34 were built and two survive in preservation.

Plzeň 106, Škoda 3Tr by RA Model Petr Došlý, 1:87, resin

Plzeň 106, Škoda 3Tr, 1941 (Škoda)

The first two series of the 3Tr had two doors and the third had three. There were several refinements to the front end – an evolution that was to be typical of Škoda until the 'quantum' leap to the 14Tr design in 1972. The front of the 3Tr.3 predicts the 6Tr, the 2 axle version. We documented Škoda's trolleybus development and use of models, such as that of the unbuilt 5Tr, in chapter 2. Plzeň, meanwhile, was the only place receiving Škoda trolleybuses in the 1940s, such was the difficulty of wartime recovery, until Brno was able to receive 16 6Trs in 1949.

Plzeň 106, Škoda 3Tr by Ivan Staněk, 1:43, wood, plastic

Plzeň 119, Škoda 3Tr by MMR Modelly, 1:87, resin

Petr Došlý has produced Plzeň 106, one of the original series 3Trs in wartime green. MMR Modely, aka. Miroslav Grisa, another artisan modeller of prodigious output, who has a shop on trolleybus routes 52, 54, 56, 58, 59 and 60 in Ústí Nad Labem, has made the 3Tr of the third series in two Plzeň liveries, red and turquoise. He has done the same with his reproduction of the two axle 6Tr, built a year after the last of the 3Trs and presumably made possible by the availability of higher load-rated axles. Neither of the 3Tr models have the four springs of the originals trolley gear. Petr Došlý typically casts 25-50 models in a batch and hand assembles and paints them. Miroslav Grisa of MMR out-sources much of the model making work.

Plzeň 119,
Škoda 3Tr by MMR Modely, 1:87, resin

Škoda 5Tr

model maker	ref.	issued	total	scale	construction	operator	fleet#	route	destination	built
Škoda				(scale?)	wood	Generic				1943

To keep continuity we've included some Škoda design models, which now only survive in photographs (see page 19). The 5Tr looks as though the intention was to have a curved windscreen, predating the 9Tr by 20 years, but it's hard to imagine the factory producing such an advanced feature in 1943. What actually followed was the more pragmatically designed 6Tr.

Škoda 6Tr

model maker	ref.	issued	total	scale	construction	operator	fleet#	route	destination	built
MMR Modely	087 118CS01			1:87	resin	Plzeň				1948
MMR Modely	087 118CS11			1:87	resin	Brno				1948

Plzeň 135, Škoda 6Tr, 1948 (Dezidor)

Plzeň 135, Škoda 6Tr by MMR Modely, 1:87, resin

Brno Škoda 6Tr by MMR Modely, 1:87, resin

Only 16 6Trs were built, 15 for Brno in 1949 and one for Plzeň, which has fortunately survived into preservation. MMR has modelled no.135, which is now kept at Brno Technical Museum in working order. Although outwardly similar in style to the 3Tr, the 6Tr was the first to have a self supporting steel body and collector equipment made by Škoda.

Tatra T400

model maker	ref.	issued	total	scale	construction	operator	fleet#	route	destination	built
IGRA	red	1954		15cm	diecast, plastic and metal	Praha	394	55		1953
IGRA	red	1960		15cm	diecast, plastic and metal	Praha	394	55		1953
IGRA	yellow	1954		15cm	diecast, plastic and metal	Praha	394	55		1953
IGRA	blue	1954		15cm	diecast, plastic and metal	Praha	394	55		1953
MHB	281			1:20	wood, metal	Praha				1948-51
RA Model Petr Došlý	1206 00			1:87	resin	Praha				1953
RA Model Petr Došlý	1206 03			1:87	resin	Bratislava				1950

Praha 26, Tatra T400/IIIA, 1953 (Petr Dadak)

Moste av Litnove Tatra T400/IIIA by Ites, (15cm), diecast, plastic & metal

Tatra T400/IIIA by Ites, (15cm), diecast, plastic & metal (Frank Wiegold)

Praha Tatra T400/IIIA by Ites, (15cm), diecast, plastic & metal

Praha Tatra T400/IIIA by Ites, (15cm), diecast, plastic & metal

Just before Škoda broke into the international market, Tatra had another go at producing trolleybuses with the imposing T400, of which 195 were built, 134 for Praha. This system expanded rapidly between 1949 and 1954, paralleling tram routes and climbing surrounding hills. The IGRA, n.p. toy factory responded to this large scale deployment with a plastic and metal 'chassised' model, powered by clockwork.

The very well engineered toy was produced in České Budějovice (home to those three trolley installations) for long enough to have had three different presentation box styles. The IGRA models are thought to date from 1954 until 1965.

Usually seen in maroon (although Praha colours are bright red) with either a single chrome band, or later, an extra embellishment at the front, echoing the white of the original, there were also yellow and blue versions (one sold recently for €320) and possibly orange, although it's hard to tell nearly 60 years later, given the instability of dyed plastic. Either way, all are of no.394 on route 55, which makes it the first T400/IIIa type, built in 1953.

Praha Tatra T400/III by RA Model Petr Došlý, 1:87, resin

Bratislava Tatra T400/III by RA Model Petr Došlý, 1:87, resin

Identifiable as one of the T400/III series because of the front panel latches being midway up the front dash, Petr Došlý has produced both Praha and Bratislava liveried versions. Ostrava also received T400s and such was local enthusiasm to preserve one, that Praha 441 was towed to the town and restored as 26. 412 was originally preserved but replaced by 431 as the Praha museum exhibit. Until restoration was completed there was a model on display at the museum, at about 1:20 scale. It doesn't look new and may date from when the vehicles were delivered.

Praha 351, Tatra T400 by MHD, 1:20, wood, metal (McMurdo)

412, despite no longer a museum exhibit, has been modeled rather successfully by HB Model, in 1:43 scale, accurately portraying the large wheels and narrow windows. Unfortunately the booms can not be raised. HB has also produced the T400/IIIa as 394, as did IGRA.

Praha Tatra T400/III by HB Model, 1:43, resin

Tatra T401

model maker	ref.	issued	total	scale	construction	operator	fleet#	route	destination	built
RA Model Petr Došlý	1209 00	2003		1:87	resin	Praha	461			1958

Before returning to the chronological history, one further Tatra was added to the Praha fleet in 1958 after three years in development. 461, built by Tatra Kopřivnice (chassis) and Karosa Vysoké Mýto (body) with ČKD Praha (electrical equipment) was the prototype for a "standard" trolley, intended to accompany T402 articulated 4 axle and T403 2 axles types. But after tests in comparison with Škoda trolleybuses, they were not proceeded with. With echoes of Russian Svarz and MTB trolleys with rooflight windows of the same period, the T401 had four tram motors and automatic starting, complex qualities that led to premature withdrawal in 1961. 461 was rescued by the Brno Technical Museum in 1975 and is not yet restored to working order. Petr Došlý's model too has difficulty, with the shape of the voluptuous windscreen and the depth of the front bumper which housed headlights, not reflecting the full size prototype. Like the real thing - a brave try.

112 5.6 Czech Republic

Praha 461, Tatra T401, 1958 (Tatra)

Praha 461, Tatra T401 by RA Model Petr Dosly, 1:87, resin

Škoda 7Tr

model maker	ref.	issued	total	scale	construction	operator	fleet#	route	destination	built
(unknown)				22cm	wood	Generic				1951
Merkur	25			56cm	metal	Generic				1951
HB Model				1:43	resin	Brno	31			1951
RA Model Petr Došlý	1207 03	2006		1:87	resin	Brno				1951
RA Model Petr Došlý	1207 00			1:87	resin	Praha				1951
Petr Kudej	PK009/etc.			1:87	card	Mariánské Lázně				1951
Willi Schincke				1:63	plasticard, tin, balsa	Gottwaldov	20			1951

John Cook, a metal construction set enthusiast from North Carolina, recently tried to recreate the Czechoslovakian Merkur 'Trolejbus' as shown in the 1950s Set No.5 Manual. It turned out to be 56mm long and used 383 parts. The Škoda 7Tr had been introduced in 1951 to the nearest town to the Merkur factory, Hradec Králové, and there was widespread introduction of trolleybuses in the former Czechoslovakia SSR from 1950 onwards.

Generic 2 axle single decker by Merkur, 56cm, metal (GirdersandGears)

5.6 Czech Republic

Generic Škoda 7Tr by (unknown), 22cm, wood

Produced for DPMB, the Brno operator, by an unknown maker, is a wooden toy trolleybus owned by the General Manager of Kummler + Matter, the trolleybus overhead suppliers. It's 22cm long and Czech, - we've (almost) arbitrarily decided it's a Škoda 7Tr. 173 7Trs were built between 1950 and 1955 and were very similar to the 6Tr. They had steel self supporting bodies and most were updated to the electrical equipment of the 8Tr. The last ran in service in 1981 in Ostrava and at least one is preserved, in Brno.

HB Models has produced a very good 0 scale model of Brno's preserved 31, although adding the fleet emblem, fleet number and darker trolley booms might have helped realism. Fox Toys in Praha have stocked versions with such improvements, added by the shop's owner. On the other hand, Petr Došlý has produced the H0 scale version with entrance graphics that haven't yet been applied to the museum trolleybus. He also produced a Bratislava version (although the operator could be Pardubice, for example; the red and cream livery was fairly universal at the time). The first Škoda trolleybuses to be exported were also red – a batch of seven 7Trs went to Warszawa in 1954. Of the other 7Tr models, we mentioned Willi Schincke's powered 7Tr on page 47 and should add Petr Kudej's card models, that show the similarity between the 7Tr and the 6Tr.

Brno 31, Škoda 7Tr by HB Model, 1:43, resin

Brno 31, Škoda 7Tr, 1951   (Dezidor)

Mariánské Lazně Škoda 7Tr by Petr Kudej, 1:87, card   (Petr Kudej)

Brno 31, Škoda 7Tr by RA Model Petr Došlý, 1:87, resin

Bratislava Škoda 7Tr by RA Model Petr Došlý, 1:87, resin

Škoda 8Tr

model maker	ref.	issued	total	scale	construction	operator	fleet#	route	destination	built
HB Model				1:43	resin	Dresden	174			1958
HB Model				1:43	resin	Praha	9482, 9470		1960	
Extra	120504/91	2004		1:87	resin	Praha			1959	
RA Model Petr Došlý	1205 04	2004		1:87	resin	Praha				1959
RA Model Petr Došlý	1205 50			1:87	resin	Dresden	174			
RA Model Petr Došlý	1205			1:87	resin	Weimar				
RA Model Petr Došlý	120500	2009		1:87	resin	Plzeň				
RA Model Petr Došlý	1202 XC	1999		1:87	resin	Ostrava				1963
V/R	266, 287			1:87	resin	Dresden, Eberswalde				1960
Petr Kudej	PK009/etc.			1:87	card	Máriesnké Lázně				1960
Willi Schincke				1:63	plasticard, tin, balsa	Gottwaldov (Zlín)	30			1958
KTU				1:20	wood, metal	Simferopol	101			1959-61

Praha 9486, Škoda 8Tr, 1960 (Škoda)

The 8Tr, a step in the evolution begun with the 3Tr, appeared in 1955. By now ruggedly practical, the Communist authorities allowed greater production and of the 742 made in only 5 years, 485 were exported to China, Georgia, Latvia, Lithuania, Germany, Poland and Ukraine.

The first went to Poland, to Warszawa and 8Trs served in seven other capitals; Beijing, Bratislava, Kiev, Riga, Vilnius and Praha. In the colours of the Czech capital, they've been modelled in 0 and H0 scales by HB Model and Petr Došlý (and also marketed by Extra). So too, have Dresden versions. Petr has also painted Weimar and the standard livery that could have been Warszawa or the 14 trolleybus cities in the then Czechoslovakia SSR. The models have no trolleyheads and have a roughness when viewed closely but manage the front rake better than the HB model which is a little upright and misses the latches of the front access panels but, as is to be expected at this larger scale, has thinner, more accurate window pillars.

Dresden and Eberswalde versions were also made some time ago by V/R with only wire trolleygear but full interior seating, like those of Petr Došlý. It has to be admitted that in cases of models that are no longer available we rely on collector's memories or better, their ability to find the box it came in, to identify who made what and even then, we're not exactly sure. But there's no doubting Willi Schincke made the fine rendering of Zlín 30 that's described on page 48. (Zlín was known, unpopularly, as Gottwaldov from 1948 to 1989.)

Praha Škoda 8Tr by RA Model Petr Došlý, 1:87, resin

Praha 9470, Škoda 8Tr by HB Model, 1:43, resin

Dresden Škoda 8Tr by HB Model, 1:43, resin

Dresden 174, Škoda 8Tr by
RA Model Petr Došlý, 1:87, resin

Weimar Škoda 8Tr by RA Model
Petr Došlý, 1:87, resin

Plzen Škoda 8Tr by RA Model Petr Došlý, 1:87, resin

Eberswalde Škoda 8Tr by V/R, 1:87, resin
(Andreas Zietemann)

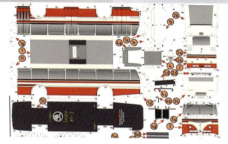

Petr Kudej has produced the 8Tr in card in most Czech liveries, including the small tourist system of Mariánské Lázně (Marienbad). His versions have just about as much detail as it's possible to get on to a card sheet and follow a traditional graphics style similar to Alphagraphix in the UK.

The last 8Tr ran in Ostrava in 1982, although one that had been rebuilt in Kiev is still running. Five 8Trs are preserved in the Czech Republic and in Ukraine, where Kiev had become the greatest adherent of Škoda trolleybuses.

Mariánské Lazně 8Tr by Petr Kudej, 1:87, card
(Petr Kudej)

Škoda 9Tr

model maker	ref.	issued	total	scale	construction	operator	fleet#	route	destination	built
RA Model Petr Došlý	1202 15			1:87	resin	Brno				1963
RA Model Petr Došlý	1202 33			1:87	resin	Dresden				1962
RA Model Petr Došlý	1201 XA	1999		1:87	resin	Teplice				1960
RA Model Petr Došlý	1202 12			1:87	resin	Praha				1961
RA Model Petr Došlý				1:87	resin	Berlin				1961
RA Model Petr Došlý				1:87	resin	Eberswalde				1961
RA Model Petr Došlý				1:87	resin	Ústi nad Labem				1961
RA Model Petr Došlý	1204 00			1:87	resin	Praha				1961
RA Model Petr Došlý	120214	2009		1:87	resin	Gera				
MMR Modelly	087 127DE10	2011		1:87	resin	Eberswalde				1962
Andreas Konz			100	1:87	resin	Magdeburg				1962-70
Andreas Konz				1:87	resin	Pardubice				1962
Andreas Konz				1:87	resin	Dresden				1962-70
Andreas Konz				1:87	resin	Lutsk				1962
Andreas Konz				1:87	resin	Rivne				1962
Andreas Konz		2010		1:87	resin	Riga				1961
HB Model				1:43	resin	Brno	40			1963
HB Model		2006		1:43	Resin	Eberswalde				1962-70
V/R	293			1:87	resin	Kiev	3606			1961
Deltax				1:120	resin	Brno				1963
Willi Schincke				1:63	plasticard,tin,balsa	Gottwaldov (Zlín)	62	B	Nemocnice	1975
Škoda Museum				1:18	metal	Plzeň			Bolevec	1963
Krementschug				1:43	resin	Crimea		5		1963
VshaCG		2010		(no scale)	virtual	Bratislava				
Škoda Museum				1:18	metal	Plzeň				1961
MMR Modely				1:87	resin	Plzeň				1961

The 8Tr had proved a great success but the culmination of Škoda's evolving engineering for trolleybuses was the 9TR. Produced between 1961 and 1982, some operators replaced 9Trs with 9Trs, such was the high regard with which they were held. It was the most numerous non-Russian trolleybus built. 7439 examples served the Communist bloc and were exported to the West; including Norway and India. Some are, just about and depending when you are reading this, still in service, including the very last with resistor control, dating from 1982.

There were two prototypes that were a little different, one of 1958, still with the 4 piece windscreen of the 8Tr and one with roof lights and two sets of doors. The distinguishing wrap-around windscreen was first seen on this 1961 trolley, but does seem a little exaggerated on Petr Došlý's model versions. The mould must have been remade to produce at least seven versions of the production 9Trs that have followed. We get a little confused here about which modeller made exactly what. With distributors claiming to be the producers and protective of actual modeller identity, we're not too sure in some cases, especially as some modellers seem shy about

Škoda 9Tr prototype, 1961 (Škoda)

Škoda 9Tr prototype by RA Model Petr Došlý, 1:87, resin

Škoda 9Tr prototype by MMR Modelly, 1:87, resin

5.6 Czech Republic   117

talking independently (unless that's us not talking Czech!). Andreas Konz has also modelled the 9Tr extensively, including the rather distinctive 9Tr wheels. In our review of the 9Tr models, we've grouped similar liveries together.

One problem with 1:87 scale models of the 9Tr is the width of the central windscreen pillar and the depth of the surround, which wasn't, in reality, very pronounced. East German Škodas were often in a uniform cream, with a differing colour midband plus the city emblem on the side, such as Berlin, Dresden, Magdeburg and Zwickau. Some places, such as Eberswalde and Gera had also been cream but managed a more distinctive livery at certain points in their history. MMR Modelly has recently issued 9Trs from Eberswalde and distinctively in blue and yellow, Yalta.

In the former Czechoslovakia and Latvia various versions of red and cream were used. The differences between Petr Došlý and Andreas Konz model versions are slight, mainly hinging on the latter having trolleyheads, but they are different castings. Apart from the boom assembly, the Konz windscreen is less raked and the roof-mounted resistance casing is of a differing pattern. Some early Došlý models exclude the box altogether and one was produced to celebrate 100 years of public transport in Ústí nad Labem in 1999.

Zwickau 311, Škoda 9Tr, 1961 (David Pearson)

Eberswalde 9Tr by RA Model Petr Došlý, 1:87, resin (Andreas Zietemann)

Gera 9Tr by RA Model Petr Došlý, 1:87, resin

Gera 9Tr by Andreas Konz, 1:87, resin

Eberswalde 9Tr by MMR Modelly, 1:87, resin

Dresden 9Tr by Andreas Konz, 1:87, resin

Dresden 9Tr by RA Model Petr Došlý, 1:87, resin (Andreas Zietemann)

Pardubice 9Tr by Andreas Konz, 1:87, resin

Magdeburg 9Tr by Andreas Konz, 1:87, resin

Berlin 9Tr by RA Model Petr Došlý, 1:87, resin (Andreas Zietemann)

Rivne 9Tr by Andreas Konz, 1:87, resin

Ustí nad Labem 9Tr by RA Model, 1:87, resin

Brno 9Tr by RA Model Petr Došlý, 1:87, resin

Brno 3076, Škoda 9Tr, 1962 (Harold17)

Brno 9Tr by HB Model, 1:43, resin

Eberswalde 9Tr by HB Model, 1:43, resin

Brno 9Tr by Deltax, 9cm, resin (TT Club)

Simferopol 9Tr by Kremenchug, 1:43, resin

Lutsk 9Tr by Andreas Konz, 1:87, resin

Kiev 9Tr by V/R, 1:87, resin (Andreas Zietemann)

At other scales, HB has produced the 9Tr realistically in both the standard liveries at 1:43 and Deltrax has produced a very creditable version in TT scale or 1:120.

Other O scale versions include the Kremenchug in Simferopol KTU livery which suffers from a little detail absence and thick window pillars. While in the Crimea, the trolleybus museum at the Simferopol depot has a 1:20 9Tr, listed on page 31. Lutsk in the Ukraine had a similar livery, as did Kiev, and both had some 2 door 9Trs. We're told Andreas Konz and V/R have modelled them at 1:87, although they appear remarkably similar and we don't think 3606 was ever assigned as a fleet number to a 9Tr in Kiev, as shown on the V/R model.

Ostrov, Škoda T11 prototype, 1964 (Sbirka M. Harak)

Ostrov Škoda T11 prototype by RA Model Petr Došlý, 1:87, resin

Škoda T11

model maker	ref.	issued	total	scale	construction	operator	fleet#	route	destination	built
RA Model Petr Došlý	1208 00			1:87	resin	Ostrov			Zkuš	1964
RA Model Petr Došlý	1208 02			1:87	resin	Plzeň	248		Škoda Ostrov	1966-70
V/R	311			1:87	resin	Plzeň				1966-70

We can't resist including two views of Petr Došlý's model of Škoda's T11, the exuberant Karosa bodied attempt at a standardized bus/trolleybus, that followed Tatra's earlier attempt. Underneath lurked a 9Tr, at least electrically. The prototype was built in 1964 and tested at Škoda's Ostrov test track and with various operators until scrapped in 1975.

Seven production versions of the T11 were built between 1966 and 1970, and delivered to Bratislava and Plzeň where the last, 248, served until 1980. Petr Došlý has had to add the central windscreen pillar, include the roof resistances and remove the 'radiator' in what would otherwise have been the same mold as the model of the prototype (despite the original being an imperceptible 55mm shorter). The real 248 has been preserved at Brno Technical Museum in working order, to be seen on open days under the wires of Brno's trolleybus system.

Ostrov Škoda T11 prototype by RA Model Petr Došlý, 1:87, resin

Plzeň 248, Škoda T11, 1966-70 (Harold17)

Plzeň Škoda T11 by RA Model Petr Došlý, 1:87, resin

Škoda 13Tr

model maker	ref.	issued	total	scale	construction	operator	fleet#	route	destination	built
Škoda				(unkown)	wood	Generic				1966

The planned 13Tr would have used a fibreglass body on a steel frame, but was not proceeded with.

The model shows a more boxy shape, in tune with 60s styling, with high windows. There's more on page 20.

Škoda-Sanos

model maker	ref.	issued	total	scale	construction	operator	fleet#	route	destination	built
MMR Modely	087 119CS02			1:87	resin	Gottwaldov (Zlín)				1986
MMR Modely	087 111CS01			1:87	resin	Ostrava				1986
Petr Kudej	PK018/etc.	2006		1:87, 120	card	Gottwaldov (Zlín)	329			1986
Willi Schincke				1:63	plasticard, tin, balsa	Gottwaldov (Zlín)	329	8		1986

Zlín 329, Škoda-Sanos S200Tr, 1986 (Škoda)

Zlín Škoda-Sanos S200Tr by MMR Modelly, 1:87, resin

Zlín Škoda-Sanos S200Tr by Willi Schincke, 1:63, plasticard, tin, balsa (Willi Schincke)

In some ways the Škoda-Sanos S200Tr that followed 16 years after the 13Tr looks like an articulated version but was a conversion of a Macedonian-built Sanos bus sold to the Yugoslavian market. The prototype was built in 1982, answering a need for articulated trolleybuses before Škoda could 'articulate' the 14Tr. Of the 77 built, one went to Beograd and 21 went to Sarajevo, but the rest, apart from one that went to Moskva, all served in former Czechoslovakia. They were well liked and survived until 2001 (in Zlín). Three have been preserved including one in Pardubice, where they never ran in service. MMR Modely has produced yellow Zlín and red standard versions that don't quite reflect the well proportioned originals. Willi Schincke, on the other hand, has achieved good evocation at 1:63 scale in the colours of Zlín, his home town. Petr Kudej has produce five permutations of the 200Tr in card, including Zlín 329, now preserved in Pardubice.

Zlín 329, Škoda-Sanos S200Tr by Petr Kudej, 1:87, card (Petr Kudej)

Brno 301 (ex-Zlín 301), Škoda-Sanos S200Tr, 1986 (Harold17)

Brno Škoda-Sanos S200Tr by MMR Modelly, 1:87, resin

Škoda 14Tr

model maker	ref.	issued	total	scale	construction	operator	fleet#	route	destination	built
Extra	872312/91			1:87	resin	Ostrava				1984
Extra	872311/91			1:87	resin	Bratislava				1980
HB Model		2006		1:43	resin	Bratislava				1990
Ivan Staněk				1:43	wood,plastic	Plzeň	88	1	Kyješovice	1981
MMR Modely	087 111CS02			1:87	resin	Ostrava				1984
Andeas Konz				1:87	resin	Potsdam				1984
Petr Kudej	PK004/etc.			1:87	card	Mariánské Lázně				1981
RA Model Petr Došlý				1:87	resin	Eberswalde				1983
Sádlo	870700-6	2004		1:87	resin	Ústí n.L,Teplice,Plzeň,Hr.Králové				
Sádlo	870700			1:87	resin	Ostrava				1984
Škoda Museum				1:16	metal	Generic				1972
Škoda Museum				1:16	metal	San Francisco				1999
Willi Schincke				1:63	plasticard,tin,balsa	Zlin	170	4	Podhar	1995

Škoda's styling of trolleybuses took a radical approach in 1972 when they first produced the very angular 14Tr – a type that had very long gestation period but which remained in production until 2004. Three trolleybus systems had closed in former Czechoslovakia in the early 1970s and Škoda had second thoughts about continuing trolleybus production until the global oil crisis and the authorities convinced them otherwise. Two prototypes, with squared windows and openings above the doors remained unique until the restoration of the project in 1980 when five similar 14Tr/0 prototypes were built. But the body was weak and the windows became radialised with no openings above the doors on the 3887 production examples that followed. Only Petr Kudej has modelled the 14Tr prototypes, rather easy to do in card, as well as subsequent types.

Mariánské Lazně 14Tr by Petr Kudej, 1:87, card   (Petr Kudej)

Villnius 1612, Škoda 14Tr, 1984   (Cmapm)

Plzen 14Tr by MMR Modelly, 1:87, resin

Bratislava 14Tr by Extra, 1:87, resin   (Andreas Zietemann)

Eberswalde 14Tr by Sadlo, 1:87, resin   (Andreas Zietemann)

Eberswalde 14Tr by RA Model, 1:87, resin   (Andreas Zietemann)

Ostrava 14Tr by MMR Modelly, 1:87, resin

Potsdam 14Tr by Andreas Konz, 1:87, resin   (Mattis Schindler)

Eberswalde 14Tr by MMR Modelly, 1:87, resin

Modelling the 14Tr in resin at 1:87 scale is not so easy, perhaps because the original is so obviously squared sheet metal on a frame of narrow dimensions. Sádlo and Extra (a distributor who has added detail) are perhaps the best and resorted to leaving the skinny windscreen pillars out altogether. So has Petr Došlý but not MMR Modelly, whose model is the least successful. The Andreas Konz version is similar and, unusually, in Potsdam livery. Sádlo made model versions of least 6 systems, including Eberswalde which only had 3 14Trs for 6 years. Došlý has done the same; perhaps it's the fan base in that town that would make painting a green version worthwhile. MMR Modelly has also followed suit recently, adding front corner pillars. Note too, the variation in door glazing and trolleyboom styles between models and makers.

Both Willi Schinke and Ivan Staněk seem to have narrowed the width and leave out the centre pillar on their scratch built powered models, even at 1:63 and 1:43 scales respectively. Was there mislabelling on the blueprints or is it an illusion? Perhaps more successful is the HB Models version, although it would have been helped by blackening the rubber glazing surrounds instead of leaving a disproportionate ridge. Had Vector Models in Ukraine modelled the 14Tr with their electroplated copper technique, one can't help thinking the result would have been more accurate. The three museum models of 14Trs that we know of, at 1:20 and 1:16 scales, certainly do accurately reflect reality if not the dents and mud of hard service now seen so often on surviving examples. The San Francisco 14Trs were the last built and differed in detail to all others. Seven 14Tr's have been preserved, including one at Eberswalde - someone there loves them!

Zlín 170, Škoda 14TrM by Willi Schincke, 1:63, plasticard, tin, balsa   (Willi Schincke)

Plzeň Škoda 14Tr by Ivan Staněk, 1:43, wood, plastic

Ústí nad Labem Škoda 14Tr by HB Model, 1:43, resin

5.6 Czech Republic

Generic 15Tr by Škoda Museum, 1:13, metal   (Škoda)

Škoda 15Tr

model maker	ref.	issued	total	scale	construction	operator	fleet#	route	destination	built
Ivan Staněk				1:43	wood, plastic	Opava	99	1	Kylešovice	1983
MMR Modely	087 114CS01			1:87	resin	Ostrava				1990
Ondřej Spáčila		2004		1:10	metal, plastic, wood	Brno	3509			1990
Petr Kudej	PK006/etc.			1:87	card	Plzeň	478			1983
Škoda Museum				1:13	metal	Generic				1983
Willi Schincke				1:63	plasticard, tin, balsa	Zlín	335	7		1990
HB Model				1:43	resin	Ústí nad Labem				1990

Škoda had planned an articulated version of the 9Tr called the 10Tr in 1958, but it was never built (although the 12Tr; pairs of coupled 9Trs, were produced for Ukraine). So Škoda came late to the articulation concept with the 15Tr prototype of 1983. Production started in 1988. They very consciously kept as many 14Tr parts as possible, to aid maintenance and keep costs down. 645 sets were built before the final batch for San Francisco in 2003. HB Model have doubtless done the same thing with their 1:43 model version, by using the 14Tr mould, and so too has MMR Modely with the only 1:87 15Tr model that we can find.

There are, inevitably, models of the 15Tr in the Škoda Museum in Plzeň and modellers Willi Schincke and Ivan Staněk have made powered versions (Ivan's is a fantasy Opava 99), but the most spectacular 15Tr model was built by Ondřej Spáčila in 2004.

We described this model on page 49, but it is worth mentioning that anything that moves, flashes or sounds on the real thing has been reproduced in 1:10 scale. A true labour of love from a country that seems to have more than its fair share of true trolleybus enthusiasts and modellers.

Ústí nad Labem 15Tr by HB Model, 1:43, resin   (HGS design)

Zlín 335 15Tr by Willi Schincke, 1:63, plasticard, (W Schincke)

Opava 99 15Tr by Ivan Staněk, 1:43, wood, plastic

Brno 3504, Škoda 15Tr, 1990   (Harold17)

Ostrava 15Tr by MMR Modelly, 1:87, resin   (Andreas Zietemann)

Ostrava 3903, Škoda 17Tr, 1987 (Harold17)

Ostrava Škoda 17Tr by MMR Modelly, 1:87, resin

Škoda 17Tr

model maker	ref.	issued	total	scale	construction	operator	fleet#	route	destination	built
MMR Modely	087 113CS01	2004		1:87	resin	Ostrava		107	Sídlištěw Fifejdy	1987
MMR Modely	087 113CS02	2004		1:87	resin	Ostrava				1987
Škoda		1987		1:16	wood	Ostrava				

Only three Škoda 17Trs were built, as part of a further attempt to unify bus and trolleybus production in Czechoslovakia. The red prototype appeared in 1987, using plastics extensively to reduce noise and small wheels to reduce boarding height without a complex chassis. The second prototype, officially designated as a Tatra TR831.03, had ČKD electrics that were replaced by a set from a 14Tr on entering service. Together with a third vehicle, which also had slight design differences, they served in Ostrava until 2007. All three are preserved, which perhaps explains why MMR Modely has produced two versions, in Škoda demonstrator livery and Ostrava's blue and white. They look like toys rather than accurate reproductions because, no doubt, of those small wheels. The project failed with the collapse of the Soviet Union and articulated (18Tr) and double articulated (19Tr) versions were never built.

Ostrava Škoda 17Tr by MMR Modelly, 1:87, resin

Škoda 21Tr

model maker	ref.	issued	total	scale	construction	operator	fleet#	route	destination	built
AM				1:87	plastic	Ostrava	3303			1997
AM				1:87	plastic	Plzeň	484			2001
AM				1:87	plastic	Brno	3042	25	St. Lískovec	2002
AM				1:87	plastic	Brno	3007	140	Královo Pole	1999
DPMB				1:87	card	Brno				1999
Petr Kudej	PK034/etc	2007		1:87	card	Ostrava				
SDV Model	230			1:87	plastic	Szeged	T801	5	Újszeged	2001
SDV Model	240			1:87	plastic	České Budějovice				1999
SDV Model	249			1:87	plastic	Brno	3018	25	Kamenny Vrch	1999
SDV Model	252			1:87	plastic	Ostrava				1997
SDV Model	230			1:87	plastic	Pardubice	397		Jesničánky	2001
Škoda Museum				1:13	metal	Demonstrator				1996
Marek Bures		2003		1:6	metal	Brno				2002
Andes Whistler				(no scale)	virtual	Bratislava	6401			2003

In the 1990s, Škoda tried to massively expand and modernize, but the capitalist reality of the period very nearly led to bankruptcy. The 21Tr, designed by architect Patrik Kotas was developed from 1991 onwards as a modern low floor trolleybus to compete throughout the world. The prototype appeared in 1995, but only 135 have been built, nearly all for use within the Czech Republic.

SDV Model, a Czech plastic kit company of mostly military models has produced 6 versions of the 21Tr, plain, Brno, Plzeň, Hradec Králové, Ostrava and Pardubice. They come self coloured,

Szeged 21Tr by SDV Model, 1:87, plastic   (Andras Ekkert)

Plzeň 483, Škoda 21Tr, 1999

Brno 3023, Skoda 21Tr, 1999   (D Lawrence)

Brno 3018 21Tr by SDV Model, 1:87, plastic (Andras Ekkert)

České Budějovice 21Tr by SDV Model, 1:87, plastic   (Andras Ekkert)

Ostrava 3303 21Tr by AM, 1:87, plastic (Mattis Schindler)

Brno 3042 21Tr by AM, 1:87, plastic (Mattis Schindler)

Plzeň 484, 21Tr by AM, 1:87, plastic   (Mattis Schindler)

but a little painting could easily make a Szeged or České Budějovice version as Andras Ekkert has done from the cheaper plain edition. Injection moulded, and not exactly well fitting, the kits are also helped by adding detail to the otherwise strange trolleygear.

Predating the SDV kits were three similar plastic models by Brno maker AM, who produced Brno, Plzeň and Ostrava liveried versions of the 21Tr in 1:87. They too had strange, but different, trolleygear.

There are virtual 21Trs, available online for the SimTr trolleybus simulator, and card models by Petr Kudej, who's covered most liveries of the 12 operators who have the 21Tr. DPMB, the Brno operator, produced a card 21TR that reduces the body and wheels to a box but adds commendable trolleygear.

Škoda, of course, have a model in their museum, at 1:13 scale, but Marek Bureš (see page 50 and also below) has been building a 1:6 scale model for a number of years out of copper and aluminium with 0.35mm tin panelling and aims ultimately to produce a rather large fully functioning scale vehicle.

Brno, Ostrava & Plzeň w21Tr by Petr Kudej, 1:87, card   (Petr Kudej)

Brno 3007, Skoda 21Tr by DPMB, 1:87, card

Ostrov 22Tr by Rietze (conversion), 1:87, resin   (Andreas Zietemann)

Škoda 22Tr

model maker	ref.	issued	total	scale	construction	operator	fleet#	route	destination	built
AM				1:87	plastic	Brno	3606			2003
AM				1:87	resin	Ústí nad Labem	601			2002
AM				1:87	resin	Škoda Ostrov				1993
Marek Bureš				1:13	metal	Brno	3609			2003
Rietze (conversion)				1:87	resin	Škoda Ostrov				2000
SDV (conversion)				1:87	injection plastic	Szeged SZKV	T650	9	Lugas Utca	2000
SDV (conversion)				1:87	injection plastic	Brno	3039	26	Novolíšeňská	2000

Brno 3609 22Tr by Marek Bures, 1:13   (Marek Bureš)

Brno 3604, Škoda 22Tr, 2002   (Harold17)

5.6 Czech Republic

The articulated 22Tr actually predates the single 21Tr by first appearing in 1993. The prototype ran for 40,000km over two years until equipment failure led to a return to Škoda's Ostrov factory, where trolleybuses were built. The second prototype lasted slightly longer, but it wasn't until 2002 that production of just 11 cars was proceeded with. Marek Bureš has built a fictitious Brno 3609 in 1:13 scale that stands direct comparison with the real thing and is described on page 50.

Andreas Zietemann has converted a Rietze Mercedes O345G to represent the original prototype in Škoda colours and Andras Ekkert has converted the SDV kits to represent Szeged T650, the asynchronous motored test vehicle of 2003 and Brno (but with the wrong fleet number).

AM of Brno also made a short run of 1:87 22Tr models. There were three versions including Ústí nad Labem 601 with overall advertising for Raiffeisen Bank and Škoda's 1993 prototype. They are a little crude but include a lot of detail.

The 22Tr coincided with the demise of the Ostrov factory and each of the 13 built were apparently different from each other. The 23Tr classification was reserved for a double articulated version but was never implemented. The 21/22Tr was Ostrov's swansong.

Szeged T650 22Tr by SDV (conversion), 1:87, injection plastic (Andras Ekkert)

Brno 3039 22Tr by SDV (conversion), 1:87, injection plastic (Andras Ekkert)

Brno 3606, Škoda 22Tr by AM, 1:87, plastic

Demonstrator 22Tr by AM, 1:87, plastic
(Mattis Schindler)

Ústí Nad Labem 601 22Tr by AM, 1:87, plastic
(Mattis Schindler)

Škoda 24Tr prototype by Ivan Staněk, 1:26, wood   (Škoda)

Škoda 24Tr prototype, 2003

Škoda 24Tr

model maker	ref.	issued	total	scale	construction	operator	fleet#	route	destination	built
Busch (conversion)				1:87	resin	Generic				2004
Petr Kudej	PK020/etc.	2006		1:87	card	Various operators,				2004
Ivan Staněk				1:26	wood	Mariánské Lázně				2003

Meanwhile, at company headquarters in Plzeň and in collaboration with Karosa, the 24Tr was launched in 2003. Using an Irisbus chassis and Renault Agora body, the design is intended for 'Central and West European' markets and was a radical departure for Škoda who, although co-ordinating production, were by now only making the electrical equipment. Škoda has their sales model of the original prototype, made by Ivan Staněk at 1:26 scale, in their museum in Plzeň, now called Technomania (see page 21). 18 full size trolleys were built before the body had to be changed in 2005 to the Citelis pattern with most noticeably a revised headlight assembly. 252 of these have been sold, with two big orders to Riga and Timisoara. There's a model of this too in Technomania (see below).

Prodigious card modeller Petr Kudej has produced both subtypes of the 24Tr with Citelis and Agora bodies, with and without remotely controlled trolley booms. Not yet produced is the articulated version, the 25Tr. And there are no commercial resin models yet of the 24Tr/25Tr.

Mariánské Lázně 51 24Tr Irisbus, 2004 (Škoda)

Škoda 24Tr Irisbus and Karosa versions by Petr Kudej, 1:87, card   (Petr Kudej)

5.6 Czech Republic

SOR TN12

model maker	ref.	issued	total	scale	construction	operator	fleet#	route	destination	built
MMR Modely		2010		1:87	resin	Ostrava	SOR1			2008
MMR Modely		2010		1:87	resin	Ostrava	3911			2008

Prototype SOR TN12C, 2008   (Aktron)

Ostrava SOR TN12C by MMR Modelly, 1:87, resin   (Mattis Schindler)

Ostrava SOR TN12A by MMR Modelly, 1:87, resin   (Mattis Schindler)

Mariánské Lázně   Škoda 24Tr wby Ivan Staněk, 1:26, wood, metal   (Herbert Slavík)

In 2008 the SOR company of Libchavy near the Polish border, made a bid to become the Czech Republic's indigenous trolleybus manufacturer with their TN12 version of their N12 bus. Both TN12 prototypes run in Ostrava and have been modelled by MMR Modely. The four door layout, but not the cranked roofline, has been inherited by the latest prototype, the TNB12 of 2010, designated the Škoda 30Tr, a further attempt to supply the expected replacement market for the 14Tr.

Škoda Ostrov had risen to be the world leader in trolleybus production, both full size and, to some extent, in miniature. The 24/25Tr is still available but the last in-house models, the 21Tr and 22Tr finished production in 2004, when Škoda Ostrov closed. New vehicles, launched in 2009, include bought-in Solaris Trollinos fitted with Škoda Electric components (the single 26Tr, articulated 27Tr and the 3 axle 28Tr) and assembled at Plzeň.

In the last 15 years nearly all Czech trolleybuses have been modelled in one or both main scales, as well as others, so there's not much that has not been miniaturised. Local enthusiasm for trolleybuses, as a means of transport, as models and in many books, continues un-abated, and long may it do so! Dagmar Braunová, webmaster of busportal.cz, covetously holding Technomania's Škoda Irisbus 24Tr is a case in point.

Electrobus Lombard-Gerin, 1901 (Spårvägsmuseet)

Chapter 5.7
Denmark

Leyland, 1930- 1939	TTB4	131
BUT, 1945 - 1964	LETB1	133
Mercedes-Benz, 1930-2008	AEG O405GTD	133

Denmark, mostly flat and historically without indigenous fuel supplies to encourage trolleybus use, nevertheless had 4 systems with 5 routes in 2 places. There had been a trial of a Lombard-Gerin trolleybus in 1902, about which little is known except the test only lasted months. There are two photographs in Stockholm's Spårvägsmuseum that show a vehicle in København that's remarkably similar to that demonstrated in Paris and Villeneuve in 1900 and Eberswalde in 1901.

Later, as a certain trolleybus mania swept northern Europe in the late 20s, the Danes ordered 5 Garrett O types from the UK followed by 3 more in 1927. Six AEC 662T vehicles started the Odense system in 1939. All of Denmark's 59 trolleybuses were from the UK except two, built of necessity during the Second World War by NESA, the København operator and Triangel, in 1946. Three motor buses were also converted to trolleybuses.

Leyland TTB4

model maker	ref.	issued	total	scale	construction	operator	fleet#	route	destination	built
Micro		1938		1:72	lead	København NESA	9	24	Jaeskerborg	1938
Modeltrafik		1950s		15cm	wood	København NESA		12	Lynoby Point	1938
Modeltrafik		1950s		15cm	wood	København KS		24	Spegersborg	1938
St.Petersburg	138	1999	25	1:43	resin	København KS	101	12	Lyngby	1938
St.Petersburg	138a	1999	25	1:43	resin	København NESA	9	12	Lyngby	1938
Kherson Models	E5600		0	1:43	resin	København NESA	9			1938

Fourteen of the export version of the TTB4 chassis were built for København with General Electric equipment in 1938 and lasted in service until 1963. Preserved no. 101 at Sporvejsmuseet Skjoldenæsholm Museum, is still operational. Historically, the oldest model Leyland TTB4 is the relatively accurate lead casting from Denmark, thought to have been made by Micro in 1938, when the stylistically brilliant KS/Scandia bodies first appeared on their Leyland chassis on the streets of København. Wooden versions, by Modeltrafik, with tiny invisible wheels and a wrap around paper print may not be so old, but, like the Micro, were available in both dark and light roof colours.

Kobenhavn Leyland TTB4/Scandia by Micro, 14cm, lead

Russian model makers, Kherson Models and St. Petersburg Tram Collection have both modeled the Danish TTB4, as from Københavns Sporveje and NESA undertakings, the joint operators of the two route system. They're in 1:43 scale. The differences between the two makers versions are minute and maybe wrongly ascribed. Unfortunately, Leonid at SPTC can't remember exactly what versions he made!

Kobenhavn Leyland TTB4/Scandia by Modeltrafik, 11cm, wood

Kobenhavn Leyland TTB4/Scandia by Kherson Models, 1:43, resin

København 101, Leyland TTB4/Scandia, 1938 (Morten E. Storgaard)

Kobenhavn Leyland TTB4/Scandia by St.Petersburg, 1:43, resin (SPTC)

BUT LETB1/SMH

model maker	ref.	issued	total	scale	construction	operator	fleet#	route	destination	built
Hanse		1950s		(no scale)	wood	København NESA				1953

BUT LETB1/SMH. (Danmarks Tekniske Museum)

Traditional Danish wooden toy manufacturers Hanse produced this classic evocation of the real thing presumably when the new BUT LETB1 trolleybuses arrived in København in 1953 to augment the Leylands on the NESA system. Today, the original is preserved in the Danmarks Tekniske Museum. The first of the batch, 31, had an East Lancashire body that was cloned in Denmark by Smith, Mygrind + Huttermeier for the remaining 19 trolleybuses.

København 112, BUT LETB1, 1950 (unkown)

At about the same time, a Dinky Leyland Royal Tiger was converted in Arnhem by a father for a trolley obsessed son who seemingly never played with it - he just stared in awe, became a trolleybus driver and has kept it ever since. He remains convinced it was inspired by the four BUT LETB1s that were delivered to Kobenhavns Sprvej in 1950. They did at least have four chrome strips at the front.

Trolleybuses in the form of two Mercedes/AEG O405GTD duo-buses, operated by NESA were trialled over parts of the original Copenhagen routes between 1993 and 1997. Despite 71% of the passengers preferring 'electric buses' the experiment was not implemented. Apparently, the City architect didn't like the wires, although I remember the overhead still being there four years later. Andreas Zietemann, on the other hand, likes O405GTD duo-buses (and overhead) and has modeled what the København versions looked like, converted from a Wiking toy bus.

Kobenhavn BUT LETB1/SMH by Hanse, 39cm wood

Kobenhavn Leyland Royal Tiger/Duple by Dinky (conversion), 12cm, diecast

Kobenhavn Mercedes Benz O405GTD by Wiking (conversion), 1:87, plastic   (Andreas Zietemann)

København NESA Leyland TTB4/Scandia/GEC by Kherson Models, 1:43, resin

Chapter 5.8
Finland

With just 5 million people, Finland has had only two of its six major cities use trolleybuses, the capital Helsinki and its "Manchester", Tampere. Three Valmet JD trolleybuses with BTH electrical equipment started services in Tampere in December 1948. The system grew to five routes but closed in 1976. Helsinki has had two trolleybus installations (and there's talk of a third) The first ran along one route from 1949 until 1974. Apart from three ex-Stockholm Scania-Vabis, three ZIU-9s and a Sisu for the second attempt between 1979 and 1985, virtually all Finland's trolleybuses were by Valmet, the state owned industrial conglomerate. They were built between 1948 and 1959 and all 32 of them were similar.

Valmet 1948-1959	JD	1

Valmet JD/BTH

model maker	ref.	issued	total	scale	construction	operator	fleet#	route	destination	built
St.Petersburg	127	1999	25	1:43	resin	Tampere	7			1949
St.Petersburg	127a	1999	25	1:43	resin	Helsinki HKL	604	14		1949

Both Helsinki and Tampere Valmet JD trolleybuses have been modelled by St. Petersburg Tram Collection, right at the beginning of their model production in 1999. If SPTC were to model them today, there are some details that would now be resolved, such as separating the trolley gantry from the roof. Tampere's 26 and 28 which differ in window detail, survive, as does 5, which is restored. (Strictly speaking the SPTC model should have a fleet number of 2 or 3, not 7 which was the first to have radialised windows, but then the roof resistances box would also have been a little different). Helsinki's 625 is stored at Ruskeasuo Depot, and 605, sister to the SPTC model, is at Helsinki Tram Museum.

Helsinki 604, Valmet JD/BTH by St.Petersburg, 1:43, resin   (SPTC)

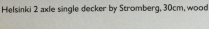

Helsinki 605, Valmet JD/BTH, 1949   (Arto Hellman)

Helsinki 2 axle single decker by Stromberg, 30cm, wood

Finland's electrical manufacturer of traction equipment, Strömberg, now part of ABB, has commissioned a toy trolleybus, with commendable Scandinavian design flare. This particular example was presented, fittingly, to the director of Salzburg's extensive trolleybus system. Strömberg supplied the electrical equipment for the single Finnish Sisu trolleybus of 1979 that ran on trial in Helsinki until 1985.

In 2009, the City of Helsinki, for what would be the third time, looked into the feasibility of introducing trolleybuses — on a network of five routes. Stating grounds for pursuing the idea, the report said the earliest they could be running was 2014. Models would doubtless play a part in the consultation process.

Paris Renault PY/STCRP by C.C.C., 1:43, resin, whitemetal

Chapter 5.9
France

Renault	PY	138
Jouet Joustra	toys	139
France Jouet	toys	143
CR	toys	143
SCMS	toys	145 (72)
Le Jouet Troll	toys	146 (73)
Vétra, 1930-1964	CS60, CB60	146
	VA3, VBB, VBR	149
	VBC-APU/Chausson	149
Renault	R4231	151
Irisbus	Civis/Cristalis	152

Rather more than other countries, France has produced a large variety of toy trolleybuses, mostly from the great producers Joustra and Charles Rossignol. But we should commence at the very beginning; at the very start of the public operation of trolleybuses (and ignore the claim that trolleybuses ran in Béthune from 1898 to 1904)

Although some sources state M.Nithard's "trolley automoteur", a system using Max Schiemann type trolley poles, as having started in January 1901, it seems likely to have been 1904, making the Lombard-Gerin installation between Fontainbleau and Samois of July 1901, France's first. It may have used the same vehicles that had been demonstrated at the Paris exposition of 1900. Either way, it appeared successful and ran until 1908 outlasting Schiemann's Bielathalbahn, also of July 1901. The next Lombard-Gerin trolleybuses to run in France went from Croix-Rouge to Allauch, near Marseilles between 1902 and 1905. The powered collector was able to run ahead of the vehicle and must have often strained the power cable. That and what must have been a heavy collector balanced precariously on the overhead wires, would surely not be acceptable today. The large headlight of the model of Lombard-Gerin's Croix-Rouge trolleybus at Marseille Noailles Metro station was added to the original after 1904.

Marseilles Electrobus Lombard-Gerin by ARTM, (unknown scale), wood, metal   (RTM)

France, like so many other countries, seemingly forgot the trolleybus until the late 20s, with some exceptions. One was a series of trials along the Enghien – Montmorency tramline of Paris in 1922 that resulted in 1925 in a trial route to Vitry-sur-Seine. Both trials used three Schneider type H trolleybuses. As converted buses they looked archetypically Parisian. They may, just, have been the inspiration for a reclusive producer of castings in Tunbridge Wells who produced fantastic, retro, almost Buck Rodgers like models in Parisian green and Lyonnaise red. Meanwhile, an inspirational Schneider H type bus is preserved at the AMTUIR museum, east of Paris.

Marseilles Electrobus Lombard-Gerin, 1902   (CGFT)

Paris 2 axle single decker by TW, 12cm, diecast

Vitry-sur-Seine Schneider H type, 1925   (AMTUIR)

Lyon 2 axle single decker by TW, 12cm, diecast

The experimental Vitry-sur-Seine line, a result of the poor reliability of buses, next received two Renault PY trolleybuses in 1929 that were very similar to those deployed in Bouches-du-Rhône and Savoie. These too were apparently not reliable, but lasted until 1934, to be replaced by petrol electric hybrids that lasted a year, after which the overhead came down. Trolleybuses didn't return to Paris until 1943. The 1929 Renaults have been accurately modelled in 1:43 scale by C.C.C. of Rouen as a resin kit with whitemetal booms and transfers of the Place Cavé to Vitry Gare route. Being a dual purpose kit, with the option to build the bus version, it

Paris Renault PY/STCRP, 1929   (RAPT)

Paris Renault PY/STCRP by C.C.C., 1:43, resin, whitemetal

looks very good but only has three window pillars instead of the requisite seven, perhaps added to take the weight of the trolleygear. A little simplified in model form, but the booms do include the unusual cantilever arrangement. The tricky-to-apply lining transfers are too thick. Four of the Electrobus de Savoie 1930 trolleybuses that ran to Villard-du-Planay were similar, and did have three pillars, but staggered trolleyboom mountings and headlights at the very front of the mudguards. The door and the windscreen were different, still, with a little surgery etc. they could be modelled - what else should kits be for?

Electrobus de Savoie Renault PY/STCRP, 1930 (coll. Lartilleux)

Before modern generation trolleybuses came to Lyon, St. Etienne and Rouen during the war, there were other isolated systems in rural areas using early Vétra trolleybuses based on the Renault PY with its distinctive bonnet. There was a very boxy 2 axle prototype Vétra in Rouen from 1933. Strange then, that Joustra should produce a 3 axle tinplate single decker before the war, not least because nothing ever looked like it and there were no electric 6 wheelers in France until the radically different Vétra VA-3 of 1948.

Joustra

"Le jouet de Strasbourg" was formed in 1934 by brothers Paul and André Kosmann and Guillaume Marx, an engineer from Bing toys of Nuremberg. They produced a wide variety of tin toys and, unlike their British contemporaries, would change toys every couple of years, either in detail or as a new toy using existing dies. By the 1970s tinplate was being increasingly usurped by plastic and Joustra adapted but couldn't stand the Far Eastern competition. By the 80s they folded, leaving a highly prolific heritage.

Jouet Joustra, Strasbourg, 1934-1987

vehicle	operator	fleet#	route	destination	model maker	ref.	issued	scale/size	construction	notes
3 axle single decker	(generic)				Joustra	439	1938	30cm	tinplate	plain in red/blue, red/yellow, blue/red, or blue/yellow
3 axle single decker	Paris		80		Joustra	442	1951	30cm	tinplate	pre war stamping, with side lining, radiator delination, route box
3 axle single decker	(generic)				Joustra	442	1953	30cm	tinplate	revised to take electric head lamps
3 axle single decker	Paris		80		Joustra	442	1954	30cm	tinplate	added roof boards, Paris and Lyon versions
3 axle single decker	Lyon		80	Mairie - Place du Marché	Joustra	442	1954	30cm	tinplate	added roof boards, Paris and Lyon versions
3 axle single decker	(generic)		80		Joustra	442	1954	30cm	tinplate	revised without radiator, blue/red
3 axle double decker	(generic)				Joustra	428	1949	33cm	tinplate	with or without headlights
Jacquemond 10-A	Paris	825	4	Gare - Hotel deVille	Joustra	444	1955	39cm	tinplate	green/cream
Jacquemond 10-A	Lyon	825	7	Gare - Marie	Joustra	450	1959	39cm	tinplate	red/cream
2 axle double decker	Lyon			Broadway	Joustra	2012	1951	13.5cm	tinplate	green, graphics and wheel variations
2 axle double decker	Paris			Broadway	Joustra	2011	1951	13.5cm	tinplate	red, graphics and wheel variations

Generic 3 axle single decker by Joustra, 30cm, tinplate

The Joustra catalogue of the late 30s shows, a little inaccurately, the first incarnation of the Joustra clockwork 3 axle single decker. It was available in at least 4 "bicoleur" schemes. Parisian green didn't, at this stage, appear to be amongst them.

After the war, the 'lined' version appeared using the same stamp press as previously but with revised lithographic printing. This green and cream "Parisian" livery seems to replace the blue and yellow version. Also new was a different pattern of wheel with lithographed tread that was to be used until the end in the 1960s (The same basic stamping was also used as a Television truck in 1962). The next iteration, in 1953, had

Generic 3 axle single decker by Joustra, 30cm, tinplate

Generic 3 axle double decker by Joustra, 33cm, tinplate

Joustra catalogue, 3 axle double decker, 1949 (Jouet Joustra)

Joustra catalogue, 2 axle single decker, 1955 (Jouet Joustra)

the headlights lowered and enlarged to take working bulbs. The following year, roof advertising boards were added and a roof route indicator. These dates assume, perhaps unwisely, that the registration plate at the rear, for example, 1951 G-67, does actually refer to the date produced. They do coincide chronologically with increasing detail. At some stage, around 1954, the crude one piece trolley booms were replaced by individual sprung types on a gantry, that, together with the roof side boards, created a more imposing model.

The last version finally does away with the anachronistic radiator and has an emblem and side lights, plus a 'V' that would have meant a third revision to the basic stamping. There were probably 3 colour schemes with each revision and so at least 9 versions of this large tinplate trolley were produced. They all had doors on both sides.

The 1949 catalogue shows a double deck trolleybus with front headlights that are absent on the two extant example we know about. One assumes an intended British market (more on page 285). Anyway, as Nicolas Léonard describes it in his tome 'Joustra: la marque française de jouet méchanique', it is an "amazing" trolleybus.

The big six wheel single decker seems to have

Strasbourg 734, Somua-SW TL-102-B, 1947 (col. CTS/Strasbourg)

Paris Jacquemond 10-A by Joustra, 39cm, tinplate

been replaced by the even bigger 4 wheeler, as Joustra brought out this much more realistic trolleybus in 1955. It has a pivoting front axle and a clockwork motor with a stop/start switch and a bell rung by the action of the wheels. Often referred to as a Vétra, I like to think of it as a Jacquemond 10-A. That front emblem just isn't a Vétra 'V' (although the original catalogue illustration looks rather more like it) and there's little about the body that truly defines it – it could even be a Somua-SW, with the forward roof mounted resistance box and the right number of doors (if not, as in Joustra models, on both sides). Five Somua TL-102-B trolleybuses were supplied to Strasbourg (the home of Joustra, Les Jouet de Strasbourg) in 1947-8, numbered 730-734 (and not tallying with the toy's 825 fleet number). Only 55 Somua trolleybuses were ever built, over a period of six years and many were for export, but we leave it to you to decide the inspirational basis.

Available in standard Paris and Lyon colours, the toy is one of, if not the largest tinplate trolleybus ever made at nearly 40cm in length. Variants of the green Joustra model include "Gare" and "Hotel De Ville" with a red "Beaumont" advert on the roof and a number 4 on the resistance box or "Gare - Marie" shown twice, a red stripe and the number 7 plus "7" on the roof resistance box. The red version has "Mon Jouet Favori" on roof boards that never seem to have appeared on the green version and, according to Nicolas Léonard, was released in 1959, not long before the trolleybuses of Strasbourg were discontinued in 1962.

Lyon Jacquemond 10-A, 1948 (Jacquemond)

5.9 France

Lyon Jacquemond 10-A by Joustra, 39cm, tinplate

Joustra's third toy trolleybus was a complete antithesis. The "Broadway" owes nothing to trolleybus practice but a lot to a toy manufacturer getting the most from his expensive dies. This strange pattern ostensibly with two decks also appeared as a bus, coach, mail truck, police car and fire engine. It was available in red and green as you'd expect and there may have been a blue version. Like the smaller Wells trolleybus of the same period in the UK, there were wind-up and 'push 'n' go' versions. There were variations in the graphics and the wheel pattern over the life of a product line that lasted into the 60s and one, regarded as rather rare, used silver paint instead of cream.

Lyon 2 axle double decker by Joustra, 13.5cm, tinplate

Paris 2 axle double deckers by Joustra, 13.5cm, tinplate

France Jouet

France Jouet (FJ) of Marseille existed from 1948 until 1972 and unusually produced diecast and plastic as well as intricate tinplate toys. But their only trolleybus, produced from 1957, following a similar bus of 1955, was a spectacular one stamp, wheel-less artefact that looks more 30s than 50s - a brilliantly evocative "Flash Gordon" trolleybus toy that owes little to reality and everything to imagination and a hopeful future. And yet it's rooted firmly in its time, which can hardly be other than the 1957 emblazoned on the registration plate. With no wheel arches but doors and the Marseille city arms proudly displayed on both sides, the graphics are wonderfully assured. This model is also a technically masterful expression of the tin plate makers art - it's not easy to achieve a full, one piece dome as deep as this. No variants of the toy have been found. The underneath wheels are powered by a friction motor. Real Marseille trolleybuses were blue and white, by the way, and long outlasted this (favourite) toy.

Marseille 2 axle single decker by FJ (France Jouet), 17cm, tinplate

Charles Rossignol

One of the oldest, certainly long surviving toy makers, was Charles Rossignol (CR) of Paris. Founded in 1868 and in existence until 1962, the company had various names but was nearly always known as CR. They made a vast array of novelties, but our interest is in the three toys they made from 1952 onwards.

CR (Charles Rossignol, Les Jouets C.Rossignal & C. Roitel) 1868-1962

vehicle	operator	destination	model maker	ref.	issued	scale/size	construction	type
2 axle single decker	Lyon	CentreVille,Aerogarde	CR (Charles Rossignol)	95	1952	10.8cm	tinplate	singlestamp double ended solid version
2 axle single decker	Paris	CentreVille,Aerogarde	CR (Charles Rossignol)	95	1952	10.8cm	tinplate	singlestamp double ended cut out version
2 axle single decker	Paris,Lyon	CentreVille,Aerogarde	CR (Charles Rossignol)	59	1952	12.5cm	tinplate	mid sized singlestamp double ended cut out version
Vétra-ChaussonVBC	Paris,Lyon	Terminus	CR (Charles Rossignol)	78	1952	26cm	tinplate	2 tone plain roof version, red or green
Vétra-ChaussonVBC	(generic)	Terminus	CR (Charles Rossignol)	78	1952	26cm	tinplate	Plain roof version, grey
Vétra-ChaussonVBC	(generic)	Terminus	CR (Charles Rossignol)	78	1952	26cm	tinplate	2 tone plain roof version, blue
Vétra-ChaussonVBC	(generic)	Terminus	CR (Charles Rossignol)	978C	1952	26cm	tinplate	2 tone, raised booms version
Vétra-ChaussonVBC	Lyon	Terminus	CR (Charles Rossignol)	78	1952	26cm	tinplate	3 tone chromed version
Vétra-ChaussonVBC	(generic)	Terminus	CR (Charles Rossignol)	78	1952	26cm	tinplate	2 tone, raised booms and/or roof headlight
Vétra-ChaussonVBC	Lyon	Terminus	CR (Charles Rossignol)	78	1952	26cm	tinplate	

Described by its owner as "the ugliest ever produced" but having "a certain charm for the fanatical collector", this small, single boomed trolleybus model seems to have been a bit of an aberration in terms of bumper to body proportion. It also appears to be double ended. As with many, if not most French toy trolleybuses, there was also a red version, with cut out rather than printed windows. Red represented the Lyon system while green was for Paris. There were friction and wind-up versions. The two versions of the smallest CR, seemingly similar, have differing wheels and bumpers and a silver or painted single boom. Like Joustra, CR made many other variants of the same die stamp, including a bank truck, an oil tanker and an ambulance. Except the first bus version, they all seem to have had an oversize bumper.

Paris 2 axle single decker by CR (Charles Rossignol), 11cm, tinplate

Lyons 2 axle single decker by CR (Charles Rossignol), 11cm, tinplate

5.9 France

The larger 12cm trolleybus seems only to have come with cut out windows. There's evidence that this is why the bumpers are oversized on the 10cm pressing – some of the 12cm truck versions had the same pattern. Perhaps not all the variants that CR produced have come down to us after 60 years and we'll never know - these 12cm trolleybuses are rarely seen. But the twin booms in either red or silver and those with a route indicator makes them rather desirable.

Lyon and Paris 2 axle single deckers by CR (Charles Rossignol), 12.5cm, tinplate (M Duprat)

Paris Vetra VBC-APU/Chausson by CR (Charles Rossignol), 26cm, tinplate

Also released in the busy year of 1952 was the much bigger 26cm toy trolleybus. Apart from the standard Paris and Lyon versions, there were blue and grey versions, the latter seemingly with windows merely cut into the lorry version, ignoring the lettering. The lime green edition has roof lights with chrome rims and a radiator stuck on the front. There are dimples for headlights and a bus version does have powered miniature bulbs. There was also a trolleybus version with a large roof mounted headlight, either with the booms atop a box or without. This model is usually regarded as based on the Vétra VBC, as, more convincingly, are the Solido diecasts (see below).

Lyon Vetra VBC-APU/Chausson by CR (Charles Rossignol), 26cm, tinplate

Generic Vetra VBC-APU/Chausson by CR (Charles Rossignol), 26cm, tinplate

Lyon Vetra VBC-APU/Chausson by CR (Charles Rossignol), 26cm, tinplate

Generic Vetra VBC-APU/Chausson by CR (Charles Rossignol), 26cm, tinplate

Generic Vetra VBC-APU/Chausson by CR (Charles Rossignol), 26cm, tinplate

La Société de construction de matériel scientifique (SCMS)

There were two slightly mysterious motorized French toy trolleybuses built in the 1950s that owed their appearance to the almost ubiquitous Vétra CS60. La Société de construction de matériel scientifique (SCMS) produced a 25cm powered toy that was steered mechanically.

Marseille 4, Vetra CB60, 1941 (col. TN Nice)

Generic Vetra CS60 by SCMS, 25cm, Aluminium

5.9 France 145

Le Jouet Troll

The quite impossible Le Jouet Troll has a single boom that is neither hinged nor sprung. Owing nothing to or even understanding of trolleybus power collection technology, this toy could only run on one straight span of wires. Large for a powered model at 28cm in length and although precisely made, was badly conceived. It has complex electrically controlled steering and was also expensive. But also impossible not to love. (See also page 72).

The small, but still continuing French trolleybus industry has spawned an almost disproportionate number of toys. There are also models, some not from France, mostly reflecting the all prevailing production of the Vétra company.

Vétra

The Société des Véhicules et Tracteurs Électrique or Vétra was an amalgamation of Als-Thom, SACM Belfort and French Thomson-Houston and was founded in 1925 to design and outsource the construction of electric mine tractors, garbage trucks and, mainly, trolleybuses. They had a near monopoly, mostly in conjunction with Renault and its subsidiary, Berliet. Between 1926 and 1958 Vétra built 1785 trolleybuses, the great majority between 1946 and 1952. Only 77 trolleybuses were built in France by other manufacturers.

Vetra CS60/Renault Scemia by Le Jouet Troll, 28cm, aluminium

Vétra CS60, CB60

model maker	ref.	issued	total	scale	construction	operator	fleet#	route	destination	built
AMTUIR				1:10(?)	metal	Paris RATP				1943
Minitrucks	24	1981		1:50	resin, whitemetal	Lyon				1943
Minitrucks	24	1981		1:50	resin, whitemetal	Paris RATP				1943
MMR Modelly				1:87	resin	Salzburg	114-7			1941
Les Éditions Atlas		2006		1:50	resin, whitemetal	Limoges				1947

The AMTUIR museum in Paris has long had a large exhibition grade model of a CS60, reflecting the 302 CS and CB60's built. The shapely and iconic wartime trolleybus, now preserved with three examples at AMTUIR, was the result of a long gestation from the boxy prototype of 1932. Vétra had a system of nomenclature that had more to do with type than design, hence, in the CS60, C meant 9m long S meant Renault Scémia and 60 passengers. B, as in the identical CB60, meant assembled by Berliet. The only CB60 scale model is by Editions Atlas, a subscription gift retailer, who produced a collection called "Bus et Trolleybus de France" which included a model Limoges Vétra CB60, made by Eligor. In service the real things were exceptionally long lived, some lasting 44 years. Limoges no.5 still runs in preservation at Sandtoft Trolleybus Museum.

Amiens Vetra CS60/Renault Scemia, 1943 (col. P.Bouillion)

Paris Vetra CS60/Renault Scemia by AMTUIR, 1:12(?), metal (R. Le Corff)

Paris Vetra CS60/Renault Scemia by Minitrucks, 1:50, resin, whitemetal

Lyon Vetra CS60/Renault Scemia by Minitrucks, 1:50, resin, whitemetal

Salzburg 114, Vetra CS60 by MMR Modelly, 1:87, resin

Between 1981 and 2001 Jacques Ehrlacher produced a resin kit for Minitrucks that was similar to the Editions Atlas model. It's rather successful and includes two clear cast front windows that work better than the usual acetate-behind-the-pillar compromise. We can't resist showing two made-up versions in Lyons and Paris colours.

Salzburg acquired four new CS60 Vetras in 1942, intended for Limoges. Called 'tin cans' locally, they were disposed of or met with accidents within a year, but that hasn't stopped MMR Modelly producing a 1:87 model. A Kapfenberg liveried version will surely follow, as that's where two of the batch served secondhand until 1948.

Vétra VBB, VBR

model maker	ref.	issued	total	scale	construction	operator	fleet#	route	destination	built
RA Model Petr Došlý	1200 00	2002		1:87	resin	Děčín		1	Chrocvince	1950
RA Model Petr Došlý	1200 01	2003		1:87	resin	České Budějovice				1948
RA Model Petr Došlý	1200 02	2003		1:87	resin	České Budějovice				1948
Willi Schincke		2007		1:63	plasticard, tin, balsa	Zlín	16	C		1949

Vetra VBR/Renault/CKD, 1948 (unknown)

České Budejovice Vetra VBR/Renault/CKD by RA Model Petr Došlý, 1:87, resin (Andreas Zietemann)

České Budějovice Vetra VBR/Renault/CKD by RA Model Petr Došlý, 1:87, resin

More numerous than the CS was the Vétra B type or 10m trolleybus, mostly produced in the boom years between 1946 and 1954. The 'standard' VBB and VBR (Berliet and Renault) and not counting later variants, numbered 533, nearly a third of all Vétra production. There seems to be no indigenous model, only those from the Czech Republic.

The prodigious Petr Došlý of Děčín in the Czech Republic has produced three versions of the Vétra VBR that was imported between 1948 and 1950 and fitted with locally produced CKD electrical equipment. These included the last four delivered to Petr's home town, just as Skoda was starting to produce the 7Tr. Apart from České Budějovice and Děčín, Petr Došlý could produce models of VBRs that ran in Hradec Králové, Jihlava and Zlín. Willi Schincke has done just that at 1:63 scale with his powered model of no.16. Unlike their French compatriots, the Czech VBRs don't seem to have lasted very long in service, around 10 years.

Děčín Vetra VBR/Renault/CKD by RA Model Petr Došlý, 1:87, resin

Zlin Vetra VBR/Renault/CKD by Willi Schincke, 1:63, plasticard, tin, balsa (Willi Schincke)

Vétra VA3

model maker	ref.	issued	total	scale	construction	operator	fleet#	route	destination	built
Volume-Trix		1955		(no scale)	card	Lyon	602	2	Hotel de Ville	1950

Lyon 601, Vetra VA3 prototype, 1950 (Adrien Gondin)

Lyon Vetra VA3 by Volume-Trix, 26.5cm, card (M Duprat)

It could almost be a tinplate, with comic passengers evocative of Wells and Betal; this large and rather faithful rendering of the Vétra VA3 in card shows it in its initial livery and, with 4 large roof ventilators, to be of the production batch, 602-654 delivered between 1950 and 1953 to Lyon. The stylish downward rear sweep and front V had gone from the full size trolleys by the time this model appeared, but the VA3 was by then the backbone of the large Lyon fleet and continued as the core form of street transport in France's second city until after the 70s. There were 141 of them and many served for three decades. 71 were exported to Madrid and Barcelona.

Vétra VBC-APU/Chausson

model maker	ref.	issued	total	scale	construction	operator	fleet#	route	destination	built
Solido	113	1954		1:72	diecast	(generic)				1955
Solido	113	1954		1:72	diecast	(generic)				1955
Solido	120	1957		1:72	diecast	(generic)	201			1955
Solido	120	1959		1:72	diecast zinc	(generic)				1955
Solido	120	1960		1:72	diecast zinc	(generic)				1955
Dinky (conversion)	29F			1:72	diecast zinc	Toulon	85	1	LaVaalette	1957

Generic Vetra VBC-APU/Chausson by Solido, 1:72, diecast

Apart from the Charles Rossignol toys above, that may be based on Chausson bodied Vétras, there's no doubting the basis of the Solido diecast that was produced for a decade from the mid-50s and doubtless resided in many a French toy cupboard. Brest, Le Havre and Toulon had 16 Chausson trolleys between them but only the 6 of Toulon had the distinctive, almost exuberant, lower ribbing and then only on the doors. The casting is an accurate modelling of the bus, which often had silver detailing as shown, but not so the (very few) equivalent trolleybuses.

Generic Vetra VBC-APU/Chausson by Solido, 1:72, diecast

Generic Vetra VBC-APU/Chausson by Solido, 1:72, diecast

Generic Vetra VBC-APU/Chausson by Solido, 1:72, diecast

Generic Vetra VBC-APU/Chausson by Solido, 1:72, diecast

According to Phillipe Morro and Mick Duprat in their "Autocars et Autobus – Les Transport Public en Minature" the Solido was released in 1954, a year before Toulon's two tone cream and sand Chausson trolleybuses were delivered. It's possible, as the real bus version with full radiator grille, first appeared in 1952. But Dave Wallace in his Diecast Collector article (issue 50, Dec. 2001) states a more tenable 1956. Solido never produced a Toulon liveried model (as far as we know), nor did they ever cover that bus grille with a plate but they did issue a series of rakish colour schemes over the years, based on a combination of maroon and a dark turquoise. There were apparently yellow and dark blue variants and grey instead of cream on some two tone editions.

Some time after 1957 Solido more realistically updated the wheels and two years later added glazing to the interior and a mid blue livery. By 1961 suspension was included. Finally, in the early 60s, there followed rather unfortunate and shorter plastic booms with bracing between them. Perhaps zealous parents had complained of possible dangers from metal 'prongs'. Production of the Solido trolleybus ceased in 1967, but not before a black boomed version was introduced.

French Dinky Toys, amongst others, have modelled the Chausson AP52 (Dinky 29F) but not as a trolleybus. That hasn't stopped Roland Le Corff from adapting said model to something he's helped restore, the only Chausson trolleybus to survive into preservation, in the livery Solido never managed, Toulon 85, kept at the MPTUR museum near Aix-en-Provence.

Toulon Vetra VBC-APU/Chausson by Dinky (conversion), 1:72, diecast (Roland La Corff)

Toulon 85, Vetra VBC-APU/Chausson, 1955 (Roland La Corff)

Generic Vetra VBC-APU/Chausson by Solido, 1:72, diecast

Generic Vetra VBC-APU/Chausson by Solido, 1:72, diecast

Renault R4231

model maker	ref.	issued	total	scale	construction	operator	fleet#	route	destination	built
St. Petersburg	192	2000	50	1:43	resin	Madrid EMT	114	101		1952/57

Madrid 105, Renault R4231, 1957 (col. Manuel Rodriguez)

Madrid 114, Renault R4231 by St.Petersburg, 1:43, resin (SPTC)

Sticking roughly to the chronology, the St. Petersburg Tram collection produced a 1:43 model of Madrid's 46 Renault R4231 diesel bus to trolley conversions that were used for the semi-interurban route 5, Atocha – Carabanchel, from 1957. Nos. 101-146 had either GEC or GEI electrical equipment and were broadly similar to the Vétra ELR. They lasted until 1966. The SPTC model skilfully has both rubber and chrome window surrounds, modelled by painting and using etched metal parts respectively. It's an excellent model of a prematurely retired trolleybus fleet.

Lyon Irisbus Cristalis by TCL, 12.6cm, card

Bologna 1101, Irisbus Civis, 2000 (Robert Renzi)

Generic Irisbus Civis by Irisbus, 1:12(?), wood, metal (Amtuir)

Nancy 13, Bombardier TVR, 2000 (Vlastimil Hutla)

Third Generation

Vétra was declared bankrupt in 1964 with no orders and it would be 10 years before a French trolleybus was built again. Renault and Berliet produced an electric version of the PR100 bus and went on to produce 326 'second generation' ER100 trolleybuses that lasted until the turn of the millennium, but we know of no French commercial models, although the Polish licensed version, the Jelcz PR100E, has been modelled – see page 234.

The 'third generation' of French trolleybuses are radically different. With hub motors and unobstructed low floors the Irisbus Civis and Cristalis designs are an attempt at a "tram sur pneus". Designed initially by Renault and tested at their Lyon test track, Irisbus has invested a decade of development in their flagship optically guided Civis concept. The only trolleybus version to be sold so far is to Bologna, although the simpler Cristalis has sold comparatively well in Metropolitan France. The original Irisbus display model was shown widely, including at the UITP show in London in 2001. It is now kept at the AMTUIR museum near Paris. The Civis trolleybuses delivered to Bologna ATC, starting with 1101 in 2004, have optical guidance via a camera housed in the extruberance above the windscreen and a livery that has since been revised. The production batch followed in 2008 and the route opens in 2011. The non-guided Cristalis trolleybus, meanwhile, has successfully replaced older generations in France, particularly in Lyon, where the operator, TCL, produced a celebratory paper model in 2002.

Also at UITP in London was a model of Nancy's slightly ill-fated 'Stan' the Bombardier TVR trolleybus system that uses a railed groove in the road centre to mechanically guide the bi-articulated vehicles. The guidance is used in the city centre's narrow streets and there were problems when a trolleybus transferred to unguided sections; a scandal that delighted more extreme tram protagonists. The system is now more reliable, but the Bombardier model has disappeared and, apart from Caen, no other installations were sold.

Arnhem Saviem SC10U by Speelgoed/Norev, 1:50, plastic

There's just one other model to mention, and we should, as 100 certified miniatures were made - a French trolleybus in Holland. Saviem never made a trolleybus, certainly not for Arnhem, but in 1987 local model maker Speelgoed Import seemed determined to cash in on the excitement of new Den Ousten Volvos that were then arriving, with an adaptation of a Norev model, complete with lever operated model doors. With the rather oversized trolleygear, it can be called a reflection of local passion for the trolleybus.

Only St. Étienne, Lyon, Limoges, and Nancy still have trolleybuses in France, but, as elsewhere, there are mutterings advocating their return, not least from EDF the state electricity company. France has seen futuristic attempts in the last decade to update the trolleybus to a true inheritor of the best of tram and bus advantages and not just a bus with poles. It's been a brave journey.

Lyon 1921, Irisbus Cristalis, 2006 (Ibou69100)

Marseille 2 axle single decker by FJ (France Jouet),
17cm, tinplate

Chapter 5.10
Germany

Günthermann	tinplate	157
Märklin etc.	kits	157
	toys	158
Büssing, 1933-1957	33F	159
	Uerdingen	160
	Uerdingen/Kiepe UBIVs	161
Henschel, 1930-1962	Gr.II/Kässbohrer	162
	Gr.II/Schumann	163
	OM 5-1/Lohner	164
	II(Krupp)/Ludewig	164
	III/NWF	165
	HS56/Gaubschat	166
	Uerdingen ÜH IIIs	167
	HS160 OSL	171
	HS160 OSL-G	171
Krauss-Maffei, 1948-1964	KME-130	173
Solingen 1968-74	TSIII	173
LOWA, 1950-1956	W600	174
	W601	175
	W602	176
	W602a	176
	IFA ES6	178
MAN, 1934-1987	36 seater/Siemens	180
	MPE1/ Schumann	180
	MKE2/3/ Kässbohrer	182
	MKE4500	182
	SG240 H	183
	SG200 HO	184
	SL172 HO	185
Daimler/Mercedes Benz, 1937-2008	O1000	187
	OE302	188
	O305	188
	O405	189
	Citaro	191

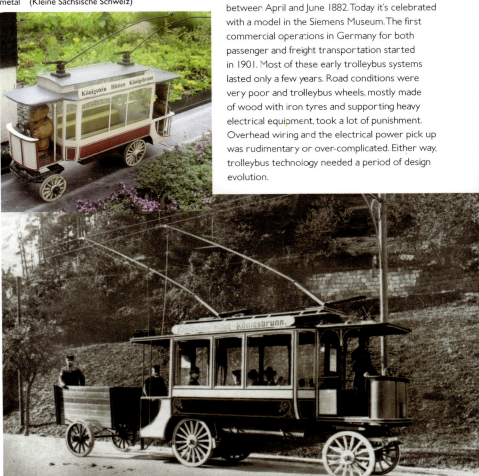

Siemens Elektromote, 1882 (Siemens)

Bielathalbahn Schiemann by Lorenz, 1:10, wood, metal (Kleine Sächsische Schweiz)

The world's first trolleybus, the "Electromote" build by Werner von Siemens made test runs between April and June 1882. Today it's celebrated with a model in the Siemens Museum. The first commercial operations in Germany for both passenger and freight transportation started in 1901. Most of these early trolleybus systems lasted only a few years. Road conditions were very poor and trolleybus wheels, mostly made of wood with iron tyres and supporting heavy electrical equipment, took a lot of punishment. Overhead wiring and the electrical power pick up was rudimentary or over-complicated. Either way, trolleybus technology needed a period of design evolution.

Bielathalbahn1, Schiemann, 1901 (werkphoto)

There are two myths about the Max Schiemann's Bielathalbahn - it wasn't the world's first passenger trolleybus service (in Germany, Eberswalde started 6 months earlier) and it didn't get to Bielatha, stopping shorter than planned at Königsbrunn. Today and 20km away, towards Dresden, Mr. Lorenz's trolleybus model of 2005 runs at Dorf Wehlen model village and has now been operating for longer than the original. The real Bielathalbahn ran from July 1901 until the bad roads and less than expected patronage led to its closure in September 1904, but it, and Schiemann's twelve or so other installations did establish the under-running trolley as the standard system for trolleybuses.

By the 1920s there were virtually no public trolleybuses in Germany and development had shifted to the United Kingdom. The modern era in Germany started in 1930 at Mettmann, with vehicles influenced by those of the United States with radically rational design. More systems followed as manufacturers sought to find replacements for trams and later, during the war, as fuel shortages became severe.

By the 1950s and 60s there were more than 70 trolleybus systems in Germany. But as buses were seen as cheaper than trolleybuses to operate and the rebuilding of streets needed expensive new overhead layouts, so systems were closed. The lack of a trolleybus lobby within the large German bus industry meant short production runs of specialist trolleybuses were seen as unviable. The trolleybus in Germany had thrived only in smaller towns and cities and those that did survive did so because of steep hills that buses couldn't easily surmount. The last new system in Hoyerswerda, in East Germany, opened in 1989 but closed in 1994. Today there are only three systems operating in Germany: Eberswalde (close to Berlin), Esslingen (close to Stuttgart) and Solingen (close to Düsseldorf).

Many German trolleybuses were made by Henschel (850, including co-builder Uerdingen and exported trolleys), although almost all major manufacturers had produced a few examples before the war. MAN built 571 including substantial exports to Spain and South America. Mercedes Benz built far more for export than for the domestic market. (591 and 113 respectively). East German GDR trolleybus manufacturers were state owned, LOWA for chassis and bodies and LEW for the electrical equipment. Because of the strictly applied COMECON regulations, trolleybus production was stopped in the GDR in 1957 and Škoda trolleybuses were imported (which are included in the Czech chapter, see page 115). Later on, Ikarus trolleybuses were bought, (see the Hungarian chapter, page 198).

There have been 71 second generation systems in Germany, nearly all small in fleet size, so, although thinly spread, they were 'normally seen' and so toys were produced of tin plate, wood and plastic. For fifty years, motorized Eheim, then Brawa model trolleybuses were available as part of the huge model train industry (see chapter 4, page 63). Today, there are resin models of many German prototypes, including those made in the Czech Republic, in small batches. And there's the Grell plastic trolleybus models produced in China in vast numbers for the Wilkinson Sword razor company. Usually in Solingen's livery, they were produced as a 'gift' within Quattro razor sets and distributed nationally by German Schlecker chemist's shops. More of these models have probably been produced than all other German trolleybus models and toys put together!

Günthermann

The name Günthermann stands, especially in Germany, for high quality tin plate toys of a huge assortment of cars, trams, buses and also three types of trolleybuses. Siegfried Günthermann started his company in 1877 to manufacture and export tin toys from his base in Nürnberg, the centre of the toy industry. The brand was known as "ASGW" in the 1900s and "SG" in the Twenties, but the full Günthermann name is always used by collectors. During the peak years, between the wars, up to 65% of production was exported to the United States. Günthermann finished production in 1965, not only because there was no family successor, but also because the time was now over for relatively expensive German tin plate toys with sharp edges that were considered unsafe. The company was apparently bought by Siemens.

Mannheim (Zwickau 20), Daimler-Benz/BBC, 1930
(Daimler Benz)

2 axle single decker by Günthermann, 22cm, tinplate

S.G. Günthermann, Nuremberg, 1877 -1965

model maker	ref.	issued	total	size	construction	operator	fleet#	route	type
Günthermann	784?	1938		22cm	Tin plate				2 axle double decker, wire booms
Günthermann	785 10	1938		33cm	Tin plate				3 axle double decker, tinplate booms
Günthermann	785 10 E	1938		33cm	Tin plate				3 axle double decker, tinplate booms, electric lights
Günthermann	525	1950s		22cm	Tin plate				2 axle single decker, wire booms

2 axle single decker by Günthermann, 22cm, tinplate

We've discussed the three double decker trolleybuses, originally produced in the 30s in the British chapter, as that was their basis and market. In the 1950s Günthermann produced a tin plate single deck, centre entrance trolleybus, reflecting the rather smaller vehicles being introduced in Germany at the time. It is archetypically a toy. The clockwork propulsion accelerated and then braked automatically, and a passenger gets out and back in again and before starting again. This trolleybus toy is rarely seen and commands a price range of between €150 to €400. Embossed as being 'Made in US Zone Germany' which means the model was manufactured in the early 1950s, although strictly, the regulation only applied between 1946 and 1947 to toys for export. Quite what trolleybus this model is based on is anyone's guess, but it is very unusual as a toy trolleybus with a tinplate passenger who jumps on (and off). The front wheels are steerable in a more realistic way than pre-war Günthermanns, but there is no connection to the trolley booms and so no intention to have any toy overhead wiring. The paint work is very precise and arguably of a higher standard than the pre-war equivalents.

Stabil and Märklin

Stabil was originally founded in 1904 by Franz Walther of Berlin whose own design of construction kits were introduced in 1911. They were similar but incompatible with Meccano or Märklin and were made up until the 1950s.

For many people "Märklin" is a synonym for model railways. The company was founded in 1859 and launched its first clockwork tin plate railway at the Leipzig toy fair of 1881. Märklin distributed the British Meccano metal sheet construction kits, that had been invented in 1901 by Frank Hornby, and then started their own production in 1919, until phased out in 2000.

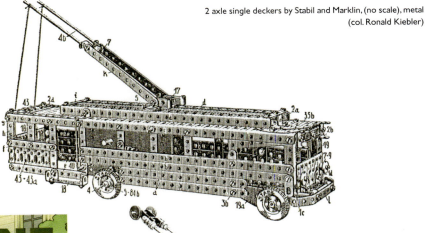

2 axle single deckers by Stabil and Marklin, (no scale), metal (col. Ronald Kiebler)

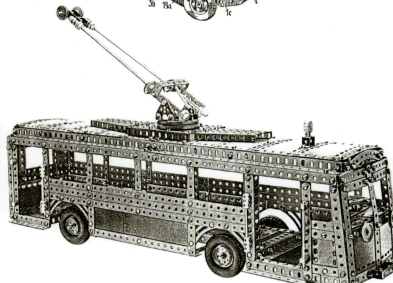

Mercedes Benz O-6000, 1937 (Daimler Benz)

Walther & Co., Berlin, 1904 -1991 (Stabil)
Gebr. Märklin & Cie. GmbH, Göppingen, 1891 to present day

model maker	ref.	issued	total	scale	construction	operator	fleet#	route	type
Stabil construction kit	350	1940			tin plate assembly				
Märklin construction kit	104-1	1949			tin plate assembly				Mercedes Benz O6000

Zwickau 8, MAN MPE1/Schumann/BBC 1938 (Freidrich Grunwald)

In 1940, Stabil illustrated an 'Obbus' (sic) that could be powered by their clockwork motor and would be 40cm long. It looks somewhat similar to the Mettmann trolleybus of 1930 that heralded the 'modern' era of trolleybuses in Germany, but has only 2 axles.

The 1949 "Märklin" construction kit catalogue showed a 2-axle trolleybus with joined booms that were sprung. The trolleybus design seems to be inspired by a Swiss original or perhaps the Mercedes Benz O6000 of 1937. It too would be impressively large, when built (see also Merkur on page 113).

Wiking-Modellbau GmbH, Lüdenscheid, 1939 to present day

model maker	ref.	issued	total	scale	construction	operator	fleet#	route	type
Wiking	Pre-series T7	1947		1:100	plastic	Zwickau	8,9		

One of the mysteries that won't go away (for us at least) is the persistent rumour of a model trolleybus made by the well known Wiking company. Up to now we haven't been able to find either an original or a photo of an original model, although we have found replica conversions of the popular streamline Wiking bus. This model bus was developed immediately after the WW2 in West Berlin where the remaining team of the Wiking company restarted with car, truck and bus models to a scale of 1:100. The Wiking owner Friedrich Pelzer lived at this time in Buer, in West Germany running a company making ship models. He wrote a letter in 1947 announcing his product portfolio and including photographs of a trolleybus with a single trolley boom. Wiking went on to became a leading model producer in Germany and still produces a huge array of models, but no further evidence of a trolleybus model has been found or is likely to be - toy producers seem rarely to preserve their company archives. Friedrich Pelzer died in 1981 leaving no further record, but a speculative reconstruction has been made.

Some people say that the Wiking streamline trolleybus has some similarities with Zwickau trolleybuses 8 and 9, which were built in 1938 using a MAN type MPE 1 chassis, a Schumann body and BBC electrical equipment. Zwickau, like Gera and Eberswalde, used the unsuccessful narrow gauge, single trolley pole system, designed by Brown Boveri in the 1940s, but later converted to standard, double poled, 600mm gauge overhead.

2 axle single decker by Wiking (conversion), 1:87, plastic

Penny Plastic Trolleybuses

Simple penny plastic toys were produced in large quantities, known in Germany as "Magarinemodelle" and have become rare collectable items – a red one, with CLEVER

2 axle single decker by Magarinemodelle, 9.5cm, polystyrene

STOLZ - MARGARINE UNION embossed on it, recently sold for €80. They were made around 1950 to 1960 and were typically packaged with margarine, coffee etc. While car and truck equivalents are frequently found at flea markets, it's not often you'll find a trolleybus.

The yellow, blue and red trolleybuses we know of are 95mm long with a one part plastic mould and 2 attached axles. It's always a challenge to try to identify the original inspiration for such trolleybus toys, but the Bielefeld trolleybuses 08-010 made in 1950 by Henschel (chassis) Wegmann (body) had a similar side window pattern to the blue and yellow examples shown here. They noticeably have only a single boom, something that wasn't unknown in Germany (see above), with the Eberswalde system, for example, using such devices up until 1945. A more likely reason, of course, is it's simpler to produce.

Wooden Trolleybuses

In the Erzgebirge area of Eastern Germany there is a long tradition of manufacturing wooden toys including a comprehensive range of miniature vehicles. For over 100 years, several specialised manufacturers and their families produced these relatively cheap toys at home. There are many well known cars, trucks, buses and some tramcars, but Erzgebirge-style trolleybuses seem to be exceptional. This trolleybus and trailer set was offered on ebay some time ago, but no further information is available. Seemingly inspired by Henschel/Schumann trolleybuses, they have doors on both sides, suitable for left and right hand traffic in typical toy making tradition.

Bielefeld 8, Henschel/Wegmann/SSW, 1949 (Werner Stock archiv)

2 axle single decker by Magarinemodelle, 9.5cm, polystyrene (Christopher Steimle)

2 axle single decker by Erzgebirge, 21cm, wood (unknown)

Rather like the dearth of real trolleybuses in Germany in the twenties, there was a dearth of miniature trolleybuses in the seventies as systems were abandoned – apart from the Eheim/Brawa models that miraculously continued production from 1950 until 2000.

By the eighties, resin models and kits were appearing, and the development of trolleybus design over the last 70 years can be traced through them. But their utility is as adjuncts to model railways and so are mainly in H0 gauge or 1:87 scale. We list them here in alphabetical order based on the chassis or lead producer.

Büssing 33F

model maker	ref.	issued	total	scale	construction	operator	fleet#	route	destination	built
Stettnitsch Modell	3030			1:87	resin	Berlin				1933
V&V Model Company	2481	2009		1:87	resin	Berlin	1001			1933
V&V Model Company	2480	2005		1:87	resin	Berlin				1933

Berlin Büssing 33F/Christoph+Unmack/AEG by Stettnitsch Modell, 1:87 resin

In 1933, a pioneer trolleybus line from Spandau to Staaken opened in Berlin. Trolleybuses 1001 – 1003 had a chassis from Büssing NAG, bodies made by Christoph & Unmack and were equipped with AEG electrical equipment. After WW2 the route was partly in the west and partly in the east, which meant, given the so-called "Cold War", that it was cut in half. In 1952 the western half of line A31 was converted to bus operation. Two trolleybuses were completely rebuilt with Henschel chassis and then used for the independently operated network in Steglitz, West Berlin. The Büssing NAG 33F type has been modelled, rather accurately by the Czech model manufacturer V&V (twice) and by Stettnitsch, who some years ago, produced a resin kit containing a body, a chassis and a plate including the seats, although side by side comparison shows disagreement over the window height dimensions and arrangement.

Berlin 1002, Büssing 33F/Christoph+Unmack/AEG, 1933, (werkphoto)

Berlin Büssing 33F/Christoph+Unmack/AEG by V&V Model Company, 1:87, resin

Büssing/Uerdingen/SSW

model maker	ref.	issued	total	scale	construction	operator	fleet#	route	destination	built
MMR Modelly	087 122DE01			1:87	resin	Leipzig	101-105			1938
MMR Modelly	087 122DE02			1:87	resin	Leipzig	101-105			1938

Leipzig had tried single boomed 1000v Schiemann trolleybuses in 1912, following a demonstration in 1907. They were Schiemann's final development but war intervened and only lasted until 1915. Twenty years later, just before the Second war, Leipzig was given permission to replace trams on the militarily expedient basis of trolleybuses needing less steel. In 1938 five Büssing/Uerdingen trolleybuses with SSW electrical equipment started service between Adler and Kochstrasse, as a demonstration provided by AEG. They lasted 28 years and usually pulled trailers. 104, used as a gazebo after retirement in 1967, has been

Leipzig Büssing/Uerdingen/SSW by MMR Modelly, 1:87, resin

preserved and is Germany's oldest surviving trolleybus. Czech model maker MMR Modelly of Ústí nad Labem has produced them in pre-war red and post war ivory liveries; a little mis-proportioned with an over-deep waistband.

Leipzig 101, Büssing/Uerdingen/SSW, 1938 (werkphoto)

Leipzig Büssing/Uerdingen/SSW by MMR Modelly, 1:87, resin

Büssing/Uerdingen/Kiepe UBIVs

model maker	ref.	issued	total	scale	construction	operator	fleet#	route	destination	built
MEK	607	2005		1:87	resin	Bonn				1957

Bonn Büssing/Uerdingen/Kiepe UBIVs by MEK, 1:87, resin (Andreas Zietemann)

Many German trolleybuses were adaptations of buses, such as the seven Büssing/Uerdingen/Kiepe UBIVs supplied to Bonn in 1957, based on the Büssing/Uerdingen 6500T, essentially Büssing axle and engine assemblies supporting Uerdingen bodies. Likewise, the large number of model buses that have been available in Germany are readily converted by such ardent trolleybus modellers as Andreas Zeitemann, a trolleybus driver in Eberswalde. MEK Modelle, of Mainz, used to make a suitable resin kit of the 6500T, making adding booms merely an extra part of the build.

Esslingen 31, Büssing/Uerdingen/Kiepe UBIVs, 1957 (W van der Plaats)

Henschel Gr.II/Kässbohrer

model maker	ref.	issued	total	scale	construction	operator	fleet#	route	destination	built
V&V Model Company	2511			1:87	resin	Neunkirchen	16			1947
V&V Model Company	2512			1:87	resin	Bochum	4			1947
V&V Model Company	2513			1:87	resin	Darmstadt	224			1947
V&V Model Company	2514			1:87	resin	Hannover	906			1947
V&V Model Company	2515			1:87	resin	Essen	21			1948

Henschel-Werke had been a locomotive builder before also moving into commercial vehicles in 1925. Their first trolleybuses were 1301-3, six wheelers for Berlin delivered in 1941 and they went on, over the next twenty years, to become the biggest supplier of trolleybus chassis and axles in Germany.

The Normgröße II - German trolleybus standard size II - was developed in 1940 and produced later on during WW2 as the KEO II design. This chassis size has a typical wheelbase of 5m and was equipped with bodies from various manufacturers. 518 trolleybuses were produced in West Germany by using a similar Henschel II chassis and a Kässbohrer body.

Hannover 908 and 90., Henschel Gr.II/Kässbohrer/BBC, 1947 (Deusche Fotothek)

Bochum Henschel Gr.II/Kässbohrer by V&V Model Company, 1:87, resin

Frantischek Vecarnik (V&V) has modelled the Henschel/Kässbohrer Gr.II in their various liveries. Bochum, located in the Ruhr area, received four trolleybuses 1 – 4 equipped with BBC electric equipment to start their trolleybus line in 1947. It was extended in 1950 to a length of 9 km. but closed in 1959 and the trolleybuses were sold to Neuwied.

Essen 21, Henschel Gr.II/Kässbohrer by V&V Model Company, 1:87, resin (V&V)

Essen, also in the Ruhr, operated a relatively short trolleybus line (40) with a gradient of up to 7.3% which replaced a former bus line. The three trolleybuses 21 – 23 served from 1949 to 1957 and were then sold to Osnabrück where they were completely rebuilt as 1½ deck trolleybuses.

Darmstadt Henschel Gr.II/Kässbohrer by V&V Model Company, 1:87, resin

Darmstadt, close to Frankfurt am Main, had two entirely separate trolleybus lines. Henschel / Kässbohrer trolleybuses 221 – 224, equipped with SSW electrics, were used only on line P. Eberstadt – Pfungstadt, until 1963 when the operation finished.

Hannover 906, Henschel Gr.II/Kässbohrer by V&V Model Company, 1:87, resin (V&V)

Hannover ran trolleybuses from 1937 until bombed, and then reopened in 1947 with six new Henschel/Kässbohrer trolleybuses. 904-906 had SSW electrics while 907 – 909 had BBC electrical equipment. The service finished in 1958 and trolleybuses 907 – 909 were sold to Osnabrück to be completely rebuilt as 1½ deck trolleybuses.

Neunkirchen in the Saarland, replaced a single track 7 km tramway in 1957 with trolleybus line 4 and extended the route a further 2km. In 1958 five second hand Henschel/Kässbohrer trolleybuses with BBC electrics and Italian CGE traction motors were acquired from Bremerhaven (51-55) and numbered 12-16. The trolleybus service was closed and all trolleybuses scrapped in 1964.

Neunkirchen 16, Henschel Gr.II/Kässbohrer by V&V Model Company, 1:87, resin (V&V)

Darmstadt Henschel Gr.II/Kässbohrer by V&V Model Company, 1:87, resin (V&V)

V&V, in a recent re-run of these models, has added rear facing roof mounted spot lights and a re-worked trolley base that matches the roof rather than as a separate, black sub-structure used previously. Despite manufacturers often having to be cajoled into producing them, usually in small numbers, the trolleybus has steadfastly survived in three towns in Germany, at Solingen, Esslingen and Eberswalde, 130 years after its invention in Berlin. his makes for a more accurate representation of, say, the Hannover trolleys, although they had their spotlights fitted to the booms. Kiel, Bremerhaven and Wilhelmshaven also had identical Henschels which V&V could also issue. They also produce the Henschel as a kit.

Henschel Gr.II/Schumann

model maker	ref.	issued	total	scale	construction	operator	fleet#	route	destination	built
(unknown)		1949		1:43	wood	Dresden	151-63			1947-9
RA Model Petr Dosly				1:87	resin	Dresden	151-63			1947-9
V&V Model Company	2431			1:87	resin	Dresden	151-63			1947-9
V&V Model Company	2432			1:87	resin	Leipzig	115-9			1944
V&V Model Company	2430			1:87	resin	Dresden	151-63			1947-9

Leipzig 119, Henschel Gr.II/Schumann, 1948 (Wolfgang Schreiner)

Dresden Henschel Gr.II/Schumann by V&V Model Company, 1:87, resin

Dresden started a second generation of trolleybus operation with Schumann bodied Henschels in 1947 with a line from Löbtau to Weißig that lasted until 1975. The chassis had been built in 1944 with existing Italian Ansaldo electrical equipment that was later exchanged for indigenously produced equipment by LEW. The trolleybuses were in use until 1969.

Presented at a public Christmas show in 1947 on an extensive snow covered model railway layout at the Louisenhof Hotel, Dresden, was a wooden O scale model trolleybus that is a good representation of the Henschel Gr.II with Schumann bodies that were running in service nearby. Forty years later local devotee Mattis Schindler bought the model from the then 75 year old hotel owner Hans-Otto Voight. It's not known who actually built the model or if it still runs, but power collection was from the overhead and steering was via guides about a roadway rail to the (correctly) double tyred front wheels.

The Czech model manufacturer V&V has modelled the subtly different Schumann model. Earlier versions include "KWU" (Kommunales Wirtschaftsunternehmen) above the logo on the side panels and a version from Leipzig. RA Dosly, also of the Czech Republic, has modelled this trolleybus, with the somewhat cruder booms than he now uses for his models (This model may have been produced by V/R, the owner is not sure!).

Henschel II chassis were also used for Vienna's trolleybuses of 1944 – see page 76.

Dresden Henschel Gr.II/Schumann by Hans-Otto Voight, 1:43, wood   (c/o Mattis Schindler)

Dresden Henschel Gr.II/Schumann by Hans-Otto Voight, 1:43, wood

Leipzig Henschel Gr.II/Schumann by V&V Model Company, 1:87, resin

Dresden Henschel Gr.II/Schumann by RA Model Petr Dosly, 1:87, resin   (Andreas Zietemann)

Henschel II(Krupp)/Uerdingen/AEG

model maker	ref.	issued	total	scale	construction	operator	fleet#	route	destination	built
PM Modellbau				1:87	resin	Mettmann Rheinbahn				1930

After the gap in the Twenties, the second trolleybus generation of Germany began in 1930 with a route from Mettmenn to Gruiten near Düsseldorf. The original trolleybuses had a 3 axle Krupp chassis, Waggonfabrik Uerdingen bodies and AEG electrical equipment. They were completely rebuilt around 1950 by using a new Henschel II chassis and a lengthened body that

Mettmann Rheinbahn Henschel II / Ueringen/AEG by PM Modellbau, 1:87, resin

added one window, but service finished two years later.

PM Modellbau, aka. the late Peter Möller, modelled the 2 axle version and said his vision was to produce a selection of trolleybus models based on rarer prototypes – perhaps he planned to produce the original 3 axle Krupp version or even, what came next.

Incredibly, having been re-chassised, these trolleybuses went on to be re-bodied. Osnabrück bought the two chassis in 1957 to build one new 1½ deck trolleybus with a Ludewig body (209) and an extra axle.

Collector Andreas Zeitmann has converted a Brekina Mercedes Benz O317 bus model to represent these uniquely German trolleybuses, one of which, from Aachen, is preserved at Sandtoft Trolleybus Museum.

Mettmann Rheinbahn Krupp/Ueringen/AEG, 1930   (GH Kohler)

Mettmann Rheinbahn Henschel II/Ueringen/AEG, 1950   (Hans-Reinhard Ehlers)

Osnabrück 209, Henschel/Ludewig/BBC, 1957   (Werner Stock arckiv)

Wuppertal Krupp/Ludewig by Brekina (converted), 1:87, resin   (Andreas Zietemann)

Henschel III/NWF

model maker	ref.	issued	total	scale	construction	operator	fleet#	route	destination	built
V&V Model Company	3431			1:87	resin	Hamburg	331-335			1952
V&V Model Company	3441			1:87	resin	Erfurt	12-16			1957

Hamburg Henschel III/NWF by V&V Model Company, 1:87, resin

Hamburg 331, Henschel III/NWF/AEG, 1952, advert.   (AEG)

In 1943 the Hamburger Hochbahn, HHA, purchased twelve 3-axle chassis, without bodies. Two were damaged in the war, five were later sold to Hildesheim and the remaining five chassis were equipped in 1953 with type 562 DD double deck bodies made by the NWF Nordwestdeutsche Fahrzeugbau GmbH with electrical equipment from AEG. These double deck trolleybuses had a roof height of 4.45m and special dispensation to exceed the German standard maximum height of 4m. But, with a change of local political control, and despite much expense and publicity, they were withdrawn only three years later. The Hamburg system closed prematurely in 1958.

The GDR Erfurt operator purchased all five Hamburg double deck trolleybuses via a dealer in 1957 (an unusual East/West trade) and converted them to single deck by removing the upper section and utilising the roof. Some of the upper deck seats were used in tramcars. In this third incarnation they lasted in service until 1961 to 1965.

V&V has modelled both versions of these trolleybuses; converting their double decker to single deck was doubtless a lot easier than rebuilding the real thing! They accurately mirror the rather subtle front end.

Erfurt 13, Henschel III/NWF/AEG, 1957 (Klaus Reichenbach)

Erfurt Henschel III/NWF by V&V Model Company, 1:87, resin

Henschel HS56

model maker	ref.	issued	total	scale	construction	operator	fleet#	route	destination	built
Stettnitsch Modell				1:87	resin	Berlin	484			1956
Stettnitsch Modell				1:87	resin	Berlin	488			1957

Berlin Henschel HS56/Gaubschat by Stettnitsch Modell, 1:87, resin

Berlin 488, Henschel HS56/Gaubschat/AEG, 1956 (Mattis Schindler)

Henschel used Gaubschat bodies and AEG equipment for a batch of 7 trolleybuses for Berlin in 1956-7. One, 488 is preserved in Eberswalde in pristine running order. Some time ago Stettnitsch Modell made the model, albeit with rather unconvincing booms. Collectors like Andeas Zeitemann and Mattis Schindler have replaced them with sprung alternatives, such as Fröwis tram trolley gear.

Henschel/Uerdingen ÜH IIIs

model maker	ref.	issued	total	scale	construction	operator	fleet#	route	destination	built
V/R				1:87	resin	Solingen				1952
Grell	7000333B	2004		1:87	plastic	Solingen	59	E2	Wald-Kirche	1959
Grell				1:87	plastic	Hartmannsdorfer Braugut				1959
Grell (repainted)				1:87	plastic	Rheydt	6		Wanlo	1959
Grell/Faller	130941	2006		1:87	plastic	Solingen	3			1959
Grell/Faller	130970	2006		1:87	plastic	Solingen	59			1959
Grell/Fleischmann		2006		1:87	plastic	Solingen	57-60			1959
Grell/Kiepe		2006		1:87	plastic	Solingen	59	E2	Wald-Kirche	1959
Grell/Roco	66485	2007		1:87	plastic	Salzburg	131		Bahrhof-Stadtmitte-Friedhof	1959
Grell/Roco	66034	2009		1:87	plastic	Moers				1960
Grell/Wilkinson	7004333L	2004		1:87	plastic	Solingen	1,3	E2	Wald-Ohlig	1959
Grell/Wilkinson	7004333T	2004		1:87	plastic	Solingen	1,3	E1	Bülowplatz	1959
MEK	635	2005		1:87	resin	Salzburg				1956,61
MEK	635	2005		1:87	resin	Aachen				1959
PM Modellbau				1:87	resin	Salzburg				1956
PS Models				1:43	resin	Aachen, Rheydt		51	Baeweiller	1959
Grell/TrainPCB				1:87	plastic/metal	Solingen	59		Schlagbaum	1959

Salzburg 123, Henschel/Uerdingen ÜH IIIs, 1959 (J Ward)

The ÜH IIIs trolleybus was a very successful German design made by Waggonfabrik Uerdingen using Henschel running gear. The self-supporting body had 3 doors with a central door, either single entrance (10,9m length) or double entrance (11,2m). The abbreviation stands for: Ü – Uerdingen, H – Henschel, III – German standard size for 11 to 12 m long trolleybuses and s – selbstragend (self-supporting). AEG, BBC, Kiepe and SSW (Siemens) provided the electrical equipment for the various batches. One of the first ÜH IIIs had a Volkswagen petrol engine driving a generator to be able to operate short distances at low speed. For instance, in Solingen, by using the auxiliary power unit, the depot had no need of overhead for all its parking places.

The first ÜH IIIs, a batch of 62, were delivered to Solingen between 1952 and 1959. 210 were built in total over a seven year period, and 53 were exported (50 to São Paulo and 3 to Salzburg). They were used by 25 West German operators. 7 are preserved, including 3 in the UK, (Solingen 1, Baden-Baden 224, Esslingen 14, 2 in Germany (Solingen 59 Obus-Museum Solingen, Kaiserslautern 1 1 Hannoversches Straßenbahn-Museum) and one in Austria that operates in service as a Museum Obus (Salzburg 123 ex-Soligen 40).

With so many ÜH IIIs, it's hardly surprising there have been many models, not least those made in plastic in China by Grell for something of an advertising blitz by a number of companies and model distributors. However, most are related to Wilkinson Sword which has a factory in Solingen.

ÜH III S Single middle entrance versions

Wilkinson started in 2006 to distribute exclusively the double door version with a trailer in a special gift box which included a Quattro Titanium razor and spare blades. The single door version followed in 2007, with a depiction of no.3 and Löhmer's Kaffee advertising, or no.1 and Solinger Tageblatt on the side..

Grell produced 50,000 of the two versions and although Wilkinson had wanted them all to reflect Solingen, many other, so called 'unofficial' versions, have been produced. For example, in September 2007, Karstadt, the locally well known German department store, started distributing a neutral version numbered 8 with a trailer.

Solingen 3, Henschel/Uerdingen ÜH IIIs by Grell/Faller, 1:87, plastic

Solingen 59 by Grell, 1:87, plastic

Solingen 3 by Grell, 1:87, plastic

Solingen 59 by Grell/Faller, 1:87, plastic   (Andras Ekkert)

Solingen 60 by Grell/Fleischmann, 1:87, plastic

Moers 104 by Grell/Roco, 1:87, plastic

Salzburg 131 by Grell/Roco, 1:87, plastic

ÜH III S double middle entrance versions

Schlecker drugstores distributed the double door version of the ÜH IIIs that had been delivered to Solingen between 1955 and 1958. It was described as "gratis" on the Quattro Titanium razor blister pack. The bath bag version includes details of the restoration of 59. (Solingen 1 is also preserved in the UK).

Faller, the German manufacturer of miniature building kits and model railway parts, launched a bus depot kit including a Solingen ÜH IIIs model trolleybus, priced at €39.95.

At the Nürnberg toy fair 2006, Fleischmann launched a 3 car set of 4-axle railway flat wagons type SSK 07 loaded with ÜH IIIs trolleybuses numbered 57, 58 and 60. The price for the single loaded cars was €29,95 and for the three car set, €84,95.

Roco launched a 2-axle railway flat wagon model in 2007, loaded with a cream and red Salzburg ÜH IIIs numbered 131 (later renumbered 121 – 123). Solingen's 40 has been repainted to this livery and now occasionally runs as museum trolleybus 123 in Salzburg). In 2009, Roco produced a version with a trailer, in Moers blue livery which finally included more realistic black booms.

The Sächsisches Nutzfahrzeugmuseum, Hartmannsdorf, close to Chemnitz, offers a blister pack of a plain cream trolleybus and trailer model with a "Harmanndorfer Braugut" advertisement but with no further indication of a real operator. And Kiepe, the manufacturer of electrical equipment for trolleybuses, had some Grell models imprinted with their logo as free give-aways at exhibitions.

Train PCB in Holland produces a motorised version of the Wilkinson Sword model which is distributed by Eichner & Stahlhaus, Solingen, more details are on page 74.

Hartmannsdorfer Braugut Henschel/Uerdingen ÜH IIIs by Grell, 1:87, plastic

Solingen 59 by Grell/Kiepe, 1:87, plastic

Aachen Henschel/Uerdingen ÜH IIIs by MEK, 1:87, resin

Salzburg Henschel/Uerdingen ÜH IIIs by PM Modellbau, 1:87, resin

Salzburg Henschel/Uerdingen ÜH IIIs by MEK, 1:87, resin

Margit Ebling, as MEK Modelle, used to produce a ÜH IIIs trolleybus as a resin kit. She produced the single central door ÜH IIIs model in Aachen's livery, but, the version produced in Salzburg colours should have a double door entrance.

A particularly fine model of the ubiquitous ÜH IIIs was made by PM Modell and has the same single door problem, but demonstrates the added quality possible in a resin model, even at 1:87 scale. The differences with the MEK casting are subtle, and differ mostly with the depth of the windows.

Larger, at 1:43, is the PS Model, which models the Aachen or Rheydt ÜH IIIs, legitimately with the single width door, but with a flatter front than the original.

Aachen, Rheydt Henschel/Uerdingen ÜH IIIs by PS Models, 1:43, resin

Esslingen 22, Henschel HS160 OSL, 1960 (Ian Hill)

Esslingen Henschel HS160 OSL by HB Model, 1:87, resin

Solingen 69, Henschel HS160 OSL by HB (conversion), 1:87, resin (Andras Ekkert)

Henschel HS160 OSL

model maker	ref.	issued	total	scale	construction	operator	fleet#	route	destination	built
HB Model		2009		1:87	resin	Solingen				1958
HB Model		2010		1:87	resin	Fribourg	64-69			1960
HB Model		2010		1:87	resin	Giessen	19-22			1961
HB Model		2011		1:87	resin	Esslingen	16-23			1960
HB (conversion)				1:87	resin	Solingen	69	E1	Schlagbaum	1960
Hammer (conversion)				1:87	resin	Esslingen	16-22		Smarckstrasse	1960

Fribourg Henschel HS160 OSL by HB Model, 1:87, resin

Henschel, apart from supplying running gear for the ÜH IIIs trolleybuses, built the HS160 OSL series between 1959 and 1963. Of aluminium chassisless construction, 35 singles and 31 artics were built for 14 operators – only Solingen had both types. Collectors adapted Hammer bus models until HB Model started producing many livery variations, especially during 2010, with more possibilities to follow. Solingen devotee Andras Ekkert has typically added detail; something that is increasingly expected by collectors in the UK.

Giessen Henschel HS160 OSL by HB Models, 1:87, resin

Solingen Henschel HS160 OSL by HB Model, 1:87, resin

Henschel HS160 OSL-G

model maker	ref.	issued	total	scale	construction	operator	fleet#	route	destination	built
Brawa	6105	1985		1:87	plastic, metal	Kaiserslautern	5	1	Vogelweh	1961
Brawa (repaint)	6104B	1967		1:87	plastic, metal	Salzburg	127	11	Bahnhof	1961
HB Model		2010		1:87	resin	Trier	26-31			1961
HB Model		2010		1:87	resin	Aachen	27-30			1961
HB Model		2010		1:87	resin	Kaiserslauten	115			1961
HB Model		2010		1:87	resin	Salzburg	124-128			1961
Hammer (conversion)				1:87	plastic	Solingen	73	E1	Bülowplatz	1962

Trier 28, Henschel HS160 OSL-G, 1961   (Berthold Werner)

Salzburg 127, Henschel HS160 OSL by Brawa (repaint), 1:87, plastic, metal

Kaiserlauten Henschel HS160 OSL by Brawa, 1:87, plastic, metal

The articulated version, the Henschel HS160 OSL-G is usually identified as the inspiration for the Eheim/Brawa articulated model (see page 66) and we can't resist putting the Kaiserslautern version next to the recent HB Model. There's windscreen wipers, commendable glazing detail and proper proportion, but none of the graphic details that appear on the 1985 Brawa version. So far, the HS160 OSL-G has appeared in Trier, Aachen and Salzburg liveries with a Solingen version due that will look like the Andras Ekkert conversion. .

Salzburg Henschel HS160 OSL-G by HB Model, 1:87, resin (Mattis Schindler)

Kaiserlauten Henschel HS160 OSL-G by HB Model, 1:87, resin

Aachen Henschel HS160 OSL-G by HB Model, 1:87, resin (Mattis Schindler)

Trier Henschel HS160 OSL-G by HB Model, 1:87, resin (Mattis Schindler)

Solingen 73, Henschel HS160 OSL-G by Hammer (conversion), 1:87, plastic   (Andras Ekkert)

Krauss-Maffei KME-130

model maker	ref.	issued	total	scale	construction	operator	fleet#	route	destination	built
V&V Model Company	2501			1:87	resin	München	9			1948
Europa		1950		1:76	plastic, metal	München				1948

München opened the first section of what was to become a 9.5km long trolleybus line in 1948 and purchased 15 locally produced trolleybuses. The type KME 130 chassis were made by Krauss Maffei and supported a central entrance body made by Rathgeber. SSW and BBC provided the electrical equipment which was re-used in the replacement vehicles, with Krauss Maffei KME 160 chassis in 1964.

München 15, Krauss-Maffei KME-130, 1948   (Ludger Kenning)

München 9, Krauss-Maffei KME-130 by V&V Model Company, 1:87, resin

V&V's model has varied in detail over the 2 editions produced by the company, with the front emblem changing style, to become more realistic on the latest attempt. Interesting to see a modeller's changing perception in action over time.

Some have argued that the Krauss Maffei KME 130 served as inspiration for the electrically powered trolleybus model from Europabahn, the precursor of Fischer, later Eheim, mainly because of the central door pattern - see page 61.

München 9, Krauss-Maffei KME-130 by V&V Model Company, 1:87, resin (V&V)

München Krauss-Maffei by Europa, 1:76, plastic, metal

TSIII

model maker	ref.	issued	total	scale	construction	operator	fleet#	route	destination	built
FMB-Unicorn	183	2006		1:87	plastic	Solingen	60	684	Hasselstrasse	1968-74
Stadtwerke Solingen		1988		1:87	card	Solingen	80	683	Graf-Wilhelm-Platz	1968-74

In 1968 – 1974 the Solingen operator put 80 new trolleybuses into service to replace their Henschel Uerdingen ÜH IIIs and HS160 OSL trolleys. The 3-axle chassis with two powered rear axles were needed as one route, the 683, uses a turntable at the Burg Brücke terminus and articulated vehicles wouldn't fit. They were also designed to be able to climb the steep hills in Solingen in sometimes severe weather conditions. Stadtwerke Solingen designed the machines and used traction equipment from earlier trolleybuses. The third series were called TS III (Trolleybus Solingen) and numbered as 46 – 80 (also known as TS3). Body maker Ludewig used the standard 3-axle Krupp truck chassis type LF 380 and completely rebuilt it to achieve a low floor entrance section of around 230mm above street level and uniquely low for the period. After nearly twenty years of operation, the TS trolleybuses were sold to Mendoza (Argentina) in 1988, where some have served another 20 years and some have now achieved over 40 years of passenger carrying.

The rugged, but essentially 'homemade' 6 wheelers served their operator well, so much so that Stadtwerke Solingen produced a card model to celebrate their 20th anniversary, just before they were exported to Argentina.

Solingen TSIII by Stadtwerke Solingen, 1:87, card

5.10 Germany

FmB-Unicorn of nearby Bergneustadt manufactures and distributes a great many car, truck and bus resin cast models including the TS III trolleybus kit which accurately portrays the unique Solingen design. The unpainted kit comes with a one piece body, the chassis, the floor with seats and model trolley boom parts. The kit cost €45. Like many a kit, it benefits from additional work, such as adding wing mirrors and, as in Andras Ekkert's rendering, fitting better booms than those supplied.

Soligen 26, TSIII, 1968-74 (Ian Hill)

Solingen TSIII by FMB-Unicorn, 1:87, plastic

LOWA W600

model maker	ref.	issued	total	scale	construction	operator	fleet#	route	destination	built
MMR Modelly	087 115DE03			1:87	resin	Erberswalde				1951
MMR Modelly	087 115DE02			1:87	resin	Magdeburg				1951
MMR Modelly	087 115DE01/5			1:87	resin	Erfurt				1950

In East Germany, LOWA (Lokomotiv Waggonbau), the state conglomerate that included the Schumann factory in Werdau (VEB Ernst Grube), displayed their first trolleybus at the Leipzig fair of 1951. The prototype W600, went to Erfurt and six more were built; three for Eberswalde and three for Magdeburg. These were testing times with fuel shortages causing towns to re-examine their trolleybus plans of the 30s and implement them. But the GDR had no ability to produce traction equipment and had to buy, for hard currency, from AEG or Siemens in West Germany or reuse BBC equipment. Miroslav Grisa of MMR Modelly has produced versions of all W600s as supplied to three operators, including both liveries that the prototype appeared in at Erfurt until retired in 1966.

Magdeburg 51, LOWA W600 Wedau, 1951 (Hans Jochim Schönitz)

Erfurt W600 Wedau by MMR Modelly, 1:87, resin

Erbswalde W600 Wedau by MMR Modelly, 1:87, resin

LOWA W601

model maker	ref.	issued	total	scale	construction	operator	fleet#	route	destination	built
MMR Modelly	087 116DE01/5			1:87	resin	Erfurt				1951
MMR Modelly	087 116DE02			1:87	resin	Berlin				1951
MMR Modelly	087 116DE03			1:87	resin	Potsdam				1951
MMR Modelly	087 116PL04			1:87	resin	Dresden				1951
MMR Modelly	087 116DE06			1:87	resin	Warszawa				1951

Berlin 1501, LOWA W601/Werdau/AEG, 1951 (col. Ludger Kenning)

The one bay longer W601 was externally very similar to the W600. Eleven were built, with electrical equipment imported from AEG, using 2×45.5kW motors. Erfurt, Eberwalde and Potsdam had 2 each and Berlin had 5. Warsaw had 30 'improved' W601s (or W602) with equipment by LEW, the by now nationalized AEG factory, and 2×60kW motors. The intention had been to use a single 90kW motor but these were not then available.

Miroslav Grisa of MMR lists Dresden, which received the type second-hand from Potsdam but not Eberswalce, otherwise he has again produced all variants, including the two liveries of Erfurt. His model of the Warszawa LOWAs has lower body panels that are a little disproportionately low, even when taking the over-thick waistband into account or perhaps it's that the wheels are too big.

Dresden W601 by MMR Modelly, 1:87, resin

Berlin W601 by MMR Modelly, 1:87, resin

Warszawa 55, LOWA W602, 1951
(Narodowe Archiwum Cyfrowe)

Potsdam W601 by MMR Modelly, 1:87, resin

Warszawa W602 by MMR Modelly, 1:87, resin

LOWA W602a

model maker	ref.	issued	total	scale	construction	operator	fleet#	route	destination	built
Axel Dopperphul			1	1:25	plasticard, metal	Dresden				1951-5
HB Model				1:87	Resin	Berlin				1952
HB Model				1:87	resin	Leipzig				1954
Kehi Modellbay	574			1:87	whitemetal	Eberswalde				1956
Krementschug				1:43	resin	Berlin BVG				1954
RA Model Petr Dosly	1200BVG	2000		1:87	resin	Dresden				1952
RA Model Petr Dosly	1200 XC	2000		1:87	resin	Generic				1952
V/R	289			1:87	resin	Zwickau				1956
V/R	292			1:87	resin	Eberswalde				1956
V/R	291			1:87	resin	Dresden				1956
VEB Dresdner Blech und Spielwarenfabrik	1955			1:87	plastic	Dresden				

The LOWA W602a design, used by all trolleybus systems in the GDR, was a development of the W602 which had been produced for Poland only. The wheelbase was lengthened to 5.74m and equipped with LEW electrical equipment and 2x60kW motors. This was the production version of the GDR's standard trolleybus and 123 were produced from 1952 to 1956, initially with no front decoration and then with chrome lining when production moved to Ammendorf, the former Lindner coachbuilders plant.

Greiz 9003, LOWA W602a, 1952 (S Hilkenbach)

Eberswalde W602a by Kehi Modellbay, 1:87, whitemetal

KEHI Modellbau produced a trolleybus model some years ago which was offered as white metal kit or as a ready built and painted model. Unfortunately it is much too short and has a front bonnet – probably because KEHI used the shorter IFA H6 B/L bus model as a basis for the trolleybus.

The Czech manufacturers HB Model and RA Model and Ukrainian modeller V/R have all produced models of the LOWA 602a, although it is a little difficult to tell them apart. The V/R and HB models are very similar but vary in the wheels fitted and the strength of the ribbing around the front lights. They have released Zwickau, Berlin, Leipzig and Eberswalde liveried versions. V/R's Dresden 602a has to be of the second batch, 166-173, built in 1955-6 at Ammendorf. RA's model is of the Werdau produced 602a with no front chrome bars, and so can be identified as Dresden 164 of 1953. Similar variants, plain or with chromed strips, from Werdau or Ammendorf respectively, were supplied to all East German systems in the early to mid-50s.

Zwickau Lowa W602a by V/R, 1:87, resin (Andreas Zietemann)

Eberswalde W602a by V/R, 1:87, resin (Andreas Zietemann)

Zwickau W602a by V/R, 1:87, resin (Andreas Zietemann)

Leipzig W602a by HB Model, 1:87, resin

Berlin W602a by HB Model, 1:87, Resin

Dresden W602a by RA Model Petr Dosly, 1:87, resin

Kremenchug has produced a 1:43 model of the Ammendorf version with the adornment of chromed bars at the front. Like many of these models, it came with a trailer, an IFA W701 type. Unfortunately the improvement in scale hasn't produced an any more accurate model, perhaps the blueprints are no longer available, but the windscreens are decidedly misleading without chrome edging.

Axel Dopperphul made a model of the 602a for the Dresden Verkehrsmuseum, without the curved side chrome strips or the more usual cascading pattern of the 'grille'. Perhaps it is Leipzig 135, the only 602a we know of to run in this condition. And there was, intriguingly, a motorized 602a that appeared in the GDR in 1955 (more on page 70). The LOWA trolleybus was usurped by the Škoda 8Tr and Comecon centralised planning, but it is one of those trolleybus icons that are fondly remembered.

Berlin W602a by Kremenschug, 1:43, resin

Dresden W602a by Axel Dopperphul, 1:25, plasticard, metal

IFA ES6

model maker	ref.	issued	total	scale	construction	operator	fleet#	route	destination	built
Beka (conversion)				1:87	resin	Berlin BVG	2001			1955
HB Model		2005		1:87	resin	Berlin BVG	2001			1955
PM Modellbau		2000		1:87	resin	Berlin BVG	2001			1955

A very unusual design of a tractor and double deck semi-trailer trolleybus was developed in East Germany for East Berlin. There was only one trolleybus prototype, built in 1955 and launched as the DoSa. Built by VEB Ernst Grube, Werdau with the tractor section based on a IFA H6 chassis equipped with LEW Henningsdorf electrical equipment. The trolleybus gained chrome strips at the front but these haven't yet been incorporated into model versions. It served until 1966/7, when the front end was converted to diesel breakdown lorry and the trailer was converted to carry horses. There were plans to build a fleet of 100 but because of the COMECON co-operation agreement, which insisted on monopolies, East Germany cancelled all further development of trolleybuses and, from 1956 onwards, committed to buy only Škoda trolleybuses from Czechoslovakia SSR. (Other Soviet bloc countries continued local trolleybus production).

Berlin 2001, IFA ES6 DoSa, 1955 (werkphoto)

Berlin 2001, IFA ES6 DoSa by PM Modellbau, 1:87, resin

Berlin 2001, IFA ES6 DoSa by HB Model, 1:87, resin

Berlin 2001, IFA ES6 Dobus by Beka (conversion), 1:87, resin   (Andreas Zietemann)

PM Modellbau of Frankfurt, used to make trolleybus models when its founder, the late Peter Möller, was the first to commercially model the imposing IFA ES6 DoSa as a kit.

Some years later the Czech model manufacturer HB selected the same original to manufacture a very fine ready built and painted resin cast model. When the model was still available, the price was around ☐80 EUR. It sold out quickly. Andreas Zeitemann couldn't resist converting Beka and SES models of the LOWA 602a (see above), on which the front tractor unit was based, into an ES6, including the huge trolley base

5.10 Germany

MAN 36

model maker	ref.	issued	total	scale	construction	operator	fleet#	route	destination	built
Eheim (conversion)				1:87	brass	Berlin	1104	32	Steglitz	1934

Berlin BVG MAN 36/ MAN/Siemens by Eheim (conversion), 1:87, brass

MAN (or Maschinenfabrik Augsburg Nürnberg AG as once known) has been Germany's second most prolific trolleybus producer, making its first in 1935 for Berlin. One of the 1101-4 batch has been modelled in brass and powered by Eheim mechanical parts, although we don't know who built it — more on page 70.

Berlin 1102, MAN 36/MAN/Siemens, 1934   (Siemens Archiv)

MAN MPE1

model maker	ref.	issued	total	scale	construction	operator	fleet#	route	destination	built
MMR Modelly	087 101AT01/2	2005		1:87	resin	Salzburg	106		Obergalel	1940
MMR Modelly	087 101DE01/5			1:87	resin	Eberswalde	40452			1940
MMR Modelly				1:87	resin	Eberswalde	40452			1940
MMR Modelly	087 101AT04			1:87	resin	Graz				1940

Despite their use in the capital, German operators perceived the trolleybus as a mode for small to medium sized towns, requiring 2 axle 9-11m vehicles. In 1939 MAN produced the MPE type trolleybus with MAN bodies and BBC equipment for Trier. The more rounded MPE1 followed in 1940 and was supplied to Eberswalde, Oldenburg and Salzburg, followed by the MPEII, again for Salzburg. The identical MPE4500 was built in 1943 for Augsburg, Gorzów and Esslingen with either Schumann or Kässbohrer bodies.

MMR Modelly has made five versions of the fairly similar wartime MAN types including two

Eberswalde MAN MPE1/Schumann/ BBC by MMR Modelly, 1:87, resin

versions of liveries and collector gear used in Eberswalde and door variants for Salzburg.

Some MAN MPE I trolleybuses went to Bratislava in 1941, fitted with Siemens equipment and local Sodomka bodies and inspired the Austrian Minobus powered models of 1948 (see page 56).

Eberswalde MAN MPE1/Schumann/BBC by MMR Modelly, 1:87, resin

Salzburg MAN MPE1/Schumann/BBC by MMR Modelly, 1:87, resin

Salzburg 108, MAN MPE1/Schumann/BBC, 1940 (Peter Wagner)

Vienna MAN MPE 1 by Minobus, 25cm, wood, metal

MAN MKE2

model maker	ref.	issued	total	scale	construction	operator	fleet#	route	destination	built
MBM by PS Model				1:43	resin	Trier			Sonderfahrt	1951

During the 50s MAN produced the MKE types including the MKE3 with shapely Kässbohrer bodies for Trier, Augsburg and Heilbronn amongst others. MBM, made by PS Model (Pereinos), produced fine 1:43 scale models in 2007 in cream and cream and green liveries. The prototype bodies are tricky to reproduce in miniature so that they don't look exaggerated - rather like painting a portrait that achieves a true likeness.

Nürnberg 657, a not dissimilar MKE with a MAN body is preserved at the Museum für Industriekultur und Verkehr, Nürnberg, where MAN was based.

Nürnberg 650, MAN MKE/MAN, 1948 (MAN)

Trier MAN MKE2/Kässbohrer by MBM by PS Model, 1:43, resin

Nürnberg MAN MKE2/Kässbohrer by MBM by PS Model, 1:43, resin

MAN MKE4500

model maker	ref.	issued	total	scale	construction	operator	fleet#	route	destination	built
Modeltrans	110	2004	300	1:43	resin	Trolebuses de Coruña-Carballo				1943-4

A specially adapted MKE variant for export was the MKE4500, built, according to Alan Murray, in 1943/4. As part of a deal between Franco and Hitler, at the behest of local promoter Enrique Rodríguez, MAN and AEG supplied vehicles and overhead for a 34km interurban line that climbed 100m between the port of La Coruña and hilltop town of Carballo. It took 5 years to build. The MAN chassis were held up in Switzerland by the UN, then stored and finally received their German designed but locally built bodies in time for the opening on February 23, 1950. The line ran until 1971, latterly with 8 ex-London Q1 class BUTs. Today, there's a motorway linking the two centres. In keeping with what was a substitute railway, the MAN/AEG's towed a large trailer for carrying goods to market and took an hour and a quarter to cover the route.

Further along Spain's northern coast is Villaviciosa where Victor Otero and Javier Castro of Modeltrans have been making impeccable 1:43 models since 1993. They cast the 300 limited edition of the Trolebuses de Coruña-Carballo S.A MAN/AEGs in 2004. It's available ready-made or as a kit and is regarded as a particular favourite of the author. Not only is the prototype especially evocative but the model is stunningly accurate, including unusually, window pillars of the correct width, although the booms don't include the cantilever detail along the top of the poles when first built.

Trolebuses Coruña-Carballo MAN MKE4500/AEG, 1950 (c/o Modeltrans)

Trolebuses Coruña-Carballo MAN MKE4500/AEG by Modeltrans, 32cm, resin

MAN SG240 H

model maker	ref.	issued	total	scale	construction	operator	fleet#	route	destination	built
Herpa (conversion)				1:87	plastic	Esslingen				1977
Wiking (conversion)				1:87	plastic	Essen		54	Hauptbahnhof	1983

MAN continued to make a few MPE and MKE trolleybuses during the 1950s but their involvement died out until the fuel crises of the 1970s caused various initiatives to try to re-invent the trolleybus as a dual propulsion 'duo-bus' that could also be guided. Most experimental vehicles were built by Mercedes-Benz but MAN tried with a MAN SÜ240/EHM that never entered service and the SG240 H which ran in Essen. Andreas Zietemann has modelled both, by adapting Herpa and Wiking models respectively.

Esslingen MAN SÜ240/EHM by Herpa (conversion), 1:87, plastic (Andreas Zietemann)

Essen MAN SG240 H EVAG duobus, 1983 (unknown)

Essen MAN SG240 H EVAG duobus by Wiking (conversion), 1:87, plastic   (Andreas Zietemann)

MAN SG200 HO

model maker	ref.	issued	total	scale	construction	operator	fleet#	route	destination	built
Herpa (conversion)				1:87	resin	Solingen				1984
Herpa (conversion)				1:87	resin	Solingen	5	682	Ohligs Bf	1984
Herpa (conversion)				1:87	plastic	Mülheim	858	27	Stadtwerke	1984
Herpa (conversion)				1:87	plastic	Solingen	18	691	Hästen	1984
Herpa (conversion)				1:87	plastic	Solingen	6	681	Hästen	1984

Only 22 SG200 HO trolleybuses were produced, specifically for Solingen, after a prototype was built in 1983 from a MAN SG200 T and tested for 3 years. The fleet served until 2003 and now runs in Sarajevo. No.5 is preserved by Obus-Museum Solingen e.V and still occasionally runs in service. Two Herpa SÜ240 bus models are required to create an articulated scale version, plus a bellows section and roof mounted electrical and trolley gear. Andras Ekkert and Mike Benkes amongst others have done just that and gone further.
An alternative reality by Andreas Soblera has a MAN 'SG260' with an additional centre axle built, as it were, for use in Mülheim, which had planned a trolleybus system in 1945. Three Henschel chassis were delivered together with traction poles and overhead wire. But nothing came of the scheme and the parts were sold to Wiesbaden and Bielefeld. Of course, if things had been different....

Solingen 1, MAN SG200 HO/Graft & Stift/Kiepe, 1984 (Andras Ekkert)

Solingen 6, MAN SG200 HO/Graft & Stift/Kiepe by Herpa (conversion), 1:87, plastic

Solingen MAN SG200 HO/Graft & Stift/Kiepe by Herpa (conversion), 1:87, resin   (Andreas Zietemann)

Solingen 5, MAN SG200 HO/Graft & Stift/Kiepe by Herpa (conversion), 1:87, resin

Solingen 18, MAN SG200 HO/Graft & Stift/Kiepe by Herpa (conversion), 1:87, plastic

Mülheim MAN SG260 HO/Graft & Stift/Kiepe by Herpa (conversion), 1:87, plastic

MAN SL172 HO

model maker	ref.	issued	total	scale	construction	operator	fleet#	route	destination	built
Grell				1:87	plastic	Solingen	64	683	SG-Burg Brücke	1986
Grell (repainted)				1:87	plastic/metal	Solingen	36	683	Krahenhome	1986-8
Herpa (conversion)				1:87	resin	Solingen	45	681	Hästen	1986-87
MEK	600	2004		1:87	resin	Solingen				1986-87
SWS / J.M.B.		1994		1:55	card	Solingen	22			1986-87

5.10 Germany   185

Solingen 64, MAN SL172 HO/Gräf & Stift, 1986

Solingen 64, MAN SL172 HO/Gräf & Stift by Grell, 1:87, plastic

Solingen 36, MAN SL172 HO/Gräf & Stift by Grell (repainted), 1:87, plastic/metal

Solingen MAN SL172 HO/Gräf & Stift by MEK, 1:87, resin

The MAN SL 172 HO was developed for Solingen as a 3-axle 12m long trolleybus to operate the Burg line, which was equipped at one end with a turntable because of limited space. The design is very much based on the VÖV-II 2-axle bus design but adapted to a 3-axle version to maximise carrying capacity on a vehicle that could use the turntable. The trolleybuses replaced the 20 year old TS trolleys which were of similar configuration (see above). ÖAF and Gräf & Stift, both Austrian MAN companies, produced the mechanical parts while the electric equipment was made by Kiepe. Between 1986 and 1987 Solingen put a total of 47 into service, numbered as 22-67. In 2010 the last 15 trolleybuses were withdrawn but many see further service in Sarajevo (Bosnia and Herzegovina). The German technical museum "Deutsches Museum" in Munich exhibits preserved Solingen 32 while 42 is preserved in Solingen.

The Solingen-based German subsidiary of the British Wilkinson Sword company launched advertising on the sides of trolleybus 64 to promote the Quattro razor in 2005, while the German Obus-Museum Solingen e.V. co-operated to produce a 1:87 scale plastic model that it hoped would promote public awareness of trolleybuses. Like the model Henschel/Uerdingen ÜH IIIs (see above), production was commissioned by Wilkinson and subcontracted to Grell in China, who mass produce truck and tramway plastic models. The Wilkinson Quattro razor sets including the trolleybus model were distributed in Germany by Schlecker chemist's shops at €9.95 and are now sold out.

The model, mounted on a diecast chassis, has a rather exaggerated curved front windscreen and avoids the moulding detail around the headlights. There's also an irritating link between the trolley booms. This hasn't stopped collectors like Andras Ekkert going to the trouble of repainting one in Solingen's traditional livery.

Before the Grell model, MEK had issued a 'traditional' resin version of the SL172, with all the signs of a 'kitchen table' producer and less of the Chinese 'industrial' miniaturisation. But in some ways, more of the character of the body design has been captured, even if there is less detail.

The Stadtwerke Solingen produced a card kit of no.22 which was printed on an A3 sheet to celebrate their 100 year anniversary in 1994. The support for the electrical equipment and the two trolley poles has to be glued separately on to the roof.

Herpa buses have also been more-or-less successfully converted, although Andreas Soblera has, perhaps, overdone the roof faring. His model is none-the-less imposing, rather like the real thing.

Solingen 22, MAN SL172 HO/ Gräf & Stift by SWS/J.M.B., 1:43, card

Solingen 45, MAN SL172 HO/Gräf & Stift by Herpa (conversion), 1:87, resin

Daimler-Benz SSW-DB45/57/Schumann/AEG

model maker	ref.	issued	total	scale	construction	operator	fleet#	route	destination	built
Sadlo				1:87	resin	Berlin BVG	1224			1947

Berlin 1224, Daimler-Benz O1000/Schumann/AEG, 1947 (Mattis Schindler)

Daimler-Benz had been involved with trolleybus development since supplying a vehicle to BBC Mannheim as a test car in 1930 followed by, for example, 12 vehicles delivered to Berlin in 1935-9 and another 15 in 1947. Large numbers of the O6600T type trolleybuses were produced mainly for Buenos Aires in 1952 and 1956. The post war order for Berlin is described as either O1000 chassis or type SSW-DB45/57, either way, they had 3 axles, a Schumann body and two 50kW AEG motors with Siemens automatic control equipment. 1224 is preserved by the Berlin Technology Museum and was restored by enthusiasts in 1998 – she's the oldest operational German trolleybus. Sadlo produced a model for MMR that captures these attractive vehicles even if the flag poles are, necessarily, a little big.

Berlin BVG Daimler-Benz O1000/Schumann/AEG by Sadlo, 1:87, resin (Mattis Schindler)

5.10 Germany

Mercedes Benz OE302

model maker	ref.	issued	total	scale	construction	operator	fleet#	route	destination	built
Brawa	6.0026E+11	1967		1:120	plastic, metal	Generic		3	Altstadt	1975
Brawa	6.0026E+11	1967		1:148	plastic, metal	Generic		3	Altstadt	1975
Brawa	6.0026E+11	1967		1:148	plastic, metal	Generic		3	Altstadt	1975
Vector Models	E5550			1:43	electroformed copper	Esslingen				1975

Esslingen Mercedes Benz OE302-12R Duo-Bus by Vector Models, 1:43, copper   (Vector)

Prototype Mercedes Benz OE302-12R Duo-Bus, 1975   (W van der Pla

Daimler had become Mercedes when an O302 bus was converted to a Duo-bus in 1975. This Esslingen prototype served as a basis for the N-gauge Eheim/Brawa models that we described on page 68. It was far more accurately recreated in 2001 by Ukrainian maker Vector Models in 0 scale and electroformed copper. Apart from the misunderstood configuration of the trolleygear, it's an excellent model of a unique experimental trolleybus.

Mercedes Benz O305

model maker	ref.	issued	total	scale	construction	operator	fleet#	route	destination	built
Vector Models	E5483			1:43	electroformed copper	Esslingen				1978
Vector Models	E5478			1:43	electroformed copper	Esslingen				1978

The experiments at Esslingen continued with single O305T and articulated O305GTD duo-buses entering service in 1979 in two configurations, trolley/battery (with black booms) or trolley/diesel (with light blue booms). They lasted under two and eight years respectively. The articulated vehicle, with a motor of only 80kW, was seriously underpowered. All were later converted to diesel power only. A second generation of O305 artics, with chopper control and 180kW motors, entered service in 1983 and ran until 1995. They ran increasingly in diesel-only mode. Vector Models has built imposing 0 scale miniatures of the first generation, which, apart from noticeably over-thick front corner pillars and trolleygear that wouldn't have worked, they convey a purposeful look.

Esslingen 301, Mercedes Benz O305T, 1978   (Daimler Benz)

Esslingen Mercedes Benz O305GTD by Vector Models, 1:43, copper

Esslingen Mercedes Benz O305T by Vector Models, 1:43, copper

Mercedes Benz O405

model maker	ref.	issued	total	scale	construction	operator	fleet#	route	destination	type	built
Speelgoed/NZG	255	1985	200	1:50	zinc diecast	Arnhem	151	1	Oosterbeck	T	1985
Andras Ekkert		2009		1:50		Esslingen	326			GT	1993
Kembel (conversion)				1:87	resin	Esslingen	326	119	Bhf. Esslingen	GT	1993
Wiking (conversion)				1:87	plastic	Esslingen			Sonderfahrt	GTD	1988
Conrad (conversion)				1:50	resin	Zürich	27		Rütihof	GTZ	1988
Conrad (conversion)		2008		1:50	resin	Winterthur	146		Oberwinterthur	GTZW	1988
Kembel (conversion)				1:87	resin	Esslingen			Muhlbachklamm	T	1987

Despite the trials and tribulations, Esslingen took a third generation of 18 Mercedes O405 articulated duo-buses between 1988 and 1995 that ran until 2008. They were progressively refined during their seven year delivery, and although they became quieter and smoother, never quite became dependable. The penultimate trolley, 327 is preserved in running order.

Esslingen 321, Mercedes Benz O405GT by Andras Ekkert, 1:50   (Andras Ekkert)

Esslingen Mercedes Benz O405GT by Kembel (conversion), 1:87, resin   (Andras Ekkert)

A single O405 was delivered in 1987 as a prototype with automatic transmission and a diesel that could only be used as an auxiliary power supply. The operator celebrated its arrival with a 1:43 scale card kit, produced by JF Schreiber of Esslingen. Both Andreas Zietemann and Andras Ekkert have converted Kembel models and painted them in liveries in which they never appeared. Duo-bus versions of the O405 were also used in Bergen, Essen, Kapfenberg, Kobenhavn and Potsdam but tended to have diesel bus service lives rather than trolleybus.

Esslingen Mercedes Benz O405T by Staedtische Strassenbahn Esslingen, 1:43, card

Zurich 27, Mercedes Benz O405GTZ by Conrad (conversion), 1:50, resin   (Andras Ekkert)

Zürich and Winterthur, amongst others, took conventional articulated trolley versions of the O405 which have been series modelled by Andras Ekkert in 1:50 scale, based on the Kembel bus model. The O405 was also supplied to Quito in Ecuador where, since 1995, it has operated probably the most intense trolleybus operation in the world.

A model of an Arnhem version of the O405 was issued locally by Wolthuis Speelgoedland in 1985. We've more on page 232.

Zurich 128, Mercedes Benz O405GTZ, 1988   (Mike Bruce)

Winterthur 146, Mercedes Benz O405GTZW by Conrad (conversion), 1:50, resin   (Andras Ekkert)

Winterthur 146, Mercedes Benz O405GTZW, 1988   (Andras Ekkert)

Mercedes Benz Citaro

model maker	ref.	issued	total	scale	construction	operator	fleet#	route	destination	built
Rietze (conversion)				1:87	resin	Szeged	T860		Probajarat	2007
Szegredi Közlekdési kft	0.530TR12EV			(no scale)	wood	Szeged	T-863			2007
WUMM	B040			1:87	resin	Szeged	T-862			2007

Szeged T-860, Mercedes Benz Citaro, 2007 (Andras Ekkert)

The most recent Mercedes 'standard' bus, the Citaro O530, has been lovingly but unofficially converted into a trolleybus no less than five times (to date) at the workshops of SZKT, the Szeged operator. They even commissioned a wooden model of one to celebrate 30 years of trolleybus services. Modellers have converted the Reitze model of the Citaro into the original conversion, no. T860, and the Hungarian model maker WUMM has produced T862 which has control equipment roof farings that extend to the front.

Despite manufacturers often having to be cajoled into producing them, usually in small numbers, the trolleybus has steadfastly survived in three towns in Germany, at Solingen, Esslingen and Eberswalde, 130 years after its invention in Berlin.

Szeged T-862, Mercedes Benz Citaro by Wumm, 1:87, resin

Szeged Mercedes Benz Citaro by Szegredi Közlekdési kft, 25cm, wood

Szeged Mercedes Benz Citaro by Rietze (conversion), 1:87, resin (Andras Ekkert)

Trolebuses Coruña-Carballo MAN MKE4500/AEG by Modeltrans, 32cm, resin

Poprad 1 and 3, Stoll/AEG, 1904. (unknown)

Chapter 5.11
Hungary

Ikarus 1952-2002,	60T	193
	T400	195
	60TCS	196
	260T	196
	280T	198
	400 series	200

In August 1904, entrepreneur Carl Stoll of Dresden opened two systems in the then Kingdom of Hungary; at Poprad, linking the town to a spa resort 13 km away and central Hermannstadt (today Sibiu in Romania), from the station to Arini Park. The two systems lasted 2 years and 2 months respectively and used 3 axle, articulated cars with AEG equipment — there's a model of the similar, possibly the same, Dresden versions in the Verkehrsmuseum. Carl Stoll's enterprise collapsed soon after, and AEG took over the assets. He committed suicide in 1907.

The business was re-launched in Vienna by his son, Hans-Ludwig, who opened a third Hungarian system in Pozsony (now Bratislava) in 1909. The trolleys were now built by Österreichische Daimler-Motoren-Gesellschaft and had hub motors by Lohner-Porsche. The 5.8km route served a hill top resort in some style until 1915 by which time Hungary was about to undergo massive change. With US president Woodrow Wilson's carve up of Hungary in 1919, these three towns became part of Czechoslovakia (later Slovakia) and Romania.

Budapest T100, Ganz/AEC, 1933. (Ganz)

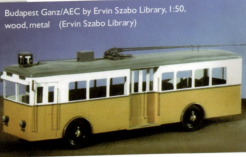
Budapest Ganz/AEC by Ervin Szabo Library, 1:50, wood, metal (Ervin Szabo Library)

Pozsony, Mercedes-Elektrique-Stoll, 1909. (unknown)

Hungary had installed a 2.7km trial route north of Budapest in 1933 with three local Ganz (using AEC chassis under licence) and Mavag trolleybuses. There's a model of one of the Ganz/AECs in the Metropolitan Ervin Szabo library. Ganz and Mavag, the two electrical, tramway and railway companies of Hungary combined in 1959 and were taken over by Škoda in 2006 to supply traction motors for trolleybuses to this day.

Like other Soviet satellite countries, Hungary after the war, at least in Budapest, had to follow policy that wanted trolleybuses on city streets, not least because imported diesel oil was scarce. After the initial route was destroyed in 1944, Budapest re-introduced trolleybuses in 1949 with 53 ubiquitous MTB-82s from both the Moskva and Engels (Uritisky) factories that took three years to deliver. Some were rebuilt with wider doors and bigger windows and have been modelled by Vector Models (see page 245). But the demand was greater than the ability of Russia

Ikarus 60T

model maker	ref.	issued	total	scale	construction	operator	fleet#	route	destination	built
										1952
HB Model				1:87	resin	Budapest				1955
WUMM				1:87	resin	Budapest	344	75		1954
Rigomodell		2010		1:24	wood, metal	Budapest	286	75	Népliget	1952
(unknown)		1961		(no scale)	plastic	Budapest				
St.Petersburg	138a	1999	25	1:43	resin	København NESA	9	12	Lyngby	
Kherson Models	E5600		0	1:43	resin	København NESA	9			

to supply so the Ikarus Bus Company, using Ganz copies of the MTB-82 electrical equipment, went on to supply 153 60T trolleybuses between 1952 and 1956.

The 60Ts were heavy vehicles with only manual steering. They took considerable effort to push across dead sections where tram overhead held precedence. Getting stuck was said to be a particular problem in Budapest, and the T60 had no batteries or auxiliary power unit. But they are fondly remembered and have been modelled by both HB Model and Kemény Gábor of WUMM in Budapest. His is the more accurate, although neither manage the silver trolleygear roof plate that seems never to have been black. The HB Model has the livery of the 1950s, although it's thought only the prototype, T200, had white wheels and wasn't fitted with a driver's kerb lookout window as shown.

Budapest Ikarus 60T by HB Model, 1:87, resin

Budapest T200, Ikarus 60T, 1952 (Németh Zoltan Ádám)

Budapest T254, Ikarus 60T, 1955 (Németh Zoltan Ádám)

Budapest 322, Ikarus 60T by Wumm, 1:87, resin

Budapest 286, Ikarus 60T by Rigomodell, 1:24, wood, metal (Endre Rigó)

Ad for Ikarus 60T toy (unknown)

Trolibusz elemes, műanyag karosszéria, áramszedővel, 25,3 ×7,3×10,7 cm .... 98,— Ft

Budapest Ikarus 60T by (unknown), 25cm, plastic

Endre Rigó of Rigomodell and a professional model maker has produced a stunning 1:24 scale model of Budapest 286 with white wheels and interior lighting to show off the impeccable inside. Perhaps the front corners aren't as rounded as the original, or the booms as thick, but an impressive model none-the-less.

Also with white wheels, is the earliest reproduction of a 60T we know of - a large plastic toy that includes a one piece metal grille and headlights and separate bumpers.

We don't know who made it but it was advertised as costing the equivalent of about one pound sterling in 1961.

Ikarus T400

model maker	ref.	issued	total	scale	construction	operator	fleet#	route	destination	built
WUMM	B 013			1:87	resin	Budapest	T400	70		1961

Budapest Ikarus T400, 1961 (Németh Zoltan Adám)

Budapest Ikarus T400 by Wumm, 1:87,

The need for greater capacity led to building trailers in 1960; altogether 59 were built and the 60Ts that were adapted to pull them were renumbered in the 300s. WUMM has faithfully reproduced 344 with a trailer (together with the driver's kerb window, which only motor bus versions had). An experimental trolleybus (trolley experimentation was to happen often in Budapest), was built in 1961 with a two axle trailer section to produce the first articulated trolley in the country. T400 was rebuilt from T283 in time for the International Fair, with white walled tyres, chrome hubs but only a 86kW motor. Thus underpowered, she survived until 1967. WUMM has produced a model version with a very flexible centre joint.

5.11 Hungary 195

Ikarus 60TCS

model maker	ref.	issued	total	scale	construction	operator	fleet#	route	destination	built
WUMM				1:87	resin	Budapest	435	75		1963

The conversion to articulated trolleybuses continued from 1962 to 1964, involving 53 cars and coincided with an attempt at route branding. Nobody seems to have modelled the short lived green/cream, orange/black and blue/orange schemes that adorned some of these "new" trolleybuses, but WUMM has produced 435 running on mainline route 75 where all were allocated, until replaced in 1976.

Operator Budapest BKV acquired 100 ZiU-5 and 172 ZiU-9 trolleybuses (see page 253) in 1967 and 1975-82 respectively. St. Petersburg Tram Collection has modelled 813 of 1976. 47 ZiU-9s also went to Hungary's second modern trolleybus system in Szeged, in 1979, and 37 went to Debrecen in 1985.

Budapest 402, Ikarus 60TCS, 1963. (Nemeth Zoltan Adam)

Budapest BKV Ikarus 60TCS by Wumm, 1:87, resin

Ikarus 260T

model maker	ref.	issued	total	scale	construction	operator	fleet#	route	destination	built
HK Modell				1:87	resin	Budapest	600	79	Garai U	1976
s.e.s modelltec		1990s		1:87	plastic	Weimar				1976
ses/Jörg Swoboda	14 1302 20	2006		1:87	plastic	Budapest	600			1976
ses/Jörg Swoboda	14 1302 01_W	2006		1:87	plastic	Weimar				1986
ses/JAndras Ekkert		2006		1:87	plastic	Budapest	600			1976
Vector Models		2006		1:43	electroformed copper	Budapest	600			1976

The 1972 oil crisis had seen off moves to scrap trolleybuses and something of a revival led to BKV buying Ikarus 260 and 280 motor buses and installing the electrical equipment from scrapped ZiU-5s.

The prototype solo 260T type trolleybus was more comfortable than the rugged ZiU-9s then being imported, but not as cheap. No.600 remained in solitary service for 19 years, and has been restored to its original yellow with white roof.

That hasn't stopped umpteen variants being produced by JS Modell (Jörg Swoboda) in different liveries based on the Modelltec (aka. s.e.s of Berlin, see below) models of Ikarus buses, with wire booms. HK Modell (Kiss Lazlo of Budapest) too has converted the same models into trolleybuses with odd but perhaps more convincing trolleygear. Modellers such Andras Ekkert have answered the obvious cry to add extra detailing to complete the models, especially

Budapest 600, Ikarus 260T, 1976 (Németh Zoltan Adám)

Budapest 600, Ikarus 260T by HK Modell, 1:87, resin

Generic Ikarus 260T by ses/Jörg Swoboda, 1:87, plastic

Budapest 600, Ikarus 260T by ses/Andras Ekkert, 1:87, resin (Andras Ekkert)

Budapest 600, Ikarus 260T, 1976 (Medium)

with various graphics.

Vector Models of Ukraine has produced a fine 1:43 model of the 260T of Budapest BKV. The great advantage of larger scale has enabled the windscreen to be properly curved and the maker's badge to be embossed, but as this is a cut down version of the articulated 280T model it has incorrectly inherited the later two piece doors of the 1980s.

A second 260T was created which was sent to Weimar (GDR), fitted with experimental Ganz electronics some ten years later than the first, in 1986. It ran until 1991. It was this vehicle that served as a basis for the conversion from the original Ikarus 260 bus model, launched 1979, by the GDR company VEB Spezialprägewerk Annaberg-Buchholz under their trade mark ESPEWE. After German unification, the model was taken over by Schmidt Electronic Systeme known as s.e.s. Berlin who developed the orange 260T trolleybus version by adding trolley booms, retriever dummies and a Weimar logo.

Many of the models have had the Weimar

5.11 Hungary 197

Budapest 600, Ikarus 260T by Vector Models, 1:43, electroformed copper

Weimar 8042, Ikarus 260T/Ganz, 1975 (Ikarus)

Gerneric Ikarus 260T by ses/Jörg Swoboda, 1:87, plastic

emblem attached but not the two tone livery or the two piece doors that the rather ill-fated prototype vehicle had. As an injection moulded plastic model, changing the die would be rather expensive. The only other 260T was converted from a 260 bus in North Korea.

Ikarus 280T

model maker	ref.	issued	total	scale	construction	operator	fleet#	route	destination	built
HK Modell				1:87	plastic	Budapest	200			1987
HK Modell (repainted)				1:87	plastic	Eberswalde	25		Ostend	1990
HK Modell (repainted)				1:87	plastic	Budapest	156	76	Baross Tsr	1978
s.e.s modelltec	14 1306 00	1990s		1:87	plastic	Eberswalde				1975
s.e.s (repaint)	14 1305	2006		1:87	plastic	Szegred	502	9	Lugas Utca	1991
s.e.s (repaint)	14 1305	2006		1:87	plastic	Budapest	100	75	Nepliget	1975
WUMM				1:87	resin	Budapest	198	80		1984
DOCA		2005		1:43	diecast zinc	Chelyabinsk	3862			1989
Vector Models	V5-40			1:43	electroformed copper	Budapest	280			1987
Vector Models	v5-40-1			1:43	electroformed copper	Moscow	0049			1989

Hoyerswerda Ikarus 280T by ses (Modelltec), 1:87, plastic

The articulated version of the 260T, the Ikarus 280T, saw something like nine variations but is generally divided into two generations, the 100 series built 1976-78 and the 200 series built 1979-93 which includes demonstrators and conversions from buses in Bulgaria, Poland and North Korea. Altogether there were 483 280Ts, depending on how you count them, as many were constantly changing test-beds to determine the best technology, at a time of change-over from resistance to electronic control. The main customers for the production 280Ts were Budapest, Sofia and the DDR. Visually the body stayed basically the same, although rooftop equipment varied considerably. One, a test bed for Finnish Strömberg AC-analog chopper control, had only three, narrower, doors and an extra window – it was designated a 284T1 and remained unique, not least because it was the only 'pusher' 280, with the motor in the rear section, ever built.

In the 1990s s.e.s developed the articulated 280 bus model, adding the rear section and the articulation. The trolleybus version, as in real life, followed. The original model is supplied in injected deep yellow, the colour of Edberswalde, Weimar, Potsdam and Hoyerswerda DDR systems at the time, with oversized external roof hinges over the articulation between body sections.

Andras Ekkert has taken the s.e.s Modelltec 1:87 280T and produced versions of the original prototype, 100, as well as Budapest 156, Szeged 502 and Eberswalde 025, all with the correct graphic detail. HK Modell has commercially repainted the model in Budapest colours as 280.91, 280.93 and 280.94 variants. The latter is with two piece doors, which has involved considerable adaptation of the injection plastic.

And local producer, WUMM, has produced a model of Budapest 198, the 284T1 testbed with its door and window differences and additional control box on the roof.

Vector Models (aka SP of Kherson, Ukraine) has produced a 1:43 version of the 280T with a rather more rounded front end than the original. Perhaps, on this now quite old electro-plating, as you can tell by the perishing tyres, the modelling was from photographs - there were no 280Ts for Vector to copy in Ukraine. Vector produced versions with the more usual 4 section doors and in blue, representing one of SVARTZ versions, part built in Moscow.

DOCA Models, of Chelyabinsk in Russia also produced a 280T in 2005 which appears more accurate with a squarer outline to the windscreen and grille. Chelyabinsk inherited 16 280T.93 trolleybuses from Germany between 1993 and 1998. They ran until 2009.

Budapest 100, Ikarus 280T by ses (repaint), 1:87, plastic

Budapest 156, Ikarus 280T by HK Modell (repainted), 1:87, plastic (Andras Ekkert)

Szegred 502, Ikarus 280T by ses (repaint), 1:87, plastic

Eberswalde 025, Ikarus 280T by HK Modell (repainted), 1:87, plastic (Andras Ekkert)

Budapest 200 Ikarus 280T by HK Modell, 1:87, plastic (Mattis Schindler)

Budapest 198, Ikarus 280T by Wumm, 1:87, resin   (Mattis Schindler)

Budapest Ikarus 280T by Vector Models, 1:43, electroformed copper

Moscow Ikarus 280T by Vector Models, 1:43, electroformed copper (Kimmeria)

Chelyabinsk Ikarus 280T by DOCA, 1:43, diecast zinc   (DOCA)

Budapest 217, Ikarus 280T, 1987 (Marc Ryckaert)

Ikarus 400 series

model maker	ref.	issued	total	scale	construction	operator	fleet#	route	destination	built
WUMM				1:87	resin	Budapest	314	80	Cseto Utca	1996
WUMM				1:87	resin	Bucharest	5280	66		1998-2002
WUMM				1:87	resin	Debrecen				1992
WUMM				1:87	resin	Budapest	713	70	Kossuth Lajos	2002

Bucharest 5108, Ikarus 415T, 2002   (Ronline)

Bucharest 5104, Ikarus 415T by Wumm, 1:87, resin

To replace the 260T/280T Ikarus produced the 415T/435T prototypes in 1992. By this time Ikarus had gone from 4th largest bus producer in the world to making only a few thousand a year and was becoming marginalised and desperate. The 415T/435T was woefully out-of-date, but 200 were built for Bucharest in 1998-2002. WUMM has produced a model of one, 5280, and another of the prototype that ended up in Debrecen, then Tallinn. In 2001 another prototype appeared with Russian IGBT control, but a large hoped for order from Moscow didn't happen.

The articulated version, the 435T has been modeled by WUMM, as one of only 15 built and sold to Budapest in 1994-6.

Debrecen Ikarus 415T by Wumm, 1:87, resin   (Lazlo Kiss)

Bucharest 312, Ikarus 435T, 1996   (Christian Pettauer)

Budapest 314, Ikarus 435T by Wumm, 1:87, resin   (Andras Ekkert)

Ikarus needed to build a low floor version and the 411T prototype followed in 1995 but no orders resulted until the length was increased by 1 metre and 20 were then sold to Tallinn and Budapest from 1999. The last 412T and the last Ikarus trolleybus, was delivered in 2002. With virtually a model of every trolleybus type to run Budapest, WUMM has loyally produced a particularly good representation of 714, the last one built.

Bucharest 710, Ikarus 412T, 2002 (Foma)

Budapest 713, Ikarus 412T by Wumm, 1:87, resin

Prototype Ikarus V.187, 2009 (SZKT)

Phantom like, Ikarus produced the controversially expensive V.187 in 2009. Obus Ltd, the company spun off from Budapest operator, city council owned BKV, and Invent Ltd, the company that had done much bus to trolleybus conversion, have again created an Ikarus trolleybus – intended for Budapest which desperately needs to replace its ageing fleet. Local modeler Endre Rigó will be adding booms to his 1:24 scale model of the bus version to create a trolleybus, with the same high quality as his Budapest Ikarus T60 model. Prototype T660, meanwhile, is now running Szegred.

Chapter 5.12
Italy

3 axle single decker	toy	203
Alfa Romeo	110AF	204
	140AF	206
Fiat	656F	210
	672F	210
	666F	211
	668F	212
	2405	212
	2401	213
	2411	214
	2472	216
	2470	217
Lancia	Esatau	217
	120.003/Dalfa	217

Cuneo 4, Fiat 635/Fiat/Marelli, 1934 (Marelli)

Desenzano 1, Guy BTX/Rees Roturbo, 1927 (Guy Motors)

In the way that technology is "of the moment", at a time of rampant nationalism throughout Europe, Italian engineers built their first trolleybus in 1903, doubtless feeling compelled to follow the example set by the German Schiemann vehicle that had been demonstrated in Roma and at the Torino Esposizone of 1902. They also felt compelled to design their own current collection system – a 4 wheeled 'trolley' pressed up against the overhead wires by a single boom. Despite a French installation by Lombard-Gérin at Gallarate in 1904, the Italian "Filovia" system was deployed at nine locations between 1906 and 1910 and was successful enough to have been seriously considered for use by Bradford Corporation in the UK. Italian model maker Giuliano Càroli has reconstructed a typical example in 1:43 scale (see page 13). Promoted by Societa per la Trazione Elettrica (STE) of Milan and thought to have been built by Turrinelli, these tiny trolleybuses ran in Siena from March 1907 to October 1917. Although most early systems failed fairly rapidly, due to poor roads and insufficient patronage, two saw second generation single boom Filovia vehicles with pneumatic tyres; at Ivrea and at Cuneo, where the narrow gauge lines were replaced in the 30s by standard gauge wiring that was then used by trolleybuses until 1968. But not, seemingly, before a single boomed Fiat 635 was delivered in 1934. Three little documented Filovia systems were built by Zaretti in the 20s at Bergamo, Châtillion and Desenzano, but Italy was suffering from the trolleybus obscurity and technical confusion that prevailed throughout the world in the mid-20s. The single boom collector gave way to the modern double variety at Desenzano where two of Zaretti's Filovia trolleys were converted in 1927. Rognini & Balbo, who had built single boomed trolley lorries for the five military installations of the First World War, built both types for Cuneo and Vicenza respectively. At Ivrea, single boomed trolleybuses survived until 1935, by which time the trolleybus in Italy was no longer the preserve of northern hilly rural communities, but was entering major urban centres. Italy is a greater pioneer and devotee of the trolleybus than is often recognised. 3916 have seen service here, so far, on 51 systems and 1350km of route.

52 Italian trolleybuses had been built by the mid-twenties. By 1927 only 15 were still in service. The arrival of two Guy BTX single deckers in that year at Desenzano heralded a new beginning, the so-called "seconde generazione". Fiat saw what was happening and trialled prototypes in Torino and Cuneo. A hybrid Tilling Stevens was imported in 1932. Much publicized at the time was the opening in 1933 of the Venezia system, using 23 Fiat 488 trolleybuses to link, in great style, the mainland to the city of canals. Perhaps because, or perhaps in spite of Benito Mussolini's official sanction of trolleybuses in 1938, 13 major systems were established by 1940 using over 540 trolleybuses.

3 axle single decker

model maker	ref.	issued	total	scale	construction	operator	fleet#	route	destination	built
Alpia		1948		(no scale)	wood, plastic	(generic)	102			

Just to demonstrate the collectability of Italian miniature trolleybuses, the only toy we know of, the 52cm Alpia clockwork 3 axle single decker, sold for £1800 in March 2008. Wooden, with opening doors this large objet d'art is, apart from a broken spring, in mint condition and supposedly dates from 1948. It has 102 on the front. There have been 11 Italian trolleybuses with that fleet number, but only one was a six wheeler, Catania's Fiat 672F of 1949, that operated with the dark green lower body half livery that was dictated by ministerial degree. We doubt Alpia was located in Sicily, as most Italian toy producers were in the north. It is, nonetheless, an evocative model of either a Fiat 672F or an Alfa Romeo 140AF.

3 axle single decker by Alpia, 52cm, wood, plastic (Galeria Navarro)

Alfa Romeo

Mussolini had dictated the saving of Alfa Romeo from certain bankruptcy in 1933 by ordering diversification into aero-engines and commercial vehicles. By 1935 Alfa was testing trolleybus versions of the Tipo 85 and alternative energy sources for buses (Italy's invasion of Ethiopia had led to global sanctions that made oil prohibitively expensive). 8 were supplied to Roma the following year.

Alfa Romeo 110AF

model maker	ref.	issued	total	scale	construction	operator	fleet#	route	destination	built
Rivarossi	Minobus	1950		1:80	plastic	(Como blue)				1945
Rivarossi	Minobus	1950		1:80	plastic	(Parma yellow)				1945
Rivarossi	Minobus	1950		1:80	plastic	(Verona red)				1945
Rivarossi	Minobus	1950		1:80	plastic	(Roma green)				1945
Vittorio Naldini		2004		1:87	resin	Roma ATAC	6001	36	Termini Tufello	1939
Mario Trinchieri				1:87	resin	Roma ATAC				1942

The 12m 3 axle 110AF type, introduced in 1938, was the sort of large capacity vehicle that was needed on major urban streets. 109 of the 320 built went to Roma between 1938 and 1942. They were ubiquitous enough to be the basis (as successive catalogues state) of Rivorossi's powered model of 1950. This beautifully engineered and now very expensive 1:80 scale trolleybus was available in at least 4 colours, red, blue and green, with a silver roof and yellow with a brown roof. Some dispensed with silver roof, but in total, not many were made. One surviving complete boxed set of 1950, with model overhead and original packaging, has £5 written on the top and sold for 200 times that amount recently, which only goes to prove that collecting model trolleybuses is a good hedge against inflation, or at least is so in the case of Rivarossi models. (More in chapter 4, page 61)

Milano 303, Alfa Romeo 110AF/Reggiane/Tibb, 1941 (ATM Photographic Archive, Milan)

Alfa Romeo 110AF by Rivarossi, 15cm, plastic, metal

Roma 6001, Alfa Romeo 110AF/Macchi/TIBB by Vittorio Naldini, 1:87, resin

Roma Alfa Romeo 110AFS/Macchi/TIBB by Mario Trinchieri, 1:87, resin   (Mario Trinchieri)

Roma 9001, Alfa Romeo 110AF/Piaggio/Ansaldo, 1942

Roma 9001, Alfa Romeo 110AF/Piaggio/Ansaldo by N3C, 1:87, resin   (N3C)

Vittorio Naldini hand builds a 1:87 resin model of his native Roma's 110AF number 6001 to order and compatriot Mario Trincheri has modeled the rather incredible 5 axle articulated 110AFS that was apparently intended for Roma. At 22m in length with a steerable 2 axle trailer unit, it was difficult to handle and evidently too unwieldy. It was lost during the war. This hasn't stopped Mario making 3 models of it!

One other 110AF should be included, partly because of it's striking stainless steel Piaggio body built in 1942 and partly because of N3C, aka. Enrico Nigrelli's intention to release a model of what became Roma 9001.

Milano 432, Alfa Romeo 140AF/SIAI Marchetti/CGE, 1950 (Milano ATM)

Alfa Romeo 140AF

model maker	ref.	issued	total	scale	construction	operator	fleet#	route	destination	built
Gila Modelli	GM266			1:43	resin	Como STECAV	87		Camerlata Cantu	1951
Gila Modelli	GM266			1:43	resin	Salerno ATACS	218	2	Fratte Porto	1951
Gila Modelli	GM266			1:43	resin, metal	Milano ATM	456	92	Montcenter	1950
Gila Modelli	GM266			1:43	resin	Milano ATM	453	90	Circolare Destra	1949
Gila Modelli	GM266			1:43	resin, metal	Ancona FPAF	16		Anacona	1949
Gila Modelli	GM266			1:43	resin	Trieste ACEGAT	706	5	Borsa	1949
Gila Modelli	GM266			1:43	resin	Roma ATAC	6647	47	Lung.T.Marzio	1949
ATM	9701	1997		1:87	resin	Trieste ACEGAT	728-758			1952-6
ATM	9713	1997		1:87	resin	Ancona FPAF	42644			1949
ATM	9711	1997		1:87	resin	Roma ATAC	6601-6655		SIAI Marchetti/TIBB	
ATM	9711	1997		1:87	resin	Milano ATM	457-476			1950-1
ATM	9712	1997		1:87	resin	Trieste ACEGAT	704		SIAI Marchetti/Marelli	
N3C	2979	2003		1:87	resin	Roma ATAC	5039	242	Tribunali	1949
N3C	2977	2003		1:87	resin	Ancona FPAF	12			1949
N3C	2980	2003		1:87	resin	Milano ATM	466		Milano	1950
N3C	2980	2003		1:87	resin	Milano ATM	462		Milano	1950
Vittorio Naldini				1:87	resin	Roma ATAC	6605	64	S.Pietro	1949

Milano 456, Alfa Romeo 140AF/SIAI Marchetti/CGE by Gila Modelli, 1:43, resin, metal

Roma 6647, Alfa Romeo 140AF/SIAI Marchetti/CGE by Gila Modelli, 1:43, resin, metal

The Alfa Romeo 140AF was essentially a development of the 110AF rather than a redesign and production overlapped between 1942 and 1949. 334 140AFs were built up until 1960 with bodies from 11 makers.

Roberto Gilardoni has produced 7 versions of the 140AF in 1:43 from his workshop at Mozzate near Como. Although absolute comparison can be a little unkind, the models are hugely impressive in the flesh. His are of SIAI Marchetti bodied variety, as supplied to Como (81-2), Ancona-Falconara (10-16), Milano (451-476), Trieste (701-707), Roma (6601-6655) and Napoli (5007-5018, 5111-5116); all built 1949-51, some with dual headlights (Milano) and some in an unusual blue livery (Ancona-Falconara). Also modelled was Salerno 218 (incorrectly numbered at the request of a customer) with a Stanga body (271), Como (83-6) with Macchi bodies and Genova 2366-2380 with Bagnara bodies, though, as standard designs, are all fairly indistinguishable from each other, unless you look at the badges. Roberto's Como 87, Milano 453 and Salerno 218 models include lower body ribbing.

Ancona 12, Alfa Romeo 140AF/SIAI Marchetti/Marelli, 1949 (Paulo Gregoris)

Ancona 16, Alfa Romeo 140AF/SIAI Marchetti/Marelli by Gila Modelli, 1:43, resin, metal (Gila Modelli)

Como 87, Alfa Romeo 140AF/Macchi/Marelli by Gila Modelli, 1:43, resin (Gila Modelli)

Milano 453, Alfa Romeo 140AF/SIAI Marchetti/CGE by Gila Modelli, 1:43, resin (Gila Modelli)

Salerno 218, Alfa Romeo 140AF/Pistoesi/CGE by Gila Modelli, 1:43, resin (Gila Modelli)

Salerno 181, Alfa Romeo 140AF/Pistoesi/CGE, 1951 (Paulo Gregoris)

The popular 140AF has been modelled in 1:87 scale by ATM (Alpadria Train Models, aka. Fabio Dobran of Trieste). They are rather smart models that look machine made, with a stout diecast chassis and were produced from 1995 to 1998. Variants include the blue Ancona FPAF (10-16), Roma ATAC (6601-6655), Milano (457-476), Trieste ACEGAT (704) and the later Trieste ACEGAT (728-758) with the pillar less front CRDA bodies.

Fabio regards his manufacturing technique as advanced for the late 90s and secret, but admits his centrifugal rubber moulds didn't last very long. He's particularly proud of the shallow wall depth he achieved in H0 scale.

Ancona Alfa Romeo 140AF/SIAI Marchetti/Marelli by ATM, 1:87, resin

Trieste Alfa Romeo 140AF/CRDA/TIBB by ATM, 1:87, resin

Roma Alfa Romeo 140AF/SIAI Marchetti/TIBB by ATM, 1:87, resin

Milano 466, Alfa Romeo 140AF/SIAI Marchetti/TIBB by N3C, 1:87, resin

Another small and rather elusive maker of Italian trolleybus models is N3C, aka. Enrico Nigrelli who similarly produces Ancona, Roma and Milano variants of the 140AF. Enrico makes to order, and includes etched windscreen frames that neatly solves the lack of realism in this area, that sometimes happens to resin models. The list of possible SIAI bodied 140AFs is long, with ribbed and non-ribbed dual and single headlight variants and can include Milan's 462 in the later orange livery. Enrico has, over the last decade, managed to make most of them.

Roma 6647, Alfa Romeo 140AF/SIAI Marchetti/TIBB by N3C, 1:87, resin

Milano 462, Alfa Romeo 140AF/SIAI Marchetti/TIBB by N3C, 1:87, resin   (Enrico Nigrelli)

Ancona 12, Alfa Romeo 140AF/SIAI Marchetti/Marelli by N3C, 1:87, resin   (Enrico Nigrelli)

Vittorio Naldini hand builds Roma 6605, an Alfa Romeo 140AF that had a SIAI Marchetti body and TIBB electrics – the same vehicle as Gila Modelli, but in 1:87 scale. Regarded as 'rough' by some, they do have their own charm.

Roma 6605, Alfa Romeo 140AF/SIAI Marchetti/TIBB by Vittorio Naldini, 1:87,

Fiat

Fiat (Fabbricca Italiana Automobili Torino) has always had a large share of the Italian automobile market and when economic realities of the early thirties hit, they diversified into commercial vehicles. Their studies of the potential trolleybus market concluded that adaptation of bus chassis was the only technical way forward. They appear to have been influenced initially, and like so many, by America's Twin Coach trolleybus of 1929. Fiat trolleybuses were based on SPA chassis (a company they had acquired), namely the 400 series, an urban bus design and the 600 series, a lorry chassis. In 1931 they supplied three experimental trolleys, the Fiat 461F, to their local city's public transport operator and three 467Fs to Cuneo in the same year. By 1933 they were able to supply 23 488Fs to inaugurate the first modern system at Venezia plus one to Milano on trial. The first real production model, the small 635F, followed in 1934, with 94 being supplied before 1941. They established the particularly Italian feature of a central driving position.

Bari 207, Fiat 656F/Varesini/CGE, 1937   (col. Francesco Rizzoli)

Fiat 656F

model maker	ref.	issued	total	scale	construction	operator	fleet#	route	destination	built
Vittorio Naldini				1:87	resin	Roma ATAC	4151	56	L.Argentina	1937

Roma 4151, Fiat 656F/Varesini/CGE by Vittorio Naldini, 1:87, resin

260 type 656Fs were produced between 1935 and 1951 and Vittorio Naldini has modelled the rather distinctive, almost gothic, Roma 4151 with a Varesini body. Most 656F trolleybuses looked somewhat plainer and one, Athens 704, is preserved.

Roma 6461, Fiat 672F/Cansa/Marelli, 1950   (Mario Diotallevi)

Fiat 672F

model maker	ref.	issued	total	scale	construction	operator	fleet#	route	destination	built
PB Models	202			1:43	resin	Roma ATAC	6707	62	S.Pistro	1950
Vittorio Naldini				1:87	resin	Roma ATAC	6701	75	Piazza Fiume	1950

Even more ubiquitous was the 672F, derived from the 656F but with a third axle. 404 were produced between 1939 and 1954 for all the major trolleybus networks, usually with a Cansa body. PB models, who mostly produce car kits, did produce a rather good 1:43 model of Roma 6707, one of 130 supplied in 4 batches between 1948 and 1952. Vittorio Naldini will also produce the same model in 1:87 scale to order, with or without the brown doors used in Milano.

Roma 6701, Fiat 672F/Cansa/Marelli by Vittorio Naldini, 1:87, resin

Roma 6707, Fiat 672F/Cansa/Marelli by PB Models, 1:43, resin

Fiat 666F

model maker	ref.	issued	total	scale	construction	operator	fleet#	route	destination	built
Gila Modelli	GM136M	50		1:43	resin, metal	Stelvio AEM	17			1943

AEM Stelvio 17, Fiat 666F/Viberti/GCE "Filocarro", 1943 (Archivo AEM)

One model we can't resist including, despite not strictly being a trolleybus is Roberto Gilardoni's very detailed Fiat Filocarro of 1943. Built to provide transport for the construction of dams in Valtellina between 1939 and 1956, were two 2 axle trolley-lorries, plus 16 3 axle Fiat 672 versions. The 750v network 'climbed' over 1100m with gradients of up to 11% and was ultimately 73km long. There had been a "Filovia" single pole installation along the same road between January and November 1918 to supply the wartime frontline. Twenty years later trolley-lorries successfully carried virtually all the cement and blocks needed to build three dams in 17 years.

AEM Stelvio 17, Fiat 666F/Viberti/GCE "Filocarro" by Gila Modelli, 1:43, resin, metal

Fiat 668F

model maker	ref.	issued	total	scale	construction	operator	fleet#	route	destination	built
Vittorio Naldini				1:87	resin	Venezia SFM	73		Mestre	1952

Venezia 73, Fiat 668F/Stanga/TIBB, 1952 (Paulo Gregoris)

Venezia 73, Fiat 668F/Stanga/TIBB by Vittorio Naldini, 1:87, resin

Vittorio Naldini's model of Venezia 73 in the unique ivory livery of the historic canal city is the final iteration of the Fiat 600 series. 375 of these iconic 4 wheelers were produced between 1945 and 1955.

Fiat 2405

model maker	ref.	issued	total	scale	construction	operator	fleet#	route	destination	built
ATM	9501	1995		1:87	resin	Verona AMT	201-226			1958-63
Jonny Porcu				1:43		Torino ATM	1200-1210		Viberti/CGE	
Mario Trinchieri				1:87	resin	Milano ATM	348	92	Via Isonzo	1957

Verona 213, Fiat 2405/Stranga/TIBB, 1953 (Paulo Gregoris)

Verona Fiat 2405/Stranga/TIBB by ATM, 1:87, resin

Torino 1204, Fiat 2405/Viberti/CGE, 1958 (Paulo Gregoris)

Fiat didn't produce its first post war trolleybus design until 1953, with the 2400 series that was to remain available in various forms until 1995. Including Iveco produced versions, 721 examples were built. They varied widely and no distinction in the classification was made between rigid and articulated variants. They were based on chassisless 400 series buses. The rigid 2405 has been modelled by Mario Trinchieri. As the first of his ATM collection of the late 1990s, Fabio Dobran modelled the imposing Fiat 2405 artic that was supplied to Verona. These trolleybuses and those supplied to Venezia were built by bodybuilder Stanga using their "Giostra" articulation system and Fiat parts (Milano's artics of the same period

Torino 1200, Fiat 2405/Viberti/CGE by Jonny Porcu, 1:43 (Jonny Porcu)

used Alfa Romeo parts).

Torino received the Viberti version of the articulated 2405. They used to pass the front door of Jonny Porcu who decided to model one in 1:43 scale instead of his usually preferred scale of 1:24. Made of balsa wood and undergoing many changes, including scrapping the initial ply base and substituting sheet copper, this 'labour of love' is powered and radio controlled with painstakingly made opening doors. The project has led to a limited edition in resin, with moulds using the original balsa model. The run comprises 15 models corresponding to the original nos. 1200-1214. It is also available in Rivoli colours as used on the straight 12km interurban route that ran into Torino and used 2 voltages, 1200 and 600v.

Brochure image, Fiat 2401/Cansa/TIBB, 1953   (TEP)

Fiat 2401

model maker	ref.	issued	total	scale	construction	operator	fleet#	route	destination	built
Simonelli		2001		1:43	resin	Milano		92	Bovisa	1953

The two axle Fiat 2401, produced between 1953 and 1958, was a 10.5 metre post war trolleybus based on the 401 bus chassis. A model maker in Milano called Simonelli produced 1:43 kits between 2000 and 2001 that included a supposed 2411 in service in Milano. The rather unflattering model can be neither a 2411 nor from Milano, although some 2401s had chrome strips at the front, such as those in Parma and Ancona

Milano Fiat 2401/Cansa/TIBB by Simonelli, 1:43, resin   (Massimo Casartelli)

Fiat 2411

model maker	ref.	issued	total	scale	construction	operator	fleet#	route	destination	built
ATM	9613	1996		1:87	resin	Modena AMCM	42-45			1958
ATM	9614	1996		1:87	resin	San Remo STEL	21-32			1957
ATM	9615	1996		1:87	resin	Venezia SFM	77-93			1953-6
ATM	9611	1996		1:87	resin	Torino ATM	1112-1121		Cansa/TIBB	1956
ATM	9612	1996		1:87	resin	Verona AMT	145-156		Cansa/CGE	1966
N3C				1:87	resin	San Remo STEL	30			1964
N3C	2981			1:87	resin	Verona AMT	225	2		1956
N3C	2982			1:87	resin	Bari AMTAB	227			1956
Gila Modelli	GM265			1:43	resin, metal	San Remo STEL	22	V	Ventimiglia	1953/5
Gila Modelli	GM265			1:43	resin, metal	Modena AMCM	33	7	Policinico	1958
Gila Modelli	GM265			1:43	resin	Torino ATM	1112	54	Lingotto	1956

Modena 43, Fiat 2411/Cansa/CGE, 1957 (Paulo Gassani)

Modena 33, Fiat 2411/Cansa/CGE by Gila Modelli, 1:43, resin, metal

Modena Fiat 2411/Cansa/CGE by ATM, 1:87, resin

For some inexplicable reason ATM, N3C and Gila Modell have all chosen to model similar variants of the 11 metre long Fiat 2411, ie. Modena 29-34, San Remo 21-32, and Torino 1112-1121.

The exceptions are ATM's Verona 145-156 (with the revised front panelling on Cansa bodies) and the N3C models of the 2411 with the unbecoming 'grille' (Verona 225-230 later Bari 225-230 with Viberti bodies). Enrico Nigrelli has produced both liveries.

Only 129 2411s were built which doesn't help explain why so many models were made – although as 52 of the real things were sold on to second operators, perhaps the opportunity for 14 livery changes does.

San Remo 22, Fiat 2411/Cansa/CGE by Gila Modelli, 1:43, resin, metal

San Remo 30, Fiat 2411/Menarini/GCE by N3C, 1:87, resin

Torino 1112, Fiat 2411/Cansa/CGE by Gila Modelli, 1:43, resin   (Gila Modelli)

Verona 226, Fiat 2411/Viberti/TIBB by N3C, 1:87, resin   (N3C)

Torino Fiat 2411/Cansa/TIBB by ATM, 1:87, resin   (Fabio Dobran)

Bari 227, Fiat 2411/Viberti/TIBB by N3C, 1:87, resin   (Enrico Nigrelli)

Fiat 2472

model maker	ref.	issued	total	scale	construction	operator	fleet#	route	destination	built
ATM	9801	1998		1:87	resin	Milano	541-580			1958-64
ATM	9811	1998		1:87	resin	Milano	541-580			1958-64
Mario Trinchieri				1:87	resin	Milano	541-580			1958-64
N3C		2010		1:87	resin	Milano	563	90		1959
Simonelli		2001		1:43	resin	Milano	541-580	93	Loreto	1958-64

Milano 548, Fiat 2472/Viberti/CGE, 1958 (Alessio Pedretti)

Milano Fiat 2472/Viberti/CGE by ATM, 1:87, resin (Fabio Dobran)

Milano Fiat 2472/Viberti/CGE by Simonelli, 1:43, resin (Massimo Casartelli)

Milano 543 Fiat 2472/Viberti/CGE by N3C, 1:87, resin   (N3C)

Easier to explain is why the imposing Fiat 2472 should be modelled. These great workhorses were the backbone of Milano's circular routes for an incredible 30+ years. 95 were delivered in 2 batches between 1958 and 1964 and were finally withdrawn in 1997. They were built by Viberti using Fiat 472 parts. Milano 548, one of the original batch, has recently been restored to pristine 'as new' condition in original green. Simonelli produced a 1:43 kit in 2001 that misses the correct proportions. Fabio Doran (ATM) produced both original and later orange liveried versions. And Enrico Nigrelli (N3C) has now produced his extremely accurate version, doubtless able to refer in detail to the real thing.

Milano ATM Fiat 2472/Viberti/CGE by ATM, 1:87, resin

Roma Lancia Esatau P101/Casaro/GCE by PB Models, 1:43, resin

Lancia Esatau

model maker	ref.	issued	total	scale	construction	operator	fleet#	route	destination	built
N3C		2004		1:87	resin	Roma ATAC	4501-4597		P101/Casaro	1957
PB Models	no.67		50	1:43	resin	Roma ATAC	4543	70	PClodio	1957

Lancia Automobiles Spa, founded in 1906 and making trucks from 1911, didn't produce a trolleybus until 1953. Production of the electric version of Esatau bus chassis continued sporadically until 1963 with a total of 95 vehicles built.

Roma received half of all Lancia Esatau trolleybuses ever made, and the 49 vehicle class has been modelled in 1:87 scale by N3C (although Enrico has only a fuzzy picture as evidence) and in 1:43 scale by PB Models as a kit as well as an impressive made up model. The three quarter front view is seemingly more shapely than the real thing!

Roma Lancia Esatau P101/Casaro, 1957 (Paulo Gregoris)

Lancia 120.003/Dalfa

model maker	ref.	issued	total	scale	construction	operator	fleet#	route	destination	built
APETc		2010		1:87	resin	Porto STC				1966

A rather spectacular export of Lancia trolleybuses was 75 120/003 types to Porto in Portugal in 1966, with bodies by local company Dalfa. The fifty that were double deckers were based on the Atlantean buses also in service with the operator and were famously the last double deck trolleys in service anywhere. The Associação Portuguesa dos Entusiastas por Troleicarros hopes to produce a model and have drawn up 3D blueprints. Meanwhile, the real no.140 is preserved in operational condition at The Trolleybus Museum at Sandtoft.

Porto 140, Lancia 120.003/Dalfa, 1966 (Sandtoft TMC)

Porto STC Lancia 120.003/Dalfa by APETc, 1:87, resin (Emídio Gardé)

Milano 927, Fiat 2470/Socimi/CGE, 1986 (Van Loon)

Milano Fiat 2470/Socimi/CGE by Simonelli, 1:43, resin (Massimo Casartelli)

Of the rather boxy, uniformly orange Italian trolleybuses of the 1980s and 90s, few seem to have been modelled. In fact, no trolleybus built since the mid-60s seem to have been made in minature, proving it would seem, that for Italy at least, trolleybus models are all about nostalgia before about 1966. The only exception we know of is a rather crude Simonelli 1:43 model of Milanos Fiat/Iveco trolleybuses with Socimi bodies.

5.12 Italy   217

Milano 456, Alfa Romeo 140AF/SIAI Marchetti/CGE by Gila Modelli, 1:43, resin, metal

Nippon Yusoki, 1928 (unknown)

Kawasaki, Mitsubishi/Tokyu Car, 1951 (unknown)

Chapter 5.13
Japan

2 axles single decker	tinplate	219
Hino/Fuji	100 series	221
	200 series	222
	300 series	222
Mitsubishi/Fuso	100 series	223
Tokyu Car	trolleybus	224

Japan's use of trolleybuses was related to oil shortages when starting its systems and a glut as the reason for dispensing with (most) of them. Today special trolleybuses only operate as tourist vehicles and attractions in their own right, within tunnels serving dams in the Japanese Alps.

Rather like America's Hollywood trolleybus of 1912, Japan's first trolley system was built to give access to attractions that were up steep hills — in this case hot springs and an amusement park. Nippon Yusoki built 2 crude, boxy trolleybuses for Hanayashiki in 1928 which lasted just 4 years. To build trolleybuses for the urban context, Kyoto imported two Guy BTs and two AEC 661Ts and then got Nippon Sharyo and Kawasaki to copy them to start their one route system in 1932. Ten years later Nagoya opened, the only other system, apart from Kyoto, that managed two generations of trolleybuses. After the war Kawasaki opened a system with Tokyu Car trolleybuses, built on Mitsubishi frames (Tokyu Car is a railway company — a trolleybus in Japan is referred to as a "non-rail train"). But the majority (210) of Japan's 390 trolleybuses used Hino bus chassis, mostly for use in Osaka and Tokyo. And most of Japan's trolleybus toys reflect these two systems.

2 axle single decker

model maker	ref.	issued	total	scale	construction	operator	fleet#	route	destination	built
Yonezawa		1960s		31cm	tinplate					
Yonezawa		1954		11cm	tinplate					
ET	123	1950s		24cm	tinplate				Express	
MToys		1950s		16cm	tinplate	Central			Central	
Daiya		1950s		36cm	tinplate	City Line	60		Citylien	1954

Yonezawa (or Y, Yone or STS) was a prodigious tin toy maker whose existence coincides with the heyday of both Japanese tin toys and trolleybus operation. More famous for tin robots that can now command thousands of dollars; they made at least two trolleybuses. One has an Osaka like livery (and a robot like windscreen) and dates from the 60s. Its strange bow collector, rather than seperate booms, is at least safe for children.

The other Y originally came with an overhead system that looks like a ski lift. The toy steers in a similar way to the Eheim and Rivarossi models, but is powered by clockwork. There's a single pole from the boom assembly that directly turns the front axle in tractor style. Although ostensibly double boomed, the mechanism follows a single wire, and looks like a tram but 'trolley bus' is what it says on the lower panels, and on the box (where the illustration looks distinctly more convincing). Perhaps it was a reworked tram made during the post war recovery of the 1950s. Again, as it says on the box, "Patent applied for, Made in Occupied Japan" which implies it was produced before 1956, although "Occupied Japan" was used by toymakers until the early 1960s.

Two tin trolleybuses have a red/yellow/blue livery. One is stamped with a logo that says "ET" but unfortunately has little else to identify it, except that "Trolley Bus", written on the side is in a distinctly 'Eagle' comic style font! The little "M Toys" (possibly Mizuno, Masudaya or Modern Toys) has the typical central entrance of Tokyo

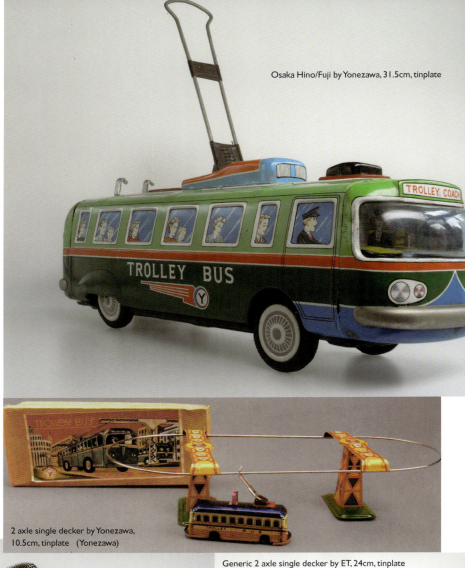

Osaka Hino/Fuji by Yonezawa, 31.5cm, tinplate

2 axle single decker by Yonezawa, 10.5cm, tinplate   (Yonezawa)

2 axle single decker by Yonezawa, 10.5cm, tinplate

Generic 2 axle single decker by ET, 24cm, tinplate

Central 2 axle single decker by M Toys, 16cm, tinplate

Tokyo Hino/Fuji by Modern Toys, 36cm, tinplate

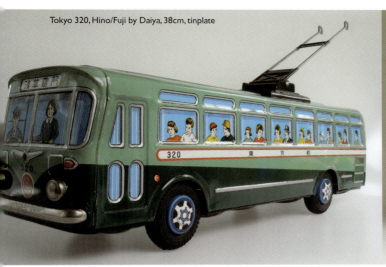
Tokyo 320, Hino/Fuji by Daiya, 38cm, tinplate

City Line 2 axle single decker by Daiya, 35cm, tinplate

trolleybuses. Masudaya of Tokyo (founded in 1923 and still trading) also produced a more recognisable Tokyo trolleybus, although real fleet numbers only went up to 358, not 3229 and trolleybuses didn't go to the zoo! Double headlights characterised buses of the early 1960s, but not trolleys.

Daiya was another large tin toy maker that was based in Tokyo from at least the late 1950s until the early 1970s. Their two trolleybuses have little in common except size – both are nearly 40cm long. The Tokyo version is quite accurate, except for the doors and the diesel APU grille at the rear which on the real dual mode 300 series was at the front. And the windscreen is too big! The wheels are very similar to the San toy (see below) and Asakusa has also been stated as the maker, but without a box it's often difficult to be sure of the manufacturer. The City Line trolley follows the side swipe style of Tokyo trolleys but looks more like an adapted coach with American GM style windows.

Hino/Fuji

model maker	ref.	issued	total	scale	construction	operator	fleet#	route	destination	built
Daiya	230			38cm	tinplate	Tokyo	320			1956
Kherson Models	E5800			1:43	resin	Tokyo				1957
St.Petersburg	186	2000	100	1:43	resin	Tokyo	205			1954
St.Petersburg	186a	2000	150	1:43	resin	Tokyo	226			1956
St.Petersburg	186b	2000	25	1:43	resin	Kawasaki	502			1955
St.Petersburg	198	2000	100	1:43	resin	Tokyo	321			1957
Glico				1:192	plastic	Tokyo	206			1954
Glico				1:192	plastic	Tokyo	206			1954
Nagano	2051-600	2007		6cm	plastic	Tokyo	226			
Marusan		1960s		36cm	tinplate	Tokyo	68	103		1952
Marusan		c.1960		28cm	tinplate	Tokyo	135			1957

Most tin trolleybuses represent the 121 Tokyo Hino/Fuji vehicles delivered in 6 batches between 1952 and 1962. The initial 50 series, intended for China, were rebuilt in 1960 to a similar specification as the subsequent 100, 200 and 300 series. They all ran on a network of 4 routes but increasing car traffic was given as the reason for prematurely scrapping the system by 1968.

Tokyo route 104 included railway crossings that had the 1957 300 series trolleys fitted with diesel engines to avoid building complex crossing overhead of differing voltages. The San (Marusan) tinplate includes the front grille but has fleet number 135, which was never used. Another Marusan is a relatively accurate tinplate toy of Tokyo's second batch of trolleybuses, the 100 series of 1952, except for the double headlights. There are "H" and "SAN" stamps at the rear but the box says "Marusan" a company founded as toy producer in 1947 Asakua, Tokyo and has reputation for high quality. Unusually the windows are cut out and lined, giving a realistic look The

Tokyo 232, Hino/Fuji 200 series, 1954 (Ishida Toshiyuki)

5.13 Japan 221

"bow collector" is similar but not the same as the Osaka Yonezawa (above). Possibly older, without wheel arches and going to "Paradise"(!) is the Ashahi (or ATC), another Tokyo toy maker of the 1950s that has since succumbed to the move to cheaper labour in China.

Tokyo 206, Hino/Fuji 200 series by Glico, 1:192, plastic

Tokyo Hino/Fuji 300 series by Marusan, 28cm, tinplate

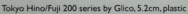

Tokyo Hino/Fuji 200 series by Glico, 5.2cm, plastic

The St Petersburg Tram Collection modelled Tokyo 205 and the similar 226 and 321 at 1:43 scale. All had the same Fuji body, apart from the addition of the front grill on the 300 series. They also sold out some time ago and are rarely seen.

Kherson Models is thought to be responsible for a model of the 300 series with its auxiliary diesel, although the Tokyo under-window red lining and destination box lettering is missing. It is otherwise an accurate model that conveys what these vehicles looked like rather better than the very few photographs of the real thing do.

Built at the same time were the 500 series for Kawasaki which were again outwardly similar and also had short lives, from 1954 to 1967. They had a rather smart grey and maroon livery, as portrayed in the fine SPTC model.

Although memories of Japanese trolleybus systems must be fading, toy maker Nagano's little creation of 2007 has sold out. Either the soppiest model or the purest toy trolleybus, depending on your point of view, the Nagano plastic kit comes ready painted in 18 parts that aren't that easy to put together. In 2001 Takara Tomy produced a Penny Racer of Osaka's 255, the preserved Hino/Fuji trolleybus that is exhibited beside a 1:12 glass cased model at the local Municipal Museum.

Tokyo 68, Hino/Fuji 100 series by Marusan, 36cm, tinplate

Tokyo 205, Hino/Fuji 200 series by St.Petersburg, 1:43, resin (SPTC)

Tokyo 226, Hino/Fuji 200 series by St.Petersburg, 1:43, resin (SPTC)

Tokyo 321, Hino/Fuji 300 series by St.Petersburg, 1:43, resin (SPTC)

Paradise Hino/Fuji by Ashahi, 30cm, tinplate

Tokyo Hino/Fuji 300 series by Kherson Models, 1:43, resin (RCForum Gregx)

Made in China for Japan are Glico's tiny 1:192 scale models of Tokyo and Osaka Hino/Fuji trolleybuses spoilt only by the strange colour choices for the liveries. Otherwise they are rather spectacular miniatures that are only 5cm long. Both are numbered 206 and were given away with Glico's sweets (Glico is a food manufacturer established in 1919 who had previously given away a tiny wood and plastic toy trolleybus around 1953).

Kawasaki 502, Hino/Fuji 200 series by St.Petersburg, 1:43, resin   (SPTC)

Tokyo 226, Hino/Fuji by Nagano, 5.2cm, plastic

Osaka 255, 4Hino/Fuji by Takara Tomy, 5.2cm, plastic (unknown)

Osaka 255, Hino/Fuji, 1956   (Rsa)

Mitsubishi/Fuso

model maker	ref.	issued	total	scale	construction	operator	fleet#	route	destination	built
KEPCO				(scale?)	not known	Kansai Electric Power Co.				1964
Takara Tomy	Choro Q	2003		5cm	plastic	Kansai Electric Power Co.			Kurobe	1964
Kanden Tunnel				16cm	card	Kansai Electric Power Co.				1994

Nagano is a city near the Kurobe Dam, Japan's largest and site of one of the two Japanese tunnel trolleybus lines currently running. Not unnaturally for a tourist attraction there's a model, available in the gift shop, made by Takara Tomy as a Choro-Q, better known in the West as a Penny Racer. It represents the first generation Fuso trolleybuses of 1964 which have also been modelled at 1:12 scale by the Kansai Electric Power Company, owners of the dam, in their exhibition area.

Kanden Tunnel Mitsubishi 100 series by Takara Tomy, 5.2cm, plastic   (Tomy)

Kanden Tunnel Mitsubishi 100 series by KEPCO, 1:50, metal   (Kepco)

5.13 Japan   223

Kurobe Dam Mitsubishi 200 series, 1994 (Querren)

Kurobe Dam Mitsubishi 200 series by Kanden Tunnel, 1:48, card

There's also a Penny Racer of the current type but as the booms are merely painted on the roof we can't bring ourselves to include it and anyway the original Fuso version seems much more popular! There are also tin and card boxes of the 'new' trolleybuses available in the Kurobe Dam gift shop.

The 15 current vehicles and their 8 sisters at the Murodo Dam were built by Mitsubishi in 1993-6 using Osaka Industrial Vehicles 'rivet-less' bodies and Toshiba electronics to run in the 5.4km and 3.7km tunnels respectively. There are 2 versions of a card kit available from the Kurobe Dam website, a simpler one for "Beginners", basically a box with trolley booms and one with more detail for "Seniors" (www.kurobe-dam.com/trolleybus/pcraft300.pdf and pcraft300_expert.pdf).

Tokyu Car

model maker	ref.	issued	total	scale	construction	operator	fleet#	route	destination	built
Sotetstu Wu				12cm	card	Yokohama	103			1959

One other preserved trolleybus and a card kit to go with it is Yokohama's 100 series, with 102 surviving as living accommodation under two roofs in a street in Yokohama and 103 having been modelled in card by Sotetstu Wu. Yokohama was Japan's last urban system, opening one route in 1959 with 15 locally built Tokyu Car trolleybuses and the only one to receive second-hand trolleybuses (4 from Kawasaki). It closed, after two route extensions, in 1972, just as the oil crisis hit, too late to make a difference to Japanese public transport planning.

Yokohama 108, Tokyu Car, 1959 (unknown)

Yokohama Tokyu Car by Sotetstu Wu, 1:87, card (unknown)

Yokohama 103, Tokyu Car by Sotetstu Wu, 1:87, card

Chapter 5.14
Mexico

Marmon-Herrington	toy	225
ACF-Brill T-46	T-46	225
MASA-Somex	4200	226

Marmon-Herrington TC44, 1950
(Robert M Campbell)

Mexico City Marmon-Herrington TC44 by Molytro, 30cm, plastic

Ciudad de México, like a number of other cities (Athens comes to mind) are geographically situated to trap air pollution and so virtually necessitate trolleybus use. The city was made more aware of the zero emission qualities of trolleybuses by such prominent sons as Dr. Mario Molina, who postulated the existence of the Ozone Hole and won a Nobel Prize for doing so. "Zero Emission Corridors" are now how trolleybus routes are branded in Ciudad de México.

The system started in 1951 and went through various crises until 1980 when MASA started locally producing 600 new trolleybuses to replace the 805 second-hand vehicles from the United States (see page 367, etc.). Locally produced toys made of plastic, however, seem to be preferred to models of the US imports. Mexico bought over 310 Marmon-Herringtons from many US operators and it's thought that's what the toy by Molytro is based on. Ciudad de México trolleybuses only had a white and red livery in the 1980s and this is presumably when the toy was produced.

Another toy by an unknown maker, looks reminiscent of the 48 Pullman Standards that came from Birmingham, Alabama in 1956. That at least is according to its owner, though even he admits that's open to interpretation!

Even more open to conjecture is the crude little toy that does at least include seats and is the right colour. Perhaps it is based on one of the 301 Brills that were imported between 1966 and 1971. Or on one of the newer MASA-Somex trolleys of 1980-1 that have a diagonal stripe.

Ciudad de México Pullman-Standard 44T by (unknown), 1:87, resin

Ciudad de México 2 axle single decker by an unknown maker, plastic

ACF-Brill T-46

model maker	ref.	issued	total	scale	construction	operator	fleet#	route	destination	built
St.Petersburg	139b	1999	25	1:43	resin	Ciudad de México				1951

Los Angeles 9123, ACF-Brill T-46 by St. Petersburg, 1:43, resin

Ciudad de México 3279, ACF-Brill T-46, 1951 (Trolleybus.net)

The only Mexican model, as opposed to toy, that we know of is the St. Petersburg Tram Collection's recreation of the ACF-Brill T-46 trolleybuses that came from Winnipeg in 1969 and were painted in the deep orange of Servico de Transportes Electricos (STE). They were partially rebuilt and survived over thirty years of hard service in two countries.

Just as legitimate would be Los Angeles ACF-Brill T-46 9123, as modelled by SPTC, which was sent as part of a batch of 28 in 1968, although a model would have to include the blanking off of half of the front doors.

MASA 4200 series/Toshiba

model maker	ref.	issued	total	scale	construction	operator	fleet#	route	destination	built
STE				1:76	card	Ciudad de México				1988

Card models are available of the current fleet, including the MASA 4200 series with electrical equipment by Toshiba in their 1980s livery and more recent green versions. We're not sure who has produced them, but it may be the operator, Servico de Transportes Elèctricos.

Ciudad de México is facing a crisis of trolleybus replacement that will test their commitment

Ciudad de México MASA 4200 series/ Toshiba by infecktedunder25, 1:76, card (infecktedunder25)

Ciudad de México 9871, MASA 500T/Misubishi, (Bdebaca)

to Zero Emission Corridors as the locally built MASA vehicles are all more than twenty years old. Mexico's only other system, Guadalajara, which opened in 1975, similarly imported redundant US trolleys and received new MASAs in the early 1980s and faces the same replacement problem.

Chapter 5.15
Netherlands

Kromhout, 1944	TB4L4/Verheul	227
BUT, 1946-1964	9721T	227
Leyland, 1968	Worldmaster	229
Den Oudsten, 1974 - 1986	DAF MB200	230
	Volvo B79T	230
Volvo, 1983-1996	B10M/Den Oudsten	231
Mercedes Benz	O405	232
Berkhof, 1998 -2001	AT18	232

Rotterdam 911, Kromhout TB4L4/Verheul, 1944 (unknown)

Groningen was the first trolleybus system of the Netherlands, starting in 1927 with 6 Associated Daimler (AEC 604T) 24 seat single deckers that replaced trams on line 2. They lasted in service until 1958. Tram line 1 was replaced by trolleybuses in 1952 using 8 DAF and 10 Kromhout vehicles which had electrical equipment taken from the trolleybuses delivered in 1944 to Rotterdam, an abortive system that saw the Maas Tunnel wired, on the orders of the Nazi authorities, but never used in public service.

Kromhout

model maker	ref.	issued	total	scale	construction	operator	fleet#	route	destination	built
Alphagrafix	AM8	1997		1:87	card	Rotterdam	124		Extra Dienst	1944
St.Petersburg	127a	1999	25	1:43	resin	Helsinki HKL	604	14		

The wartime Rotterdam trolleybuses, converted from 1939 motor buses, have been modelled in card by Alphagraphix for Attic Models of Amsterdam, in 1:87 scale. After the war they had replacement Verheul bodies fitted before entering service in Groningen to a similar style to those that inaugurated the Arnhem system in 1949.

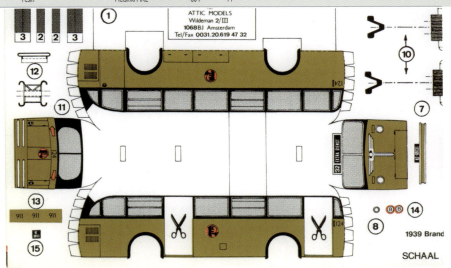

Rotterdam 911, Kromhout TB4L4/Verheul by Alphagrafix, 1:87, card   (Alphagraphix)

BUT 9721T

model maker	ref.	issued	total	scale	construction	operator	fleet#	route	destination	built
(unknown)				(no scale)	card	Arnhem	101	1	Velp	1949
Alphagrafix	AM3	1996	1	1:87	card	Arnhem	101	1	Oosterbeek	1949
HB Model				1:87	resin	Arnhem	137-143			1955
HB Model	MBM			1:43	resin	Arnhem	137-143			1955
Jansen de Koning		1992		(no scale)	card	Arnhem	101	2	Geitenkamp	1949
Tippco				(no scale)	tinplate	Arnhem	101	2	Station	1949
Verheul		1949		1:12	wood,metal	Arnhem	101	1	Velp	1949

British United Traction's 97 series chassis, built between 1949 and 1957, were all exported; 55 type 9711Ts (right hand drive) went to Auckland and 67 type 9721Ts (left hand drive) went to Arnhem, Nijmegen and Sao Paulo. The only ones to be modelled commercially are the Arnhem BUTs, the longest British built trolleybuses, at 36'11" or 11.26m. An unknown maker produced a charming card model and so too has Alphagraphix in 1:87 scale of the first Arnhem trolley especially for Attic Models of Amsterdam. The first of the batch, Arnhem 101, is preserved in pristine running condition.

Such is the fond regard with which Arnhemians lavish on their trolleybuses, especially the first,

Arnhem 101, BUT 9721T/Verheul/EE by (unknown), (no scale), card

Arnhem 101, BUT 9721T/Verheul/EE, 1949 (Ans Nillson)

that local family bakery shop, Jansen de Koning, produced a cake box of 101. And the original 1:12 scale model by the bodybuilder, Verheul, still resides in operator Gemeente Arnhem's canteen and bar. The 5 visible sides are carved in wood, with the windows represented by printed graphics, and chrome work, bumpers and trolley gear attached. The wheels are integrally carved with the body sides. Local fathers converted toy buses for their sons, such as this Tippco Japanese tinplate at a time when trolleybuses were still new in Arnhem. But strangely, there's never been a proper scale of model of this first batch, only the next, which were delivered in 1955.

Arnhem BUT 9721T/Verheul/EE by Jansen de Koning, 23cm, card

Arnhem 101, BUT 9721T/Verheul/EE by Verheul, 80cm, wood, metal

228   5.15 Netherlands

HB Model, a prolific producer from the Czech Republic, has produced both 1:87 and 1:43 versions of BUT 9721T/Verheul/EE nos. 137-143 which, side by side, is a great way to test a modellers skill. Interestingly the smaller one comes off best in this case, not least because the 6 part windscreen is particularly tricky. At O scale, HB has included window rubbers, a detail that, unpainted, makes the framing look too thick..

Arnhem 101, BUT 9721T/Verheul/EE by Tippco, 15cm,

Arnhem 137, BUT 9721T/Verheul/EE, 1955 (Carl Isgar)

Arnhem BUT 9721T/Verheul/EE by HB Model, 1:87, resin

Arnhem BUT 9721T/Verheul/EE by HB Model, 1:43, resin

Leyland Worldmaster

model maker	ref.	issued	total	scale	construction	operator	fleet#	route	destination	built
HB Model		2009		1:43	resin	Arnhem	159-66			1968
HB Model		2009		1:87	resin	Arnhem	159-66			1968

Arnhem 161, Leyland Worldmaster/Verheul LVB6T, 1968 (Carl Isgar)

Arnhem Leyland Worldmaster/Verheul LVB6T by HB Model, 1:87, resin

Arnhem Leyland Worldmaster/Verheul LVB6T by HB Model, 1:43, resin

The very last BUTs were built for Wellington, New Zealand in 1964 at the Scammell lorry factory and so when Gemeente Arnhem wanted to maximize utilization of the English Electric equipment in their BUTs, they had Veheul, then a Leyland subsidiary, import Leyland Worldmaster VBW10 integrated chassis as a basis for their bodies. The resulting 16 trolleybuses ran until 1985, by which time some of the electrical sets were 35 years old. HB Model has produced versions of the last batch 159-66, again in 1:43 and 1:87 scales. Again the window rubber problem rather spoils the O scale version and the booms could have done with painting a darker grey, but the overall impression is evocatively accurate. The previous batch were similar but with 5 piece windscreens, like the earlier BUTs.

Despite importing British chassis in earlier years, including to Nijmegen in 1952 and 1957, operators after the 1960s had to turn increasingly to Dutch manufacturers that were later able to export trolleybuses. But by 1964 Groningen and then by 1969, Nijmegen, had both closed, leaving Arnhem the only system operating in the country.

As Arnhem's residents have always appreciated their trolleybuses, so a number have always demanded models. With a population of less than 150,000 the market is small but determined with local suppliers adapting models from neighbouring France and Germany to the distinctive blue livery and adding trolley booms.

Den Oudsten

model maker	ref.	issued	total	scale	construction	operator	fleet#	route	destination	built
Mastica		1986		1:87	resin	Arnhem	128	1	Velp	1979
(unknown)				1:30	card	Arnhem	131			1979

Arnhem 167 DAF MB200/Den Ousten/Kiepe, 1974 (Carl Isgar)

Arnhem 128, DAF MB200/Den Ousten/Kiepe by Mastica, 1:87, resin

Den Oudsten was a bus body builder that built Arnhem's 121-171 between 1974 and 1986 to replace BUTs and Leylands and provide for route extensions. A model of the 121-130 batch, with DAF chassis, has been produced in Arnhem colours in a number of variants, all a little inaccurate, either with doors in the wrong place or missing window detail. Some have been altered, and Bennie Aalbers example, in his Trolleybus Museum at Westervoortsedijk Depot, has carefully re-made the booms. The model is stamped 'Den Oudsten' on the base but was made by Mastica of the Netherlands. 174 (now renumbered 128) is preserved at the DAF Museum in Eindhoven.

Arnhem 131, Den Oudsten B79T/Den Oudsten/Kiepe, 1979. (Carl Isgar)

Arnhem Den Oudsten B79T/Den Oudsten/Kiepe by unknown maker, 1:30, card

TraWos, a Dutch model maker produced a DAF SB200 for Modelbouwcentrum in Hilversum and doubtless collectors created Arnhem trolleybus versions. But arguably more accurate is a large 1:30 scale card model by an unknown maker of the 131-171 batch of Den Oudsten trolleybuses. Den Oudsten provided their own chassis frame and used Gräf & Stift rear axles. They were delivered in 4 batches over a seven year period in the then new all-over blue livery.

After taking over New Flyer in Canada (who have also produced trolleybuses), Den Oudsten was declared bankrupt in 2002. Many of its Arnhem trolleybuses went on to Sarajevo and Rostov to see further service.

Volvo B10M

model maker	ref.	issued	total	scale	construction	operator	fleet#	route	destination	built
AHC Models				1:87	resin	Arnhem	142			1983

Arnhem 180, Volvo B10M/Den Oudsten/Kiepe, 1990. (Mauritsvink)

Arnhem 142, Volvo B10M/Den Oudsten/Kiepe by AHC Models, 1:87, resin

Arnhem's commitment to using trolleybuses has been driven by its demanding population, so the need for new vehicles in 1989 saw Volvo B10M chassis being used by Den Oudsten and Kiepe to produce 11 trolleybuses. Local company AHC Models (Johannes van Rijn of nearby Epe) had made models of the very similar B88 bus but got the doors wrong with their model of trolleybus 142; the second entrance should be between the axles. The 1989 Volvo trolleybuses of Arnhem to which this model is adapted, were numbered 172-182 and had VH##PH registrations – the 142 fleet number on the model was actually a Den Oudsten B79T of 1982 and looked rather different. But the windscreen is right and there's the definitive Volvo diagonal across the front air intake.

Arnhem Mercedes Benz O405T by Speelgoed/NZG, 1:50, zinc diecast

Mercedes Benz O405

model maker	ref.	issued	total	scale	construction	operator	fleet#	route	destination	built
Speelgoed/NZG	255	1985	200	1:50	zinc diecast	Arnhem	151	1	Oosterbeek	1985

An edition of 200 certified models that were repainted by NZG Modelle of a Mercedes O405 - a model never operated by Arnhem - were issued in 1985, just after the second and just before the third batches of Den Oudsten B79T-KM560 trolleybuses were being delivered. Wolthuis Speelgoedland of Arnhem produced the rather over-engineered model trolley gear and added it to the roof. Benny Albers has certificated model no. 199 in his Trolleybus Museum inside Gemeente Arnhem depot, with added detail, including fleet number 151, which actually belonged to one of the 1984 Den Oudsten B79Ts and which saw later service in Rostov. The museum, more a shrine to trolleybuses, is well worth a visit.

Arnhem Mercedes Benz O405T by Speelgoed/NZG, 1:50, zinc diecast

Berkhof

model maker	ref.	issued	total	scale	construction	operator	fleet#	route	destination	built
Speelgoed/NZG	255	1985	200	1:50	zinc diecast	Arnhem	151	1	Oosterbeek	1985

For a small but densely populated country, it is perhaps surprising (if you include DAF and Den Oudsten as separate manufacturers) that a fourth producer started making trolleybuses in 1998. Berkhof was independent until, in 1998, it became part of the VDL group that had inherited DAF buses. Apart from Škoda traction motors the two Berkhof trolleybus prototypes were entirely Dutch with electrical equipment from Traxis. After prolonged testing 20 more entered service between 2000 and 2002. Andras Ekkert has modeled the Solingen examples that had been built at the same time. He took two Den Oudsten bus kits made by Vemi Miniaturen of Holland and joined them together, but as he says, it took many long hours and, he thinks, is not entirely successful. Despite the step at the top of the windscreen, on my collectors shelf, it looks rather precise. No more Berkhof trolleybuses have been built since the joint Arnhem/Solingen order and both operators have since ordered Hess vehicles from Switzerland.

Holland has produced 92 indigenous trolleybuses and imported 118 that had considerable local input. Arnhem, despite only gentle hills to justify its trolleybuses, remains wedded to them as fumeless and quiet transport that enhances their city.

Solingen 171, Berkhof AT18 by Andras Ekkert, 1:87, resin, plastic

Chapter 5.16
Poland

Jelcz, 1975-1999,	PR series	233
Solaris, 2001 – current	Trollino	235

Poland's first trolleybus system was really German, and is interesting as one of only five that used the vertically arranged overhead of the Lloyd-Kohler system. The Brockau system opened in 1912 but closed in 1914. After WW2, Brockau became part of Poland and in the same region is the Jelcz bus factory that led a revival of Polish trolleybus systems in the 1980s.

Independent between the wars, Poland had no trolleybuses until Poznań, the fifth city, bought three Ransomes, Sims and Jefferies trolleybuses in 1929 following the exhibition of ex-Ipswich 6

Brockau 1, Lloyd-Kohler, 1912 (public domain)

in 1926. War intervened and the system closed in 1939. It re-opened under German occupation in 1943 on different routes with Kiev and Henschel trolleybuses but closed again in 1945. It re-opened again, within the Soviet Union, in late 1946 and added new MAN trolleys. The system finally closed in 1970. Today, not far away, is the Solaris factory that has had great success at exporting trolleybuses during the last decade. Historically, systems in Gdynia, Gorzów, Legnica, Lublin, Wałbrych and Warszawa followed a similar intermitant pattern of operation using imported trolleys from all over Europe, but predominately trolleybuses by Škoda and ZiU. Two new systems opened in the 80s and Warszawa saw a second attempt, but only Gdynia, Lublin and Tychy still operate trolleybuses today.

In 1975, the Jelcz Bus Company had signed a licence with Berliet to produce the PR100 bus and, like the French, made a trolleybus version, the PR100E. Between 1975 and 1992, 152 were built in various versions, the E, UE, and T types reflecting their transition from electric to electronic control. Their availability enabled the creation of systems in Debica (1988-90), Słupsk (1985-99), Tychy (1982 to date) and Warszawa for a second time (1983-95).

Poznań 402, Ransomes, Sims and Jefferies, 1929 (Ransomes)

Lublin 754, Jelcz PR110T, 1988 (Michał Krupinski)

Jelcz PR series

model maker	ref.	issued	total	scale	construction	operator	fleet#	route	destination	built
Andreas Konz				1:87	resin	Lublin				1980
W.Goerke		2005		1:72	card	Gdynia	10110	21	Sopot	1982
W.Goerke		2007		1:72	card	Gdynia	3372	27	Kacze Buki	1992
Carta		2005		1:87	card	Gdynia	3367	28		1997
Carta		2005		1:87	card	Gdynia	3374			1999

Lublin Jelcz PR110T by Andreas Konz, 1:87, resin

The original Jelcz PR110 trolleybuses had motors from scrapped Škoda 9Trs and it's this first batch that have been modelled by Andras Konz. There are (as so often in Europe) card models of the local trolleybuses, produced in Poland's case by Carta (Maciej Beister) and rather more attractively by W.Goerke at www.600v.org. The scale of card models is a little arbitary, but standard printing from these downloaded files gives 1:72.

Gdynia 3310, Jelcz PR110UE, 1997 (Michael Marszandt)

Gdynia Jelcz PR110UE by W. Goerke, 1:72, card (W. Goerke)

Jelcz started producing the PR120MTE in 1992 which incorporated plastic parts to reduce weight. Including the similar PR120M, only 25 were built. Both card kits by Carta and Goerke are described as 120MTs but are, in fact 120MTEs.

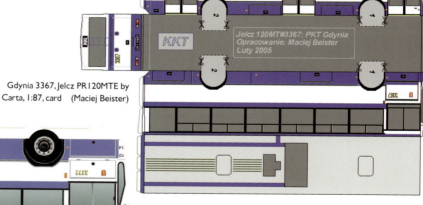

Gdynia 3367, Jelcz PR120MTE by Carta, 1:87, card (Maciej Beister)

Another ten years and Jelcz introduced the low floor M121MT trolleybus of which only three have been built. But the card model is available to download free from www.600v.org or www.zkmgdynia.com.pl.

Jelcz, as a trolleybus manufacturer, was completely eclipsed by Solaris, which originated as Neoplan Polska in 1994. The first of the 'Trollino' brand, a 12m single, was tested in Gdynia in 2001. Since then over 500 of 12m, 15m and 18m types

Gdynia 3372, Jelcz PR120MTE by W. Goerke, 1:72, card   (W Goerke)

Gdynia 3004, Jelcz M121MT, 1999 (NDT)

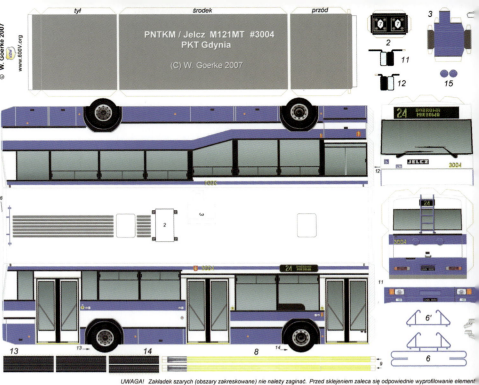

Gydnia 3004, Jelcz M121MT by W. Goerke, 1:72, card (W Goerke)

have been supplied throughout Europe, plus over 50 Skoda-branded versions (26Tr, 27Tr and 28Tr). Solaris has achieved a high profile that has involved a lot of exhibition attendance with promotional models to accompany their displays.

Solaris

model maker	ref.	issued	total	scale	construction	operator	fleet#	route	destination	built
Mattis Schindler				1:87	card	Ostrava	XI	108	Hlavi nadrazi	2002
Mattis Schindler				1:87	card	Opava		203	Globus	2002
GanzTranselektro				1:30	wood	Budapest		76	Jaszai MariTer	2002
GanzTranselektro				1:30	wood	Roma ATAC		90	Stazione Termini	2003
Rietze (conversion)				1:87	resin	Winterthur Stadbus	172	1	Toss	2004
VK Modelle	08701133a	2009		1:87	plastic	Salzburg	301	3	Salzburg Sud	2009
VK Modelle	08701133b	2009		1:87	plastic	Salzburg	302	4	Mayrwies	2009
VK Modelle	08701133c	2009		1:87	plastic	Salzburg	303	3	Salzachsee	2009
VK Modelle	08701144	2010		1:87	plastic	Eberswalde	051,2	862	Ostend	2010
VK Modelle	08701188	2010		1:87	plastic	Solaris	301		Trollino	2010
VK Modelle	08701177	2011		1:87	plastic	Bologna	1057		Trollino	2010
VK Modelle	08701166	2011		1:87	plastic	Roma			Trollino	2005
VK Modelle	08701155	2011		1:87	plastic	Winterthur			Trollino	2005
VK Modelle	08701911	2011		1:87	plastic	Solaris	301		Trollino	2010
WUMM	B024		150	1:87	plastic	Budapest	602	76	Jaszai Mari	2003
WUMM	B024		150	1:87	plastic	Debrecen	341	2	SegnerTer	2003
Solaris		2009		1:22.5	wood	Salzburg				2002
Solaris		2008		1:30	wood	Generic				2002

Ganz Transelektro of Hungary has supplied many of the electric traction component sets for Solaris trolleybuses and, before being taken over by Škoda in 2006, exhibited 1:30 models of the 12T and 18T. Solaris themselves, especially their Swiss operation, are only too pleased to show their more detailed model, as salesman Hans Thommen demonstrated at the 2008 Zürich Trolleybus Conference (see page 22).

WUMM have modelled the second generation Trollinos of Debrecen and of Budapest, which are also available with added detail from Andras Ekkert. The real nos. 601-16, built 2004-7, are said to cope well with the poor roads of Hungary's capital.

Solaris did well to sell to Switzerland, in the

Hans Thommen with exhibition Solaris Trollino SGT 12 by Solaris, 1:30, wood

Debrecen DKV Solaris Trollino SGT 12 by Wumm, 1:87, resin (Mattis Schindler)

Budapest 603, Solaris Trollino SGT 12, 2003 (Foma)

Budapest 602, Solaris Trollino SGT 12 by Wumm, 1:87, resin

Winterthur 179, Solaris Trollino 18T by Rietze (conversion), 1:87, resin (Andras Ekkert)

Winterthur 178, Solaris Trollino 18T, 2004 (Andras Ekkert)

shape of ten second generation Trollino 18Ts (171-180) in 2005. There are many more models of the Urbino bus version, but Andras Ekkert has converted the Rietze model, despite its being third generation, with the fuller curve to the bottom of the asymmetric windscreen.

The manager of Salzburg's trolleybuses, Gunter Mackinger, encouraged VK Modelle (aka. Veit Kornburger) to produce a third generation Trollino 18AC version of their Solaris model to represent the 301-23 batch of 2009-12. For an injection moulded model the result is highly successful and makes a reproduction of a current, state of the art, trolleybus more readily available than the more usual small batch artisan resin models that can cost twice or even three times the price (€30). So far there are three versions - 301, on route 3 with additional graphics, 302, which comes with 2 sets of trolleybooms, in raised and lowered positions and 303 enroute to Salzachsee.

Salzburg 303, Solaris Trollino 18T, 2009 (Alex7771)

Salzburg 302, 301, Solaris Trollino 18T by VK Modelle, 1:87, plastic

Eberswalde 052, Solaris Trollino 18T by VK Modelle, 1:87, plastic

Eberswalde BBG has also commissioned VK Modelle to produce two versions of their new Trollinos, delivered in 2010; one of 051 on route 861 to Nordend and other of 052 on route 862 to Ostend. The actual delivery, the first of 12 new trolleys, was celebrated in the town square with the inclusion of Solaris's resin model in 1:24 scale made by Modellbau Buxbaum of Waidhofen in Austria for Eberswalde.

Eberswalde 051, Solaris Trollino 18T, 2010 (Solaris)

Solaris demonstrator, Solaris Trollino 18T by VK Modelle, 1:87, plastic

Ostrava Solaris Trollino 12T by Mattis Schindler, 1:87, card

Solaris themselves, with their unusual support for bus enthusiasts, also commissioned VK Modelle to produce an all-white Trollino version. Due are versions from Bologna, Roma and Winterthur and a 12T single version (see page 380).

For those with virtually no budget, there is a good number (at least 36) of card Trollinos depicting many of the operators that have them. Some are special occasion issues, such the first Czech Trollino, Opava X1 of 2002, which was fitted with traditional DC equipment. W. Goerke at www.600v.org has drawn Lublin 836, one of three model Trollino 12Ts he has online.

There are only 32 Solaris trolleybuses in Poland out of a total of 164 trolleybuses available for service nationally (2010). Gdynia finds it cheaper to convert Mercedes O405 buses to trolleybuses and Lublin now seems to prefer the cheaper Russian MAZ-103T, but it remains true that one of the world's leading trolleybus manufacturers is based in Poland.

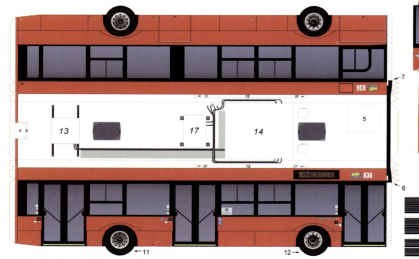

Lublin 836, Solaris Trollino SGT 12 by W.Goeke, 1:72, card   (W.Goeke)

Chapter 5.17
Russia

SVARTZ, 1933-1941	LK-1	240
	LK-5	242
Yaroslavsl, 1936-1958	YaTB-1	242
	YaTB-3	244
Tushino/Uritskiy 1946-1961	MTB-82	245
SVARTZ, 1933-1941	MTB-ES	248
	TS-1/2	249
Uritskiy/Trolza	ZiU-5	250
1959-current	ZiU-9/682	253
	ZiU-10/683	257
	ZiU-11/681	257
Moskva Trolleybus Plant	MTrZ-5279	258
1981-current	MTrZ-6232	259

Russia, or rather, in this context, the former Soviet Union, has had far more trolleybuses than anywhere else. So many, in fact, it's hard to put figures on them, especially as the countries of the former Soviet Union still use and produce so many. Moskva at the time of writing has 1750 trolleybuses on 85 routes, while Minsk, a tenth the geographical size, has 1050 trolleybuses on 60 routes. But this chapter is about Russia – we have separate chapters for former Soviet republics of Belarus and Ukraine.

There appear to be rather more trolleybus model makers in the Ukraine than in Russia but both countries have produced a plethora of models, replicating the huge number of operators rather than the relatively few chassis types. As the models are mainly produced by small "cottage" producers, we are bound to have made mistakes here, as it's often hard to discover exactly who is the maker and who the distributor. Russian trolleybus toys seem confined to crude versions of the once ubiquitous MTB-82 and so are included under that model's listing rather than at the beginning of this chapter.

A note about nomenclature. Because of the vast number of Russian and Soviet trolleybuses, but relatively few designs, we're using the titling system adopted by Alan Murray in the "World Trolleybus Encyclopaedia (1st edition, Trolleybooks, 2000) and also by Aare Orlander, partly because of our need, in the West at least, to ascribe a manufacturing company, although in communist times, state ownership prevailed, and partly to identify the originating factory. This last point is complicated by designs with various differences being assembled at more than one works. Rather than sticking rigidly to supposed 'manufacturers', we've ordered this chapter chronologically. There are thought to have been about 85,000 trolleybuses produced in Russia so far, so neither before the collapse of communism nor since has it been straight forward to chronicle vehicle details. Constant detailed improvements over long periods to standard trolleybus designs at different factories all over the country, driven more by necessity than economics, are only now being chronicled in what remains the world's most enthusiastic trolleybus user.

Russian trolleybus history started with a short demonstration of a Czarist copy of Siemens Elecktromote in 1902, at the St.Petersburg car factory of Petr Frese in front of Prince MI Hilkova, but the subsequent revolutionary turmoil meant no other trolleybuses were built in Russia for another 30 years, despite plans in the twenties.

Although there had been trials in Rostov, trolleybus operation in the Soviet Union started on 15th November 1933 in Moskva. The first two vehicles, classified LK-1, were locally assembled by the SVARZ factory on chassis supplied by Yaroslavl Automobile Plant with electrical equipment by Dinamo and bodies by ZIS. 68 LK-series trolleybuses were delivered to Moskva in three years and including 3-axle LK-2 types in 1934. Kiev and St. Petersburg had locally assembled LK trolleybuses, but none lasted beyond 1941 – they were apparently not up to the task of presenting the thrusting image of Communist industrial progress and the electric future on the streets of the capital. But the concept of trolleybus technology certainly fitted the political ideology. The LK series was named after politician Lazar Kaganovich, whose protégé was Nikita Khrushchev, then in charge of Moskva, and thus its transport. He was a particular fan, liking the quietness of trolleybuses, their pollution free qualities and their 'progressiveness'. Stalin hesitantly approved them but was sceptical about the six-wheel double deckers based on one of two AEC 664Ts that had been imported in 1937. Khrushchev claimed credit for successfully introducing trolleybuses, but perhaps it was the failure of the LK series that motivated the import of AECs to learn of the very latest in trolleybus technology and copy it.

Trial vehicle, Petr Frese, 1902   (public domain)

Rostov-na-Donu prototype, 1932   (public domain)

Moskva 10, Svarz LK-2, 1934   (public domain)

SVARZ LK-1

model maker	ref.	issued	total	scale	construction	operator	fleet#	route	destination	built
RK				1:87	resin	Moskva	9			1933
RK				1:87	resin	Moskva	1			1933
RK				1:87	resin	Moskva	2			1933
RK				1:87	resin	Moskva	1			1933
Vector Models	P1-10	2009		1:43	resin	Moskva	17			1934
Vector Models	P1-00	2009		1:43	resin	Moskva	2			1933
Kherson Models (?)				1:43	resin	Moskva	5			1933
Kremenchug				1:43	resin	Moskva	7			1933

There have been at least four 1:43 scale models of the Moskva LK-1, by Vector Models, Kherson Models and Kremenshug. They're all 'cottage' artisan modellers of Ukraine, from Kiev and Kherson, who produce for various distributors. The quality of the models has steadily improved since the late 90s, when these modellers started producing cars, trucks and buses. Vector Models has produced the original, rather ornate, LK-1 in Moskva blue, representing prototype no.2. The ornate front decoration surely reflects political

Moskva 16, Svarz LK-1, 1933 (unkown)

Moskva 5, Svarz LK-1 by Kherson Models (?), 1:43, resin

Moskva 7, Svarz LK-1 by Kremenschug, 1:43, resin

Moskva 17, Svarz LK-1 by Vector Models, 1:43, electroformed copper

Moskva 2, Svarz LK-1 by Vector Models, 1:43, electroformed copper   (Vector)

exuberance and homage by Nikita Krushchev to his mentor, Lazar Kaganovich. The 3 axle LK-2 that followed, also had a very ornate front and but has yet, as far as we know, to be modelled.

Somewhat cruder are the resin 1:87 scale models produced by RK of Russia in various colour schemes of the production LK-1s. Most display fleet number 1 but at least one displays no.9 and has a slightly more realistic wire bumper. Photographs of Russia's first trolleybus are surprisingly rare, but seem to show a less than practical front route indicator, that is more faithfully reproduced on the RK models than on some of the larger scale models.

Moskva 1, Svarz LK-1 by RK, 1:87, resin

Moskva 1, Svarz LK-1 by RK, 1:87, resin

Moskva 1, Svarz LK-1 by RK, 1:87, resin

Moskva 9, Svarz LK-1 by RK, 1:87, resin

SVARZ LK-5

model maker	ref.	issued	total	scale	construction	operator	fleet#	route	destination	built
St.Petersburg	36	1997	100	1:43	resin	Leningrad	9			1936

Apart from the 3 axle LK-2 trolleybus, there is little visually to distinguish the production LK types, except for the revised front route indicator. The LK-5 was built, presumably to common Soviet blueprints sent from Moskva, by the Leningrad Municipality Workshops in 1936. 7 LK-5s were also built locally in Kiev in 1939, but were withdrawn by 1941, suffering from being heavy with poor brakes. Also, there was only one door, opened manually.

Leningrad 9, Svarz LK-5 by St.Petersburg, 1:43, resin

Yaroslavl YaTB-1

model maker	ref.	issued	total	scale	construction	operator	fleet#	route	destination	built
DNK		2007		1:43	resin	Leningrad	44			1936
St.Petersburg	37		100	1:43	resin	Leningrad	91	4		1936
V/R				1:43	resin	Moskva				1936
Laboratory 57		2010		1:43	resin	Leningrad	55			1936
RK				1:87	resin	Moskva				1936
RK				1:87	resin	Kiev				1936
RK				1:87	resin	Generic				1936

In August 1936, the Yaroslavl Automobile Plant north of Moskva unveiled their first trolleybus, the YaTB-1, at the same time as they were ordering 2 AECs from Britain. The lessons of the LK series had been learnt and the YaTB series were regarded as comfortable but still heavy vehicles that evolved through 4 versions, becoming progressively lighter and faster, but outwardly looking the same. Some remained in service until 1962 (in Odessa). 100 initially went

Leningrad 44, Yaroslavl YaTB-1, 1936 (Kaverzin Andrey)

Leningrad Yaroslavl YaTB-1 by DNK (Nizhny Novgorod), 1:43, resin

Leningrad Yaroslavl YaTB-1 by St. Petersburg, 1:43, resin

Moskva Yaroslavl YaTB-1 by V/R, 1:43,

to Moskva, followed by 249 of the improved but similar YaTB-2. With the YaTB-4 and YaTB-4a, 900 examples of the YaTB series were plying the streets of 11 cities by 1944. Like the LK series the bodies were of wood. In 1996, no. 44 of Leningrad, (now St Petersburg), a YaTB-1 of 1936 was discovered, rebuilt as new and is kept at the St. Petersburg Museum of Public Transport.

DNK of Nizhny Novgorod, (known as Gorky until 1990) has produced a fairly accurate model of preserved 44, in 1:43 scale, but, as with other Russian trolleybuses, the production of so many in widely varying factories across the country leads to local variations. The front of the St. Petersburg Tram Collection model, for example, has atypical body shaping at the front and a higher gutter line than the model by V/R. Both are, however, YaTB-1s with the characteristic central route number indicator window that subsequent variants didn't have. New maker, Laboratory 57, an architectural model producer of Oryol, near Moskva, has managed to get all the details rights with their limited edition of Leningrad 55. But then, as they admit, there are at least 10 variations possible.

Like the LK series, RK have produced a number of variously liveried YaTB-1 models, that are not quite realistic. They may have been produced before preserved 44 surfaced as an example to follow. In particular, the waist band shouldn't rise at the front, something that may have resulted from only being able to consult poor photographic reproductions rather than blueprints.

Leningrad Yaroslavl YaTB-1 by Laboratory 57, 1:43, resin (Laboratory 57)

Moskva Yaroslavl YaTB-1 by RK, 1:87, resin

Generic Yaroslavl YaTB-1 by RK, 1:87, resin

Yaroslavl YaTB-3

model maker	ref.	issued	total	scale	construction	operator	fleet#	route	destination	built
Kremenchug				1:43	resin	Moskva				1938
St.Petersburg	111/II	2009	75	1:43	resin	Moskva	1002	3		1938
St.Petersburg	111	1998	100	1:43	resin	Moskva				1938

Moskva Yaroslavl YaTB-3, 1938 (Peter Greaves)

The Yaroslavl Automobile Plant claimed to have cloned the imported AEC 664T double decker (see page 300) in 4 days, such was the Communist Party pressure for results that could be used as propaganda. In fact, the ten Soviet versions took 8 months to build, being delivered to Moskva from June 1938 onwards. After body strengthening and despite Stalin's protestations about their safety, they outlasted the AEC by five years and were scrapped in the year of the dictator's death, 1953. The YaTB-3 has been a particular favourite of Leonid Khoykhin of the St. Petersburg Tram Collection, who's managed to model it twice - once when he started commercial modelling in 1998 and again in 2009. The improvement is palpable and the latest versions are so accurate that they offer better historic evidence of the subtle differences between the AEC and the clones than the few surviving photographs. The 1998 version includes the second door added at the front in 1940, whereas the new version reflects the as-built condition.

Kremenchug has also modelled the YaTB-3, albeit some time ago, with similar debateable interpretation of the photographic evidence. The front is wrongly pointed, the body is too narrow and the wheels are too small and thin, but it looks more realistic than Leonid's first attempt. Individual modellers have displayed 1:12 scale models wrongly reproducing the split front, perhaps they took the Kremenchug model as gospel, but it does demonstrate the fascination Russians have for their only double deckers.

Moskva 1002, Yaroslavl YaTB-3 by St. Petersburg, 1:43, resin (SPTC)

Moskva 1010, Yaroslavl YaTB-3 by St.Petersburg, 1:43,

Moskva Yaroslavl YaTB-3 by Kremenschug, 1:43, resin

Tushino/Uritskiy MTB-82

model maker	ref.	issued	total	scale	construction	operator	fleet#	route	destination	built
Minsk Radio Technical Factory		1950		22cm	tinplate	Minsk				1946
Minsk Radio Technical Factory		1950		22cm	tinplate	Moskva				1946
MGF		1950s		13cm	tinplate	Odessa				1948
RK (?)				1:87	resin	Moskva				1950
Oleksandr Krasnov		2009		1:87	resin	Moskva	174			1950
St.Petersburg	40		100	1:43	resin	Leningrad	26			1946
St.Petersburg	44		100	1:43	resin	Leningrad				1955
V/R				1/43	resin	Moskva				1950
Kherson Models	2477		0	1:43	diecast	Moskva	30			1948
Vector Models	B-2101	2008		1:43	electroformed copper	Moskva	256			1946
Vector Models	B-2340	2009		1:43	electroformed copper	Budapest	T134	72		1952
Vector Models	B-2100	2006		1:43	electroformed copper	Moskva	70			1946
Vector Models	B-2102	2001		1:43	electroformed copper	Moskva	70			1946
Vector Models		2001		1:43	electroformed copper	Kherson	76	1	Vokel	1948
Vector Models		2009		1:43	electroformed copper	Moskva				1950
Vector Models		2010		1:43	electroformed copper	Kiev	215			1950

Russia, or rather the USSR's, next trolleybus was a fresh start, at least externally, after the desperate tribulations of war. The MTB-82, in production at two factories from 1946 to 1961 and virtually the only trolleybus manufactured in the Soviet Union between 1948 and 1958, numbered over 4,270 examples at a time when the trolleybus became the officially preferred street transport mode. The first, the MTB-82A and M types, were rebuilt YaTB-2s and 4s and were developed from a YaTB-5 prototype that had created the precedent of an all-metal body and chassis design. Developed at Plant No.82 in Toshino, the "Moscow Trolleybus" project moved to the Uritiskiy plant in Engels, whence the production version, the MTB-82D entered service from 1951 onwards, following an initial batch of 372 of a slightly different version for Moskva, the MTB-10. The body was less of a direct copy of America's General Motors 'old-look' monocoque than Russia's diesel bus version, but the influence is none-the-less strong.

Not surprisingly with such a large number of 'standard' trolleybuses, there have been many toy and model versions. The earliest we know of is the crude tinplate made by MGF, supposedly in Odessa. 12.7cm long with protruding wheels, it has its own charm and despite not looking much like a MTB-82, it can't, at a time when only the MTB-82 was in use, have been anything else.

Much more recognisable, with rather short booms, is the Minsk Radio Technical Factory's version, that was available in at least two colours, had a clockwork motor and a body made from a single pressing.

There have been at least two 1:87 scale models of the MTB-82. A not very realistic one, especially at the front, is thought to have been made by RK in Russia. A more recent attempt by Oleksandr Krasnov of the Ukraine, is of Moskva's 174, which would make it a MTB-10, the original production batch for the capital, of 1948-52.

Nizhny Novgorod 57, MTB-82, 1952 (Serge Filatov)

Odessa MTB-82 by MGF, 12.7cm, tinplate

Moskva MTB-82M by Minsk Radio Technical Factory, 22cm, tinplate

Moskva 174, MTB-82 by Oleksandr Krasnov, 1:87, resin

Moskva MTB-82 by RK, 1:87, resin

The same model was an early creation of the St Petersburg Tram Collection with a smooth finish uncharacteristic of the rugged prototype, whose bodywork looked a little battered even when new! A Leningrad version with trailers built from retired MTB-82s has also been modelled by SPTC. V/R and Kherson Models, both of the Ukraine, have also made resin versions. But perhaps the most consistent producer of MTB-82 miniatures is Vector Models (also, confusingly, of Kherson in Ukraine) who make reassuringly heavy electroformed 1:43 scale versions. Just a small number of a type are made every few months, and one gets the impression that every MTB-82 variant is being made, which will take a few more years to achieve.

Leningrad 26, MTB-82 by St.Petersburg, 1:43, resin

Budapest FVV MTB-82FVV by Vector Models, 1:43, copper (Vector)

Moskva MTB-82D by Vector Models, 1:43, copper (Vector)

Moskva MTB-82M by Vector Models, 1:43, copper (Vector)

Zkskursiya MTB-82M by Vector Models, 1:43, copper (Vector)

Kiev MTB-82M by Vector Models, 1:43, copper (Vector)

Moskva MTB-82 by V/R, 1/43, resin

Apart from standard versions, including a Kiev trolley-train and a bizarrely decorated sight-seeing (ЗКСКУРСNЯ as it says on the side) MTB-82, there's the 'wide-eyed' version, based on a batch of 80 that were built for Moskva and which have subsequently appeared in a number of liveries. And there's exported MTB-82s. Five of Budapest's MTB-82FVVs were rebuilt by the operator with wider doors and a new route indicator box and at least one, T134, had a front grille added. Vector Models seems to have fitted standard square mirrors rather than the round ones seen in surviving photographs. And details at the front differ from the original in an otherwise fine model. The grille gives a very distinct 'face' that the model, rather like a portrait, nearly, but doesn't quite, have. Vector has also modelled T143, of Budapest's standard MTB-82s.

Moskva MTB-82M by Kherson Models, 1:43, resin

Kherson 76, MTB-82M by Vector Models, 1:43, copper

Budapest T134, MTB-82FVV, 1952 (Németh Zoltan Adám)

Budapest FVV MTB-82FVV by Vector Models, 1:43, copper

Svartz MTB-ES

model maker	ref.	issued	total	scale	construction	operator	fleet#	route	destination	built
Mungojerrie		2010		1:87	card	Moskva	701	14		1963

Chronologically, the next Soviet trolleybuses were the brilliantly 'retro' TB-ES and MTB-ES types, but their acrylic roof windows leaked and they were cold in winter. 'Only' 480 were built and, in the event, were not to be the intended replacement for the MTB-82. Two superbly restored examples regularly run on the streets of Moskva and 701, the preserved MTB-ES, has been modelled in paper by Mungojerrie, aka. Andrey Kuznetsov.

Moskva 701, Svartz MTBES by Mungojerrie, 1:87, card

Moskva 421, Svarz TB-ES, 1957 (Valey Zenkow)

Moskva 701, Svarz MTB-ES, 1963 (Valey Zenkow)

Yaroslavsl YaTB-3

model maker	ref.	issued	total	scale	construction	operator	fleet#	route	destination	built
HB Model				1:43	resin	Moskva				1959
St.Petersburg	113		100	1:43	resin	Moskva				1959

Moskva Svarz TS-1 by St.Petersburg, 1:43, resin

Moskva 1, Svarz TS-1, 1959 (public domain)

A 4 axle articulated version of the TB-ES, produced in response to the growing need for greater capacity on trolleybuses, certainly in the larger cities and especially in Moskva, was the SVARTZ TS series which could officially carry 224 people. One is reported to have once carried 402! 48 of the more ornate TS-1 were produced between 1959 and 1964, but they were under-powered and caused traffic jams by their slowness. SPTC produced a duly impressive model in the late 90s celebrating the indulgence of Soviet engineers, who had originally specified a large, impractical two piece windscreen which gave way to a 4 piece version after the first batch. They steered through 3 axles and the rear two were powered by two motors. The prototype, built to serve the permanent economic exhibition, had even more chrome than the 1:43 scale model and, at inauguration, white walled tyres.

Moskva Svarz TS-2 by HB Model, 1:43, resin

Moskva 51, Svarz TS-2, 1959 (R Makewell)

Relative practicality dawned with the TS-2. The motors went from 110Kw to 136Kw, the chrome disappeared as did the headlights from within the bumpers and the white wheel paint was only applied to trolleys that served international exhibitions. HB Model of Czech Republic has modelled the TS-2 but has strangely included the discredited two piece windscreen in an otherwise accurate creation. 87 real TS-2s were produced between 1964 and 1967, but the whole series were out of service by 1975. One survives with (very) long term hopes of restoration.

Uritskiy ZiU-5

model maker	ref.	issued	total	scale	construction	operator	fleet#	route	destination	built
Finoko	6335			1:43	diecast	generic				1961
Finoko	7135			1:43	diecast	Moskva				1961
Finoko	6334?			1:43	diecast	Leningrad				1961
Kremenchug				1:43	resin	Moskva	2			1961
Moshimvolokno	mhv-10-04	2010		1:43	resin	generic		35		1961
Moshimvolokno	mhv-10-01	2010		1:43	resin	generic				1961
Mungojerrie		2008		1:87	card	Moskva	2323	19		1960
St.Petersburg	41		100	1:43	resin	Leningrad				1961
Vector Models	B2120	2008		1:43	electroformed copper	Moskva	84			1961
Vector Models	B2122	2008		1:43	electroformed copper	Moskva	2409	30		1969
Vector Models	B2122a	2008		1:43	electroformed copper	Moskva	366	4		1969
Vector Models		2010		1:43	electroformed copper	Kherson	17	1		1969
Vector Models	B2121	2008		1:43	electroformed copper	Moskva	2672			1966
Vector Models		2010		1:43	electroformed copper	Stravropol	11	4		1964
Z-tanks				1:43	metal	generic				1961

Leningrad Uritsky ZiU-5 by Finoko, 1:43, diecast

By the late 1950s the need to replace the 'standard' MTB-82 was becoming paramount. Trolleybus technology was regarded as highly applicable and successful in the Soviet Union and was the preferred way to replace 'out-moded' trams and to provide public transport to vast new housing areas. The SVARTZ TS series hadn't proved too practical compared to the rugged but dated MTB-82 which, in lieu of a replacement, remained in production until 1961. The Uritskiy factory tried a replacement design with the TBU-1 in 1955, but the motor was at the extreme rear and caused severe handling problems. After 11 prototypes the design was replaced by the TBU-5, better known as the ZiU-5. Outwardly similar, with large windows but wider doors and the motor moved ahead of the rear axle, 200 were built for extensive tests between 1959 and 1961.

Leningrad 143, Uritsky ZiU-5, 1967 (Stas Davydov)

Moskva 59, Uritsky ZiU-5B by Vector Models, 1:43, copper (Vector)

Moskva 355, Uritsky ZiU-5D by Vector Models, 1:43, copper (Kimmeria)

The design was highly successful and over 20,000 were built until replaced by the ZiU-9 in 1971. Far and away the most numerous type of trolleybus of the 1960s, it inaugurated many new systems all over the Soviet sphere of influence.

As far as we know, the ZiU-5 has only been modelled in 1:43 (apart from card models in 1:87), and our list is probably not exhaustive. Some of

250 5.17 Russia

Moskva 2409, Uritsky ZiU-5D by Vector Models, 1:43, copper (Kimmeria)

Moskva 2672, Uritsky ZiU-5G by Vector Models, 1:43, copper (Vector)

Stravropol 11, Uritsky ZiU-5G by Vector Models, 1:43, copper (Vector)

Kherson 17, Uritsky ZiU-5D by Vector Models, 1:43, copper (Vector)

Moskva 2323, Uritsky ZiU-5, 1961 (Aleksandr Konov)

the models included here are merely discoveries from the web, images from which don't enable fair commentary. Z-tanks, for example, who make military models, is twice listed as making a diecast ZiU-5, but it's too poor an image on which to make judgement or reproduce here.

All the main Russian and Ukrainian 0 scale model producers have at some time made various versions of the ZiU-5 as it evolved through its 15 year production period, in various liveries in both resin and metal. Finoko Models are diecast whilst Vector Models are electroplated copper. Vector is known to have produced more variants than are included here — they have listed ten variations of the ZiU-5. Unfortunately all have less than accurate front bumpers that seem mounted too high. Both the Kremmenchug and the St. Petersburg models of the 1990s are simplifications of the real thing, especially around the front windscreen. Unfortunately Leonid of SPTC hasn't kept pictures that can be reproduced here. The recently produced models by Moshimvolokno are better and include rubber window sealing that adds realism.

Moskva Uritsky ZiU-5 by Kremenschug, 1:43, resin

Moskva Uritsky ZiU-5 by Moshimvolokno, 1:43, resin   (Kimmeria)

Of the card models, one, by Mungojerrie and freely available on the net (http://papertrolley.110mb.com) is of completely rebuilt Moskva 2323, one of the original trial ZiU-5s. With the real thing regularly seen during street rallies, the model is photographic rather than the traditional graphic style.

It's not really known if Meccano (UK) ever planned a Dinky trolleybus push along, but the drawing office produced plans for a Moskva trolleybus in July, 1977. We have created a 'what might have been' image, care of Dave Wilsher's 3-D computing skills. It's not recognisably any particular Soviet trolleybus although it looks somewhat like an early ZiU-5 or the ill-fated TBU-1 that preceded it.

Moskva 2323 Uritsky ZiU-5 by Mungojerrie, 1:87, card (Mungojerrie)

Volgograd 24. Uritsky ZiU-5, 1961   (official image)

Moscow 2 axle trolleybus by Meccano, 10cm   (col. Jan Verner)

Moskva 2 axle single decker by Dinky, 10cm, virtual   (Dave Wilsher)

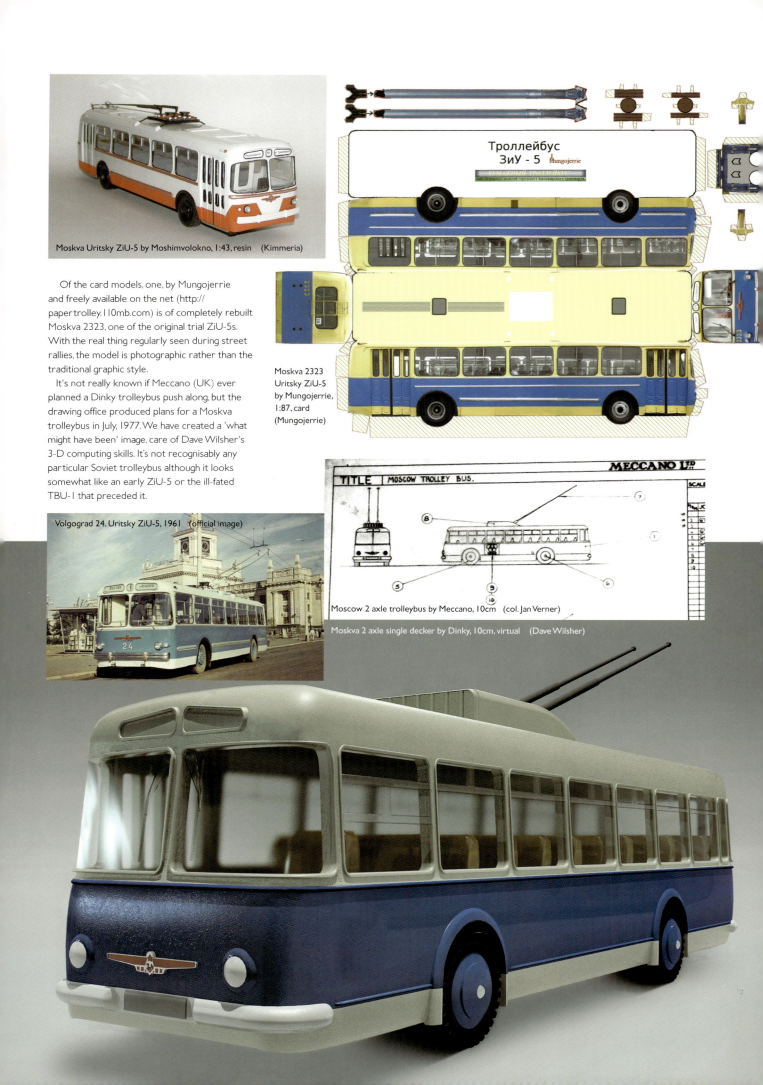

Uritskiy ZiU-9/ZIU682

model maker	ref.	issued	total	scale	construction	operator	fleet#	route	destination	built
Finoko	6333			1:43	diecast	Novokuibyshevsk				1972
Finoko	7025			1:43	diecast	Cheboksary				1972
Konka		2009		1:43	resin	generic				1972
Rigomódell		2010		1:24	wood, metal	Szeged	9-11	5	Odessza	1985
Kremenchug				1:43	resin	Severodontetsk	507			2000
Moshimvolokno	mhv-10-02	2010		1:43	resin	Moskva		42	Rizhskaya	1974
Moshimvolokno	mhv-20-01	2009		1:43	resin	Moskva		54		1974
Moshimvolokno	mhv-10-01	2009		1:43	resin	Moskva		42	Rizhskaya	1974
St.Petersburg	38		100	1:43	resin	Leningrad	4856	41		1972
St.Petersburg	146		25	1:43	resin	Helsinki	601-603			1973
St.Petersburg	42		100	1:43	resin	Leningrad				1982
St.Petersburg	146a	1999	25	1:43	resin	Budapest				1975
St.Petersburg	146b	1999	25	1:43	resin	Córdoba				1989
St.Petersburg	146c	1999	25	1:43	resin	Athens	3001-3132		ZiU-682	
St.Petersburg	146e	2000	25	1:43	resin	Bogota	2000-2074		ZiU-682	
St.Petersburg	146d	1999	25	1:43	resin	Beograd				1979
Vector Models	V-10-37	2009		1:43	electroformed copper	Kherson	196	2	Station	1974
Vector Models				1:43	electroformed copper	Athens	262	4		1974
Vector Models				1:43	electroformed copper	Kirovgrad	246	1		1974
Vector Models				1:43	electroformed copper	Kremmenchug	173	1		1974
Denis Dolgushev		2011		1:87	resin	Dnepropetrovsk	2143		ZiU-682g	
Denis Dolgushev		2011		1:87	resin	Tolyatti	3332	7	Sotsogrod ZiU-682g	
(unkown)				24cm	wood	Beograd		22	Station	1984

Not dissimilar to the ZiU-5, ZiU-9, introduced in 1971, included a third door, a steel instead of aluminium body and dispensed with a chassis, using an integral structure that sagged with age. It was designed with a high carrying capacity for large cities. Its electrical equipment was evolved from the Ziu-5. On starting mass production in 1972 the model designation became Ziu-682 but the 9 label also continued to be used. This trolleybus design is rugged, simple and cheap and has been cloned in many factories across Russia and Belarus. It remains in production, albeit with updated styling. The most poplar current version is the Trolza ZiU-682G-016, successor to an estimated 45,000 examples, the most numerous trolleybus ever built, by a considerable margin.

Like the ZiU-5, models, excepting card versions,

Donetsk 1642, Uritsky ZiU-9, 1988 (Maximiljan)

Novokuibyshevsk Uritsky ZiU-9 by Finoko, 1:43, diecast

Leningrad 4856, Uritsky ZiU-9 by St.Petersburg, 1:43, resin

Moskva Uritsky ZiU-682 by Moshimvolokno, 1:43, resin (Kimmeria)

Cheboksary Uritsky ZiU-9 by Finoko, 1:43, diecast (Constantin Levin)

Moskva Uritsky ZiU-682 by Moshimvolokno, 1:43, resin (Kimmeria)

Kherson 196, Uritsky ZiU-682 by Vector Models, 1:43, copper (Vector)

Moskva Uritsky ZiU-682 by Moshimvolokno, 1:43, resin (Kimmeria)

Kirovgrad 246, Uritsky ZiU-682 by Vector Models, 1:43, copper (Vector)

Moskva Uritsky ZiU-682 by Moshimvolokno, 1:43, resin (Kimmeria)

Kremmenchug 173, Uritsky ZiU-682 by Vector Models, 1:43, copper (Vector)

all seem to be at 1:43 scale. Prominent makes are St.Petersburg Tram Collection, Finoko and Moshimvolokno of Moskva. Vector Models seems to have only issued ZiU-682 models recently, and four variants came out in 2010. But the duplication of models is surprising and sometimes catches the dealers out, who then mislabel who the maker is and thus confuse us!

Both Vector and Moshimvolokno have produced very similar variants of the Soviet red livery of the 1970s, ostensibly from Kherson and Moskva respectively, but there's little to tell them apart, just the indicator lights at the front and the chrome gutter present on the more typical Moskva version. Otherwise the detailing is remarkably similar. So too are the pair from Moshimvolokno and Finoko, although the former, being a more recent model, includes rubber beading around the glazing. Omsk producer Alexander Kobrits, aka Finoko, produces kits and parts of his zinc diecast models and customers have probably produced every production variant and a number of the conversions, such as those to lorries. New maker Konka has added another ZiU-682 model that doesn't quite have the detail of the Moshimvolokno's similar generic blue version. Perhaps it's right that there's such a plethora of models to reflect the absolute ubiquitousness of the real thing. Like its predecessor and the Škoda 9TR, the ZiU-9 replaced itself in many fleets. It had a near monopoly of design during the world's greatest expansion of trolleybus transport. We should also add that St Petersburg has modelled all the exported ZiU-682s; to Argentina, Columbia, Hungary and Greece. An Athens ZiU-9 was virtually rebuilt as new and donated to the East Anglia Transport Museum in the UK.

Greek ZiU-9s were also donated to Beograd where they run in Athens orange. Gunter Mackinger, manager of Salzburg's trolleybuses has a Serbian wooden toy that we assume is based on the ZiU-9. At 1:24 scale, where accuracy is even more possible, Endre Rigo of Hungary has produced wood and metal models of the ZiU-9 in Szeged colours. We're into public display quality here, and museums (and board rooms) are the usual recipients of Endre's fine models. There's a similar model of Budapest 026 in the city museum.

Kursk 262, Uritsky ZiU-682 by Vector Models, 1:43, copper   (Vector)

Belgrade Uritsky ZiU-9 by (unknown), 26cm, wood

Athens 5088, Uritsky ZiU-682, 1989

Cordoba, Bogata, Budapest & Athens Uritsky ZiU-682 by St.Petersburg, 1:43, resin (SPTC)

Szegred 9-111, Uritsky ZiU-9M by Rigomódell, 1:24, wood, metal   (Endre Rigo)

5.17 Russia 255

Just recently the first H0 models of the ZiU-9 have appeared, made by Denis Dolgushev of Tolyatti in southern Russia. If, like the real things, rugged is a euphemism for rough, then these models fit the bill. They are however accurately scaled, and Denis's local inspiration for one, Tolyatti 3332, is currently still in service.

One mystery is the basis for a model by Kremenchug; called by dealer Konrad Pernetta a ZiU-9 and indeed having a fine ZiU badge on the front, but with lower headlights and an untraced fleet number of 507. Trawls through the massive online Russian tram and trolleybus database revealed no equivalent, although Budapest ZiUs had lower but protruding headlights (the ZiU-682UV variant). Kirov's 507 has standard headlights while the Vologda VMZ-5298 and the YuuzMash YMZ-T2 trolleybuses look similar but are 'boxier'. As Konrad Pernetta commissioned the model in the mid 90s and now can't remember what it was, we may never know.

Tolyatti 3332, Uritsky ZiU-682G, 1992   (Alexander Zelentsov)

Dnepropetrovsk Uritsky ZiU-682G by Denis Dolgushev, 1:87, resin   (Mattis Schindler)

Tolyatti 3332, Uritsky ZiU-682G by Denis Dolgushev, 1:87, resin

Severodontetsk(?) 507, Uritsky ZiU-9 by Kremenschug, 1:43, resin

Uritskiy ZiU-10/ZiU683

model maker	ref.	issued	total	scale	construction	operator	fleet#	route	destination	built
Kremenchug				1:43	resin	Tolyatti				1990
St.Petersburg	39		100	1:43	resin	Leningrad				1990
St.Petersburg	177	1999	25	1:43	resin	Cordoba EMIR				1991

Tolyatti 2436, Uritsky ZiU-683, 1991 (Artem Veselov)

Krementshug is actually a place of heavy industry, in central Ukraine, where the modeller lives, rather than being the name of a model making company. (Dealers are understandably secretive about real identities). The city has had over 200 trolleybuses, including many ZiU-682s (and YMZ-T2s) but never a ZiU-683, the articulated variant (also known as the ZiU-10). The local maker has produced a model however, and this time, got the headlight height right. St Petersburg Tram Collection has also produced the ZiU-683, including the exported Córdoba versions. The original ZiU-10 was produced between 1986 and 1995, but less than a thousand were produced (!).

Tolyatti Uritsky ZiU-10 by Kremenschug, 1:43, resin

Uritskiy ZiU-11/681

model maker	ref.	issued	total	scale	construction	operator	fleet#	route	destination	built
Kherson Models (?)		2009		1:43	resin	Volgograd				1973

There was a shortened wheelbase variant of the ZiU-9, the ZiU-11, only known to have been used in Volgograd, where there were about 15 (some say 5). It was also known as a ZiU-681. (There was also a short ZiU-5, known as a ZiU-7 also with a truncated front overhang). Anyway, Volgograd 4001, the only example chronicled, was in service between 1973 and 1979 when it caught fire. A strange choice then for a model, except Kherson Models had only to do some simple carpentry to a ZiU-9 and voilà. At least, we think the maker is Kherson, again the dealer isn't too sure. The small but secretive Russian/Ukrainian model network includes a wholesale market in Moskva, where the probity of models tends, like the traceability of Russian sustainably grown hardwoods, to get lost, especially on the journey to the West. The model isn't particularly noteworthy but does correctly include the straight edged wheel arches of the original, an echo of early ZiU-9 prototypes.

Volgograd Uritsky ZiU-11 by Kherson Models (?), 1:43, resin

Although the days of extreme uniformity, when thousands of ZiU-9s metaphorically stretched from Budapest to Vladivostok, are now gone, replaced by a far richer diversity of trolleybus types, there are still many of them, together with their clones and direct descendants, still doggedly carrying passengers in all conditions right across Russia. For many operators there is no other choice – ZiU-9s are cheap and cheerful.

MTrZ-5279

model maker	ref.	issued	total	scale	construction	operator	fleet#	route	destination	built
Kimmeria		2009		1:43	electroformed copper	Moskva		42		2004
Kimmeria		2009		1:43	electroformed copper	Moskva		17		2003
Vector Models	P9-23	2010		1:43	electroformed copper	Moskva	2028			2006

Moskva 2028, MTrZ-52791 'Sadovoye Koltso', 2006 (Evginiy Akinfeev)

With the fall of Communism and Russia's near financial meltdown in 1998, little progress was made in developing indigenous trolleybus design in the two decades up to the new millennium and since. For instance, moves to low floor configurations were to happen only after the mid-naughties. Factory structures remained essentially the same, despite privatisation, with trolleybus designations being somewhat confusing. Take the Moskva Trolleybus Plant which introduced the high floor 5279 type in 2003, a design that follows the tradition of the ZiU-9. The following year, the front was radically changed. Four years later the 5279 becomes a low floor design with little, externally at least, to relate it to previous 5279s. The official designations are 5279.0000010, 5279.0000012, 52791.0000010 respectively.
At least model makers have kept track with Kimmeria modelling the high floor and Vector Models the low floor versions. Model accuracy is now very good and manufacturers supply current blueprints to model makers, perhaps, in these competitive times, to encourage scale production and help win real orders.

Moskva MTrZ-52791 'Sadovoye Koltso' by Vector Models, 1:43, copper

Moskva 8007, MTrZ-5279, 2003 (Shurik)

Moskva MTrZ-5279 by Kimmeria, 1:43, copper (MTC)

Moskva MTrZ-5279 by Kimmeria, 1:43, copper (MTC)

Moskva 6006, MTrZ-5279, 2004 (Artyom Svetlov)

MTrZ-6232

model maker	ref.	issued	total	scale	construction	operator	fleet#	route	destination	built
Kimmeria		2009		1:43	electroformed copper	Moskva				2008
Kimmeria		2009		1:43	electroformed copper	Moskva				2008

Kimmeria has modelled the low floor articulated version of the 5279, the MTrZ-6232 (based on the LiAZ 6212 bus) that so far amounts to only one prototype in service. Perhaps getting ahead of the game, Kimmeria has also produced a variant in traditional Moskva livery, before any real production version has been so painted. Perhaps the Moskva Trolleybus Plant encouraged them. The model could do with some lettering detail, especially as the original makes particular claims to easy access for wheelchair users, and has its fleet number prominently displayed.

Like current Russian trolleybuses, indigenous models have incrementally improved. They are considerably more accurate than they were only a few years ago. The developing heritage of large models from the Ukraine as well as Russia that are expensive to buy and continue to be issued is showing no signs of diminishing. It says something about nostalgia, not to say pockets of considerable wealth that must be making it all worthwhile, in these post-Soviet times.

Moskva MTrZ-6232 by Kimmeria, 1:43, copper (Kimmeria)

Moskva 3690, MTrZ-6232, 2008 (Artyom Kovalevskiy)

Moskva MTrZ-6232 by Kimmeria, 1:43, copper (Kimmeria)

Moskva 1001, AEC 664T/English Electric/EE by St.Petersburg, 1:43, resin

Chapter 5.18
Spain

Tilling-Stevens	TS4X	261
Rico	AR 140AF	262
Jugettes Y Estuches	toy	263
Denia	toy	264
Maquitrans, 1945-1954	500B	265
MAN, 1934-1987	MKE4500	265 (182)
BUT, 1945-64	9614T	265 (ch.5.22)

Spain, ravaged by civil war and economic poverty following political instability had been in no position to play any part in trolleybus development until the 1940s. Even then trolleybuses were initially a 'make do and mend' solution to problems of fuel oil shortages.

The first Spanish system was in Bilbao, starting, as was to become a frequent occurrence, with imported trolleybuses. Three Vétra CS60s were the first of 467 imports out of a total of 636 trolleybuses that ran in Spain. Next came Barcelona, with the conversion of 38 Tilling-Stevens petrol-electric buses during a long period of hardship, material shortages and frequent power cuts that followed the civil war.

Barcelona Tillings Stevens/CGA, 1941 (Dewi Williams)

Tilling-Stevens

model maker	ref.	issued	total	scale	construction	operator	fleet#	route	destination	built
Albert Gonzalez				1:16	wood, card	Barcelona	511	FP	Provenza P.Nuevo	1941
Rico?				30cm?	tinplate	Barcelona	537	FC	San Andres	1941
Unknown				15cm	glass	Barcelona				1941

Albert Gonzales of Catalonia has two Tilling-Stevens model trolleybuses. One is a straightforward 1:16 model of Barcelona 511 (see page 31), the other is an "eau-de-cologne" bottle in the shape of a Tilling-Stevens. Such, presumably, was the regard in which the eccentric double deckers were held that a perfume manufacturer thought it worth investing in a production run. Whether the gift was intended for a man or woman is not known, nor, because Albert has never opened it, is the quality or otherwise of the scent! Tinplate Tillings trolleybuses have been made too, although it's not known by whom, possibly Rico. 15 of the 38 Tilling Stevens, originally built as buses between 1932 and 1940, lasted until 1964, including at least 3 that had run as trolleybuses since 1941. The conversion was carried out by the operator, including moving the cab to the centre of the locally built CGA body and rebuilding the chassis to take Maquitrans motors, but the chassis frames were from the UK.

For a country that made so few of its own trolleybuses, it's a little surprising that two toy trolleys were produced in the 1950's.

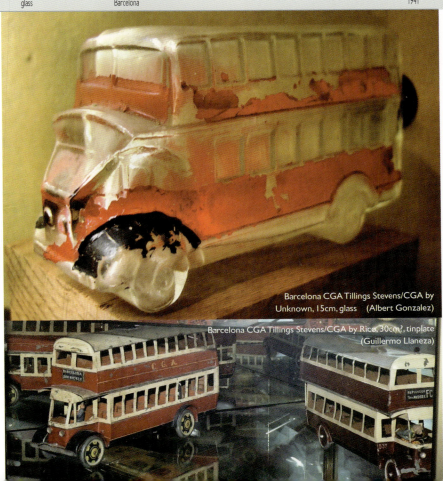
Barcelona CGA Tillings Stevens/CGA by Unknown, 15cm, glass (Albert Gonzalez)

Barcelona CGA Tillings Stevens/CGA by Rico, 30cm?, tinplate (Guillermo Llaneza)

Rico

Rico had made tin toys before moving over to plastic in the late 1950s, typically making novelty figures, themed vehicles and penny toys. Just before they changed technique, they produced a trolleybus that seems to owe its appearance to an Italian Alfa Romeo with fluted body sides, which, for a Spanish toy maker, might seem odd as no indigenous manufacturer ever made a 3 axle trolleybus and no Italian trolleybuses were ever imported! Rico was part of the concentration of toy manufacturers around Ibi near Alicante that at one time numbered over 250 'factories' employing over 6,000 people. But the nearest trolleybus system was at Valencia, 120km away, the one city in Spain to have come near to having Italian trolleybuses when it ordered Fiats that, in the event, were never delivered because of the war. The one route that opened in 1951, with 10 Vétras, may have been the spur to make the toy, although the locally bodied, and rather boxy 4 wheel trolleybuses of Valencia's first series didn't look much like the Rico. Looking only vaguely similar were secondhand 6 wheeled trolleys in the shape of BUTs and Vétras that arrived in 1970 from Barcelona.

Italian ad, 3 axle trolleybus, 1939 (CGE)

Generic 3 axle single decker by Rico, 15cm, tinplate

Rico SA, Ibi, Alicante, 1912-1984

model maker	ref.	issued	total	size	construction	operator	fleet#	route	destination	built
Rico	129	1950		15cm	tinplate	(generic)				1942-60
Rico	129	1950		15cm	tinplate	(generic)				1942-60
Rico	129	1950		15cm	tinplate	(generic)				1942-60

The two standard Rico toy trolleybuses, in red and yellow are mirror images, even down to yellow headlights becoming red on the yellow lower body version. They have a clockwork motor and an adjustable, tractor style, front axle. There is in existence a blue and white version. Although first glance would suggest this is a conversion of a Rico to motorized version using Rivarossi parts, there are aspects that suggest it might have been a factory "trial" – the motor is different, the wheelbase shorter, the wheels are not Rivarossi, the tyres are Rico and the baseplate is well engineered. Finally, the roof has no slots for the usual trolley base and the paint job looks original and is, as far as we know, unique, (although a red and white motorized version has also been seen}. The trolleygear mounting on both examples, although on pressings in the roof, is off centre. So, dear reader, apart from telling you that Rico did go on to make electric toy buses, we leave it to you to decide whether Rico really was intending to sell an electric version.

Generic 3 axle single decker by Rico, 15cm, tinplate

Generic 3 axle single decker (motorized) by Rico, 15cm, tinplate

Jugettes Y Estuches

Near the Rico factories in the small town of Ibi in the hills above Alicante, Jugettes Y Estuches SA was similarly set up by ex-employees of Paya, the original toy maker, in the early 20th century. Better known as Jyesa or JYE, the company went on to make H0 model railways, but, at the same time as Rico, they too produced a toy trolleybus in the early 50s with JYE on the front grille.

Jugettes Y Estuches SA, Ibi, Alicante, 1925-1980 (JYE and Jyesa brands)

model maker	ref.	issued	total	scale	construction	operator	fleet#	route	destination	built
Jugettes Y Estuches	253	1950		(no scale)	tinplate	Barcelona			Circunvalcion	n/a
Jugettes Y Estuches	253	1950		(no scale)	tinplate	Madrid			Circunvalcion	n/a

While the wheel arches have similarities to Pegaso trolleybuses the overall look is more of a coach. With a clockwork motor and four piece tinplate construction, versions have blue or red liveries that perhaps relate to Madrid and Barcelona in the same way that French models relate to Paris and Lyon. But the prototype is hard to identify, perhaps it was the prototype Hispano-Suiza trolleybus of 1944 or based on the advertisement by the body builder, Seida. It could also, just as easily, have been based on a bus, certainly Jugettes Y Estuches made such variants (including a crude double deck version with a strange half height deck stuck on top).

Santander 13, Pegaso/Macosa/Cenemesa, 1955 (unknown)

San Sebastion 16, Hispano-Suiza/Seida 1948 (Metalbloc)

Barcelona 2 axle single decker by Jugettes Y Estuches, 20cm, tinplate

Madrid 2 axle single decker by Jugettes Y Estuches, 20cm, tinplate

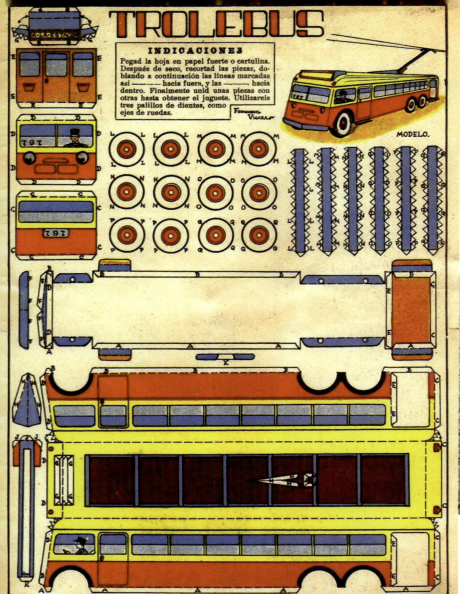

A couple of other Spanish trolleybus toys have been found. A pattern for a paper model, signed by Fernandez Vigaro and stated to be from 1945, interestingly has twin booms be-topped with a pantograph type contact shoe and the doors on both sides. No trolleybus ever wore the fleet number 797 in Spain, the nearest was Barcelona 725, a 1959 Vétra VA3 B2 and rather different in styling to Vigaro's 40s post-war 'trolebus'. Madrid's versions had Seida bodies with chrome adornments that somehow evoke M. Vigaro's exuberant cutout paper model, even if they aren't what he based it on.

3 axle single decker by Fernandez Vigaro, 21cm, card (Gottfried Kure)

Generic 3 axle single decker by Fernandez Vigaro, 21cm, card

The other toy trolleybus is 38cm long, dated 1945, has a clockwork motor and is wooden with tin wheels, headlights and booms. Made by Denia, a co-operative of small toy producers, based at Denia near Ibi but on the coast, with a label saying Iaucco of Valencia which was the retail outlet. It looks to be based on Barcelona's single deck Maquitrans 500B. Denia also made a double deck bus that looks surprisingly like those Tilling Stevens of Barcelona at the top of this chapter, but without booms.

Maquitrans

The Maquitrans 500B is rather more accurately modeled by Modeltrans of Asturias in Northern Spain. The Barcelona operator Tranvías de Barcelona formed the Maquitans company during the war as a somewhat desperate way of obtaining new or at least rebuilt trams and trolleybuses. They started in 1940 by rebuilding Tilling Stevens buses as trolleybuses and then the following year introduced a 2 axle single decker (and a PCC style tram). Incredibly, both types (A and B, as they were designated) were in 'production' for 13 years until 1954, as new routes opened, constituting the 3rd and 4th biggest batches of trolleybuses ever supplied in Spain (40 and 38 vehicles respectively).

Madrid 201, Vetra VA3B2/Seida, 1957 (Seida)

Barcelona CGA Maquitrans 500B by Denia, 38cm, wood/tin (Galeria Navarro)

Maquitrans 500B

model maker	ref.	issued	total	scale	construction	operator	fleet#	route	destination	built
Dentia	445	late 1940s	38cm	wood	Barcelona				500B "Gilda"	
Modeltrans	114	2007	300	1:43	resin	Barcelona	574	FH	Rocafort P.Catalana	1941-54

Barcelona 569, Maquitrans 500B, 1950   (Dewi Williams)

The impeccable Modeltrans replica represents 572 built in 1950 and painted dark green experimentally for a short while. Like many of this period, the roof top resistances were later refitted inside the body which is thought to have been built by Carde y Escoriaza, who were also rebuilding Barcelona's trams at the same time.

Modeltrans have also modeled the wonderful MAN/AEGs of Trolebuses Coruña-Carballo SA, described on page 182. Of the great number of imported trolleybuses, the Renault R4231s of Madrid, which were converted buses, have been modeled by the St. Petersburg Tram Collection, see page 151.

Barcelona 574, CGA Maquitrans 500B by Modeltrans, 1:43, resin

Trolebuses Coruña-Carballo, MAN MKE4500/AEG by Modeltrans, 32cm, resin

Of the British imports, there's the Zaragoza models of the BUT 9641Ts mentioned on page 31. Barcelona received 27 BUT 9651Ts between 1953 and 1956 which were fitted with Material y Construcciones double deck bodies. These seem to have been troublesome as the whole batch was withdrawn in 1962 and rebuilt with single deck Macosa bodies. It's in this form that Editions Roma issued a tinplate-like card model in 1984, by which time the prototypes had been sold to Valencia and then Pontevedra to join ex-London trolleybuses and finally scrapped after 32 years of hard service. 102 (ex-610) was acquired for preservation in 1992 and has since returned to Barcelona and public exhibition, still in Pontevedra colours.

At least one collector has converted a Dinky 29c bus to a Pontevedra Electric Tramway Q1 trolleybus. Pontevedra was the last Spanish trolleybus system, closing in 1989, until that is, three Irisbus Cristalis optically guided trolleybuses were introduced to Castellón de la Plana in 2008. Strangely in San Sebastian livery, where it never ran, Zaragoza 73 is immaculately preserved at Museo del Ferrocarril de Azpeteiia.

Pontevedra 102 (ex-Barcelona 610), BUT 9651T/Material y Construcciones, 1955 (chausson bs)

Pontevedra BUT 9641T/MCCW by Dinky (conversion), 1:72, diecast

Zaragoza 73, BUT 9641T/MCCW/EE, 1948 (Josep Pratel)

Barcelona BUT 9651T/Material y Construcciones by Editorial Roma, 1:43, card (Gottfried Kuře)

Castellón de la Plana Irisbus Crystalis, 2007 (Siemens)

Chapter 5.19
Sweden

Scania-Vabis, 1973-1989	T30	267
Volvo, 1983-1996	B10M	268 (231)
	B7	268

Rather like neighbour Finland, Sweden's two main cities had trolleybus systems; both opened in 1940 and had closed by the 1960s. Like Belgium and Van Hool, the country has since had an indigenous producer, Volvo, who has only manufactured trolleybuses for export. And environmentally aware Sweden re-introduced trolleybuses in 2003 to the small town of Landskrona.

Göthenburg started using 10 locally built Lindholmen T40 trolleybuses in 1940, but the 192 subsequent trolleys were mostly for Stockholm and built by Scania-Vabis in two batches, starting in 1940 and then 1947. All 202 had bodies by AB Hagglund and ASEA electrical equipment. ASEA had a trolleybus wired test track between 1938 and 1942 at its Västerås factory.

Scania-Vabis

model maker	ref.	issued	total	scale	construction	operator	fleet#	route	destination	built
St.Petersburg	142	1999	50	1:43	resin	Stockholm SS		91		1947

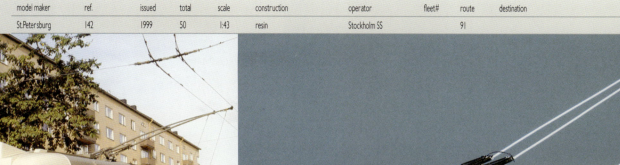

Stockholm 4036, Scania-Vabis T30, 1947 (Svenska Spårvägssällskapet)

The post war Scania-Vabis T30s were a large batch of 113 trolleys that were needed for major tram replacement in Stockholm and enabled the trolleybus network to evolve into 12 routes. But as car ownership etched away at ridership so contraction set in, starting in 1955 and completed by 1964.

Thirty five years later the St Petersburg Tram Collection chose the Stockholm Scanias as the basis for one of their first trolleybus models. And it looks smarter than the real thing often did. Even when new a white roof and booms were unlikely to stay that way in service. The 1947-49 batch were classified F3 by the operator and were distinguished from the 1940 F1 and F2 classes by radialised windows at the front. Four survive into preservation and one, 4038, has been tested using a pantograph trailer on tram tracks to gauge the possibility of a installing a 2km heritage trolleybus line between two Stockholm tourist attractions.

There's a model of an F1 class at Stockholms Spårvägsmuseet. It's 50cm long, of wood and simplistic, without the radialised windows, but the booms are in a different league and rather accurate. The museum houses a preserved F1 class of 1940, 30505, a Scania-Vabis with Hägglunds body and ASEA electrical equipment. A preserved F3, 1585, has also run over Stockholm's tramlines using a pantograph equipped trailer.

Stockholm 1528, Scania-Vabis T30 by St.Petersburg, 1:43, resin (SPTC)

Stockholm Scania-Vabis T30 by Svenska Spårvägsmuseet, wood, metal (Gottfried Kuře)

Volvo

Volvo, headquartered in Gothenburg, is claimed to be the world's second largest bus manufacturing company. Their city bus chassis, especially the B58 and B10 types were used for 184 trolleybuses for Holland, Switzerland, New Zealand and Italy between 1973 and 1989 - a time when trolleybus manufacturers were thin on the ground but operators, reacting to oil crises and environmental awareness, wanted vehicles. Volvo's involvement was more as subcontractor, either to the bodybuilder or the electrical supplier. Such were the B10M chassis supplied for Arnhem in 1989. We describe the model based on them in chapter 5.15, on page 231.

Linz 212, Volvo B7/Kiepe by Andras Ekkert, 1:87, plastic   (Andras Ekkert)

Volvo B7

model maker	ref.	issued	total	scale	construction	operator	fleet#	route	destination	built
Andras Ekkert		2009		1:87	resin	Linz ESG	212	43	Stadtfriedhof	2000

Volvo subsidiaries have since made trolleybuses for Linz (built in Poland) and Shanghai (built in China) using the B7 chassis design but whether we should include them here is debatable. We've included details of the Sunwin Shanghai trolleybus on page 104 - Sunwin is half owned by Volvo.

The Linz Volvos have been modelled, by Andras Ekkert, as one of his masterful conversions, that involved considerable rebuilding of the WUMM bus model equivalent.

As if to prove the current non-production of Volvo trolleybuses in Sweden, the latest system, in Landskrona, uses Polish Solaris trolleybuses. This almost heroic network added a fourth vehicle to its fleet in 2010, such was the demand of residents travelling by trolleybus between the recently moved railway station and their little town. Someone has doubtless adapted Landskrona green to one of the many Solaris Urbino bus or even Trollino trolleybus models made by Rietze or VK Modelle. Meanwhile, many in Sweden would be pleased to see trolleybuses return to Stockholm.

Linz 219, Volvo B7/Kiepe, 2000

Landskrona 6993, Solaris Trollino 12T, 2003 & Kobenhavn 101, Leyland TTB4/Scandia, 1938 (Thomas Johanson)

Linz 212, Volvo B7/Keipe by Andras Ekkert, 1:87, plastic   (Andras Ekkert)

Chapter 5.20
Switzerland

FBW/BBC	T51	270
FBW/SAAS	91 GTS	270
Saurer/Sécheron	3TP	271
Hess	Swisstrolley	271
	LighTram	272

Writing in 1872, Henry James described the Hotel Byron, at Villeneuve beside Lake Geneva, as having mellow gentility and being rather empty, perhaps due to the lack of "what is technically termed a "feature". In 1888, Switzerland's first tramway, built by Siemens, arrived at nearby Chateau Chillon from Vevey, using double overhead wires and an insulated double bow collector. Henry James might have missed this "feature" but double wires arrived at his "charming" hotel in December 1900 in the shape of a Lombard-Gerin Trolley Automoteur. This undoubted "feature" seems to have been sadly unnoticed by most trolleybus histories, perhaps because no photograph has yet been found. It was mentioned in the 1912 Enzyklopädie des Eisenbahnwesens as being part of the marketing of the Hotel Byron and implying that it remained in service until 1903 as a feeder to the tram, to be replaced when the Chillon line was reconstructed to standard single overhead and extended to Villeneuve. This would make it not only the first Swiss trolleybus system but the first commercial trolleybus operation in the world.

It is more likely that the apparently converted horse bus of 1889 was exhibited at the 1900 Paris Exposition as one of two trolleybuses, whence it came to a trial installation between Chillon station and Hotel Byron, Villeneuve, on 900 metres of overhead wires before going to Eberswalde in March 1901. But trolleybuses did return, replacing the tram in 1957 and passing over the same road that the trial took place and where the Hotel Byron had stood until 1933.

Where the French system (and the Hotel Byron) had not succeeded, the Austrian did, with the installation of a 13.3km rural route from nearby Friburg to Farvagny, one of the last Mercedes-Stoll systems to be built, in 1912, and incredibly lasting until 1932, the same year that trolleybuses started the first modern Swiss system in Lausanne. At Fribourg, three Daimlers served remote villages along roads that took 4 years to install with overhead wires and which took 50 minutes to ride the route when finally completed. The original hub motors were replaced between 1917 and 1920 with a chain drive on cars 1-2 and a cardan shaft on car 3, critical improvements for longevity. It must have taken dedication to keep Switzerland's first real trolleybus system going for 20 years. Trolleys returned to Friburg in 1949.

If Germany invented the trolleybus and Britain legitimised it then Switzerland refined it. A specialist industry grew up that took advantage of cheap hydro-electricity to provide trackless public transport often over steep hills. Meticulous operation saw reliability and long vehicle life helped by careful engineering of trolleybus overhead that had been revolutionised by Kummler and Matter in 1938. The large Swiss electric traction industry, including Brown Boveri (BBC), Oerlikon (MFO) and Sécheron (SAAS) had no trouble providing electrical components. Truck and bus manufacturers Berna, Saurer and FBW (Franz Brozincevic et Cie) produced most of the chassis including the first refined and practical articulated trolleybuses - demonstrated by their still being in service in Valparaíso, Chile, 50 years later.

But, and this is surprising, for a country so dedicated to trolleybuses, there are, as far as we can find, no indigenous Swiss toy or model trolleybuses, apart from one manufacturer's exhibition models and two abortive attempts at commercial motorised models (see page 74).

Vevy, Montreux, Chillon and Villeneuve 4, Berna/Moser/Sécheron, 1957 (SAAS)

Fribourg 1 & 3, Cedes-Stoll, 1912 (Club du Tramway de Fribourg)

FBW/BBC

model maker	ref.	issued	total	scale	construction	operator	fleet#	route	destination	built
Willi Schincke				1:63	plasticard, tin, balsa	Zlin	6	A		1944

Switzerland has had 1665 trolleybuses in service, of which 651 were built by FBW (Franz Brozincevic of Wetzikon) who also exported 8 to Zlin in Czechoslovakia in 1943, together with overhead by Kummler+Matter. This installation was half paid for by the local and socially conscious Bata shoe factory. These particular trolleybuses were the childhood favourites of Willi Schincke who has modelled no.6 in 1:63 scale. (see also page 46). The real FBWs lasted until 1965 and were popular enough to be used for at least one wedding!

Zlin FBW/BBC by Willi Schincke, 1:63, plasticard, tin, balsa   (Willi Schincke)

Zlin 4, FBW/BBC, 1944   (Zlinska Dopravni AS.)

FBW/Hoch/SAAS

model maker	ref.	issued	total	scale	construction	operator	fleet#	route	destination	built
Mobatech		1981		1:87	brass	Basle	911-920			1975
Basle BVB		2000		1:55	card	Basle	915			1975

Leaping two trolleybus generations, the FBW 91 GTS/GTL was supplied to Basel, Berne, Geneva, La Chaux-de-Fonds, Lausanne and Neuchatel from 1975 onwards. As a 'typical' trolleybus of the period, it was an obvious candidate for a miniature and was to have been the basis of a powered model by Mobatech (see page 74). What would have been Switzerland's only indigenous commercial model faded into obscurity, unlike the real things, a number of which lasted more than 35 years in service.

Ploeisti 5216 (ex-Geneve 637), FBW 91 GTS/Hess/SAAS 1975   (John Zebedee)

One operator whose FBWs lasted well (and always looked new) were the 1975 batch supplied to Basle which were sold on to Romania in 2000, to run a further 8 years. Basle BVB produced a giveaway celebratory card model at the time of their departure.

Berne 915, FBW 91 GTS/Hoch/SAAS by Berne SVB, 1:55, card   (Gottfried Kuře)

Saurer/Sécheron

model maker	ref.	issued	total	scale	construction	operator	fleet#	route	destination	built
APETc		2007		1:87	resin	Coimbra				1947

The second largest chassis supplier in Switzerland was Saurer (307) which had acquired Berna in 1929 but used both names to badge their trolleybuses. They exported two diminutive 3TP types to Coimbra, Portugal, in 1947 to inaugurate the system which crossed the frail Montegro river bridge and climbed the hill to Santa Clara. They are fondly remembered doing this for 37 years until 1984 when they were replaced by local Caetano trolleybuses which run to this day. To celebrate the 60th anniversary of the system, Emídio Gardé of the Associaçao Portuguesa dos Entusiastas por Troleicarros commissioned MR Modelly in the Czech Republic to make an 1:87 scale model of resin, the only known commercial model of a Swiss trolleybus. Just 60 models were produced in 2007.

Coimbra Saurer/Sécheron 3TP by APETc, 1:87,

Coimbra 21, Saurer/Sécheron 3TP, 1947
(Centre d'Iconographie Genovoise)

Saurer and FBW merged in 1982 to form NAW (Nutzfahrzeuggesellschaft Arbon & Wetzikon) and were almost instantly taken over by Daimler-Benz. NAW, nearly always in conjunction with Hess and ABB (Brown Boveri), built 205 trolleybuses. In 1991 their 'Swisstrolley' the first low floor trolleybus, was introduced. But with many Swiss systems having (relatively) recently renewed their fleets and the price of oil dropping, sales weren't enough and the company was liquidated in 2002. Hess has been able to carry on, introducing the Swisstrolley2 in 1996 and the Swisstrolley3 in 2003. However, all-Swiss construction has ceased, despite the consolidation of electrical contractors Brown Boveri with Oerlikon in 1967 and with Sécheron in 1969. Today Swiss trolleybuses use German electrical equipment.

Hess SwissTrolley

model maker	ref.	issued	total	scale	construction	operator	fleet#	route	destination	built
Vossloch		2008		1:20	wood	Generic				2008
Hess		2005		1:20	wood	Generic				2005

Hess SwissTrolley3/1 by Hess, 1:20, wood, metal

Lucerne 209, Hess SwissTrolley3/1, 2005
(Lucerne Trolley)

Hess first built trolleybus bodies for Basel and Biel in 1940 and went on to produce over 750, including 250 as manufacturer of the entire vehicle. Hess produces the world's only production bi-articulated trolleybus, the 'LighTram' and since 2006, the re-styled Swisstrolley3. But in a small, cost conscious market, Hess has its work cut out and uses models to publicise its case. Surprising then that they were still displaying the 'old' version of the Swisstrolley at 2007 exhibitions - possibly it was the original styling concept model with round headlights. At the same convention, Vossloh/Kiepe, now the usual electrical supplier, showed the 'new' version, but without the standard roof cowling, presumably to show off their otherwise hidden components. Both models are largely of wood at 1:20 scale. There have been further exhibition models since.

Solingen 961, Hess SwissTrolley3/2, 2009

Hess SwissTrolley3/2 by Vossloch, 1:20, wood

Hess lighTram

model maker	ref.	issued	total	scale	construction	operator	fleet#	route	destination	built
Robin Male				1:30	wood, metal	London				2008

Robin Male has modelled Hess's bi-articulated version of the Swisstrolley, the 'lighTram3'. Motorised to two axles, with dual steering and, optimistically in London colours, the 1:30 scale model has taken 2 years to build. Seeing it drive around Robin's impeccable overhead equipped layout is uncanny and faultless. As far as we know, there isn't another model of the 24.7m originals, which have been highly successful as people movers in Geneva, Zürich, St.Gallen and Luzerne.

Switzerland's small trolleybus industry continues to refine the mode, through careful evolution of the engineering. But such sophistication has a cost and it takes appreciative operators to pay the premium for quality that enables the rest of the world to see how good trolleybuses can be.

London Hess lighTram3 by Robin Male, 1:30, wood, metal (Jane Saker)

Zurich 62, Hess lighTram3, (Micha L Reiser)

Chapter 5.21
Ukraine

KZET	KTB-4	273
	K5-LA/695	274
	K-6	275
LAZ	52522	276

Kiev Yaroslavly YaTB-1 by RK, 1:87, resin

Kiev, the capital of Ukraine, had trolleybuses from 1935, two years after Moskva. Six LK-5 trolleybuses were assembled from Russian parts at the Dabal factory in Kiev, following delivery of the first, supplied in knockdown form from Moskva. Typically, Ukrainians went their own way and installed regenerative braking, unlike the Russian examples. This was to be the history of trolleybus development in Ukraine, engineering alternatives to the prescribed Soviet diktat. The LK-5, as supplied to Leningrad, has been modelled by St.Petersburg Tram Collection (see page 242).

Kiev's trolleybus system expanded rapidly, often without enough vehicles to ply newly wired streets. The YaTB series, in their various iterations, followed the impractical single door LK-5 from 1937 onwards, totalling 40 examples by 1940. Again, these have been modelled, including one in Kiev livery by RK. More were ordered and built but the war intervened and they were diverted to Alma-Ata. 18 of the best Kiev YaTB-4s were sent by occupying Nazi forces to Poznań, Gdynia and Königsberg.

Kiev struggled mightily to return 12 trolleybuses to service from 1944 onwards, although at times only three were on the roads. Five MANs from Chernivtsi arrived by way of reparation in 1945. They were not dissimilar to those modelled by MMR Modelly (see page 180) except they had three doors and no front grille. But things only started looking up as MTB-82Ms arrived from 1947 and the D variant from 1950 onwards. Kievans enjoyed the new trolleybuses, being especially fond of riding on the large rear chrome bumpers, which led to police riding shotgun by the rear door. Kiev had virtually no other sort of trolleybus from 1948 until 1959 and owned 238 of them. Vector Models, of Kherson in Ukraine has modelled Kiev MTB-82 70. No. 50 is preserved.

Kharkiv in Ukraine followed a similar history from 1939 onwards, as did Odessa, but most Ukrainian systems started after 1960, when locally designed trolleybuses, built in Kiev, became available. Central Soviet authorities had sent the TBE-S to Ukraine in 1957 but they were none too successful and designers at KZET, as the Dabal factory was now known, started to re-engineer a combination of the MTB-82 and the TBE-S. After experiments, the KTB-4 evolved, not to be used much in Kiev, but at the emerging systems of Ukraine. The capital preferred the larger and dependable Škoda 9Tr from the then SSR of Czechoslovakia. But the Kiev-built KTB series was a success and represented a certain independence from Moskva.

KZET KTB-4

model maker	ref.	issued	total	scale	construction	operator	fleet#	route	destination	built
Vector Models	2448	0		1:43	diecast	Kirovograd	42			1962
Vector Models	B2110			1:43	diecast	Kiev	10			1962
Vector Models	B2111			1:43	diecast	Kherson	102			1964

Kiev 492, Kzet KTB-4, 1962 (public domain)

Kiev 10, Kzet KTB-4 by Vector Models, 1:43, copper (ritmonexx.ru)

Kirovograd 12, Kzet KTB-4 by Vector Models, 1:43, copper

The KTB-4 had a more raked windscreen than the KTB-2 and a more rounded front, but was otherwise similar. Altogether nearly a thousand of the two types were built between 1960 and 1963. It's the KTB-4 that has been modelled by Vector Models, as Kirovograd 12 (or 91, also available). And they've modelled what seems to be the prototype KTB-4 with exposed trolley base and three part destination window, but running in Kirovograd as no. 10. Vector Models also issued the trolleybus train version, where two trolleybuses are semi-permanently coupled with the lead vehicle attached to the overhead. (This was also true of MTB-82 train-sets, but not Skoda 9Trs which used the trailing vehicle's booms). There was a vogue in the Soviet Union for this arrangement between 1970 and 1990, using various types of trolleybus, until articulated vehicles became more dependable.

The KTB-4 models, although often listed as

Kherson 107, Kzet KTB-4 by Vector Models, 1:43, copper   (Vector)

diecast, are of electroformed copper, plated on to a "mandrel" master, which is then removed so that plastic interior details can be added. Vector and Kherson Models grew out of Techno Exclusive, a modelling company that was founded in Kherson in 1992 and is now known as Kimmeria. Kimmeria not only makes model trolleybuses but sells those of Vector and Kherson as well – they obviously all know each other! And the common metal making technique is used by all three modelling companies on most of their model trolleybuses, although some are in resin.

K5-LA/LAZ 695T

model maker	ref.	issued	total	scale	construction	operator	fleet#	route	destination	built
Alexei Vorobiev				1:43	plasticard, wood	Kiev				1963
Finoko	695T			1:43	diecast	Odessa				1963
Vector Models	B2111			1:43	diecast	Kherson	102			1963
Oleksandr Krasnov		2011		1:87	resin	Kiev				1963

The small KTB-5. was developed from the popular LAZ-695E bus, and designated the K5-LA by KZET. The prototype was tested on Kiev route 20 for a month, never to return there. KZET however went on to build 159 for the many new small systems of Ukraine (including, by the way, Kherson). The design was then outsourced to OdAZ in Odesa who produced a further 478 and called them LAZ-695T. For some reason they didn't last long. Built between 1963 and 1967, they are thought to have all been taken out of service by 1972. Finoko (aka. Omsk producer Alexander Kobrits) has made a wonderful metal model of this much publicised design, although the trolleygear is supplied loose and tends to fall on to the upper windows – with these regularly failing on the real thing, is this a case of art imitating life? Alexei Vorobiev, typical of enthusiasts for the ill-fated K5, has created his own late OdAZ-695 variant. And Oleksandr Krasnov has recently produced a 1:87 resin model.

Odessa LAZ-695T by Finoko, 1:43, diecast

Kiev KZET K5-LA, 1963 (Kzet)

Kiev LAZ-695T by Oleksandr Krasnov, 1:87, resin.

Sevastapol 83 LAZ-695T by Alexei Vorobiev, 1:43, plasticard, wood (Alexei Vorobiev)

KZET K-6

model maker	ref.	issued	total	scale	construction	operator	fleet#	route	destination	built
MBM by Krementchug				1:43	resin	Kiev				1966
St.Petersburg	118		100	1:43	resin	Kiev	546			1966

By the 1960s the rush to replace the standard MTB-82, in production since 1947, had resulted in the Uritsky ZiU-5 (see page 250) but despite its ubiquitousness elsewhere in the Soviet Union, it found no favour in Kiev. The 60 that came, broke down often on the steep gradients and were soon disposed of. The Škoda 9Tr was much preferred but the local KZET factory determinedly set out to design a high capacity trolleybus in 1965. The K-6 incorporated ideas from the KTB-4, Skoda and ZiU-5 trolleybuses and one was the first Soviet trolleybus to use thyristor control. But this caused ire in Moskva, and Kiev was ordered to stop producing "competitor" vehicles. Before the order came, 336 had been distributed to all Ukrainian systems and some remained in service until the mid-80s.

Both St.Petersburg Tram Collection and Kremenchug have modelled the K-6. Unfortunately we don't have a proper image of the SPTC version, and neither has Leonid at SPTC, but it looks very similar to the model made by Kremenchug for MBM, as fleet no. 546. It was one of only two that ran in Kiev. KZET had to wait until 1989 before being able to build Ukrainian trolleybuses again, although they had been building trolley lorries in the interim. But the K-11 type was none too successful and production shifted to the Yuzmash factory where the design, looking like a rounded Skoda 14 or 15Tr, evolved into the YuMZ-T1. Meanwhile KZET produced the K-12 with interesting expertise from the Antonov aircraft factory – Ukrainian trolley production now came potentially from three factories producing two designs and still can to this day, in theory, although there are a lot more "competitors" from Eastern Europe today.

Kiev KZET KTB-6 by MBM by Krementchug, 1:43, resin

Kiev 546, KZET KTB-6, 1966 (Kzet)

Nikolaev 3160, LAZ 52522, 1998
(Aleksey Vorobev)

LAZ 52522

model maker	ref.	issued	total	scale	construction	operator	fleet#	route	destination	built
Vector Models		2010		1:43	electroformed copper	Nikolaev	3160			1998

Ukrainian bus builder LAZ or Lviv Bus Plant, formed in 1945, built 133 trolleybus versions of their 52528 city bus between 1993 and 1998, mainly for use in their home town, but also on smaller Ukrainian systems. Vector has chosen Niklolaev 6130 as its prototype, one of the last built, and still in service. The highly detailed model is in its original livery, something that very few of the real LAZ52522s still have.

Perhaps more models of the recent, wider variety in Ukraine will follow in due course, particularly the rather stylish, if noisy, LAZ E301 trolleybuses that are inspired by the Neoplan Electroliner. Local model makers Vector, Kherson and Kimmeria are all able to do so, but they know their main market is Russian trolleybus models for Russian collectors, either across the border or in the United States.

Nikolaev 3160 LAZ 52522 by
Vector Models, 1:43, copper   (Petr Babayev)

Kiev 2604, LAZ-E301, 2007   (Ivan Gricenko)

Chapter 5.22
United Kingdom

Taylor and Barrett	diecasts	280
Wells-Brimtoy	tinplate	281
Betal	tinplate	281
	Q type	283
Günthermann	tinplate	284
Joustra	tinplate	285
Tri-ang Minic	tinplate	286 (55)
(unknown)	wood	287
Stonebridge Toy Products	tinplate	287
Turner & Sanders	diecast	287 (73)
Modelcraft Ltd.	Leyland TTB4	287
Boomaroo	Leyland TTB1	288
AEC, 1922-1942	663T	289
	661T	290
BUT, 1946-1964	9611T	294
AEC, 1922-1942	662T	299
	664T	300
BUT, 1946-1964	9641T	305
	9712T	313, (227)
	L/RETB1T	313, (133)
Crossley, 1935-1958	TDD6	315
Daimler, 1936-1951	CTE6	316
Dennis, 1985-2000	Dominator	317
English Electric, 1926-1931	SD6W	318 (39)
Garrett, 1924-1931	OS	318
Guy, 1926-1948	BT	318
Karrier, 1933-1946	E4	319
	E6	320
	MS2	325
Leyland, 1931-1969	TBD1	326
	TB2	327
	TB5/7	328
	TTBD2	327
	TTB2	329
	TTB4	329 (278)
	TTB5	332
	Twin steer	333
Railless, 1909-1926	trolleybus	334
Ransomes, Sims & Jefferies, 1924-1948	C & D types	335
Sunbeam, 1931-1966	MS2	336
	S7	339
	W	340
	F4	347
	MF2B	352
	MF2C	353
Tilling-Stevens, 1923-1931	TS4X	353 (261)

Although William Siemens, founder of Siemens Bros. in the United Kingdom, wrote of the trolleybus concept in the Royal Society of Arts Journal of 1880, it is his brother Werner who is credited with the invention of the trolleybus. The two were close and worked together - William supplied 50 'iron telegraph posts of largest size' for the Halensee, Berlin experiments of 1882. He died the following year while his Portrush electric tramway, the first of any real length, was being built. Perhaps there would have been trials with an electric omnibus with 'contact-rollers' and 'without the necessity of running upon rails at all' at his home in Tunbridge Wells, had he lived. As it was, Britain followed the German lead and the first trolleybus in the UK was based on Max Schiemann's under running trolley, although Edward Munro's design has similarities to the Italian Filovia system.

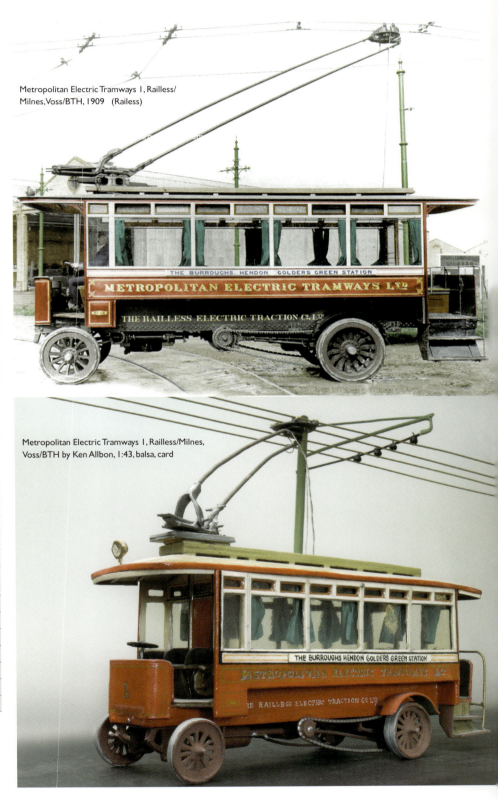

Metropolitan Electric Tramways 1, Railless/Milnes, Voss/BTH, 1909 (Railless)

Metropolitan Electric Tramways 1, Railless/Milnes, Voss/BTH by Ken Allbon, 1:43, balsa, card

Retired teacher, Ken Allbon has been making model trolleybuses since he was 11, albeit with a career gap. He's made at least 27 since 1977 and can trace the history of British trolleybuses with representations in 1:43 scale, starting with Metropolitan Electric Tramway's no.1. This Railless trolleybus of 1909 was designed by Edward Munro, who patented a whole series of current collectors and was still refining his designs in 1923 when he retired.

His trolleygear for the first public service trolleybuses in Leeds and Bradford appear over-designed, but Ken has valiantly reflected the complexity, albeit with compression springs to achieve upward thrust. His model is now 30 years old and suffers from some warping – the real things lasted a lot shorter period of time and had their trolleygear and bodies replaced within 5 years

Bradford 240, Railless/Hurst, Nelson/Siemens by Ken Allbon, 1:43, balsa, card

Railless/Hurst Nelson/Siemens, 1911 (Bradford Corporation)

Hove 1, Cedes/Dodson/Johnson&Phillips by Ken Allbon, 1:43, balsa, card

Hove 1, Cedes/Dodson/Johnson&Phillips, 1914 (Hove Borough Library)

In 1914 the Austrian Mercedes-Elektrique-Stoll over-running system was tried in Hove between September and November; built and installed by Cedes Electric Traction Ltd. Ken, who lives nearby, could also have produced his model in Keighley colours, which is where the trolleybus served on the Sutton route for 8 years until 1924.

Keighley 10, Straker Squire A/Brush/BTH, 1924 (BTH)

Keighley 5, Straker Squire A/Brush/BTH by Ken Albon, 1:43, balsa, card

While the rest of the world faltered, Britain can fairly be said to be the flag bearer for the trolleybus in the 1920s when 800 were built, of which 123 were double-deckers. Incredibly, one survives - Keighley no.5 is a Brush bodied Straker Clough A type that's stored at Keighley Bus Museum. Ken, who lived in Yorkshire in his teens 'discovered' this eccentric system with under and over running trolleybuses and built an evocative model of under- running no.5 in 1984.

Rotherham 53, AEC 664T/East Lancs/EE, 1939 (unknown)

Rotherham 74, Sunbeam MS2C/East Lancs/BTH by Ken Allbon, 1:43, balsa, card

By the end of the twenties, Britain had more trolleybuses than anywhere else and by 1939 had the largest (London) and the fastest (Rotherham) systems in the world. The streamlined livery of Rotherham's high powered AEC, Guy and Sunbeam single-deckers typified the 'modern electric' age. Ken's model of preserved 73, a Sunbeam MS2C, shows her as modernised in 1950, with additional roof faring to enclose the resistances and new trolleygear.

London Transport's staggering deployment of 1660 trolleybuses on 256 miles of route in only six years between 1933 and 1940, has never been equalled. Suddenly they were everywhere and throughout the country trolleybuses had gone from 684 in service in 1933 to 2462 in service in 1940, a 360% increase. No wonder toy makers felt compelled to introduce commercial trolleybus toys. There were at least 4 makers in the 30s - Betal, Taylor & Barrett and Wells who were all in London and Güntherman whose toys were imported from Germany. There was very nearly a fifth, the Minic, but it was not be, as the war intervened. Before looking at models, we'll examine these toys and those that followed after the war.

London Transport 664, Leyland TTB4/Leyland/MV by St.Petersburg, 1:43, resin

Taylor & Barrett (1929-1941, East Finchley)

ref.	issued	construction	size or scale	route destination	note
197	1936	cast lead	9cm long	617 Holborn	"Travel in Comfort" or "Use Dominion Petrol"
204	1936	cast lead	13cm long	621 Finchley	"Champions Malt Vinegar" or "Use Dominion Petrol"

A Barrett & Sons (1945-1982, Finsbury Park)

ref.	issued	construction	size or scale	route destination	note
197	1945	cast lead	9cm long	617 Holborn	"Travel in Comfort" or "Use Dominion Petrol"
204	1945	cast lead	13cm long	621 Finchley	"Champions Malt Vinegar" or "Use Dominion Petrol" or "Exide Batteries"

London 3 axle double decker by Taylor & Barrett, 13cm, cast lead

The Taylor and Barrett trolleybus, cast in lead, is referred to in the encyclopaedic 'British Tin Toys' as produced in the '1930's, but others state 1936, making it the first British commercial model trolleybus. With a driver and conductor, and 'Use Dominion Petrol', "Champions Malt Vinegar", 'Ramsgate' or "Exide Batteries" adverts, this 127mm toy was, apart from the war years, to be produced until at least the late 1950s. A boxed, pre-war mint example sold for £1000 in 1995. They have convincing sprung booms and were sometimes crudely sprayed. Repainted examples miss details like the oversize 'Trolleybus' logo. The 621 route to Finchley, emblazoned on the front, passed by the Taylor & Barrett factory and started operating in 1938, which might be a clue to when the toy was first produced. On the same date, March 3rd, the 617 to Holborn opened and this route destination is cast into the front of the smaller 88mm version. But exactly when the toys were introduced is open to speculation; the pre-war box doesn't help, as no date is given by the copyright notice.

The factory was bombed in 1941 and Fred Taylor, an engineer, and Alfred Barrett, a lead caster, went their separate ways after 1945, with A Barrett & Sons (Toys) Ltd. taking the trolleybus model moulds. The 'T' in 'T&B' cast into the base was erased, giving a convenient way of identifying the age of surviving examples, which are otherwise indistinguishable (except for the lack of conductor, after the war). With the Coronation of 1953, the bigger model was given editorial space in the US journal 'House Beautiful' as a worthy souvenir 'of the wonderful trolley bus', suitable for domestic display.

YOU'VE BEEN TO LONDON TO SEE THE QUEEN? Then we bet the thing you remember with the warmest affection in all of England is the wonderful Trolley Bus. Remember how the conductor pointed out all the sights like a genial host? So here is an engaging miniature to bring back happy memories, to show your little Piggy who stayed home. 5", $1.25 ppd. J. J. Anthony, Box 402, Milwaukee, Wis.

Ad for 3 axle double decker model trolleybus, 1953

London 3 axle double decker by Barrett and Sons, 13cm, cast lead

London 3 axle double decker by Barrett and Sons, 13cm, cast lead

London 3 axle double decker by Barrett (repaint), 9cm, cast lead

Bournemouth 2 axle double decker by Barrett (repaint), 9cm, cast lead

London 3 axle double decker by Taylor & Barrett, 9cm, cast lead

The smaller version is all together more crude, but at least it has 6 wheels. Some collectors seem to have an irresistible urge to repaint (especially as the mouldings are already in place on the casting) or even adapt the model, such as a 4 wheel Bournemouth representation. Legitimate examples carry 'Travel in Comfort', or smaller versions of the Dominion or Champions ads on the side, but don't have route blinds, the London Transport logo and air intake painted black, cream linings with gold fleet name and headlights painted white.

Wells-Brimtoy (A Wells &Co. 1919-1932, then Wells-Brimtoy Ltd 1932–1965, Walthamstow)

ref.	issued	construction	size or scale	route destination	note
105	1938? to 1940	tin plate	17cm long	804 (fictitious)	clockwork, pressed 'wire' wheels, red booms, full front mudguards
105	1945 to early 1960s	tin plate	17cm long	804 (fictitious)	clockwork or friction drive, pressed bucket or plastic wheels, red, black or silver booms, truncated mudguards
131	1938? to early 1960s	tin plate	21cm long	657 (real)	red booms, clockwork
111	1949-1955	tinplate	10cm long	516 (fictitious)	'Pocketoy' clockwork drive Black boom, plastic wheels
516	1955-65	tin plate	10cm long	516 (fictitious)	'Welsotoy' friction drive. Black boom, plastic wheels

Betal (JH Glasman, 1918-1951, Plaistow)

ref.	issued	construction	size or scale	route destination	note
	1938? to 1950s	tin plate	18cm long	691 (real) Central Station	clockwork, pressed wheels, silver booms
	1938? to 1950s	tin plate	22cm long	693 (real) Central Station	clockwork, pressed 'wire' wheels, silver booms
	1938 or 1948 to early 1950s	tin plate	28cm long	25 (real bus route) Piccadilly	clockwork, pressed 'wire' wheels, silver booms. Also with electric lights. Based on AEC 'Q' type.

Because of their marked similarity, though there's no known commercial linkage between the two London toy makers of Wells and Betal, the tinplate trolleybuses of both companies are dealt with together.

According to Marguerite Fawdry, the author of 'British Tin Toys', both the 'Betal' Glasman and the Wells-Brimtoy 4 wheel London style trolleybuses were both first produced in 1938. Confusingly, she then goes on to state that JH Glasman Ltd., of 'Betal Works', Plaistow Road, London dates from 1948 (there is elsewhere reference to Glasmans being founded in 1918). This contradiction has since been repeated in many articles and perpetuates the difficulties of dating. Trolleybuses had arrived in Walthamstow, where Wells-Brimtoy Ltd. had their factory, in October 1936 and it's possible the tinplates date from the same year. Real trolleybuses started running past the Betal Works in June 1937 (as the 669, not the 691 or 693 depicted). But such pedantry, as our wanting to know precisely when they were first produced doesn't sit well with mercurial manufacturers wanting to stack 'em high and shift 'em out the door. The idea that toy ephemera had any historic significance would have been looked upon with total bewilderment by producers. Even the catalogues weren't dated and as all these companies are now defunct, it's rather doubtful we'll ever know, although a recent sale of a trade box of 6 Wells trolleybuses was stated to be of 1938. (The lot sold for £320). What is known is that makers wanted to minimise tooling and printing, so wire wheels on a trolleybus, inherited from a 1929 saloon car, were not seen as anachronistic. Both Wells and Betal were guilty on their pre-war versions. Like anything else that has been collected for a long time, variants abound and the details of what is genuine become confused. On the smaller 17cm Wells, there were black or red booms, balloon, red or black plastic wheels and subtle differences in the lithographic printing of the tin. The black booms and balloon tyres are supposed to denote pre-war, while red booms and red wheels are supposed to have been made after 1945. Some versions have 'droopier' front mudguards which may well be pre-war. Maguiritte Fawdry implies the '804' routed toy dates from 1945. Presumably the litho plates wore out and had to be re-drawn. Three versions are known – perhaps the moustached

Two 2 axle double deckers by Wells-Brimtoy, 17cm, tinplate

2 axle double decker comparison by Wells-Brimtoy, 17cm, tinplate

driver was rather too reminiscent of a familiar dictator to have survived for long, and again, it's not possible to date the graphics.

The larger Wells, seems always to have had 'dish' tin wheels (made on German ALBA machines) and red booms but no conductor. Its catalogue number was 131 and cost 12 shillings (60p) per dozen wholesale in 1938.

The two Betals are taller, share the same sized conductor and are arguably less 'lowbridge' looking, but are in many ways very similar to the Wells. The different styles of the artists producing the litho print plates is obvious; one is much more cartoon like (on the bigger model) than the more jovial and colourful depiction on the other. Both are similar to the drawings of passengers on the Wells toys. It's always been surprising that two seemingly unconnected toy manufacturers should both choose to produce two versions each of essentially the same thing, even down to similar trolley booms.

2 axle double decker by Wells-Brimtoy, 17cm, tinplate

2 axle double decker by Wells-Brimtoy, 21cm, tinplate

No. 131 Trolley Bus

Wells-Brimtoy Trade Catalogue 1951, item 131, TrolleyBus, (Wells-Brimtoy Distributors Ltd.)

2 axle double decker by Betal, 22cm, tinplate

2 axle double decker by Betal, 18cm, tinplate

Wells brought out a new small tinplate trolleybus in 1949, initially with a clockwork motor and later with a friction drive. It was part of the new 'Pocketoy' range with wheels benefiting from newly installed plastic injection machinery. The rather plain 3 colour lithography included no passengers. It was re-branded as a 'Welsotoy' in 1955 but Japanese competition was making supposedly cheap British tinplates expensive, not to say anachronistic. Novelty toy representations needed to become scale models.

Betal and the AEC 'Q' type

Betal did go its own way with a trolleybus version of the famous AEC 'Q' type bus, which had attracted so much attention as a 'vision of the future' both within the transport industry and the toy trade. (The first Dinky Toys bus was a 'Q'.) AEC produced a styling model 1932 which shows what a radical design the Q was. Betal issued both bus and trolleybus versions, with, it has to be said, little difference apart from the booms. Both share the same bus route, the 25, going through such never electrified streets as Piccadilly, Leicester Square and the Haymarket. Even the side radiator was inherited, which of course, the trolleybus didn't have or need. But it is a fine toy none-the-less and probably the biggest commercial British toy trolleybus made. It's not clear when Betal made their Qs. On the evidence of surviving specimens it's hard to believe their issue was coincident with the real launch in 1932. Auctioneers rarely seem to date it, but references in the literature vary from 1937 to 1948. Some versions had working front headlights. There has been rumour that there was a green bus version; there were, after all, a few real ones. But of the only five real Q type trolleybuses, three went to Sydney, Australia (they were painted a blue-green colour), one went to Southend-on-Sea (a lowbridge version) and the prototype went to Bradford as a demonstrator, on loan.

It's hard not to include a conversion here, though purists may complain, but the urge to add booms to an existing model was compelling. A Corgi Original Omnibus model of Bradford no.393 has been converted to no.633 with the addition of trolleybooms made by Terry Russell and judicious covering of the side radiator and fuel entry. Originally in an all white livery, and delivered with additional cowling to the trolley

2 axle double decker by Wells-Brimtoy, 15cm, tinplate

AEC 'Q' type by Betal, 28cm, tinplate

5.22 United Kingdom 283

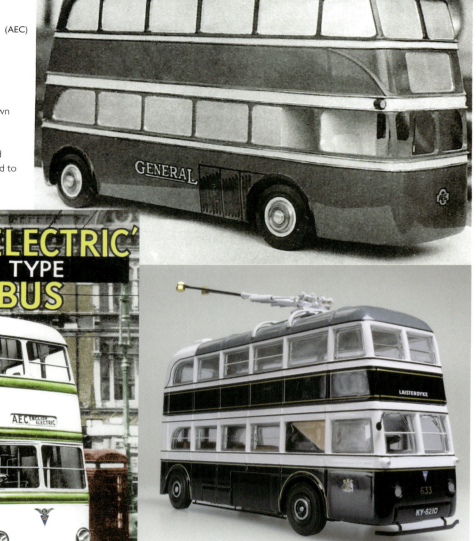

AEC 'Q' type by AEC, (scale?), wood?   (AEC)

base, the original Bradford Q trolleybus was exhibited at Olympia in 1933 on the English Electric stand. Interestingly, the passengers in the AEC/EE advert of the time have a distinct similarity to the tinplate bus passengers! Known in Bradford as "Queenie", no.633 was bought by the Corporation in September 1934 and, according to an undated photograph, received standard Prussian blue livery before being sold to South Shields in 1942.

Bradford AEC 'Q' type by Corgi (conversion), 1:76, diecast

Ad for AEC 'Q' type, 1933   (AEC)

Siegfried Günthermann (1887-1965, Nuremberg)

ref.	issued	construction	size or scale	route destination	note
784	1938	tin plate	22cm long	none	2 axle double-decker, wire booms
785 10	1938	tin plate	33cm long	none	3 axle double-decker, tinplate booms
785 10E	1938	tin plate	33cm long	none	3 axle double-decker, tinplate booms, electric lights
525	1950s	tin plate	22cm long	none	2 axle single-decker, wire booms

Siegfried Günthermann had long exported toys to Britain and the US. They were making tinplate London buses from 1910 and, by 1930, a six wheeler carried the General fleet name and a LS class label on the forward control bonnet (There was also a cream Berlin version). They must have started to look rather old fashioned by the later thirties at Gamages, where they sold, so this famous toy maker produced two sizes of trolleybus, the very latest thing on the roads and appearing in large numbers in London at the time. The toy is also thought to have been exported to the United States (65% of production had been going to the US), where it was reminiscent of New York's Fifth Avenue double-deckers, though these exports were unlikely to have been of trolleybuses. They are now very rare, perhaps because of the 1932 Import Duties Act that

Generic 2 axle double decker by Günthermann, 22cm, tinplate

3 axle double decker by Günthermann, 33cm, tinplate

restricted imports, their large size and thus cost, and because Wells and Betal undercut them with their locally produced versions. The trolleybus version inherits the rear two thirds of the LS bus, rather crudely cut, and the eccentric detail in the heavily sloped upper front and a plethora of livery lining. There were versions with and without working headlights. The 4 wheel version is all the more coherent with the remnants of a 'piano' front. Günthermann's smaller trolleybus is still odd, with oversize wheels, a split in the body sides and a grill at the upper front corners. The booms are wire rather than the pressings design used on the 6 wheeler. They were copied later by Betal, Wells and Joustra in France. Günthermann had another go at a trolleybus in the 1950s with a novelty toy that includes a passenger jumping on (and off) through the centre door – see Germany for more details.

3 axle double decker by Joustra, 33cm, tinplate

Jouet Joustra, Strasbourg, 1934-1987

ref.	issued	construction	size or scale	route destination	note
428	1948 - 1951	tin plate	33cm long	none	3 axle double-decker, tinplate booms

At around this time, during the late 40s, the French company, Joustra, produced a clone of the Günthermann. It's mentioned here because it has 'British Patent applied for' embossed on the bottom and a nearside open entrance. Perhaps Joustra had got hold of the presses from Germany and although different – there's a more realistic treatment of the upper front windows – the toy still inherits the Günthermann split, a third of the way along the side. There are no headlights though. The toy is rather rare.

London 3 axle double decker by Minic (Tri-ang), 18cm, tinplate

Minic (Lines Bros. Ltd, 1919-1970, Merton)

ref.	issued	construction	scale or size	route destination	note
77m	planned 1939	tinplate	18cm long	177 Mitcham	3 axle double-decker, wire booms, wooden seats

As noted in on page 55, there was a patent, granted in 1938, to George Edward Smallwood of London for a powered toy trolleybus with a steering mechanism at the front and a motor drive to the rear wheels. Given the size of the motor and the form of the half cab bus, it's hard not to attribute the patent to Lines Bros., makers of Minic toys at their Tri-ang works. Despite nearly all their wheeled toys being clockwork powered, some, such as the Fire Engine, issued in 1937, had electric lights and Lines Bros. at this time certainly were into innovation – their Barrage Balloon 'flew' when assembled. Announced in the same catalogue as the balloon, no. 43, of 1939, was toy 77M, a 7" long double deck trolleybus. All these circumstantial facts lead, far from conclusively, to the supposition that, had the war not intervened, Minic would have gone on to produce the world's first electrically powered toy trolleybus. In the event, 77M, despite reappearing in catalogue 50 of 1947, was never produced. According to Sue Richardson in her book on Minic tinplate vehicles, Mr. HR Lines himself confirmed this. But this hasn't stopped the belief that conversions of the Minic bus to trolleybus, of which there are at least 4 in existence, were somehow salesmen's prototypes. Presumably at least one was made by Minic, not least to be photographed for the catalogue, and perhaps to test manufacturing. Of the four conversions known, three show route 177 (as originally shown in the catalogue and which didn't exist until 1952 as a tram replacement bus route from Victoria Embankment to Abbey Wood) and another shows route 654. Two of the route 177 examples have recently appeared on eBay, one with black tyres and the other with white. Another example has a London Transport roundel on the front. All were apparently made in 2002 from post war Minic motor buses, have Bovril/Ovaltine ads and "look like new". Although one example fetched $950 in a

The story of British trolleybus toys and models comes to halt with World War 2. The toy factories that produced them, all in London, gradually turned over to war work and by 1942 the Government banned toy production. After the war Betal resumed production with minor changes. Taylor and Barrett lost Taylor and so smudged the logo on the dies, but otherwise carried on as before. Günthermanns were imported, but the Minic never appeared. Apart from these well known makes, there were other post war toy trolleybuses.

London 3 axle double decker by Minic (Tri-ang), 18cm, tinplate

Double-deckers

model maker	ref.	issued	total	scale	construction	operator	fleet#	route	destination	built
(unknown)		1950s		(no scale)	wood	Generic		135		
Stonebridge Toy Products		Late 1940s		(no scale)	tinplate	London				
Turner & Sanders		1956?		1:72	plastic, metal	London				
Modelcraft Ltd.		1940s		1:72	card	London	1273			

During "these war-times" as it says in the instructions, Modelcraft Ltd. (aka. JT Hill of Victoria, London) produced plans for a London Transport "AEC-Weymann" 00 scale model with, strangely, a Q1 fleet number of 1775.

We found a similar wood, card and acetate model of the 1950s with fleet number 1273, making it an all-Leyland TTB4 of 1939. A little the worst for wear after nearly 60 years, the springs have wrenched the booms from their bases and the red has faded badly on one side. Also listed by Modelcraft was a Bournemouth AEC 661T Weymann as a "full colour card cut out kit", although we've only seen black and white plans with details, amongst other things, on how to make wheels without a lathe.

There was one very crude tinplate toy produced by Stonebridge Toy Products, who were presumably near Stonebridge Park in London and the 662 trolleybus route. All 3 examples we know of have differing cut-cut alignments but at least it has 6 wheels.

Also thought to have been produced commercially was a stylish wooden 'trolley bus', owing something to the 1951 Festival of Britain design ethic, but little else is known about its history.

Brighton AEC 661T/Weymann/CP by Modelcraft Ltd, 1:72, card (JT Hill)

London 1273, Leyland TTB4/Leyland by Modelcraft Ltd, 1:72, card

London 3 axle double decker by Stonebridge Toy Products, 18cm, tinplate

2 axle double decker by (unknown), 10cm, wood

Another mystery is the Turner and Sanders motorized London trolleybus of around 1957 that was recently discovered at auction. We've described the model on page 73, in the powered model chapter.

London 3 axle double decker by Turner & Sanders, 1:72, plastic

5.22 United Kingdom 287

Perth Leyland TTB1/Park Royal by Boomaroo(?), 30cm, tinplate

Perth 1, Leyland TTB1/Park Royal, 1933 (Leyland)

The first miniature we can relate to a real prototype, is a wonderful Australian tinplate model of a Perth Leyland TTB1 single-decker. Perth's first three trolleybuses were built in 1933 and survived until 1960. A second batch, delivered in 1938 were identical apart from having conventional trolleybases instead of the 'one-on-top-of-the- other' Estler bases of the first batch. The maker of the toy is unknown but speculation suggests Boomaroo Toys who manufactured between 1947 and 1970 and are known to have produced a stylistically similar toy tram.

The famous Matchbox trolleybus of 1958 was unmistakably a London Q1 trolleybus and all subsequent UK models were based, more realistically than previously, on real prototypes. Tinplates now gave way completely to zinc alloy diecasts and so began a particularly British tradition.

Because, by the 1960s and 1970s, models began to proliferate, the history of scale trolleybuses can now be told by chassis type rather than miniature producer, not least because comparisons become more interesting. Included here are conversions and scratchbuilt models; not to claim to be definitive in our listings but as an indication of the variety that exists and model collectors need to enrich their hobby.

One senses frustration at this time as model diesel buses were starting to proliferate in the late 1960s, but as some were in plastic, they could more easily be converted to trolleybuses. Not only to full fronted, but, by cutting up two buses, as Gregg Diffen did, to 3 axles as well. Dollops of filler and added plasticard made passable toys, but the real wish was for real scale models of recognisable marques.

London BUT 9641T/MCCW/EE by Lesney Products, 1:137, diecast

Manchester 3 axle double decker by Gregg Diffen, 1:76, plastic

AEC and BUT

The Associated Equipment Company, despite its solidly bus heritage was the largest trolleybus supplier in the UK, a fact that was true even without the massive order for 218 vehicles for Shanghai, built between 1924 and 1930 or the joint production with Leyland to form British United Traction after the war. In 1930 English Electric entered into a strategic partnership with AEC that resulted in the end of the experimental era and the perfection of dependable trolleybuses. "Regent" and "Renown" bus chassis were adapted to become the 661T and the 664T models that continued in production, as BUT products, until 1957.

London AEC 663T/Union Construction/EE by Matchbox Collectibles, 1:76, diecast

.AEC 663T

model maker	ref.	issued	total	scale	construction	operator	fleet#	route	destination	built
John Edgar		1971	1?	1:76	plasticard, metal	London Transport	1	604	Hampton Court	1931
London Transport		c.1951	1	1:8	wood, metal	London United	1	1	Tolworth	1931
Matchbox Collectibles	Y10	1988		1:76	diecast	London Transport	1	604	Hampton Court	1931
Matchbox Collectibles	YET03M	1996		1:76	diecast	London United	1	4	Wimbledon	1931
Matchbox Collectibles (conversion)				1:76	diecast	London United	1	10	Tolworth	1931
Terry Russell		c.1972		1:43	wood, metal	London Transport	12	604	Hampton Court	1931

The best known early London trolleybus both in full and miniature sizes is arguably the 663T "Diddler" that grew out of the slightly troublesome development of 3 prototypes that had full width cabs and upper decks which were too low and soon to be illegal (under the Road Transport Act of 1930) that resulted in re-bodying within months. One had been demonstrated to London United Tramways in October 1930 and was sufficiently impressive for an order for 60 to follow, but with distinctive bodies by Union Construction instead of English Electric. The Matchbox 'Yesteryear' model of 1988 was a landmark eye opener amongst bus modellers and apparently sold out in weeks, such was the appreciation of the heightened level of detail and accuracy on a commercially available "toy". It had been specifically intended to be that way by designer Jack Odell, joint managing director at Lesney who had also designed the Matchbox toy in 1958 and went on to design the Lledo trolleybus in 1990 (see below, under BUT9641T and Karrier E6). Those that couldn't face precision white metal construction could now buy into model, as opposed to toy, trolleybus collecting. Matchbox rather spoilt the act with a strange decision to add gold plated booms to their London United version of 1996, but some, such as Colin Lawrence, have put things right, at least for their own collections, with conversions to accurate renderings of the "Diddler" No.1 as she was when first entering service.

Other models of the "Diddler" are included on page 29 (LT's wonderful 1/8th scale model) and page 41 (John Edgar and Terry Russell's motorized versions).

Lonon United 1, AEC 663T/Union Construction/EE, 1931   (LT Museum)

London United AEC 663T/Union Construction/EE by Matchbox Collectibles (conversion), 1:76, diecast (Colin Lawrence)

London AEC 663T/Union Construction/EE by Matchbox Collectibles, 1:76, diecast

AEC 661T

model maker	ref.	issued	total	scale	construction	operator	fleet#	route	destination	built
Corgi (conversion)			1?	1:76	diecast	London Transport	63	654	Crystal Palace	1934
Corgi OOC	40102	1996	5000	1:76	diecast	Hastings Tramways Co	20	6	Silverhill	1940
Corgi OOC	40107	2000	2600	1:76	diecast	Brighton, Hove & District	6340	41	Circular	1939
Ken Allbon				1:43	wood, metal	Brighton	38	43A	Race Hill	1939
Modelcraft Ltd	9	1970s		1:43?	card	Brighton, Hove & District				1939
Graham Bilbé		1970		1:72	wood	Reading	113	A	Three Tuns	1938
Alphagraphix		1992		1:76	wood	Reading	113		Tilehurst	1938
Solido (conversion)			1?	1:50	diecast	London Transport	63			1934
Tony Chlad			1	1:76	plastic	London Transport	63			1934
Varney Transport Replicas	35	1980		1:76	diecast	Hastings Tramways Co	12	5	Bexhill	1940

382 of AEC's 1,837 trolleybuses were 661Ts, built between 1931 and 1941. A further 344 BUT 9611, 2 or 3T trolleybuses were built between 1947 and 1957, including 8 foot wide versions. Not surprising then, that with 21 operators in the UK, including some that took two generations of the design, there have been quite a few models.

Purists will argue that, in the case of the Corgi 661T, a Park Royal body isn't a Weymann, and despite the flare, the same casting misses the subtlety. Despite having the trolley base cowling of the real Hastings trolleys, the Hastings Tramways model is the least successful of these two Corgis, not helped by the older, less familiar, version of the livery. The Brighton version, no.6340, works well, but never had wrap around adverts, only Corporation vehicles did and this is a Brighton Hove & District company version. It should be noted that the Corgi casting also "does" for BUT 9611T and Sunbeam W chassis and Weymann, Park Royal and Northern Coachbuilders bodies.

Hastings 20, AEC 661T/Park Royal/EE by Corgi OOC, 1:76, diecast

Brighton, Hove & District 6340, AEC 661T/Weymann/CP by Corgi OOC, 1:76, diecast

Hastings 8, AEC 661T/Park Royal/BTH, 1940 (H Luff)

Brighton 20, AEC 661T/Weymann/CP, 1939 (Geoff Lumb)

9 Brighton, Hove & District models, AEC 661T/Weymann/CP by Ken Allbon, 1:43, balsa, card (Andrew Henbest)

Ken Allbon has given himself the luxury of building Brighton's trolleys to 1:43 scale, in card, not once, but at least five times. The comparison in scales with 2 Corgis and two more at 5.5mm to the foot scale could unfairly be said to amount to an obsession, but Ken has since moved on to building London trolleybuses(!) Author Andrew Henbest, who owns a number of the 1:43 models says, "The chassis of each trolleybus is made from balsa wood and card. The wheels are taken from the tractor units of suitable scale plastic lorries. The body is made from card covered with varnish to make it rigid, with transparent plastic windows. The seats are made from card and balsa wood while the handrails, fully sprung trolley equipment and painted bamboo pole (carried in a paper tube underneath) are made from wire. There is wooden flooring, Alhambrinal ceiling covers (on Corporation trolleybuses only), light fittings and vents. In the lower saloon on Corporation trolleybuses, there are five advertisements in a cabinet above the windows of the front bulkhead. The Company trolleybuses did not have the cabinet, but two advertisements. On the front bulkhead, there is also a bell, Bus Number plaque (Corporation only) and a central advertisement at about waist height. The rear bulkhead carries a faretable on the offside, while on the platform is a used ticket box. Each AEC trolleybus even carries a "Vokins" advertisement in the window behind the longitudinal seats over the rear wheels. In the driver's cab, as well as the driver's seat, steering wheel, and handbrake, there is a resistance box and licence discs."

Before the Corgi range was issued, Jim Varney of Transport Replicas started, like a number of enthusiasts, producing diecast kits from his proverbial kitchen table. His 35th was another Hastings 661T, though, as a kit, the owner could of course paint it in any livery he liked. The kits add exaggerated ribs or linings, but were the epitome of modelling in the early 80s. Enthusiasts of a certain generation were demanding more and more accurate variety in their models and were adapting what was available to their own tastes and predilections.

Brighton, Hove & District 391, BUT 9611T/Weymann/CP by Ken Allbon, 1:43, balsa, card

Hastings 12, AEC 661T/Park Royal/EE by Varney Transport Replicas, 1:76, diecast

5.22 United Kingdom 291

Conversions started appearing at markets including one recently picked up at an annual LOTS sales fest for £25. London's only 4 wheeler, no.63, had an English Electric body that didn't look much like the flared Weymann body of the Corgi casting, but needs must! 63 also had her booms mounted over the first bay rather than the second, no trolley base cowling and a waistband that was deeper, higher up and cream not yellow! And the headlights are a bit low on the model - perhaps these are all reasons why Corgi hasn't released a London version, or, for that matter, a Reading version, the only other contender with a Park Royal body.

The amount of work needed to convert a Corgi to London Transport 63 is considerable, involving dismantling down to the bare casting, removing the booms and the original paint. Then repainting, including in this case, the brown roof, and applying transfers, adverts and, it seems, trickiest of all, the cream bands. All a labour of love, as the subsequent value is rarely greater than that of the original model.

Slightly more convincing is the conversion of a Solido RT type bus, but it is at 1:50 scale. Of course, 63's very forward booms make it ideal for an Eheim conversion, which has been attempted.

Tony Chlad's scratchbuilt motorised model of 63 is considerably more accurate, including the booms — still a little oversized, like the Eheim, but much better than the doomed Corgi conversions above.

London 63, AEC 661T/EE by Corgi (conversion), 1:76,

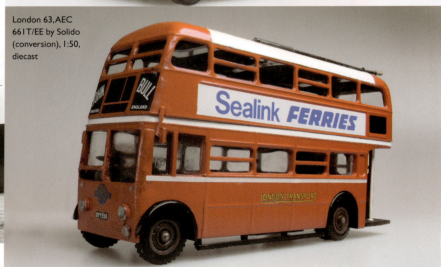

London 63, AEC 661T/EE by Corgi (conversion), 1:76,

London 63, AEC 661T/EE by Solido (conversion), 1:50, diecast

London 63, AEC 661T/EE, 1934 (AEC/LT Museum)

London 63, AEC 661T/EE by Eheim (conversion), (unknown)

London 63 (with 64), AEC 661T/EE by Tony Chlad, 1:76, plasticard, (Bob Heathcote)

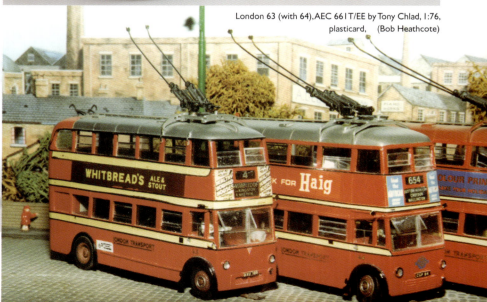

Supposedly produced for an exhibition and certainly made in small numbers was a conversion from a Dinky 289 Routemaster with an added third axle. With differing side ads but usually on route 654, the models are an interesting 'bodge'.

Not really attempting to be deadly accurate is Graham Bilbé's model of Reading 113 made 'long ago' as a money box that 'tings' when money is inserted. It's all the more evocative for being over-rounded and more sloping than the original. Not displaying such foibles is Alphagraphix's card representation of 113 and neither could it, given it's 2D translation into 3D.

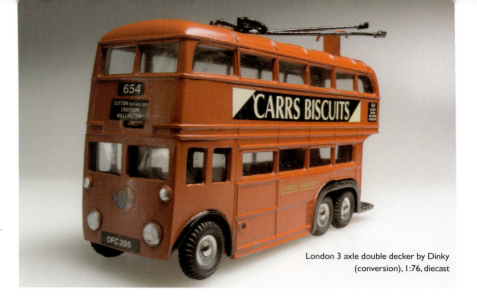

London 3 axle double decker by Dinky (conversion), 1:76, diecast

Reading 113, AEC 661T/Park Royal/EE by Graham Bilbé, 1:72, wood

Reading 112, AEC 661T/Park Royal/EE, 1938 (Geoff Lumb)

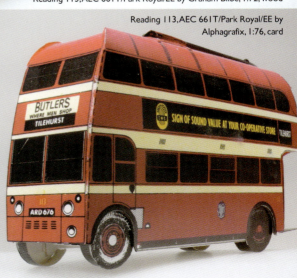

Reading 113, AEC 661T/Park Royal/EE by Alphagrafix, 1:76, card

Bradford 754, BUT 9611T/Weymann/EE by Bradford City Transport, 1:12, wood, metal   (Mike Bruce)

BUT 9611T

model maker	ref.	issued	total	scale	construction	operator	fleet#	route	destination	built
Corgi OOC	40101	1996	8100	1:76	diecast	Maidstone	51	-	Barming	1947
Corgi OOC	40104	1997	4000	1:76	diecast	Bradford	803	89	Thornbury	1948
Corgi OOC	40105	1998	4700	1:76	diecast	Bradford	769	8	Duckworth Lane	1949
Corgi OOC	45001	1996	10500	1:76	diecast	Bournemouth	294	21	Christchurch	1948
Corgi OOC	97811	1995	9500	1:76	diecast	Notts and Derby	357	A1	Ripley	1948
Corgi OOC	97813	1995	13500	1:76	diecast	Brighton, Hove & District	46	42	Brighton Stn	1948
K&B Models		1981		1:76	diecast	Bournemouth				1948
K&B Models		1982		1:76	diecast	Bradford	831			1948
K&B Models		1982		1:76	white metal	Bradford	746	19	Dudley Hill	1949
Pirate Models	4909	1970s		1:76	white metal	Bradford	743			1949
Little Bus	TNB2	2005		1:76	resin	Newcastle	560	42	Heaton Rd	1949
Kieth Turner		1980s		1:76	balsa, card	Nottingham	493	39	Woolaton Park	1948
TiNY Bus and Coach		2010		1:76	resin	Nottingham	493	39	Woolaton Park	1948
Reading Trolleybus Society		1972		1:76	card	Reading	144			1949
Bradford City Transport		1956		1:12	wood, metal	Bradford	754	25	Bradford	1950
Tony Chlad				1:76	plasticard, filler	Bournemouth	294	21	Old Christchurch	1948
Ken Allbon		2008		1:43	balsa, card	Brighton Hove & District	391	44	Seven Dials	1948
Ken Allbon				1:43	balsa, card	Portsmouth	313	6	Dockyard	1950
Ken Allbon		1988		1:43	balsa, card	Bradford	746	24	Crossflatts	1949

Bradford 754, BUT 9611T/Weymann/EE by Bradford City Transport, 1:12, wood, metal (Mike Bruce)

The Science Museum's model of Bradford 754 is staggeringly detailed and comes apart to reveal a complete chassis, upper and lower body sections. It was built in 1956 by Bradford City Transport, paid for by British Electrical and Allied Manufacturers Association and is arguably the finest model trolleybus ever made. Sister vehicle 758 is preserved and undergoing restoration - she was the last traditional rear entrance, open platform trolleybus to operate in the British Isles. The BUT 9611T model, meanwhile, is almost indistinguishable from the real thing and needs no criticism. There's more on page 30.

Bradford 758, BUT 9611T/Weymann/EE, 1950 (Gary Wilkinson)

Pirate Models, started by Guy Harrison and Peter Cox in late 60s, didn't strictly produce a BUT 9611T as they'd taken over K&B Model Manufacturing of Bradford, who did, from the early 80s. One was a rear entrance Roe bodied variant and the other has the front entrance of East Lancashire bodies. Pictures and model precision can play havoc with impressions and so it is with these two examples that appear unrelated, despite coming from the same kit maker. Bradford's diverse fleet underwent a large rebodying scheme during 1956-63 and the new bodies seem difficult to model. The third K&B, a Bournemouth Weymann is, from the fuzzy picture we've seen, rather simplistic, which is a kind way of saying even worse. K&B also advertised an N gauge BUT9611T. By the way, the original Pirate partnership of Messrs Harrison and Cox started when the former was the trying to re-discover the Taylor and Barrett trolleybus diecast of his youth and the latter had just bought some of the last stock from the factory. Meanwhile, a full size rear entrance Roe variant can be seen on the magnificently restored Bradford 746, a BUT 9611T at The Trolleybus Museum at Sandtoft. Ken Allbon has modelled 746 rather better with the hindsight of studying the real thing and a bigger scale.

Keith Turner's scratch built model of a Roe bodied BUT 9611T, in original livery, is of Nottingham 493. Made in the 80s, with the contactor housing correctly in place, the front corner curvature and trolley gantry fixing points are details to be corrected, but the overall look of these attractive bodies is very convincing. The original is now preserved in full running order at Sandtoft.

Bradford 672, BUT 9611T/Roe/EE by K&B Models, 1:76, whitemetal

Bradford 831, BUT 9611T/East Lancashire/EE by K&B Models, 1:76, diecast

Bradford 746, BUT 9611T/Roe/EE by Ken Allbon, 1:43, balsa, card

Bradford 746, BUT 9611T/Roe/EE, 1949

Nottingham 493, BUT 9611T/Roe/EE, 1948   (Neil Lewin)

Nottingham 493, BUT 9611T/Roe/EE by Keith Turner, 1:76, balsa, card   (Keith Turner)

The original issue of Corgi Original Omnibus Company trolleybuses in 1995 were of the Bournemouth Corporation, Notts and Derby Traction and Brighton, Hove and District BUT 9611Ts issued as reference numbers 401a, b and c, according to 'The Complete World of Little Buses'. The Brighton ones tend to suffer from cream paint that cracks or crazes with age, and shouldn't have a trolleybase shroud.

Corgi's Bournemouth 9611T came to be packaged with a Bristol L ECW in a "Dorset Delights" set. The late Tony Chlad motorised one using non-swivelling trolleyheads on his booms that only provide slight deviation from the overhead. His Faller guide wire, embedded in the roadway, had to be positioned directly under the wires to avoid dewirement. But living in Luton and remembering only once seeing a trolleybus in service, the finer points of trolleybus operation were, understandably, not slavishly followed!

Brighton 46, BUT 9611T/Weymann/CP by Corgi OOC, 1:76, diecast

Bournemouth 294, BUT 9611T/Weymann/CP, 1948 (Fred Ivey)

Bournemouth 294, BUT 9611T/Weymann/CP by Corgi OOC, 1:76, diecast

Bournemouth 294, BUT 9611T/Weymann/CP by Corgi OOC (motorised), 1:76, diecast   (Tony Chlad)

Notts and Derby 353, BUT 9611T/Weymann, 1948 (C Carter)

Notts and Derby 357, BUT 9611T/Weymann/EE by Corgi OOC (rebuild), 1:76, diecast zinc (Keith Turner)

The Notts and Derby Corgi is superficially rather impressive but, to someone who knows, the details niggle. Keith Turner has had a go, by removing the trolley shroud, adding chrome to the windscreen and black lining the windows. The effect is a considerable improvement but, as he says, "I did a lot of work on it to get to this stage, although it doesn't show as much as I would like".

Corgi next produced two Bradfords, including the wonderfully exuberant Coronation livery of 1953, followed by the first of 3 Maidstone incarnations of the Weymann/Park Royal casting. Preserved examples of Weymann bodied BUT 9611Ts include Notts and Derby 353 and 357 and Maidstone 52.

A note here about the vexed subject of subjective colour. Even if you don't agree about the hue on Bradford 803, which to me isn't cyan enough, then you have to agree the tone is too dark on the model, except, of course if you want to argue that this is supposed to be Bradford's short lived post-war darker blue livery, in which case it needs more magenta and is not nearly dark enough! Surviving images of Bradford's Coronation livery, and there are but few, show it to be a very pale shade of blue and seemingly cream, not white. Maidstone 51, on the other hand, appears spot on, colour wise.

Corgi had used the Weymann/Park Royal 2 axle casting from 1995 to 2000 (with a final fling in 2004). They had produced 63,400 models (including 2 Sunbeam Ws, see later) so examples remain readily available to buy at around their original price or less.

Notts & Derby 357, BUT 9611T/Weymann by Corgi OOC, 1:76, diecast

Bradford 803, BUT 9611T/Weymann by Corgi OOC, 1:76, diecast

Bradford 769, BUT 9611T/Weymann/EE by Corgi OOC, 1:76, diecast

Bradford 769, BUT 9611T/Weymann/EE, 1949 (J Copland)

298 5.22 United Kingdom

Maidstone 51, BUT 9611T/Weymann/CP, 1947 (Fred Ivey)

Maidstone 51, BUT 9611T/Weymann/CP by Corgi OOC, 1:76, diecast

Although nominally a model of a Sunbeam F4 with a Northern Coachbuilders body, this example of the Little Bus kit has been built as Newcastle 560, BUT 9611T with a 1949 version of the Northern Coachbuilders body that was virtually identical to those fitted to Sunbeams 529-53.

Reading Trolleybus Society produced a card model of Reading 144, just before they became the British Trolleybus Society in 1972. Surviving examples are a little faded, but are more accurate than they first appear.

Newcastle 560, BUT 9611T /Northern Coachbuilders/EE by Little Bus Co., 1:76, resin (David Bowler)

Reading 144, BUT 9611T/Park Royal/EE by Reading Trolleybus Society, 1:76, card

AEC 662T

model maker	ref.	issued	total	scale	construction	operator	fleet#	route	destination	built
EFE conversion		1970's		1:76	diecast zinc	Notts and Derby	306		Ripley	1932

Specifically a single deck design, just 28 662T chassis were built between 1932 and 1935, for Notts & Derby, Darlington, Odense and Milan. Based on the Regal motor bus chassis, which was vastly more numerous both in the number built and the models made, it's not surprising that the EFE replica has been converted to an interurban Notts and Derby Traction Co trolleybus, especially as the Corgi trolley shroud is rather similar to the originals. The model is on public display at Sandtoft Trolleybus Museum.

Notts & Derby 306, AEC 662T/English Electric by EFE (conversion), 1:76, diecast

AEC 664T

The 3-axle AEC, produced between 1935 and 1941 and numbering 827 examples, was based on the Renown motor bus chassis, strengthened to take the additional starting torque of increasingly powerful traction motors. The chassis was a development of the 663T, mentioned above, and came to represent, in its BUT 8' wide incarnation, the pinnacle of British twentieth century trolleybus engineering.

London 1521, AEC 664T/MCCW/MV, 1940

AEC 664T

model maker	ref.	issued	total	scale	construction	operator	fleet#	route	destination	built
Alphagrafix	DB105	1992		1:76	card, cutout sheet	London Transport	260	628	Clapham Junction	1936
Bribec		c.1972		1:87	vacuum formed plastic	Cardiff				1941
CMA		1998		1:76	resin	London Transport				
CMA		1998		1:76	resin	London Transport	1368		Tottenham Crt Rd	1939
CMA		1999		1:76	resin	London Transport	1763	693	Barking Broadway	1941
Corgi OOC	OM43701	2001	2700	1:76	diecast	Belfast	16	8	Cregagh	1940
Corgi OOC	43704	1998	4100	1:76	diecast	Cardiff	203	5A	Beda Road	1941
Corgi OOC	43706	1999	6200	1:76	diecast	Cardiff	201	6A	Cathedral Rd	1941
Corgi OOC	OM43702	2002	2900	1:76	diecast	Cardiff	204	6	Cathedral Rd	1941
WLC Jeffery		1965		1:7.5	wood, metal	London Transport	1525	601	Fulwell Depot	1939
Little Bus	TBL3	2005		1:76	resin	London Transport	1521	601	London's Last	1939
Meccano	MB132	1946		#1.9	metal	London Transport	284-383	623	Epping Forest	1936
St Petersberg	III/IIa	1998 and 2009		1:43	resin	Moskva	1001	1		1937
Oxford Diecast	NQ1005	2011		1:148	diecast	Cardiff	207	11	Sutton	1941
Pirate Models	4901	1980s		1:76	diecast kit	London Transport	132-383			1935-6
St Petersberg	III/IIa	1998, 2009		1:43	resin	Moskva	1001	1		1937

The 3-axle AEC models are inevitably dominated by London Transport who owned 899 of the 1058 domestically sold 6 wheelers (663T and 664T) built at Southall. The most spectacular model of a London AEC is a hand-built no.1525, an L3 class of 1940. Sold at a Phillips auction in 1998, the model is 122cm. long with electric running gear, lighting, operating windows, working wipers and tyres that look like those that surrounded ashtrays in garages after the war. This fine, but irritatingly flawed, model came up again for auction in 2008, looking a little the worst for wear, with a reserve of £6,000. The catalogue claimed that it, together with 2 others, may have been built by Bassett-Lowke as 'prototypes' in the late 30s, though this would seem unlikely. Why would AEC, MCCW (the body builders) or London Transport need models of a 'standard' L3 class of 1940? It came up again at auction, without the builder claims, and sold for £3,000. Although the model is very impressive, the lower upper front window radius is too large, the rear dome 'droops' and the side lights are too near the front corner. The roof is of wood and none too smooth - something that, to my mind at least, precludes the likelihood of a professional model. It's also difficult to imagine scale electrics being specified by the supposed clients, the full scale makers, or that the modeller was using real plans. It's much more likely to be a lovingly hand-built model, perhaps constructed after the war, by someone devoted to his local trolleybuses. Dating this model would be problematic. As brown rear domes were specified for all repaints after 1946, a red rear dome would suggest the model dates from before the mid fifties, as does the trolleybus emblem over the bogie (a practice that finished in 1955) but then No.1525 was based in West Ham and didn't work the 601 route until after 1961! Some suggested that the model was built by apprentices at Chiswick as a training exercise in either 1939 or 1940. But the mystery has been solved by discovering a letter from W.L.C. Jeffery of Teddington to Model Engineer magazine in 1965, together with a picture. Mr Jeffery built the model between 1960 and 1964, saying, rhetorically, that his effort took four years to complete, adding "Or is any model complete to the maker's satisfaction?" (More on page 38).

London 1525, AEC 664T/MCCW/MV by WLC Jeffery, 1:6, wood, metal

More accurate and at a much smaller scale, is Little Bus's kit. An evocative model for many, especially for those that were at Fulwell Depot when London trolleybus operation ended in 1962, this model of an AEC L3 class trolleybus has been executed in final day appearance by the kits master mould maker, Rod Blackburn.

Getting ahead of ourselves slightly, but Paul Bennett of West Molesey does extremely well executed 'Code 3' conversions of Corgi OOC London trolleybuses, such as 1521, as she finally ran into Fulwell Depot on 8 May 1962. ('Code 3' is the modification of available models). Paul's favourite basis for conversion is OM43703 and his least favourite is OM43707, but more of this subtlety later, under the BUT 9641T section.

Of the other AEC models, nothing is really known about the Bribec kit, apart from the fact that it existed, but CMA kits, also known as Wheelbase Models and made by Olaf Olsen, were comprehensive, if not very finely detailed – more details under the Sunbeam section.

The real variety of AEC 6 wheeler models is in the Pirate Kits range, still available from John Gay in Sittingbourne. The Pirate kits, like any white metal kit, take skill to build well. There's sometimes a difficulty in getting the roof to sit properly that can result in a front protuberance, but it can be done. Apart from livery variants decided by the builder, kit 4902 can be adapted to C, D, E, F, H, J or K classes with all the necessary optional parts provided.

London 1521, AEC 664T/MCCW/MV by Little Bus Co., 1:76, resin (Rod Blackburn)

London 1521, AEC 664T/MCCW/MV by Corgi OOC (code3), 1:76, diecast

London AEC 664T/MCCW/MV by CMA, 1:76, resin

London C1 class, AEC 664T/MCCW/EE by Pirate Models, 1:76, whitemetal

London 214, AEC 664T/BRCW/EE by Pirate Models, 1:76, whitemetal

London Transport's X4 class, 754, was the first chassisless trolleybus but is included here as it used AEC components. Graham Hawkyard's model, at his Uxbridge terminus, stands beside a Corgi Q1. John Gay's 'official' model is in pre-war livery.

London 754 (with 1768), AEC chassisless/LPTB by Pirate Models, 1:76, whitemetal

London 754, AEC chassisless/LPTB/MV, 1937 (London Transport)

London 754, AEC chassisless/LPTB by Pirate Models, 1:76, whitemetal

1379, the X5 class built to test clearances in Kingsway's tram subway, also used AEC parts. The Pirate model is available with the unique offside door open or closed. Although 1379 had a roof route indicator aperture that is faithfully reproduced in the casting, what isn't is her straighter rear profile and rounded roof dome that distinguished her from the rest of the L1 class to which she was related.

London 1379, AEC chassisless/MCCW, 1939 (London Transport)

London 1379, AEC chassisless/MCCW by Pirate Models, 1:76, whitemetal

London 1379, AEC chassisless/MCCW by Pirate Models, 1:76, whitemetal

Corgi's AEC 664T models use the same casing as the 8' (2.44m) wide Q1 to represent 7'6" (2.23m) wide trolleybuses from Cardiff and Belfast. The model width is 1.2635 inches (32.1mm) which, if you want to be precise, is 8.0021 feet (2439.6mm). So bit of a cheat here – Corgi could have modelled the post war 8' wide Cardiff fleet but they had dual entrances. Still, being able to compare the look of the same vehicle (available as 201, 203 or 204) as a model has its benefits.

The Northern Counties bodies of Cardiff's first ten trolleybuses were the only ones built for all-electric chassis and were carried on the last 664Ts constructed. Their skirt flare and 6-bay design rather differentiate them from the Corgis. No.203 was preserved at the Trolleybus Museum, Sandtoft, in wartime grey, but is now restored to the streamline livery that adorned her between 1946 and 1949. Oxford Diecast has taken similar liberties with a Q1 casting in N scale, with the livery used from 1950 until 1965.

Cardiff 204, AEC 664T/Northern Counties/EE by Corgi OOC, 1:76, diecast

Cardiff 201, AEC 664T/Northern Counties/EE, 1941 (Transport World)

Cardiff 203, AEC 664T/Northern Counties/EE, 1941

Cardiff 201, AEC 664T/Northern Counties/EE by Corgi OOC, 1:76, diecast

Cardiff 203, AEC 664T/Northern Counties/EE by Corgi OOC, 1:76, diecast

Cardiff 209, AEC 664T/Northern Counties/EE by Oxford Diecast, 1:148, diecast

The width problem is also true for the Corgi AEC 664T of Belfast. The casting has the Q1 curved drop down line from under the lower windows to the bottom windscreen corners which, unlike the real thing, has been highlighted in black – a creative decision by the Corgi modeller, who also couldn't add the missing front pillar. The casting is, of course, the same as Corgi use for the Q1.

Belfast 16, AEC 664T/Harkness/GEC, 1940
(PRO Northern Ireland)

Belfast 16, AEC 664T/Harkness/GEC
by Corgi OOC, 1:76, diecast

Moskva 1001, AEC 664T/English Electric/EE by St.Petersburg, 1:43, resin

Moskva 1001, AEC 664T/English Electric/EE, 1937 (AEC)

The finest model AEC 664T is the St Petersburg Tram Collection's new rendering of Moscow's imported no.1001. Double-deckers were the initiative of Nikita Khrushchev, then in charge of Moscow's transport. In November 1936 an order was placed with AEC and English Electric for sample trolleybuses, which were built by April 1937 and shipped to Leningrad on board SS Luga.

Trials in Moscow began in July 1937 at depot 2. Higher wiring had to be erected. In October 1937 no.1001 was towed to the Yaroslavl factory where its design was copied and ten YaTB-3 trolleybuses were built for "double deck" route 12. 1001 was withdrawn from service in 1948. Rumours persist of BUT 9641T chassis being imported after the war, but there is no evidence.

BUT 9641T

model maker	ref.	issued	total	scale	construction	operator	fleet#	route	destination	built
Alphagrafix	DB113	1996		1:76	card,	Cardiff	262	4	Roath Park	1949
Alphagrafix	DB101	1990		1:76	card,	London Transport	1812	604	Wimbledon	1948
Alphagrafix	DB111	1992		1:76	card,	Bournemouth	212	25	Central Station	1950
Carde y Escoriaza		1951			metal sheet	Zaragoza T.SS.T.	10-14		Terminalls	1951
Corgi OOC	43713	2000	2600	1:76	diecast	Nottingham	568	43	Trent Bridge	1952
Corgi OOC	43711	2000	3100	1:76	diecast	Huddersfield	626	44	Deighton	1956
Corgi OOC	43702	1998	4200	1:76	diecast	Belfast	203	30	Bloomfield	1950
Corgi OOC	43701	1998	12200	1:76	diecast	London Transport	1768	667	Fulwell Depot	1948
Corgi OOC	43703	1998	5700	1:76	diecast	Glasgow	TB4	102	Hampden Garage	1949
Corgi OOC	43705	1999	6500	1:76	diecast	Newcastle	628	32	Fenham	1950
Corgi OOC	43707	1999	4000	1:76	diecast	Glasgow	TB4	102	Hampden Garage	1949
Corgi OOC	43708,-2,-3	1999	9700	1:76	diecast	London Transport	1830	6E+08	Kingston,	1948
Corgi OOC	43709	1999	1000	1:76	diecast	Glasgow	TB4	101	Rutherglen	1949
Corgi OOC	43710	1999	3750	1:76	diecast	(Chrome)	-	-	-	
Corgi OOC	43712	2000	4000	1:76	diecast	London Transport	1842	607	Shepherds Bush	1952
Corgi OOC	OM43704	2003	2300	1:76	diecast	Bournemouth	240	25	Central Station Square	1950
Corgi OOC	OM43706	2004	2000	1:76	diecast	Glasgow	TB4	101	Rutherglen	1949
Corgi OOC	OM43707	2004	2900	1:76	diecast	London Transport	1812	601	Twickenham	1948
Corgi OOC	OM43709	2010	1400	1:76	diecast	London Transport	1879	607	Hanwell Broadway	1952
Dave Wood				1:76	card, wood, & metal	Cardiff	243	14	Beresford Sq.	1955
Dave Wall				1:18	card, wood, & metal	Cardiff	243	14	Pier Head	1955
Dave Wall				1:24	card, wood, & metal	Bournemouth	246	28	Cricket	1950
Fanfare Transport Models		2001		1:76		Bournemouth	200-23	25	Bournemouth Square	1950
Ken Allbon				1:43	balsa, card	London/Transport	1812	604	Wimbledon	1952
Langley	E11			1:148	diecast	London/Newcastle/Glasgow				1948-52
Lesney Products	56A	1958		1:137	diecast	London Transport	1765-1840	667	Hampton Court	1948
Lesney Products (repaint)	56b	2008		1:137	diecast			72	Lesney Factory	
Oxford Diecast	NQ1001	2010		1:148	diecast	London Transport	1808	667	Hampton Court	1948
Oxford Diecast	NQ1002	2010		1:148	diecast	Belfast	208	11	Falls Rd	1950
Oxford Diecast	NQ1003	2010		1:148	diecast	Newcastle	487	31A	Central Stn	1948
Oxford Diecast	NQ1004	2010		1:148	diecast	Glasgow	TB9	101	Shawcross	1948
Oxford Diecast	NQ1006	2011		1:148	diecast	Nottingham	590	43	Bulwell Market	1951
P&D Marsh				1:152	diecast	London Transport	1765-1840			1948
Pirate Models	406/4906	1980s	1000+	1:76	White metal	London Transport	1765-1840	613	Holborn Circus	1948
SOES		1966		1:76	vacuum formed plastic	London Transport	1765-1840	613	Holborn Circus	1948
Terry Russell				1:43	plastic, wood	Newcastle	620	39	Denton	1950
Terry Russell				1:43	plastic, wood	London Transport	1772	604	Hampton Court	1948
Varney Transport Replicas		1970s		1:76	diecast	London/Glasow/Newcastle				1948-52

This has to be the most modelled trolleybus type, especially if the AEC 664Ts are included. And included here are a number of scratch built models on public display (see page 26 etc.) and conversions.

We should start with Matchbox (Lesney Products) no.56a, the 1:137 scale diecast that is so well known and arguably symbolised the move toward more realistic trolleybuses when it was issued in 1958. It was designed by Jack Odell, then Joint Managing Director at Lesney. (He went on to retire in 1973 and set up Lledo, where he designed another model trolleybus). Originally with black trolleybooms, most of the production run featured red booms. The value of the former is said to be five times greater than the less realistic latter (and later) version, though a rare edition with 'BP Visco-Static' ads, possibly because the factory had run out of 'Peardrax' adverts, sold for £1200 with red trolleybooms. The value also depends on the type of box supplied - the scarce 'type C' version, with the offside three quarters view, commanding higher prices. Such are the number of Matchbox Q1s that are around, there's a maker in Roswell, New Mexico who produces the booms for the restoration of those that have lost them! Andy McCoy of Cheshire sells and refurbishes Matchbox Q1s to a very high standard with his own livery variations; not for purists, but to my mind, they're endearing.

London 1812, BUT 9641T/MCCW/EE, 1948

London BUT 9641T/MCCW/EE by Lesney Products, 1:137, diecast

Generic BUT 9641T/MCCW/EE by Lesney Products (repaint), 1:137, diecast

As a comparison with the Lesney product is the series of five Oxford Diecast 1:148 scale Q1 castings that include London, Belfast, Newcastle, Glasgow, Nottingham and, as an AEC 664T, Cardiff. These are a mark of production progress in the intervening 30 years of small scale British diecast trolleybus models; available ready built and somewhat miraculous miniaturisations that are only possible by computer and machine. As Oxford's head of production was at Corgi, the models are like half size versions of the OOC Q1 models.

London 1808, BUT 9641T/MCCW/EE by Oxford Diecast, 1:148, diecast

London 1832, BUT 9641T/MCCW/EE by Langley, 1:148, diecast

London BUT 9641T/MCCW/EE by SOES, 1:76, vacuum formed plastic

Still available, at the time of writing, is the Langley N scale Q1 kit of the 1970s, that, even in the expert hands of the late Bill Avery, is now a little crude, with disproportioned windows. Bill's wheels are not as supplied in the kit.

Some of the earlier kit models were probably not produced in great numbers. Jim Varney's kit of a Q1 is reported but not yet seen and so, too is P&D Marsh's Q1 in 2mm scale or 1:152. One of the earliest kits, indicative of enthusiasts not wanting to wait for commercial producers, is that of SOES (Sheffield Omnibus Enthusiasts Society) produced in 1966 by Dennis Vickers. Vacuum forming the model in clear plastic has its advantages from a production point of view, but requires great skill and dedication to paint. The kit came in 2 halves. (see also Crossley TDD64 and Daimler CTE6, below)

Pirate's models take skill too, especially in fine tuning the assembly of the body, which buyers need to adjust to get a tight fit. Some would not expect to fine file and fill but just glue together straight out of the box, but such is the nature of these kits. The Q1 kit, a revelation when it came out around 1973, actually needs exhibition standard construction to really look good. It has been one of the two most popular Pirates ever, selling over a thousand units. The kit can be finished in London, Glasgow or Newcastle liveries. Further fiddling could give you Nottingham, Bournemouth or Cardiff, although surgery to alter the headlight positions would be necessary, strictly speaking.

Bournemouth BUT 9641T/Weymann/CP by Fanfare Transport Models, 1:76, diecast (Fanfare)

One person who performed such surgery a number of times was the late Norman Clay. Or rather he has done to Corgis, to produce "Code 3" conversions to achieve the characteristic top curve of the front panelling of Bournemouth's BUT 9641T trolleybuses. Mike Pannell used to similarly market such conversions, though to make Portsmouth 4 wheelers.

London BUT 9641T/MCCW/EE by Pirate Models, 1:76, whitemetal

While we're at Bournemouth and with individual modellers, Dave Wall of Birmingham, (who built the Aston Manor display, see page 28) has built a 1:24 (or ½" to the foot in old money) scale model of No.246. Of course, building at this scale makes for much greater opportunities for accuracy, but can also be inhibiting, with details, such as front grilles, left out.

Terry Russell has made non-powered 1:43 scale trolleybuses, including what's often called the Rolls-Royce of trolleybuses, the Q1. Commissioned as a pair for a family in Kingston in 1968, Terry used Airfix racing car wheels and hand built everything else. With hindsight (and better technology) he now thinks the transfers could have been better. But the proportion of this model is wonderfully evocative and has survived 40 years surprisingly well.

Bournemouth 246, BUT 9641T/Weymann/CP by Dave Wall, 1:24, card, wood, plastic & metal (Dave Wall)

Bournemouth 212, BUT 9641T/Weymann by Alphagrafix, 1:76, card

London 1772, BUT 9641T/MCCW/EE by Terry Russell, 1:43, wood, card

London 1812, BUT 9641T/MCCW/EE by Alphagrafix, 1:76, card

A rather pure way of modelling is from card, requiring only a knife, nimble fingers and glue. Roger Crombleholme of Alphagrafix has produced 3 BUT 9641Ts, from Bournemouth, Cardiff and London. Each has the advantage of individual accuracy that is not possible on an expensive diecast master mould that needs to be re-used for different versions to make commercial sense.

Cardiff 262, BUT 9641T/East Lancashire by Alphagrafix, 1:76, card (Alphagraphix)

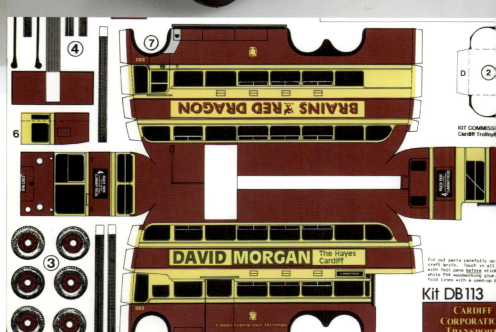

London 1768, BUT 9641T by Corgi OOC, 1:76, diecast

London 1830, BUT 9641T by Corgi OOC, 1:76, diecast

London 1812, BUT 9641T by Corgi OOC, 1:76, diecast

London 1777, BUT 9641T by Corgi OOC, 1:76, diecast

London 1842, BUT 9641T by Corgi OOC, 1:76, diecast

London 1891, BUT 9641T by Corgi OOC, 1:76, diecast

London 1886, BUT 9641T by Corgi OOC (code3), 1:76, diecast

London 1879, BUT 9641T by Corgi OOC, 1:76, diecast

The Corgi OOC models have shown variable detail over the six years they produced BUT 6 wheelers, especially the London ones. Between 1998 and 2004 Corgi has produced six London Q1s (including two commissioned versions for the Ramblers Association). Between all these, there was an accurate model aching to get out, but all had their good and bad points. Take the recent Corgi Q1, OM43707, no.1812, accurately portrayed as preserved at Sandtoft. even down to the missing running number plate! But the mid band is too thick and the front emblem too small, which is a shame as Corgi got it so nearly right on ref.43712, the model of the first vehicle of the last batch of London trolleybuses (so far), 1842. But the big problem here is the wrong shade of red, which is noticeably too bright. Purists also bemoaned the lack of upper rain shield detail but they like the "Aldenham" destination blinds. The second issue, of 1830, has a strange drop shadow on the side logo and fleet number. But, viewed from a distance (and in the right light), all the Corgis look highly detailed and absolutely of the right overall proportions.

London Buses and Replica Transfers of Hailsham, in the form of Paul Bennett, have repainted Corgi Q1s, not just to give alternative routeings but also right some of those niggling wrongs – though the between decks cream band remains too deep! Paul regards OM43703, Leyland TTB4, 1253, as the best Corgi rendition and thus the preferred base for his Code3 conversions. Very nostalgic for those who where present at the end of London's trolleys, is his conversion of 1521 (see above). Paul particularly dislikes OM43707 (1812, a recent Corgi Q1, see above) saying "The booms are much thinner than used on previous releases thus they do not sit flush in their brackets, they either sit on the roof or hang over the side of the bus. The Trolleybus logo on the front of the bus is too small, the front ads are far too big and the destination screen runs into the ads. It really is a rubbish bus!" Such is the passion generated on the road to perfection.

The latest (at the time of writing) Corgi Q1 is OM43709, 1879 on route 607 to Hanwell Broadway. A lot has been put right here, except the irritating mismatch at the front of the cream waist band, where the black ribbing doesn't follow either the cream or moulding itself. And the LT trolleybus logo is too small, again. Oh well!

Atlas Editions (De Agostini), the European direct marketing company, had Corgi produce a version of 1891 in 2010, that misses the black line under the windscreen that all other versions have and puts the white legal lettering too high but does manage the two tone brown of the roof and a front logo of the right size.

David Wood has successfully motorized a standard Corgi Q1 (43708) by using BEC tram motor units and converted David Voice trolley gear. What had been seen as a technical difficulty of getting 'heavy' diecasts to run successfully with the Faller guidance system has been brilliantly and meticulously achieved by David Wood on his "West Porton" layout. Fittingly, West Porton Corporation has embarked on a tram to trolleybus conversion and is about half way through.

London 1830, BUT 9641T/MCCW/EE by Corgi OOC (motorised), 1:76, diecast

London 1891, BUT 9641T/MCCW/EE by Atlas Editions, 1:76,

Doubtless someone in Spain has repainted his model Q1 to Coruña Tramways blue or Zaragoza two tone green. And added front bumpers. Or perhaps Corgi will. The exported Q1s of London were to last in service until the mid-70s in Spain. One, no.1812, that flawed Corgi model, has returned to Britain to join no.1768 in preservation, leaving nos.1836, 1837 and 1839 preserved to varying degrees in Spain.

In 1950, when London Transport was considering buying a second batch of Q1s, Newcastle was receiving its second batch and Glasgow too had received virtually identical trolleybuses. Inevitably, Corgi followed suit as it were, modelling all variants of the liveries applied by these two operators. In the Newcastle model, Corgi faithfully reproduced such detail as the maroon splash top on the front mudguards.

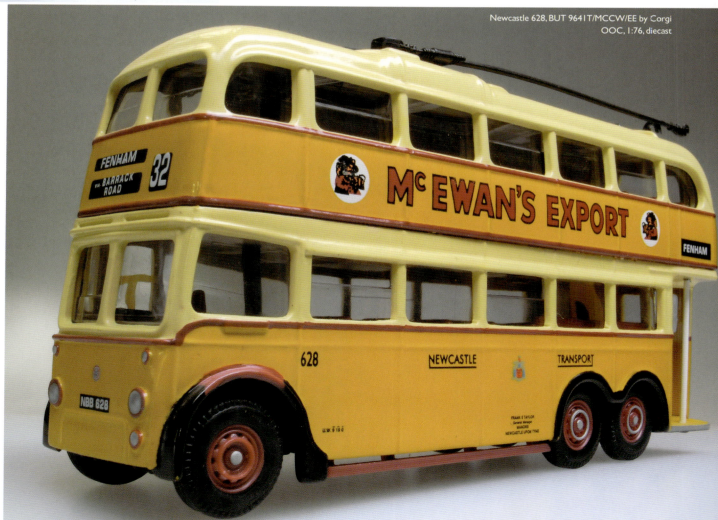

Newcastle 628, BUT 9641T/MCCW/EE by Corgi OOC, 1:76, diecast

Glasgow has warranted three livery variants over four models. They could also have included the original version with its cream roof and 'illegal' trolleybus emblem on the front, quickly removed after protests from London Transport. The original model of TB4 with orange lower panels doesn't have its lower window frames properly painted green, but has inherited the livery of buses and trams of the time – something the double deck trolleys never had.

Glasgow TB9, BUT 9641T/MCCW/EE, 1949 (C Carter)

Glasgow TD18, Daimler CTM6/MCCW/MV, 1950 (Marcus Eavis)

Glasgow TD16, Daimler CTM6/MCCW/MV, 1949 (Fred Ivey)

Glasgow TB4, BUT 9641T/MCCW/EE by Corgi OOC, 1:76, diecast

Glasgow TB4, BUT 9641T/MCCW/EE by Corgi OOC, 1:76, diecast

Glasgow TB4, BUT 9641T/MCCW/EE by Corgi OOC, 1:76, diecast

Chrome BUT 9641T/MCCW/EE by Corgi OOC, 1:76, diecast

Belfast 203, BUT 9641T/Harkness/GEC by Corgi OOC, 1:76, diecast

Love it or hate it, for the Millennium, Corgi released a rather bizarre chrome version of the Q1 casting in 2000. No detailed criticism of livery details here! At the same time, Corgi released three "cheats"; Belfast, Nottingham and Huddersfield "Q1s" with Harkness, Brush and East Lancashire bodies. (the biggest cheats of all are Reading's S7, a Sunbeam and Rotherham's Daimler – see under Daimler and Sunbeam). Doubly confusing is Corgi giving Huddersfield 626, a BUT 9641, the red wheels of sister vehicles 631-40, which were Sunbeam S7s, instead of silver ones. The bodies, however, were virtually the same.

It rather depends on your point of view – would you prefer to have a large variety of classic British 30' 3 axle trolleybus models or just three, from London, Newcastle and Glasgow? Not only have Corgi "cheated" with scale width, body skirts and body builders, they went on to include different chassis builders as well. But let's not get into how the Q1 casting includes the London running plates that become odd bumps on Belfast's 203 or the strange trolley gantry on Nottingham's 568. Conversion to quarter light windows did at least make an appearance on Huddersfield's 626 even if the squared, upright front of the original is hardly Q1-like. The five bays of the model don't tally with the six of the real thing either.

Nottingham 568, BUT 9641T/Brush/CP by Corgi OOC, 1:76, diecast

Belfast 207, BUT 9641T/Harkness/GEC, 1950 (GEC)

Nottingham 566, BUT 9641T/Brush/CP, 1952 (Mike Russell)

Huddersfield 631, BUT 9641T/East Lancashire/EE, 1956

Huddersfield 626, BUT 9641T/East Lancashire/EE by Corgi OOC, 1:76, diecast

Perhaps the most dubious use of Corgi's Q1 casting was to try to make a full blown Weymann body with bottom skirt curves, front door and bottom curved windscreen all missing, though an attempt is made with the door! One can say that this Corgi looks nothing like the original but then Bournemouth is, for many, such a powerful evoker of childhood memories that Corgi can be understood for wanting to produce another Bournemouth model, safe in the knowledge that it's bound to sell.

Bournemouth 249, BUT 9641T/Weymann/CP, 1950 (B S Watson)

Bournemouth 240, BUT 9641T/Weymann/CP by Corgi OOC, 1:76, diecast

Nottingham 601, BUT 9641T/Brush/MV by Keith Turner, 1:76, diecast (Keith Turner)

Keith Turner of TiNY Bus and Coach has gone to the considerable trouble of chopping up two OOC two axle Weymanns to properly achieve the six bay Brush bodies of Nottingham's highest numbered trolleybus, 601. It's hardly something Corgi could do in production, but maybe, in recycling molds.........

BUT 97 series

British United Traction's 97 series chassis, built between 1949 and 1957, were all exported; 55 type 9711Ts went to Auckland and 67 type 9721Ts went to Arnhem, Nijmegen and São Paulo. The only ones to be modelled commercially are the Arnhem BUTs, the longest British trolleybuses built, see page 227.

BUT RETB1

model maker	ref.	issued	total	scale	construction	operator	fleet#	route	destination	built
St.Petersburg	112	1998	150	1:43	resin	Glasgow	TBS13	108	Mount Florida	1958
EFE (conversion)	16317			1:76	diecast	Glasgow	TBS21	109	Linthorpe	1958
Dave Wall				1:18	card, wood, plastic & metal	Glasgow	TBS13	108	Mount Florida	1958

431 BUT ETB series trolleybuses were built, between 1950 and 1964 and some remained in service until 1989 (in Coimbra). Many are preserved; in Holland, New Zealand, Portugal and Scotland. They were the Leyland single deck, forward entrance design for export, as the LETB1 type (see page 133) or RETB1 with right hand drive, as sold to Auckland, Dunedin, Hobart, Launceston and, in both long and short versions, to Glasgow.

Glasgow TBS13, BUT RETB1/Burlingham/MV, 1958 (Martin Smith)

Glasgow TBS13, BUT RETB1/Burlingham/MV by St.Petersburg, 1:43, resin

Of the few known models, only one, from the St. Petersburg Tram Collection, can be said to be a commercial model, despite only 150 being produced. It is beautifully accurate, down to the wheels that appeared on the exhibited prototype at the Commercial Motor show in 1952.

Other models include a careful conversion from an Exclusive First Editions (EFE) Bristol LS model, with inevitably, detailed differences from the Burlingham body of the full scale original. All of which perhaps explains why the registration plate has been given a number that is 2 higher than the last of the real batch, a useful protection for purist criticisms. TBS21 actually carried FYS996 and was 34 feet (10.2m) long, something that required special legal dispensation at the time. A Bristol LS is 30 feet long and has pronounced indicator housings that have been removed on the model. The drop windscreen has had to be painted over. The well made trolley base carries Corgi OOC booms. A conversion to a TBS trolleybus was reported in Model Buses magazine that involved joining 2 dissected EFE BET single-deckers to achieve the correct scale length.

Dave Wall's large model of Glasgow TBS13 is the right length and can often be seen passing along a 1:18 scale terrace at Aston Manor Road Transport Museum (for more, see page 28). The real TBS13 is preserved at the Museum of Transport in Glasgow.

Glasgow BUT RETB1/Burlingham/MV by EFE (conversion), 1:76, Diecast

Glasgow TBS13, BUT RETB1/Burlingham/MV by Dave Wall, 1:18, card, wood, plastic & metal

Crossley TDD6

model maker	ref.	issued	total	scale	construction	operator	fleet#	route	destination	built
Alphagrafix	DB108	1992		1:76	card,	Manchester	1081	28	Piccadilly	1938
Anbrico (conversion)					diecast	Kingsland				
SOES		1968		1:76	vacuum formed plastic	Manchester	1250	205	Exchange	1951
Keith Turner		1970s		1:76	balsa, card	Manchester	1250	210	Picadilly	1951

Manchester 1250, Crossley TDD64 'Dominion'/MV by SOES, 1:76, vacuum formed plastic

Manchester 1250 Crossley TDD64 'Dominion'/MV by Keith Turner, 1:76, balsa, card (Keith Turner)

Manchester 1081, Crossley TDD6/MV by Alphagrafix, 1:76, card

Manchester 1240, Crossley TDD64 'Dominion'/MV, 1951 (R Brook)

Manchester 1055, Crossley TDD6/MV, 1938 (Crossley)

Kingsland Corporation Crossley TDD6/MV by Anbrico (conversion), 1:76, diecast

Although trolleybuses were built at the Crossley factory after 1951, Manchester's batch of 16 TDD64/1 six wheelers were the last 'proper' Crossley trolleybuses ever built. A rare breed, only 189 such vehicles were constructed over a 15 year period. No. 1250 is preserved, at the Museum of Transport, Manchester. The SOES kit of 1250 was produced in 1968 and shows a detail over scaling that could perhaps have been avoided on a vacuum forming mould. Here, because the decks are one piece, the window bars don't need to be as wide as they do on a diecast or resin model. They could have been wafer thin as they are on the prototype, especially around the windscreen. Keith Turner, a professional kit maker, who has worked on the real 1250, realised these problems when scratch building his model in the 70s. The result, though not to his perfectionist satisfaction, is impressive.

Unless and until Corgi produces a trolleybus variant of its DD42 bus, either the Alphagrafix card or a newly found SOES vacuum formed kit from the 1970s are the only options to produce a model of Manchester, Ashton under Lyne or Belfast versions of the magnificent pre-war Crossley 6 wheelers. Others couldn't resist the temptation to attempt surgery. In Keith Jackson's case, by combining two Anbrico DD42 kits and scratchbuilding a full front. Immediately apparent is that this isn't a real representation. "Kingsland Corporation" is Keith's 76th scale world where the red of Manchester becomes a sort of South Shields blue! And it's an excuse to apply a streamline livery to the post war 1240-55 batch, that never had it.

5.22 United Kingdom 315

Daimler CTE6

model maker	ref.	issued	total	scale	construction	operator	fleet#	route	destination	built
Corgi OOC	OM43705	2003	2300	1:76	diecast	Rotherham	37	6	Kimberworth	1950
SOES	R1/72/***	1968	300+	1:76	plastic	Rotherham	7-18			1950
Keith Turner		2008		1:76	balsa, card	Rotherham	84	9	Mexborough	1950
Wakey Models	14	2010		1:76	resin	Rotherham	17	49	Silverwood	1950

Another 6 bay trolleybus 'given' 5 bays by Corgi, is their Rotherham 37, the fleet number corresponds to Sandtoft Trolleybus Museum's preserved 1950 vehicle. Adding the missing bumper shouldn't be too difficult and a touch of orange glass paint would make the fog lamp more accurate. Sheffield Omnibus Enthusiasts Society's 1968 kit of a Rotherham double-decker had the difficulty of having to cut vacuum formed body parts, something that needed great accuracy to get the halves to fit well together and for the wheel arches to look right. It could be done - see also the London Q1 version above. The trolley booms used rubber bands instead of springs. SOES (Dennis Vickers) helpfully provided notes on how to build overhead and each kit had a "chassis number".

Rotherham's double deck Daimlers all started life as single-deckers, with the operator's characteristic roof farings. Wakey Models produces a 4mm scale resin kit that could be any one of 44 delivered in 1949-50. We've chosen 17, as 37 was when she had an East Lancashire body. Graham Dowson of Mexborough, aka Wakey Models, casts his kits to order and uses a whiter resin than many that is easy to carve and sand. And considerable dedication and care is needed to make a first class model, which exactly what Keith Turner has done with his scratch build of 84. No. 84, later no.9 in Tranvía de San Sebastian a Tolosa's fleet is undergoing restoration by José Saurez, as the only surviving single deck Rotherham Daimler.

Rotherham 37, Daimler CTE6/Roe/EE by Corgi OOC, 1:76,

Rotherham Daimler CTE6/Roe/EE by SOES, 1:76, vacuum formed plastic

Rotherham 37, Daimler CTE6/Roe/EE, 1950 (Peter Swift)

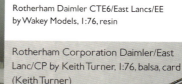

Rotherham Daimler CTE6/East Lancs/EE by Wakey Models, 1:76, resin

Rotherham Corporation Daimler/East Lanc/CP by Keith Turner, 1:76, balsa, card (Keith Turner)

Rotherham 11, Daimler CTE6/East Lancs/EE, 1950 (R Brook)

Dennis

model maker	ref.	issued	total	scale	construction	operator	fleet#	route	destination	built
80M Bus Model Shop	88001	2001	800	1:76	diecast zinc	Citybus	701	2001	Environmental bus	1994
Ken Allbon		1985		1:43	balsa, card	South Yorkshire PTE	2450	163	Doncaster	1985
Anbrico	29	1988			diecast	South Yorkshire PTE	2450			1985

Anbrico announced a model of the South Yorkshire PTE Dennis Dominator 2450 that had been converted to a trolleybus in 1985 (and which is currently at The Trolleybus Museum at Sandtoft), but the model unfortunately never appeared. Ken Allbon did produce a model in 1985, in his inimitable style and at 1:43 scale, just after seeing the real thing running at Doncaster Racecourse to demonstrate trolleybus feasibility. Another, in fact the only other Dennis trolleybus, was also a demonstrator conversion. Citybus, one of Hong Kong's major operators, spent a lot of time and effort proposing a major trolleybus scheme and testing a prototype. The side banner on the model says "Pollution free Trolley Buses for a cleaner tomorrow". Unfortunately the Chinese authorities of Hong Kong didn't get the message and the plan for the huge network came to naught. The model, produced for 80M Bus Model Shop, predates the real prototype, hence the different livery. It's a reminder of a brave proposal.

South Yorkshire 2450, Dennis Dominator/Alexander/GEC by Ken Allbon, 1:43, balsa, card

South Yorkshire 2450, Dennis Dominator/Alexander/GEC, 1985

Hong Kong 701, Dennis Dragon/Duple-Metsec/Ansaldo by 80M Bus Model Shop, 1:76, diecast zinc

Hong Kong 701, Dennis Dragon/Duple-Metsec/Ansaldo, 1994   (Tim Runaccles)

English Electric

model maker	ref.	issued	total	scale	construction	operator	fleet#	route	destination	built
Peter Smith				1:76	diecast and plastic	Cardiff	231-7		Cardiff	1930

The only known modeller of an English Electric trolleybus, of which only 82 were ever made, is Peter Smith, who cut down a double deck Corgi 'Q' type. More about Peter's layout is on page 45.

Garrett

model maker	ref.	issued	total	scale	construction	operator	fleet#	route	destination	built
Garrett		1927	1	1:10	wood, metal	Southend	104			927

An historically very significant model is that built by Garrett to about 1:10 scale in 1927. The exact purpose of the model is not known, but it resided in the company boardroom for many years until the company was broken up in 1960. Today, it's back where it belongs, in the Long Shop Museum in Leiston, Suffolk, in the same room it had always been. There's more about Garrett and this model on page 15.

Garrett OS demonstrator by Garrett, 1:10, wood, metal

Hastings 3, Guy BT, 1928 (J Thompson)

Guy BT

model maker	ref.	issued	total	scale	construction	operator	fleet#	route	destination	built
Alphagrafix	DB116	1994		1:76	card, cutout sheet	Hastings Tramways Co	3	6	Circular	1928
Mick Sherwood			1	1:18	wood, plasticard	Hastings Tramways Co	45			1929

Hastings Tramways Company's first generation of Guy trolleybuses have been modelled by Alphagraphix, as "Happy Harold", the open top double-decker and by Mick Sherwood, of the Hastings Trolleybus Restoration Group as way of raising money for the single-decker, no.45. Both trolleybuses are preserved.

Hastings Guy BT by Alphagrafix, 1:76, card. (Alphagraphix)

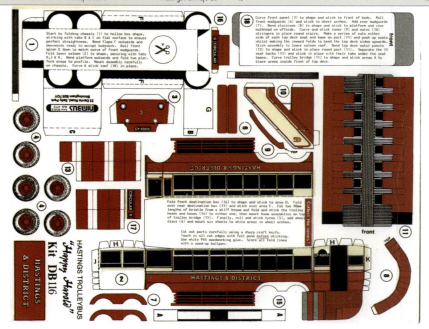

Karrier E4

model maker	ref.	issued	total	scale	construction	operator	fleet#	route	destination	built
Anbrico	26			1:76	whitemetal	Bradford	677	4	Centre	1938
Anbrico (conversion)	26			1:76	whitemetal	South Shields	204	2	Tyne Dock	1937
Model Bus Company				1:76	whitemetal	Bradford	677			1938

It's a little difficult to identify exactly which Karrier E4 the Anbrico model is based on. The best bet seems to be 692, the last E4 built, in 1940, although the route indicator configuration was horizontal. Earlier Bradford trolleybuses that had very distinctive V shaped rain deflectors above the windows include AEC 661Ts 634 and 635 with English Electric bodies but they, and the production batch, 636-676, have the typical straight slope at the top of the driver's side windows. It could be based on the previous batch, 677-691, but the upper band is much thinner, until that is, you discover the slightly faded official Bradford Corporation photographs and all is clear. That suspicious front badge is indeed the wings of the English Electric logo but with Karrier and not the usual AEC emblem. When new, these Karriers had ultramarine blue panels, primrose bands and gold lining - by 1942 that became a brighter "Bradford" blue and yellow lining, but still with grey roofs. By 1951 the lining and the wide bands were gone, in the interests of saving money, and roofs became blue. At some time between 1942 and 1952, the front fog lamp was added.

One problem with diecast models is the propensity to massively emboss the casting with ribbing where painted lines go, making it hard to disregard them. That's particularly true of the Anbrico (or the Model Bus Company as it was known for a while) rendering of the Karrier E4.

Peter Short, with strong feelings of nostalgia for his home town of South Shields took this to heart. As he says of his model of 204, "The panel joins were far too fat, and there were some where 204 didn't have any, so I filed them off completely, then stuck narrow tape on instead - the kind you use to stick on the copper side of blank printed circuit panels to define where the tracks will be after etching. There's no sign of vents at the front on any photos of 204 so they went too."

Bradford 677, Karrier E4/Weymann by Model Bus Company, 1:76, whitemetal

Bradford Karrier E4/Weymann by Anbrico, 1:76, whitemetal

Bradford 690, Karrier E4/Weymann/EE, 1938 (J Copland)

South Shields 204, Karrier E4/Weymann/MV, 1937

South Shields 204, Karrier E4/Weymann/MV by Anbrico (amended), 1:76, diecast

Karrier E6

model maker	ref.	issued	total	scale	construction	operator	fleet#	route	destination	built
Lledo	DG41-000a	1990		1:76	diecast	County Borough of Doncaster				1928
Lledo	DG41-001a	1990		1:76	diecast	City of Nottingham				1928
Lledo	DG41-002a,b,c			1:76	diecast	London Transport				1928
Lledo	DG41-003a			1:76	diecast	London Transport				1928
Lledo	DG41-004a			1:76	diecast	London Transport				1928
Lledo	DG41-005a			1:76	diecast	North Yorks Moors Railway				1928
Lledo	DG41-006a			1:76	diecast	London Transport		12	South Croydon	1928
Lledo	DG41-007a			1:76	diecast	City of Nottingham				1928
Lledo	DG41-008a,b		5000	1:76	diecast	London Transport				1928
Lledo	DG41-009a			1:76	diecast	General		11A	Strand, Aldwych	1928
Lledo	DG41-010a			1:76	diecast	Newcastle		31	Gosforth	1928
Lledo	DG41-011a			1:76	diecast	London Transport		604	Wimbledon	1928
Lledo	DG41-012a			1:76	diecast				Huis Ten Bosch	1928
Lledo	DG41-013a		2000	1:76	diecast	London Transport		567	Barking	1928
Lledo	DG41-014a	1997		1:76	diecast	Autumn 1997			Enfield	1928
Lledo	DG41-015a			1:76	diecast	London Transport		660	North Finchley	1928
Lledo	DG41-016a,b			1:76	diecast	London Transport			Finsbury Park, Wood Green	1928
Lledo	DG41-017a			1:76	diecast	London Transport		667	Hammersmith Bdy	1928
Lledo	DG41-020a			1:76	diecast	London Transport		621	Holborn	1928
Lledo	DG41-021a			1:76	diecast	Nottingham City Transport	513	43	Trent Bridge	1928
Sunnyside	yellow			1:76	zamac					1928
Sunnyside	white			1:76	zamac					1928
Sunnyside	blue			1:76	zamac					1928
Sunnyside	red			1:76	zamac					1928

Usually described as 1:76 scale, the Lledo E6 model is nearer to 1:87 (the real length, 28', divided by the model length, 97mm) and were, in any case, designed to fit a box rather than be accurate in scale. Altogether there are 150 variants (depending on how you count; there's 215 if you include all the destination options). We've only listed the original 'Days Gone' versions above, the Promotional E6 Lledos are all listed in the appendix. We do illustrate all the type variants here.

The omnipresent Lledo diecast trolleybus was based on the Roe bodied Karrier chassis design supplied by Clough, Smith to Doncaster Corporation in 3 batches between 1928 and 1931, by which time they were decidedly dated in appearance. London, Newcastle and many of the other operators depicted, of course, had nothing like them. Nottingham, Bradford and Maidstone vaguely had.

The 'DG' in the Lledo reference number, by the way, stands for Days Gone, LP for Lledo Promotional and SP for Stevelyn Promotional (a company in Watford who were sub-contracted by Lledo). The 'DG' numbers were allocated at conception and appear in Lledo catalogues but not on the model itself or its packaging. 'SL' was the Special License range, introduced in 1997 - there are only two of the trolleybus. None of the LP or SP promotional numbers were allocated by LLedo but have been by Ray Dowding in his RDP Lledo Collector Guides and are universally used by collectors. The "a" and "b" suffix is also an unofficial RDP designation, where there are, in the case of the trolleybus, variant route destinations on the front. There is doubt whether one or two models are official or Code 3.

Jack Odell, after becoming a millionaire at Lesney Products (Matchbox, see above) couldn't resist setting up Lledo in 1983 and designing the E6 trolleybus in 1990. Only by tapping into the promotional market did he again survive and prosper, until selling up in 1996 after 50 years in the toy trade. He died in 2007. Lledo was taken over by Corgi in 2000.

Despite the 'Days Gone' trolleybuses theoretically being the 'proper' models, as Jack intended, SP41-34a was arguably the most reminiscent of the original, despite being in Maidstone Corporation livery. Maidstone had eight Ransomes, Sims and Jefferies trolleybuses that were similar to the Doncaster Karriers. As a promotional model, the livery is part applied

Doncaster 8, Karrier E6/Roe/BTH, 1928 (Roe)

as a vinyl sticker and part printed directly by the Tampo or pad technique. The first Lledo, DG41-000a, strangely emblazoned with 'County Borough of Doncaster', rather than 'Doncaster Corporation' was replaced with a second casting with vents over the windscreen but none on the roof, and became the basis for all subsequent models.

DG41-021a, last of the 'Days Gone' series and issued after Corgi took over, was also one of the more realistic model Lledos, with scale lettering, detailed destination indicators and a good representation of Nottingham's livery. Like Maidstone, Nottingham had RSJ and English Electric trolleybuses with the protruding drivers cab and roof. The fleet number, 513, was actually owned by one of the first batch of BUT 9641T six wheelers, of which 502 and 506 are preserved at The Trolleybus Museum at Sandtoft. Nottingham did own a total of 36 Karrier E6 trolleybuses (1, 51-85), although none were old enough to have the stepped body style of the model. No.67, from 1934, is preserved.

We could go on about how utterly mistaken many, if not all, Lledo E6s were as models, but, luckily, many a youngster got hooked on them in the 1990s - they might not otherwise have known what a trolleybus was. Collecting them is still very possible today as there'll be at least one on any given day on ebay; very probably many more. They're likely to cost between £2 and £12. Some are regarded as rare, such as LP41-60a the second Anadin version or DG41-019a Huis Ten Bosch, issued for the Japanese market. (Huis Ten Bosch is a Dutch Royal Palace and a Japanese residential resort). Quite why these rarities are described as such isn't obvious as there were 1300 of the Anadin version made and 6500 of the Huis Ten Bosch versions. Perhaps, now that international bidding on the internet is possible, knowledge of their whereabouts will become a lot easier. And, of course, ascribing rarity is a good way of upping the price.

Copying is the greatest form of flattery, which is what Sunnyside of Hong Kong has done, adding an anachronistic radiator, 'mag' wheels and psychedelic livery to their clone. The toy was available in 4 colours, and is the same size as the Lledo.

Maidstone 25, Karrier E6/Roe/BTH by Lledo, 1:76, diecast

Doncaster Karrier E6/Roe/BTH by Lledo, 1:76, diecast

Nottingham 513, Karrier E6/Roe/BTH by Lledo, 1:76, diecast

Generic Karrier E6/Roe/BTH by Sunnyside, 1:76,

Models DG41000 - LP41022, Karrier E6/Roe/BTH by Lledo, 1:76, diecast zinc

Models LP41023 - LP41095, Karrier E6/Roe/BTH by Lledo, 1:76, diecast zinc

Models LP41096 – SP41028, Karrier E6/Roe/BTH by Lledo, 1:76, diecast zinc

Models SP41029 – SP41041 etc., Karrier E6/Roe/BTH by Lledo, 1:76, diecast zinc

Karrier MS2/Weymann

model maker	ref.	issued	total	scale	construction	operator	fleet#	route	destination	built
Corgi OOC	OM43708	2009	1200	1:76	diecast zinc	South Lancs	71		Leigh	1948
Ken Allbon		1986		1:43	balsa, card	South Lancs	69		Leigh	1948

After a five year lull, Corgi, now owned by Hornby, released a new version of the Q1 casting in 2009. Described on the box as a Sunbeam S7 and on the "Collectors Card" as (correctly) a Karrier MS2, this model is really a bit bizarre if not desperate, with little but superficial similarity between model and the original. No Weymann "skirt", but with nut guards on the wheels where SLT had never found the need and a blob under the side cab windows that had been running plates on the original LTE models. And awful painted-on window opener frames, that don't hide the fact that this a 5 bay model of an 6 bay trolleybus. Fortunately, this hasn't proved to be "The Last Trolley Bus" from Corgi. Just to show what the rather curvy SLT Weymann bodied Karrier MS2 should look like at 1:43 scale, Ken Allbon's scratch built model has characteristic overall accuracy.

Karrier W models are included in the Sunbeam W section below.

South Lancs 71, Karrier MS2/Weymann by Corgi OOC, 1:76, diecast

South Lancs 69, Karrier MS2/Weymanns by Ken Allbon, 1:43, balsa, card

South Lancs 71, Karrier MS2/Weymann, 1948 (J Saunders)

Leyland

Leyland Motors had been publicly anti-trolleybus during the Twenties, when the mode was barely a threat to their petrol buses, but with technological refinement and a lot of trams to replace, they changed their tune in 1930 and entered into a strategic partnership with GEC to supply electrical components for their chassis. Leyland, with their breakthrough order for London in 1936, and despite a poor reputation for all-metal bodies, went on to supply 1400 trolleybus chassis and 445 trolleybus bodies.

Leyland TBD1

model maker	ref.	issued	total	scale	construction	operator	fleet#	route	destination	built
EFE (conversion)				1:76	diecast	Birmingham	19		Nechells	1930

It wasn't known what colour the prototype Leyland trolleybus was originally painted, until diligent research by David Harvey established from the records that it was green, not red, as most thought. It only ran in Birmingham as a demonstrator for three months, but it did lead to an order for 11 electrified Titan chassis to replace the first generation Railless trolleys. After going to Chesterfield for further demonstration, the prototype had a petrol engine (rudely) inserted under the bonnet, where the contactors and traction motor had been. Incredibly, she then went to Jersey to be preserved on withdrawal in 1958 after 27 years of service. The power cables that came through the roof and down the central front pillar can still be seen as they go through the upper panelling of the 'piano front'. EFE produces the model in JMT livery, possibly without realizing they've made a trolleybus! An Exclusive First Edition TD1 has been converted to depict the prototype with trolley booms and gantry by Terry Russell, correctly showing the Brecknell, Willis 'Low Type' or 'Bradford' collector mechanism as they were known, before the better known 'Lightweight' type appeared in 1933.

Birmingham 19, Leyland TBD1/Shorts/GEC by EFE (conversion), 1:76,

Coventry Leyland Titan by Copycat Models/Lesney, 1:72, diecast

Leyland TBD1/Shorts/GEC, 1931 (GEC)&(Jon Bennett)

Copycat Models (Jim Varney) produced a trolleybus conversion kit for Lesney 'Yesteryear' Titan models, making it fully fronted and with an impressive trolley gantry. It's not altogether clear what prototype the resulting model is supposed to be as the front has a distinctly Guy BTX look about it and there were no fully fronted Leyland piano fronts, unless you count the residual curve of Leyland's next prototype, the TTBD1 of 1932, designed from the ground up as a trolleybus. There is, despite the inaccuracy (Coventry never had trolleybuses) a poetic justice in being able to hack off the radiator, insert a full front and add rather fine sprung trolleybooms.

326   5.22 United Kingdom

Leyland TB2

model maker	ref.	issued	total	scale	construction	operator	fleet#	route	destination	built
Pirate Models	452/4907	1990s		1:76	white metal	Birmingham	1-11	7	Nechells	1932

For some reason, Pirate call their ref. 4907 a Leyland TB2 when it is in fact a TBD1 based on the Leyland TD1 'Titan' chassis (The designation became TB2 after the Birmingham production batch of 1-11 had been delivered). Leyland sub-contracted the bodies for Birmingham's second generation of trolleybuses to Short Bros. who came up with one of the last 'piano front' designs built, with expensive curves, in 1932. Although the first one failed the tilt test and so all had to be lightened, the batch received larger trolley gantries in 1938, as can be seen in the model. These 11 vehicles only ran on the Nechells route. There were only ever a few half-cab trolleybuses, built in the early 30s by AEC and Leyland as almost a 'quick and dirty' way of entering the trolleybus market.

But getting back to the model. What happens when you let a Londoner and one from Southall, home of AEC, loose on a Birmingham Leyland – you get a spectacular piece of fantasy as if London Transport never existed and trolleybuses in the capital were operated by "Red and White". The famous LT trolleybus roundel seems to have made it into Grahame Hawkyard's alternative universe however, as does 513 route numbering.

Birmingham 1, Leyland TB2/Shorts/GEC by Pirate Models, 1:76, whitemetal

Red & White, Leyland TB2/Shorts/GEC by Pirate Models, 1:76, whitemetal

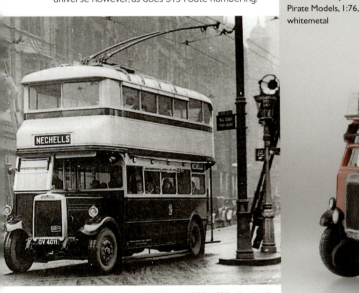

Birmingham 11, Leyland TB2/Shorts/GEC, 1932 (Leyland)

Leyland TTBD2

model maker	ref.	issued	total	scale	construction	operator	fleet#	route	destination	built
CMA		1998		1:76	resin	Birmingham	17-66	92	Yardley	1933

One of the largest trolleybus orders of its time, Birmingham's 50 Leyland TTBD2 vehicles of 1933, were for the Coventry Road routes and their smart modernity caused a considerable increase in ridership. Olaf Olsen's CMA model was not quite so successful and suffers from a rough casting which needs a lot of cleaning up before assembly.

Birmingham 31, Leyland TTBD2/MCCW/GEC, 1933 (C Carter)

Leyland TTBD2 by CMA, 1:76, resin (R Edmundson)

Leyland TB5/7

model maker	ref.	issued	total	scale	construction	operator	fleet#	route	destination	built
Pirate Models	4900			1:76	diecast	Birmingham	67-78			1937
Laurence Ahearn		2010		1:43	wood, metal	Perth	27			1939
Dave Wall				1:18	plastic & metal	Birmingham	90	93	Yardley	1940

Leyland designed a trolleybus from the ground up after they head-hunted T.A. Garrett from Ransomes, Sims and Jefferies in 1932. The TB and TTB series of 4 and 6 wheelers numbered nearly 1,300 before the war stopped production. They were one of the most common of British trolleys. Of the 2 axle type, of which 260 were built, Birmingham had 24 and they've been faithfully modelled by Pirate and Dave Wall. Many, 110, were exported and Laurence Ahearn has modelled Perth's 27 for use on his large layout that includes a wired turntable - more on page 53.

Birmingham Leyland TB5/MCW/GEC by Pirate Models, 1:76, diecast

Perth Leyland TB5/WAGT/GEC by Laurence Ahearn, 1:43, wood, metal   (Laurence Ahearn)

Birmingham Leyland TB7/MCCW/GEC by Dave Wall, 1:18, card, wood, plastic & metal

Leyland TTB2

model maker	ref.	issued	total	scale	construction	operator	fleet#	route	destination	built
Little Bus	TBB1	2004		1:76		London Transport	65	696	Dartford	1935
Terry Russell			1	1:43		London Transport	76	654	Sutton	1935

Most of Leyland's 1930s output was of the 3 axle type and most went to London, starting with the B1 class. Master builders Terry Russell (see page 40) and Rod Blackburn (for Little Bus) have both modelled the class in post war livery, in 0 and 00 scales respectively, and Rod has additionally demonstrated the look before the war, when roofs were silver and windscreen frames were chrome plated.

London Transport 85 and 106, Leyland TTB2/BRCW/MV by Little Bus Co., 1:76, resin   (Rod Blackburn)

London Transport 79, Leyland TTB2/BRCW/MV, 1935   (David Bradley)

Leyland TTB4

model maker	ref.	issued	total	scale	construction	operator	fleet#	route	destination	built
CMA		1998		1:76	resin	London Transport				1935
Corgi OOC	OM43703	2002	4000	1:76	diecast	London Transport	1253	677	West India Docks	1938
Little Bus	TBK2	2005		1:72	resin	London Transport	1273	628	Clapham Junction	1939
Modelcraft Ltd		1950s		1:72	card	London Transport	1273		Depot	1939
St.Petersburg	434	2004	10	1:43	resin	London Transport	1248	647	Stamford Hill	1238
St.Petersburg	434-1	2004	25	1:43	resin	London Transport	1121	630	West Croydon	1938
St.Petersburg	434a	2004	10	1:43	resin	London Transport	1672	649	Ponders End	1940
St.Petersburg	435	2004	10	1:43	resin	London Transport	753	607	Shepherds Bush	1937
St.Petersburg	435-1	2004	15	1:43	resin	London Transport	664	607	Uxbridge	1937
St.Petersburg	434m	2004		1:43	resin	London Transport	1121	630	West Croydon	1938
Rod Blackburn				1:76	resin	London Transport	422	628	Clapham Junction	1936
Kherson Models	E5600			1:43	resin	København NESA	9-17			1938
Micro		1938		1:72	lead	København NESA	9-17	24	Jaeskerborg	1938
Modeltrafik		1938		no scale	wood	København NESA		12	Lynoby Point	1938
St.Petersburg	138	1999	25	1:43	resin	København KS	101	12	Lyngby	1938
St.Petersburg	138a	1999	25	1:43	resin	København NESA	9-17	12	Lyngby	1938

The TTB4 is rightfully one of the most modelled of trolleybuses, certainly of the UK. Let's start with the St. Petersburg Tram Collection models of London's F and K classes. They're available in pre, post and wartime liveries, with detail differences, such as exterior and inset sidelights, open or cowled airvents, and even the correct depot allocation plates depending on their date.

The SPTC models are beautifully accurate and detailed, In fact, it's hard to see how they could be bettered, so any attacks, which would probably need a magnifying glass to spot, on Leonid Khoykhin and his team's considerable efforts seem irrelevant. They are, of course expensive, over €300, and rarely if ever come up for sale second-hand. Ordering from Leonid can mean a wait of a year, but it is well worth it.

London 1121, Leyland TTB4/Leyland/MV by St.Petersburg, 1:43, resin   (SPTC)

London 1248, Leyland TTB4/Leyland/MV by St.Petersburg, 1:43, resin (David Bradley)

London Transport 753, Leyland TTB4/Leyland/MV by St.Petersburg, 1:43, resin

London 1121, Leyland TTB4/Leyland/MV by St.Petersburg, 1:43, resin (David Bradley)

London 1253, Leyland TTB4/Leyland/MV, 1938

London 422, Leyland TTB4/MCCW/MV by Rod Blackburn, 1:76, resin   (Rod Blackburn)

Two K2 Little Bus kits have been made up as a P1 class on route 630 and as a K2 class on route 628 by Rod Blackburn. The Little Bus K2 kit is itself an adaptation of the L3 kit and cast from Rod's master mould. His model of a London D2 class Leyland was practically a prototype for his models for the Little Bus Company. Scratch built from plastic card, Rod admits it's not as accurate has it might have been, though it's not too easy to see how - perhaps the depth of the lower windows is a little too generous.

The earliest kit, from the 1950s, is thought to be by Modelcraft, details are discussed above. 60 years of trolleybus kits have seen more than progress, more a quantum leap in quality and critical debate can centre on minutiae. Corgi have made a slightly dubious claim for a model of K2 class, 1253, using the Q1 casting with the trolley base support integrated into the roof, rather than as it should be, carried on the standard pre-war gantry assembly. But then 1253 is preserved at London Transport Museum, and so the model is assured of sales. 1201 is resident at East Anglia Transport Museum and 1348 is at Sandtoft.

The 14 Leyland TTB4 chassis that were export to København in 1938 and the various models of them are described in chapter 5.7, on page 131.

London 1701 and 1273, Leyland TTB4/Leyland/MV by Little Bus Co., 1:72, resin   (Rod Blackburn)

København NESA Leyland TTB4/Scandia/GEC by Kherson Models, 1:43, resin

London 1253, Leyland TTB4/Leyland/MV by Corgi OOC, 1:76, diecast

Leyland TTB5

model maker	ref.	issued	total	scale	construction	operator	fleet#	route	destination	built
Little Bus	TBSA	2006		1:76	resin	London Transport	1742	693	Barking Broadway	1941
Little Bus	TBSA	2006		1:76	resin	London Transport	1742	693	Barking Broadway	1941
Ken Allbon		1988		1:43	balsa, card	London Transport	1748	691	Fairlop	1942

Famous, amongst London trolleybus aficionados anyway, are the 43 8' wide Leyland TTB5s of the SA classes that were diverted from delivery to South Africa during the war to spend their lives working out of Ilford depot. The Little Bus kit can make SA1 or SA2 versions but Rod Blackburn has also built one to show how the TTB5 model would have appeared had they been delivered to Durban as intended in 1942. With the likelihood of life reflecting art and the return of an identical Johannesburg BUT, currently in Durban colours, to the UK for restoration, possibly as an SA3 London trolleybus, it's likely the SA class will be further modelled, not least to raise funds. Ken Allbon made his SA3 in 1988.

London 1742, Leyland TTB5/MCCW/MV by Little Bus Co., 1:76, resin (Rod Blackburn)

Durban Leyland TTB5/MCCW/BTH by Little Bus Co., 1:76, resin (Rod Blackburn)

London 1739, Leyland TTB5/MCCW/MV, 1942 (David Bradley)

Leyland TTB6

In the interests of completeness mention can be made that Leonid Khoykhin at St. Petersburg did intend to make 0 scale models of Belfast's 2 prototype Leyland TTB6 double-deckers in the 3 liveries that they wore during their lives. He still might, if there is sufficient interest. Doubtless the task is made easier by their similarity to London's K class that he has already made; they had the same distinctive low doorway, although they were higher than any other British trolleybuses as there was no need to adhere to the British 16ft 6ins clearance maximum. As he says of their first appearance in 1938, 'The trolleybuses were painted in a very attractive streamlined blue and white livery, lined out in gold.' There are at least the Corgi Belfast AECs that look similar.

London 1748, Leyland TTB5/MCCW/MV by Ken Allbon, 1:43, balsa, card

Leyland Twin Steer

model maker	ref.	issued	total	scale	construction	operator	fleet#	route	destination	built
Pirate Models	4905		0	1:76		London Transport	1671	654	Sutton	1939
Southern Miniature Models				1:76		London Transport	1671	607	Shepherds Bush	1939
Tony Chlad				1:87	scratchbuilt	London Transport	1671	607	Shepherds Bush	1939

London 1671, Leyland Twin Steer/ Leyland/MV, 1939 (Leyland Motors)

London 1671, Leyland Twin Steer/ Leyland/MV by Tony Chlad, 1:76, plasticard (Tony Chlad)

London 1671, Leyland Twin Steer/Leyland/MV by Pirate Models, 1:76, diecast

London 1671, Leyland Twin Steer/Leyland/MV by Southern Miniature Models, 1:76, diecast

Conceived as an answer to the rear bogie tyre scrub problem, and designed as giving greater tyre mileage, a better turning circle and less likelihood of front wheel skids, London's 1671 always turned heads whenever she passed. With two front steering axles and one axle at the rear, albeit using doubles, she had eight tyres in all. This was Leyland's state-of the-art thinking for 1939 and their first attempt at a chassisless trolleybus. She apparently gave a rougher ride at the rear and wore the front tyres quicker than expected but could out-brake any standard trolleybus. She gave 16 years of service, without any recorded major problems. And inevitably, she has been modelled. The late Tony Chlad built a powered 00 scale version from scratch, complete with 4 wheel steering and Faller guidance.

Static models of 1671 include an accurate Pirate Models kit and an adaptation by Southern Miniature Models, that involved cutting up two Corgi AEC 661Ts that you preferably sent to them for conversion.

Railless

model maker	ref.	issued	total	scale	construction	operator	fleet#	route	destination	built
Alphagrafix	DB114	1993		1:76	card	Ipswich Corporation	2	-	-	1923
Ken Allbon		1981		1:43	balsa, card	Bradford Corporation	240		Dudley Hill	1911
Ken Allbon		1984		1:43	balsa, card	Metropolitan Electric Tramways	1		The Burroughs	1909
Ken Allbon				1:43	balsa, card	Brighton Corporation	50			1914
Eric Thornton		1948		1:30	wood, metal	Bradford Corporation	240		Laisterdyke, Dudley Hill	1911

Ipswich 2, Railless/Shorts/EE, 1923
(Alan B Thompson)

Ipswich 2, Railless/Shorts/EE by Alphagrafix, 1:76, card (detail)
(Alphagraphix)

Railless Electric Traction Co., was, in its three incarnations following two restructurings, the great trolleybus pioneer company in the UK between 1908 and 1926. So much of its production was an ever changing development, that the designation of 'type' was barely something that could be applied, although the last 28 vehicles, built in the last two years of the company, were of the 'LF30' type with (comparatively) low floors. A Railless of 1923 miraculously survives in Ipswich Transport Museum and is the basis for an Alphagrafix card model. Mentioned in Model Engineer magazine in 1948 is the model of Bradford 240, one of the first Railless to be used in public service. Neither the real thing nor the model seem to have survived, but Ken Allbon of Sussex has recently completed his model of Brighton 50, the first ever double deck trolleybus, as she ran in 1913-14. He's also, as mentioned at the top of this chapter, built MET 1, Bradford 240 and Leeds 501 (now lost).

Brighton 50, Railless/RET/Siemens by Ken Allbon, 1:43, wood, metal, plastic   (Andrew Henbest)

Ipswich 41, Ransomes, Sims + Jefferies D type by Percy Wilby, 1:12, tin, ply

Ipswich 47, Ransomes, Sims + Jefferies D type by Percy Wilby, 1:12, tin, ply

Ransomes, Sims & Jefferies

model maker	ref.	issued	total	scale	construction	operator	fleet#	route	destination	built
Alphagrafix	DB115	1993		1:76	card	Ipswich Corporation	46	7A	Royal Show	1933
André Dessart				1:30	wood, metal	Liège TULE	402	20		1930
Percy Wilby				1:12	tin, ply	Ipswich Corporation	41	8	Adair Road	1928
Percy Wilby				1:12	tin, ply	Ipswich Corporation	47	9	Whitton	1933
Percy Wilby				1:9	tin, ply	Ipswich Corporation	68	1	Bourn	1937
Percy Wilby		1948		1:9	tin, ply	Ipswich Corporation	6	8	Adair Road	1926

Percy Wilby, a railway engineer of Ipswich, built a series of four models of his beloved local trolleybuses between 1948 and 1955 (more details from page 38 onwards). Ransomes, Sims and Jeffries, as the local agricultural engineers, had diversified into electric vehicles at the turn of the century and so inevitably built trolleybuses for their local operator, Ipswich Corporation, after they first adopted the mode with Railless trolleys in 1923. Apart from Percy's model of no.47, Alphagrafix has produced a card kit of no.46, a sister Ransomes of 1933, which is preserved in Ipswich Transport Museum.

Similar to Ipswich's single deckers and tested under the corporations wires, were Liège 401-5, exported in 1930. With new bodies after war, they lasted in service until 1961. Not long after, Liège resident, the late André Dessart, built a 1:30 scale model of 402, resplendent with Estler trolleybases, and made of wood, sheet metal and clear plastic. The model, together with representations of later generations (see page 89), now resides in the Musée des Transports en commun du Pays de Liège, in glass cases between full size trams and trolleybuses.

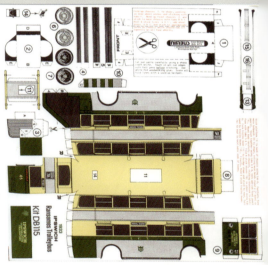

Ipswich 46, Ransomes, Sims + Jefferies D type by Alphagrafix, 1:76, card   (Alphagraphix)

Liège 404, Ransomes/RSJ/EMB, 1930   (Ransomes)

Liège 402, Ransomes/RSJ/EMB by André Dessart, 1:30, wood, metal   (André Corteil)

Sunbeam

The Sunbeam Trolleybus Co Ltd., built as many trolleybuses as Leyland Motors, although, unlike Leyland, most were built after the war. From 1935 onwards they also built all Karrier trolleybuses, which arguably made Sunbeam's factory in Wolverhampton the largest trolleybus production facility in the UK. The MS series of chassis began production in 1931 and was followed by the MF series, originally intended for single deck bodies, in 1934.

Wolverhampton 206 Sunbeam MF1/Park Royal/ BTH, scratchbuilt, 1:72, wood, card

Sunbeam MS2

model maker	ref.	issued	total	scale	construction	operator	fleet#	route	destination	built
Little Bus (conversion)	TMS2	2006		1:76	resin	Bournemouth	201	20	Square	1935
Little Bus	TMS2	2006		1:76	resin	London Transport	87	691	Barking Broadway	1935
Little Bus	TMS2	2006		1:76	resin	Bournemouth	208	25	Westbourne	1935
Dave Wall				1:24	card, wood, plastic & metal	Bournemouth	202	39	Circular Service	1935
Robin Male		2009		1:30	metal, plasticard	Bournemouth	99	21	Boscombe Square	1935
Ken Allbon		1986		1:43	balsa, card	South Lancs	69		Leigh	1948
CMA		2000		1:76	resin	Bournemouth				1935
CMA		1998		1:76	resin	Huddersfield	595	90	Longwood	1950

A loving conversion of a Little Bus resin kit to an open top Bournemouth MS2 has been built, though still with a front entrance, that, admits the builder, was a little beyond him. Nigel Leahy is a vehicle paint supplier in the south west of England so he's able to get the correct Bournemouth Corporation yellow enamel. He could also produce the necessary graphics on his computer. It was then merely a question of taking a miniature saw to the kit, cutting through all the window struts, bar those that hold the trolley base aloft and those that support the boom retaining hooks. The rest was brushing on 'in flooding' technique to get the high gloss plus a bit of judicious fine body filler here and there. Someone you'd expect to get the front door right is David Bowler, author of the definitive history of Bournemouth's Trolleybuses, though for him, paint was a problem. "Although the considerable amount of reconstruction came out to my complete satisfaction, the spray painting unfortunately was not as successful as that with the covered top MS2".

Bournemouth 202, Sunbeam MS2/Park Royal/ BTH by Little Bus Co., 1:76, resin (Nigel Leahy)

Bournemouth 201 and 213, Sunbeam MS2/Park Royal/BTH by Little Bus Co., 1:76, resin (David Bowler)

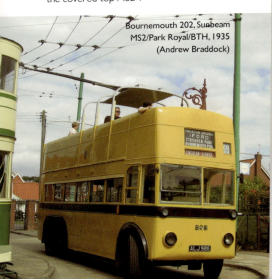

Bournemouth 202, Sunbeam MS2/Park Royal/BTH, 1935 (Andrew Braddock)

Dave Wall has also built Bournemouth 202 in 1:24 scale, the extremely popular open top Sunbeam MS2, preserved by the National Trolleybus Association, that regularly runs at the East Anglia Transport Museum in Suffolk. Rod Blackburn, using his MS2 master moulds, (as everybody modelling Sunbeam MS2s in 1:76 scale has), made 208 in standard Bournemouth livery and painted a version of 87, in wartime colours, as she appeared on route 691, on loan to London Transport in 1941. So too has the late Graham Hawkyard, additionally adding headlight blackout covers to his 72.

Rather more eccentrically, David Wood's motorized Little Bus MS2 kit is in fictitious West Porton Corporation colours with a cheeky LT trolleybus roundel on the side. Robin Male has modelled a motorized Bournemouth 99 in 1:30 scale on his extensive layout in Somerset, using Meccano wheels and a 'wire in road' steering system (more on page 53). 99 is preserved at Sandtoft.

Bournemouth 202, Sunbeam MS2/Park Royal/BTH by Dave Wall, 1:24, card, wood, plastic & metal (Dave Wall)

Bournemouth 208, Sunbeam MS2/Park Royal/BTH by Little Bus Co., 1:76, resin (Rod Blackburn)

Bournemouth 72, Sunbeam MS2/Park Royal/BTH by Little Bus Co., 1:76, resin

Bournemouth 99, Sunbeam MS2/Park Royal/BTH, 1935 (Bruce Lake)

West Porton Corporation Sunbeam MS2/Park Royal/BTH by Little Bus Co., 1:76, resin

Bournemouth 99, Sunbeam MS2/Park Royal/BTH by Robin Male, 1:30, metal, plasticard

CMA (Olaf Olsen, Wheelbase Models) produced a Bournemouth Sunbeam kit and one of Huddersfield 595. The prototypical Sunbeams had 6-bay Roe bodies from new, in 1950-52 and were originally fitted with bumpers. The kit does have particularly oversize lining edges that could be reduced to make a more accurate model. The upper front corners are too rounded, looking suspiciously like the London L1 class kit that CMA also produced. But stood against the real thing, perhaps such 76th size detail pales to insignificance!

Huddersfield Sunbeam MS2/Roe/MV by CMA, 1:76, resin, beside Huddersfield 619 rear wheel bogie   (Bruce Lake)

Huddersfield Sunbeam MS2/Roe/MV by Wheelbase Models, 1:76, resin

Sunbeam S7, 7A

model maker	ref.	issued	total	scale	construction	operator	fleet#	route	destination	built
Corgi OOC	43714	2000	2700	1:76	diecast	Reading	174	17	Cemetery Junction	1950
Ken Allbon		1979		1:43	balsa, card	Reading	181	15	Caversham Br.	1950
Scratchbuilt		1960's		1:32	wood, metal	Reading	170	17	Tilehurst	1950
Bruce Lake		2005	1	1:76	plasticard	Huddersfield	631	6	Birkby	1959
Neil Mortson		2008		1:43	diecast and plastic	Huddersfield	631		Almondbury	1959

Sunbeam introduced the S7 replacement for the MS2 at the 1948 Commercial Motor Show, although only 83 were built and the MS2 continued in production. 30 went to South Africa while Newcastle, Huddersfield and Reading were the main users in Britain. Corgi created Reading 174 out of the Q1 casting in 2000, resorting to painted-on cab window bars and ignoring the completely different upper deck styling of the Park Royal original. Better reflecting the character of the class, if not the Corgi polish, is Ken Allbon's recreation of 181. 181 and 174 are preserved in running order at The Trolleybus Museum at Sandtoft where there is also a large 1:32 model of 170.

Huddersfield 631, a Sunbeam 7A, is a stalwart of the museum and owned by Bruce Lake, whose motorised model is detailed from page 50. Also at Sandtoft is Neil Morston's stylishly impeccable model of 631, in the same scale as the Corgi Classics, and commissioned by the Model Bus Federation for its founder, Bob Heathcote, on the occasion of the MBF 40th anniversary.

Reading 174, Sunbeam S7/Park Royal/BTH by Corgi OOC, 1:76, diecast

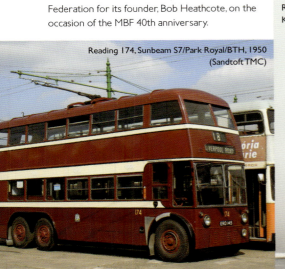

Reading 174, Sunbeam S7/Park Royal/BTH, 1950 (Sandtoft TMC)

Reading 181, Sunbeam S7/Park Royal/BTH by Ken Allbon, 1:43, balsa, card

Huddersfield 631, Sunbeam S7A/East Lancs/MV, 1959

Huddersfield 631, Sunbeam S7A/East Lancs/MV by Neil Mortson, 1:43, diecast and plastic

Sunbeam W

model maker	ref.	issued	total	scale	construction	operator	fleet#	route	destination	built
Alphagrafix	DB102	1991		1:76	card	Nottingham	460	39	Carlton	1945
Alphagrafix	DB104	1992		1:76	card	Bradford	737	40	Greengates	1945
Alphagrafix	DB110	1992		1:76	card	Derby	172	-	Victoria Street	1944
Atlas Editions	GBB015	2011		1:76	diecast	Teeside	T294		North Ormesby	1944
Corgi Classics	97801	1995	5500	1:50	diecast	Maidstone	55		Barming	1945
Corgi Classics	97800	1993	12750	1:50	diecast	Reading	132		Norcot Junct.	1943
Corgi Classics	97871	1994	6500	1:50	diecast	Bradford	715	24	Bingley	1945
Corgi Classics	34701	1996	7300	1:50	diecast	Nottingham	454	43	Trent Bridge	1944
Corgi Classics	34702	1996	5500	1:50	diecast	Ashton-under-Lyne	61		Manchester Picadilly	1944
Corgi Classics	97870	1994	5500	1:50	diecast	Newcastle	125	3A	Delaval Rd via Elswick Rd	1944
Corgi Classics	97316	1995	5500	1:50	diecast	Ipswich	102		Electric House	1945
Corgi Classics	34703	1997	4100	1:50	diecast	Derby	172		Midland Station via London Road	1944
Corgi Classics (conversion)				1:50	diecast	London Transport		693	Chadwell Heath	
Corgi Classics (repaint)				1:50	diecast	Belfast	130	33	Cregah	1943
Corgi Classics (repaint)				1:50	diecast	Southend	138	28B	West Circular	1945
Corgi OOC	OM40101	2004	1500	1:76	diecast	Maidstone	72	-	Park Wood via Sutton Road	1946
Corgi OOC	OM41405	2006	2260	1:76	diecast	Maidstone	56	-	Sutton Road (Grove Road)	1944
Corgi OOC	OM40102a,b	2010	1000	1:76	diecast	Wolverhampton	455	8	Fighting Cocks	1947-8
Corgi OOC	40103	1997	3600	1:76	diecast	Walsall	306	-	Bloxwich	1946
Corgi OOC	40106	1999	4000	1:76	diecast	Maidstone & District	34	-	Trolleys Last Run	1947
Corgi OOC (repaint)				1:76	diecast	Doncaster	392		Race Course	1945
Pirate Models	433/4908	1981		1:76	diecast	South Shields	237			1946
TiNY Bus and Coach	TK2	2006		1:76	resin	Nottingham	478	49	Carlton	1946
TiNY Bus and Coach	TK2	2006		1:76	resin	Pontypridd	9		Treforest	1946
TiNY Bus and Coach	TK14	2010		1:76	resin	Nottingham	459			1945
Tony Chlad		1990's		1:76	resin	Derby	172		Derby	1944
Wakey Models	8A/11	2005		1:76	resin	Mexborough & Swinton	18	A	Mexborough	1947
Westward	45	1978		1:76	diecast	Derby			Grove Park	1946

Alphagrafix have issued 3 editions and Corgi have produced three different versions of the Sunbeam/Karrier W, the utility vehicle that was the only trolleybus that could be ordered by UK operators between 1942 and 1946. The W proved rather robust and continued in production until 1949. 467 were built for 26 operators and many were sold on and rebodied, finally lasting in service until 1971 in Bradford.

Nottingham 460, Sunbeam W/Park Royal by Alphagrafix, 1:76, card

Maidstone 56, Sunbeam W/Roe/BTH, 1944   (Marcus Eavis)

Maidstone 72, Sunbeam W/Northern Coachbuilders/BTH by Corgi OOC, 1:76, diecast

Maidstone 56, Sunbeam W/Roe/BTH by Corgi OOC, 1:76, diecast

There are two Corgi 1:76 versions, typified by the Maidstone models. The 1996 casting, used for no.72 with a Northern Coachbuilders body, has also been used for BUT 9611Ts with Weymann bodies and AEC 661Ts with Harkness, Park Royal and Weymann bodies. The 2006 casting, used for no.56 with a Roe body, has also been used as Sunbeam F4s with Roe bodies. This casting incorporates the new idea of individually inserted windows that give an arguably more realistic appearance by visually reducing the window pillar depth. Wolverhampton 455, W type Sunbeam of 1947, was rebodied by Roe in 1961 and was modelled with the casting in 2010.

Wolverhampton 455, Sunbeam W/Roe/BTH by Corgi OOC, 1:76,

Sunbeam W/Roe/BTH, 1947-8   (Fred Ivey)

Atlas Editions has employed the Corgi casting to model Teesside Municipal Transport T294 in the final, some say lurid, livery used by the undertaking from 1968 until closure in 1971. The colour is difficult to reproduce and often looks bluer. The model doesn't include wing mirrors or, correctly, the boom base cowling.

Teeside T294, Sunbeam W/Roe/BTH by Atlas Editions, 1:76,

Maidstone & District 34, Sunbeam W/ Weymann/BTH by Corgi OOC, 1:76, diecast

Walsall 306, Sunbeam W/Weymann/BTH by Corgi OOC, 1:76, diecast

Two other Sunbeam Ws have been modelled by Corgi using the 1996 casting, Hastings last trolleybus, no. 34, that later operated in Maidstone, now thankfully preserved at Carlton Colville and Walsall 306, bought second-hand from Hastings in 1959, and surviving in service until 1970, when she was 24 years old.

The 'proper' Sunbeam/Karrier W4 chassis had utility bodywork with wooden slatted seats, built by Park Royal or Weymann or in the case of single-deckers, Brush. Roe and others also built utility bodies later and after the war. Corgi went to town with a Park Royal model, producing a larger diecast in 1:50 scale, rather than O gauge (1:43) or American O (1:48).

Perhaps the best preserved W is Derby 172 at The Trolleybus Museum at Sandtoft and the Corgi (in the last in the series so far) accurately replicates the adverts on each side, the wartime white mudguards and the headlight 'black out' shades. Tony Chlad's scratch built model shows how it ought to be done however, with the correct side shape over the cab. Alphagraphix has also produced a model of 172 in card.

Derby 172, Sunbeam W/Weymann/ BTH by Corgi Classics, 1:50, diecast

Derby 172, Sunbeam W/Weymann/BTH, 1944 (A Murray)

Derby 172, Sunbeam W/Weymann/BTH by Tony Chlad, 1:76, resin

The first Corgi Classic W is of a trolleybus long gone, Reading 132, scrapped with rest of the batch after just 8 years in 1951. Pity the top and bottom cream bands couldn't have been wider on the model – it seems a thick black lining always has to compromise the appearance.

Reading 132, Sunbeam W/Park Royal/EE, 1943   (WJ Haynes)

Maidstone's Ws were rebodied by Roe in 1960 and modelled thus by Corgi in their OOC range, but the original Park Royal body is reproduced in the Classics range and painted in the darker tan of the immediate post war years.

Maidstone 51, Sunbeam W/Park Royal/BTH, 1945   (H Luff)

Bradford had received Roe bodied Ws immediately after the war, without the characteristic drop to the windscreen, but the second batch had Park Royal bodies with the front slope. This and the identical Newcastle version were issued by Corgi in 1994. There are no less than 10 preserved Bradford W's, in various states of repair, though none have their original utility bodywork.

Reading 132, Sunbeam W/Park Royal/EE by Corgi Classics, 1:50, diecast

Maidstone 55, Sunbeam W/Park Royal/BTH by Corgi Classics, 1:50, diecast

Newcastle 125, Sunbeam W/Park Royal/MV by Corgi Classics, 1:50, diecast

Bradford 715, Sunbeam W/Park Royal/EE by Corgi Classics, 1:50, diecast

5.22 United Kingdom   343

Nottingham 454, Sunbeam W/Park Royal/EE by Corgi Classics, 1:50, diecast

Nottingham 454, Sunbeam W/Park Royal/EE, 1944 (Nottingham Library)

Nottingham had Ws bodied by Brush, Roe, Weymann and Park Royal. All except the latter had straight sided bodies, but 452-454 and 469-478 had the windscreen droop and also a thicker first pillar to the upper deck which most Park Royal W bodies had. The detail doesn't make it on to the Corgi model.

Corgi's eight 1:50 scale W trolleybuses include Ashton under Lyne and Ipswich versions (No.105 is preserved at the Ipswich transport Museum). They could equally produce models in the liveries of Belfast, Doncaster, Grimsby, Llanelly, Pontypridd, Southend, Walsall or Wolverhampton; all operators who had deliveries with the characteristic body before Park Royal revised the design in 1947.

Some collectors have jumped the gun and had Belfast and Southend versions expertly created by professional modellers.

Ashton-under-Lyne 61, Sunbeam W/Park Royal/EE by Corgi Classics, 1:50, diecast

Ipswich 102, Sunbeam W/Park Royal/MV by Corgi Classics, 1:50, diecast

Southend 138, Sunbeam W/Park Royal/BTH by Corgi Classics (repaint), 1:50, diecast

Belfast 130, Sunbeam W/Park Royal/BTH by Corgi Classics (repaint), 1:50, diecast

Some have gone further. Two Corgi Classics models of Sunbeam Ws have been rather expertly joined together to make a London 6 wheeler but is it a SA3 or a W6, as if there had ever been a utility specification for a three axle trolleybus? It's known that at least 4 of these rather imposing conversions were made for sale.

One obviously huge advantage of kits is that you're forced to paint them and so choose the livery. John Gay's Pirate W model, with the slightly odd alignment between lower windows is in Southend colours and from Norman Dickenson's collection.

Another W model was the Westward kit. These early, if not the earliest, white metal kits show the learning curve that master modellers had embarked on in the early 80s. Aspects of the casting show commendable likeness to the real thing, but getting the thing to align is tricky and the roof is just plain too flat! The booms show that the width is too great, almost like a 8 footer and the technique for smooth body sides had yet to be learnt.

The TiNY Bus and Coach resin kit version of the Park Royal W can be in Nottingham green, does include that thicker upper front pillar, has smooth body panels and aligns the drivers and passenger windows. Perhaps getting all that right is why Keith Turner decided to produce the model, even though so many, including Corgi, had tried before. Arnold Chave has built the kit in the livery of that obscure system, Pontypridd, with characteristic 'weathering'. Keith Turner, Rob Nicholson and Peter Yates, the TiNY team, now produce a W kit with a Roe body.

London Sunbeam W6/Park Royal/MV (fictitious) Sunbeam MS2C (fictitious) by Corgi Classics (conversion), 1:50, diecast

Southend Sunbeam W/Park Royal/BTH by Pirate Models, 1:76, whitemetal

Derby Sunbeam W/Park Royal/BTH by Westward, 1:76, whitemetal

Southend 132, Sunbeam W/Park Royal/BTH, 1945 (C Carter)

Nottingham 478, Sunbeam W/Park Royal/BTH by TiNY Bus and Coach, 1:76, resin (Doug Nicholson)

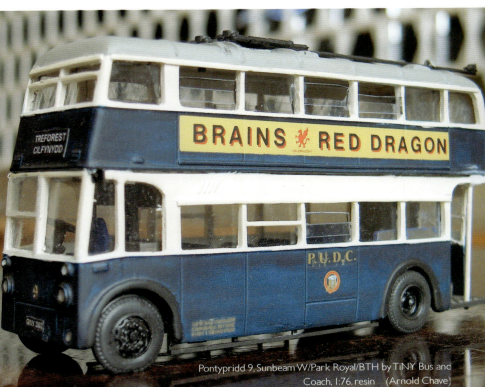

Pontypridd 9, Sunbeam W/Park Royal/BTH by TiNY Bus and Coach, 1:76, resin (Arnold Chave)

Finally we should mention that many Ws were re-bodied and had considerable service lives. For instance, Bradford's Karriers of 1946 lasted, with new bodies by East Lancashire, until the end in 1972. Alfagrafix has modelled 737 which is preserved at the Bradford Industrial Museum. 704 of a similar but earlier batch, has been impeccably modelled from scratch by Tony Chlad, who managed the subtlety of the East Lancashire body rather better than other attempts (see below). 704 herself is preserved in Cardiff, while her sister 706 runs at Sandtoft Museum.

Bradford 737, Sunbeam W/Roe (Karrier) by Alphagrafix, 1:76, card

Bradford 704, Karrier W/East Lancs by Tony Chlad, 1:76, resin

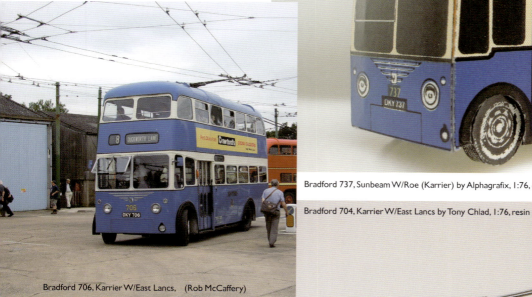

Bradford 706, Karrier W/East Lancs, (Rob McCaffery)

Sunbeam F4

model maker	ref.	issued	total	scale	construction	operator	fleet#	route	destination	built
Alphagrafix	DB106	1992		1:76	card, cutout sheet	Ipswich	126	5	Foxhall Road	1950
Alphagrafix	DB107	1992		1:76	card, cutout sheet	Walsall	347	-	Walsall	1950
Bob Heathcote				1:76	plasticard	Bradford	844		City Centre	1948
Corgi OOC	OM41401a,b	2006	3220		diecast	Teesside	2	-	North Ormesby, South Bank	1950
Corgi OOC	OM41407a,b	2007	1005		diecast	Derby	237	22,11	Midland Station	1960
Dave Wall				1:18	card, wood, plastic & metal	Walsall	353	32	Lower Farm Estate	1950
K&B Models		1970s		1:76	diecast	Bradford	844			1948
Little Bus	TNB"	2005		1:76	resin	South Shields	257	12	Marsden	1947
Mike Skeggs				1:43	plastic	Derby	201-15			1949
Peter Lepino		1964-7	1	1:3	aluminium, steel and wood	Reading	187	A	Tilehurst	1961
Pirate Models	4910			1:76	white metal	Bradford	844			1948
Tony Chlad				1:76	plasticard	Reading	184			1961
Tont Chlad				1:76	plasticard	Walsall				1954
Wakey Models				1:76	resin kit	Island Traction				

The Corgi OOC W casting of 2006 allowed the maker legitimately to produce versions of Sunbeam's F4 trolleybus that was the post war adaptation of, or replacement for the W chassis. Like the W, the very first F4s were Brush bodied single-deckers, for the Mexborough and Swinton Traction Company and were externally indistinguishable from the previous Ws.

The fictitious 'Island Traction Co.,' a Tilling company, 'operates' Sunbeam F4 single-deckers that Keith Jackson has produced from Wakey Models kits in his preferred colours of French blue and ivory. In reality, the olive and cream single-deckers of Mexborough and Swinton, the only F4 single-deckers in the UK, were sold to Bradford and were variously rebodied, although one, T.403, famously survived for a number of years with its original body.

Island Traction Sunbeam F4/Brush/BTH by Wakey Models, 1:76, resin

Mexborough & Swinton 18, Sunbeam W/Brush/BTH by Wakey Models, 1:76, resin (Wakey Models)

Bradford 844, Sunbeam F4/East Lancs/BTH, 1948 (Howard Piltz)

Bradford 844, Sunbeam F4/East Lancs/BTH by Bob Heathcote, 1:76, plasticard (R Heathcote)

Bradford 844, Sunbeam F4/East Lancs/BTH by Pirate Models, 1:76, whitemetal

Britain's last trolleybus to run in public service so far is Bradford's 844, preserved at The Trolleybus Museum at Sandtoft. Originally a Sunbeam F4 single-decker, she was rebodied by East Lancashire in 1961 and is seemingly difficult to get right as a model. Bob Heathcote's scratch built model was made by laminating a scale drawing directly on to plasticard, which should make it correct. The Pirate (ex-K&B Models) kit has a problem of the front being too curved and wheels appearing too small, giving it a 'toy' look. Ken Allbon has managed a true likeness however, modelling 847 in 1:43 scale.

Park Royal bodied F4s are typified by Ipswich 126, the very last new trolleybus delivered to the town in 1950, at which time the Corporation owned only trolleys. Eight of the batch were sold to Walsall in 1963, but 126 has since returned home to the Ipswich Transport Museum, where you can buy the Alphagrafix card kit in either Ipswich or Walsall livery. Dave Wall has similarly modelled Walsall 353 (ex-Ipswich 121) with all the accuracy that a 1:18 scale more capaciously allows. The motorized model, together with others, can be seen running at Aston Manor Road Transport Museum.

Bradford 847, Sunbeam F4/East Lancs/BTH by Ken Allbon, 1:43, balsa, card

Ipswich 125, Sunbeam F4/Park Royal/MV, 1950 (John Law)

Ipswich 126, Sunbeam F4/Park Royal/MV by Alphagrafix, 1:76, card

Walsall 347, Sunbeam F4/Park Royal/MV by Alphagrafix, 1:76, card

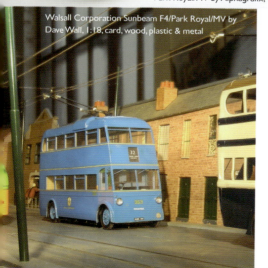

Walsall Corporation Sunbeam F4/Park Royal/MV by Dave Wall, 1:18, card, wood, plastic & metal

Vic Franklin has been making model trolleybuses from cereal packets for years, often displaying them at the Model Bus Federation's annual exhibition. Typical of his longstanding output is a Sunbeam F4 of Newcastle, one of the 443-78 batch of 1948-9.

Newcastle 443, Sunbeam F4/Northern Coachbuilders by Vic Franklin, 1:76, Balsa, card

Derby 201, Sunbeam F4/Brush/BTH by Mike Skeggs, 1:43, plastic (Simon Cole)

Mike Scraggs has built a motorized Derby Brush bodied F4 from a plastic bus for use on Terry Russell's kerb guidance layout (more in chapter 3, page 40).

The Roe body style on Derby's 1960 vehicles was traceable back to the first double deck Utility body of 1944, owing much to the Park Royal design. Nos.236-243 were only in service for seven years but one, 237, is preserved, almost like new, at the East Anglia Transport Museum. The Corgi model adds the gloriously appropriate advert "Live wires prefer electricity". And David Wood has successfully motorized one.

Derby 237, Sunbeam F4/Brush/BTH, 1949   (Irvine Bell)

Derby 237, Sunbeam F4/Roe/BTH by Corgi OOC, 1:76, diecast

Derby 237, Sunbeam F4/Roe/BTH by Corgi OOC (motorised), 1:76,

Teesside Railless Traction Board too, had Sunbeam F4s that were rebodied by Roe to a very similar style in 1962. Ashton under Lyne and Doncaster had trolleybuses that were rebodied with the same Roe design between 1957 and 1965, so there's still potential life in the Corgi 2006 casting for new issues. Keith Turner has already shown how one could look.

Tees-side 2, Sunbeam F4/Roe/BTH by Corgi OOC, 1:76, diecast

Tees-side 5, Sunbeam F4/Roe/BTH, 1950 (Sandtoft TMC)

Doncaster 392, Sunbeam W/Roe/BTH by Corgi OOC (repaint), 1:76, diecast   (Keith Turner)

The Little Bus kit of the Northern Coachbuilders bodied F4 makes for possibilities in Maidstone, Newcastle, and South Shields liveries. Peter Short, in wanting to evoke childhood memories, chose 257 and added the characteristic mounting for the trolley recovery pole, above the lower windows. But why 257, when it had caused a bloody nose? Lunch time from school was huge crush, when, says Peter, "the conductor decided enough was enough and dinged the bell. 257 took off with me still holding the handle, running to try and jump on, but unsuccessfully. It dragged me off my feet and I arrived on my nose in the middle of the road, somewhat sore, slightly bleeding, and left with a 20-minute wait." None the less, the 251-60 and 261-70 batches were Peter's favourites and the last new trolleybuses supplied to South Shields.

South Shields 257 Sunbeam F4/Northern Coachbuilders/MV by Little Bus Co., 1:76, resin

South Shields 256, Sunbeam F4/Northern Coachbuilders/MV, 1947   (Geoff Lumb)

Reading 182, Sunbeam F4A/Burlingham/AEI by Peter Lepino, 1:3, Aluminium and wood

Surely the most magnificent Sunbeam F4 model, (strictly a F4A) has to be Peter Lepino's 1:3 scale Reading 182, built when the real things were still in service. Built in 1961, they were the last F4s and the only Sunbeams to receive bodies by HV Burlingham Ltd. Five of the batch went to Tees-side in 1969 for another four years of service. Two are preserved, 186 (as T291, in Tees-side colours) and 193. Peter's model, meanwhile, is also still running and is described on page 35.

Skilled and prodigious modeller Tony Chlad also modelled a Reading Burlingham F4A and a Walsall Willowbrook bodied F4A. These 'Liners' or 'Goldfish bowls' seem to divide opinion, some even saying the bodies were fitted the wrong way round, but they were innovative in the mid-50's and the first 30' 2 axle double deckers to run in the UK. These unique, lightweight trolleybuses were a typical product of the pioneering general manager at Walsall, Ronald Edgley-Cox. Although 864 now languishes somewhat at Sandtoft museum and 872 has been static at Aston Manor Museum, 862 regularly carries passengers at Black Country Museum – the inspiration for the late Tony Chlad's wonderfully accurate model.

Walsall 862, Sunbeam F4A/Willowbrook/BTH, 1954 (Gary S Crutchley)

Walsall 862, Sunbeam F4A/Willowbrook/BTH by Tony Chlad, 1:76, plasticard, wood (Tony Chlad)

Sunbeam MF2B

model maker	ref.	issued	total	scale	construction	operator	fleet#	route	destination	built
Dave Wall				1:24	card, wood, plastic & metal	Bournemouth	258	21	Old Christchurch Rd	1959
(unknown)					plastic	Bournemouth		20	Bournemouth	
Robin Male				1:30	metal, plasticard	Bournemouth	303			1962
Terry Russell				1:43	wood, card	Bournemouth	303			1962
TiNY Bus and Coach				1:76	resin	Hull	111		Newland Avenue	1954

The Sunbeam chassis that offered the option a front entrance ahead of the front axle was the MF2B, first produced for export to Coimbra in 1950. Sunbeam exported most of the MF2Bs built, including the very last, again to Coimbra in 1966. In the UK, the "Coronations" of Kingston upon Hull and the last new domestic trolleybuses, those built for Bournemouth, are the ones remembered by many as innovative, as almost 'the shape of things to come' in trolleybus design.

Terry Russell has converted and motorized a plastic bus to fairly represent Bournemouth 303 (see page 40) and Dave Wall has scratch-built, with a lot of detail, especially to the booms, no.258. Others have tried, if for no other reason than to evoke memories of seaside summers under the wires. Typically, a 1970s Hong Kong copy of an Atlantean Dinky Toy has been repainted and 'electrified' to represent the design.

2010 saw TiNY Bus and Coach announce their kit of Hull's 'Coronation' Roe bodied Sunbeam MF2B, admirably produced specifically to fund trolleybus preservation. Doubtless X-Acto saws will be inventively employed to create a Bournemouth version, with the rather different Weymann body.

Bournemouth 258, Sunbeam MF2B/Weymann/CP by Dave Wall, 1:24, card, wood, plastic & metal (Dave Wall)

Sunbeam MF2B/Weymann/CP, 1958 (Black Country Museum Transport Group)

Bournemouth Sunbeam MF2B/Weymann/CP by Dinky (conversion), (no scale), Plastic

Hull 103, Sunbeam W/Park Royal/BTH, 1946 (FW Ivey)

Sunbeam MF2C (fictitious)

model maker	ref.	issued	total	scale	construction	operator	fleet#	route	destination	built
Dave Wall				1:24	plastic & metal	Bournemouth	304	23	Tuckton Bridge	1981
David Bowler				1:76	plastic	Bournemouth	350	43	Winton	1980

Bournemouth 350, Sunbeam MF2C/MCW/AEI by David Bowler, 1:76, plastic (David Bowler)

Bournemouth 304, Sunbeam MF2C/MCW/AEI by Dave Wall, 1:24, plastic & metal (Dave Wall)

While discussing obscure one-offs and Bournemouth, there are two models by two modellers acting completely independently of each other who have both come to similar solutions to the vexed question (amongst some, anyway) of what would have replaced the Sunbeam MF2Bs in Bournemouth during the late 1970s, when some would be due for retirement.

Described as a Sunbeam MF2C with a MCW H39/26D body, this flight of fancy by modeller and author David Bowler is said to have been delivered in the spring of 1980. Such wishful thinking is described by the writer thus - "Following the "oil shock" of the early 1970s the UK adopted a policy of reducing its dependence on imported fossil fuels and Bournemouth, together with a number of other municipalities, dropped its trolleybus abandonment programme. Encouraged by government grants towards both new vehicles and infrastructure, electric operation was both continued and expanded".

David is not alone in his thinking as modeller Dave Wall came to much a similar conclusion, but at three times the scale. His has converted a red bus bought in Woolworths with added booms made in part from Meccano. Five bay, dual entrance 1980s British trolleybuses running in service - if only, as many would say.

Tilling-Stevens

Hybrid bus maker Tilling-Stevens supplied TX4X petrol-electric chassis to Barcelona between 1929 and 1940 of which 38 were converted into trolleybuses between 1941 and 1954 – more in chapter 5.18, on page 261.

Possibly the most wonderfully bizarre casting in this book, made in Tunbridge Wells by a reclusive maker and sold, according their owner collector, by his brother. The models have a retro Buck Rodgers feel, and are rather difficult to relate to a prototype, though there's definitely a French connection, green for Paris and red for Lyon (see page 137). The double-decker is almost a latter day clone of the Taylor & Barrett London 6 wheeler trolleybus, with which we started this chapter, complete with driver but no conductor. Although crude, there's a charm about these zinc creations, that shows great creative individuality. And that as they say, is what it is all about.

Britain has had no service trolleybuses for four decades, despite the brave but hopeless South Yorkshire initiative of 1985 – stalled because the short-termist Government de-regulation caused a free-for-all on bus routes. Government policy will also decide whether Leeds again (re-) starts trolleybus operation in the UK (see page 379).

London Transport 3 axle double decker by TW, 15cm, cast lead

Bradford 754, BUT 9611T/Weymann/EE by Bradford City Transport, 1:12, wood, metal   (Mike Bruce)

Chapter 5.23
United States

Versare	Model 3880	356
ACF-Brill	T-40	357
	T-30	358
	T-44	358
	TC-44	359
	T-46	363
	TC-46	364
Mack	CR3S	366
Marmon-Herrington	TC-44	366
	TC-46,48,49	367
Pullman-Standard	40CX	367
	43CX	368
	44CX,AS	369
	45CX	371
Twin Coach	40TT	372
	G series	373
	44TTW	374
Yellow Coach	1208	376
St Louis	W600	376

Laurel Canyon Oldsmobiles, 1910 (unknown)

One thing was certain about the United States in the early 20th century – if it didn't make a profit, it didn't run. So something must have been right about the trolleybus mode to have enabled very nearly ten thousand of them to have run in the land of the dollar. Starting in 1903, AB Upham finally built the very first US trial trolleybus line in New Haven, Conn. after 2 years of trying elsewhere. He moved it a few months later to private land in Scranton Pa. where the open fronted, solid tired and twin boomed trolleybus ran until 1904. It must have looked something like one of Max Schiemann's vehicles then being tried in Germany.

What is frequently referred to as the first public trackless trolley in the United States ran from the end of the Los Angeles Pacific streetcar line to Lookout Mountain at the head of Laurel Canyon. Promoter Charles S. Mann, apparently inspired by a Swiss trolleybus of the time, trumpeted the two converted Oldsmobile buses as the first of their kind, while using them to open up his "Bungalow Land" residential development. But the winding track, wired for ascending only, was unpaved and the service was replaced after 5 years, in 1915, by a Stanley Steamer.

The trolleybus was re-invented in 1913 in Merrill, Wisc. when manager ES King, needing a feeder to his streetcar line beyond Cottage Street, noticed the Field Electric Bus Co. battery bus and got the company to make him an 18 passenger overhead wire version. Despite looking rather well engineered, but weighing three tons and only having a 15hp motor, it lasted 18 months and was sold to Fairhaven, Mass. where it lasted a month and a half.

From 1915 to 1921 there were no trolleybuses in the USA. Then, suddenly, New York City introduced seven Atlas "Trollibuses" to Staten Island. Similar "RailLess" cars by Brill were tried in Los Angeles, Baltimore and Minneapolis. And the following year, a home made TCRT trolleybus was built in the Twin Cities that had flanged wheels for travelling to the railed depot. America was, initially at least, emulating the mistakes of Britain, by building trolleybuses that followed tramway practice. Some of these early vehicles had a single boom, with a "T" or "Y" arrangement to hold the trolley wheels. There were one or two bonneted, bus-like Packards at this time, but what's interesting is the possibility of a model of one of those streetcar-like vehicles.

In Model Auto Review 4, Geoff Price lists a toy trolleybus by Dayton Friction Toy Co. in sheet steel that's 340mm long and c.1920. Unfortunately it's not true. The actual "trolley" is a trolley car with open platforms at each end, but there was a tin trolley emblazoned with "Twin Trolleys – The Trackless Trolley", made by Ferdinand Strauss of New Jersey before 1922 when he went bankrupt. There was also supposed to be an O scale trolleybus by Iron Art which is just as likely to

Merrill Field Electric Bus, 1913 (Jownie)

Staten Island Atlas Trollibus, 1921 (Duraduct)

Los Angeles Brill RailLess, 1921 (Brill)

Twin Cities TCRT, 1922 (TCRT)

Trackless Trolley by Ferdinand Strauss, (12cm?), tinplate (unknown)

Chicago CSL Twin Coach 40TT by Arcade, 25cm, cast iron

Brooklyn & Queens 1001, Twin Coach 40TT, 1930 (OB)

have been a trolley car.

But this desperation to find toy trolleybuses in the United States is born of the surprising lack of them from an otherwise vibrant and inventive indigenous toy industry. Arcade of Illinois for instance, and typical of the many cast iron toy makers of the 20s and 30s could easily have produced a trolleybus version of their Twin Coach, based on the 40TT trolleybuses being tried at nearby Chicago and Brooklyn. The New York – Chicago side lettering of the 10" version might have been a bit optimistic for a trolleybus, however. A 5" AC Williams version might have been easier, but for the obvious gas engine grille. As it is, nearly all models of American trolleybuses, including the Twin Coach 40TT, are made in Russia, at Leonid Khoykin's St. Petersburg Tram Collection (SPTC) workshops.

By 1930 the American trolleybus had grown up, in the same way it had in the rest of the world; past the experimental stage and matured into a highly dependable public service vehicle that could stand the rigors of service for more than 20 years. The revolution started in Salt Lake City and because SPTC has modelled the historic vehicles concerned, we'll start with Versare (and continue with makers alphabetically thereafter).

Versare Model 3880

model maker	ref.	issued	total	scale	construction	operator	fleet#	route	destination	built
St.Petersburg	416	2002	25	1:48	resin	Salt Lake City UL&T Co.	300			1928
St.Petersburg	416a	2002	special	1:48	resin	Salt Lake City PCL	311	21	Wasatch Springs	1928

Salt Lake City 300, Versare Model 3880 by St.Petersburg, 1:48, resin

356   5.23 United States

Salt Lake City 311, Versare Model 3880 by St. Petersburg, 1:48, resin

Salt Lake City 300, Versare Model 3880, 1928 (Bradley H Clarke)

Utah Light & Traction Co's manager Edward A. West had been to Europe and saw thriving trolleybus services that convinced him that trolleys could replace streetcar lines. He convinced Versare of Albany, NY to build an all-electric version of their large hybrid bus and so began the modern era of "trolley coach" operation in the States. SPTC has produced both the original 3 axle version and the 2 axle conversion, which was the result of drive shaft breakage and rough riding. Despite this initial hiccup, the 43 seat coaches could run a four minute headway and so successfully replaced streetcars. Trolleybuses went on to replace three more lines and Edward West found himself proselytising the new mode around the country.

ACF-Brill

The history of ACF-Brill is complex and included the American Car Foundry, American Car Company, Brill Ohio, Brill Missouri, Canadian Car & Foundry, Kuhlman and JG Brill. All had made streetcars and are generically referred to as ACF-Brill (or CCF-Brill in the Canadian chapter). ACF, which had acquired Fageol and Hall Scott bus builders, was associated with Brill from 1926 onwards and so there was a background of both streetcar and bus building that inevitably lead to trolleybus production. ACF and Brill merged in 1944 and went on to be most prodigious of trolleybus makers, producing over two thousand within the group (over three thousand if you include Canadian Brills).

ACF-Brill T-40

model maker	ref.	issued	total	scale	construction	operator	fleet#	route	destination	built
Roberts Miniature Transports				1:87	plaster	Generic		21		1940

ACF-Brill T-40 by Roberts Miniature Transports, 1:87, plaster (Retsch)

Duluth ACF-Brill 40SMT, 1940 (OB)

The first 'modern' Brill was the T40 of 1930, based on the famous Fageol bus. As is US industry practice, chassis were made in one factory and bodied at another. Type designations could remain but body styling evolved and the last T40, built in 1946, looked considerably different to the first. Surprisingly, considering the volumes built, only one T-40 has been modelled – by David Roberts of Florida, in his inimitable plaster-cast manner, as a small series.

ACF-Brill T-30

model maker	ref.	issued	total	scale	construction	operator	fleet#	route	destination	built
Modern Traction Supply Co.	505-3002	1980s		1:87	diecast zinc	Providence				1936
Modern Traction Supply Co.	505-3002	1980s		1:87	diecast zinc	generic				1936

The 30 seat version, the T30, was introduced in 1931. Perhaps the only indigenous commercial American trolleybus model was advertised in the huge Walthers Model Railroad catalogue of 1986. Based on a Brill, it was made by Modern Traction Supply Co. of Middletown, New York, who had produced an ACF Brill H-17S bus as a metal kit since the 1970s. The 'freelanced trolleybus' kit perhaps represents the smallest Brill. T-30s only found homes in Shreveport, Topeka, St. Joseph, Columbus, Greenville and Philadelphia but none had the pronounced front roofline of some model versions.

Shreveport 302; ACF-Brill T-30, 1936 (OB)

ACF-Brill T-30 by Modern Traction Supply Co., 1:87, zinc

St. Joseph ACF-Brill T-30 by Modern Traction Supply Co., 1:87, zinc

ACF-Brill T-44

model maker	ref.	issued	total	scale	construction	operator	fleet#	route	destination	built
Miniatures by Eric	BUST44	2009		1:87	urethane	generic				1946
St. Petersburg	168	1999	80	1:48	resin	Chicago	9306	76	Diversy	1948
St. Petersburg	168a	1999	50	1:48	resin	Chicago	9261	74	Fullerton	1948
St. Petersburg	168b	1999	50	1:48	resin	Wilkes-Barre	849			1948
St. Petersburg	168c	1999	25	1:48	resin	St Joseph	#860			1948

Brill's T-44 had been introduced in 1938 but was considerably redesigned in 1946 with a lot of aluminium in the body. The first of the "New Look" T44s went to Chicago in May 1948 where they lasted in service until 1970. SPTC has modelled these and the batch that went to Wilkes-Barre, following Brill's demonstration in 1947. They were all sold to St. Joseph, Miss. in 1958.

Eric Courteney of Alberta produces a one piece body T-44 kit for $35 which is intended to be motorised by using a Faller bus but the process does involve a lot of surgery to elongate the wheelbase and reposition the electrics – not for the faint hearted! Eric's booms though, are ideal.

ACF-Brill T-44, 1946 (Brill)

ACF-Brill T-44 by Miniatures by Eric, 1:87, urethane

Chicago 9306, ACF-Brill T-44 by St.Petersburg, 1:48, resin

ACF-Brill TC-44

model maker	ref.	issued	total	scale	construction	operator	fleet#	route	destination	built
St.Petersburg	424	2002	25	1:48	resin	Oakland	2015	7	Euclid Avenue	1946
St.Petersburg	424a	2002	25	1:48	resin	Los Angeles	8001		Not in Service	1946
St.Petersburg	424a-1	2002	10	1:48	resin	Los Angeles	8015	2	Union Station	1946
St.Petersburg	424b	2002	25	1:48	resin	New Orleans	1214	1	Station	1945
St.Petersburg	424c1	2002	10	1:48	resin	Dallas	1001			1945
St.Petersburg	424d	2002	10	1:48	resin	Kansas City	2420	41	Union Station	1945
St.Petersburg	424d-1	2002	10	1:48	resin	Kansas City	2405	41	Union Station	1945
St.Petersburg	424e	2002	10	1:48	resin	Honolulu Rapid	600		Iilha School	1945
St.Petersburg	424f	2002	5	1:48	resin	Denver	563			1945
St.Petersburg	424h	2002	10	1:48	resin	Fort Wayne	170		Oxford	1946
St.Petersburg	424g	2002	5	1:48	resin	Memphis	1000	31	Crosstown	1945
St.Petersburg	424j	2002	5	1:48	resin	Ankara	171-180			1945
St.Petersburg	425	2002	50	1:48	resin	Philadelphia	262			1947/48
St.Petersburg	425a	2002	25	1:48	resin	Philadelphia	222	29		1947/48
St.Petersburg	425b	2002	50	1:48	resin	Philadelphia	249	61	Manayunk	1947/48
St.Petersburg	426	2002	25	1:48	resin	Akron	170		East Market	1948
St.Petersburg	426a	2002	25	1:48	resin	Wilkes-Barre	846		West Pittston	1947
St.Petersburg	426b	2002	25	1:48	resin	Dayton City	61	5	Hillcrest	1947
St.Petersburg	426c	2002	10	1:48	resin	Des Moines	225-244			1948
St.Petersburg	426d	2002	10	1:48	resin	Denver	642		Union Station	1948
St.Petersburg	426e	2002	10	1:48	resin	São Paulo	3128			1948
St.Petersburg	427	2002	25	1:48	resin	Baltimore	2190	2		1948
St.Petersburg	427-1	2002	50	1:48	resin	Baltimore	2136	10	Highlandtown	1948
St.Petersburg	427a	2002		1:48	resin	Calgary	485-504			1948
St.Petersburg	428	2002	50	1:48	resin	Los Angeles	9025	2	Union Station	1948
St.Petersburg	428-1	2002	50	1:48	resin	Los Angeles	9028	2	Union Station	1948
St.Petersburg	424c	2002	10	1:48	resin	Dallas	1001	34		1945
St.Petersburg	424n	2002		1:48	resin	Edmonton	129		Low Level Bridge	1945

The first TC-44 variants were delivered in 1944 to Fort Wayne and the type constituted all of the Philadelphia factory's post war production until 1948; a total of 665 trolley coaches to 19 operators. SPTC has modelled 17 of those operators and added reproductions of secondhand sales to Dayton, Calgary and São Paulo. Also modelled is the abortive delivery to Oakland's Key System, revised liveries at Los Angeles, Kansas City and Baltimore and additional batches to Flint, Denver and Des Moines amongst others. Unusually two ACF-Brill TC-46s were supplied to Edmonton, Canada, in 1945. The design was revised in 1947 with a larger windscreen and the adding of a trolleybase shroud. Los Angeles had both types.

The delivery to Memphis in 1946, originally intended for Oklahoma City, appears to have been a hybrid design with trolleybase farings but the original style narrow windscreen, perhaps it was a condition of the sale – all other trolleys delivered to Memphis around this time were so fitted.

Fort Wayne 170, ACF-Brill TC-44, 1946 (GE)

Fort Wayne 170, ACF-Brill TC-44 by St.Petersburg, 1:48, resin (SPTC)

Los Angeles TL. 2001, ACF-Brill TC-44 by St.Petersburg, 1:48, resin

Baltimore 2136, ACF-Brill TC-44 by St.Petersburg, 1:48, resin

Models 424a,b,c1,c,426a,425a,b,d,e, ACF-Brill TC-44 by St.Petersburg, 1:48, resin (SPTC)

360   5.23 United States

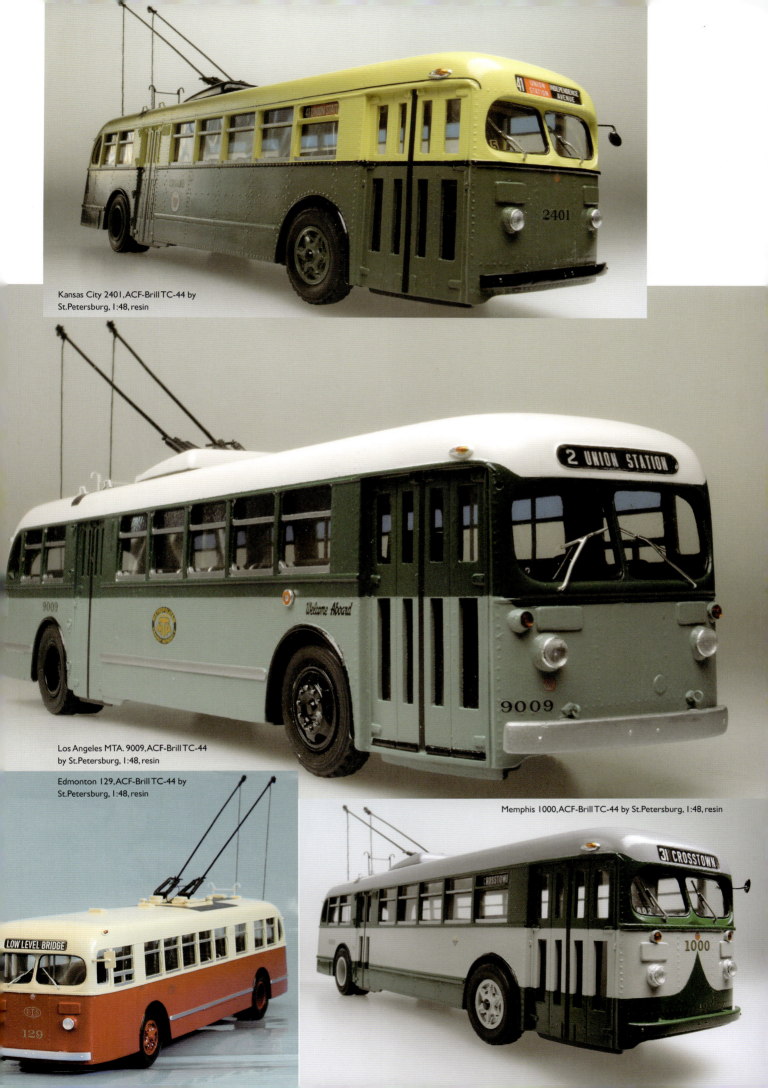

Kansas City 2401, ACF-Brill TC-44 by St.Petersburg, 1:48, resin

Los Angeles MTA. 9009, ACF-Brill TC-44 by St.Petersburg, 1:48, resin

Edmonton 129, ACF-Brill TC-44 by St.Petersburg, 1:48, resin

Memphis 1000, ACF-Brill TC-44 by St.Petersburg, 1:48, resin

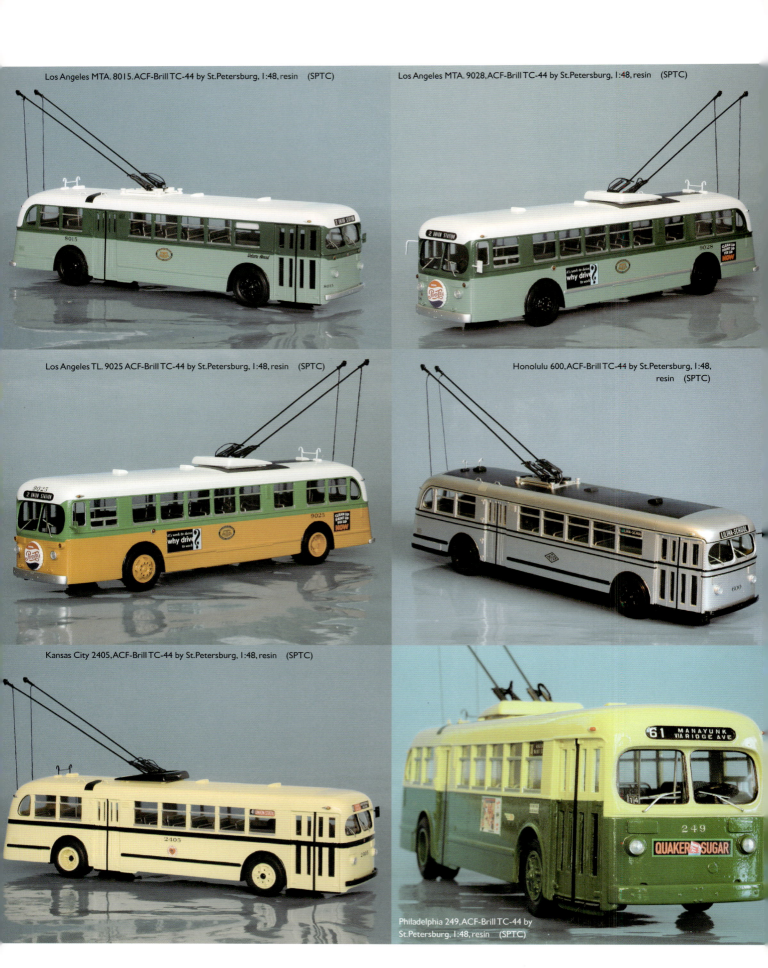

Los Angeles MTA. 8015. ACF-Brill TC-44 by St.Petersburg, 1:48, resin   (SPTC)

Los Angeles MTA. 9028, ACF-Brill TC-44 by St.Petersburg, 1:48, resin   (SPTC)

Los Angeles TL. 9025 ACF-Brill TC-44 by St.Petersburg, 1:48, resin   (SPTC)

Honolulu 600, ACF-Brill TC-44 by St.Petersburg, 1:48, resin   (SPTC)

Kansas City 2405, ACF-Brill TC-44 by St.Petersburg, 1:48, resin   (SPTC)

Philadelphia 249, ACF-Brill TC-44 by St.Petersburg, 1:48, resin   (SPTC)

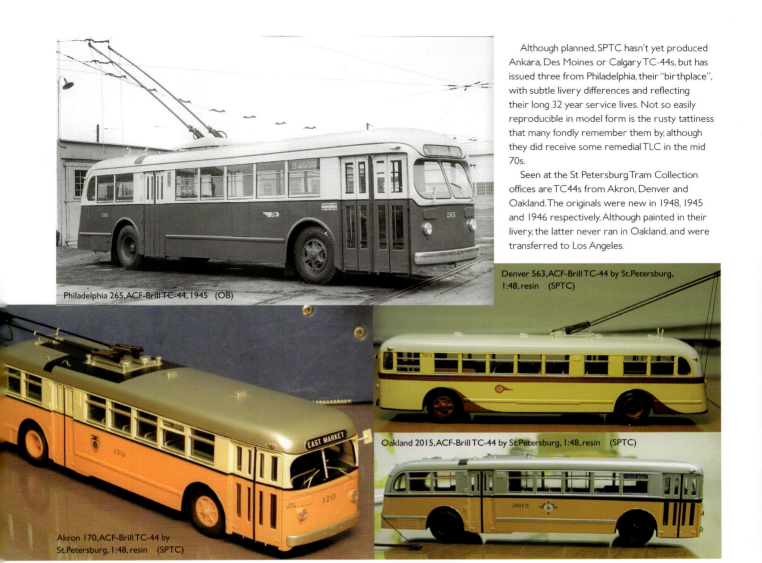

Philadelphia 265, ACF-Brill TC-44, 1945 (OB)

Denver 563, ACF-Brill TC-44 by St.Petersburg, 1:48, resin (SPTC)

Oakland 2015, ACF-Brill TC-44 by St.Petersburg, 1:48, resin (SPTC)

Akron 170, ACF-Brill TC-44 by St.Petersburg, 1:48, resin (SPTC)

Although planned, SPTC hasn't yet produced Ankara, Des Moines or Calgary TC-44s, but has issued three from Philadelphia, their "birthplace", with subtle livery differences and reflecting their long 32 year service lives. Not so easily reproducible in model form is the rusty tattiness that many fondly remember them by, although they did receive some remedial TLC in the mid 70s.

Seen at the St Petersburg Tram Collection offices are TC44s from Akron, Denver and Oakland. The originals were new in 1948, 1945 and 1946 respectively. Although painted in their livery, the latter never ran in Oakland, and were transferred to Los Angeles.

ACF-Brill T-46

model maker	ref.	issued	total	scale	construction	operator	fleet#	route	destination	built
St.Petersburg	139	1999	100	1:43	resin	Los Angeles	9123	2	City Terrace	1948
St.Petersburg	139-1	1999	10	1:43	resin	Los Angeles	9130			1948
St.Petersburg	139a	1999	25	1:43	resin	Winnipeg				1951
St.Petersburg	139b	1999	25	1:43	resin	Mexico City				1951
St.Petersburg	139c	1999	50	1:43	resin	Wilkes-Barre	863			1950
St.Petersburg	139d	1999	25	1:43	resin	Flint	867-876			1951
St.Petersburg	139e	1999	25	1:43	resin	St Joseph	281-285			1950
St.Petersburg	139f	1999	50	1:43	resin	Des Moines	245			1949

Models 139f,c,e,d,a,b, ACF-Brill T-46 by St.Petersburg, 1:43, resin (SPTC)

ACF-Brill's 46 passenger T-46 type had wider front doors as well as 2 extra seats and 4 inches of extra length when compared to the otherwise identical T-44. The first customer was Los Angeles in 1948, followed by Des Moines in 1949, Wilkes-Barre in 1950 and Flint in 1951. The 16 Wilkes-Barre T-46s were sold to St.Joseph in 1959 and the 10 that went to Flint were sold to Winnipeg and then Mexico City, the only US built trolleybuses to operate in the USA, Canada and Mexico. SPTC has modelled all the combinations, including liveries for Los Angeles Transit Lines and Los Angeles Metropolitan Transit Authority. Unusually, the models are in 1:43 scale rather than the usual 1:48.

Los Angeles 9123, ACF-Brill T-46, 1948 (GE)

Los Angeles 9123, ACF-Brill T-46 by St.Petersburg, 1:43, resin

ACF-Brill TC-46

model maker	ref.	issued	total	scale	construction	operator	fleet#	route	destination	built
St.Petersburg	159/11	-		1:43	resin	Boston	8700		Linden	1950
St.Petersburg	159a		80	1:43	resin	Johnstown	731		Morrellville	1952
St.Petersburg	159b		50	1:43	resin	Covington	661			1952
St.Petersburg	159b-1		10	1:43	resin	Covington	664			1952

The TC-46 variant, supplied to Boston and Covington in 1950 and 1952 had a more upright destination box, lifting instead of sliding windows and more aluminium in the bodywork than the T-46. Only 31 vehicles were built. Those of the Cincinnati, Newport & Covington Railway Co. after receiving two liveries, were sold to Johnstown Traction Co. in 1958. They were the last Brills built. Like SPTC's T-46 models, the TC-46s are in 1:43 scale rather than the usual 1:48.

Not yet modelled is the T-48 sold only to Chicago and Memphis, although 431 of the Canadian version went to 9 other operators.

Boston 8722, ACF-Brill TC-46, 1950   (GE)

Johnstown 731, ACF-Brill TC-46 by St. Petersburg, 1:43, resin

Boston 8700, MTA ACF-Brill TC-46 by St. Petersburg, 1:43, resin   (Richard Romagnoli)

Mack

model maker	ref.	issued	total	scale	construction	operator	fleet#	route	destination	built
Roberts Miniature Transports		1980s		1:87	plaster	Portland				1937

David Roberts of Florida has reputedly produced a plaster model of the Mack CR3S trolleybus in Portland colours. Unfortunately, we've never seen one. There were 290 real Mack trolleybuses, built between 1934 and 1943, at their Allentown, Penn. truck factory. They were built like proverbial trucks, strong but heavy, and that penalty probably accounted for their comparative rarity. there were only 11 users, with Portland being by far the largest, with 141 delivered between 1936 and 1937.

Marmon-Herrington

model maker	ref.	issued	total	scale	construction	operator	fleet#	route	destination	built
St.Petersburg	471			1:48	resin	San Francisco	552	22	Fillmore	1948
St.Petersburg	471-1			1:48	resin	San Francisco	566	30	Stockton	1949
St.Petersburg	470	2009		1:48	resin	San Francisco	756	30	Stockton	1950-1
St.Petersburg	470-0	2009		1:48	resin	San Francisco	842	41	Union	1950-1
St.Petersburg	470-1	2009		1:48	resin	San Francisco	845	21	Hayes	1950-1
St.Petersburg	422	2011		1:48	resin	Chicago	9580	81	Lawrence	1951-2
Molytro				30cm	plastic	Mexico City				

San Francisco 756, Marmon-Herrington TC48 by St.Petersburg, 1:48, resin

4x4 truck builder Marmon-Herrington was persuaded by ACF-Brill's mid-west sales manager Charles Guernsey that there would be a huge post war market in trolleybuses. M-H achieved a 10% weight reduction with a radical, monocoque, aeroplane like body design that translated into power, maintenance and journey time savings. It sold like hot cakes – in only eight years they produced 1,513 trolleys. Chicago, in the largest US trolleybus order, had 349 in one go. The modular design was stretched and even shrunk to order, San Francisco had TC40, TC44 and TC48 types.

At least seven Marmons are preserved, including Dayton's 515 in working order. SPTC has so far produced the TC48 and TC44, and has recently released the TC49 that ran in Chicago. Coming is the shortened TC-40. As the TC48 is available as a kit, it can be reproduced in any one of the 17 US operators' liveries. Ready built models of all three variants of the SF Municipal Railways livery have been produced as well as two Chicago types and Toronto. The real Marmons served the hilly city for up to 28 years and many saw further service in Mexico City.

Produced in considerable numbers, by Molytro, is a Mexican plastic toy trolleybus, that is usually ascribed to Marmon-Herrington although it could be a St.Louis car. Mexico City bought 805 secondhand US trolleys, between 1956 and 1977. It's a generic 'pull-along' toy, that has taken liberties with the look, although, compared to many toys produced in Mexico, is fairly accurate and surprisingly solid. Repainted (and re-boomed) examples can look imposing. Shreveport had a batch of five Marmons, 423-427, in 1947 that were sold to Mexico City in 1966.

San Francisco 689, Marmon-Herrington TC44, 1948 (GE)

Marmon-Herrington TC48, 1950-1 (Steve Morgan)

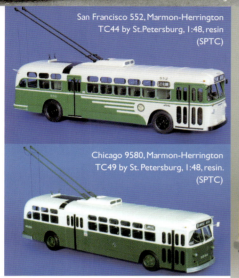

San Francisco 552, Marmon-Herrington TC44 by St.Petersburg, 1:48, resin (SPTC)

Chicago 9580, Marmon-Herrington TC49 by St.Petersburg, 1:48, resin. (SPTC)

Pullman-Standard

Chicago's Pullman-Standard built 1,906 trolleybuses at its Osgood Bradley plant in Worcester, Mass. Nearly as many as Brill in Philadelphia. SPTC has modelled many, but Pullman records have left gaps in type nomenclature and so are grouped here more by passenger capacity than model number.

Shreveport 427, Marmon-Herrington TC44 by Molytro, 30cm, plastic

Pullman-Standard 40CX

model maker	ref.	issued	total	scale	construction	operator	fleet#	route	destination	built
St.Petersburg	406	2000	50	1:48	resin	Boston	8001			1936
St.Petersburg	406a	2000	50	1:48	resin	Providence	818-850			1936

Boston El.Ry. Pullman-Standard 40CX by St.Petersburg, 1:43, resin

The smallest modelled Pullman trolleybus is of their first batch to be supplied to Boston, in 1936, the first of many. Their other stalwart customer, Providence United Electric Railways Co. received the same model in 1936, a much improved version of that supplied in 1935. STPC's model, now long out of production, sold recently on eBay for over $600.

Boston 8002, Pullman-Standard 40CX, 1936 (Westinghouse)

Pullman-Standard 43CX

model maker	ref.	issued	total	scale	construction	operator	fleet#	route	destination	built
St.Petersburg	154	1998	50	1:48	resin	Boston	8433			1947
St.Petersburg	155-1		5	1:48	resin	Boston	8522		Harvard	1951
St.Petersburg	169		50	1:48	resin	Boston	8567		Harvard	1951
St.Petersburg	163	1998	50	1:48	resin	Valparaíso	814			1947
(unkown)				(no scale)	wood	Valparaíso				1947
St.Petersburg	163a		50	1:48	resin	Santiago	801-900			1947/48

Boston 8567, Pullman-Standard 43CX by St.Petersburg, 1:43, resin (SPTC)

Valparaíso 714, Pullman-Standard 43CX, 1947 (friendsofnails)

Valparaiso 814, Pullman-Standard 43CX by St.Petersburg, 1:43,

Boston had 17 batches of Pullmans over a 15 year period (including two batches that were secondhand). Three were 43CXs and one, 8522, appeared in two liveries of the Metropolitan Transit Authority. Some lasted 20 years in service. Boston 8361 is preserved at the Seashore Trolley Museum, Maine, alongside 8490, a 44CX.

Pullman-Standard supplied 30 43CXs to Santiago, some of which were sold to Valparaíso in 1978 when already 31 years old. They joined 30 that had been supplied in 1952. Incredibly, 814, built in 1947, is, at the time of writing, the oldest trolleybus without body modification to remain in service in the world. 14 more, variously modified, are also in service. Valparaíso's Pullmans have become famous and are modelled not only by SPTC but also by Chilean producers as tiny wooden souvenirs for tourists. A trial run of wooden model 43CX Pullmans (if that indeed is what they were) was produced in 1986 for dealer Konrad Pernetta, but the identity of the maker is now lost. They would have taken considerable effort to manufacture.

Boston 8522, Pullman-Standard 43CX by St.Petersburg, 1:43, resin (SPTC)

Valparaiso Pullman-Standard 43CX by (unknown), 9cm, wood

Pullman-Standard 43CX by (unknown), 1:87, wood

Pullman-Standard 44CX, AS

model maker	ref.	issued	total	scale	construction	operator	fleet#	route	destination	built
St.Petersburg	189	1999	50	1:43	resin	Birmingham	103	15	Norwood	1945/46
St.Petersburg	189a	1999	50	1:43	resin	Vancouver	2501-2524			1947
St.Petersburg	130	1998	200	1:43	resin	Providence	1345		Providence	1947
St.Petersburg	130a	1998	50	1:43	resin	Boston	8593		Clarendon Hill	1947
St.Petersburg	130b	1998	50	1:43	resin	Cleveland	850-899			1947
St.Petersburg	130c	1998	50	1:43	resin	Winnipeg	1560-1594			1947
St.Petersburg	130d	1998	50	1:43	resin	Halifax	282-287			1947
St.Petersburg	130e	1999	5	1:43	resin	Greenville	146		Overbrook	1948
St.Petersburg	130f	1999	25	1:43	resin	Bogota	21-30			1948
St.Petersburg	155	1999	80	1:43	resin	Boston	8598		Arlington Centre	1951
St.Petersburg	187	1999	80	1:43	resin	Chicago	9323-9367			1948
St.Petersburg	187a	1999	50	1:43	resin	Chicago	323-367			1948
St.Petersburg	190	1999	50	1:43	resin	Memphis	1100-1226			1947
St.Petersburg	193	1999	50	1:43	resin	São Paulo	3004-3009			1947
(unknown)				1:87	resin	Mexico City	3185-3247			

Providence 1345, Pullman-Standard 44CX by St.Petersburg, 1:43, resin

Birmingham Electric Pullman-Standard 44AS by St.Petersburg, 1:43, resin (SPTC)

Boston 8598, Pullman-Standard 44CX by St.Petersburg, 1:43, resin (SPTC)

Greenville 146, Pullman-Standard 44CX by St.Petersburg, 1:43, resin (SPTC)

The subtle differences between 44AS and 44CX models (front styling and door outline, amongst others) haven't led SPTC to produce two patterns. Thus, all customers are represented, if technically inaccurately, plus the secondhand sales to Canada and Bogata. The exports to Winnipeg and São Paulo are modelled but not those that went to Mexico City, although they have been modelled locally and a little crudely, in 1:87 scale.

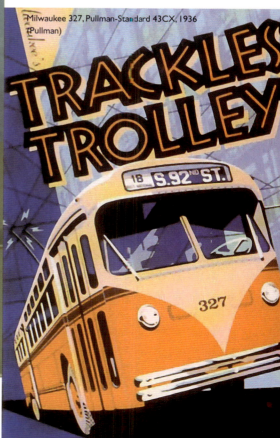

Milwaukee 327, Pullman-Standard 43CX, 1936 (Pullman)

Pullman-Standard 45CX

model maker	ref.	issued	total	scale	construction	operator	fleet#	route	destination	built
St.Petersburg	144	1998	80	1:43	resin	Milwaukee	350-423		Wilson Park	1948
St.Petersburg	188		50	1:43	resin	Dayton City Railway	401-445			1947
St.Petersburg	188a		25	1:43	resin	Dayton City Transit	401-445			1947
St.Petersburg	188b		25	1:43	resin	Dayton & Xenia Rly	62	10	Ewalt Circle	1947
St.Petersburg	188c		25	1:43	resin	Oakwood	#35			1947
St.Petersburg	196		50	1:43	resin	Atlanta	1235-1334			1946/47

Milwaukee 350, Pullman-Standard 45CX by St.Petersburg, 1:43, resin

Dayton & Xenia 62, Pullman-Standard 45CX by St.Petersburg, 1:43, resin   (SPTC)

Dayton 445, Pullman-Standard 44T, 1947   (Cliff Scholes Collection)

The 45CX was sold to Atlanta, Milwaukee and Dayton, where the 46 Pullmans had a complex history of ownership. SPTC, again able to use the same patterns as the 44AS and 44CX models and by varying headlight positions, has produced all four Dayton liveries in which they appeared and the Atlanta and Milwaukee schemes. One prototype, Milwaukee 350 survives in preservation at the Illinois Railway Museum along with Cleveland 874, a 44CX.

5.23 United States   371

Twin Coach

Frank and William Fageol were innovative designers, who'd changed bus design with their 1922 Safety Coach and did it again with their revolutionary twin rear engine design of 1927, with its double ended look, curved corner glass and easy adaptability to a trolley coach. The first such electric Twin Coaches went to Salt Lake City in 1928 followed by deliveries to New Orleans. The design was copied by the American Car Foundry, Brill, Cincinnati Car and St. Louis. In fact, the design was so influential that it did much to legitimize the trolleybus as a viable mode. Virtually all of the 178 trolleys delivered to American operators in the seminal years of 1930-31 were Twin Coach 40TTs or copies thereof.

Detroit 401, Twin Coach 40TT (GE)

Twin Coach 40TT

model maker	ref.	issued	total	scale	construction	operator	fleet#	route	destination	built
St.Petersburg	183	2000	50	1:48	resin	Detroit Street Railway	401			1930
St.Petersburg	183a	2000	50	1:48	resin	Cincinnati Street Ry.	599			1930
St.Petersburg	183b	2000	50	1:48	resin	Brooklyn & Queens Transit	1001			1930
St.Petersburg	184	1999	80	1:48	resin	Chicago CSL	64		Central	1930
St.Petersburg	184a	1999	10	1:48	resin	Chicago CTA	9063	85	Central	1930
St.Petersburg	184b	1999	50	1:48	resin	Chicago CTA	9051-9079		40TT	

Detroit 401, Twin Coach 40TT by St.Petersburg, 1:48, resin   (SPTC)

Chicago 9063, Cincinnati 599, Chicago 64 and Brooklyn 1001 Twin Coach 40TT by St.Petersburg, 1:48, resin   (SPTC)

SPTC has modeled Brooklyn, Chicago and Cincinatti Twin coach 40TTs but it's the Detroit version that has an iconic air, with "Electric Coach" emblazoned on the side.

The motor city had intended to convert more bus routes but the depression stalled the idea and the isolated Plymouth line ran until 1937, whereupon the six Detroit built Twin Coaches were sold to Cincinnati, to run for a further seven years.

Twin Coach G series

model maker	ref.	issued	total	scale	construction	operator	fleet#	route	destination	built
St.Petersburg	197a	1999	specia	1:48	resin	Seattle	875	10	Mercer St.	1940
St.Petersburg	197	1999	80	1:48	resin	Milwaukee	164-173			1939
St.Petersburg	114	1999	50	1:48	resin	Seattle	976	7	Prentice St.	1943
St.Petersburg	114-2	1999	specia	1:48	resin	Seattle				1943
St.Petersburg	114-3	1999	specia	1:48	resin	King County Metro				1943
St.Petersburg	114a	1999	50	1:48	resin	Atlanta	1043	20	College Park	1943
St.Petersburg	114b	1999	25	1:48	resin	Akron	113-132			1942
Seattle Transit		1952	1	1:87	metal, wood	Seattle				1943

Twin Coach had to redesign it's trolleybus by 1936, such was the fast moving evolution of vehicle styling in the 30s, with what might be called the R (rear engined) series and then again by 1939 with the G ("gravity" suspension) series. They were essentially modernized versions of the 40TT but carried more passengers, weighed less and, finally, had lower floors. Of the 41GTT and the 44GTT, Seattle had by far the most. At the 1952 city centennial celebrations, employees of Seattle Municipal Railway built a powered model layout including a scale Twin Coach 40GWFT with slot steering and especially accurate Ohio Brass overhead (see page 27). Of the prototypes, 636 and 643, are preserved by the Metro Employees Historic Vehicle Association and 633 is at the Illinois Railway Museum. SPTC hasn't modeled the R series but many of the wartime G series have been, exceptions at the moment, are Youngstown, Kansas, Cincinnati and Greenville.

Seattle 802, Twin Coach 40GWFT, 1940 (unknown)

Seattle 875, 40GWFT by St.Petersburg, 1:48, resin (SPTC)

Seattle 955, Twin Coach 44GTT by St.Petersburg, 1:48, resin

Twin Coach 40TT

model maker	ref.	issued	total	scale	construction	operator	fleet#	route	destination	built
St.Petersburg	183	2000	50	1:48	resin	Detroit Street Railway	401			1930
St.Petersburg	183a	2000	50	1:48	resin	Cincinnati Street Ry.	599			1930
St.Petersburg	183b	2000	50	1:48	resin	Brooklyn & Queens Transit	1001			1930
St.Petersburg	184	1999	80	1:48	resin	Chicago CSL	64		Central	1930
St.Petersburg	184a	1999	10	1:48	resin	Chicago CTA	9063	85	Central	1930
St.Petersburg	184b	1999	50	1:48	resin	Chicago CTA	9051-9079		40TT	

Twin Coaches penchant for innovative design saw an unsuccessful attempt at an articulated trolleybus in 1940 that, articulating only vertically, caused traffic hold-ups. But it symbolised the hope that there would be a public transit boom; instead people bought cars and operators tried to compete. Immediately after the war Twin Coach's final fling was the rather exuberantly styled T series that was based on the S (single-engined) bus. The aluminium fluting, ornate insignia and front roof mounted "flashes" were slightly bizarre art deco embellishments that looked derived from 30s cinemas but added a certain panache to the otherwise dreary 40s and 50s. In 1949, Detroit had 60 and San Francisco had 90, one of which, 614 is at Illinois Railway Museum. SPTC has faithfully reproduced all three variants of San Francisco Municipal Railways green and cream livery including the experimental, mostly cream version of 1963. No.570 was painted in the new red and yellow livery of 1969. The SF Twins were in service until the mid 70s. Detroit's Twins lasted until 1961, when they were scrapped, despite a rider poll that showed 87% preferred trolleys to diesels.

San Francisco 593, Twin Coach 44TTW, 1949 (Scalzo col. trolleybus.net)

San Francisco 621, Twin Coach 44TTW by St.Petersburg, 1:48, resin

San Francisco 570, Twin Coach 44TTW by St. Petersburg, 1:48, resin

San Francisco 656, Twin Coach 44TTW by St. Petersburg, 1:48, resin (SPTC)

San Francisco 614, Twin Coach 44TTW by St. Petersburg, 1:48, resin (SPTC)

Detroit 9003, Twin Coach 48TT2 by St. Petersburg, 1:48, resin (SPTC)

Yellow Coach

Yellow Truck & Coach Mfg. Co., a division of General Motors in Pontiac, Michigan, produced only 455 trolleybuses between 1932 and 1938 and nearly half were "All Service Vehicles" or trolley hybrids for New Jersey. Milwaukee's 40 1208 type Yellow Coaches were the last they built, designed in conjunction with the operator and perhaps intended as a precursor for more, but the following year Yellow introduced diesel-hydraulic transmission and GM abandoned all-electric trolleys.

Yellow Coach 1208

model maker	ref.	issued	total	scale	construction	operator	fleet#	route	destination	built
St.Petersburg	401		80	1:48	resin	Milwaukee Electric Lines	124	14	E.Capital	1938
St.Petersburg	401a		25	1:48	resin	Milwaukee Electric Lines	136			1938

SPTC has produced the Yellow Coach in Milwaukee standard livery plus an edition of 136, which appeared in a special red livery for the local Fire Department, just after the war, with fire prevention slogans.

In the realms of hyper-critique, it's perhaps worth noting that the front roof lights and wing mirrors are too big, as are the front bumper uprights but there are limits to resin imitating steel. It might also be a little unfair to show a 48th scale model at twice the size of the full size version!

Milwaukee 127, Yellow Coach 1208, 1938 (OB)

Milwaukee 124, Yellow Coach 1208 by St.Petersburg, 1:48, resin

St. Louis

Surprisingly, or should that be still to come, are models of the St. Louis Car Company. Of American trolleybus producers, St. Louis was the 4th largest, producing 1,119 vehicles, and was an early pioneer, building the "Trackless-Trollicar", based on a bus chassis, in 1921. There is a model of New York 3124, a St.Louis trolleybus of 1948, in the local transit museum (see page 26). Perhaps, in the fullness of time, Leonid Khoykin of the St. Petersburg Tram Collection will get around to it – he's certainly done a sterling job of representing America's trolleybus history in miniature so far.

Also due to be modelled are the 4th generation Flyers of the energy conscious 70s that were imported from Canada and newer trolleybuses currently in service in Boston, Dayton, Philadelphia, Seattle and San Francisco (see pages 95 and 122). Modelled, but hardly representative, is Silvine's "American" powered trolleybus, included in chapter 4, page 71.

America was pivotal in the development of the trolleybus. Standardisation and mass production made it a reliable and efficient form of public transit that quietly and without fuss moved millions just before the car became dominant. It might again when the oil runs out. As it was, many operators were subsidiaries of power companies often using inherited and worn tramcar equipment. They were separated by anti-trust laws and only remained solvent by converting to fewer and smaller diesel buses in times of hugely increasing car use. Only five operators remain, each with special reasons for keeping trolleybuses long after the majority, sometimes reluctantly, had abandoned them.

Metro Transit Lines Trolley Coach by Lurelle Guild, US advertisement, 1944 (Timken Axles)

Chapter 6
New Directions

In some ways a chapter about the future is anathema in a book about the certainty of nostalgia. But hopefully, there will be a nostalgia for what is yet to come which, like that of the past, depends on enthusiasm for surviving and new trolleybuses, real or miniature.

During the 130 years since Werner Von Siemens invented the trolleybus, the largest numbers of trolleys ran in the 1940s, 50s and 60s - within living memory of many readers of this book. The great majority of trolleybus models were produced in the 1990s and 2000s, perhaps coinciding for some readers with our looking back to our childhoods, 40 years before. Trolleybus operation slowed after the 60s but rose again following the 1973 oil crisis. Alleviating street level air pollution and the global climate crisis have become reasons for the trolleybus to continue but equally, lack of finance, especially in former Communist countries has been a reason for system closures. The audience for trolleybuses and so for models, has never-the-less increased, especially east of the old "iron curtain" where trolleybus use proliferated to the extent that it's

Super Trolley, in children's colouring book, Soviet Union, 1937 (Azcherizdat)

become nearly impossible to state just when the peak period of trolleybuses in service was or is.

In recent years more and more resin cast models have been released; a technique that supports reasonable production costs for perhaps 20 to 50 models from one mould, that can then be painted to represent the liveries of various operators. Card kits are easier and can be produced with great graphic accuracy by computer and given away by operators and manufacturers as well as by online enthusiasts.

Production techniques in China are now making shorter metal diecast runs more viable and enabling models with ever greater detail.

We hope this book has demonstrated that it is still just about possible to include the majority the world's toy and model trolleybuses, or at least give an inclusive view of what is and has been available. The size of this catalogue, however, is about to change, if the potential for new ways of making models comes about.

New Directions 377

Predicting the future with models

In Pescara, on Italy's Adriatic coast, the 'Filo – L'antitraffico' trolleybus scheme has been planned for a number of years. Public consultations in Pescara to present the rather delayed scheme, see presentations to re-assure potential passengers use the Lion-Toys model of the ordered APTS Phileas vehicle to show them what the trolleybus will look like.

But the scheme has been so long coming that public meetings have had to change to a newer, restyled version. The original Lion-Toys model faithfully reproduced the 1999 Eindhoven, Holland, bus rapid transit vehicles with a magnetic stud guidance that has since been all but abandoned. The model is easily converted into a trolleybus for showing at meetings (no full size Phileas trolleybus has yet been built). The stalled futuristic guidance technology seems to have delayed bringing the first Phileas trolleybuses to Pescara where they would run, for the most part, on a ready built reserved roadway. Meanwhile, Lion-Toys have made models of the new 2004 version of the Phileas with a restyled front end and continuing meetings in Pescara now use the new model, suitably converted to a trolleybus.

Virtual 3D simulation

Using models to visualise the future is nothing new, either to test what looks best or to help sell an idea or product – in the case of trolleybuses, Garrett in the UK, was doing it in 1927 (see chapter 1). But the ways that models can be

Eindhoven 1201, APTS Phileas, 1999   (Antick)

Pescara APTS Phileas by Lion-Toys 1:50, diecast zinc   (GTM SpA.)

Einhoven APTS Phileas by Lion-Toys (conversion), 1:50, diecast zinc

Bratislava Skoda 9Tr by VshaCG, virtual (VshaCG)

achieved is now changing. Virtual 3D computer 'models', like card models, are available free on the internet, needing only the right software to 'render' them to the screen or as a file to print in two dimensions. 3dTransit.com, for instance. produces a model of Boston's Canadian built Flyer E800 4002 which ran on the Harvard Square tunnel routes until 2004 (see chapter 5.4).

Producing ultra realistic virtual models takes considerable time and effort and the most accurate don't come cheap. There's a very detailed Skoda 14TR at the3dStudio.com, made with 139,000 polygons that costs $150. And there's a Skoda 9TR with full interior detail in 460,00 polygons built by VshaCG from turbosquid.com at $199. For illustrators this a boon, with views and colour schemes that can be re-configured almost instantly.

At a necessarily cruder level, there's a LK-1 from Perrette Auguste and all sorts of trolleybus models for Transport Tycoon games and the trolleybus simulator, SimTr, written by Andes in Slovakia in 2004. With only keyboard keys to use, it's tricky to drive a trolleybus on a computer, but enthusiasts have re-created whole trolleybus systems, such as Chelyabinsk near the Urals. A successor, Trancity, has a growing following in Russia, with (slightly) more realistic models, such

London Transport Leyland TTB4/Leyland/MV by Jason Noakes, virtual (KaiShikisai)

as Volograd's shortened ZiU-9, the ZiU-11. In London, Jason Noakes has been working on a Trainz simulator Leyland TTB4 L3 class, based on the 694 Plumstead to Erith route.

3D modelling

Virtual model trolleybuses have other uses – helping to visualise schemes such as the Leeds New Generation Transport for instance, to test acceptability or to help plan installation. Such models are created in 3d software usually by joining boxes, cones and cylinders and then, with a great deal of trial and error, refining them into polygons. Materials are assigned with reflections or transparency and the result is then lit, viewed by a virtual camera and 'rendered' or

Lectroliner model within 3D Studio Max software

'photographed' to the screen.

Models can be created in 3d for fun or fantasy but they can also test concepts, branding and passenger approval. Such ability makes raising funds easier and final reality less of a surprise.

3d modelling has become essential to the automotive industry where producing a physical prototype model is becoming less essential, such is the realism and real time ability to move around the 'virtuality' during screen based approval consultations. Company bosses can give a confident go-ahead, leading to the investment of billions, without seeing a physical model at all. But not everybody is so enamoured or prepared to take such risks. And for those wanting to contribute who don't have the massive computing power still necessary to present 1:1 virtual reality, then it's easier to make a model to show to industry. Marcelo Ballonga's industrial design thesis project for a new, highly manoeuvrable trolleybus for Mendoza's polluted streets involved both, and it takes a bit of looking at to tell them apart. The physical model is 1:10 scale and shows a different handling of the windscreen. The virtual model is more sculptural. It remains a pity that Argentina's finances are unlikely to afford 1:1 versions. so Mendoza will continue to use trolleys that are 40 years old, such as the just retired ex-Solingen TSIII's.

Viet Kornberger, aka VK-Modelle, employs SolidWorks, an industry standard 3D CAD program used by over a million engineers worldwide, to generate 'instructions' for his

Moskva Svarz LK-1 by Perrette Auguste, virtual (Sergej)

Volgograd Uritsky ZiU-11 by Slastenin Sasha, virtual (trancity)

Leeds NGT Lectroliner by Ashley Bruce, virtual

New Directions 379

Salzburg Ebus by Dave Wilsher, virtual

Mendoza Ballonga, 2010   (Marcelo Ballonga)

Mendoza Ballonga by Marcelo Ballonga, 1:10, resin, metal   (Marcelo Ballonga)

by modelling the vehicle in virtual 1:1 using Catia 3d software. The 'model' can then be sent to a computer controlled '3D shaper' and be automatically milled, in this case, into a physical, as opposed to virtual, 1:10 scale model. It's remotely carved from a single block of Necurite, a specially formulated polyurethane that's rather like wood. Viseon then painted the body white, but rather than line out and add painted details, they printed high gloss and very precise decals that create a better representation of the windows and windscreen. By laser cutting, the white parts were deleted, leaving only the black detail to be applied as a transfer film to the model.

The bellows are made by casting polyurethane foam in a mould. Almost untouched by human hand, the models (there are two) represent a Saudi version and one for Europe. 'Rendered' screen images were then output to further 'sell' the concept, and resulted in a contract worth €13 million for the trolleybuses which presumably plastic injection mouldings. His latest model is a 12m Solaris Trollino for which he has yet to decide a livery – Landskrona is one thought. His SolidWorks is admittedly an old version as this sort of 'universal' software is not cheap, but it does include PhotoWorks that can output realistic impressions of what the model will look like in various liveries.

Money is less of a problem in Saudi Arabia where 12 futuristic trolleybuses are to arrive at Riyad Medical University in 2011. To design them, Viseon (inheritors of Neoplan's trolleybus division) used standard automotive techniques,

generic Solaris Trollino 12T by VK Modelle, 1:87, plastic

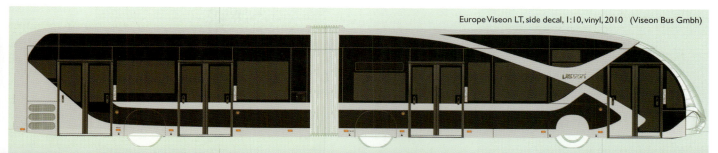

Europe Viseon LT, side decal, 1:10, vinyl, 2010 (Viseon Bus Gmbh)

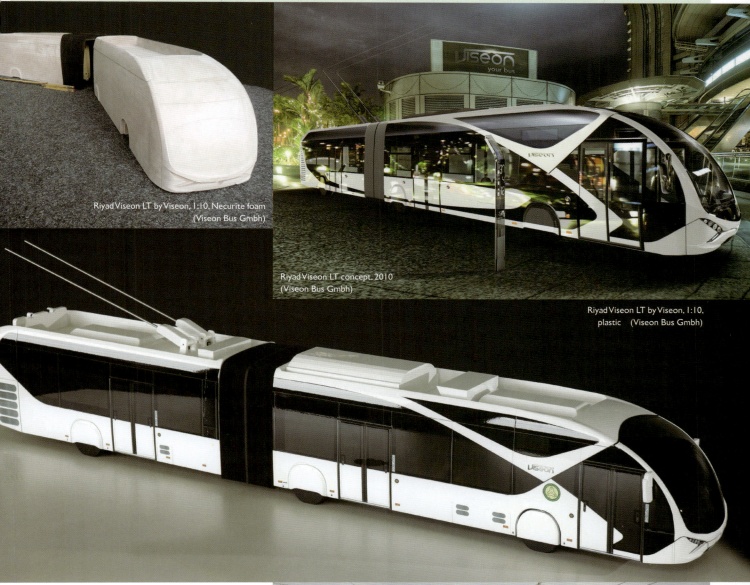

Riyad Viseon LT by Viseon, 1:10, Necurite foam (Viseon Bus Gmbh)

Riyad Viseon LT concept, 2010 (Viseon Bus Gmbh)

Riyad Viseon LT by Viseon, 1:10, plastic (Viseon Bus Gmbh)

Riyad prototype Viseon LT, 2011 (Marcus Fey)

includes the air conditioning, double glazing and air curtains needed to cope with extreme desert temperatures.

These professional model-making processes are expensive and not intended as a way of batch producing models. But the future (as always) promises new technologies that could be used to produce small model runs for collectors. Many will still want to cast resin trolleybuses and the Ukrainians of Kherson have a particular fondness for electroforming copper, but it is now possible to use a '3d printer', which has the advantage of being able to build the exterior, the interior and the glazing all at the same time.

Beyond convention

A group of people near Bath in the UK, the Rapman community, have a mission to make 3d printing more affordable. Their software is free. All that is needed is a virtual 3D model which can then be converted into thousands of horizontal slices, depending on the required accuracy, and fed as instructions into a 3d printer. With two filament heads, one for clear and one for opaque plastic of any colour, the printer squirts out the less than 0.1mm layers to recreate the model, albeit rather slowly. The printer costs £750 as a kit and can make anything that's smaller than

Generic Lectroliner within Nettfabb software, by Ashley Bruce, virtual, plastic

Rapman 3d printer head (Adrian Bowyer)

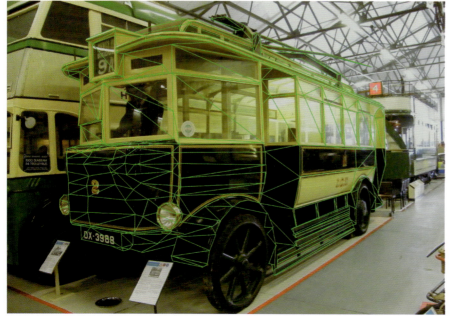

Ipswich 3, Railless cartoon by Googles, 1923 (c/o Ipswich Transport Museum)

275x205x210mm - big enough for a bi-articulated model trolleybus in 0 scale. With perhaps seven sales, the printer would have paid for itself, although painting and adding transfers would still be necessary.

It would be possible today without human intervention to use a 3d scanner to input the 1923 Railless trolleybus in Ipswich Transport Museum and output perfectly scaled miniature reproductions. A great deal has changed since Ipswich residents were waiting for their turn to play with the new 'toy' trolleybus with which we began this book.

Ipswich 2, Railless/Shorts/EE, 1923, with 3D polygon grid (Alan B Thompson)

Bibliography

A selected bibliography that includes publications referenced rather than a definitive list. Books that relate to the world are on the next page, followed by magazine publications. The list of model and toy publications also follows on the next page.

Trolleybus history

Argentina
Trolebuses Rosarinos, Mariano Antenore, Arar, 2004, ISBN.9879734912

Austria
Busbewegtes Linz an der Donau, Horst Schaffer et al, Linz AG, 2004, ISBN.3950185429
Der Obus in Salzburg, Gunter Mackinger, Verlag Kenning, 2005, ISBN.3933613744
Frühe Obusse 1907-1938, Herbert Wöber, Wöber, 1994, ISBN.none
Wiener Oberleitungsbusse, Herbert Wöber, Bahn im Film, 2008, ISBN.9783950225068

Belgium
425, RS Ledgard, Bobtail Press, 2005, ISBN.0951101323
Liège, Aux Fils des Trolleybus, Jean-Géry Godeaux et al, Editions du GTF, 2001, ISBN.none

Czech Republic
50 Let Trolejbusu v Ostava Ales Stejskal et al, Dopravni Podnil Ostrava, 2002, ISBN.8023886347
Atlas Trolejbusu, Ladislav Holub, Nadas, 1986, ISBN.none
Encyklopedie Československých Autobusu a Trolejbusu, Martin Harak, Corona, 2005, ISBN.8086116301 etc.
Mesto v Pohybu, Jiri Rieger et al, Stary Most, 2009, ISBN.9788087338018
MPK Lublin, Bohdan Turzanshki, Wyawnictwo Eurosprinter, 2009, ISBN.9788392604649
Skoda-Sanos Monografie, Martin Harak et al, DPZO, 2003, ISBN.none
Trolejbusové Dopravy v Ústí nad Labem, Petr Sasek, Dopravni Podnik, 2008, ISBN.none
Trolejbusy Chomutov-Jirkov, Vojtech Wolf, Pragprojekt, 1996, ISBN.8090218083
Trolejbusy Most-Litvinov, Ivan Grisa, Vydavatelstvi Cada, 2005, ISBN.8086765032
Trolejbusy v Bratislave, Jan Horník, Dopravný Podnik Bratislava, 2009, ISBN.none
Trolejbusy v Praze, Jan Cech et al, Solecnost mestske dpravy, 1994, ISBN.8090106765
Trolejbusy v Pražských Ulicích, Jan Arazim et al, Atlas Vozidel, 2002, ISBN.none
Trolleybuses in Brno, Vojtěch Wolf, Vydavatelstvi Wolf, 2001, ISBN.none
Zlatá Éra Trolejbusu, Radovan Rebstock, Nakladatelstvi, 2009, ISBN.9788086876184

France
Berliet, Cristophe Puvilland, Histoire & Collections, 2008, ISBN.9782352500599
France by Trolleybus, Martin Nimmo, Trolleybooks, 1988, ISBN.0904235114
Le Trolleybus à Lyon, Jacues Perenon et al, Les Editions du Cabri, 2002, ISBN.2914603010
Les Transports en Commun a Lyon, Roland Racine, Alan Sutton, 2008, ISBN.0782849107430
Les Trolleybus Français, René Courant, Presses et Editions Ferroviaires, 1985, ISBN.290544701X
Mulhouse sur Rails, Eugene Riedweg et al, La Nuee Bleue, 2006, ISBN.2716506892
Trolleybus Marseillais, Marc Bargier, Alan Sutton, 2005, ISBN.2849102792

Germany
DDR-Omnibusse, Chrisitan Suhr, Motorbuch Verlag, 2007, ISBN.9783613027091
Der Oberleitungs-Omnibus, Sigfrid Matthes, Verkehrsmuseum Dresden, 1979, ISBN.none
Der Obus in Oldenburg, Klaus-Dieter Stolle, Verlag Kenning, 2007, ISBN.9783933613
Mit Straßenbahn und Obus durch Trier, Joachim Gilles, Sutton Verlag, 2007, ISBN.9783866802230
Obus-Anlagen in Deutschland, Werner Stock, Hermann Busch Verlag, 1987, ISBN.392688200X
Obusse in Deutschland, vol. I, Mattis Schindler, Verlag Kenning, 2008, ISBN.9783933613349
Obusse in Deutschland, vol. II, Jürgen Lehmann, Verlag Kenning, 2010, ISBN.9783933613318
Obusse in Kapfenberg und Bruck a.d. Mur, Hans Lehnhart, Verlag Kenning, 2009, ISBN.9783933613646
Stadtverkehr in Gießen, Dietrich Augstein et al, Verlag Kenning, 2009, ISBN.9783933613967
Straßenbahn und Obus in Solingen, Jürgen Lehmann, Verlag Kenning, 2007, ISBN.9783933613868
Von der Gleislossen zum Oberleitungsomnibus, Gerhard Bauer, Bauer Verlag fur Verkehrsliteratur, 1997, ISBN.3980430316

Hungary
év az áramszedök alatt 1933-2008, Jakab Làszló, BKV, 2008, ISBN.9789630654449

Italy
Alfa Romeo Trolleybussen, Patrick Italiano, Klaverblaadje, 2005, ISBN.none
Giro d'Italia in Filobus, Paulo Gregoris, Calosci-Cortona, 2003, ISBN.8877851937
Il Filobus a Roma, Vittorio Formigari, Calosci Cortona, 1980, ISBN.none
La filovia dello Stelvio, Alessandro Albé, Macchione Editore, 2006, ISBN.8883402715
La Filovia Milanese, Gianni Pola et al, ATM, 2009, ISBN.none
Oltre lo Stretto in Filobus, Giuseppe dei Lorenzo, Calosci Cortona, 1991, ISBN.8877850574
Trieste in Filovia, Roberto Carmeli, Edioriale Danubio, 1995, ISBN.none

Netherlands
Langs gouden draden, Ferry Bosman, Connexxion, 1999, ISBN.9789090130545
tussen Arnhemse lijnen, Ferry Bosman, Studio Vervoer Nderland, 2009, ISBN.9789090245652

Russia
Empire of the Trolleybus vol. 1, Sergei Tarkhov, Rapid Transit Publications, 2000, ISBN.0948619023

Spain
Tranvías de Barcelona S.A., César Ariño, Maketa2, 2004, ISBN.none

Sweden
Trådbuss Landskrona, Per Andersson, Trivector, 2005, ISBN.916315367X

Switzerland
Der Trolleybus in Zürich, Peter Kamm, Tram-Museum Zürich, 2007, ISBN.9783909062065
Les trolleybus régionaux en Suisse, Jean-Philippe Coppex, Editions Endstation Ostring, 2008, ISBN.9783952254530
Swiss Trolleybus Systems, JR Scraggs, Scraggs, 1975, ISBN.none
Tram und Trolleybus in Basel, Dominik Madörin, Sutton Verlag, 2009, ISBN.9783866805323

Ukraine
Kiev Trolleybus, S Mashkevich, Kiy Publishing, 2009, ISBN.9789668825583
Electro Transport Ukrainiy, S Tarkov, K Kozlov, A Olander, Bapto Kyiv, 2010, ISBN 9789662321111

United Kingdom
A Nostalgic look at Birmingham Trolleybuses, David Harvey, Silver Link Publishing, 1997, ISBN.1857940695
Beneath the Wires of London, Charlie Wyatt, Capital Transport, 2008, ISBN.9781854143259
Bournemouth Trolleybuses, David Bowler, Trolleybooks, 2001, ISBN.090423519X
Bradford 758, MJ Leak, Bradford Trolleybus Association, 2010, ISBN.none
Bradford Corporation Trolleybuses, JS King, Venture Publications, 1994, ISBN.1898432031
British Trolleybuses 1911-1972, Geoff Lumb, Ian Allan, 1995, ISBN.0711023476
British Trolleybuses in Colour, Kevin McCormack, Ian Allan, 2004, ISBN.0171103008 1
Chesterfield Trolleybuses, Barry Marsden, Tempus Publishing, 2002, ISBN.0752427601
Doncaster's Electric Transport, Peter Tuffrey, Amberley, 2010, ISBN.9781445601168
Garrett Wagons part 3 Electrics & Motors, RA Whitehead, RA Whitehead & Partners, 1996, ISBN.0950829870
Ipswich and Its Trolleybuses, a personal story, Brian Cobb, Cobb, 1998, ISBN.none
Karrier and Sunbeam Trolleybuses of Ipswich, Mike Abbot, Ipswich Transport Museum, 2010, ISBN.9781904640172
Keighley Corporation Transport, JS King, Advertiser Press, 1964, ISBN.none

Keighley Tramways and Trolleybuses, Barry Marsden, Middleton Press, 2006, ISBN.1904474837
Leyland Bus MK2, Doug Jack, Transport Publishing, 1984, ISBN.none
London Trolleybus Routes, Hugh Taylor, Capital Transport, 1994, ISBN.1854141554
London Trolleybuses, Mick Webber, Capital Transport, 2009, ISBN.9781854143334
Newcomen Society transactions vol.68, F Dittman, The Science Museum, 1996, ISBN.03720187
Nottingham Trolleybuses, David Bowler, Trolleybooks, 2006, ISBN.9780904235203
The Best of British Buses, various, Transport Publishing Company, 1981-, ISBN.903839571
The Electric Trolley Bus, RA Bishop, Dover, 1931, ISBN.none
The Heyday of the Trolleybus, Howard Piltz, Ian Allan, 1994, ISBN.0711022712
The Heyday of the Trolleybus - 2, Geoff Lumb, Ian Allan, 1996, ISBN.0711024634
The London Trolleybus vols 1 & 2, Keb Blacker, Capital Transport, 2002-4, ISBN.1854142607 etc.
The Trolley-Bus, Harold Brearley, Oakwood Press, 1966, ISBN.none
The Trolleybuses of Huddersfield, Roy Brook, Manchester Transport Museum Soc, 1976, ISBN.none
The Weymann Story, John Senior, Venture Publications, 2002, ISBN.1898432368
Trolleybus Classics nos.1-25, various, Middleton Press, 1995-2010, ISBN.1873793669 etc.
Trolleybus Memories series, Glyn Kraemer-Johnson etc., Ian Allan, 2007-, ISBN.0711031991 etc.
Trolleybus to the Punch Bowl, Phillip Taylor, Triangle Publishing, 2002, ISBN.09252933373

USA
Buses of ACF, William Luke, Iconografix, 2003, ISBN.1583881018
Faegol & Twin Coach Buses, William Luke, Iconografix, 2002, ISBN.1583880755
History of the JG Brill Company, Debra Brill, Indiana University Press, 2001, ISBN.0253339499
New York City Transit System, James Greller, Xplorer Press, 2008, ISBN.0964576570
Seattle Trolley Coaches, Harre Demoro, Interurbans, 1971, ISBN.none
The Trolley Coach in North America, Mac Sebree, Interurbans, 1974, ISBN.7420367
Trackless Trolley Years - Milwauke, Russell Schulz, Interurbans, 1980, ISBN.0916374432
Trackless Trolleys of Boston, Bradley Clarke, Boston Street Railway Association, 1970, ISBN.none
Trackless Trolleys of Fitchburg & Leominster, Bradley Clarke, Boston Street Railway Association, 1975, ISBN.none
Transit's Stepchild The Trolley Coach, Paul Ward, Interurbans, 1973, ISBN.7384356
Trolley Buses, William Luke, Iconografix, 2001, ISBN.1583880577

World
A Hundred Years of Development of Electric Traction, J Graeme Bruce, The Electric Railway Society, 1985, ISBN.0855340231
Double-Deck Trolleybuses of the World, Brian Patton, Adam Gordon, 2004, ISBN.1874422508
Trams and Trolleybuses Worldwide, Paul Heywood, DTS, 2006, ISBN.1900515415
Trolleybuses Around the World, William Luke, Iconografix, 2006, ISBN.1583881751
World Trolleybus Encyclopaedia, Alan Murray, Trolleybooks, 2001, ISBN.0904235181

Magazines
Buses, World
Classic Bus, UK
Omnibus Spiegel, Germany
TransUrban, Czech Republic
Trolleyberichten, Netherlands
Trolleybus (BTS), UK
Trolleybus Magazine (NTA), UK
Vintage Roadscene, UK

Toy and Model references
France
Joustra, Nicolas Léonard, Du May, 2003, ISBN.2841020819
Les Jouet C.R, Mick Duprat, Massin, 1998, ISBN.2707203335

Japan
Tinplate Toy Cars, Andrew Raston, Veloce, 2008, ISBN.9781845841263
Toys from Occupied Japan, Anthony Marsella, Schiffer, 1995, ISBN.0887408753

UK
British Tin Toys, Marguerite Fawdry, New Cavendish Books, 1990, ISBN.0904568865
Collecting & Constructing Model Buses, Michael Andress, Ducimus Books, 1974, ISBN.0903234238
Corgi Toys, Edward Force, Schiffer, 2005, ISBN.0764322532
EFE & Corgii OOC Model Buses, Anne Letch, Anne Letch, 2008, ISBN.0954262883
Lledo Toys, Edward Force, Schiffer, 1996, ISBN.076430013X
Minic Tinplate Vehicles, Sue Richardson, Mikansue, 1981, ISBN.0904338010
Model Car Rail Racing, JD Laidlaw Dickson, Model Aeronautical Press, 1959, ISBN.none
Painting and Detailing Model Buses, Chris Hall, Almark Publishing, 1978, ISBN.0855242922
Ramsey's British Diecast Model Toys Catalogue, John King, Warners, varios, ISBN.9780955619403
Road Vehicles for Model Railways, Ian Morton, Ian Allan, 2007, ISBN.0711031541
Scale Model Tramways, E Jackson-Stevens, David & Charles, 1972, ISBN.0715354809
The British Toy Business, Kenneth Brown, Hambledon Press, 1996, ISBN.1852851368
The Illustrated Directory of Toys, David Wallace, Colin Gower, 2007, ISBN.0681636149
Toy and Model Bus Handbook, Roger Bailey, British Bus Publishing, 1996, ISBN.1897990316
Whitemetal Locos, Iain Rice, WIld Swan Publications, 1989, ISBN.0906867770

USA
Traction Guidebook for Model Railroaders, Mike Schafer, Kalmbach Books, 1974, ISBN.7476225

World
A World of Bus Toys and Models, Kurt Resch, Schiffer, 1999, ISBN.0764308149
Autocars & Autobus, Phillipe Morro, Retro Viseur, 1995, ISBN.2840780275
Christie's Automotive Toys, Mike Richardson, Pavilion, 1998, ISBN.1862050848
Collecting Tin Toys, Jack Tempest, Collins, 1987, ISBN.0004122755
Collector's Guide to Transport Toys, Gordon Gardiner, Salamander Books, 1997, ISBN.0861019423
Collectors Guide to Bus Toys and Models, Kurt Resch, Schiffer, 2002, ISBN.0764316311
Complete World of Little Buses, Vic Davey, Northcord Transport, 1999, ISBN.9629200252
Illustrated Directory of Toys, David Wallace & Bruce Wexler, Colin Gower Enterprises, 2007, ISBN.0681636149
International PSV Models, CE Moate, Emaodes, 1973, ISBN.none
Model Bus Assemblage, Peter Cox, Model Buses, 2008, ISBN.none
Model Bus Review etc., John Gay etc., Pirate Models, 1970s, ISBN.none
Model Commercial Vehicles, Cecil Gibson, Viking, 1971, ISBN.670482455
Plastic Toy Cars, Andrew Raston, Veloce, 2007, ISBN.9781845841256
The Art of the Tin Toy, David Pressland, New Cavendish Books, 976, ISBN.0904568040
The History of Toys, Deborah Jaffé, Sutton Publishing, 2006, ISBN.0750938501
Toy and Model Trams of the World vol. 1, David Voice, Gottfried Kuře, Adam Gordon, 2001, ISBN.1874422354
Toy and Model Trams of the World vol. 2, David Voice, Gottfried Kuře, Adam Gordon, 2001, ISBN.1874422419

Magazines
Classic Toys, World
Diecast Collector, UK
Eisenbahn und Modelbahn, Germany
La Vie du Jouet, France
Meccano Magazine, UK
Model Auto Review, World
Model Bus Journal, UK
Model Buses, World
Model Collector, World
Model Engineer, UK
Model Railway Constructor, UK
Railway Modeller, UK

Appendix 1
Model makers

All 1281 minatures mentioned in this book are included here, whether commercially produced or as one-offs.

A list of suppliers in included at the end.

model maker	ref.	issued	total	scale	construction	country	vehicle	operator	fleet#	route	built	page
unknown				10cm	wood	gbr	2 axle double decker	Generic		135	n/a	287
unknown				1:87	injection plastic	gbr	2 axle double decker	London Transport			n/a	286
unknown				14cm	wood, metal	gbr	2 axle double decker	London Transport		25	n/a	40
unknown				100cm	wood	fra	2 axle single decker	Generic			n/a	138
unknown				13cm	injection plastic	mex	2 axle single decker	Ciudad de México			n/a	225
unknown				18cm	card	gbr	BUT 9721T/Verheul/EE	Arnhem	101	1	1949	227
unknown				1:30	card	nld	Den Oudsten B79T/Den Oudsten/Kiepe	Arnhem	131		1979	230
unknown				1:87	resin	aut	Gräf & Stift GE 110M16	Salzburg	136-47/161-78		1982-85	79
unknown		1949		1:43	wood	deu	Henschel Gr.II/Schumann	Dresden	151-63		1947-9	163
unknown		1961		25cm	injection plastic	hun	Ikarus 60T	Budapest			1952	193
unknown				9cm	wood	usa	Pullman-Standard 43CX	Valparaiso			1936	368
unknown		1986		1:87	wood	usa	Pullman-Standard 43CX	Generic			1936	368
unknown				1:87	resin	usa	Pullman-Standard 44T	Ciudad de México	3185-3247		1947	225
unknown				22cm	wood	cze	Škoda 7Tr	Generic			1951	113
unknown				24cm	wood	rus	Uritsky ZiU-9	Beograd		22	1984	253
unknown				1:87	injection plastic	bel	Van Hool AG 300T	Solingen	268	684	2002	89
3dTransit.com				virtual	virtual	can	Flyer E800	Boston	4002	73	1979	95
52Bus	52002-A	2009	1000	1:76	diecast	chn	Shanghai SK5105GP	Shanghai	100	14	1997	102
52Bus	52002-B	2009	1000	1:76	diecast	chn	Shanghai SK5105GP	Shanghai	1	15	1997	102
52Bus	52002-C	2010	1000	1:76	diecast	chn	Shanghai SK5105GP	Shanghai	80	11	1997	102
80M Bus Model Shop	88001	2001	800	1:76	diecast	gbr	Dennis Dragon/Duple-Metsec/Ansaldo	Citybus	701	2001	1994	317
ACP				1:43	wood, metal	bel	Brossel Frères/D'Heure	Liège RELSE	402		1936	87
AEC		1932	1	?	plaster?	gbr	AEC 'Q' type	General			1932	281
AEC		1937		1:8	wood, metal	gbr	AEC chassisless/MCCW/MV	London Transport	953		1938	17
AHC Models				1:87	resin	swe	Volvo B10M/Den Oudsten/Kiepe	Arnhem	142		1990	231
Albert Maslip			1	1:16	wood, card	gbr	Tillings Stevens/CGA	Barcelona	511	FP	1941	31
Axel Vorobiev				1:43	plasticard, wood	ukr	LAZ-695T	Sevastapol	83		1963	274
ALO Alexander Olajos	ALO700-01	2005		1:87	resin, metal	aut	Gräf & Stift EO I	Salzburg	122		1948	77
ALO Alexander Olajos	ALO700-02	2005		1:87	resin, metal	aut	Gräf & Stift EO I	Linz	700-2		1950	77
ALO Alexander Olajos	ALO7000/01	2010		1:87	resin	aut	Gräf & Stift EO II	Salzburg	128-30		1956	77
ALO Alexander Olajos	ALO900-01			1:87	resin	aut	Gräf & Stift OE 105/54	Salzburg	102	3	1974	79
ALO Alexander Olajos	ALO500-01	2004		1:87	resin, metal	deu	Henschel OM 5-1/Lohner	Wien	6390-9	22	1946	76
ALO Alexander Olajos	ALO200-01	2004		1:87	resin	aut	Steyr STS 11HU	Linz		45	1988	81
ALO Alexander Olajos	ALO200-02	2004		1:87	resin	aut	Steyr STS 11HU	Salzburg	107-114	1	1989-90	81
ALO Alexander Olajos (repaint)	ALO200-02			1:87	resin	aut	Steyr STS 11HU	Salzburg		1	1989-90	81
ALO Alexander Olajos (repaint)	ALO200-02			1:87	resin	aut	Steyr STS 11HU	Salzburg		6	1989-90	81
Alphagrafix	DB109	1992		1:76	card	gbr	AEC 661T/Park Royal/EE	Reading	113	-	1938	290
Alphagrafix	DB105	1992		1:76	card	gbr	AEC 664T/MCCW/MV	London Transport	260	628	1936	300
Alphagrafix	DB113	1996		1:76	card	gbr	BUT 9641T/East Lancashire/GEC	Cardiff	262	4	1948	305
Alphagrafix	DB101	1990		1:76	card	gbr	BUT 9641T/MCCW/EE	London Transport	1812	604	1948	305
Alphagrafix	DB111	1992		1:76	card	gbr	BUT 9641T/Weymann/CP	Bournemouth	212	25	1950	305
Alphagrafix	AM3	1996	1	1:87	card	gbr	BUT 9721T/Verheul/EE	Arnhem	101	1	1949	227
Alphagrafix	DB108	1992		1:76	card	gbr	Crossley TDD6 'Dominion'/MV	Manchester	1081	28	1938	315
Alphagrafix	DB116	1994		1:76	card	gbr	Guy BT	Hastings	3	6	1928	318
Alphagrafix	AM8	1997		1:87	card	nld	Kromhout TB4L4/Verheul	Rotterdam	124		1944	227
Alphagrafix	DB114	1993		1:76	card	gbr	Railless/Shorts/EE	Ipswich	2	-	1923	334
Alphagrafix	DB115	1993		1:76	card	gbr	Ransomes, Sims + Jefferies D type	Ipswich	46	7A	1933	335
Alphagrafix	DB106	1992		1:76	card	gbr	Sunbeam F4/Park Royal/MV	Ipswich	126	5	1950	347

model maker	ref.	issued	total	scale	construction	country	vehicle	operator	fleet#	route	built	page
Alphagrafix	DB107	1992		1:76	card	gbr	Sunbeam F4/Park Royal/MV	Walsall	347	-	1950	347
Alphagrafix	DB102	1991		1:76	card	gbr	Sunbeam W/Park Royal/BTH	Nottingham	460	39	1945	340
Alphagrafix	DB104	1992		1:76	card	gbr	Sunbeam W/Roe/MV	Bradford	737	40	1945	340
Alphagrafix	DB110	1992		1:76	card	gbr	Sunbeam W/Weymann/BTH	Derby	72	-	1944	340
Alpia		1948		52cm	wood, plastic	ita	3 axle single decker	Generic	102		n/a	203
AM				1:87	injection plastic	cze	Škoda 21Tr	Ostrava	3303		1997	125
AM				1:87	injection plastic	cze	Škoda 21Tr	Plzen	484		2001	125
AM				1:87	injection plastic	cze	Škoda 21Tr	Brno	3042	25	2002	125
AM				1:87	injection plastic	cze	Škoda 22Tr	Brno	3606		2003	127
AM				1:87	injection plastic	cze	Škoda 22Tr	Ustí nad Labem	601		2002	127
AM				1:87	injection plastic	cze	Škoda 22Tr	Škoda Ostrov			1993	127
AMTUIR				1:12(?)	metal	fra	Vetra CS60/Renault Scemia	Paris			1943	146
Anbrico	29	1988		1:76	diecast	gbr	Dennis Dominator/Alexander/GEC	South Yorkshire PTE	2450		1985	317
Anbrico	26			1:76	diecast	gbr	Karrier E4/Weymann/EE	Bradford		4	1938	319
Anbrico	26			1:76	diecast	gbr	Karrier E4/Weymann/MV	South Shields	211	11	1937	319
Anbrico (amended)	26			1:76	diecast	gbr	Karrier E4/Weymann/MV	South Shields	204	2	1937	319
Anbrico (conversion)				1:76	diecast	gbr	Crossley TDD6 'Dominion'/MV	Kingsland Corporation			1938	315
Andes Whistler				virtual	virtual	cze	Škoda 21Tr	Bratislava	6401		2003	125
Andras Ekkert				1:87	resin, plastic	nld	Berkhof AT18	Solingen	171	682	2001	232
Andras Ekkert		2009		1:87	resin	swe	Volvo B7/Kiepe	Linz	212	43	2000	268
Andreas Konz				1:87	resin	pol	Jelcz PR110T	Lublin			1980	234
Andreas Konz				1:87	resin	cze	Škoda 14Tr	Potsdam	401		1983	122
Andreas Konz			100	1:87	resin	cze	Škoda 9Tr	Magdeburg			1962-70	116
Andreas Konz				1:87	resin	cze	Škoda 9Tr	Pardubice			1962	116
Andreas Konz				1:87	resin	cze	Škoda 9Tr	Dresden			1962-70	116
Andreas Konz				1:87	resin	cze	Škoda 9Tr	Lutsk			1962	116
Andreas Konz				1:87	resin	cze	Škoda 9Tr	Rivne			1962	116
Andreas Konz		2010		1:87	resin	cze	Škoda 9Tr	Riga			1961	116
Andreas Konz				1:87	resin	cze	Škoda 9Tr	Gera			1962	116
André Deassart				1:30	wood, metal	fra	Brossel Frères 500/D'Heure/CEBT38	Liège TULE	499	35	1939	89
André Deassart				1:20	wood, metal	bel	FNT54	Liège TULE	523	8	1954	89
André Deassart				1:30	wood, metal	gbr	Ransomes/RSJ/EMB	Liège TULE	402	20	1930	335
APETc	Emidio Garde	2008		1:87	resin	ita	Lancia 120.003/Dalfa	Porto			1966	210
APETc		2007	60	1:87	resin	che	Saurer/Sécheron 3TP	Coimbra	21		1947	271
Arcade		1930		25cm	cast iron	usa	Twin Coach 40TT	Chicago			1930	356
ARTM				?	wood, metal	fra	Electrobus Lombard-Gerin	Marseilles	1,2		1902	137
Ashahi	A310	1950s		30cm	tinplate	jpn	Hino/Fuji	Paradise			1955	221
Ashley Bruce				virtual	virtual	gbr	Lectroliner	Leeds NGT			2014	379
Ashley Bruce				virtual	injection plastic	gbr	Lectroliner	Generic			2014	382
Ashley Bruce		1972		1:9	wood, metal	gbr	Railless 6 wheeler	South Yorkshire Transport		1	1932	43
Atlas Editions	GBB004	2010		1:76	diecast	gbr	BUT 9641T/MCCW/EE	London Transport	1891	657	1952	305
Atlas Editions	GBB015	2011		1:76	diecast zinc	gbr	Sunbeam W/Roe/BTH	Teeside	T294		1944	340
ATM	9701	1997		1:87	resin	ita	Alfa Romeo 140AF/CRDA/TIBB	Trieste	728-758		1952-6	206
ATM	9713	1997		1:87	resin	ita	Alfa Romeo 140AF/SIAI Marchetti/Marelli	Ancona	Oct-16		1949	206
ATM	9712	1997		1:87	resin	ita	Alfa Romeo 140AF/SIAI Marchetti/Marelli	Trieste	704		1949	206
ATM	9711	1997		1:87	resin	ita	Alfa Romeo 140AF/SIAI Marchetti/TIBB	Roma	6601-6655		1949	206
ATM	9501	1995		1:87	resin	ita	Fiat 2405/Stranga/TIBB	Verona	20-226		1958-63	212
ATM	9613	1996		1:87	resin	ita	Fiat 2411/Cansa/CGE	Modena	42-45		1958	214
ATM	9614	1996		1:87	resin	ita	Fiat 2411/Cansa/CGE	San Remo	21-32		1957	214
ATM	9615	1996		1:87	resin	ita	Fiat 2411/Cansa/CGE	Venezia	77-93		1953-6	214
ATM	9612	1996		1:87	resin	ita	Fiat 2411/Cansa/CGE	Verona	145-156		1966	214
ATM	9611	1996		1:87	resin	ita	Fiat 2411/Cansa/TIBB	Torino	1112-1121		1956	214
ATM	9801	1998		1:87	resin	ita	Fiat 2472/Viberti/CGE	Milano	541-580		1958-64	216

model maker	ref.	issued	total	scale	construction	country	vehicle	operator	fleet#	route	built	page
ATM	9811	1998		1:87	resin	ita	Fiat 2472/Viberti/CGE	Milano	541-580		1958-64	216
Axel Dopperphul			1	1:25	wood, plastic	deu	Cedes-Stoll	Dresdner Haide-Bahn			1903	32
Axel Dopperphul			1	1:25	plasticard, metal	deu	Lowa W602a	Dresden			1951-5	176
Axel Dopperphul				1:43	resin	deu	Lowa W602a	Dresden			1951-5	31
Barrett and Sons	197?	1945		9cm	cast lead	gbr	3 axle double decker	London Transport		617	n/a	280
Barrett and Sons	204/819	1945		13cm	cast lead	gbr	3 axle double decker	London Transport		621	n/a	280
Barrett and Sons	204/819	1945		13cm	cast lead	gbr	3 axle double decker	London Transport		621	n/a	280
Basle BVB				1:55	card	che	FBW 91 GTS/Hoch/SAAS	Basle	915		1975	270
Beijing Public Transport Group		2010		1:64	diecast	chn	Beijing BD562	Beijing	2819	111	1978	101
Beijing Public Transport Group		2009	1000	1:64	diecast	chn	Beijing BK540	Beijing	1039		1956	101
Beijing Public Transport Group		2010		1:64	diecast	chn	Beijing BK560	Beijing	1128		1958	100
Beijing Public Transport Group		2010		1:64	diecast	chn	Shanghai SK561	Shanghai			1983	102
Beijing Public Transport Group		2010		1:64	diecast	chn	Shanghai SK561G	Shanghai			1980	102
Beka (conversion)				1:87	resin	deu	IFA ES6 Dobus	Berlin	2001		1955	178
Beka (conversion)				1:87	injection plastic	hun	Ikarus 180T	Tallinn			1970	205
Belgium Trucks	57	1980	100	1:43	diecast	bel	Brossel/ACEC	Bruxelles	6023	54	1956	88
Belgium Trucks		1980		1:43	diecast	bel	FNT54	Liège TULE	544	12	1954	89
Belkommunmash		2006		1:20	plastic, wood, metal	blr	Belkommunmash AKSM-331	Minsk			n/a	85
Betal		c.1938,		18cm	tinplate	gbr	2 axle double decker	General Transport		691	n/a	281
Betal		c.1938,		22cm	tinplate	gbr	2 axle double decker	General Transport		693	n/a	281
Betal		c.1938		1:30	tinplate	gbr	AEC 'Q' type	General Transport	Q2	25	1933	283
Bill Avery				1:160	balsa, card	gbr	Bradford-Brown	Bradford	522		1922	43
Bob Heathcote				1:76	plasticard	gbr	Sunbeam F4/East Lancs/BTH	Bradford	844		1948	347
Boomaroo (?)				30cm	tinplate	gbr	Leyland TTB1/Park Royal/GEC	Perth	1		1933	288
Bradford City Transport		1956		1:12	wood, metal	gbr	BUT 9611T/Weymann/EE	Bradford	754	25	1950	294
Brawa	6.09861E+11	1967		1:87	plastic, metal	deu	Büssing	Generic		21	1950	68
Brawa	6107G,R,B	1967		1:87	plastic, metal	deu	Büssing	Generic			1950	68
Brawa	6100	1963		1:87	injection plastic	deu	Büssing	Generic			1950	68
Brawa	6104G,R,B	1967		1:87	plastic, metal	deu	Henschel HS160 OSL	Generic		11	1955	68
Brawa	6105	1985		1:87	plastic, metal	deu	Henschel HS160 OSL	Kaiserslauten	5	1	1959	68
Brawa	6.0026E+11	1967		1:160	plastic, metal	deu	Mercedes Benz OE302-12R Duo-Bus	Generic		3	1975	68
Brawa				1:160	injection plastic	deu	Mercedes Benz OE302-12R Duo-Bus	Generic		3	1975	68
Brawa				1:160	injection plastic	deu	Mercedes Benz OE302-12R Duo-Bus	Generic		3	1975	68
Brawa (conversion)				1:87	injection plastic	deu	3 axle articulated single decker	West Porton			n/a	52
Brawa (repaint)				1:87	plastic, metal	deu	Henschel HS160 OSL	Salzburg	127	11	1959	171
Brawa/Brekina (conversion)				1:87	plastic, metal	deu	Büssing 6500T	Deutsche Bundesbahn			1954	70
Brekina (conversion)				1:87	resin	deu	Krupp/Ludewig	Wuppertal			1960	162
Bribec		c.1972		1:87	vacuum formed plastic	gbr	AEC 664T/Northern Counties/EE	Cardiff	201-10		1941	300
Bruce Lake		2005	1	1:76	plasticard	gbr	Sunbeam S7A/East Lancs/MV	Huddersfield	631	6	1959	50
Busch				1:87	injection plastic	can	GM/Brown Boveri	Edmonton	158		1982	94
Busch (conversion)				1:87	resin	cze	Škoda 24Tr Irisbus	Škoda Ostrov			2004	129
BW Francis		1950	1	1:43	wood	gbr	Leyland TB10	Horam Transport			1934	38
C.C.C.	P28b	1988		1:43	resin, whitemetal	fra	Renault PY/STCRP	Paris			1929	138
Carde y Escoriaza		1950		1:43	metal	gbr	BUT 9641T/Escoriaza	Zaragoza	10-14		1951	31
Carta				1:87	card	pol	Jelcz M121IMT	Gdynia	3374	28	1999	234
Carta		2005		1:87	card	pol	Jelcz PR120MTE	Gdynia	3367	22	1997	234
China Model		2010	1000	1:76	diecast	chn	Shanghai SK561G	Shanghai			1980	102
CM Model		2010		1:64	diecast	chn	Beijing BJD-WG120EK	Beijing			2007-8	105
CM Model		2007	3000	1:64	diecast	chn	Beijing-Neoplan WG120N	Beijing	852200	103	2006	104
CMA		1998		1:76	resin	gbr	AEC 664T/MCCW/MV	London Transport			1935	300
CMA		1998		1:76	resin	gbr	AEC 664T/MCCW/MV	London Transport	1368		1939	300
CMA		1999		1:76	resin	gbr	AEC 664T/MCCW/MV	London Transport	1763	693	1941	300
CMA		1998		1:76	resin	gbr	Leyland TTB4/Leyland/MV	London Transport			1938	329

model maker	ref.	issued	total	scale	construction	country	vehicle	operator	fleet#	route	built	page
CMA		1998		1:76	resin	gbr	LeylandTTBD2/MCCWGEC	Birmingham	17-68	94	1933	304
CMA		2000		1:76	resin	gbr	Sunbeam MS2/Park Royal/BTH	Bournemouth			1935	336
CMA		1998		1:76	resin	gbr	Sunbeam MS2/Roe/MV	Huddersfield	595	90	1950	336
Conrad (conversion)				1:50	resin	deu	Mercedes Benz O405GTZ	Zurich	27		1988	189
Conrad (conversion)		2008		1:50	resin	deu	Mercedes Benz O405GTZW	Winterthur	145		1988	189
Copycat Models		1980's		1:72	diecast	gbr	LeylandTitan	Coventry			n/a	326
Corgi (conversion)	C469			1:64	diecast	gbr	2 axle double decker	LondonTransport		24	n/a	283
Corgi (conversion)	OM45702	2008	1	1:76	diecast	gbr	AEC 'Q' type	Bradford	633		1933	281
Corgi (conversion)	OM45702	2008		1:76	diecast	gbr	AEC 'Q' type	West Porton		81	1933	284
Corgi (conversion)	OM45702	2008		1:76	diecast	gbr	AEC 'Q' type	West Porton		64	1933	52
Corgi (conversion)			1?	1:76	diecast	gbr	AEC 661T/English Electric/EE	LondonTransport	63	654	1934	290
Corgi (conversion)				1:76	diecast	gbr	AEC 661T/English Electric/EE	LondonTransport	63	607	1934	290
Corgi Classics	97801	1995	5500	1:50	diecast	gbr	SunbeamW/Park Royal/BTH	Maidstone	55		1945	340
Corgi Classics	97800	1993	12750	1:50	diecast	gbr	SunbeamW/Park Royal/EE	Reading	132		1943	340
Corgi Classics	97871	1994	6500	1:50	diecast	gbr	SunbeamW/Park Royal/EE	Bradford	715	24	1945	340
Corgi Classics	34701	1996	7300	1:50	diecast	gbr	SunbeamW/Park Royal/EE	Nottingham	454	43	1944	340
Corgi Classics	34702	1996	5500	1:50	diecast	gbr	SunbeamW/Park Royal/EE	Ashton-under-Lyne	61		1944	340
Corgi Classics	97870	1994	5500	1:50	diecast	gbr	SunbeamW/Park Royal/MV	Newcastle	125	3A	1944	340
Corgi Classics	97316	1995	5500	1:50	diecast	gbr	SunbeamW/Park Royal/MV	Ipswich	102		1945	340
Corgi Classics	34703	1997	4100	1:50	diecast	gbr	SunbeamW/Weymann/BTH	Derby	172		1944	340
Corgi Classics (conversion)				1:50	diecast zinc	gbr	SunbeamW6/Park Royal/MV	LondonTransport		693	n/a	340
Corgi Classics (repaint)				1:50	diecast	gbr	SunbeamW/Park Royal/BTH	Belfast	130	33	1943	340
Corgi Classics (repaint)				1:50	diecast	gbr	SunbeamW/Park Royal/BTH	Southend	138	28B	1945	340
Corgi OOC	40102	1996	5000	1:76	diecast	gbr	AEC 661T/Park Royal/EE	Hastings	20	6	1940	290
Corgi OOC	40107	2000	2600	1:76	diecast	gbr	AEC 661T/Weymann/CP	Brighton, Hove & District	6340	41	1939	290
Corgi OOC	OM43701	2001	2700	1:76	diecast	gbr	AEC 664T/Harkness/GEC	Belfast	16	8	1940-3	300
Corgi OOC	43704	1998	4100	1:76	diecast	gbr	AEC 664T/Northern Counties/EE	Cardiff	203	5A	1941	300
Corgi OOC	43706	1999	6200	1:76	diecast	gbr	AEC 664T/Northern Counties/EE	Cardiff	201	6A	1941	300
Corgi OOC	OM43702	2002	2900	1:76	diecast	gbr	AEC 664T/Northern Counties/EE	Cardiff	204	6	1941	300
Corgi OOC	40101	1996	8100	1:76	diecast	gbr	BUT 961T/Weymann/CP	Maidstone	51	-	1947	294
Corgi OOC	45001	1996	10500	1:76	diecast	gbr	BUT 961T/Weymann/CP	Bournemouth	294	21	1948	294
Corgi OOC	97813	1995	13500	1:76	diecast	gbr	BUT 961T/Weymann/CP	Brighton, Hove & District	46	42	1948	294
Corgi OOC	40104	1997	4000	1:76	diecast	gbr	BUT 961T/Weymann/EE	Bradford	803	89	1948	294
Corgi OOC	40105	1998	4700	1:76	diecast	gbr	BUT 961T/Weymann/EE	Bradford	769	8	1949	294
Corgi OOC	97811	1995	9500	1:76	diecast	gbr	BUT 961T/Weymann/EE	Notts and Derby	357	A1	1948	294
Corgi OOC	43713	2000	2600	1:76	diecast	gbr	BUT 964T/Brush/CP	Nottingham	568	43	1952	305
Corgi OOC	43711	2000	3100	1:76	diecast	gbr	BUT 964T/East Lancashire/EE	Huddersfield	626	44	1956	305
Corgi OOC	43702	1998	4200	1:76	diecast	gbr	BUT 964T/Harkness/GEC	Belfast	203	30	1950	305
Corgi OOC	43701	1998	12200	1:76	diecast	gbr	BUT 964T/MCCW/EE	LondonTransport	1768	667	1948	305
Corgi OOC	43703	1998	5700	1:76	diecast	gbr	BUT 964T/MCCW/EE	Glasgow	TB4	102	1949	305
Corgi OOC	43705	1999	6500	1:76	diecast	gbr	BUT 964T/MCCW/EE	Newcastle	628	32	1950	305
Corgi OOC	43707	1999	4000	1:76	diecast	gbr	BUT 964T/MCCW/EE	Glasgow	TB4	102	1949	305
Corgi OOC	43708	1999	9700	1:76	diecast	gbr	BUT 964T/MCCW/EE	LondonTransport	1830	603	1948	305
Corgi OOC	43709	1999	1000	1:76	diecast	gbr	BUT 964T/MCCW/EE	Glasgow	TB4	101	1949	305
Corgi OOC	43710	1999	3750	1:76	diecast	gbr	BUT 964T/MCCW/EE	Generic	-	-	1948	305
Corgi OOC	43712	2000	4000	1:76	diecast	gbr	BUT 964T/MCCW/EE	LondonTransport	1842	607	1952	305
Corgi OOC	OM43706	2004	2000	1:76	diecast	gbr	BUT 964T/MCCW/EE	Glasgow	TB4	101	1949	305
Corgi OOC	OM43707	2004	2900	1:76	diecast	gbr	BUT 964T/MCCW/EE	LondonTransport	1812	601	1948	305
Corgi OOC	43708-3	1999	1000	1:76	diecast	gbr	BUT 964T/MCCW/EE	LondonTransport	1777	645	1948	305
Corgi OOC	43708-2	1999	1000	1:76	diecast	gbr	BUT 964T/MCCW/EE	LondonTransport	1891	602	1948	305
Corgi OOC	OM43709	2010	1400	1:76	diecast	gbr	BUT 964T/MCCW/EE	LondonTransport	1879	607	1952	305
Corgi OOC	OM43704	2003	2300	1:76	diecast	gbr	BUT 964T/Weymann/CP	Bournemouth	240	25	1950	305
Corgi OOC	OM43705	2003	2300	1:76	diecast	gbr	Daimler CTE6/Roe/EE	Rotherham	37	6	1950	316

model maker	ref.	issued	total	scale	construction	country	vehicle	operator	fleet#	route	built	page
Corgi OOC	42201	1997	4900	1:76	diecast	gbr	Guy Arab Tower Wagon	Birmingham	64		1936	14
Corgi OOC	OM43708	2009	1200	1:76	diecast	gbr	Karrier MS2/Weymann/MV	South Lancs Transport	71		1948	325
Corgi OOC	OM43703	2002	4000	1:76	diecast	gbr	Leyland TTB4/Leyland/MV	London Transport	1253	677	1938	329
Corgi OOC	OM41401a,b	2006	3220	1:76	diecast	gbr	Sunbeam F4/Roe/BTH	Teesside F.ailless Traction	2	-	1950	347
Corgi OOC	OM41407a,b	2007	1005	1:76	diecast	gbr	Sunbeam F4/Roe/BTH	Derby	237	22,11	1960	347
Corgi OOC	43714	2000	2700	1:76	diecast	gbr	Sunbeam S7/Park Royal/BTH	Reading	174	17	1950	339
Corgi OOC	OM40101	2004	1500	1:76	diecast	gbr	Sunbeam W/Northern Coachbuilders/	Maidstone	72	-	1946	340
Corgi OOC	OM41405	2006	2260	1:76	diecast	gbr	Sunbeam W/Roe/BTH	Maidstone	56	-	1944	340
Corgi OOC	OM40102a,b	2010	1000	1:76	diecast	gbr	Sunbeam W/Roe/BTH	Wolverhampton	455	8	1947-8	340
Corgi OOC	40103	1997	3600	1:76	diecast	gbr	Sunbeam W/Weymann/BTH	Walsall	306	-	1946	340
Corgi OOC	40106	1999	4000	1:76	diecast	gbr	Sunbeam W/Weymann/BTH	Maidstone & District	34	-	1947	340
Corgi OOC (code3)		2009		1:76	diecast	gbr	AEC 664T/MCCW/MV	London Transport	1521	601	1939-40	300
Corgi OOC (code3)	OM43703	2009		1:76	diecast	gbr	BUT 9641T/MCCW/EE	London Transport	1886	657	1952	305
Corgi OOC (motorised)	43708			1:76	diecast	gbr	BUT 9641T/MCCW/EE	London Transport	1830	603	1948	305
Corgi OOC (motorised)	OM41407b	2007	1005	1:76	diecast	gbr	Sunbeam F4/Roe/BTH	Derby	237	11	1960	347
Corgi OOC (repaint)				1:76	diecast	gbr	BUT 9611T/Weymann/EE	Notts and Derby	357	A1	1949	294
Corgi OOC (repaint)				1:76	diecast	gbr	Sunbeam W/Roe/BTH	Doncaster	392		1945	340
CR (Charles Rossignol)	95	1952		11cm	tinplate	fra	2 axle single decker	Lyon			n/a	143
CR (Charles Rossignol)	59	1952		12.5cm	tinplate	fra	2 axle single decker	Paris, Lyon			n/a	143
CR (Charles Rossignol)	95	1952		11cm	tinplate	fra	2 axle single decker	Paris			n/a	143
CR (Charles Rossignol)	78	1952		26cm	tinplate	fra	Vetra VBC-APU/Chausson	Paris			1955	143
CR (Charles Rossignol)	78	1952		26cm	tinplate	fra	Vetra VBC-APU/Chausson	Lyon			1955	143
CR (Charles Rossignol)	78	1952		26cm	tinplate	fra	Vetra VBC-APU/Chausson	Generic			1955	143
CR (Charles Rossignol)	78	1952		26cm	tinplate	fra	Vetra VBC-APU/Chausson	Generic			1955	143
CR (Charles Rossignol)	78	1952		26cm	tinplate	fra	Vetra VBC-APU/Chausson	Generic			1955	143
CR (Charles Rossignol)	978C	1952		26cm	tinplate	fra	Vetra VBC-APU/Chausson	Lyon			1955	143
Creative Master Northcord	CN2005	2004	2000	1:76	diecast	chn	Sunwin SWB5115GP-3	Shanghai	166	20	2001	104
Daiya		1950s		36cm	tinplate	jpn	2 axle single decker	City Line	60		n/a	226
Daiya	230			38cm	tinplate	jpn	Hino/Fuji	Tokyo	320		1956	221
Dave Wall				1:18	card, wood, plastic	gbr	BUT 9641T/East Lancashire/GEC	Cardiff	243	14	1955	27
Dave Wall				1:24	card, wood, plastic	gbr	BUT 9641T/Weymann/CP	Bournemouth	246	28	1950	305
Dave Wall				1:18	card, wood, plastic	gbr	BUT RETB1/Burlingham/MV	Glasgow	TBS13	108	1958	313
Dave Wall				1:18	card, wood, plastic	gbr	Leyland TB7/MCCW/GEC	Birmingham	90	93	1940	281
Dave Wall				1:18	card, wood, plastic	gbr	Sunbeam F4/Park Royal/MV	Walsall	353	32	1950	347
Dave Wall				1:24	card, wood, plastic	gbr	Sunbeam MF2B/Weymann/CP	Bournemouth	258	21	1958	352
Dave Wall				1:24	card, wood, plastic	gbr	Sunbeam MF2C/MCW/AEI	Bournemouth	304	23	1980	353
Dave Wall				1:24	card, wood, plastic	gbr	Sunbeam MS2/Park Royal/BTH	Bournemouth	202	39	1935	336
David Bowler				1:76	injection plastic	gbr	Sunbeam MF2C/MCW/AEI	Bournemouth	350	43	1980	353
David Wood				1:76	wood, metal	gbr	BUT 9641T/East Lancashire/GEC	Cardiff			1955	305
Dayton		c.1920		1:18	sheet steel	usa	2 axle single decker	Staten Island			1920s	356
Deltax				1:120	resin	cze	Škoda 9Tr	Brno			1963	116
Denia	45	1940s		38cm	wood	esp	Maquitrans 500B	Barcelona			1941-54	264
Denis Dolgushev		2011		1:87	resin	rus	Uritsky ZiU-682G	Dnepropetrovsk	2143		2006	253
Denis Dolgushev		2011		1:87	resin	rus	Uritsky ZiU-682G	Tolyatti	3332	7	1992	253
Dinky				10cm	virtual	rus	2 axle single decker	Moskva			n/a	246
Dinky (conversion)				1:76	diecast	gbr	3 axle double decker	London Transport		654	n/a	286
Dinky (conversion)				1:72	diecast	gbr	BUT 9641T/MCCW/EE	Pontevedra			1948	305
Dinky (conversion)				12cm	diecast	gbr	Leyland Royal Tiger/Duple	Kobenhavn KS		6	1950	133
Dinky (conversion)			5500		injection plastic	gbr	Sunbeam MF2B/Weymann/CP	Bournemouth		20	1962	352
Dinky (conversion)	29F			1:72	diecast	fra	Vetra VBC-APU/Chausson	Toulon	85	1	1955	149
DNK (Nizhny Novgorod)		2007		1:43	resin	rus	Yaroslavly YaTB-1	Leningrad	44		1936	242
DOCA		2005		1:43	diecast	hun	Ikarus 280T	Chelyabinsk	3862		1989	198
DPMB				1:87	card	cze	Škoda 21Tr	Brno	3007	140	1999	125

model maker	ref.	issued	total	scale	construction	country	vehicle	operator	fleet#	route	built	page
Editorial Roma		1984		1:43	card	gbr	BUT 965IT/Material y Construcciones	Barcelona	608		1955	262
EFE (conversion)		1970's		1:76	diecast	gbr	AEC 662T/English Electric/EE	Notts and Derby	306		1932	299
EFE (conversion)	16317			1:76	Diecast	gbr	BUT RETB1/Burlingham/MV	Glasgow	TBS21	109	1958	313
EFE (conversion)				1:76	diecast	gbr	Leyland TBD1/Shorts/GEC	Birmingham	19		1931	326
Eheim	100	1954		1:87	plastic, metal	deu	Büssing	Generic			1950	63
Eheim	101	1954		1:87	plastic, metal	deu	Büssing	Generic			1950	63
Eheim	6100	1963		1:87	plastic, metal	deu	Büssing	Generic		21	1950	63
Eheim	6100	1963		1:87	injection plastic	deu	Büssing	Generic			1950	63
Eheim	108	1956		1:87	plastic, metal	deu	Henschel	Generic			1950	64
Eheim	110	1956		1:87	plastic, metal	deu	Henschel	Generic			1956	64
Eheim	6110	1963		1:87	plastic, metal	deu	Henschel	Generic			1950	64
Eheim	110	1956		1:87	plastic, metal	deu	Henschel	Generic			1956	64
Eheim	110	1956		1:87	plastic, metal	deu	Henschel	Generic			1956	64
Eheim	6104	1963		1:87	plastic, metal	deu	Henschel HS160 OSL	Generic		11	1955	171
Eheim	6104	1963		1:87	injection plastic	deu	Henschel HS160 OSL	Generic		11	1955	171
Eheim	6104	1963		1:87	injection plastic	deu	Henschel HS160 OSL	Generic			1955	66
Eheim	5100, 5102	1964		1:160	plastic, metal	deu	Mercedes Benz O321	Generic			1975	67
Eheim (Aristocraft)				1:87	plastic, metal	deu	Büssing	Generic			1950	69
Eheim (conversion)				1:87	injection plastic	gbr	AEC 661T/English Electric/EE	London Transport	13		1934	290
Eheim (conversion)				1:87	brass	deu	MAN 36/MAN/Siemens	Berlin	104	32	1934	70
Eric Chambers		1929		1:6	wood	gbr	Straker Squire	Chesterfield	7		1927	35
Eric Thornton		1948		1:30	wood, metal	gbr	Railless/Hurst Nelson/Siemens	Bradford	240		1911	334
Ervin Szabo library				1:50	wood, metal	hun	Ganz/AEC	Budapest		T	1933	203
Erzgebirge					wood	deu	2 axle single decker	Erzgebirge			n/a	159
ET		1950s		24cm	tinplate	jpn	2 axle single decker	Generic			n/a	220
ETS				1:48	card	can	CC&F-Brill T-44	Edmonton	148		1947	92
Europa		1950		1:76	plastic, metal	deu	Krauss-Maffei	München			1950	61
Europa		1950		1:76	plastic, metal	deu	Krauss-Maffei	München			1950	173
Extra	872312/91			1:87	resin	cze	Škoda 14Tr	Ostrava			1984	122
Extra	872311/91			1:87	resin	cze	Škoda 14Tr	Bratislava			1980	122
Extra	120504/91			1:87	resin	cze	Škoda 8Tr	Praha			1960	115
F Toys	F1208			19cm	tinplate	chn	2 axle single decker	Generic			n/a	98
Fairylite	MS705	1960s		27cm	tinplate	chn	2 axle single decker	Generic			n/a	98
Fairylite	MS705	1960s		27cm	tinplate	chn	2 axle single decker	Generic			n/a	98
Fanfare Transport Models		2001		1:76	diecast	gbr	BUT 9641T/Weymann/CP	Bournemouth	200-23	25	1950	305
Ferdinand Strauss		1922		12cm?	tinplate	usa	2 axle single decker	The Trackless Trolley			n/a	356
Fernandez Vigaro		1945		21cm	card	esp	3 axle single decker	Generic			n/a	267
Finoko	695T			1:43	diecast	ukr	LAZ-695T	Odessa			1963	274
Finoko	6335			1:43	diecast	rus	Uritsky ZiU-5	Generic			1961	250
Finoko	7135			1:43	diecast	rus	Uritsky ZiU-5	Moskva			1961	250
Finoko	6334?			1:43	diecast	rus	Uritsky ZiU-5	Leningrad			1961	250
Finoko	6333			1:43	diecast	rus	Uritsky ZiU-9	Novokuibyshevsk			1972	253
Finoko	7025			1:43	diecast	rus	Uritsky ZiU-9	Cheboksary			1972	253
FJ (France Jouet)		1957		17cm	tinplate	fra	2 axle single decker	Generic			n/a	143
FMB-Unicorn	183	2006		1:87	injection plastic	deu	TS111	Solingen	60	684	1968-74	173
Ganz Transelektro				1:50	wood	pol	Solaris Trollino 12T	Budapest		76	2002	23
Ganz Transelektro				1:50	wood	pol	Solaris Trollino 18T	Roma		90	2003	23
Garrett		1927		1:10	wood, metal	gbr	Garrett OS	Southend	104		1927	318
Gila Modelli	GM266			1:43	resin	ita	Alfa Romeo 140AF/Macchi/Marelli	Como STECAV	87		1951	206
Gila Modelli	GM266			1:43	resin	ita	Alfa Romeo 140AF/Pistoesi/CGE	Salerno	218	2	1951	206
Gila Modelli	GM266			1:43	resin, metal	ita	Alfa Romeo 140AF/SIAI Marchetti/CGE	Milano	456	92	1950	206
Gila Modelli	GM266			1:43	resin	ita	Alfa Romeo 140AF/SIAI Marchetti/CGE	Milano	453	90	1949	206
Gila Modelli	GM266			1:43	resin, metal	ita	Alfa Romeo 140AF/SIAI Marchetti/Marelli	Ancona	16		1949	206

model maker	ref.	issued	total	scale	construction	country	vehicle	operator	fleet#	route	built	page
Gila Modelli	GM266			1:43	resin	ita	Alfa Romeo 140AF/SIAI Marchetti/Marelli	Trieste	706	5	1949	206
Gila Modelli	GM266			1:43	resin	ita	Alfa Romeo 140AF/SIAI Marchetti/TIBB	Roma	6647	47	1949	206
Gila Modelli	GM265			1:43	resin, metal	ita	Fiat 2411/Cansa/CGE	San Remo	22	V	1953/5	214
Gila Modelli	GM265			1:43	resin, metal	ita	Fiat 2411/Cansa/CGE	Modena	33	7	1958	214
Gila Modelli	GM265			1:43	resin	ita	Fiat 2411/Cansa/CGE	Torino	1112	54	1956	214
Gila Modelli	GM136M		50	1:43	resin, metal	ita	Fiat 666F/Viberti/GCE "Filocarro"	AEM Stelvio	17		1943	211
Giuliano Caroli				1:43	wood, plasticard	ita	Turrinelli	Siena	12		1907	198
Glico				1:192	injection plastic	jpn	Hino/Fuji 200 series	Tokyo	206		1954	222
Glico				1:192	injection plastic	jpn	Hino/Fuji 200 series	Tokyo	206		1954	222
Gottfried Kure				1:87	injection plastic	deu	Lohner	Dynamit Nobel AG			1945	75
Graham Bilbé		1970		1:72	wood	gbr	AEC 661T/Park Royal/EE	Reading	113	A	1938	290
Gregg Diffen				1:76	injection plastic	gbr	2 axle double decker	Manchester		210	n/a	288
Gregg Diffen				1:76	injection plastic	gbr	3 axle double decker	Manchester		218	n/a	288
Grell	7000333B	2004		1:87	injection plastic	deu	Henschel/Uerdingen ÜH IIIs	Solingen	59	E2	1959	167
Grell		2004		1:87	injection plastic	deu	Henschel/Uerdingen ÜH IIIs	Hartmannsdorfer			1959	167
Grell				1:87	injection plastic	aut	MAN SL172 HO/Gräf & Stift	Solingen	64	683	1986	185
Grell (repainted)		2008		1:87	injection plastic	deu	Henschel/Uerdingen ÜH IIIs	Rheydt	16	6	1959	167
Grell (repainted)				1:87	plastic/metal	deu	MAN SL172 HO/Gräf & Stift	Solingen	36	683	1986-8	185
Grell/Faller	130941	2006		1:87	injection plastic	deu	Henschel/Uerdingen ÜH IIIs	Solingen	3	E2	1959	167
Grell/Faller	130970	2006		1:87	injection plastic	deu	Henschel/Uerdingen ÜH IIIs	Solingen	59		1959	167
Grell/Fleischmann		2006		1:87	injection plastic	deu	Henschel/Uerdingen ÜH IIIs	Solingen	60		1959	167
Grell/Kepe		2006		1:87	injection plastic	deu	Henschel/Uerdingen ÜH IIIs	Solingen	59	E2	1959	167
Grell/Roco	66485	2007		1:87	injection plastic	deu	Henschel/Uerdingen ÜH IIIs	Salzburg	131		1959	167
Grell/Roco	66034	2009		1:87	injection plastic	deu	Henschel/Uerdingen ÜH IIIs	Moers	104		1960	167
Grell/Wilkinson	7004333L	2004		1:87	injection plastic	deu	Henschel/Uerdingen ÜH IIIs	Solingen	1,3		1959	167
Günthermann	784?	1938		22cm	tinplate	deu	2 axle double decker	Generic			n/a	284
Günthermann	525	1950s		22cm	tinplate	deu	2 axle single decker	Generic			n/a	157
Günthermann	785 10	1938		33cm	tinplate	deu	3 axle double decker	Generic			n/a	284
Günthermann	785 10E	1938		33cm	tinplate	deu	3 axle double decker	Generic			n/a	157
Hammer (conversion)				1:87	resin	deu	Henschel HS160 OSL	Esslingen	16-22		1960	171
Hammer (conversion)				1:87	injection plastic	deu	Henschel HS160 OSL-G	Solingen	73	E1	1962	171
Hanse		1950s		39cm	wood	gbr	BUT LETB1/SMH	Kobenhavn NESA			1953	133
HB (conversion)				1:87	resin	deu	Henschel HS160 OSL	Solingen	69	E1	1960	171
HB Model				1:43	resin	bel	Brossel Frères/D'Heure	Liège RELSE	402		1936	87
HB Model				1:87	resin	gbr	BUT 9721T/Verheul/EE	Arnhem	137-143		1955	227
HB Model	MBM			1:43	resin	gbr	BUT 9721T/Verheul/EE	Arnhem	137-143		1955	228
HB Model		2010		1:87	resin	aut	Gräf & Stift GE 105M16	Kapfenburg	20-24		1978	79
HB Model		2010		1:87	resin	aut	Gräf & Stift GE 110M16	Salzburg	136-47/161-78		1982-85	79
HB Model		2010		1:87	resin	aut	Gräf & Stift GE 110M16	Salzburg	129-135		1978-80	79
HB Model		2010		1:87	resin	aut	Gräf & Stift GE 150M16	Linz			1979	80
HB Model		2010		1:87	resin	aut	Gräf & Stift GEO I	Leoben	8		1961	78
HB Model		2010		1:87	resin	aut	Gräf & Stift GEO II	Salzburg			1961	78
HB Model		2010		1:87	resin	deu	Henschel HS160 OSL	Solingen	64-69		1960	171
HB Model		2010		1:87	resin	deu	Henschel HS160 OSL	Fribourg	43-46		1958	171
HB Model				1:87	resin	deu	Henschel HS160 OSL	Esslingen	16-23		1960	171
HB Model		2010		1:87	resin	deu	Henschel HS160 OSL-G	Trier	26-31		1961	171
HB Model		2010		1:87	resin	deu	Henschel HS160 OSL-G	Aachen	29-30		1961	171
HB Model		2010		1:87	resin	deu	Henschel HS160 OSL-G	Kaiserslauten	115		1961	171
HB Model		2010		1:87	resin	deu	Henschel HS160 OSL-G	Salzburg	124-128		1961	171
HB Model		2005		1:87	resin	deu	IFA ES6 Dobus	Berlin	2001		1955	178
HB Model				1:87	resin	hun	Ikarus 60T	Budapest			1952	193
HB Model		2009		1:43	resin	gbr	Leyland Worldmaster/Verheul LVB6T	Arnhem	159-66		1968	229
HB Model		2009		1:87	resin	gbr	Leyland Worldmaster/Verheul LVB6T	Arnhem	159-66		1968	228

model maker	ref.	issued	total	scale	construction	country	vehicle	operator	fleet#	route	built	page
HB Model				1:87	resin	deu	Lowa W602a	Berlin			1952	176
HB Model				1:87	resin	deu	Lowa W602a	Leipzig			1954	176
HB Model				1:43	resin	cze	Praga TOT 430 3 axle	Praha	303		1936	107
HB Model		2010		1:43	resin	cze	Praga TOT 430 3 axle	Praha	308		1936	108
HB Model		2006		1:43	resin	cze	Škoda 14Tr	Ustí nad Labem			1990	122
HB Model				1:43	resin	cze	Škoda 15Tr	Ustí nad Labem			1990	124
HB Model		2007		1:43	resin	cze	Škoda 7Tr	Brno	31		1951	113
HB Model				1:43	resin	cze	Škoda 8Tr	Praha	9462, 9470		1960	115
HB Model				1:43	resin	cze	Škoda 8Tr	Dresden	17		1958	115
HB Model		2006		1:43	resin	cze	Škoda 9Tr	Eberswalde			1962-70	116
HB Model				1:43	resin	cze	Škoda 9Tr	Brno	40		1963	116
HB Model				1:43	resin	rus	Svarz TS-2	Moskva			1959	249
HB Model		2011		1:43	resin	cze	Tatra T400/III	Praha	42		1953	111
HB Models		2010		1:87	resin	deu	Henschel HS160 OSL	Giessen	15-22		1961	171
Herpa (conversion)				1:87	resin	deu	MAN SG200 HO/Graft & Stift/Kiepe	Solingen			1984	184
Herpa (conversion)				1:87	resin	deu	MAN SG200 HO/Graft & Stift/Kiepe	Solingen	5	682	1984	184
Herpa (conversion)				1:87	injection plastic	deu	MAN SG200 HO/Graft & Stift/Kiepe	Mülheim	68	27	1984	184
Herpa (conversion)				1:87	injection plastic	deu	MAN SG200 HO/Graft & Stift/Kiepe	Solingen	3	691	1984	184
Herpa (conversion)				1:87	injection plastic	deu	MAN SG200 HO/Graft & Stift/Kiepe	Solingen		681	1984	184
Herpa (conversion)				1:87	resin	deu	MAN SL172 HO/Gräf & Stift	Solingen	5	681	1986-87	185
Herpa (conversion)				1:87	injection plastic	deu	MAN SU240/EHM	Esslingen			1977	183
Hess		2005		1:20	wood, metal	che	Hess Swiss Trolley 3/1	Geneva			2005	271
HK Modell				1:87	resin	hun	Ikarus 260T	Budapest	600	79	1976	196
HK Modell				1:87	injection plastic	hun	Ikarus 280T	Budapest	200		1987	196
HK Modell (repainted)				1:87	injection plastic	hun	Ikarus 280T	Eberswalde	25		1990	196
HK Modell (repainted)				1:87	injection plastic	hun	Ikarus 280T	Budapest	156	76	1978	196
IGRA		1954		15cm	plastic, metal	cze	Tatra T400/IIIA	Praha	394	55	1953	111
IGRA		1960		15cm	plastic, metal	cze	Tatra T400/IIIA	Praha	394	55	1953	111
IGRA		1954		15cm	plastic, metal	cze	Tatra T400/IIIA	Praha	394	55	1953	111
IGRA		1954		15cm	plastic, metal	cze	Tatra T400/IIIA	Most A Litnov	394	55	1953	111
Imperssion Model	imbus1001	2010	150	1:76	resin	chn	Shanghai SK561G	Guangzhou	1-151	101	1980	102
Irisbus		2000		1:12(?)	wood, metal	fra	Irisbus Civis	Generic			2000	144
Ites		1954		15cm	plastic, metal	cze	Tatra T400/IIIA		394	55	1953	111
Ivan Staněk				1:43	wood, plastic	cze	Škoda 14Tr	Plzen	88	1	1981	122
Ivan Staněk				1:43	wood, plastic	cze	Škoda 15Tr	Opava	99	1	1983	124
Ivan Staněk				1:26	wood, metal	cze	Škoda 24Tr Irisbus	Mariánské Lázne			2006	129
Ivan Staněk				1:26	wood	cze	Škoda 24Tr prototype	Mariánské Lázne			2003	129
Ivan Staněk				1:43	wood, plastic	cze	Škoda 3Tr	Plzen	106		1941	109
J. Meir		1905		10cm	tinplate	gbr	Penny toy	The Electric Omnibus Co.			n/a	13
Jansen de Koning		1992		23cm	card	gbr	BUT 9721T/Verheul/EE	Arnhem	101	2	1949	228
Jason Noakes				virtual	virtual	gbr	Leyland TTB4/Leyland/MV	London Transport	1358	694	1939	379
JF Schreiber				1:43	card	deu	Mercedes Benz O405T	Esslingen	205	101	1986	189
John Edgar		1971	1?	1:76	plasticard, metal	gbr	AEC 663T/Union Construction/EE	London Transport	1	604	1931	42
Joustra	2011	1951		13.5cm	tinplate	fra	2 axle double decker	Paris			n/a	139
Joustra	2012	1951		13.5cm	tinplate	fra	2 axle double decker	Lyon			n/a	139
Joustra	428	1949		33cm	tinplate	fra	3 axle double decker	Generic			n/a	285
Joustra	442	1951		30cm	tinplate	fra	3 axle single decker	Paris		80	n/a	139
Joustra	442	1953		30cm	tinplate	fra	3 axle single decker	Generic			n/a	139
Joustra	442	1954		30cm	tinplate	fra	3 axle single decker	Lyon		80	n/a	139
Joustra	442	1954		30cm	tinplate	fra	3 axle single decker	Generic		80	n/a	139
Joustra	439	1938		30cm	tinplate	fra	3 axle single decker	Generic			n/a	139
Joustra	442	1954		30cm	tinplate	fra	3 axle single decker	Paris		80	n/a	139
Joustra	439	1938		30cm	tinplate	fra	3 axle single decker	Generic			n/a	139

model maker	ref.	issued	total	scale	construction	country	vehicle	operator	fleet#	route	built	page
Joustra	439	1938		30cm	tinplate	fra	3 axle single decker	Generic			n/a	139
Joustra	439	1938		30cm	tinplate	fra	3 axle single decker	Generic			n/a	139
Joustra	444	1955		39cm	tinplate	fra	Jacquemond 10-A	Paris	825	4	1948	139
Joustra	450	1959		39cm	tinplate	fra	Jacquemond 10-A	Lyon	825	7	1948	139
Jugettes Y Estuches	253	1950		20cm	tinplate	esp	2 axle single decker	Generic			n/a	263
Jugettes Y Estuches	253	1950		20cm	tinplate	esp	2 axle single decker	Generic			n/a	263
K&B Models		1982		1:76	diecast	gbr	BUT 9611T/East Lancashire/EE	Bradford	831		1948	294
K&B Models		1970s		1:76	diecast	gbr	BUT 9611T/Roe/EE	Bradford	746	19	1949	294
K&B Models		1970s		1:76	diecast	gbr	BUT 9611T/Weymann/CP	Bournemouth			1948	294
K&E Models		1970s		1:76	diecast	gbr	Sunbeam F4/East Lancs/BTH	Bradford	844		1946	347
Kanden Tunnel				1:48	card	jpn	Mitsubishi 200 series	Kansai Electric Power			1994	223
Kehi Modellbay	574			1:87	diecast	deu	Lowa W602a	Eberswalde			1956	176
Keith Turner				1:76	balsa, card	gbr	BUT 9611T/Roe/EE	Nottingham	493	39	1948	294
Keith Turner		2010		1:76	diecast	gbr	BUT 9641T/Brush/MV	Nottingham	601		1952	305
Keith Turner		1970's		1:76	balsa, card	gbr	Crossley TDD64/1/MV	Manchester	1250	210	1951	315
Keith Turner		2008		1:76	balsa, card	gbr	Daimler/East Lancs/CP	Rotherham	84	9	1949	316
Keith Turner		1980's		1:76	balsa, card	gbr	Sunbeam F4/Brush/BTH	Mexborough & Swinton	27		1947	347
Kembel (conversion)				1:87	resin	deu	Mercedes Benz O405GT	Esslingen	326	119	1993	189
Kembel (conversion)				1:87	resin	deu	Mercedes Benz O405T	Esslingen			1987	189
Kembel (conversion)				1:87	resin	deu	Mercedes Benz O405T	Esslingen	205	118	1986	189
Ken Allbon				1:43	balsa, card	gbr	AEC 661T/Weymann/CP	Brighton, Hove & District	38	43A	1939	290
Ken Allbon				1:43	balsa, card	gbr	BUT 9611T/Burlingham/EE	Portsmouth	313	6	1950	294
Ken Allbon		1988		1:43	balsa, card	gbr	BUT 9611T/Roe/EE	Bradford	746	24	1949	294
Ken Allbon		2008		1:43	balsa, card	gbr	BUT 9611T/Weymann/CP	Brighton, Hove & District	391	44	1948	294
Ken Allbon		1981-4		1:43	balsa, card	gbr	BUT 9641T/MCCW/EE	London Transport	1812	604	1948	305
Ken Allbon		2008		1:43	balsa, card	gbr	Cedes-Stoll	Hove			1914	278
Ken Allbon		1985		1:43	balsa, card	gbr	Dennis Dominator/Alexander/GEC	South Yorkshire PTE	2450	163	1985	317
Ken Allbon		1986		1:43	balsa, card	gbr	Karrier MS2/Weymann/MV	South Lancs Transport	69		1948	325
Ken Allbon		1988		1:43	balsa, card	gbr	Leyland TTB5/MCCW/MV	London Transport	1748	691	1942	332
Ken Allbon		1981		1:43	balsa, card	gbr	Railless/Hurst Nelson/Siemens	Bradford	240		1911	334
Ken Allbon		1984		1:43	balsa, card	gbr	Railless/Milnes,Voss/BTH	Metropolitan Electric	1		1909	334
Ken Allbon				1:43	balsa, card	gbr	Railless/RET/Siemens	Brighton Corporation	50		1914	334
Ken Allbon		1984		1:43	balsa, card	gbr	Straker Squire A/Brush/BTH	Keighley	5		1924	278
Ken Allbon		1981		1:43	balsa, card	gbr	Sunbeam F4/East Lancs/BTH	Bradford	847		1950	347
Ken Allbon		1984		1:43	balsa, card	gbr	Sunbeam MS2C/East Lancs/BTH	Rotherham	74		1942	336
Ken Allbon		1979		1:43	balsa, card	gbr	Sunbeam S7/Park Royal/BTH	Reading	181	15	1950	339
Ken Allbon				1:43	balsa, card	fra	Vetra CS60	Paris		164	n/a	146
KEPCO				?	not known	jpn	Mitsubishi 100 series	Kansai Electric Power			1964	223
Kherson Models	E5800		0	1:43	resin	jpn	Hino/Fuji 300 series	Tokyo			1957	222
Kherson Models	E5600		0	1:43	resin	gbr	Leyland TTB4/Scandia/GEC	Kobenhavn NESA	9		1938	278
Kherson Models	2477		0	1:43	resin	rus	MTB-82M	Moskva	30		1948	245
Kherson Models (?)				1:43	resin	rus	Svarz LK-1	Moskva	5		1933	240
Kherson Models (?)		2009		1:43	resin	rus	Uritsky ZiU-11	Volgograd			1973	257
Kimmeria		2008		1:43	electroformed copper	blr	MAZ 103T	Minsk			2004	85
Kimmeria		2008		1:43	electroformed copper	blr	MAZ 103T	Moskva			2002	84
Kimmeria		2009		1:43	electroformed copper	rus	MTrZ-5279	Moskva	2004	42	2004	258
Kimmeria		2009		1:43	electroformed copper	rus	MTrZ-5279	Moskva	2003	17	2003	258
Kimmeria		2009		1:43	electroformed copper	rus	MTrZ-6232	Moskva			2008	259
Kimmeria		2009		1:43	electroformed copper	rus	MTrZ-6232	Moskva			2008	259
Konka		2009		1:43	resin	rus	Uritsky ZiU-682	Moskva			1972	253
Kremenschug				1:43	resin	deu	Lowa W602a	Berlin			1954	176
Kremenschug				1:43	resin	cze	Škoda 9Tr	Simferopol		5	1963	116

model maker	ref.	issued	total	scale	construction	country	vehicle	operator	fleet#	route	built	page
Kremenschug				1:43	resin	rus	Svarz LK-1	Moskva	7		1933	240
Kremenschug				1:43	resin	rus	Uritsky ZiU-10	Tolyatti			1990	257
Kremenschug				1:43	resin	rus	Uritsky ZiU-5	Moskva	2		1961	250
Kremenschug				1:43	resin	rus	Uritsky ZiU-9	Severodontetsk	507		2000	253
Kremenschug				1:43	resin	rus	Yaroslavly YaTB-3	Moskva			1938	244
KTU				1:20	wood,metal	cze	Škoda 14Tr	Simferopol	1990		1984	33
KTU				1:20	wood,metal	cze	Škoda 8Tr	Simferopol	101		1959-61	115
KTU				1:20	wood,metal	cze	Škoda 9Tr	Simferopol	181		1962-81	32
Laboratory 57		2010		1:43	resin	rus	Yaroslavly YaTB-1	Leningrad	55		1936	242
Langley	E11			1:148	diecast	gbr	BUT 9641T/MCCW/EE	London/Newcastle/Glasgow	1822	654	1948	305
Laurence Ahearn		2010		1:43	wood,metal	gbr	Leyland TB5/WAGT/GEC	Perth	27		1939	53
Le Jouet Troll		1950		28cm	aluminium	fra	Vetra CS60/Renault Scemia	Generic			1943	72
Les Brunton				1:50	wood,metal	gbr	Crossley TDD42/2	Ashton-under-Lyne	77		1949	45
Les Éditions Atlas		2006		1:50	resin,whitemetal	fra	Vetra CB60/Berliet	Limoges			1947	146
Lesney Products	56A	1958		1:137	diecast	gbr	BUT 9641T/MCCW/EE	London Transport	1765-840	667	1948	305
Lesney Products (repaint)	56b	2008		1:137	diecast	gbr	BUT 9641T/MCCW/EE	Generic		56b	1948	305
Lesney Products (repaint)	56b	2008		1:137	diecast	gbr	BUT 9641T/MCCW/EE	Generic		56b	1948	305
Lesney Products (repaint)	56b	2008		1:137	diecast	gbr	BUT 9641T/MCCW/EE	Generic			1948	305
Lesney Products (repaint)	56b	2008		1:137	diecast	gbr	BUT 9641T/MCCW/EE	Generic		72	1948	305
Lion-Toys		2003		1:50	diecast	nld	APTS Phileas	Einhoven			1999	378
Little Bus Co.	TBL3	2005	0	1:76	resin	gbr	AEC 664T/MCCW/MV	London Transport	1521	601	1939-40	300
Little Bus Co.	TNB2	2005		1:76	resin	gbr	BUT 9611T/Northern Coachbuilders/EE	Newcastle	560	42	1949	294
Little Bus Co.	TBB1	2004		1:76	resin	gbr	Leyland TTB2/BRCW/MV	London Transport	65	696	1935	329
Little Bus Co.	TBK2	2005		1:72	resin	gbr	Leyland TTB4/Leyland/MV	London Transport	273	628	1938	329
Little Bus Co.	TBSA	2006		1:76	resin	gbr	Leyland TTB5/MCCW/BTH	Durban			1942	332
Little Bus Co.	TBSA	2006	0	1:76	resin	gbr	Leyland TTB5/MCCW/MV	London Transport	742	693	1942	332
Little Bus Co.	TNB2	2005		1:76	resin	gbr	Sunbeam F4/Northern Coachbuilders/MV	South Shields	257	12	1947	347
Little Bus Co.	TMS2	2006	0	1:76	resin	gbr	Sunbeam MS2/Park Royal/BTH	Bournemouth	202	20	1935	336
Little Bus Co.	TMS2	2006		1:76	resin	gbr	Sunbeam MS2/Park Royal/BTH	London Transport	37	691	1935	336
Little Bus Co.	TMS2	2006		1:76	resin	gbr	Sunbeam MS2/Park Royal/BTH	Bournemouth	208	25	1935	336
Little Bus Co.	TMS2	2006		1:76	resin	gbr	Sunbeam MS2/Park Royal/BTH	West Porton		62	1935	336
Lledo	DG41-000a	1990		1:76	diecast	gbr	Karrier E6/Roe/BTH	Doncaster			1928	320
Lledo	DG41-001a	1990		1:76	diecast	gbr	Karrier E6/Roe/BTH	Nottingham			1928	320
Lledo	DG41-002a,b,c	1990		1:76	diecast	gbr	Karrier E6/Roe/BTH	London Transport			1928	320
Lledo	DG41-003a	1991		1:76	diecast	gbr	Karrier E6/Roe/BTH	London Transport			1928	320
Lledo	DG41-004a	1991		1:76	diecast	gbr	Karrier E6/Roe/BTH	London Transport			1928	320
Lledo	DG41-005a	1991	6500	1:76	diecast	gbr	Karrier E6/Roe/BTH	Scarborough			1928	320
Lledo	DG41-006a	1992		1:76	diecast	gbr	Karrier E6/Roe/BTH	London Transport		12	1928	320
Lledo	DG41-007a	1992		1:76	diecast	gbr	Karrier E6/Roe/BTH	Nottingham			1928	320
Lledo	DG41-008a,b	1992	5000	1:76	diecast	gbr	Karrier E6/Roe/BTH	London Transport			1928	320
Lledo	DG41-009a	1992		1:76	diecast	gbr	Karrier E6/Roe/BTH	General		11A	1928	320
Lledo	DG41-010a	1994		1:76	diecast	gbr	Karrier E6/Roe/BTH	Newcastle		31	1928	320
Lledo	DG41-011a	1994		1:76	diecast	gbr	Karrier E6/Roe/BTH	London Transport		604	1928	320
Lledo	DG41-012a	1994		1:76	diecast	gbr	Karrier E6/Roe/BTH	Huis Ten Bosch			1928	320
Lledo	DG41-013a	1994	2000	1:76	diecast	gbr	Karrier E6/Roe/BTH	London Transport		567	1928	320
Lledo	DG41-014a	1997		1:76	diecast	gbr	Karrier E6/Roe/BTH	Autumn 1997			1928	320
Lledo	DG41-015a			1:76	diecast	gbr	Karrier E6/Roe/BTH	London Transport		660	1928	320
Lledo	DG41-016a,b			1:76	diecast	gbr	Karrier E6/Roe/BTH	London Transport		629	1928	320
Lledo	DG41-017a	2000		1:76	diecast	gbr	Karrier E6/Roe/BTH	London Transport		667	1928	320
Lledo	DG41-020a	2001		1:76	diecast	gbr	Karrier E6/Roe/BTH	London Transport		621	1928	320
Lledo	DG41-C3			1:76	diecast	gbr	Karrier E6/Roe/BTH	Holt			1928	320
Lledo	SL41-000	1997		1:76	diecast	gbr	Karrier E6/Roe/BTH	London Transport		96	1928	320

model maker	ref.	issued	total	scale	construction	country	vehicle	operator	fleet#	route	built	page
Lledo	SL41-001	1998		1:76	diecast	gbr	Karrier E6/Roe/BTH	Guinness		12	1928	320
Lledo	LP41-001a	1990	1000	1:76	diecast	gbr	Karrier E6/Roe/BTH	Birmingham	12		1928	320
Lledo	LP41-002a	1990	1000	1:76	diecast	gbr	Karrier E6/Roe/BTH	London United			1928	320
Lledo	LP41-003a,b	1990	250	1:76	diecast	gbr	Karrier E6/Roe/BTH	Bournemouth			1928	320
Lledo	LP41-004a,b	1990	250	1:76	diecast	gbr	Karrier E6/Roe/BTH	Bournemouth			1928	320
Lledo	LP41-005a	1990	?	1:76	diecast	gbr	Karrier E6/Roe/BTH	Colchester			1928	320
Lledo	LP41-006a	1990	550	1:76	diecast	gbr	Karrier E6/Roe/BTH	Nottingham			1928	320
Lledo	LP41-007a	1990	3500	1:76	diecast	gbr	Karrier E6/Roe/BTH	Doncaster		5	1928	320
Lledo	LP41-008a	1990	1260	1:76	diecast	gbr	Karrier E6/Roe/BTH	Nottingham			1928	320
Lledo	LP41-009a	1990	1260	1:76	diecast	gbr	Karrier E6/Roe/BTH	Kingston Upon Hull			1928	320
Lledo	LP41-010a	1990	1000	1:76	diecast	gbr	Karrier E6/Roe/BTH	Wolverhampton	98		1928	320
Lledo	LP41-011a	1990	3000	1:76	diecast	gbr	Karrier E6/Roe/BTH	Grimsby			1928	320
Lledo	LP41-012a,b	1991	1100	1:76	diecast	gbr	Karrier E6/Roe/BTH	Derbyshire Constabulary			1928	320
Lledo	LP41-013a	1991	1000	1:76	diecast	gbr	Karrier E6/Roe/BTH	National Trolleybus Assoc.			1928	320
Lledo	LP41-014a,b	1991	550	1:76	diecast	gbr	Karrier E6/Roe/BTH	Donington Park			1928	320
Lledo	LP41-015b	1991	500	1:76	diecast	gbr	Karrier E6/Roe/BTH	Maidstone	24		1928	320
Lledo	LP41-016a,b	1991	500	1:76	diecast	gbr	Karrier E6/Roe/BTH	Gordon			1928	320
Lledo	LP41-017a,b	1991	500	1:76	diecast	gbr	Karrier E6/Roe/BTH	Ipswich			1928	320
Lledo	LP41-018a,b	1991	504	1:76	diecast	gbr	Karrier E6/Roe/BTH	Valerie & Brian Glover			1928	320
Lledo	LP41-019a,b	1991	1000	1:76	diecast	gbr	Karrier E6/Roe/BTH	Bridgend & District	91		1928	320
Lledo	LP41-020a	1991	1000	1:76	diecast	gbr	Karrier E6/Roe/BTH	London Transport			1928	320
Lledo	LP41-021a,b	1991	1000	1:76	diecast	gbr	Karrier E6/Roe/BTH	London Transport			1928	320
Lledo	LP41-022a,b	1991	500	1:76	diecast	gbr	Karrier E6/Roe/BTH	Walsall		30	1928	320
Lledo	LP41-023a,b	1991	1050	1:76	diecast	gbr	Karrier E6/Roe/BTH	Cleethorpes			1928	320
Lledo	LP41-024a,b	1991	1000	1:76	diecast	gbr	Karrier E6/Roe/BTH	EFTU			1928	320
Lledo	LP41-025 (cut)	1991	-	1:76	diecast	gbr	Karrier E6/Roe/BTH	Reeder			1928	320
Lledo	LP41-026 (cut)	1991	-	1:76	diecast	gbr	Karrier E6/Roe/BTH	Triton			1928	320
Lledo	LP41-027a	1991	1300	1:76	diecast	gbr	Karrier E6/Roe/BTH	Whitehall			1928	320
Lledo	LP41-028a	1991	1000	1:76	diecast	gbr	Karrier E6/Roe/BTH	Walsall			1928	320
Lledo	LP41-029a	1992	1000	1:76	diecast	gbr	Karrier E6/Roe/BTH	Coventry			1928	320
Lledo	LP41-030a,b	1991	1000	1:76	diecast	gbr	Karrier E6/Roe/BTH	Bournemouth			1928	320
Lledo	LP41-031 (cut)	1991	-	1:76	diecast	gbr	Karrier E6/Roe/BTH	Mullion			1928	320
Lledo	LP41-032a	1991	1000	1:76	diecast	gbr	Karrier E6/Roe/BTH	Walsall	860		1928	320
Lledo	LP41-033a,b	1991	?	1:76	diecast	gbr	Karrier E6/Roe/BTH	Bradford			1928	320
Lledo	LP41-034 (cut)	1991	-	1:76	diecast	gbr	Karrier E6/Roe/BTH	St. Julians			1928	320
Lledo	LP41-035 (cut)	1991	-	1:76	diecast	gbr	Karrier E6/Roe/BTH	Walsall			1928	320
Lledo	LP41-036 (cut)	1991	-	1:76	diecast	gbr	Karrier E6/Roe/BTH	Stoneleigh			1928	320
Lledo	LP41-037a	1991	1500	1:76	diecast	gbr	Karrier E6/Roe/BTH	Rotherham			1928	320
Lledo	LP41-038a	1991	1500	1:76	diecast	gbr	Karrier E6/Roe/BTH	Doncaster			1928	320
Lledo	LP41-039a	1991	?	1:76	diecast	gbr	Karrier E6/Roe/BTH	London Transport		604	1928	320
Lledo	LP41-040 (cut)	1991	-	1:76	diecast	gbr	Karrier E6/Roe/BTH	Sandown			1928	320
Lledo	LP41-041a,b	1991	1000	1:76	diecast	gbr	Karrier E6/Roe/BTH	Bradford			1928	320
Lledo	LP41-042a,b	1991	1000	1:76	diecast	gbr	Karrier E6/Roe/BTH	Leeds			1928	320
Lledo	LP41-043a	1991	2500	1:76	diecast	gbr	Karrier E6/Roe/BTH	Derby	101		1928	320
Lledo	LP41-044a	1991	2500	1:76	diecast	gbr	Karrier E6/Roe/BTH	Birmingham	31		1928	320
Lledo	LP41-045a	1991	2500	1:76	diecast	gbr	Karrier E6/Roe/BTH	Walsall	872		1928	320
Lledo	LP41-046a	1991	2500	1:76	diecast	gbr	Karrier E6/Roe/BTH	Wolverhampton	74		1928	320
Lledo	LP41-047a	1991	2500	1:76	diecast	gbr	Karrier E6/Roe/BTH	Newcastle			1928	320
Lledo	LP41-048 (cut)	1991	-	1:76	diecast	gbr	Karrier E6/Roe/BTH	Glasgow			1928	320
Lledo	LP41-049 (cut)	1991	-	1:76	diecast	gbr	Karrier E6/Roe/BTH	Birmingham			1928	320
Lledo	LP41-050 (cut)	1992	-	1:76	diecast	gbr	Karrier E6/Roe/BTH	Silver Queen			1928	320
Lledo	LP41-051a,b	1992	500	1:76	diecast	gbr	Karrier E6/Roe/BTH	Huddersfield			1928	320
Lledo	LP41-052 (cut)	1992	-	1:76	diecast	gbr	Karrier E6/Roe/BTH	British Gas			1928	320

model maker	ref.	issued	total	scale	construction	country	vehicle	operator	fleet#	route	built	page
Lledo	LP41-053 (cut)	1992	-	1:76	diecast	gbr	Karrier E6/Roe/BTH	Canterbury			1928	320
Lledo	LP41-054a	1992	1500	1:76	diecast	gbr	Karrier E6/Roe/BTH	Beamish Tramways			1928	320
Lledo	LP41-055a	1992	1000	1:76	diecast	gbr	Karrier E6/Roe/BTH	Coaster City			1928	320
Lledo	LP41-056a	1992	5000	1:76	diecast	gbr	Karrier E6/Roe/BTH	London Transport			1928	320
Lledo	LP41-057 (cut)	1992	-	1:76	diecast	gbr	Karrier E6/Roe/BTH	Farnham			1928	320
Lledo	LP41-058 (cut)	1992	-	1:76	diecast	gbr	Karrier E6/Roe/BTH	Heathrow			1928	320
Lledo	LP41-059a	1992	?	1:76	diecast	gbr	Karrier E6/Roe/BTH	London Transport			1928	320
Lledo	LP41-060a	1992	1300	1:76	diecast	gbr	Karrier E6/Roe/BTH	Whitehall			1928	320
Lledo	LP41-061a	1992	1100	1:76	diecast	gbr	Karrier E6/Roe/BTH	Nottingham			1928	320
Lledo	LP41-062a,b	1992	500	1:76	diecast	gbr	Karrier E6/Roe/BTH	Cardiff	2	5	1928	320
Lledo	LP41-063a (cut)	1992	-	1:76	diecast	gbr	Karrier E6/Roe/BTH	Phonecard			1928	320
Lledo	LP41-064a (cut)	1992	-	1:76	diecast	gbr	Karrier E6/Roe/BTH	Kent Kids			1928	320
Lledo	LP41-065a (cut)	1992	-	1:76	diecast	gbr	Karrier E6/Roe/BTH	Northampton			1928	320
Lledo	LP41-066a,b	1992	1050	1:76	diecast	gbr	Karrier E6/Roe/BTH	Nottingham			1928	320
Lledo	LP41-067a (cut)	1992	-	1:76	diecast	gbr	Karrier E6/Roe/BTH	QE			1928	320
Lledo	LP41-068a (cut)	1992	-	1:76	diecast	gbr	Karrier E6/Roe/BTH	Watsons			1928	320
Lledo	LP41-069a	1992	1000	1:76	diecast	gbr	Karrier E6/Roe/BTH	Newport			1928	320
Lledo	LP41-070a,b	1992	1000	1:76	diecast	gbr	Karrier E6/Roe/BTH	North Western	1		1928	320
Lledo	LP41-071a	1992	?	1:76	diecast	gbr	Karrier E6/Roe/BTH	Doncaster			1928	320
Lledo	LP41-072a,b	1992	1000	1:76	diecast	gbr	Karrier E6/Roe/BTH	St. Georges			1928	320
Lledo	LP41-073a,b	1992	1000	1:76	diecast	gbr	Karrier E6/Roe/BTH	Fleetwood			1928	320
Lledo	LP41-074 (cut)	1992	-	1:76	diecast	gbr	Karrier E6/Roe/BTH	Bury			1928	320
Lledo	LP41-075a	1992	2000	1:76	diecast	gbr	Karrier E6/Roe/BTH	Bournemouth			1928	320
Lledo	LP41-076a,b	1992	2000	1:76	diecast	gbr	Karrier E6/Roe/BTH	Bradford			1928	320
Lledo	LP41-077a	1992	500	1:76	diecast	gbr	Karrier E6/Roe/BTH	Mexborough & Swinton		7	1928	320
Lledo	LP41-078 (cut)	1992	-	1:76	diecast	gbr	Karrier E6/Roe/BTH	Scalextric			1928	320
Lledo	LP41-079a	1992	?	1:76	diecast	gbr	Karrier E6/Roe/BTH	London Transport			1928	320
Lledo	LP41-080 (cut)	1992	-	1:76	diecast	gbr	Karrier E6/Roe/BTH	NEC		3	1928	320
Lledo	LP41-081 (cut)	1992	-	1:76	diecast	gbr	Karrier E6/Roe/BTH	NEC			1928	320
Lledo	LP41-082a	1992	2500	1:76	diecast	gbr	Karrier E6/Roe/BTH	Teesside Railless Traction			1928	320
Lledo	LP41-083 (cut)	1992	-	1:76	diecast	gbr	Karrier E6/Roe/BTH	Bradford			1928	320
Lledo	LP41-084 (cut)	1992	-	1:76	diecast	gbr	Karrier E6/Roe/BTH	Maidstone			1928	320
Lledo	LP41-085 (cut)	1992	-	1:76	diecast	gbr	Karrier E6/Roe/BTH	Toytown			1928	320
Lledo	LP41-086a,b	1992	1000	1:76	diecast	gbr	Karrier E6/Roe/BTH	Grimsby			1928	320
Lledo	LP41-087a	1993	1350	1:76	diecast	gbr	Karrier E6/Roe/BTH	Beamish Tramways			1928	320
Lledo	LP41-088 (cut)	1991	-	1:76	diecast	gbr	Karrier E6/Roe/BTH	Bradford			1928	320
Lledo	LP41-089a	1993	1000	1:76	diecast	gbr	Karrier E6/Roe/BTH	Birmingham	16		1928	320
Lledo	LP41-090a	1993	?	1:76	diecast	gbr	Karrier E6/Roe/BTH	Doncaster			1928	320
Lledo	LP41-091a	1993	3000	1:76	diecast	gbr	Karrier E6/Roe/BTH	London Transport			1928	320
Lledo	LP41-092a	1994	?	1:76	diecast	gbr	Karrier E6/Roe/BTH	London United		4	1928	320
Lledo	LP41-093a	1994	1000	1:76	diecast	gbr	Karrier E6/Roe/BTH	St. David's Foundation			1928	320
Lledo	LP41-094a	1994	1000	1:76	diecast	gbr	Karrier E6/Roe/BTH	Mansfield & District			1928	320
Lledo	LP41-095a	1994	2600	1:76	diecast	gbr	Karrier E6/Roe/BTH	Barclays			1928	320
Lledo	LP41-096a,b	1994	1000	1:76	diecast	gbr	Karrier E6/Roe/BTH	Walsall	152	29	1928	320
Lledo	LP41-097a	1994	1000	1:76	diecast	gbr	Karrier E6/Roe/BTH	Birmingham	15		1928	320
Lledo	LP41-098a	1994	?	1:76	diecast	gbr	Karrier E6/Roe/BTH	Weatherfield		694	1928	320
Lledo	LP41-099a	1995	5000	1:76	diecast	gbr	Karrier E6/Roe/BTH	British Lung Foundation			1928	320
Lledo	LP41-100a	1995	1000	1:76	diecast	gbr	Karrier E6/Roe/BTH	Cardiff			1928	320
Lledo	LP41-101a	1995	1000	1:76	diecast	gbr	Karrier E6/Roe/BTH	Llanelly		1	1928	320
Lledo	LP41-102a	1997	1000	1:76	diecast	gbr	Karrier E6/Roe/BTH	London Transport			1928	320
Lledo	LP41-103a	1997	?	1:76	diecast	gbr	Karrier E6/Roe/BTH	Guinness			1928	320
Lledo	LP41-104a	1998		1:76	diecast	gbr	Karrier E6/Roe/BTH	Walsall			1928	320
Lledo	LP41-106a	1998	1000	1:76	diecast	gbr	Karrier E6/Roe/BTH	Notts and Derby	334	A1	1928	320

model maker	ref.	issued	total	scale	construction	country	vehicle	operator	fleet#	route	built	page
Lledo	LP41-108a	1998		1:76	diecast	gbr	Karrier E6/Roe/BTH	Folkestone			1928	320
Lledo	LP41-109a	1998		1:76	diecast	gbr	Karrier E6/Roe/BTH	London Transport			1928	320
Lledo	LP41-No Iss		-	1:76	diecast	gbr	Karrier E6/Roe/BTH	Coventry			1928	320
Lledo	LP41-No Iss		-	1:76	diecast	gbr	Karrier E6/Roe/BTH	Evening News			1928	320
Lledo	SP41-001a,b	1991	500	1:76	diecast	gbr	Karrier E6/Roe/BTH	Triton			1928	320
Lledo	SP41-002a,b	1991	500	1:76	diecast	gbr	Karrier E6/Roe/BTH	London Transport			1928	320
Lledo	SP41-003a,b	1991	500	1:76	diecast	gbr	Karrier E6/Roe/BTH	Mullion			1928	320
Lledo	SP41-004a	1991	1000	1:76	diecast	gbr	Karrier E6/Roe/BTH	Lloyds			1928	320
Lledo	SP41-005a,b	1991	500	1:76	diecast	gbr	Karrier E6/Roe/BTH	Walsall	4		1928	320
Lledo	SP41-006a,b	1991	500	1:76	diecast	gbr	Karrier E6/Roe/BTH	Leicester			1928	320
Lledo	SP41-007a,b	1991	500	1:76	diecast	gbr	Karrier E6/Roe/BTH	London United			1928	320
Lledo	SP41-009a,b	1992	500	1:76	diecast	gbr	Karrier E6/Roe/BTH	Pilgrim Hospital			1928	320
Lledo	SP41-010a	1992	500	1:76	diecast	gbr	Karrier E6/Roe/BTH	Silver Queen			1928	320
Lledo	SP41-011a,b	1992	500	1:76	diecast	gbr	Karrier E6/Roe/BTH	Donington Park			1928	320
Lledo	SP41-012a,b	1992	506	1:76	diecast	gbr	Karrier E6/Roe/BTH	Eltham School			1928	320
Lledo	SP41-013a,b	1992	500	1:76	diecast	gbr	Karrier E6/Roe/BTH	London United	24	92	1928	320
Lledo	SP41-014a,b	1992	550	1:76	diecast	gbr	Karrier E6/Roe/BTH	London Transport			1928	320
Lledo	SP41-015a	1992	504	1:76	diecast	gbr	Karrier E6/Roe/BTH	Phonecard			1928	320
Lledo	SP41-016a,b	1992	500	1:76	diecast	gbr	Karrier E6/Roe/BTH	Kent Kids			1928	320
Lledo	SP41-017a	1992	500	1:76	diecast	gbr	Karrier E6/Roe/BTH	Northampton			1928	320
Lledo	SP41-018a,b	1992	500	1:76	diecast	gbr	Karrier E6/Roe/BTH	QE			1928	320
Lledo	SP41-019a,b	1992	500	1:76	diecast	gbr	Karrier E6/Roe/BTH	Newcastle			1928	320
Lledo	SP41-020a,b	1992	500	1:76	diecast	gbr	Karrier E6/Roe/BTH	Pilkington			1928	320
Lledo	SP41-021a,b	1992	500	1:76	diecast	gbr	Karrier E6/Roe/BTH	Scalextric			1928	320
Lledo	SP41-022a,b	1992	500	1:76	diecast	gbr	Karrier E6/Roe/BTH	Birmingham		3	1928	320
Lledo	SP41-023a,b	1992	500	1:76	diecast	gbr	Karrier E6/Roe/BTH	Birmingham			1928	320
Lledo	SP41-024a,b	1992	500	1:76	diecast	gbr	Karrier E6/Roe/BTH	Bradford			1928	320
Lledo	SP41-025a,b	1992	500	1:76	diecast	gbr	Karrier E6/Roe/BTH	London Transport		601	1928	320
Lledo	SP41-026a,b	1992	500	1:76	diecast	gbr	Karrier E6/Roe/BTH	Bridlington Corporation			1928	320
Lledo	SP41-027a,b	1993	500	1:76	diecast	gbr	Karrier E6/Roe/BTH	Bradford			1928	320
Lledo	SP41-028a,b	1993	500	1:76	diecast	gbr	Karrier E6/Roe/BTH	Revell			1928	320
Lledo	SP41-029a,b	1993	500	1:76	diecast	gbr	Karrier E6/Roe/BTH	Hornby Railways			1928	320
Lledo	SP41-030a,b	1993	500	1:76	diecast	gbr	Karrier E6/Roe/BTH	Lancaster			1928	320
Lledo	SP41-031a,b	1993	500	1:76	diecast	gbr	Karrier E6/Roe/BTH	South Wales	92		1928	320
Lledo	SP41-032a,b	1993	500	1:76	diecast	gbr	Karrier E6/Roe/BTH	SIS			1928	320
Lledo	SP41-033a,b	1993	500	1:76	diecast	gbr	Karrier E6/Roe/BTH	Bradford			1928	320
Lledo	SP41-034a,b	1995	550	1:76	diecast	gbr	Karrier E6/Roe/BTH	Maidstone	25		1928	320
Lledo	SP41-035a	1996	500	1:76	diecast	gbr	Karrier E6/Roe/BTH	St. David's Foundation			1928	320
Lledo	SP41-036a	1997	500	1:76	diecast	gbr	Karrier E6/Roe/BTH	St. David's Foundation			1928	320
Lledo	SP41-037a,b	1997	550	1:76	diecast	gbr	Karrier E6/Roe/BTH	Nottingham			1928	320
Lledo	SP41-038a	1998	500	1:76	diecast	gbr	Karrier E6/Roe/BTH	St. David's Foundation			1928	320
Lledo	SP41-039a	1998		1:76	diecast	gbr	Karrier E6/Roe/BTH	Nottingham			1928	320
Lledo	SP41-040a,b	1998	550	1:76	diecast	gbr	Karrier E6/Roe/BTH	Nottingham			1928	320
Lledo	SP41-041a	1999	600	1:76	diecast	gbr	Karrier E6/Roe/BTH	St. David's Foundation			1928	320
Lledo	DG41-021a	2004		1:76	diecast	gbr	Karrier E6/Roe/BTH	Nottingham	513	43	1928	320
Lledo	SP41-008a,b	1992	500	1:76	diecast	gbr	Karrier E6/Roe/BTH	Glasgow			1928	320
Lledo	DG41-018a	2001		1:76	diecast	gbr	Karrier E6/Roe/BTH	Huis Ten Bosch			1928	320
Lledo	DG41-019a	2001		1:76	diecast	gbr	Karrier E6/Roe/BTH	Huis Ten Bosch			1928	320
Lledo	LP41-105a	1998		1:76	diecast	gbr	Karrier E6/Roe/BTH	Huis Ten Bosch			1928	320
Lledo	LP41-c3	1994		1:76	diecast	gbr	Karrier E6/Roe/BTH	London Transport			1928	320
Lledo	LP41-110a	1998		1:76	diecast	gbr	Karrier E6/Roe/BTH	EISL			1928	320
Lledo	LP41-107a	1998		1:76	diecast	gbr	Karrier E6/Roe/BTH	Bentalls			1928	320
London Transport		c.1951	1	1:8	wood, metal	gbr	AEC 663T/Union Construction/EE	London United	1	1	1931	29

model maker	ref.	issued	total	scale	construction	country	vehicle	operator	fleet#	route	built	page
Lorenz				1:10	wood, metal	deu	Schiemann	Bielathalbahn			1901	159
Lurelle Guild		1944		print	print	usa	Trolley Coach	Metro Transit Lines			1944	377
MToys	123	1950s		16cm	tinplate	jpn	2 axle single decker	Central			n/a	219
M.F		1968		37cm	tinplate	chn	2 axle single decker	Shanghai	425		n/a	98
Magarinemodelle				9.5cm	polystyrene	deu	2 axle single decker	Generic			n/a	158
Magarinemodelle				9.5cm	polystyrene	deu	Henschel/Wegmann	Bielefeld	08-010		1950	159
Marcelo Ballonga		2010		1:10	resin, metal	arg	Ballonga	Mendoza			2010	380
Marek Bures		2003		1:6	metal	cze	Škoda 21Tr	Brno			1999	50
Marek Bures				1:13	metal	cze	Škoda 22Tr	Brno	3609		2003	127
Mario Trinchieri				1:87	resin	ita	Alfa Romeo 110AFS/Macchi/TIBB	Roma			1942	220
Mario Trinchieri				1:87	resin	ita	Alfa Romeo 85AF/Macchi/CGE	Mainz		22	1936	220
Mario Trinchieri				1:87	resin	ita	Fiat 2405/Viberti/CGE	Milano	348	92	1957	212
Mario Trinchieri				1:87	resin	ita	Fiat 2472/Viberti/CGE	Milano	541-580		1958-64	216
Marks Metallmodellclassics		2006		1:160	plastic	deu	Henschel/Uerdingen ÜH IIIs	Generic				74
Marusan		1960s		36cm	tinplate	jpn	Hino/Fuji 100 series	Tokyo	58	103	1954	221
Marusan		c.1960		28cm	tinplate	jpn	Hino/Fuji 300 series	Tokyo	135		1954	222
Mastica		1986		1:87	resin	nld	DAF MB200/Den Ousten/Kiepe	Arnhem	128	1	1974	230
Matchbox Collectibles	Y10	1988		1:76	diecast	gbr	AEC 663T/Union Construction/EE	London Transport	1	604	1931	289
Matchbox Collectibles	YET03M	1996		1:76	diecast	gbr	AEC 663T/Union Construction/EE	London United	1	4	1931	289
Matchbox Collectibles (code3)				1:76	diecast	gbr	AEC 663T/Union Construction/EE	London United	1	10	1931	289
Mattis Schindler		2002		1:87	card	pol	Solaris Trollino 12T	Ostrava	X1	203	2002	235
MBM by Krementchug				1:43	resin	ukr	Kzet KTB-6	Kiev			1966	275
MBM by PS Model				1:43	resin	deu	MAN MKE2/Kässbohrer	Trier			1951	182
MCW		1937		1:5	wood, metal	gbr	AEC chassisless/MCCW/MV	London Transport	954		1938	18
Meccano				1:9	metal	gbr	2 axle single decker	Arnhem			n/a	43
Meccano	MB132	1946		1:9	metal	gbr	AEC 664T/BRCW/EE	London Transport	284-383	623	1936	43
MEK	607	2005		1:87	resin	deu	Büssing/Uerdingen/Kiepe UBIVs	Bonn			1957	161
MEK	635	2005		1:87	resin	deu	Henschel/Uerdingen ÜH IIIs	Salzburg			1956,61	167
MEK	635	2005		1:87	resin	deu	Henschel/Uerdingen ÜH IIIs	Aachen			1959	167
MEK	600	2004		1:87	resin	deu	MAN SL172 HO/Gräf & Stift	Solingen			1986-87	185
Merkur	25			56cm	metal	cze	2 axle single decker	Generic			n/a	113
MGF		1950s		12.7cm	tinplate	rus	MTB-82	Odessa			1948	245
MHD				1:20	wood, metal	cze	Tatra T400	Praha	361		1948	111
Mick Sherwood			1	1:18	wood, plasticard	gbr	Guy BT	Hastings	45		1929	33
Micro		1938		1:72	lead	gbr	Leyland TTB4/Scandia/GEC	Kobenhavn NESA	9	24	1938	131
Mike Skeggs				1:43	injection plastic	gbr	Sunbeam F4/Brush/BTH	Derby	201-15		1949	347
Miniatures by Eric	BUST-44	2009		1:87	urethane	usa	ACF-Brill T-44	Generic			1946	358
Minic (Tri-ang)	77M	1939		18cm	tinplate	gbr	3 axle double decker	London Transport		177	n/a	56
Minitrucks	24	1990s		1:50	resin, whitemetal	fra	Vetra CS60/Renault Scemia	Lyon			1943	146
Minitrucks	24	1990s		1:50	resin, whitemetal	fra	Vetra CS60/Renault Scemia	Paris			1943	146
Minobus		1948		25cm	wood, metal	aut	MAN/Siemens	Wien			1940	56
Minsk Radio Technical Factory		1950		22cm	tinplate	rus	MTB-82M	Minsk			1946	245
Minsk Radio Technical Factory		1950		22cm	tinplate	rus	MTB-82M	Moskva			1946	245
MMR Modelly		087 122DE01		1:87	resin	deu	Büssing/Uerdingen/SSW	Leipzig	101		1938	160
MMR Modelly		087 122DE02		1:87	resin	deu	Büssing/Uerdingen/SSW	Leipzig	101		1938	160
MMR Modelly		087 115DE03		1:87	resin	deu	Lowa W600 Wedau	Eberswalde			1951	174
MMR Modelly		087 115DE01		1:87	resin	deu	Lowa W600 Wedau	Erfurt			1950	174
MMR Modelly		087 116DE02		1:87	resin	deu	Lowa W601	Berlin			1951	175
MMR Modelly		087 116DE03		1:87	resin	deu	Lowa W601	Potsdam			1951	175
MMR Modelly		087 116DE04		1:87	resin	deu	Lowa W601	Dresden			1951	175
MMR Modelly		087 116PL06		1:87	resin	deu	Lowa W602	Warszawa			1951	176
MMR Modelly		087 101AT02	2005	1:87	resin	deu	MAN MPE1/Schumann/BBC	Salzburg	106		1940	180
MMR Modelly		087 101DE01		1:87	resin	deu	MAN MPE1/Schumann/BBC	Eberswalde	01-Oct		1940	180

model maker	ref.	issued	total	scale	construction	country	vehicle	operator	fleet#	route	built	page
MMR Modelly	087 101AT04			1:87	resin	deu	MAN MPE1/Schumann/BBC	Eberswalde			1940	180
MMR Modelly	087 111CS02			1:87	resin	cze	Škoda 14Tr	Ostrava			1984	122
MMR Modelly	087 111DE06	2010		1:87	resin	cze	Škoda 14Tr	Eberswalde			1984	122
MMR Modelly	087 112CS12	2009		1:87	resin	cze	Škoda 14Tr	Plzen			1984	122
MMR Modelly	087 114CS01			1:87	resin	cze	Škoda 15Tr	Ostrava			1990	124
MMR Modelly	087 113CS01	2004		1:87	resin	cze	Škoda 17Tr	Ostrava		107	1987	125
MMR Modelly	087 113CS02	2004		1:87	resin	cze	Škoda 17Tr	Ostrava			1987	125
MMR Modelly	087 117CS01			1:87	resin	cze	Škoda 3Tr	Plzen			1941	109
MMR Modelly	0871 117 CS02			1:87	resin	cze	Škoda 3Tr	Plzen			1941	109
MMR Modelly	087 118CS01			1:87	resin	cze	Škoda 6Tr	Plzen			1948	110
MMR Modelly	087 118CS11			1:87	resin	cze	Škoda 6Tr	Brno			1948	110
MMR Modelly	087 127DE10	2011		1:87	resin	cze	Škoda 9Tr	Eberswalde			1962	116
MMR Modelly				1:87	resin	cze	Škoda 9Tr prototype	Plzen			1961	116
MMR Modelly	087 119CS02			1:87	resin	cze	Škoda Sanos S200Tr	Zlin			1986	121
MMR Modelly	087 111CS01			1:87	resin	cze	Škoda Sanos S200Tr	Ostrava	301		1986	121
MMR Modelly		2010		1:87	resin	cze	SORTN12A	Ostrava	SOR1		2008	130
MMR Modelly		2010		1:87	resin	cze	SORTN12C	Ostrava	3911		2008	130
MMR Modelly				1:87	resin	fra	Vetra CS60	Salzburg	114-7		1941-2	146
Mobatech		1981		1:87	brass	che	FBW/Hoch/SAAS	Basle			1975	74
Model Bus Company				1:76	diecast	gbr	Karrier E4/Weymann/EE	Bradford	677		1938	319
Modelcraft Ltd	9	1940s		1:72	card	gbr	AEC 661T/Weymann/CP	Brighton Corporation			1939	290
Modelcraft Ltd		1950s		1:72	card	gbr	LeylandTTB4/Leyland/MV	London Transport	1273		1939	329
Modeltrafik		1938		15cm	wood	gbr	LeylandTTB4/Scandia/GEC	Kobenhavn NESA		12	1938	131
Modeltrafik		1938		15cm	wood	gbr	LeylandTTB4/Scandia/GEC	Kobenhavn NESA		24	1938	131
Modeltrans	110	2007	300	1:43	resin	deu	MAN MKE4500/AEG	Trole Coruña-Carballo			1950	182
Modeltrans	114	2007	300	1:43	resin	esp	Maquitrans 500B	Barcelona	574	FH	1941-54	265
ModernToys		1960s			tinplate	jpn	Hino/Fuji	Tokyo	3229		1954	221
Modern Traction Supply Co.	505-3002	1980s		1:87	diecast	usa	ACF-BrillT-30	St. Joseph RLHP			1936	358
Modern Traction Supply Co.	505-3002	1980s		1:87	diecast	usa	ACF-BrillT-30	Generic			1936	358
Molytro				30cm	injection plastic	usa	Marmon-HerringtonTC44	Ciudad de México			1950	226
Moshimvolokno	mhv-10-04	2010		1:43	resin	rus	Uritsky ZiU-5	Generic		35	1961	250
Moshimvolokno	mhv-10-01	2010		1:43	resin	rus	Uritsky ZiU-5	Generic			1961	250
Moshimvolokno	mhv-10-02	2010		1:43	resin	rus	Uritsky ZiU-682	Moskva		42	1974	253
Moshimvolokno	mhv-20-01	2009		1:43	resin	rus	Uritsky ZiU-682	Moskva		54	1974	253
Moshimvolokno	mhv-10-01	2009		1:43	resin	rus	Uritsky ZiU-682	Moskva		42	1974	253
Mungojerrie		2008		1:87	card	blr	Belkommunmash AKSM-101	Moskva	1806	70	1995	83
Mungojerrie		2008		1:87	card	blr	Belkommunmash AKSM-201	Moskva	1815	70	1996	84
Mungojerrie		2010		1:87	card	rus	Svartz MTBES	Moskva	701	14	1963	248
Mungojerrie		2008		1:87	card	rus	Uritsky ZiU-5	Moskva	2323	19	1960	250
Märklin				?	metal	deu	2 axle single decker	Generic				157
N3C		2010		1:87	resin	ita	Alfa Romeo 110AF/Piaggio/Ansaldo	Roma	9001		1942	204
N3C	2979	2003		1:87	resin	ita	Alfa Romeo 140AF/SIAI Marchetti/CGE	Roma	5039	64	1949	206
N3C	2977	2003		1:87	resin	ita	Alfa Romeo 140AF/SIAI Marchetti/Marelli	Ancona	12		1949	206
N3C	2980	2003		1:87	resin	ita	Alfa Romeo 140AF/SIAI Marchetti/TIBB	Milano	466		1950	206
N3C				1:87	resin	ita	Alfa Romeo 140AF/SIAI Marchetti/TIBB	Milano	462	92	1950	206
N3C	A051	2010		1:87	resin	ita	Alfa Romeo 140AF/SIAI Marchetti/TIBB	Roma	6647	64	1949-50	206
N3C				1:87	resin	ita	Fiat 2411/Menarini/GCE	San Remo	30		1964	214
N3C	2981			1:87	resin	ita	Fiat 2411/Viberti/TIBB	Verona	225	2	1957	214
N3C	2982			1:87	resin	ita	Fiat 2411/Viberti/TIBB	Bari	227		1956	214
N3C		2010		1:87	resin	ita	Fiat 2472/Viberti/CGE	Milano	563	90	1959	216
N3C	Emidio Garde	2004		1:87	resin	ita	Lancia Esatau P101/Casaro/GCE	Roma	4501-4597		1957	210
Nagano	2051-600	2007		6cm	injection plastic	jpn	Hino/Fuji	Tokyo	226		1954	221

model maker	ref.	issued	total	scale	construction	country	vehicle	operator	fleet#	route	built	page
Neil Mortson		2008		1:43	diecast,plastic	gbr	Sunbeam S7A/East Lancs/MV	Huddersfield	631		1959	339
Nigel MacMillan		1955		1:72	diecast	gbr	BUT 9641T/MCCW/EE	Glasgow			n/a	40
NY Transit Museum				1:12	wood,metal	usa	St Louis Car Job 1754	New York	3④	63	1948	26
Oleksandr Krasnov		2009		1:87	resin	rus	MTB-82	Moskva	17		1950	245
Oleksandr Krasnov		2011		1:87	resin	ukr	LAZ-695T	Kiev			1963	275
Ondreje Spáaila		2004		1:10	metal,plastic,wood	cze	Škoda 15Tr	Brno	3409		1990	49
Oxford Diecast	NQ1005	2011		1:148	diecast	gbr	AEC 664T/Northern Counties/EE	Cardiff	19	6	1941	300
Oxford Diecast	NQ1006	2011		1:148	diecast	gbr	BUT 9641T/Brush/MV	Nottingham	30	43	1951	305
Oxford Diecast	NQ1002	2011		1:148	diecast	gbr	BUT 9641T/Harkness/GEC	Belfast	208	11	1950	305
Oxford Diecast	NQ1001	2011		1:148	diecast	gbr	BUT 9641T/MCCW/EE	London Transport	1508	667	1948	305
Oxford Diecast	NQ1003	2011		1:148	diecast	gbr	BUT 9641T/MCCW/EE	Newcastle	487	31A	1948	305
Oxford Diecast	NQ1004	2011		1:148	diecast	gbr	BUT 9641T/MCCW/EE	Glasgow	TB9	101	1949	305
P&D Marsh				1:152	diecast	gbr	BUT 9641T/MCCW/EE	London Transport	765-840		1948	305
PB Models	202	2001		1:43	resin	ita	Fiat 672F/Cansa/Marelli	Roma	5707	62	1950	210
PB Models	no.67		50	1:43	resin	ita	Lancia Esatau P101/Casaro/GCE	Roma	4543	70	1957	210
Percy Wilby		1948		1:9	tin,ply	gbr	Ransomes,Sims + Jefferies C type	Ipswich	6	8	1926	25
Percy Wilby				1:12	tin,ply	gbr	Ransomes,Sims + Jefferies D type	Ipswich	41	8	1928	25
Percy Wilby				1:12	tin,ply	gbr	Ransomes,Sims + Jefferies D type	Ipswich	47	9	1933	335
Percy Wilby				1:9	tin,ply	gbr	Ransomes,Sims + Jefferies Light 2	Ipswich	68	1	1937	21
Perrette Auguste		2010			virtual	rus	Svarz LK-1	Moskva			1933	379
Peter Lepine-Smith		1964	1	1:3	aluminium,wood	gbr	Sunbeam F4A/Burlingham/AEI	Reading	187	A	1961	35
Peter Smith				1:76	diecast,plastic	gbr	English Electric SD6W/English Electric	Cardiff			1930	45
Petr Kudej	PK004/etc.			1:87	card	cze	Škoda 14Tr	London Transport			1981	122
Petr Kudej	PK006/etc.			1:87	card	cze	Škoda 15Tr	Opava	478		1983	124
Petr Kudej	PK034/etc	2007		1:87	card	cze	Škoda 21Tr	Ostrava			1999	125
Petr Kudej	PK020/etc.	2006		1:87	card	cze	Škoda 24Tr Irisbus	Various			2004	129
Petr Kudej	PK032/etc	2007		1:87	card	cze	Škoda 24Tr Irisbus	Various			2005	129
Petr Kudej	PK009/etc.			1:87	card	cze	Škoda 7Tr	Mariánské Lázne			1951	113
Petr Kudej	PK009/etc.			1:87	card	cze	Škoda 8Tr	Mariánské Lázne			1960	115
Petr Kudej	PK018/etc.	2006		1:87	card	cze	Škoda Sanos S200Tr	Zlin	329		1986	121
Pirate Models	461/4902	1980s		1:76	diecast	gbr	AEC 664T/MCCW/MV	London Transport	142-1354	654	1936-9	300
Pirate Models	4901	1980s		1:76	diecast	gbr	AEC 664T/Weymanns/EE	London Transport	132-383		1935-7	300
Pirate Models	4903	1980s		1:76	diecast	gbr	AEC chassisless/LPTB/MV	London Transport	754		1937	290
Pirate Models	4904	1980s		1:76	diecast	gbr	AEC chassisless/MCCW/MV	London Transport	1379	613	1939	290
Pirate Models	4904	1980s		1:76	diecast	gbr	AEC chassisless/MCCW/MV	London Transport	1379	613	1939	290
Pirate Models	4909	1970s		1:76	diecast	gbr	BUT 9611T/Roe/EE	Bradford	743		1949	294
Pirate Models	406/4906			1:76	diecast	gbr	BUT 9641T/MCCW/EE	London Transport	1765-840	613	1948	305
Pirate Models	452/4907		0	1:76	diecast	gbr	Leyland TB2/Shorts/GEC	Birmingham	01-Nov	7	1932	327
Pirate Models	4900		0	1:76	diecast	gbr	Leyland TB5/MCW/GEC	Birmingham	67-78		1937	327
Pirate Models	4905		0	1:76	diecast	gbr	Leyland Twin Steer/Leyland/MV	London Transport	1671	654	1939	333
Pirate Models	4910			1:76	diecast	gbr	Sunbeam F4/East Lancs/BTH	Bradford	844		1948	347
Pirate Models	433/4908	1981	0	1:76	diecast	gbr	Sunbeam W/Park Royal/BTH	South Shields	237		1946	340
PM Modellbau		2002		1:87	resin	deu	Henschel/Uerdingen ÜH IIIs	Salzburg			1956	167
PM Modellbau				1:87	resin	deu	IFA ES6 Dobus	Berlin	2001		1955	178
PM Modellbau				1:87	resin	deu	Krupp/Ueringen/AEG	Mettmann Rheinbahn			1930	162
PS Models		2002		1:43	resin	deu	Henschel/Uerdingen ÜH IIIs	Aachen		51	1959	167
RA Model Petr Dosly				1:87	resin	deu	Henschel Gr.II/Schumann	Dresden	151-63		1947-9	163
RA Model Petr Dosly	1200BVG	2000		1:87	resin	deu	Lowa W602a	Dresden			1952	176
RA Model Petr Dosly	1200 XC	2000		1:87	resin	deu	Lowa W602a	Generic			1952	176
RA Model Petr Dosly				1:87	resin	cze	Škoda 14Tr	Eberswalde			1983	122
RA Model Petr Dosly	1210 00	2006		1:87	resin	cze	Škoda 1Tr	Praha			1936	108
RA Model Petr Dosly	1212 00			1:87	resin	cze	Škoda 3Tr	Plzen	106		1941	109
RA Model Petr Dosly	1207 03	2006		1:87	resin	cze	Škoda 7Tr	Brno	31		1951	113

model maker	ref.	issued	total	scale	construction	country	vehicle	operator	fleet#	route	built	page
RA Model Petr Dosly	1207 00			1:87	resin	cze	Škoda 7Tr	Bratislava			1951	113
RA Model Petr Dosly	1205 04	2004		1:87	resin	cze	Škoda 8Tr	Praha			1959	115
RA Model Petr Dosly	1202 XC	1999		1:87	resin	cze	Škoda 8Tr	Ostrava			1963	115
RA Model Petr Dosly	1205 50			1:87	resin	cze	Škoda 8Tr	Dresden	174		1958	115
RA Model Petr Dosly	1205			1:87	resin	cze	Škoda 8Tr	Weimar			1958	115
RA Model Petr Dosly	120500	2009		1:87	resin	cze	Škoda 8Tr	Plzen			1957	115
RA Model Petr Dosly	1202 15			1:87	resin	cze	Škoda 9Tr	Various			1963	116
RA Model Petr Dosly	1202 33			1:87	resin	cze	Škoda 9Tr	Dresden			1962	116
RA Model Petr Dosly	1201 XA	1999		1:87	resin	cze	Škoda 9Tr	Teplice			1960	116
RA Model Petr Dosly	1202 12			1:87	resin	cze	Škoda 9Tr	Praha			1961	116
RA Model Petr Dosly				1:87	resin	cze	Škoda 9Tr	Berlin			1961	116
RA Model Petr Dosly				1:87	resin	cze	Škoda 9Tr	Eberswalde			1961	116
RA Model Petr Dosly				1:87	resin	cze	Škoda 9Tr	Esslingen			1961	116
RA Model Petr Dosly	120214	2009		1:87	resin	cze	Škoda 9Tr	Gera			1964	116
RA Model Petr Dosly				1:87	resin	cze	Škoda 9Tr	Ústí nad Labem		100	1961	116
RA Model Petr Dosly	1204 00			1:87	resin	cze	Škoda 9Tr prototype	Praha			1961	116
RA Model Petr Dosly	1208 02			1:87	resin	cze	Škoda T11	Plzen	248		1966-70	120
RA Model Petr Dosly	1208 00			1:87	resin	cze	Škoda T11 prototype	Ostrov			1964	120
RA Model Petr Dosly	1206 03			1:87	resin	cze	Tatra T400	Bratislava			1950	111
RA Model Petr Dosly	1206 00			1:87	resin	cze	Tatra T400/III	Praha	394-468		1953	111
RA Model Petr Dosly	1209 00	2003		1:87	resin	cze	Tatra T401	Praha	461		1958	112
RA Model Petr Dosly	1200 00	2002		1:87	resin	fra	Vetra VBR/Renault/CKD	Décin			1950	149
RA Model Petr Dosly	1200 02	2003		1:87	resin	fra	Vetra VBR/Renault/CKD	Ceské Budejovice			1948	149
RA Model Petr Dosly	1200 01	2003		1:87	resin	fra	Vetra VBR/Renault/CKD	Ceské Budejovice			1947	149
Reading Trolleybus Society		1972		1:76	card	gbr	BUT 9611T/Park Royal	Reading	144		1949	294
Rico	129	1950		15cm	tinplate	esp	3 axle single decker	Generic			n/a	262
Rico	129	1950		15cm	tinplate	esp	3 axle single decker	Generic			n/a	262
Rico	129	1950		15cm	tinplate	esp	3 axle single decker	Generic			n/a	61
Rico?				30cm?	tinplate	gbr	Tillings Stevens/CGA	Barcelona	537	FC	1928	261
Rietze (conversion)				1:87	resin	deu	Mercedes Benz Citaro	Szeged	T860		2007	191
Rietze (conversion)				1:87	resin	cze	Škoda 22Tr	Škoda Ostrov			2000	127
Rietze (conversion)				1:87	resin	pol	Solaris Trollino 18T	Winterthur	179	1	2004	235
Rigomódell		2010		1:24	wood,metal	hun	Ikarus 60T	Budapest	286	75	1954	193
Rigomódell		2010		1:24	wood,metal	rus	Uritsky ZiU-9M	Szeged	9-111	5	1985	253
Rivarossi	Minobus	1950		1:80	injection plastic	ita	Alfa Romeo 110AF	Generic			1945	61
Rivarossi	Minobus	1950		1:80	injection plastic	ita	Alfa Romeo 110AF	Generic			1945	61
Rivarossi	Minobus	1950		1:80	injection plastic	ita	Alfa Romeo 110AF	Generic			1945	61
Rivarossi	Minobus	1950		1:80	injection plastic	ita	Alfa Romeo 110AF	Generic			1945	204
RK				1:87	resin	rus	Svarz LK-1	Moskva	9		1933	240
RK				1:87	resin	rus	Svarz LK-1	Moskva	1		1933	240
RK				1:87	resin	rus	Svarz LK-1	Moskva	2		1933	240
RK				1:87	resin	rus	Svarz LK-1	Moskva	1		1933	240
RK				1:87	resin	rus	Yaroslavly YaTB-1	Moskva			1936	242
RK				1:87	resin	rus	Yaroslavly YaTB-1	Kiev			1936	242
RK				1:87	resin	rus	Yaroslavly YaTB-1	Generic			1936	242
RK (?)				1:87	resin	rus	MTB-82	Moskva			1950	245
Roberts Miniature Transports				1:87	plaster	usa	ACF-Brill T-40	Denver		21	1940	357
Roberts Miniature Transports				1:87	plaster	can	CC&F-Brill T-44	Toronto	1925		1948	92
Roberts Miniature Transports				1:87	plaster	can	Flyer E700	Toronto	9232	76	1979	95
Roberts Miniature Transports		1980's		1:87	plaster	usa	Mack CR3S	Portland			1937	366
Robin Male				1:30	wood,metal	che	Hess Light-am	London Transport			n/a	52
Robin Male				1:30	metal,plasticard	gbr	Sunbeam MF2B/Weymann/CP	Bournemouth			1962	53
Robin Male		2009		1:30	metal,plasticard	gbr	Sunbeam MS2/Park Royal/BTH	Bournemouth	99	21	1935	336

model maker	ref.	issued	total	scale	construction	country	vehicle	operator	fleet #	route	built	page
Rod Blackburn				1:76	resin	gbr	Leyland TTB4/MCCW/MV	London Transport		628	1936	329
s.e.s (Modelltec)	14 1306 00	1986		1:87	injection plastic	hun	Ikarus 280T	Budapest	0355		1975	196
s.e.s (repaint)	14 1305	2006		1:87	injection plastic	hun	Ikarus 280T	Szeged		9	1991	196
s.e.s (repaint)	14 1305	2006		1:87	injection plastic	hun	Ikarus 280T	Budapest		75	1975	196
s.e.s/Andras Ekkert		2009		1:87	resin	hun	Ikarus 260T	Budapest	0	78	1976	196
s.e.s/Jörg Swoboda	14 1302 20	2006		1:87	injection plastic	hun	Ikarus 260T	Budapest		24	1975	196
s.e.s/Jörg Swoboda	14 1302 01_W	2006		1:87	injection plastic	hun	Ikarus 260T	Generic			1975	196
Sadlo				1:87	resin	deu	Daimler-Benz O1000/Schumann/AEG	Berlin	224		1947	187
Sadlo	870700-6	2004		1:87	resin	cze	Škoda 14Tr	Various			1982	122
Sadlo	870700			1:87	resin	cze	Škoda 14Tr	Ostrava			1984	122
Sakai		1958		1:87	injection plastic	usa	2 axle single decker	Philadelphia	133		n/a	71
Salzburger Stadtwerke				1:50	card	aut	Gräf & Stift GE 110M16	Salzburg	129-135	6	1978-80	79
Salzburger Stadtwerke				24cm	card	aut	Gräf & Stift GE 110M16	Salzburg	178		1985	79
Salzburger Stadtwerke				1:32	card	aut	Gräf & Stift GE 112M16	Salzburg	179		1986	81
Salzburger Stadtwerke				1:87	card	aut	Steyr STS 11HU	Salzburg			1989-90	81
Salzburger Stadtwerke				1:87	card	bel	Van Hool AG 300T	Salzburg			2000-5	89
Salzburger Stadtwerke				1:87	card	bel	Van Hool AG 300T	Salzburg			2000-5	89
SCMS		1950		25cm	aluminium	fra	Vetra CS60	Generic		117	1943	71
SCMS		1950		25cm	aluminium	fra	Vetra CS60	Generic		119	1943	146
scratchbuilt				1:72	wood, card	gbr	Sunbeam MF1/Park Royal/BTH	Wolverhampton	206		1934	336
scratchbuilt		1960's		1:32	wood, metal	gbr	Sunbeam S7/Park Royal/BTH	Reading	170	17	1950	339
SDV (conversion)				1:87	injection plastic	cze	Škoda 22Tr	Szeged	T650	9	2000	127
SDV (conversion)				1:87	injection plastic	cze	Škoda 22Tr	Brno	3039	26	2000	127
SDV Model	230			1:87	injection plastic	cze	Škoda 21Tr	Szeged	T801	5	1999	125
SDV Model	240			1:87	injection plastic	cze	Škoda 21Tr	České Budejovice			1999	125
SDV Model	249			1:87	injection plastic	cze	Škoda 21Tr	Brno	3018	25	1999	125
SDV Model	252			1:87	injection plastic	cze	Škoda 21Tr	Ostrava			1997	125
SDV Model	230			1:87	injection plastic	cze	Škoda 21Tr	Pardubice	397		2001	125
Seattle Transit		1952	1	1:87	metal, wood	usa	Twin Coach 44GTT	Seattle Transit			1943	27
Shanghai Living Museum				1:1	fibreglass	gbr	AEC 603T	Shanghai		14	1925	97
Siemens				1:10	wood, metal	deu	Elektromote	Siemens			1882	158
Simonelli		2001		1:43	resin	ita	Fiat 2401/Cansa/TIBB	Milano		92	1953	208
Simonelli		2000		1:43	resin	ita	Fiat 2470/Socimi/CGE	Milano	901-970		1986	217
Simonelli		2001		1:43	resin	ita	Fiat 2472/Viberti/CGE	Milano	541-580	93	1958-64	216
Škoda				?	wood	cze	Škoda 13Tr	Generic			1966	121
Škoda				?	wood	cze	Škoda 16Tr	Generic			1980	18
Škoda		1987		1:16	wood	cze	Škoda 17Tr	Ostrava			1987	125
Škoda				?	wood	cze	Škoda 5Tr	Generic			1943	110
Škoda Museum				1:16	metal	cze	Škoda 14Tr	Generic			1972	122
Škoda Museum				1:16	metal	cze	Škoda 14Tr	San Francisco			1999	122
Škoda Museum				1:13	metal	cze	Škoda 15Tr	Generic			1983	124
Škoda Museum				1:13	metal	cze	Škoda 21Tr	Demonstrator			1996	125
Škoda Museum				1:18	metal	cze	Škoda 9Tr	Plzen			1963	116
Škoda Museum				1:18	metal	cze	Škoda 9Tr prototype	Plzen			1961	116
Slastenin Sasha				virtual	virtual	rus	Uritsky ZiU-11	Volgograd			1974	379
SOES		1968		1:76	vacuum formed plastic	gbr	BUT 9641T/MCCW/EE	London Transport	1765-840	613	1948	305
SOES		1968		1:76	vacuum formed plastic	gbr	Crossley TDD6 'Dominion'/MV	Manchester	1240	205	1951	315
SOES	R1/72/***	1968	300+	1:76	vacuum formed plastic	gbr	Daimler CTE6/Roe/EE	Rotherham	Jul-18		1950	316
Solaris		2008		1:30	wood	pol	Solaris Trollino SGT 12	Generic			2002	235
Solido	113	1957		1:72	diecast	fra	Vetra VBC-APU/Chausson	Generic			1955	149
Solido	120	1960		1:72	diecast	fra	Vetra VBC-APU/Chausson	Generic			1955	149
Solido	113	1954		1:72	diecast	fra	Vetra VBC-APU/Chausson	Generic		201	1955	149
Solido	113	1954		1:72	diecast	fra	Vetra VBC-APU/Chausson	Generic			1955	149

model maker	ref.	issued	total	scale	construction	country	vehicle	operator	fleet#	route	built	page
Solido	120	1959		1:72	diecast	fra	Vetra VBC-APU/Chausson	Generic			1955	149
Solido	113	1954		1:72	diecast	fra	Vetra VBC-APU/Chausson	Generic			1955	149
Solido	120	1962		1:72	diecast	fra	Vetra VBC-APU/Chausson	Generic			1955	149
Solido (conversion)			1?	1:50	diecast	gbr	AEC 661T/English Electric/EE	London Transport	63		1934	290
Sotetstu Wu				12cm	card	jpn	Tokyu Car	Yokohama	103		1959	224
Southern Miniature Models				1:76	diecast	gbr	Leyland Twin Steer/Leyland/MV	London Transport	1671	607	1939	333
Speelgoed/Norev	1984			1:50	injection plastic	fra	Saviem SC10U	Arnhem			1957	153
Speelgoed/NZG	255	1985	200	1:50	diecast	deu	Mercedes Benz O405T	Arnhem	151	1	1985	232
Spårvägsmuseet					wood, metal	swe	Scania-Vabis T30	Stockholm SS		96	1947	267
St.Petersburg	422-1	2011	25	1:48	resin	usa	Marmon-Herrington TC49	Chicago	9631	54	1951-2	367
St.Petersburg	422	2011	75	1:48	resin	usa	Marmon-Herrington TC49	Chicago	9580	81	1951-2	367
St.Petersburg	168	1999	80	1:48	resin	usa	ACF-Brill T-44	Chicago	9306	76	1948	358
St.Petersburg	168a	1999	50	1:48	resin	usa	ACF-Brill T-44	Chicago	9261	74	1948	358
St.Petersburg	168b	1999	50	1:48	resin	usa	ACF-Brill T-44	Wilkes-Barre	849		1948	358
St.Petersburg	168c	1999	25	1:48	resin	usa	ACF-Brill T-44	St Joseph	#860		1948	358
St.Petersburg	139	1999	100	1:43	resin	usa	ACF-Brill T-46	Los Angeles Transit Lines	9123	2	1948	363
St.Petersburg	139-1	1999	10	1:43	resin	usa	ACF-Brill T-46	Los Angeles MTA	9130		1948	363
St.Petersburg	139a	1999	25	1:43	resin	usa	ACF-Brill T-46	Winnipeg			1951	363
St.Petersburg	139b	1999	25	1:43	resin	usa	ACF-Brill T-46	Ciudad de México			1951	363
St.Petersburg	139c	1999	50	1:43	resin	usa	ACF-Brill T-46	Wilkes-Barre	863		1950	363
St.Petersburg	139d	1999	25	1:43	resin	usa	ACF-Brill T-46	Flint	867-876		1951	363
St.Petersburg	139e	1999	25	1:43	resin	usa	ACF-Brill T-46	St Joseph	281-285		1950	363
St.Petersburg	139f	1999	50	1:43	resin	usa	ACF-Brill T-46	Des Moines	245		1949	363
St.Petersburg	424	2002	25	1:48	resin	usa	ACF-Brill TC-44	Oakland	2015	7	1946	359
St.Petersburg	424a	2002	25	1:48	resin	usa	ACF-Brill TC-44	Los Angeles Transit Lines	8001	5	1946	359
St.Petersburg	424a-1	2002	10	1:48	resin	usa	ACF-Brill TC-44	Los Angeles MTA	8015	2	1946	359
St.Petersburg	424b	2002	25	1:48	resin	usa	ACF-Brill TC-44	New Orleans	1214	1	1945	359
St.Petersburg	424c1	2002	10	1:48	resin	usa	ACF-Brill TC-44	Dallas Railway & Co.	1001		1945	359
St.Petersburg	424d	2002	10	1:48	resin	usa	ACF-Brill TC-44	Kansas City	2420	41	1945	359
St.Petersburg	424d-1	2002	10	1:48	resin	usa	ACF-Brill TC-44	Kansas City	2405	41	1945	359
St.Petersburg	424e	2002	10	1:48	resin	usa	ACF-Brill TC-44	Honolulu Rapid Transit Co.	600		1945	359
St.Petersburg	424f	2002	5	1:48	resin	usa	ACF-Brill TC-44	Denver	563		1945	359
St.Petersburg	424h	2002	10	1:48	resin	usa	ACF-Brill TC-44	Fort Wayne Transit Inc.	170		1946	359
St.Petersburg	424g	2002	5	1:48	resin	usa	ACF-Brill TC-44	Memphis	1000	31	1945	359
St.Petersburg	424j	2002	5	1:48	resin	usa	ACF-Brill TC-44	Ankara	171-180		1945	359
St.Petersburg	425	2002	50	1:48	resin	usa	ACF-Brill TC-44	Philadelphia	262		1947/48	359
St.Petersburg	425a	2002	25	1:48	resin	usa	ACF-Brill TC-44	Philadelphia	222	29	1947/48	359
St.Petersburg	425b	2002	50	1:48	resin	usa	ACF-Brill TC-44	Philadelphia	249	61	1947/48	359
St.Petersburg	426	2002	25	1:48	resin	usa	ACF-Brill TC-44	Akron	170		1948	359
St.Petersburg	426a	2002	25	1:48	resin	usa	ACF-Brill TC-44	Wilkes-Barre	846		1947	359
St.Petersburg	426b	2002	25	1:48	resin	usa	ACF-Brill TC-44	Dayton City Transit	61	5	1947	359
St.Petersburg	426c	2002	10	1:48	resin	usa	ACF-Brill TC-44	Des Moines	225-244		1948	359
St.Petersburg	426d	2002	10	1:48	resin	usa	ACF-Brill TC-44	Denver	642		1948	359
St.Petersburg	426e	2002	10	1:48	resin	usa	ACF-Brill TC-44	Sao Paulo	3128		1948	359
St.Petersburg	427	2002	25	1:48	resin	usa	ACF-Brill TC-44	Baltimore	2190	2	1948	359
St.Petersburg	427-1	2002	50	1:48	resin	usa	ACF-Brill TC-44	Baltimore	2136	10	1948	359
St.Petersburg	427a	2002		1:48	resin	usa	ACF-Brill TC-44	Calgary Transit System	485-504		1948	359
St.Petersburg	428	2002	50	1:48	resin	usa	ACF-Brill TC-44	Los Angeles Transit Lines	9025	2	1948	359
St.Petersburg	428-1	2002	50	1:48	resin	usa	ACF-Brill TC-44	Los Angeles MTA	9028	2	1948	359
St.Petersburg	424c	2002	10	1:48	resin	usa	ACF-Brill TC-44	Dallas Railway & Co.	1001	34	1945	359
St.Petersburg	424n	2002		1:48	resin	usa	ACF-Brill TC-44	Edmonton	129		1945	359
St.Petersburg	159/11		-	1:43	resin	usa	ACF-Brill TC-46	Boston	8700		1950	364
St.Petersburg	159a		80	1:43	resin	usa	ACF-Brill TC-46	Johnstown	731		1952	364

model maker	ref.	issued	total	scale	construction	country	vehicle	operator	fleet#	route	built	page
St.Petersburg	159b		50	1:43	resin	usa	ACF-Brill TC-46	Cincinnati, Newport & Co	661		1952	364
St.Petersburg	159b-1		10	1:43	resin	usa	ACF-Brill TC-46	Cincinnati, Newport & Co	664		1952	364
St.Petersburg	111/11a	2009		1:43	resin	gbr	AEC 664T/English Electric/EE	Moskva	IC01	1	1937	300
St.Petersburg	112	1998	150	1:43	resin	gbr	BUT RETB1/Burlingham/MV	Glasgow	TB513	108	1958	313
St.Petersburg	175	1999	100	1:48	resin	can	CC&F-Brill T-44	Toronto	9000-9049		1947	92
St.Petersburg	175-1	1999	50	1:48	resin	can	CC&F-Brill T-44	Toronto	9073	61	1947	92
St.Petersburg	175a	1999	25	1:48	resin	can	CC&F-Brill T-44	Edmonton	131-177		1947	92
St.Petersburg	175b	1999	50	1:48	resin	can	CC&F-Brill T-44	Vancouver	2001		1947	92
St.Petersburg	175c	1999	5	1:48	resin	can	CC&F-Brill T-44	Bogota	Jan-20		1947	92
St.Petersburg	175d	1999	12	1:48	resin	can	CC&F-Brill T-44	Vancouver	2042	25	1947	92
St.Petersburg	175d-1	1999	12	1:48	resin	can	CC&F-Brill T-44	Vancouver	2040	10	1947	92
St.Petersburg	175e	1999	50	1:48	resin	can	CC&F-Brill T-44	Montreal	4042	26	1947	92
St.Petersburg	175f	1999	25	1:48	resin	can	CC&F-Brill T-44	Halifax	201	10	1948	92
St.Petersburg	175g	1999	10	1:48	resin	can	CC&F-Brill T-44	Calgary Transit System	422		1947	92
St.Petersburg	175h	1999	special	1:48	resin	can	CC&F-Brill T-44	Winnipeg	1600		1947	92
St.Petersburg	186	2000	100	1:43	resin	jpn	Hino/Fuji 200 series	Tokyo	205		1954	222
St.Petersburg	186a	2000	150	1:43	resin	jpn	Hino/Fuji 200 series	Tokyo	226		1956	222
St.Petersburg	186b	2000	25	1:43	resin	jpn	Hino/Fuji 200 series	Kawasaki	502		1955	222
St.Petersburg	198	2000	100	1:43	resin	jpn	Hino/Fuji 300 series	Tokyo	321		1957	222
St.Petersburg	118		100	1:43	resin	ukr	Kzet KTB-6	Kiev	546		1966	275
St.Petersburg	434	2004	10	1:43	resin	gbr	Leyland TTB4/Leyland/MV	London Transport	1248	647	1938	329
St.Petersburg	434-1	2004	25	1:43	resin	gbr	Leyland TTB4/Leyland/MV	London Transport	1121	630	1938	329
St.Petersburg	434a	2004	10	1:43	resin	gbr	Leyland TTB4/Leyland/MV	London Transport	1672	649	1940	329
St.Petersburg	435	2004	10	1:43	resin	gbr	Leyland TTB4/Leyland/MV	London Transport	753	607	1937	329
St.Petersburg	435-1	2004	15	1:43	resin	gbr	Leyland TTB4/Leyland/MV	London Transport	664	607	1937	329
St.Petersburg	434m	2004		1:43	resin	gbr	Leyland TTB4/Leyland/MV	London Transport	1121	630	1938	329
St.Petersburg	138	1999	25	1:43	resin	gbr	Leyland TTB4/Scandia/GEC	Kobenhavn KS	101	12	1938	131
St.Petersburg	138a	1999	25	1:43	resin	gbr	Leyland TTB4/Scandia/GEC	Kobenhavn NESA	9	12	1938	277
St.Petersburg	437		-	1:43	resin	gbr	Leyland TTB6/Leyland/GEC	Belfast	T11-T12		1938	332
St.Petersburg	437-1		-	1:43	resin	gbr	Leyland TTB6/Leyland/GEC	Belfast	T1-T12		1938	332
St.Petersburg	437-2		-	1:43	resin	gbr	Leyland TTB6/Leyland/GEC	Belfast	T11-T12		1938	332
St.Petersburg	471	2009	75	1:48	resin	usa	Marmon-Herrington TC44	San Francisco	552	22	1948	366
St.Petersburg	471-1	2009	25	1:48	resin	usa	Marmon-Herrington TC44	San Francisco	566	30	1949	366
St.Petersburg	470	2009	100	1:48	resin	usa	Marmon-Herrington TC48	San Francisco	756	30	1950-1	367
St.Petersburg	470-0	2009		1:48	resin	usa	Marmon-Herrington TC48	San Francisco	842	41	1950-1	367
St.Petersburg	470-1	2009	25	1:48	resin	usa	Marmon-Herrington TC48	San Francisco	845	21	1950-1	367
St.Petersburg	40		100	1:43	resin	rus	MTB-82	Leningrad	26		1946	245
St.Petersburg	44		100	1:43	resin	rus	MTB-82	Leningrad			1955	245
St.Petersburg	406	2000	50	1:43	resin	usa	Pullman-Standard 40CX	Boston	8001		1936	367
St.Petersburg	406a	2000	50	1:43	resin	usa	Pullman-Standard 40CX	Providence	818-850		1936	367
St.Petersburg	154	1998	50	1:43	resin	usa	Pullman-Standard 43CX	Boston	8433		1947	368
St.Petersburg	155-1		5	1:43	resin	usa	Pullman-Standard 43CX	Boston	8522		1951	368
St.Petersburg	163	1998	50	1:43	resin	usa	Pullman-Standard 43CX	Valparaiso	814		1947	368
St.Petersburg	163a		50	1:43	resin	usa	Pullman-Standard 43CX	Santiago	301-900		1947/48	368
St.Petersburg	169		50	1:43	resin	usa	Pullman-Standard 43CX	Boston	8567		1951	368
St.Petersburg	189	1999	50	1:43	resin	usa	Pullman-Standard 44AS	Birmingham Electric	103	15	1945/46	369
St.Petersburg	189a	1999	50	1:43	resin	usa	Pullman-Standard 44AS	Vancouver	2501-2524		1947	369
St.Petersburg	130	1998	200	1:43	resin	usa	Pullman-Standard 44CX	Providence	1345		1947	369
St.Petersburg	130a	1998	50	1:43	resin	usa	Pullman-Standard 44CX	Boston	8593		1947	369
St.Petersburg	130b	1998	50	1:43	resin	usa	Pullman-Standard 44CX	Cleveland Transit System	850-899		1947	369
St.Petersburg	130c	1998	50	1:43	resin	usa	Pullman-Standard 44CX	Winnipeg	1560-1594		1947	369
St.Petersburg	130d	1998	50	1:43	resin	usa	Pullman-Standard 44CX	Halifax	282-287		1947	369
St.Petersburg	130e	1999	5	1:43	resin	usa	Pullman-Standard 44CX	Greenville	146		1948	369

model maker	ref.	issued	total	scale	construction	country	vehicle	operator	fleet#	route	built	page
St.Petersburg	130f	1999	25	1:43	resin	usa	Pullman-Standard 44CX	Bogota	21-30		1948	369
St.Petersburg	155	1999	80	1:43	resin	usa	Pullman-Standard 44CX	Boston	8598		1951	369
St.Petersburg	187	1999	80	1:43	resin	usa	Pullman-Standard 44CX	Chicago	9323-9367		1948	369
St.Petersburg	187a	1999	50	1:43	resin	usa	Pullman-Standard 44CX	Chicago	323-367		1948	369
St.Petersburg	190	1999	50	1:43	resin	usa	Pullman-Standard 44CX	Memphis	1100-1226		1947	369
St.Petersburg	193	1999	50	1:43	resin	usa	Pullman-Standard 44CX	Sao Paulo	3004-3009		1947	369
St.Petersburg	144	1998	80	1:43	resin	usa	Pullman-Standard 45CX	Milwaukee	350-423		1948	371
St.Petersburg	188		50	1:43	resin	usa	Pullman-Standard 45CX	Dayton City Railway	401-445		1947	371
St.Petersburg	188a		25	1:43	resin	usa	Pullman-Standard 45CX	Dayton City Transit	401-445		1947	371
St.Petersburg	188b		25	1:43	resin	usa	Pullman-Standard 45CX	Dayton & Xenia Rly	62	10	1947	371
St.Petersburg	188c		25	1:43	resin	usa	Pullman-Standard 45CX	Oakwood	35 (62)		1947	371
St.Petersburg	196		50	1:43	resin	usa	Pullman-Standard 45CX	Atlanta	1235-1334		1946/47	371
St.Petersburg	192	2000	50	1:43	resin	fra	Renault R4231	Madrid	114	101	1952/57	151
St.Petersburg	142	1999	50	1:43	resin	swe	Scania-Vabis T30	Stockholm SS		91	1947	267
St.Petersburg	36	1997	100	1:43	resin	rus	Svarz LK-5	Leningrad	9		1936	242
St.Petersburg	113		100	1:43	resin	rus	Svarz TS-1	Moskva			1959	249
St.Petersburg	197a	1999	specia	1:48	resin	usa	Twin Coach 40GWFT	Seattle Transit	875	10	1940	372
St.Petersburg	183	2000	50	1:48	resin	usa	Twin Coach 40TT	Detroit	401		1930	372
St.Petersburg	183a	2000	50	1:48	resin	usa	Twin Coach 40TT	Cincinnati	599		1930	372
St.Petersburg	183b	2000	50	1:48	resin	usa	Twin Coach 40TT	Brooklyn & Queens	1001		1930	372
St.Petersburg	184	1999	80	1:48	resin	usa	Twin Coach 40TT	Chicago	64		1930	372
St.Petersburg	184a	1999	10	1:48	resin	usa	Twin Coach 40TT	Chicago	9063	85	1930	372
St.Petersburg	184b	1999	50	1:48	resin	usa	Twin Coach 40TT	Chicago	9051-9079		1930	372
St.Petersburg	197	1999	80	1:48	resin	usa	Twin Coach 41GTT	Milwaukee	164-173		1939	373
St.Petersburg	114	1999	50	1:48	resin	usa	Twin Coach 44GTT	Seattle Transit	976	7	1943	373
St.Petersburg	114-2	1999	specia	1:48	resin	usa	Twin Coach 44GTT	Seattle Transit			1943	373
St.Petersburg	114-3	1999	specia	1:48	resin	usa	Twin Coach 44GTT	King County Metro			1943	373
St.Petersburg	114a	1999	50	1:48	resin	usa	Twin Coach 44GTT	Atlanta	1043	20	1943	373
St.Petersburg	114b	1999	25	1:48	resin	usa	Twin Coach 44GTT	Akron	113-132		1942	373
St.Petersburg	404	2001	100	1:48	resin	usa	Twin Coach 44TTW	San Francisco	614	5	1949	374
St.Petersburg	404-1	2001	5	1:48	resin	usa	Twin Coach 44TTW	San Francisco	656		1949	374
St.Petersburg	404-2	2001	10	1:48	resin	usa	Twin Coach 44TTW	San Francisco	621	21	1949	374
St.Petersburg	404a	2001	25	1:48	resin	usa	Twin Coach 44TTW	San Francisco	570	30	1949	374
St.Petersburg	404d	2001		1:48	resin	usa	Twin Coach 48TT2	Detroit	9003		1949	374
St.Petersburg	39		100	1:43	resin	rus	Uritsky ZiU-10	Leningrad			1990	257
St.Petersburg	41		100	1:43	resin	rus	Uritsky ZiU-5	Leningrad			1961	250
St.Petersburg	146a	1999	25	1:43	resin	rus	Uritsky ZiU-682	Budapest			1975	253
St.Petersburg	146b	1999	25	1:43	resin	rus	Uritsky ZiU-682	Cordoba EMIR			1989	253
St.Petersburg	146c	1999	25	1:43	resin	rus	Uritsky ZiU-682	Athens	3001-3132		1984	253
St.Petersburg	146e	2000	25	1:43	resin	rus	Uritsky ZiU-682	Bogota	2000-2074		1975	253
St.Petersburg	146d	1999	25	1:43	resin	rus	Uritsky ZiU-682B	Belgrade			1979	253
St.Petersburg	177	1999	25	1:43	resin	rus	Uritsky ZiU-683	Cordoba EMIR			1991	257
St.Petersburg	38		100	1:43	resin	rus	Uritsky ZiU-9	Leningrad	4856	41	1972	253
St.Petersburg	146		25	1:43	resin	rus	Uritsky ZiU-9	Helsinki	601-603		1973	253
St.Petersburg	42		100	1:43	resin	rus	Uritsky ZiU-9M	Leningrad			1982	253
St.Petersburg	127	1999	25	1:43	resin	fin	Valmet JD/BTH	Tampere	7		1949	135
St.Petersburg	127a	1999	25	1:43	resin	fin	Valmet JD/BTH	Helsinki	604	14	1949	135
St.Petersburg	416	2002	25	1:48	resin	usa	Versare Model 3880	Salt Lake City	300		1928	356
St.Petersburg	416a	2002	specia	1:48	resin	usa	Versare Model 3880	Salt Lake City	311	21	1928	356
St.Petersburg	37		100	1:43	resin	rus	Yaroslavly YaTB-1	Leningrad	91	4	1936	242
St.Petersburg	111	1998	100	1:43	resin	rus	Yaroslavly YaTB-3	Moskva	1010		1938	244
St.Petersburg	111/II	2009	75	1:43	resin	rus	Yaroslavly YaTB-3	Moskva	1002	3	1938	244
St.Petersburg	401		80	1:48	resin	usa	Yellow Coach 1208	Milwaukee	124	14	1938	376

model maker	ref.	issued	total	scale	construction	country	vehicle	operator	fleet#	route	built	page
St.Petersburg	401a		25	1:48	resin	usa	Yellow Coach 1208	Milwaukee	136		1938	376
Stabil				?	metal	deu	2 axle single decker	Generic			n/a	157
Stadtwerke Solingen		1988		1:87	card	deu	TSIII	Solingen	8C	683	1968-74	173
STE				1:76	card	mex	MASA 4200 series/Toshiba	Ciudad de México			1988	226
Stettnitsch Modell	3030			1:87	resin	deu	Büssing 33F/Christoph+Unmack/AEG	Berlin	1002		1933	159
Stettnitsch Modell				1:87	resin	deu	Henschel HS56/Gaubschat/AEG	Berlin	484		1956	166
Stettnitsch Modell				1:87	resin	deu	Henschel HS56/Gaubschat/AEG	Berlin	488		1957	166
Stonebridge Toy Products		1950s		18cm	tinplate	gbr	3 axle double decker	London Transport			n/a	287
Stromberg				30cm	wood	fin	2 axle single decker	Helsinki			n/a	135
Sunnyside	yellow			1:76	diecast	gbr	Karrier E6/Roe/BTH	Generic			1928	320
Sunnyside	white			1:76	diecast	gbr	Karrier E6/Roe/BTH	Generic			1928	320
Sunnyside	blue			1:76	diecast	gbr	Karrier E6/Roe/BTH	Generic			1928	320
Sunnyside	red			1:76	diecast	gbr	Karrier E6/Roe/BTH	Generic			1928	320
SWS/J.M.B.		1994		1:55	card	deu	MAN SL172 HO/Gräf & Stift	Solingen	22		1986-87	185
Szegedi Közlekdési kft	0.530TR12EV			25cm	wood	deu	Mercedes Benz Citaro	Szeged	T-863		2007	191
Takara Tomy	Choro Q	2001		5.2cm	injection plastic	jpn	Hino/Fuji	Osaka	255		1956	221
Takara Tomy	Choro Q	2003		5.2cm	injection plastic	jpn	Mitsubishi 100 series	Kansai Electric Power			1964	223
Taylor & Barrett	197	1936		9cm	cast lead	gbr	3 axle double decker	London Transport		617	n/a	280
Taylor & Barrett	204	1936		13cm	cast lead	gbr	3 axle double decker	London Transport		621	n/a	280
Taylor & Barrett	197	1945		9cm	cast lead	gbr	3 axle double decker	London Transport		617	n/a	280
Taylor & Barrett (repaint)	197			9cm	cast lead	gbr	2 axle double decker	Bournemouth		21	n/a	280
Taylor & Barrett (repaint)	197			9cm	cast lead	gbr	3 axle double decker	Newcastle		35	n/a	280
TCL		2002		12.6cm	card	fra	Irisbus Cristalis	Lyon			2002	152
Technische Museum Wien		1953		1:10(?)	wood,metal	deu	Henschel OM 5-1/Lohner	Wien		3	1943	76
Terry Russell		1960s		1:43	injection plastic	gbr	2 axle double decker	Hastings		2	n/a	40
Terry Russell		c.1972		1:43	wood,metal	gbr	AEC 663T/Union Construction/EE	London Transport	2	604	1931	41
Terry Russell				1:43	wood,card	gbr	BUT 9641T/MCCW/EE	Newcastle	520	39	1950	305
Terry Russell				1:43	wood,card	gbr	BUT 9641T/MCCW/EE	London Transport	1772	604	1948	305
Terry Russell				1:43	wood,card	gbr	Leyland TTB2/BRCW/MV	London Transport	76	654	1935	329
Terry Russell				1:43	wood,card	gbr	Sunbeam MF2B/Weymann/CP	Bournemouth	303		1962	352
TiNY Bus and Coach	TK40	2010		1:76	resin	gbr	Sunbeam MF2B/Roe/MV	Kingston Upon Hull			n/a	352
TiNY Bus and Coach	TK2	2006		1:76	resin	gbr	Sunbeam W/Park Royal/BTH	Nottingham	478	49	1946	340
TiNY Bus and Coach	TK2	2006		1:76	resin	gbr	Sunbeam W/Park Royal/BTH	Pontypridd	9		1946	340
TiNY Bus and Coach	TK14	2010		1:76	resin	gbr	Sunbeam W/Roe/BTH	Nottingham	459		1945	340
Tippco				15cm	tinplate	gbr	BUT 972IT/Verheul/EE	Arnhem	101	2	1949	228
Tony Chlad			1	1:76	balsa,card	gbr	AEC 661T/English Electric/EE	London Transport	63	4	1934	51
Tony Chlad		1996		1:76	balsa,card	gbr	AEC 664T/Northern Counties/EE	Cardiff	201	1	1941	300
Tony Chlad				1:76	balsa,card	gbr	BUT 9611T/WeymannCP	Bournemouth	294	21	1948	294
Tony Chlad		1990's		1:76	balsa,card	gbr	Karrier W/East Lancs/MV	Bradford	704	8	1945	340
Tony Chlad				1:76	balsa,card	gbr	Leyland Twin Steer/Leyland/MV	London Transport	1671	607	1939	333
Tony Chlad				1:76	balsa,card	gbr	Sunbeam F4/Northern Coachbuilders/MV	Newcastle	551	42	1949	347
Tony Chlad				1:76	plasticard,Milliput filler	gbr	Sunbeam F4A/Burlingham/AEI	Reading	184	11	1961	347
Tony Chlad				1:76	plasticard,wood	gbr	Sunbeam F4A/Willowbrook/BTH	Walsall	862	30	1954	347
Tony Chlad		1990's		1:76	resin	gbr	Sunbeam W/Weymann/BTH	Derby	172		1944	340
TrainPCB		2006		1:87	plastic/metal	deu	Henschel/Uerdingen ÜH IIIs	Solingen	59		1959	74
Turner & Sanders		1958?		1:72	injection plastic	gbr	3 axle double decker	London Transport			n/a	73
TW	2000			12cm	diecast	fra	2 axle single decker	Lyon			n/a	137
TW				12cm	diecast	fra	2 axle single decker	Paris			n/a	137
TW	2000			15cm	cast lead	gbr	3 axle double decker	London Transport			n/a	353
Unknown				15cm	glass	gbr	Tillings Stevens/CGA	Barcelona			1941	261
V&V Model Company	2481	2009		1:87	resin	deu	Büssing 33F/Christoph+Unmack/AEG	Berlin	1001		1933	159
V&V Model Company	2480	2005		1:87	resin	deu	Büssing 33F/Christoph+Unmack/AEG	Berlin	1001		1933	159
V&V Model Company	2511			1:87	resin	deu	Henschel GrII/Kässbohrer	Neunkirchen	16		1947	162

model maker	ref.	issued	total	scale	construction	country	vehicle	operator	fleet#	route	built	page
V&V Model Company	2512			1:87	resin	deu	Henschel GrII/Kässbohrer	Bochum	4		1947	162
V&V Model Company	2513			1:87	resin	deu	Henschel GrII/Kässbohrer	Darmstadt	224		1947	162
V&V Model Company	2514			1:87	resin	deu	Henschel GrII/Kässbohrer	Hannover	906		1947	162
V&V Model Company	2515			1:87	resin	deu	Henschel GrII/Kässbohrer	Essen	21		1948	162
V&V Model Company	2431			1:87	resin	deu	Henschel GrII/Schumann	Dresden	151-63		1947-9	163
V&V Model Company	2432			1:87	resin	deu	Henschel GrII/Schumann	Leipzig	115-9		1944	163
V&V Model Company	2430			1:87	resin	deu	Henschel GrII/Schumann	Dresden	151-63		1947-9	163
V&V Model Company	3431			1:87	resin	deu	Henschel III/NWF	Hamburg			1952	165
V&V Model Company	3441			1:87	resin	deu	Henschel III/NWF	Erfurt			1957	165
V&V Model Company	2501			1:87	resin	deu	Krauss-Maffei KME-130	München	9		1948	173
V/R	320			1:87	resin	deu	Henschel/Kässbohrer	Generic			1947	164
V/R		1999		1:87	resin	deu	Henschel/Uerdingen ÜH IIIs	Solingen			1952	167
V/R	289			1:87	resin	deu	Lowa W602a	Zwickau			1956	176
V/R	292			1:87	resin	deu	Lowa W602a	Eberswalde			1956	176
V/R	291			1:87	resin	deu	Lowa W602a	Dresden			1956	176
V/R				1/43	resin	rus	MTB-82	Moskva			1950	245
V/R	266,287			1:87	resin	cze	Škoda 8Tr	Eberswalde			1960	115
V/R	293			1:87	resin	cze	Škoda 9Tr	Kiev	3606		1961	116
V/R	311			1:87	resin	cze	Škoda T11	Plzen			1966-70	120
V/R	281			1:87	resin	cze	Tatra T400	Praha			1948-51	111
V/R				1:43	resin	rus	Yaroslavly YaTB-1	Moskva			1936	242
V/R (conversion)				1:87	resin	aut	Gräf & Stift EOVI	Linz	43		1960	78
Varney Transport Replicas	35	1980		1:76	diecast	gbr	AEC 661T/Park Royal/EE	Hastings	12	5	1940	290
Varney Transport Replicas		1970s		1:76	diecast	gbr	BUT 9641T/MCCW/EE	London/Newcastle/Glas			1948	305
VEB Dresdner Spielwarenfabrik		1955		1:87	injection plastic	deu	Lowa W602a	Dresden			1955	70
Vector Models		2006		1:43	electroformed copper	hun	Ikarus 260T	Budapest			1975	196
Vector Models	V5-40			1:43	electroformed copper	hun	Ikarus 280T	Budapest			1987	196
Vector Models	v5-40-1			1:43	electroformed copper	hun	Ikarus 280T	Moskva			1989	196
Vector Models	V1-21		0	1:43	electroformed copper	ukr	Kzet KTB-4	Kirovograd	42	2	1962	273
Vector Models	V1-20			1:43	electroformed copper	ukr	Kzet KTB-4	Kiev	10		1962	273
Vector Models	VE21+VE22			1:43	electroformed copper	ukr	Kzet KTB-4	Kherson	102		1964	273
Vector Models		2010		1:43	electroformed copper	ukr	LAZ 52522	Nikolaev	3160		1998	276
Vector Models	E5483			1:43	electroformed copper	deu	Mercedes Benz O305GTD	Esslingen			1978	188
Vector Models	E5478			1:43	electroformed copper	deu	Mercedes Benz O305T	Esslingen			1978	188
Vector Models	E5550			1:43	electroformed copper	deu	Mercedes Benz OE302-12R Duo-Bus	Esslingen			1975	188
Vector Models	B-2101			1:43	electroformed copper	rus	MTB-82D	Moskva	256		1946	245
Vector Models	B-2340	2009		1:43	electroformed copper	rus	MTB-82FVV	Budapest	T134	72	1952	245
Vector Models	B-2100	2006		1:43	electroformed copper	rus	MTB-82M	Moskva	70		1946	245
Vector Models	B-2102	2001		1:43	electroformed copper	rus	MTB-82M	Moskva	70		1946	245
Vector Models		2001		1:43	electroformed copper	rus	MTB-82M	Kherson	76	1	1948	245
Vector Models		2009		1:43	electroformed copper	rus	MTB-82M	Zkskursiya			1950	245
Vector Models		2010		1:43	electroformed copper	rus	MTB-82M	Kiev	215		1950	245
Vector Models	P9-23	2010		1:43	electroformed copper	rus	MTrZ-52791 'Sadovoye Koltso'	Moskva	2028		2006	258
Vector Models	P1-10	2009		1:43	electroformed copper	rus	Svarz LK-1	Moskva	17		1933	240
Vector Models	P1-00	2009		1:43	electroformed copper	rus	Svarz LK-1	Moskva	2		1934	240
Vector Models	B2120	2008		1:43	electroformed copper	rus	Uritsky ZiU-5B	Moskva	84		1961	250
Vector Models	B2122	2008		1:43	electroformed copper	rus	Uritsky ZiU-5D	Moskva	2409	30	1969	250
Vector Models	B2122a	2008		1:43	electroformed copper	rus	Uritsky ZiU-5D	Moskva	366	4	1969	250
Vector Models		2010		1:43	electroformed copper	rus	Uritsky ZiU-5D	Kherson	17	1	1969	250
Vector Models	B2121	2010		1:43	electroformed copper	rus	Uritsky ZiU-5G	Moskva	2672		1966	250
Vector Models	V-10-37	2009		1:43	electroformed copper	rus	Uritsky ZiU-682	Kherson	196	2	1974	253
Vector Models				1:43	electroformed copper	rus	Uritsky ZiU-682	Kursk	262	4	1974	253
Vector Models				1:43	electroformed copper	rus	Uritsky ZiU-682	Kirovograd	246	1	1974	253

model maker	ref.	issued	total	scale	construction	country	vehicle	operator	fleet#	route	built	page
Vector Models				1:43	electroformed copper	rus	Uritsky ZiU-682	Kremmenchug	173	1	1974	253
Verheul	1949			1:12	wood,metal	gbr	BUT 9721T/Verheul/EE	Arnhem	101	1	1949	229
Vic Franklin				1:76	balsa,card	gbr	AEC 691T/London General/EE	London Transport	61		1933	288
Vic Franklin				1:76	balsa,card	gbr	Sunbeam F4/Northern Coachbuilders/MV	Newcastle	535		1949	347
Viseon				1:10	injection plastic	deu	Viseon LT	Riyad			2010	380
Viseon				1:10	Necurite	deu	Viseon LT	Riyad			2010	378
Vittorio Naldini	Emidio Gardé	2004		1:87	resin	ita	Alfa Romeo 110AF/Macchi/TIBB	Roma	6001	36	1939	204
Vittorio Naldini				1:87	resin	ita	Alfa Romeo 140AF/SIAI Marchetti/TIBB	Roma	6605	64	1949	206
Vittorio Naldini				1:87	resin	ita	Fiat 656F/Varesini/CGE	Roma	4151	56	1937	210
Vittorio Naldini				1:87	resin	ita	Fiat 668F/Stanga/TIBB	Venezia	73		1952	212
Vittorio Naldini				1:87	resin	ita	Fiat 672F/Cansa/Marelli	Roma	6701	75	1950	210
Viva Scale Models				1:20	plastic,wood,metal	blr	Belkommunmash AKSM-321	Minsk			2004	85
Viva Scale Models		2008		1:20	plastic,wood,metal	blr	Belkommunmash AKSM-333	Minsk			2007	85
Viva Scale Models		2008		1:20	plastic,wood,metal	blr	Belkommunmash AKSM-420	Minsk	2500		2007	86
VK Modelle	8701911	2011		1:87	injection plastic	pol	Solaris Trollino 12T	Generic			2009	380
VK Modelle	8701133	2009		1:87	injection plastic	pol	Solaris Trollino 18T	Salzburg	301,2,3	3	2009	235
VK Modelle	8701144	2010		1:87	injection plastic	pol	Solaris Trollino 18T	Eberswalde	051,52	862	2010	235
VK Modelle	8701188	2010		1:87	injection plastic	pol	Solaris Trollino 18T	Solaris			2010	235
Volume-Trix		1955		26.5cm	card	fra	Vetra VA3	Lyon	602	2	1950	149
Vossloch		2008		1:20	wood	che	Hess Swiss Trolley3/2	Generic			2008	272
VshaCG		2010		virtual	virtual	cze	Škoda 9Tr	Bratislava			1963-81	379
W.Goerke				1:72	card	pol	Jelcz M121MT	Gydnia	3004	24	1999	234
W.Goerke				1:72	card	pol	Jelcz PR110UE	Lublin	10110	21	1982	234
W.Goerke				1:72	card	pol	Jelcz PR120MTE	Gdynia	3372	27	1992	234
W.Goerke		2008		1:72	card	pol	Solaris Trollino SGT 12	Lublin	836	153	2004	235
Wakey Models	14	2010		1:76	resin	gbr	Daimler CTE6/East Lancs/EE	Rotherham	17	9	1950	316
Wakey Models				1:76	resin	gbr	Sunbeam F4/Brush/BTH	Island Traction			1947	347
Wakey Models	8A/11	2005		1:76	resin	gbr	Sunbeam W/Brush/BTH	Mexborough & Swinton	18	A	1947	340
Wang Feng	SH-860			20cm	injection plastic	chn	2 axle single decker	Generic	860		n/a	98
Wang Feng				30cm	injection plastic	chn	3 axle double decker	Generic			n/a	99
Wang Feng				35cm	injection plastic	chn	3 axle single decker	Generic			n/a	99
Wang Feng				35cm	injection plastic	chn	3 axle single decker	Generic			n/a	99
Wang Feng				60cm	injection plastic	chn	4 axle single decker	Generic			n/a	100
Wells-Brimtoy	516	1955		15cm	tinplate	gbr	2 axle double decker	Transport		516	n/a	281
Wells-Brimtoy	111	1949		15cm	tinplate	gbr	2 axle double decker	Transport		516	n/a	281
Wells-Brimtoy	105	c.1945		17cm	tinplate	gbr	2 axle double decker	Transport Bus		804	n/a	281
Wells-Brimtoy	131	1950s		21cm	tinplate	gbr	2 axle double decker	Transport Bus		657	n/a	281
Wells-Brimtoy	105	1938		17cm	tinplate	gbr	2 axle double decker	Transport Bus		804	n/a	281
Wells-Brimtoy	105	1950s		17cm	tinplate	gbr	2 axle double decker	Transport Bus		804	n/a	281
Westward	45	1978		1:76	diecast	gbr	Sunbeam W/Park Royal/BTH	Derby			1946	340
Wheelbase Models				1:76	resin	gbr	Sunbeam MS2/Roe/MV	Huddersfield			1950	336
Wiking (conversion)	T7	1948		1:87	injection plastic	deu	2 axle single decker	Zwickau	8,9		1938	158
Wiking (conversion)				1:87	injection plastic	aut	Gräf & Stift NGE 152M17	Eberswalde		861	1994	77
Wiking (conversion)				1:87	injection plastic	aut	Gräf & Stift OE 112M11	Kapfenburg	15,16		1986	81
Wiking (conversion)				1:87	injection plastic	deu	MAN SG240 H EVAG duobus	Essen		54	1983	183
Wiking (conversion)				1:87	injection plastic	deu	Mercedes Benz O405GTD	Kobenhavn			1988	189
Willi Schincke				1:63	plasticard,tin,balsa	che	FBW/BBC	Zlin	6	A	1944	270
Willi Schincke				1:63	plasticard,tin,balsa	cze	Škoda 14TrM	Zlin	170	4	1995	48
Willi Schincke				1:63	plasticard,tin,balsa	cze	Škoda 15Tr	Zlin	335	7	1990	46
Willi Schincke				1:63	plasticard,tin,balsa	cze	Škoda 7Tr	Zlin	20		1951	47
Willi Schincke				1:63	plasticard,tin,balsa	cze	Škoda 8Tr	Zlin	30		1958	48
Willi Schincke				1:63	plasticard,tin,balsa	cze	Škoda 9Tr	Zlin	62	B	1975	116
Willi Schincke				1:63	plasticard,tin,balsa	cze	Škoda Sanos S200Tr	Zlin	329#	8	1986	121

model maker	ref.	issued	total	scale	construction	country	vehicle	operator	fleet#	route	built	page
Willi Schincke		2007		1:63	plasticard,tin,balsa	fra	Vetra VBR/Renault/CKD	Zlin	16	C	1949	149
WLC Jeffery				1:6	wood,metal	gbr	AEC 664T/MCCW/MV	London Transport	1525	601	1940	38
Wumm				1:87	resin	hun	Ikarus 280T	Budapest	198	80	1984	196
Wumm				1:87	resin	hun	Ikarus 412T	Budapest	713	70	2002	200
Wumm				1:87	resin	hun	Ikarus 415T	Bucharest	5280		2002	200
Wumm				1:87	resin	hun	Ikarus 415T	Debrecen			2002	200
Wumm				1:87	resin	hun	Ikarus 435T	Budapest	314	80	1996	200
Wumm				1:87	resin	hun	Ikarus 60T	Budapest	344	75	1955	193
Wumm				1:87	resin	hun	Ikarus 60TCS	Budapest	435	75	1963	195
Wumm	B013			1:87	resin	hun	Ikarus T400	Budapest	T400	70	1961	195
Wumm	B040			1:87	resin	deu	Mercedes Benz Citaro	Szeged	T-862		2007	191
Wumm	B024		150	1:87	resin	pol	Solaris Trollino SGT 12	Budapest	602	76	2003	234
Wumm				1:87	resin	pol	Solaris Trollino SGT 12	Debrecen	341	2	2005	234
Yonezawa		1954		10.5cm	tinplate	jpn	2 axle single decker				n/a	219
Yonezawa		c.1960		31.5cm	tinplate	jpn	Hino/Fuji	Osaka			1956	221
Z-tanks				1:43	metal	rus	Uritsky ZiU-5-264	Generic			1961	250

Boston 8001, Pullman-Standard 40CX by St.Petersburg, 1:43, resin

Appendix 2
Suppliers

This is a list of some of the suppliers who stock or have supplied model trolleybuses.

name	address	country	website	phone	contact
ALO Busmodelle	Perfektastraße 19/28 A-1230 Wien	Austria	http://www.busmodelle.at/	+43 1 955 37 46	Alexander Olajos
80m Bus Model	302-304, 3/F, Pioneer Shopping Centre 750 Nathan Road, MongKok, Kowloon.	China	http://www.80mbusmodel.com/	+852 2381 8168	
DP Modely-shop	U Továren 662/16, 102 00 Praha 10-Hostivar	Czech Republic	http://www.dpmodely-shop.eu/	+420 739 245 197	Daniel Pilar
Foxtoys Modely	Pøikopi 12, 110 00 Prag 1	Czech Republic	http://www.foxtoys.eu/	+420 221 014 400	Martin Kot
ModelTrain s.r.o.	Slovanská 154, 326 00 Plzen	Czech Republic	http://www.modelauto.cz/	+420 377 457 146	
Modelly MMR	Masarykova 90, 400 01 Ustí nad Labem	Czech Republic	http://www.modelymmr.cz/	+420 603 547 703	
V+V model	Kmochova 1353, 40747 Varnsdorf	Czech Republic	http://www.vvmodel.cz	+420 412 372 084	Frantischek Vecarnik
Modell Bus Markt	Schmädlgasse 8, 82487 Oberammergau	Germany	https://modellbusmarkt-oberammergau.de/	+49 (0) 8822 6127	Konrad Pernetta
VK Modelle	Bellscheider Weg 33, D-40883 Ratingen	Germany	http://www.vkmodelle.de	+49 2 02 66921	Veit Kornburger
Ho-Ki Modell bt.	1073 Budapest Erzsébet krt. 51	Hungary	http://www.hokimodell.hu/	+36 1 351 2335	
Gila Modelli s.a.s.	Via Guglielmetti 4/B - 22076 Mozzate	Italy	http://www.gilamodelli.com/	+39 (3) 331 833 262	Roberto Gilardoni
Moscow Tram Collection	Ganetsky Square 1, Moscow	Russia	http://www.moscow-tram-collection.ru/	+7 8 (926) 881 66 66	
St.-Petersburg Tram Colle	PO Box No.16, 196158 St.-Petersburg	Russia	http://www.sptc.spb.ru/	+7 (812) 961 63 34	Leonid Khoykin
ModelTrans	Apdo. 31 - 33300 Villaviciosa, Asturias	Spain	http://www.modeltrans.com/	+34 985 140 346	
Daves Die Cast Models	Consett, County Durham	UK	http://www.davesdiecastmodels.co.uk	+44 1207 544743	Dave Herron
Diecast Devon	Unit 3, Grange Way Business Park, Colchester, CO2 8HF	UK	http://www.diecastdevon.co.uk/	+44 (0) 845 6432346	Ian Dawson
Hattons Model Railways	364-368 Smithdown Road, Liverpool L15 5AN	UK	http://www.hattons.co.uk/	+44 (0)151-733-3655	
Hornby Hobbies	Westwood, Margate, Kent, CT9 4JX	UK	http://www.corgi.co.uk/	+44 1843 233525	
Little Bus	6 Appleyard, Haworth Close, Halifax, HX1 2NN	UK	http://www.little-bus.com/	+44 (0) 1422 301600	Tony Asquith
Oxford Diecast	PO Box 62, Swansea UK SA1 4YA	UK	http://www.oxforddiecast.co.uk/	+44 (0)1792 643500	
Pirate Models	7 Horsham Lane, Upchurch, Sittingbourne, Kent, ME9 7AL	UK	johngay@aol.com	+44 (0) 1634 233144	John Gay
The Model Store	Boundary Elms, Burchetts Green Lane, Maidenhead, SL6 3QP	UK	http://www.modelstore.co.uk	+44 (0) 845 6806795	
TiNY Bus & Coach Kits	Willow House, 3 Mellor Brow, BB2 7EX	UK	http://www.themodelbus.com/kits/tiny.htm		Keith Turner
Wakey Models	Mexborough, Yorkshire	UK	wakeymodels@talktalk.net		Graham Dowson

Giessen Henschel HS160 OSL by HB Models, 1:87, resin

Frantischek Vecarnik of V&V with his production of Darmstadt 224, Henschel Gr.II/Kässbohrer by V&V Model Company, 1:87, resin

Appendix 411

Display of model trolleybuses and toys at The Trolleybus Museum, Sandtoft

Underside and mechanics of London Transport Hess LighTram by Robin Male, 1:30, wood, metal (see page 52)

Generic Vetra CS60 by SCMS, 25cm, aluminium

Barcelona 574, Maquitrans 500B by Modeltrans, 1:43, resin

Moskva MTrZ-52791 'Sadovoye Koltso' by Vector Models, 1:43, electroformed copper

Salt Lake City 311, Versare Model 3880 by St.Petersburg, 1:48, resin

London trolleybuses by Pirate Models, 1:76 cast,
Taylor & Barrett, 13cm, cast,
Betal, 18cm, tinplate and
St. Petersburg Tram Collection, 1:43, resin.